# PSYCHOTHERAPY AND CONFIDENTIALITY

# PSYCHOTHERAPY AND CONFIDENTIALITY

*Testimonial Privileged Communication,*
*Breach of Confidentiality,*
*and Reporting Duties*

*By*

## RALPH SLOVENKO

**CHARLES C THOMAS • PUBLISHER, LTD.**
*Springfield • Illinois • U.S.A.*

*Published and Distributed Throughout the World by*

CHARLES C THOMAS • PUBLISHER, LTD.
2600 South First Street
Springfield, Illinois 62794-9265

*With* THOMAS BOOKS *careful attention is given to all details of manufacturing
and design. It is the Publisher's desire to present books that are satisfactory as to their
physical qualities and artistic possibilities and appropriate for their particular use.*
THOMAS BOOKS *will be true to those laws of quality that assure a good name
and good will.*

*Printed in the United States of America*
*CR-R-3*

*Library of Congress Cataloging in Publication Data*

Slovenko, Ralph.
    Psychotherapy and confidentiality : testimonial
privileged communication, breach of confidentiality, and
reporting duties / by Ralph Slovenko.
        p.    cm.
    Includes bibliographical references and index.
    ISBN 0-398-06827-5 (cloth)
    1. Psychotherapist and patient--Moral and ethical aspects.
    2. Interpersonal communication--Moral and ethical aspects.
    3. Confidential communications--Physicians.  I. Title.
    RC480.8.S59  1998
    616.89'14--dc21

*Dedicated*
*to the memory of*
*Dr. Maurice Grossman*

*And whatsoever I shall see or hear in the course of my profession, as well as outside my profession in my intercourse with men, it if be what should not be published abroad, I will never divulge, holding such things to be holy secrets.*
                                        –Hippocratic Oath


*Wishes often exceed what later actually happens.*
                                        –Alexander Solzhenitsyn


*For every complex social problem there's a simple solution that is quick, easy...and wrong.*
                                        –H.L. Mencken

# INTRODUCTION*

Confidentiality is an implicit assumption in every professional relation-ship. We expect that a professional will maintain a professional standard of both ethical conduct and technical competency. The term "professional" derives from the Latin *profitere*, which means to make an oath or vow, to "profess" in the old sincere sense (the word is not rooted in "profit," the making of which we daily witness).

A professional is expected to be a confidant, and a confidant does not divulge confidences. In the words of Lord Riddell, secrecy is an "implied term of a contract for professional or confidential services."[1] Sissela Bok put it thus: "As codes of ethics take form in old and new professions, the duty of confidentiality serves in part to reinforce their claim to professional status, and in part to strengthen their capacity to offer help to clients."[2]

In the fourteenth century, Chaucer observed: "Faith in the doctor is one of the greatest aids to recovery. A doctor should be careful never to betray the secrets of his patients, either men or women, or belittle some to others, for if a man knows that other men's secrets are well kept, he will be the readier to trust you with his own."

The expectation of confidentiality is embedded not only in custom and in the codes of ethics of various professional societies, but also, to some degree, in codes of laws. In some countries, a breach of confidentiality is a violation of the criminal law.[3] In others, it may be the basis of a civil suit or ground for revocation or suspension of license. However, oft-times, the law itself may authorize or require testimony of the professional person in which confidences may be divulged. In the latter case, detriment to the professional relationship or other consequences may ensue.

There are fashions and trends in how or what we keep secret, or hope to keep secret. In 18th-century Europe, in upper-middle class society, people talked about their mistresses much more openly than today, although that appears to be changing. The "sexual revolution" has removed the compul-

---

*For the sake of simplicity, unless the contrary is indicated, the term "psychiatrist" includes psychologists and other mental health professionals, and the masculine includes the feminine. No offense is intended.

sions of secrecy regarding many aspects of sexual behavior (homosexuality, for example, is now more openly acknowledged). Kinsey researchers, after eliciting intimate details of some housewife's sex life, would ask about the husband's salary, and often the answer was, "That's rather personal, isn't it?" A woman, after performing coitus on stage, later that evening is mindful about her dress covering her knee. A person on the beach may wear next to nothing, but not in the center of town. Thus, the claim to secrecy, or privacy, is specific to location and instance.

In a relationship with a physician, a patient assumes that his disclosures will not be passed on to others except for the specific purpose of lending necessary help, and then only with consent. Confidentiality is especially expected of physicians, as the patient submits and bares himself to a physician in the professional relationship unlike in any other. Professor Joseph Grano, a leading authority on constitutional law and criminal procedure, writes:[4]

> Doctors and psychiatrists have traditionally earned the public's trust by respecting the confidences of their patients, and largely because of this trust, a substantial segment of the public will reveal secrets to these professionals that it will not reveal to others. Indeed, some commentators have gone so far as to suggest that the expectations of privacy in these relationships are sufficiently great to justify constitutional protection for private communications.

People generally feel that anything can be said or shown to a doctor. The comedian Jackie Mason quipped that a physician tells a woman to undress and she quickly does so (and a bill is sent to the husband).[5] Literally speaking, the physician is granted admission to body and home. One physician expressed it thus:[6]

> The special thing that the doctor contributes to his community is the care of the sick. For this reason, the physician has been given special privileges through the centuries: he may enter the most private boudoir and indulge in the most searching physical examination, and no stigma of trespass or adultery need arise; he may enter a battlefield or a prison or a dark neighborhood on his professional mission and he should be protected against violence; he enters a house with secrets, and the secrets should be opened to him if they will help in his special healing role. That the privileges carry responsibilities is unarguable.

In the report of the Privacy Protection Study Commission it is observed:[7]

> The physician-patient relationship is an inherently intrusive one in that the patient who wants and needs medical care must grant the doctor virtually unconstrained discretion to delve into the details of his life and his person. As a practical matter, because so much information may be necessary for proper diagnosis and treatment, no area of inquiry is excluded. In addition to describ-

ing the details of his symptoms, the patient may be asked to reveal what he eats, how much he drinks or smokes, whether he uses drugs, how often he has sexual relations and with whom, whether he is depressed or anxious, where and how long he has worked, and perhaps what he does for recreation. Moreover, he is expected to submit to as much direct observation and recording of what is observed as his condition suggests and as the confines of the medical-care setting permit. As the Executive Director of the American Medical Record Association observed to the Commission, "a complete medical record [today] may contain more intimate details about an individual than could be found in any single document."

The patient often feels that the physician, invested with secrets and special data, has gained power over him and his family. The physician has "something on them." The dignity of the patient and his family lies at the mercy of the physician's ethics. Fear of the physician, and especially of the psychiatrist ("the head shrinker"), is therefore easily aroused. Quite often in the media, the psychiatrist is portrayed as mind-controlling or sinister. This fear of the physician or psychiatrist goes back to the time when the physician was, to all intents and purposes, the witch-doctor, the possessor of esoteric knowledge, which gave him power over people. Sherlock Holmes saw the physician as the potential master criminal, with his trained powers turned from good to evil purposes. Hence, the physician must be extraordinarily careful to safeguard confidences entrusted to him. Responsibilities come with intimacy.[8]

The delineation of the responsibility of the physician on confidentiality brings to mind a legend about a stranger who came to Shammai, an interpreter of law, and asked to be taught the entire Torah very quickly, while he was standing on one foot. Shammai chased him away. He went to Hillel, another interpreter of law, who said, "If that is what you wish, so be it. This is the substance of the law: 'Do not do unto others what you do not want them to do unto you.' All the rest is commentary—now go and study."[9]

The classic delineation of the responsibility of the physician on confidentiality is the oath of Hippocrates. It says it all, albeit in a generalization, and all else is a footnote. It is one of the oldest statements of an ethical code, and is still administered, albeit with variations, to graduating classes of most colleges of medicine. In it, the physician pledges that "whatsoever I shall see or hear in the course of my profession, as well as outside my profession in my intercourse with men, if it be what should not be published abroad, I will never divulge, holding such things to be holy secrets."[10] Implicit, in this most popular version of the oath, is that there are matters that should be spoken of abroad. According to this version of the oath, Hippocrates did not consider confidentiality absolute.

Codes of ethics or codes of practice have multiplied in the last decades, not only in the professions but also in business and industry, largely in response to consumer movements and their demand for accountability. The professions call their codes "oaths" or "codes of ethics" or "guidelines," but these terms are virtually interchangeable. Some codes have a "code of conduct" supplementing a code of ethics to give guidance on how a principle should operate in particular situations. In regard confidentiality, many of the grounds for exception to confidentiality are specified in the codes, but they are exceptions to be justified through a process of moral deliberation, and that not all of them can be specified in advance of particular circumstances.[11]

A recent version of the Code of Medical Ethics of the American Medical Association, in a modern restatement of that part of the Hippocratic oath relating to professional confidence, states: "A physician may not reveal the confidence entrusted to him in the course of his medical attendance, or the deficiencies he may observe in the character of his patients, unless he is required to do so by law, or unless it becomes necessary in order to protect the welfare of the community."[12]

The World Medical Association, in 1949, published an ethical principle which omitted any condition on absolute secrecy by the physician. It provided: "A doctor owes to his patient absolute secrecy on all which has been confided to him or which he knows because of the confidence entrusted to him." In an interpretive statement made in 1954, the WMA stated: "Professional secrecy by its very nature must be absolute. It must be observed in all cases. A secret which is shared is no longer a secret. Exceptions to the rule of professional secrecy can be made only in special cases such as reporting the incidence of epidemic or communicable diseases."

The World Psychiatric Association in its Declaration of Madrid in 1996 stated: "Information obtained in the therapeutic relationship should be kept in confidence and used, only and exclusively, for the purpose of improving the mental health of the patient. Psychiatrists are prohibited from making use of such information for personal reasons, or financial or academic benefits. Breach of confidentiality may only be appropriate when serious physical or mental harm to the patient or to a third person could ensue if confidentiality were maintained; in these circumstances, psychiatrists should whenever possible, first advise the patient about the action to be taken." The Declaration follows the Declaration of Hawaii in 1977 and the Declaration of Vienna in 1983.

In a "Bill of Rights for Patients Undergoing Mental Health Treatment" drafted in 1996 by various mental health associations, it is stated: "Patients shall be guaranteed the confidentiality of their relationship with their mental health professional except when ethics and good clinical judgment and/or law dictate otherwise to assure their safety or the safety of others."[13] It is the "otherwise" or exceptions that give rise to controversy.

As commonly understood, secrecy or privacy is necessary to spare shame and humiliation. Some phenomena are intrinsically private affairs, which cannot be displayed publicly without alteration, adulteration, or violation.[14]

But Suzanne Brogger writes, "Let us abolish private life."[15] And in Mike Leigh's prize-winning film "Secrets and Lies," Maurice, the portrait photographer, bemoans, "Secrets are lies. Why the secrets? Why can't we share our pain?" And, it is to be especially noted, the professional's urging of confidentiality allegedly on behalf of patients is often a facade to serve self-interest.[16]

In the trial of cases, jurors are sworn to secrecy regarding their deliberations, and the law protects them from all investigation and inquiry "as fully as the temple authorities protected the priestess who spoke to the suppliant votary at the shrine."[17] The author of a book on his experience as a law clerk to the U.S. Supreme Court says about the constraint of confidentiality: "Much of what goes on with the Supreme Court must be kept in confidence if the spirit of frank and informal exchange there is to continue to prevail. The need for such confidence in the Court's deliberations will always be important, and I have tried in every instance to respect it."[18]

In the history of the law, privacy as a concept developed in the latter part of the 19th century. According to French social historian Philippe Ariès, the origin of privacy is closely linked to the breakup of large households. There was little room for privacy in communal living. The concept developed during the industrial age, and reflects an alienation and isolation of that style of life. With the breakup of communal living, the existential situation imposed privacy on people, then it was used as a protective device, and became a treasured value. In a way, the group therapy process is a form of communal living where there is little privacy among its members, and privacy is not valued. Outside the group, however, isolation and privacy prevail. Group therapy is thus tribal in nature—both inclusive and exclusive—trusting those within the group and not those outside.[19]

In a number of decisions, the Supreme Court has said that the "right to privacy" is a fundamental right, implicitly enshrined in the Constitution, and on that right many other rights are being based. An increasing number of decisions have been based on the right to privacy. For example, the Supreme Court in 1973 determined that the "right to privacy" is "broad enough to encompass a woman's decision whether or not to terminate her pregnancy." The Court categorized the right as fundamental, and therefore could only be infringed upon if a state could demonstrate a "compelling interest" in regulating the activity. The central citadels of privacy are said by many to be marriage, the relation of client and attorney, penitent and priest, and patient and physician; and if the law does not protect them, then, *a fortiori*, it is claimed, little of human privacy would warrant protection.

With certain exceptions, no duty is imposed on a therapist to report to law enforcement officials.[20] Like any other citizen, a therapist is not obliged to be an informer. In the absence of a special relationship, there is no duty to rescue. Thus, a man may decline with impunity to aid another dying from an overdose of sleeping pills.[21] Likewise, an individual who overhears a plan to rob a store or knowing of the danger of rape in an area is under no duty to warn even though the individual may be uniquely positioned and could offer help without any risk to his own safety. However, under the law of torts, the duty of care owed by a therapist to his patient has been expanded to include individuals who might be harmed by the patient.

For the general welfare of society, the law, in certain matters, demands that the physician under penalty come forward and make known his patient's condition. Most of the conditions under which the law requires exposure involve matters related to public health or crime. In the area of public health, statutes in many states impose a positive legal duty on the physician to report cancer, contagious and infectious diseases, epilepsy, drug addiction, tuberculosis, and to file certificates of death or stillbirth along with such medical data as can be furnished. These laws are considered to be in full accord with the doctor's professional role of healing the sick. The doctor's duty to heal the sick implies an obligation to prevent others from becoming ill. Thus, a physician who faces a food handler with typhoid fever sees no conflict in ethical standards in reporting the danger to the appropriate authority.

A conflict may occur between the physician's professional duty to his patient and his role as a citizen. In matters relating to crime, the physician has a duty, as a citizen, to render aid and assistance in enforcing the criminal laws. Beyond this duty, several states have statutes specifically requiring physicians who treat persons suffering an injury which may have been received in an unlawful manner to report the facts to the police. Most physicians feel that compliance with these specific laws is not a violation of medical ethics. The rationale behind this is the public's awareness in such cases of the physician's legal responsibility to make a report.

But suppose there is no specific law requiring a report. What if a subpoena is issued or an investigator appears demanding the disclosure of information that was considered confidential by both physician and patient? There are many exceptions to the rules of confidentiality and privileged communication. There is no liability for invasion of the right to privacy or for defamation when a physician does that which the law requires.[22] Compliance is also in accord with official medical ethics of the American Medical Association, which provides that confidences entrusted to a physician shall be revealed when disclosure is required by law.

The privilege not to make disclosure in a legal proceeding is, generally speaking, a right existing only by statute. If there is such a statute, a patient may prevent his physician from testifying about his treatment and the disclosures which are an integral part of it, or the patient may oblige the physician to disclose.

Outside the judicial process, even in the absence of testimonial privilege, society has a strong interest in protecting confidentiality. For example, society may wish to assure the personal development of individuals by safeguarding confidential discussions with career advisors or teachers, though these relationships traditionally have not enjoyed a testimonial privilege. Society also has an interest in promoting relationships beneficial to commerce. Thus it may seek to protect the confidentiality of bank records. The Alabama Supreme Court aptly stated that "whether or not testimony may be barred at trial does not necessarily control the issue of liability for unauthorized extra-judicial disclosures."[23] A mnemonic device distinguishes testimonial privilege and the duty of confidentiality of a clinician (or other professional): PRivilege is the Patient's Right; COnfidentiality is the Clinician's Obligation.

In the legal process witnesses are called to establish facts, or to challenge or refute testimony of another witness, or to offer character evidence about a litigant or witness. In any of these situations, a mental health professional may be called as a fact witness or as an expert. A fact witness testifies on the basis of personal knowledge about the issues in the case. Thus, a clinician may be called to testify about a patient's condition before or after an alleged traumatic event. An expert may testify not only on the basis of personal knowledge but also on the basis of information provided by others or on the basis of an investigation or a hypothetical question. In addition, the expert may draw conclusions from the data and is compensated for his participation as a witness. The expert witness usually appears voluntarily. Attorneys often try to get a therapist involved as a witness so as to avoid the expense of getting and paying for an examination.[24]

## NOTES

1. "The Law and Ethics of Medical Confidence," *Lancet*, 1927, p. 4.
2. S. Bok, "The Limits of Confidentiality," *Hastings Center Report*, Feb. 1983, p. 24; adapted from her book *Secrets* (New York: Pantheon Books, 1982).
3. Arkansas is one state making disclosure of a patient's confidence a crime. Ark. Stat. Ann. (1974) 72-516.
4. J.D. Grano, *Confessions, Truth, and the Law* (Ann Arbor: University of Michigan Press, 1993), p. 111.
5. Unauthorized persons in the presence of the undressing gives rise to a cause of concern. In DeMay v. Roberts, 9 N.W. 146 (Mich. 1881), a case which has since come to stand for the right to privacy, a physician brought a young man without medical qualifications to the plaintiff's home to assist him while the plaintiff gave birth. The assistant's lack of training was not disclosed;

hence the court held that the plaintiff's consent to his presence and touching of her was invalid to bar a tort action. A person of reasonable sensibilities tolerates more from qualified medical professionals or intimate friends than from strangers.

6. V. Sidel, "Confidential Information and The Physician," *New Eng. J. of Med.* 264:1133, 1961.

7. Report of the Privacy Protection Study Commision, *Personal Privacy in an Information Society* (Washington, D.C.: U.S. Govt. Ptg. Off., 1977), p. 282.

8. One of Woody Allen's recurring story ideas, according to a book about the film-maker, involves a man who eavesdrops on a woman's psychotherapy sessions through thin walls between offices or a similar inadvertent opportunity. Armed with secret knowledge of her intimate fantasies and desires, he contrives to meet her and become her "dream lover." Once when he tried this concept in a film script a few years ago, however, Allen "began to question the eavesdropping idea on grounds of taste," writes Julian Fox in *Woody: Movies from Manhattan* (Woodstock, N.Y.: Overlook Press, 1996), "since, even in the most benign Chaplinesque way it seemed wrong." But this story line drives Allen's recent movie, "Everyone Says I Love You." The eavesdropper is not the man in question but his daughter, who peers through a peephole at a therapy patient and relays the secrets to her father, who has women troubles. They meet, and he beguiles her with his uncanny capacity to do the right thing and they become lovers, but then she tires of him because he is so predictablty perfect in anticipating her wishes. R. Sklar, "Woody Allen's True Confections," *Forward,* Dec. 6, 1996, p. 15.

9. E. Wiesel, *Sages and Dreamers* (New York: Simon & Schuster, 1991), p. 169.

10. The addition "as well as outside my profession in my intercourse with men" is worthy of note. The physician must not gossip, no matter how or where the subject matter for gossip may have been acquired; whether it be in practice or in private life makes no difference. Hippocrates appears to have been instructing physicians to restrict the dissemination of information to professional purposes.

11. M. Coady & S. Bloch, *Codes of Ethics and the Professions* (Melbourne: Melbourne University Press, 1996).

12. The American Medical Assocaition in Section 4 of its current "Principles of Medical Ethics" states: "A physician shall respect the rights of patients, of colleagues and of other health professionals, and shall safeguard patient confidences within the constraints of the law."

13. H.I. Eist, "From the Presidency/Interdisciplinary Meetings," *Psychiatric News,* July 19, 1996, p. 3. There is, however, divided opinion about secrets. Following Watergate, it has been said that all secrets are bad secrets. Considering that disclosure is salutary in the political arena in order to maintain representative or accountable government, the justification of a shield in other areas is questioned as well. The advertisement of a laundry soil and stain remover, *Shout,* said it "will get out stains you couldn't get out before." It is time, those who are opposed to secrets say, that we be shown

for what we are—warts and all.

14. C.D. Schneider, *Shame, Exposure, and Privacy* (New York: W.W. Norton, 1992; originally published: Boston: Beacon Press, 1977).

15. *Deliver Us From Love* (New York: Delacorte, 1976). See also S.C. Heilman, *Synagogue Life* (Chicago: University of Chicago, 1976); R. Bar-Levav, "The Stigma of Seeing a Psychiatrist,": *Amer. J. Psychotherapy* 30:473, 1976; D. Gould, "To Hell With Medical Secrecy!" *New Statesman*, March 3, 1967, p. 290; G. Medini & E.H. Rosenberg, "Gossip and Psychotherapy," *Amer. J. Psychotherapy* 30:473, 1976; J. Morgan, "The Case for Gossip," *New Statesman*, Sept. 24, 1965, p. 433.

16. H.C. Modlin, "How Private is Privacy?" *Psychiat. Digest*, Feb. 1969, p. 13. For discussion, see Part V, Chapter 2.

17. Skidmore v. Baltimore & O.R.R., 167 F.2d 54, 60 (2d Cir.), *cert. denied*, 335 U.S. 816 (1948).

18. J.H. Wilkerson, *Serving Justice: A Supreme Court Clerk's View* (New York: Charterhouse, 1974), p. xiii. He notes further: "The Supreme Court is remarkable in the extent to which it takes law clerks into its trust" (p. 40).

19. The more one feels in danger, the more one is wary, the more one demands privacy. One may note the parallels between contemporary man and the timid and furtive savage of primitive society. The savage feared revelation of his name; contemporary man fears a psychiatric label. The savage feared the witch doctor; contemporary man fears his colleagues. In Joseph Heller's novel *Something Happened* each of the 120 people in the office is depicted as afraid of the other 119. Savage man was enmeshed in a nightmare of fears; so too is contemporary man. Disaster films – "Jaws," "Towering Inferno" "Earthquake," "Two Minute Warning"– apparently touched a responsive chord and reflected contemporary man's state of fear and trembling. With a few changes in terminology, one would think that a description of primitive man is that of contemporary man. See J.G. Frazer, *The Golden Bough* (New York: Macmillan, 1960); see also H. Smith, *The Russians* (New York: Quadrangle, 1976), p. 801.

20. In the public interest, physicians are obliged to report communicable diseases (*e.g.*, venereal diseases), medical disability related to possible criminal behavior (gunshot and knife wounds, possession of narcotics), and child abuse. During the McCarthy period, the Federal Bureau of Investigation requested psychiatrists to report subversive activities and sentiments of their patients; and today, the F.B.I. sends out notices to medical clinics on wanted criminals soliciting information on their whereabouts.

21. People v. Beardsley, 150 Mich. 206, 113 N.W. 1128 (1907).

22. Boyd v. Wynn, 150 S.W.2d 648 (Ky. 1941).

23. Horne v. Patton, 291 Ala. 701, 287 So.2d 824 (1973).

24. For an overview, see M. Smithbell & W.J. Winslade, "Privacy, Confidentiality, and Privilege in Psychotherapeutic Relationships," *Am. J. Orthopsychiat.* 64:180, 1994.

# ACKNOWLEDGMENTS

It seems that it was just yesterday, but it was in the early 1960s when my friend Dr. Gene L. Usdin of New Orleans suggested that I write an article on psychiatry and testimonial privilege. That initiated my interest in the topic; then followed a small book and other articles on the topic.

In the years that followed, Dr. Maurice Grossman asked that I serve on the American Psychiatric Association's task force on confidentiality which he chaired. Thereafter, until his recent passing, we had many interesting conversations about confidentiality. He made physician-patient confidentiality one of his causes as a long-time psychiatrist on the Stanford faculty. He testified regularly before Congress on the need to protect confidentiality. He was critical of the landmark *Tarasoff* ruling in 1976 of the California Supreme Court that as a matter of law a psychotherapist must reveal a patient's threats. He contended that the ruling was unnecessary. He said, "If there is danger and the psychotherapist knows it, he is not violating any code by a warning and common sense would dictate such a warning." This book is dedicated to Dr. Grossman.

For reading drafts of earlier versions and offering suggestions, I want to thank Dr. Joseph Fischoff, Julie Hathaway, David Palmiere, Dr. Sara Feldman-Schorrig, and Professor Daniel W. Shuman. I am immensely grateful to Dr. Abraham L. Halpern, professor emeritus at New York Medical College and a past president of the American Academy of Psychiatry and Law. Dr. Halpern has an acute ability for noting omissions and catching miscues and I have benefited from his talent.

I am grateful to Dr. Elliot Luby, my colleague at Wayne State University, for our interesting discussions through the years.

I want to thank Dr. Raman N. Bhavsar, Director of Psychiatric Education at Northville Psychiatric Hospital, for his many invitations to me to discuss with members of the staff the issue of confidentiality as well as other issues in psychiatry and law.

Portions of this book are adapted and revised from articles I have published in professional journals. Personal communications are quoted with permission as are the drawings that appear herein.

I want also to thank the staff of the Wayne State University Law Library for their helpful assistance in obtaining articles and books.

I will never be able to adequately thank my secretary, Ms. Lorraine Lorenger. Through the years, Ms. Lorenger has been most dependable and gracious in her assistance. I also want to thank Ms. Paula Green for her secretarial assistance.

R.S.

# CONTENTS

Page

*Introduction*                                                    vii

*Acknowledgments*                                                xvii

## PART I - TESTIMONIAL PRIVILEGED COMMUNICATION

Chapter 1.    Relational Privileges in General                     5

Chapter 2.    The Medical Privilege and Its Criticisms            16

Chapter 3.    Restrictions on the Medical Privilege               25

Chapter 4.    The Case for Psychotherapy                          35

Chapter 5.    Misguided Hope in Psychotherapist-                  57
              Patient Privilege

## PART II - PSYCHOTHERAPY AND PRIVILEGE PROBLEMS

Chapter 1.    Therapists Under the Privilege                      79

Chapter 2.    Divorce and Alienation of Affections               91

Chapter 3.    Child Custody                                      106

Chapter 4.    Tort Cases                                         115

Chapter 5.    Identity of Patient                                139

Chapter 6.    Criminal Cases                                     150

Chapter 7.    Proceedings to Hospitalize                         186

Chapter 8.    Hospital and Office Records                        191

Chapter 9.    Group Therapy                                      200

              Interview of Group on Confidentiality             219

## PART III - TERMINATION OF PRIVILEGE

Chapter 1.    Waiver of Privilege                                239

Chapter 2.    The Self-defense Exception                         251

## PART IV - PSYCHOTHERAPY AND CONFIDENTIALITY

| Chapter 1. | Introduction | 259 |
| Chapter 2. | Jeopardy to Patient or Others | 270 |
| Chapter 3. | "Very Important Persons" | 342 |
| Chapter 4. | Teaching and Writing | 359 |
| Chapter 5. | Treatment of Minors and Young Adults | 386 |
| Chapter 6. | Hospital Care, Supervision and Research | 403 |
| Chapter 7. | Communications to Nonmedical Persons in Response to Inquiries | 412 |
| Chapter 8. | Fee Collection | 435 |
| Chapter 9. | Consent to Release of Information | 439 |

## PART V - RECORDKEEPING AND ACCOUNTABILITY

| Chapter 1. | Recordkeeping | 449 |
| Chapter 2. | Accountability and Abuse of Confidentiality | 481 |
| Chapter 3. | The Stigma of Psychiatric Discourse | 503 |

## PART VI - EVIDENTIAL VALUE OF THERAPIST VERSUS FORENSIC EXPERT TESTIMONY — 521

## CONCLUSION — 545

Appendix

| Statutes on Medical and Psychotherapy Privilege | 559 |
| Oral Argument in U.S. Supreme Court in *Jaffee v. Redmond* | 565 |
| U.S. Supreme Court Decision in *Jaffee v. Redmond* | 587 |

Indices

| *Table of Cases* | 603 |
| *Name Index* | 611 |
| *Subject Index* | 627 |

*About the Author* — 639

# PSYCHOTHERAPY AND CONFIDENTIALITY

# Part I

# TESTIMONIAL PRIVILEGED COMMUNICATION

Chapter 1. Relational Privileges in General
Chapter 2. The Medical Privilege and Its Criticisms
Chapter 3. Restrictions on the Medical Privilege
Chapter 4. The Case for Psychotherapy
Chapter 5. Misguided Hope in Psychotherapist-
        Patient Privilege

# Chapter 1

# RELATIONAL PRIVILEGES IN GENERAL

Evidence is the basis for justice. It is the very essence of a fair trial. Unless judge and jury have all of the relevant evidence, the decision will be based on a distorted presentation of the facts. The law, therefore, gives to the tribunal the power to summon witnesses and to make them answer, as a rule, any question. The only specific exception provided in the Constitution is the privilege not to give evidence against oneself.

A full and fair trial, however, is impossible to achieve as a matter of practice. There are always difficulties in carrying out the ideal. One might consider the difficulties involved in arranging an ordinary meeting or conference; such difficulties are multiplied in arranging a trial. For example, material witnesses may be unavailable or dead. Cases may be frequently postponed or continued for so long that the memory of many of the available witnesses has dimmed. In view of this, when relevant and material evidence is also excluded for whatever reason, there remains even less basis for a decision.

Without an explicit constitutional mandate, the courts and the legislatures have allowed witnesses to keep secret evidence acquired through certain confidential relationships. These so-called confidential communication or relational privileges (because they derogate from the duty of the witness to disclose matters within his knowledge) are granted only "when some competing public policy is considered to be more important than disclosing the information."[1] The U.S. Supreme Court admonished that privileges "are not lightly created nor expansively construed, for they are in derogation of the search for truth."[2] Privileges permit the exclusion of relevant evidence, on the theory that the search for truth is not as important as some other social value which is served by suppressing the evidence. Some years ago Raymond Peters, Associate Justice of the California Supreme Court, observed:[3]

The search for truth is the basic aim of our law. Truth, like motherhood, should be sacrosanct. Yet the law, in many of its rules of evidence, treats the search for the truth in a cavalier fashion and as being far from sacred. Many rules of evidence result in the suppression rather than in the ascertainment of the truth. Nowhere is this better demonstrated than in the field of the testimonial privileges afforded several relationships. Every testimonial privilege afforded a party or witness necessarily and inevitably results in the suppression of material and relevant, and in some cases of basic, facts. Thus any testimonial privilege constitutes a legislatively created barrier to the search for truth. The public policy behind some of these privileges is so apparent and basic that it outweighs the public policy behind the unfettered search for the truth. But as to other testimonial privileges the public policy behind them is not so apparent or basic. The existence or continuance of such privileges presents a highly debatable and controversial question.

As any book on evidence will point out, the law is concerned not only with truth but also with the manner of its ascertainment. The Supreme Court has rendered innumerable decisions based on this philosophy. For example, the law excludes evidence obtained by illegal search and seizure or by a coerced confession. The proper administration of justice involves the rejection of relevant evidence when its reception would be unduly offensive to contemporary public opinion. Hence, as public opinion changes, that which was the subject of privilege at one time may not necessarily be privileged at a different time.

A privilege of nondisclosure applies in all states to communications (and observations) between a client and his attorney; to communications between husband and wife; in some jurisdictions to communications between a penitent and priest; and between patient and physician. In recent years, the number of privileges has increased. Journalists, broadcasting and television newscasters, accountants, social workers, detectives, "confidential" clerks, and trust companies have succeeded, in a number of states, in obtaining special legislation granting a privilege to their professional relationships. The counseling profession believes that a privilege should also be established for secondary school and college counseling personnel.

Architects feel the same way about their professional role. Scientists and investigators ask for privileged communication in research. They say, "Freedom of scholarship (to investigate) without fear to the investigated is of paramount importance."[4] The sex researcher A.C. Kinsey, in order to obtain the confidence of his subjects, developed elaborate techniques, including the development of a code with the guidance of an experienced cryptographer.[5] Kinsey stated:[6]

> If we were brought before a court we would have to hope that such precedents would be extended to scientists involved in the investigation of such a subject

as human sex behavior. If the courts of all levels were to refuse to recognize such a privilege, there would be no alternative but to destroy our complete body of records and accept the consequences of such defiance of the courts. If law enforcement officials, students of law, and persons interested in social problems want scientific assistance in understanding such problems, they will have to recognize a scientist's right to maintain the absolute confidence of his records; for without that it would be impossible to persuade persons to contribute to this sort of study.

Even call girls, when questioned by law enforcement officials, declare roundly: "It's a matter of honor that you don't name your clients. My business depends on trust. It takes a long time to build up a clientele of standing." When $200-an-hour call girl Sherry Rowlands told the tabloid *Star* about her affair with President Clinton's chief campaign adviser, Dick Morris, Margo St. James, a member of a new association of sex professionals in San Francisco, said, "Most hookers have a code of ethics—they wouldn't run to the *Star*. If she were in our guild, she would be censured. I'd suspend her for ten days."[7] William Safire of the *New York Times* commented that by breaching confidentiality she gave prostitution a bad name.[8]

Obviously, if all groups desiring a privilege were granted one, little evidence would remain in the trial of a case. The right to a fair trial includes the right to have a witness disclose matters which are relevant to the determination of the issue. It is true that guarantees of confidence are vital to the achievement of the purposes of certain relationships. The crucial question, however, is whether the expected injury to the relationship through fear of later disclosure in court is greater than the expected benefit to justice in obtaining the testimony. The problem is establishing the line separating the privileged from the non-privileged.

In answer to the various professional groups seeking a confidential communication privilege, the late Dean John Wigmore of the Northwestern University School of Law, renowned for his work on evidence, formulated four conditions which should be satisfied in order to warrant creating a class of privileged communications. These criteria are oft-quoted. They are:[9]

(1) Does the communication in the usual circumstances of the given professional relation originate in a confidence that it will not be disclosed?
(2) Is the inviolability of that confidence essential to the achievement of the purpose of the relationship?
(3) Is the relation one that should be fostered?
(4) Is the expected injury to the relation, through the fear of later disclosure, greater than the expected benefit to justice in obtaining the testimony?

Wigmore's criteria are concerned with the general rather than the particular case. That is, they determine whether a privilege should be adopted for a given professional relationship as, for example, the physician-patient relationship. The determination of whether an individual or communication in a particular case falls under an enacted privilege depends upon its scope, as interpreted by the court.

Justifying a privilege for the legal profession is the social good derived from the proper function of attorneys acting for their clients. It is believed to outweigh the harm that may come from the suppression of evidence in specific cases. It is said to promote freedom of consultation with legal advisers. A client would tend to keep secret from his counsel anything that might appear to him to be unfavorable to the case if the attorney could be required to disclose the communications. The confidential communication privilege plays a more important role in civil cases than in criminal cases, as pretrial discovery procedures are usually not allowed in criminal cases.

The purpose of the confidential communications privilege for husband and wife is allegedly to promote confidence between the spouses by assuring them that their communications will never be revealed without their consent. During a marriage, when the spouses are in harmony, one spouse will presumably not wish to testify against the other. However, when marital problems or separation or divorce occur, a spouse feeling vindictive may wish to reveal confidential communications made during the marriage. The husband-wife privilege protects against such disclosure and to that extent promotes the marital relation. It assures others in marriage that anything said between them during the marriage remains inviolate: once privileged, always privileged.[10]

At common law a spouse was deemed incompetent to testify either for or against the other (the rule was based on the idea of family unity); it was not until the incompetency of a spouse to testify was removed that legislation was passed making confidential communications between husband and wife privileged.[11] The privilege is inapplicable in proceedings between the parties such as divorce or where one spouse is charged with a crime or tort against the person or property of the other or a minor child of either.[12] In the case of all privileges, they do not apply as far as necessary in resolving a dispute between the parties to the privilege.

The First Amendment of the United States Constitution on the free exercise of religion is said to justify the protection afforded the priest-penitent communication. Secrecy is essential to a religious confessional system. However, the privilege of nondisclosure was not extended to the priest-penitent relationship by the common law of England. The antipathy of the English courts to the Roman Catholic Church prevented the priest-penitent privilege from ever becoming a part of the common law. Many states, by statute, have changed the common law rule, but even without such legislation, a discreet practitioner would hesitate before putting a priest to a claim of privilege.[13]

Legislation providing a penitential privilege, where it exists, typically provides that a priest "shall not without the consent of the party making the confession, be allowed to disclose a confession made to him in his professional character in the course of discipline enjoined by the rules or practice of the religious body to which he belongs." The courts have held that this privilege is not limited to Roman Catholic priests, but applies to all who may stand as spiritual representatives of their churches. Pastoral counseling, which to some extent has been supplanted by psychiatry, relies on secrecy of communication.[14]

On numerous occasions, newsmen have urged protection against testimonial compulsion as a necessary safeguard for the preservation of the freedom of the press. It is said that effective news-gathering depends largely on the preservation of the confidential sources of information.[15] However, many policy considerations have been expressed in opposition to this privilege. Gallup observed that "the protection of an innocent person from slander and libel by unscrupulous newsmen seems more compelling in the public interest than the protection of equally unscrupulous informants." A study by the American Civil Liberties Union concluded that "the legislative approach in this field is neither necessary nor at the present time desirable."

The enactment of some of the newer privileges in the law of evidence is said to be the result of efforts of organized occupational groups to obtain special legislation. Some groups feel that it is an unfair discrimination against their profession if secrets of other professions are protected from disclosure in court while their secrets must be revealed. In reply to such demands, it may well be said that the administration of justice cannot be influenced by interprofessional jealousies.

In 1960, a report of the Group for the Advancement of Psychiatry (GAP) made a recommendation of privilege for psychiatrists; it did not argue on behalf of psychologists, social workers, counselors, or other psychotherapists. Through lobbying efforts of their own, psychologists and social workers in a number of states have obtained a privilege as part of their licensing or certification law.

The fact that a communication is made in confidence is not enough for privilege, though Judge Henry Edgerton of the D.C. Court of Appeals in 1958 recommended that "a communication made in reasonable confidence that it will not be disclosed, and in such circumstances that disclosure is shocking to the moral sense of the community, should not be disclosed in a judicial proceeding, whether the trusted person is or is not a wife, husband, doctor, lawyer, or minister."[16]

That view has not prevailed as a matter of law, but it was raised again in 1996 during oral argument in *Jaffee v. Redmond* (hereinafter discussed). In that case the U.S. Supreme Court considered issues involving confidential relations and privileged communications, to wit: (1) Do the Federal Rules of Civil Procedure provide trial judges with adequate tools to protect privacy interests involved in confidential communications with a psychotherapist without creation of new evidentiary psychotherapist-patient privilege under the Federal Rules of Evidence? (2) Should any privilege for psychotherapist-patient communications be extended to social workers, rather than being limited to psychiatrists and clinical psychologists? (3) Should a psychotherapist-patient privilege be recognized in federal law, and, if so, what would be the scope of the privilege?

In the course of oral argument, Justice Scalia asked: "If somebody comes up to me and, let's say, my nephew comes up to me and says, you know, Unc, I want to tell you something in strictest confidence, and I say yes, you tell me that, I promise you I won't tell this to anybody. Is that enough that I've undertaken a duty of confidentiality to justify the creation of a privilege?" And Justice Breyer asked whether there is any reason in logic or policy to distinguish between physicians who treat physical problems and psychotherapists.

The Supreme Court, by 7-2, recognized a psychotherapist-patient privilege in federal law. Justice Scalia dissented and suggested that people would be better advised to seek advice from their mothers than from psychiatrists, yet there is no mother-child privilege.[17] Justice Scalia wrote, "When is it, one must wonder, that the psychotherapist came to play such an indispensable role in the maintenance of the citizenry's mental health? For most of history, men and women have worked out their difficulties by talking to, *inter alios*, parents, siblings, best friends and bartenders—none of whom was awarded a privilege against testifying in court. Ask the average citizen: Would your mental health be more significantly impaired by preventing you from seeing a psychotherapist, or by preventing you from getting advice from your mom? I have little doubt what the answer would be. Yet there is no mother-child privilege."[18] He contended that the privilege would interfere with the truth-finding function of the courts and cause the courts "to become themselves the instruments of wrong."[19]

While Judge Edgerton's suggestion fell on deaf ears when he made it, probably because it was subject to abuse, something like it held sway centuries ago. In the book *How the Irish Saved Civilization*, Thomas Cahill points out:[20]

> The Irish developed a form of confession that was exclusively private and that had no equivalent on the continent. In the ancient church, confession of one's sins...had always been public. Sin was thought to be a public matter, or crime against the church...

The Irish innovation was to make all confession a completely private affair between penitent and priest...This adaptation did away with public humiliation out of tenderness for the sinner's feelings....

One did not necessarily choose one's "priest" from ordained professionals: the act of confession was too personal and too important for such a limitation. One looked for an *anmchara*, a soul-friend, someone to be trusted over a whole lifetime. Thus, the oft-found saying "anyone without a soul-friend is like a body without a head," which dates from pagan times.

In recent decades, proposals have been made for a privilege not for certain popularly labeled professions such as "psychiatrists," "psychologists," or "social workers," but rather for a privilege to protect the performance of a particular type of function when exercised by "duly qualified persons."[21] Increasingly, just as in matters of insurance or licensing, it is asked: Is there justification for extending privilege status to one profession and denying it to another that is functionally accomplishing the same thing? Where, as a practical matter, would the line be drawn? For group therapy, would it be limited to groups conducted by a licensed or certified therapist, or by the size of the group?

In defining the therapist, it is pertinent to note that, according to the National Association for Mental Health, groups of barbers, beauticians, bartenders, taxi drivers, and other occupations in social listening posts have set out informal curricula to sensitize their members to the mental health needs of their patrons.[22] The hairdresser may be the closest confidant; says one hairdresser, "With me, women really let their hair down."[23] To be sure, divulging of confidences is not vital in cosmetology, as it is in psychotherapy, nor does it deal with deep-seated conflicts, but therapy of a sort takes place.

Today, among various treatment modalities, there is "music therapy," "art therapy," "poetry therapy," "dance therapy," "recreation therapy," "occupational therapy," and "horticultural therapy," indicating therapy may arise out of a myriad of activities. Where to draw the line? Assuredly, under Wigmore's criteria, the Mafia would not be covered, though its get-togethers may be therapeutic for its members. Privileges do not shield the planning of antisocial activities.

In his dissent, Justice Scalia accused the majority of ignoring the "traditional judicial preference for the truth" by creating a privilege for psychotherapy. For Justice Scalia, access to "the truth" is more important than protecting confidentiality in psychotherapy. He was not impressed that various professional organizations filed amicus briefs supporting the privilege, including the American Psychiatric Association and the American Psychoanalytic Association. He said, "There is no self-interested organization out there devoted to pursuit of the truth in federal courts."[24] Is there, though, "a silent majority" out there (to paraphrase President Nixon) to support a privilege? And should that be a reason for a decision?

# NOTES

1.  The following quotation from Wigmore sets out the philosophy of the law: For more than three centuries it has now been recognized as a funda- mental maxim that the public (in the words sanctioned by Lord Hardwicke) has a right to every man's evidence. When we come to examine the various claims of exemption, we start with the primary assumption that there is a general duty to give what testimony one is capable of giving, and that any exemptions which may exist are dis- tinctly exceptional, being so many derogations from a positive gene- ral rule...The investigation of truth and the enforcement of testimoni- al duty demand the restriction, not the expansion, of these privileges. They should be recognized only within the narrowest limits required by principle. Every step beyond these limits helps to provide, without any real necessity, an obstacle to the administration of justice. J.Wigmore, *Evidence in Trials at Common Law* (Boston: Little, Brown, 3d ed. 1940), J. McNaughton rev. ed. 1961, vol. 8, § 2192, pp. 64, 67, hereinafter cited as *Evidence.*
2.  United States v. Nixon, 418 U.S. 683, 710 (1974).
3.  Book review, *Calif. L. Rev.* 47:783, 1959.
4.  Typically, writers or researchers promise confidentiality to their informants. For example, here's an author's query: "For a book about sexual abuse, I am looking for letters that victims have written, or are willing to write, to their abusers. Confidentiality is assured." *New York Times Book Review,* June 18, 1995, p. 21. See R.N. Butler, "Privileged Communication and Confidentiality in Research," *Arch. Gen. Psychiat.* 8:139, 1963; R.D. Schwartz, "Field Experimentation in Sociolegal Research," *J. Legal Ed.* 13:401, 1961.
5.  Sex researcher Gene Abel's techniques for preserving confidentiality are set out in G.G. Abel & J.L. Rouleau, "The Nature and Extent of Sexual Assault," in W.L. Marshall, D.R. Laws & H.E. Barbaree (eds.), *Handbook of Sexual Assault* (New York: Plenum Press, 1990), and, he has stated, he stores his records on a Caribbean island.
6.  A.C. Kinsey, W.B. Pomeroy & C.E. Martin, *Sexual Behavior in the Human Male* (Philadelphia: Saunders, 1948), p. 47.
7.  "Quotable," *Chicago Tribune,* Sept. 1, 1996, p. 6. See also A. Mitchell, "Ex- Aide to Clinton Rejects Defeat," *New York Times,* Sept. 2, 1996, p. 8.
8.  W. Safire, "Morris vs. Clinton," *New York Times,* Sept.12, 1996, p. 19. Michael Thomas of the *New York Observer* said, "If you can't trust a hooker, who can you trust?" M.M. Thomas, "Nowadays, You Just Can't Trust a Hooker Any- more!", *New York Observer,* Sept. 16, 1996, p. 1.

9.   J. Wigmore, *Evidence*, vol. 8, § 2285.

10.  This privilege does not cover the situation in which one or other of the spouses consults a physician, clergyman or marriage counselor with regard to his or her matrimonial problems; it covers only direct communications between husband and wife.

11.  C.L. Black, "The Marital and Physician Privileges–A Reprint of a Letter to a Congressman," *Duke L.J.* 1975:51; M.C. Regan, "Spousal Privilege and the Meanings of Marriage," *Va. L. Rev.* 81:2044, 1995. In ancient law a person could not give testimony which would disgrace his master. In Japan, a person can be prohibited from testifying about that which would bring disgrace to any member of his family (within the third degree) .

12.  Trammel v. United States, 445 U.S. 40, 46 n. 7 (1980).

13.  In Oregon, a 20-year-old suspected of murdering three children asked, in jail, to see a priest. The suspect told the priest he wished to make a confession, the priest recited the introductory rites, heard the man's confession, granted (contingent) absolution, and left. The prosecutor taped the exchange and announced his intention to present it to the grand jury. The archdiocese cited an Oregon statute that all exchanges between priests and their consultants are confidential. The attorney general cited another statute that all conversations except those between lawyers and their clients can be recorded, even if surreptitiously. William Buckley wrote, "This is an absolutely clear-cut case that justifies civil disobedience....A movement should instantly be organized in Oregon to impeach and disbar the district attorney." W.F. Buckley (syndicated column), "Priestly confessions are sacred–even in prison," *Detroit Free Press*, May 16, 1996, p. 11. A month later the district attorney apologized for recording the confession and asked that the tape be sealed. "An Inmate's Talk With a Priest, Taped Secretly, Is Repudiated," *New York Times*, May 24, 1996, p. C-20.

14.  A pastoral counselor had this to say:
     In the course of my ministry, I have been sought out by many men, women, and youths, both members of the churches in the communities where I served, and non-members, who in trouble sought the aid, comfort and counsel of a clergyman. In all kinds of pastoral counseling the clergyman seeks information from all sides. His usefulness depends upon his impartiality and therefore he refrains from being judgmental, and seeks to reconcile the parties to each other and to the God of all mankind. To be forced to testify for public record in a court would tend to destroy his impartial position as a reconciler of person to person and persons to God. Whether or not a state has a law regarding "privileged communication," the people have a right to discuss their problems with an ordained clergymen without fear that the clergyman can or will be forced to reveal for public record that which they have revealed in confidence. The granting of privileged communication to an ordained clergyman in respect to his function as a pastor may make the work of legal counsel more difficult in a given case.

However, privileged communication to ordained clergyman is a refuge for people in trouble, acknowledged by all men of good will, many courts and lawyers, and is inherent in the pastoral ministry ordained by God.

Statement by Rev. Percy F. Rex, rector of Trinity Church in Wilmington, Delaware, made in Civil Action No. 154, Superior Court, June 26, 1961. See further discussion in the chapter on waiver or termination of privilege.

15. "News Shield Bill Spurred in House," *New York Times*, Jan. 4, 1974, p. 41.

16. Judge Edgerton quoted what Justice Holmes said of wiretapping, "We have to choose, and for my part, I think it a less evil that some criminals should escape than that the Government should play an ignoble part." Mullen v. United States, 263 F.2d 275 (D.C. Cir. 1958).

17. The parent-child relationship has a policy base that is closely aligned to the husband-wife privilege but few jurisdictions provide a privilege for the relationship. For a commentary urging the privilege, see L.M. Bauer, "Recognition of a Parent-Child Testimonial Privilege," *St. Louis U.L. Rev.* 23:676, 1979. For a decision upholding the privilege, see People v. Fitzgerald, 101 Misc. 2d 712, 422 N.Y.S.2d 309 (1979). The Michigan Court of Appeals in People v. Dixon, 161 Mich. App. 388, 411 N.W.2d 760 (1987) stated that Michigan does not recognize such a privilege and that the recognition of a new privilege should be left up to the legislature.

18. 116 S. Ct. 1923 at 1932 (1996). Justice Scalia's suggestion that people would be better advised to seek advice from their mothers rather than from psychiatrists prompted the comment that apparently he never heard the old story of the mother who boasted about the devotion of her son: "Not only did he buy me a condo, a Cadillac and a mink coat, but he also pays a psychiatrist $250 for a visit every week and all he talks about is me." E. Muravchik (ltr.), *New York Times*, June 19, 1996, p.14.

19. 116 S. Ct. at 1932.

20. New York: Doubleday, 1996, pp. 176-177.

21. R.M. Fisher, "The Psychotherapeutic Professions and the Law of Privileged Communications," *Wayne L. Rev.* 10:609, 1964. See also A. Fischer, "Nonmedical Psychotherapists," *Arch. Gen. Psychiat.* 5:7, 1961. In Allred v. State, 554 P.2d 411 (Alaska 1976), the case where the Alaska Supreme Court by judicial decision adopted a psychiatrist-patient privilege, the author of the lead opinion, Justice Roger G. Connor, contended that it should apply only to psychiatrists and licensed psychologists and to communications made in the course of psychotherapeutic treatment, and not to such unlicensed practitioners as psychiatric social workers. In a concurring opinion, however, Chief Justice Robert Boochever said: "It is not necessarily relationships with psychiatrists or licensed psychologists that ought to be sedulously fostered; rather, what should be fostered is the therapeutic relationship which looks toward improvement of mental health." 554 P.2d at 425-426.

22. A.H. Malcolm, "Bartenders Being Trained to Provide Counseling as well as Drinks," *New York Times*, Oct. 13, 1974, p. 75. One bar in New York has a

sign: "Giving advice, $10 per hour; Taking advice, $15 per hour; Listening to argument, $25 per hour. By appointment only." Said one patient to his doctor: "This will be my last visit, doctor. I've found a bartender who's cheaper." In a moment of personal crisis, how much help can you expect from a taxi driver? After watching HBO's series of documentaries "Taxicab Confessions," John Tierney was persuaded to experiment with taxicab therapy. He found the results varied according to the type of treatment being sought. J. Tierney, "The Yellow Couch," *New York Times Magazine*, Aug. 11, 1996, p. 22.

23.   N. Lupos, *The Happy Hairdresser* (New York: Simon & Schuster, 1973). Psychologist Lew Losoncy, after studying client-hairdresser relationships and surveying clients, determined that four out of five women say they would trust the advice of their hairdresser over the advice of a therapist and many women use their hair appointments almost as therapy sessions to discuss personal problems with their hairdressers. He foresees the return of "the old private styling station," with partitions between chairs, making it more conducive to private conversation than open styling stations where clients are in clear view of others in the salon. He says his research gives credence to the old adage that "only her hairdresser knows." L. Losoncy, *Salon Psychology: How to Succeed With People and Be a Positive Person* (Solon, Ohio: Matrix University Press, 1988).

Ron Alexander of the *New York Times* reports a continuing conversation in a beauty salon between a woman and the manicurist. With each visit, they discuss the woman's deteriorating relationship with her husband. Finally, the woman says she is considering divorce. "What do you think?" she asks. The manicurist is taken aback. "That's a very serious matter," she says. "I think you should consult another manicurist." R. Alexander, "Metropolitan Diary," *New York Times*, Sept. 8, 1996, p. 22.

24.   116 S. Ct. at 1932.

# Chapter 2

# THE MEDICAL PRIVILEGE AND
# ITS CRITICISMS

In the absence of special legislative enactment, it is generally assumed that the courts will not recognize a privilege protecting confidentiality of communications (the federal courts develop privileges on the basis of reason and experience). At common law, the physician had no legal right or privilege to remain silent on the witness stand.[1] The first formal announcement of the common-law rule came in 1776, in the trial for bigamy of the notorious Elizabeth, Duchess of Kingston. In this case, a surgeon who had attended the defendant in his professional capacity was called to the stand and asked if the accused had informed him of a previous marriage. The court ruled that the question had to be answered, and said: "If a surgeon was voluntarily to reveal these secrets, to be sure he would be guilty of a breach of honour, and of great indiscretion; but to give that information in a court of justice, which by the law of the land he is bound to do, will never be imputed to him as any indiscretion whatsoever."[2]

English law has never abandoned this statement of the legal obligation of the physician to testify when he is called to the witness stand; however, today, as a result of the National Health Service, the privilege of the minister may protect communications from disclosure in court. The only relationships protected by a testimonial privilege at common law were the attorney-client relationship and the husband-wife relationship.

The medical privilege is an American statutory innovation originating in New York in 1828.[3] Since that time it has been enacted in approximately thirty-nine more states and the District of Columbia.[4] At present, every state and the District of Columbia has enacted some kind of statute covering testimony by psychiatrists, psychologists, social workers, or other psychotherapists, but they vary widely as to the therapists who are covered.[5] Some states have a broad psychotherapist-patient privilege but not a physician-patient privilege. And the states vary on the circumstances under which the privileges will be respected. As will be discussed, Georgia gives broad scope to its psychotherapy privilege.

The law of the forum governs the conduct of proceedings in court and, generally speaking, determines the admissibility of evidence. Thus, if no privilege exists in the state where the legal action is brought, the physician or other professional may be called to testify and disclose confidential information acquired in a state where there is a privilege.[6]

In federal courts, Rule 501 of the Federal Rules of Evidence (adopted in 1975) provides that privileges are to be governed by "principles of the common law as they may be interpreted... in the light of reason and experience," except that in civil actions, as to claims or defenses grounded in state law, the federal courts are to decide questions of privilege in accordance with applicable state law.[7] Federal law in cases where state law does not apply is discussed in Chapter 5 of this section. Several federal statutes also accord rights similar to privileges in certain circumstances.[8]

Amidst legislative activity in the nineteenth century, which led to many reforms in procedural law, the state of New York enacted its medical privilege. According to the Reports of the Commissioners on Revision of the Statutes of New York, the purpose of the statute was to encourage the patient to disclose to his physician all information necessary to effectuate proper treatment without the fear of later disclosure before a public tribunal and consequent embarrassment or disgrace. In the 1820s and 1830s, people sedulously concealed from the community the fact that they were the victims of some "dreadful" disease which was rampant at the time. With confidence protected by the law, people were encouraged to have checkups, and better public health was envisioned.[9]

From the viewpoint of litigation, the medical privilege was of comparatively little importance when most of these statutes were enacted. At the turn of the twentieth century, however, the increase in personal injury litigation rapidly expanded the role of the medical privilege and came into conflict with the privilege. The number of states having the medical privilege came to be misleading as to its acceptability or effectiveness. The confidentiality protected by the medical privilege was not substantial. Indeed, a survey of decisions by the highest court of one state showed that, for one reason or another, the privilege in every case on appeal was interpreted so as not to shield the physician-patient communication.[10] The medical privilege statutes closely resembled a sieve—they let through more than they keep out.

With the increase in personal injury litigation arose strong antipathetic comment toward the privilege on the part of authorities in the law of evidence, the Hippocratic oath notwithstanding. Other privileges too (with the possible exception of the attorney-client privilege) were subjected to criticism. As a result, the general tendency in the various states has been to delimit or restrict the scope of the privileges—particularly the medical privilege—either by judicial or legislative action. As one court noted: "[There has been] considerable criticism of physician-patient privilege statutes in recent years, on the ground that such statutes [have] but little justification for their existence and that they [are] often prejudicial to the cause of justice by the suppression of useful truth, 'the disclosure of which ordinarily [can] harm no one.'"[11] Professor Zechariah Chafee of the Harvard Law School wrote in an oft-cited article:[12]

> Physicians and surgeons are required by the ethics of their profession to preserve the secrets of their patients which have been communicated to them or learned from the inspection of symptoms and other bodily conditions. How far this ethical requirement should be enforced by law is a question on which there is much difference of opinion among both lawyers and doctors...
>
> The reasons usually advanced for extending the privilege of silence to the medical profession are not wholly satisfactory. First, it is said that if the patient knows that his confidences may be divulged in future litigation he will hesitate in many cases to get needed medical aid. But although the man who consults a lawyer usually has litigation in mind, men very rarely go to a doctor with any such thought. And even if they did, medical treatment is so valuable that few would lose it to prevent facts from coming to light in court. Indeed, it may be doubted whether, except for a small range of disgraceful or peculiarly private matters, patients worry much about having a doctor keep their private affairs concealed from the world. This whole argument that the privilege is necessary to induce persons to see a doctor sounds like a philosopher's speculation on how men may logically be expected to behave rather than the result of observation of the way men actually behave. . . .
>
> The same a priori quality vitiates a second argument concerning the evils of compelling medical testimony, namely, that a strong sense of professional honor will prompt perversion or concealment of the truth. . . .

Wigmore contended that only the attorney-client, priest-penitent, and husband-wife relationships satisfy the basic considerations justifying legislation for privileged communication. Wigmore maintained that a negative answer to any of the four criteria that he set out would leave a privilege without support.[13] With the exception of the third criterion ("Is the relation one that should be fostered?"), Wigmore, like Chafee and others, was of the opinion that little can be said in favor of the view that the physician-patient relationship satisfies these conditions.[14] More recently, California Superior Court Judge B. Abbott Goldberg echoed the same sentiments.[15]

First of all, it was said by these various commentators, a communication of a patient to a physician rarely originates in a confidence that it will not be disclosed. The Hippocratic oath is apparently based on the idea that confidence is intended, but, it was said, this is contrary to the reality of the situation. Wigmore caustically wrote: "From asthma to broken ribs, from ague to tetanus, the facts of the disease are not only disclosable without shame, but are in fact often publicly known and knowable by everyone excepted the appointed investigators of truth."

Except in cases of syphilis and other loathsome diseases, many individuals seek a chance to discuss their ailment with family, friends, neighbors, and, in fact, with anyone who will listen. Some people injure themselves or develop symptoms for the purpose of gaining attention and affection. The United States has been called "hypochondriacal U.S.A.," with good reason. Frequent subjects of conversation at social gatherings are cholesterol levels, gallbladder operations, and other tales of illness.

Moreover, various commentators claimed that physicians no longer have time to talk to their patients, and hence there is little verbal communication between physician and patient. It is verbal communication for which confidentiality is now mainly desired. Crowded schedules or HMOs limit a physician's contact with a patient to a few minutes—the next patient is always waiting. The old "bedside manner" is now a luxury.

Patients with emotional problems are often regarded as "hypochondriacs" to be gotten out of the office as soon as possible. The "family doctor" is very much a thing of the past. Matters that were once brought to the attention of a family doctor are now brought to psychiatrists, Christian Science practitioners, marriage counselors, social workers, chiropractors, or naturopaths. It is sardonically stated that developments in medical science have provided a new type of medical relationship: the doctor-patient-computer relationship.

Second, according to the critics, confidence is not considered essential for the achievement of the purposes of the relationship. To be sure, a patient does not ordinarily hesitate revealing his symptoms of distress to a physician from fear of disclosure in court. The privilege is not necessary to persuade persons to see a physician. People seek medical advice even where the privilege does not exist. As one legal scholar noted, the hospitals are as full and doctors as busy in those states which do not have the physician-patient privilege as in those that do.[16]

Finally, in weighing "truth versus privilege," or better put, in balancing the unbalanceables, it is considered that the injury to the physician-patient relationship by disclosure is not greater than the social benefit gained by the disposal of litigation based on all of the evidence. The injury which the relationship may suffer from the physician's testimony is thought to be outweighed by the benefit to society derived from his assistance in the administration of justice. Professor Chafee wrote in the aforementioned article that the medical privilege has fostered fraudulent claims in the field of personal injury litigation, permitted unwarranted recovery on insurance policies, and interfered with the proper determination of mental capacity of decedents where that fact is disputed.[17]

The litigant claiming personal injury while trying to conceal his medical history brought disrepute to the medical privilege. Charles McCormick, a leading authority in evidence, wrote in 1954: "More than a century of experience with the [medical privilege] statutes has demonstrated that the privilege in the main operates not as a shield of privacy but as the protection of fraud. Consequently the abandonment of the privilege seems the best solution."[18]

The only support for the privilege seemed to be mainly the weight of professional medical opinion, pressing upon the legislature. "The real reason today for the privilege," Wigmore said, "is professional jealousy on the part of medical men."[19] In 1938, the American Bar Association's Committee on Improvements in the Law of Evidence considered these criticisms of the medical privilege, but made a recommendation which was conciliatory in nature. It stated:[20]

> The amount of truth that has been suppressed by this statutory rule must be extensive. We believe that the time has come to consider the situation. We do not here recommend the abolition of the privilege, but we do make the following recommendation: the North Carolina statute allows a wholesome flexibility. Its concluding paragraph reads: "Provided that the presiding judge of a superior court may compel such a disclosure if in his opinion the same is necessary to the proper administration of justice." This statute has needed but rare interpretation. It enables the privilege to be suspended when suppression of a fraud might otherwise be aided.

The National Conference of Commissioners on Uniform State Laws, which seeks to promote uniform legislation throughout the country, voted in 1950 that the physician-patient privilege should not be recognized. However, in 1953 the Conference reversed its previous action and by a close vote decided to recommend the privilege as optional. The recommendation, however, contained so many exceptions, as those made by the various states in its privilege, that it was difficult to imagine a case in which it might be applied.

The Federal Rules of Evidence, adopted in 1975, omitted a physician-patient privilege. The Advisory Committee to the Rules explained that no general physician-patient privilege was proposed because "the exceptions which have been found necessary in order to obtain information required by the public interest or to avoid fraud are so numerous as to leave little if any basis for the privilege."[21] The Advisory Committee took the position that, while the privilege reflects the sentiment that a physician should honor the confidences of a patient, this consideration is adequately protected by the medical code of ethics and must yield to the overriding need for full disclosure when litigation arises.[22]

It is noteworthy that about a half-century earlier, the drafting committee of the American Law Institute intentionally omitted the medical privilege in its final draft of the Model Code of Evidence. The membership, after much debate, restored the privilege (in Rules 220-223 of the Model Code of Evidence of 1942). In 1950, the National Conference of Commissioners on Uniform Laws voted to abolish the privilege, but three years later, after protests by the medical profession, voted to recommend it (Rule 27), and was adopted by several states.

No medical privilege statute has been repealed in any state, but as a result of the adverse criticism, legislatures and courts together have seriously undercut and restricted the practical value of the statutes. The various legislatures have added amendments or exceptions which restrict the scope of the privilege.

As a rule of judicial interpretation, statutes that depart from the common law are narrowly construed, but courts often fail to show ordinary deference in their interpretation of the medical statute.[23] More often than not, the privilege is circumvented by an exception.

The restrictions on the medical privilege do not result from any animosity between the professions of law and medicine, but rather out of the belief that the privilege unnecessarily excludes evidence which is often essential for the administration of justice.

It is to be noted that when an attorney refers a client to a physician for examination, the attorney-client privilege protects a report made by the physician to the attorney. This is especially important in jurisdictions where there is no medical privilege. In cases of referral for examination, the physician acts as the agent of the attorney. In this situation, the physician is serving as an examining physician, rather than as a treating physician, and is performing the examination on behalf of the attorney in the preparation of a case. The physician, as he is acting as an agent of the attorney, falls under the umbrella of the attorney-client privilege.[24] The attorney will call upon the physician to testify if the physician's opinion is favorable to the attorney's theory of the case, but if the opinion is unfavorable, the attorney will discharge him and seek another expert or will drop the case.[25]

# NOTES

1.   "Common law" means the law produced by courts in the process of deciding cases, in absence of applicable constitutional or statutory provisions.

"Statutory" means a law established by the legislature. At one time, custom sufficed to determine people's rights and duties.

2.   20 How. St. Trials 355 (1776). In this case, the confidence which the surgeon tried to keep secret was as to a first marriage having taken place. The court might have said that such a fact was irrelevant to the health of the Duchess, and therefore not privileged, but it decided the case on a more basic ground, namely, that there is no physician-patient privilege.

3.   The New York statute read: "No person duly authorized to practice physic or surgery shall be allowed to disclose any information which he may have acquired in attending any patient, in a professional character, and which information was necessary to enable him to prescribe for such patient as a physician, or to do any act for him, as a surgeon." N.Y. Rev. Stat. pt. 3, ch. 7, § 73, at 406 (1828).

4.   The states that do not have a statutory physician-patient privilege are Alabama, Connecticut, Florida, Georgia, Kentucky, Maryland, Massachusetts, New Mexico, South Carolina, Tennessee and West Virginia. The statutes adopted in the other states and the District of Columbia vary widely in their formulation and exceptions. See S.H. Stone & R.K. Taylor (eds.), *Testimonial Privileges* (Colorado Springs: Shepard's/McGraw-Hill, 1994); "Developments–Privileged Communications/Medical and Psychological Counseling Privileges," *Harv. L. Rev.* 98:1450 at 1532, 1985; E.Z. Ferster, "Statutory Summary of Physician-Patient Privileged Communication Laws," in R.C. Allen, E.Z. Ferster & J.G. Rubin (eds.), *Reading in Law and Psychiatry* (Baltimore: Johns Hopkins, 1975), p. 329.

5.   See Appendix.

6.   To illustrate: In a suit for divorce in one state, which does not have a privilege, a physician who treated one of the parties in another state, which has a privilege, can be called to testify as to confidential communications. See Doll v. Equitable Life Assur. Soc., 138 Fed. 705 (1905); Abety v. Abety, 10 N.J. Super. 287, 77 A.2d 291 (1950). There are contrary holdings, which in effect provide that privilege is a matter of substantive rather than procedural law and hence is governed by the jurisdiction where the communication is made. For example, in Application of Queen, 233 N.Y.S.2d 798 (1962), the New York court held that a New York psychologist (privileged) could not be compelled to testify in a custody suit in Massachusetts, which has no privilege. In this case, the petitioner sought to obtain from the defendant-wife, the custody of their minor child. The petitioner contended "that his wife is not mentally fit to care for the infant child," and the New York psychologist who saw the wife, was asked to answer interrogatories pursuant to an order issued out of a Massachusetts probate court. The New York court, upholding privilege, said "that to grant the relief sought would be violative of the rights of a citizen of our state."

7.   See, *e.g.*, Hancock v. Dodson, 958 F.2d 1367 (6th Cir. 1992); United States v. Bercier, 848 F.2d 917 (8th Cir. 1988); United States v. Burzynski Cancer Research Inst., 819 F.2d 1301 (5th Cir. 1987), *cert. denied*, 484 U.S. 1065

(1988); United States v. Lindstrom, 698 F.2d 1154 (11th Cir. 1983); United States v. Meagher, 531 F.2d 752 (5th Cir.), *cert. denied,* 429 U.S. 853 (1976).

8. See, *e.g.,* 18 U.S.C. § 4244 (pretrial examinations of defendants' competency to stand trial are privileged); 21 U.S.C. § 1175, 42 U.S.C. § § 260, 290ee 3(a), 4582 (records of drug and alcohol abuse programs that are federally conducted, regulated, and assisted are privileged); 42 U.S.C. § 242a (names of subjects in federally-conducted mental health research are privileged). *See also* United States v. Eide, 875 F.2d 1429 (9th Cir. 1989) (results of urinalysis test given to pharmacist at Veteran's Administration hospital considered "records within meaning of federal statute protecting confidentiality of alcohol and drug abuse program records"); Whyte v. Connecticut Mut. Life Ins. Co., 818 F.2d 1005 (1st Cir. 1987) (patient's statements made during treatment excluded under federal regulations limiting disclosure of hospital records regarding treatment for alcoholism).

9. The purpose of the original New York statute was explained in 1836: "The ground on which communications to counsel are privileged, is the supposed necessity of a full knowledge of the facts, to advise correctly, and to prepare for the proper defense or prosecution of a suit. But surely the necessity of consulting a medical advisor, when life itself may be in jeopardy, is still stronger. And unless such consultations are privileged, men will be incidentally punished by being obliged to suffer the consequences of injuries without relief from the medical art, and without conviction of any offence." *Extracts from the Original Reports of the Revisers,* 3 N.Y. Rev. Stat. App. pt. 3, ch. 7, § 73, at 737 (1836).

10. R. Slovenko, "The Physician and Privileged Communications," *J. La. State Med. Soc.* 110:39, 1958.

11. Boyles v. Cora, 232 Iowa 822, 6 N.W.2d 401, 414 (1942), quoted in Van Wie v. United States, 77 F. Supp. 22 (N.D. Iowa 1948).

12. "Privileged Communications: Is Justice Served or Obstructed by Closing the Doctor's Mouth on the Witness Stand?," *Yale L.J.* 52:607, 1943.

13. See Chapter 1.

14. J. Wigmore, *Evidence,* vol. 8, §§ 2380-91. See also, *e.g.,* C.C. Callahan & E.E. Ferguson, "Evidence and the New Federal Rules of Civil Procedure," *Yale L.J.* 47:194, at 207, 1937; T.H.S. Curd, "Privileged Communications between the Doctor and His Patient—An Anomaly of the Law," *W. Va. L.Q.* 44:165, 1937; H. Duque, "Interpretation of Statutes Making Communications between Physician and Patient Privileged," Proceedings of A.B.A. Section of Insurance Law, 1952, p. 137; H.S. Lipscomb, "Privileged Communications Statute—Sword and Shield," *Miss. L.J.* 16:181, 1944; E. Morgan, "Suggested Remedy for Obstructions to Expert Testimony by Rules of Evidence," *U. Chi. L. Rev.* 10:285, 1944; W.A. Purrington, "An Abused Privilege," *Colum. L. Rev.* 6:388, 1906.

15. "Physician-Patient Privilege—An Impediment to Public Health," *Pac. L.J.* 16:787, 1985.

16. To quote: "Physicians at Massachusetts General Hospital or at Johns Hopkins Hospital, for example, have not been kept from doing creditable

work and patients have not remained away from these institutions because Massachusetts and Maryland lack privilege." Argument quoted in M. Guttmacher, *The Mind of the Murderer* (New York: Farrar, Straus, 1960), p. 170. See also M. Ladd, "A Modern Code of Evidence," *Iowa L. Rev.* 27:214, 1942.

17. Z. Chafee, *op. cit. supra.*
18. C. McCormick, *Handbook of the Law of Evidence* (St. Paul, MN.: West, 1954), §108 at p. 224 (2d ed. 1972, §105 at p. 228).
19. J. Wigmore, *Evidence,* vol. 8, § 2380a.
20. A.L.I. Model Code of Evidence, Rules 220-223 (1942). Virginia, following the recommendation, included this flexibility in its statute. Code of Va. § 8-289.1 (1956, c. 446).
21. Supreme Court Standard 504, Advisory Committee Note.
22. J.B. Weinstein & M.A. Berger, *Weinstein's Evidence Manual* (New York: Matthew Bender, 2d ed. 1995), sec. 18.04(01).
23. "At common law, communications between a physician and his patient were not privileged. Therefore, the statute creating the privilege, being in derogation of the common law, should be construed strictly." Randa v. Bear, 50 Wash.2d 415, 312 P.2d 640 (1957).
24. Antrade v. Superior Court of Los Angeles County, 54 Cal. Rptr.2d 504 (Cal. App. 1996); City & County of San Francisco v. Superior Court, 37 Cal.2d 227, 231 P.2d 26 (1951); Lindsay v. Lipson, 116 N.W.2d 60 (Mich. 1962); Comment, "Function Overlap Between the Lawyer and Other Professionals: Its Implications for the Privileged Communication Doctrine," *Yale L.J.* 71:1226, 1962.

    With the possible exception of Ohio and Mississippi, confidential communications made to an attorney or someone retained to assist the attorney are not obligated to report acts of child abuse that would otherwise be required. However, concerning threats or future acts of violence that may result in serious injury or death to others, many states require attorneys to disclose this information. D. Shuman, "Reporting of Child Abuse During Forensic Evaluations," American Psychology-Law Society, Division 41, American Psychological Association 15:3, 1995.
25. The question sometimes arises as to whether the opponent may make use of the first expert. Unless there are special circumstances, such as the unavailability of other experts, he may not, as a general rule, since he has been made privy to the opposing attorney's case. In United States v. Talley, 790 F.2d 1468 (9th Cir. 1986), the court held that the government should not have been allowed to call as a rebuttal witness a psychiatrist, appointed for the defendant's benefit, but who was not called as a witness by the defendant.

# Chapter 3

# RESTRICTIONS ON THE
# MEDICAL PRIVILEGE

The word "privilege" stems from the Latin "privata lex," a prerogative given to a person or to a class of persons. The word is a composite derived from the words "privus" and "lex." The privilege here under discussion affords a right to bar a witness from testifying. However, because the privilege is that of a particular person or class, matters covered by it may always be proved by evidence of other witnesses. Furthermore, because a privilege is contrary to the general law, it is strictly construed and (except in federal courts) does not exist apart from statute.[1] As has been pointed out, other than the common-law, attorney-client privilege, no privilege has been extended in the various states to other professions except by statute.[2]

Military law does not recognize a medical (or psychotherapy) privilege, though it does recognize the attorney-client, husband-wife, and priest-penitent privileges.[3] The Manual for Courts-Martial specifically removes communications to medical officers from the privileged category.[4] Military officials can also have access to the mental health records of civilian family members treated by the military; there are times when the military may seek a spouse's records for insights into whether an armed services member is having any personal problem.[5] According to one survey, most military officers prefer civilian to military psychiatrists, primarily for the reason that there is no privilege under military law.[6] The civilian psychiatrist does not have the obligation to report adverse matters to appropriate authorities.[7] The American Psychiatric Association has urged the Pentagon to provide confidentiality safeguards for individuals treated in the military health care system.[8]

The determination of which relationships give rise to a privilege is, by and large, a legislative policy decision. Moreover, in some ways, judicial interpretations of the laws reflect almost the same diversity as the language of the statutes. In many respects, there is uniformity among the laws, but the differences may loom important in a particular case. It is therefore necessary in any given case to examine both the scope and meaning of the particular statute which is involved.[9] In general, while privacy is heralded in the United States, there is greater entrenchment of medical privacy in many countries than in the United States.[10]

The scope of many of the early statutes in the United States on medical privilege were and many remain very limited in application. Most states excluded criminal cases from the scope of its privilege,[11] but Louisiana's was applicable only in criminal cases.[12] Kentucky limited its medical privilege to vital statistics.[13] New Mexico limited its medical privilege to venereal or loathsome diseases and workers' compensation claims. North Carolina and Virginia compelled disclosure when "necessary to a proper administration of justice." Pennsylvania's statute extended only to information which tends "to blacken the character of the patient."[14] More recently, these and the other states have enacted a psychotherapist-patient privilege.

Generally speaking, the courts usually construe the term "physician" in the medical statute to exclude from the privileged class medical students, chiropractors, pharmacists, psychologists, social workers, dentists, Christian Science practitioners, and veterinarians. The Model Code of Evidence of the American Law Institute recommended that a "physician" be defined as a person authorized by the state licensure act (or reasonably believed by a patient to be authorized) to practice medicine, but apparently no cases expressly accept this definition as controlling.

Some states expressly extended the medical privilege to the physician's stenographer or confidential clerk (Iowa) or to nurses (Arkansas, Iowa, Mexico, New York), but in many states, these attendants to the physician are not included within the privilege. The medical privilege statute covers communications between "physician and patient"—and an attendant is not a "physician, but rather is a "third party" to the relationship.[15]

Communications between a physician and patient are not privileged when a "third party" is present.[16] Take the example: a patient is brought to the physician's office by a housekeeper-companion and, for emotional support, the patient requests that the housekeeper be present during the examination. The office nurse is often also present. As a practical matter, such persons are not strangers to the relationship—but legally, they are often held to be a "third party." In general, the presence of a "third party" is said to "pollute" confidentiality. As a result, the information may not be held privileged and both the physician and such third person may be called to testify about the communications.[17]

Obviously, the purpose and policy of the medical privilege is undercut when a court requires evidence from those assisting the patient or from persons who gather and record information while acting for and in conjunction with the physician. This restrictive approach to the privilege is contrary to the modern day practice of medicine. As medical science becomes more complicated, more people are involved in the treatment of a single patient. The physician is no longer an isolate but part of a complex system providing health services—he works with specialists, technicians, nurses, social workers, social scientists, administrators, and others, in the care and study of sick persons and in the prevention of illness. Ironically, information to an insurer is not deemed to "pollute" confidentiality as the insurer is regarded as a facilitator of treatment.

A psychiatrist, holding a medical degree, is included within the scope of medical statutes which grant the privilege to "physicians." Such statutes, however, offer no protection for nonmedical therapists (clinical psychologists, psychiatric social workers, lay analysts and others who may practice psychotherapy).[18]

The role of nonphysician therapists in all forms of psychotherapy is a much debated issue. In recent years there has been an increase in the number of nonmedical people engaged in psychotherapy, both privately and in an institutional setting. Psychologists, social workers, and even nurses conduct private or largely independent practices.[19]

With the revolutionary spirit and intellectual ferment that marked the opening of the 19th century, physicians and reformers began for the first time to consider the possibility of a cure for mental illness. Until the late 18th century, mental affliction was generally considered to be God's punishment for trafficking with the devil. Medical treatment was limited largely to cathartics, emetics, bleeding, and physical restraints, all concerned mainly with subduing the patient, and "beating the devil out of him."[20]

The New York statute of 1828, which served as a model for other states, preceded by almost three-quarters of a century the systematic body of knowledge and technique introduced by Freud. The treatment of physical or emotional disorders by psychotherapy was not considered by legislators of the time. The legislators also failed to consider the psychological aspects involved in all medical practice. Thus, focusing on the physical, the Arizona statute provided that "a physician or surgeon shall not, without the consent of his patient, be examined as to any communication made by his patient with reference to any physical or supposed physical disease or any knowledge obtained by personal examination of the patient."

The United States are fifty and, in such a large country, many types of decisions may be anticipated. In some jurisdictions, statements to a physician which lack pertinency to treatment are held not privileged. The communication must be "necessary" to discharge the physician's function in the usual course of practice. In medical care the identity of an assailant is seldom relevant to diagnosis or treatment, but usually it is in psychotherapy. Thus, for medical treatment, it is relevant to know that the patient stepped on a rusty nail, but not who put it in his pathway. The physician could be compelled to testify to the latter fact.[21] Some courts have limited the medical privilege to conditions related to the particular ailment for which the patient sought or was being given treatment.[22] And as the privilege only covers confidential communications made in the course of professional treatment, information obtained in social contacts is not privileged. The judge (not the jury) decides whether a privilege applies, *e.g.*, whether the appropriate relationship existed or whether the communication was confidential.

The privilege was established to promote ends deemed medically and ethically desirable and not to aid in the commission of a crime. The privilege is not extended to communications made in the effort to procure the commission of a crime as in cases of unlawful abortion or unlawful purchase of a narcotic drug or in cases where reporting is required.[23] State statutes require any physician called upon to treat a gunshot wound or any wound inflicted by a deadly weapon to report the case to a law-enforcement officer.[24]

It has been argued, however, that a physician should not be compelled to incriminate or inform on his patients under the general rule of criminal law which distinguishes between active concealment and passive nonrevelation. In years gone by, the crime which most frequently came to the attention of physicians was that of illegal abortion. In such cases, however, the crime had already been committed—the patient went to a legitimate practitioner for the treatment of the condition which was the aftermath of the operation (only the abortionist was criminally liable).

It is only the physician who actively assists a patient, for example, in concealing his identity or aiding him to escape arrest, who would be guilty of crime; a physician who helps a known criminal to escape would be guilty of the crime of accessory after the fact. John Dillinger, a public enemy No. 1, when fleeing from prison, went to Dr. Clayton May to be treated for gunshot wounds incurred during his escape. Dr. May neglected to inform the police of his ministrations and was consequently imprisoned for two years for harboring a fugitive wanted under a federal warrant. In another notable case, Dr. Samuel Mudd was convicted for treating and harboring a fugitive in failing to report that he set the fractured leg of John Wilkes Booth, after he had assassinated President Abraham Lincoln. Mudd was one of the eight persons charged and convicted, by military tribunal, in the assassination of President Lincoln (Mudd was given a life sentence, but was released by President Andrew Johnson after serving four years in desolate Fort Jefferson).[25]

The medical privilege has been invoked most often in three areas, to wit: contested will cases where the testamentary capacity of the patient is under inquiry; actions for bodily injuries where the plaintiff's prior physical condition is at issue; and actions on life and accident insurance policies where misrepresentations of the insured as to state of personal health are at issue. In all of these situations, in one way or another, the privilege can be circumvented by an exception.

In contested will cases, the legal representative, the administrator, or the patient's heir is given the power to waive the privilege. The California statute provides that either before or after probate, upon the contest of any will, the attending physician may testify to the mental condition of the deceased patient and may disclose information acquired by him in his professional capacity.

In suits for personal injuries, the privilege is considered waived by the patient by instituting litigation.[26] In such cases, the patient is using the privilege aggressively. As Professor Chafee stated, the patient cannot make the medical statute both a sword and a shield.[27] The confidence of the medical consultation is no longer considered necessary because, in bringing suit, the patient offers his physical or mental health as a matter of public record. Moreover, it is considered that a good-faith claimant suing for personal injuries would not object to the testimony of any physician who examined or treated him, but rather would wish him to testify.

This view is exemplified by specific legislation or court decision that suit for personal injury or wrongful death waives the medical privilege for that injury. The privilege is not urged in these cases because its exercise, even if permitted, would adversely influence the decision. The traditional position in lawsuits is that a party who fails to bring in available information needed for an enlightened decision deserves to lose the case. It is similarly presumed that the evidence must be unfavorable or it would have been produced. Workers' compensation legislation usually provides that a physician can be required to testify to information procured in attending the claimant.

In actions on life and accident insurance policies wherein the truth of the insured's representations as to his health are vital, the insurer may desire to introduce testimony of the insured's physician to show fraud on the part of the insured in making his application. The medical privilege may be circumvented quite easily by the insurer by inserting a provision in the application whereby the insured waives his right to the privilege, both for himself and his beneficiary. The same procedure is often followed in employment applications, and also for disability benefits, pensions, and compensation claims. Such a waiver by contract is generally but not always upheld.[28]

Waiver by contract is particularly useful to the insurer in those states where the termination-by-death rule does not prevail. For large life insurance policies, the insured is required to undergo a medical examination by the company's physician. As a result, most undesirable risks are eliminated and the problem of the medical privilege is diminished in importance.

## NOTES

1.  Opponents to privileges argue that privileges give first consideration to the individual client or patient, doctor or lawyer, as against the public interest or the welfare of the community as a whole. See, *e.g.*, R.W. Baldwin, "Confidentiality between Physician and Patient," *Md. L. Rev.* 22:181, 1962. But why identify a trial with the public interest and privileges with individual interest? It is just as logical to say that a trial concerns only the immediate litigants, and that a privilege concerns a broad class of persons (all patients and all clients–past, present and future).

2.  See Dyer v. State, 241 Ala. 679, 4 So.2d 311 (1941); C. Joiner, "Uniform Rules of Evidence for the Federal Courts," 20 F.R.D. 429 (1957). In Michigan, under its constitution, the state supreme court adopts rules of evidence and any legislation in conflict, unless it is of a substantive nature, is void. M.C.L.A. Const. Art. 6, §5; McDougall v. Eliuk, 554 N.W.2d 56 (Mich. App. 1996).

3.  J.H. Munster & M.A. Larkin, *Military Evidence* (Indianapolis: Bobbs - Merrill (2d ed. 1978); T.C. Oldham, "Privileged Communications in Military Law," *Military L. Rev.*, July 1959, p. 17.

4.  § 151c (2).

5.  E.J. Pollock, "Mother Fights to Keep Daughter's Records in Rape Case Secret," *Wall Street Journal*, Aug. 22, 1996, p. 1. Protesting the military's position requiring psychiatrists to turn over patient records–including those of nonactive duty dependents–in the case of a forensic investigation, Air Force psychiatrist Jay Weiss resigned. It is believed that the resignation may prompt the Department of Defense to reconsider its policy regarding privilege in cases involving nonactive-duty dependents of active-duty personnel. "Air Force Psychiatrist to Retire Early Over Ethical Dilemma," *Psychiatric News*, Dec. 20, 1996, p. 1.

6.  J.F.T. Corcoran, J. Breaskin & H.L. Court, "Absence of Privileged Communications and Its Impact on Air Force Officers," *Air Force L. Rev.* 19:51, 1977.

7.  National Public Radio in 1994 reported a case in which as active-duty soldier told his therapist that he was having homosexual feelings (not that he was homosexual). The therapist felt obligated to report this, and as a result, the patient was discharged from the military for homosexuality. The case brought forth comment in the American Psychiatric Association's *Psychiatric News* that patients should be informed about what type of information will be reportable, that is, the limits of physician-patient confidentiality. D.W. Hicks (Ltr.), "Military and Gays," *Psychiatric News*, July 15, 1994, p. 18. See J.A. Knight, "Divided Loyalties in Mental-Health Care," in W.T. Reich (ed.), *Encyclopedia of Bioethics* (New York: Macmillan, rev. ed. 1995), vol. 2, pp. 629-633. Typically, when a serviceman is sent to a psychiatrist by a commanding officer, he is informed that a report will be made.

8.  "Confidentiality Concerns Prompt Meeting Between APA and Pentagon Officials," *Psychiatric News*, Sept. 6, 1996, p. 1.

9. The various statutes on the medical privilege are discussed in C. DeWitt, *Privileged Communications Between Physician and Patient* (Springfield, IL: Thomas, 1958). "Certainly the United States must furnish a fascinating laboratory to students of the law because of the marked differences in legal structure under which persons of similar origin and makeup live. A variegated legal panoply is found when one reviews the state laws dealing with the physician-patient privilege and the diverse ways in which these statutes have been interpreted by the courts." M. Guttmacher, *The Mind of the Murderer* (New York: Farrar, Straus 1960), p. 176.

10. D.W. Shuman, "The Origins of the Physician-Patient Privilege and Professional Secret," *Sw. L. J.* 39:661, 1985.

11. For example, in regard medical privilege, the California Code of Evidence states: "There is no privilege under this article in a criminal proceeding." Cal. Evid. Code § 998. Numerous California decisions have accordingly ruled that there is no physician-patient privilege in criminal cases. See, *e.g.*, People v. Ditson, 20 Cal. Rptr. 165, 369 P.2d 714, 57 Cal.2d 415 (1962); People v. Combes, 14 Cal. Rptr. 4, 56 Cal.2d 135 (1961).

12. Shortly before the adoption of the Code of Criminal Procedure containing rules of evidence, the Louisiana Supreme Court said that the rules of evidence are the same in Louisiana in civil and criminal cases. State v. Wilson, 163 La. 29, 111 So. 484 (1927). But there was question as to the effect of the adoption of the Code of Criminal Procedure on civil evidence rules. Comment, *La. L. Rev.* 14:568, 1954. In civil cases involving the problem of medical privilege, the courts do not decide the matter by saying that there is no privilege in civil cases but rather decide on some other ground. R. Slovenko, "The Physician and Privileged Communication," *J. La. State Med. Soc.* 110:39, 1958.

13. Boyd v. Wynn, 150 S.W.2d 648 (Ky. 1941).

14. R.C. Turkington, "Legal Protection for the Confidentiality of Health Care Information in Pennsylvania: Patient and Client Access; Testimonial Privileges; Damage Recovery for Unauthorized Extra-Legal Disclosure," *Villanova L. Rev.* 32:259, 1987.

15. The attorney-client privilege includes the attorney's secretary, but if any of the attorney's or client's documents or verbal statements are disclosed to third parties (*i.e.*, anyone other than the attorney, his secretary or the client), then those documents or statements are no longer regarded as confidential. In the language of the old common law, the confidence has been "profaned" or "polluted" and the privilege terminated. Such pollution could occur either at the source of the information, or it could take place later on. At common law, the client's and the attorney's necessity of allowing immediate office personnel access to documents without destroying their confidential nature is accepted and approved.

16. On whether nurses are included within the medical privilege, one court observed: "It is true the authorities on the question appear to be divided. A number of courts hold that the statutory privilege does not exclude the tes-

timony of a nurse attending the physician. Other courts have permitted such testimony where it appears the information sought to be elicited was acquired from sources separate and distinct from action in concert with a physician against whom the claim of privilege is made. On the other hand, some jurisdictions take the view that the privilege extends by implication to nurses or attendants who are employees or acting under the direction of the physician examining or treating the patient. In our opinion, the latter view to a greater extent carries out the intent and purport of the statute creating the privilege." Ostrowski v. Mockridge, 242 Minn. 265, 65 N.W.2d 185, 190 (1954). On other attendants, see Prudential Life Ins. Co. v. Koslowski, 226 Wis. 641, 276 N.W. 300 (1937).

17. The rulings on the medical privilege vary from state to state. Some courts allow the privilege when the third party is related to the holder of the privilege insofar as the testimony of the physician is concerned but not, oddly, as to the third party. The court in Denaro v. Prudential Ins. Co., 154 App. Div. 840, 139 N.Y.S. 758, 761 (1913), said: "When a physician enters a house for the purpose of attending a patient, he is called upon to make inquiries, not alone of the sick person, but of those who are about him and who are familiar with the facts, and communications necessary for the proper performance of the duties of a physician are not public, because made in the presence of his immediate family or those who are present because of the illness of the person. Of course, the persons who are present are not denied the right to testify. It is only the physician who is bound by the rule."

18. Griggs v. Griggs, 707 S.W.2d 488 (Mo. App. 1986).

19. The term "psychotherapy" includes all modes of psychological treatment. The forms of psychotherapy are various but may be expressed with reference to two extremes: psychotherapy may seek improvement of the adaptive capacity of the individual or it may seek to modify the environmental stresses. In the first, the patient seeks knowledge about himself (psychoanalysis is the most intensive form). In the second form, the therapist, aided by the patient's family or other interested persons, strives to alter the patient's behavior (*e.g.*, environmental manipulation or directive psychotherapy).

20. See N. Dain, *Concepts of Insanity in the United States, 1786-1830* (New Brunswick: Rutgers University Press, 1964); G. Grob, *Mental Institutions in America: Social Policy to 1875* (New York: Free Press, 1973).

21. This is the way one court expressed it: "Statements of an injured person to his physician as to matters connected with the occasion out of which the injuries arose and observations by a physician of the patient and of the facts surrounding the injury would seem to stand or fall as privileged communcations on their possible relevancy to treatment or on their relevancy as reasonably believed by either the physician or patient or both of them... While it is realized that it is common and natural human behavior for one in recounting a series of events which gave rise to an injury of a certain nature to include much data irrelevant to the ascertainment of the correct

type of treatment to be administered, and while it is perhaps desirable that much latitude be allowed these statements as privileged communications to encourage disclosure of all facts necessary for treatment, an extension of the privilege to circumstances related by the patient which could have no possible bearing on the treatment of the injury or other professional service is beyond the plain language of the statute and the most liberal construction of it." Van Wie v. United States, 77 F. Supp. 22 (N.D. Iowa 1948). Professor Thomas Krattenmarker provides this illustration: If the family doctor inquires, "How did you sprain you ankle?" and the response is, "While walking my mistress home from a date," the response is not privileged. If the family doctor asks, "Why are you depressed?" and the patient says, "Because I just murdered my mistress," the patient's statement is privileged. T.G. Krattenmarker, "Testimonial Privileges in Federal Courts: An Alternative to the Proposed Federal Rules of Evidence," *Geo. L.J.* 62:61, at 70, 1973.

22.  See Carson v. Beatley, 82 N.E.2d 745 (Ohio Ct. App. 1948), noted in *W. Res. L. Rev.* 1:142, 1949.

23.  Many states require the reporting of gun or knife wounds. See, *e.g.*, Ariz. Code Ann. § 43-2208 (1939); Cal. Gen. Laws § 3431 (1) (1943). It is a criminal offense for any individual who knows of treasonous activities not to notify the proper authorities. La. R.S. 14:25, 115. In various states, a physician is required to report suspicious death to proper authorities. La. R.S. 15:39. Under the Uniform Narcotic Drug Act, sec. 17, adopted by approximately half of the states, a physician can be compelled to testify in the court room concerning communications made "in an effort unlawfully to procure a narcotic drug, or unlawfully to procure the administration of any such drug." See H.J. Anslinger, "The Physician and the Federal Narcotic Law," *Tul. L. Rev.* 20:309, 1946.

24.  In State v. Antill, 197 N.E.2d 548 (1964), the Ohio Supreme Court ruled the physician-patient privilege to be inapplicable to medical testimony regarding the condition of a person assaulted with a dangerous weapon. In this criminal case, the patient in the course of a violent argument with her husband sustained a puncture-type chest wound, certain other cuts, and bruises on her arm and upper body. The husband was indicted on a charge of assaulting his wife with a dangerous weapon or instrument likely to produce great bodily harm. At the trial, the wife refused to testify against her husband (the court found her in contempt and ordered her confined to jail until she agreed to testify). The physician who treated her was called as a witness and was advised by the court that his testimony would not violate the physician-patient privilege. He then testified as to the condition in which he found the patient and gave his opinion as to the cause of her injuries. The jury found the husband guilty as charged. On appeal, to no avail, the husband contended that the physician's testimony ought to have been excluded by the physician-patient privilege. His conviction was affirmed.

25.  N. Mudd, "Life of Dr. Samuel A. Mudd," *AMA News*, April 12, 1965, pp. 8-9. Salmon Raduyev, a Chechen military commander who was wanted by

Russian authorities for the attack he led in Dagestan in January 1996, went to Germany where he underwent plastic surgery after losing an eye when hit by a sniper bullet. Upon his return he carried out bombings of busses in Moscow. He called the bombings "in honor of my return." Though his wound was suspicious, the physician performing the plastic surgery made no report.

26. Randa v. Bear, 50 Wash.2d 415, 312 P.2d 640 (1957); Anno., 25 A.L.R.2d 1429. Likewise, claimants for benefits under workers' compensation laws waive the privilege by making a claim. Trotta v. Ward Baking Co., 21 A.D.2d 701, 249 N.Y.S.2d 262 (1964).

27. Z. Chafee, "Privileged Communications: Is Justice Served or Obstructed by Closing the Doctor's Mouth on the Witness Stand?," *Yale L.J.* 52:607, 1943.

28. The Michigan Supreme Court has held that a waiver of the privilege in an application for insurance is against public policy. Gilchrist v. Mystic Workers, 188 Mich. 466, 154 N.W. 575 (1915).

# Chapter 4

# THE CASE FOR PSYCHOTHERAPY

Evaluating the case for the medical privilege calls for the consideration that medicine consists of various specialties, and, also, that methods of practicing medicine change with great rapidity. On the other hand, law attempts to regulate behavior by general principles, and by nature, law is conservative, not pioneering in spirit, as it must rely on knowledge developed in other fields. Based on precedent, law moves slowly (in many areas of the law, the essential concepts remain the same as they were at the end of the last century).

How should "medicine" be defined for purposes of privilege? Should the privilege apply to all members of what might broadly be called the "care-taking" professions? As we have noted, commentators have questioned the need of privilege for practitioners treating physical or organic disorders solely by drugs or surgery. However, all practitioners of medicine are now trained, to some extent, in psychiatry. General practitioners of medicine prescribe psychiatric medications (such as Prozac for depression) and engage in counseling.

While some physicians do not regard psychiatry with much esteem, and many do not have time for it, a psychological basis is involved in all medical practice and treatment. Through choice or necessity, at least in theory, if not in practice, a physician must serve as a counselor. Even if a definite organic cause for distress can be detected, there is usually a functional overlay. For example, women who suffer from dysmenorrhea have a low pain threshold. To take another example, a different psychological reaction to a drug is elicited when it is purchased over the counter than when obtained with a prescription. The physician is often consulted regarding marital and sexual difficulties, now more than ever, because patients tend to be less defensive and more open about these matters.

Until about the last 50 years, medical science did not have much to offer most people. Physicians mostly provided a bedside manner, and as one practitioner said:

As a general practitioner, I find that the most gratifying aspect of my practice is the priceless opportunity to be an integral part of the lives of many families. As their family physician, I am often called upon not only as a doctor but also as a friend, teacher, adviser, or counselor. Resulting from this relationship are the mutual trust and respect so necessary to any stay-well or get-well process.

A patient's complaint is more extensive than his symptoms. In a Jewish story, a patient complains, "Doctor, my bowels are sluggish, my feet hurt, my heart jumps–and you know, Doctor, I myself don't feel so well either." Many patients offer their physicians an option of a medical complaint or a perplexity in living as their reason for consulting him, but most physicians today choose to treat the medical complaint, usually because they do not have the time to talk with the patient. Moreover, in today's age of specialization, various physicians take care of different parts of the patient's body with none taking care of the entire patient. Clinics are dubbed, *e.g.*, "Knees 'R' Us."

The psychiatrist, on the other hand, remains the physician who uses words and listens. Hence, the psychiatrist has a distinct and unique need to preserve the confidence of his patient. While psychiatrists want to be identified with medicine ("a psychiatrist must be a good physician first and always"), strict identification works to a disadvantage insofar as the traditional medical privilege is concerned. Some say the name "Louisiana Psychiatric Medical Association" is a redundancy, which it is, but it serves to accentuate the identification of psychiatry with medicine.

In jurisdictions where the statute grants the privilege to "physicians" without qualifying the word, there is little doubt that psychiatrists are included within the scope of the statute, but these statutes, as we have noted, have been the subject of so much criticism and qualification that they are of little value to psychiatry. From the viewpoint of jurisprudence, the court is not in a position to interpret the statute broadly when a patient in psychotherapy is involved in a case, yet construe the same statute narrowly when a patient of a surgeon is concerned. It is a strained interpretation of a statute which produces opposite effects as applied to subjects governed by the same language. Hence, the call went out for a special statute for the psychiatrist-patient relationship in states not having a medical statute as well as in those that do.

Existing statutes on the medical privilege were for the most part adopted before psychotherapy had any significant degree of acceptance. Wigmore in his critical evaluation of the medical privilege omitted discussion of psychiatry. The first edition of Wigmore's work on evidence appeared in 1904, the second in 1923, and the third in 1940 (later editions were by others). In his latest work, Wigmore recognized the value of psychiatric testimony on the issue of credibility (he advocated the use of psychiatric testimony in cases in which a woman charges a man with sexual crime), but he failed to discuss psychotherapy in connection with privileged communication.

Operationally, psychotherapy is conversation, but it is conversation in which one is encouraged to let down one's guard and to reveal one's inmost thoughts and feelings. "It is in the trusting sanctuary of the 'magic room' as one patient called the office in which his psychoanalytic unfolding has taken place, that the carefully guarded deeper feelings of a person's love, or hate, or greed, or ambition, hostility, and frustration emerge and then become a conscious reality."[1]

As we have noted, commentators generally agree, but without empirical proof, that Wigmore's four tests of legitimate privilege are met in the case of psychotherapy.[2] Each of the tests appears to be satisfied. While Wigmore did not comment on psychotherapy, his argument on behalf of a priest-penitent privilege is applicable. While psychiatry and religion do not share the same orientation or basic assumptions, many of their basic concerns are the same. Fundamentally, both attempt to minister to people. Psychiatrists J.R. Ewalt and Dana Farnsworth put it this way:[3]

> Both disciplines begin with the desire to help people; their views of the nature of the trouble, and of the means of assistance, differ. The relationship of psychiatrists and clergymen to those they help is based on concern, sensible involvement, sympathy, and a respect for the dignity of the individual. This latter element is expressed in part in the tradition of privileged communication, a tradition long upheld by custom, although seldom by law. The patient or parishioner is encouraged to place full confidence in the psychiatrist or clergyman—in fact, this confidence is almost absolutely necessary to effective treatment—and he may rest assured that what he discloses in the course of consultation will remain completely confidential.

Questions are raised: Does the psychotherapist-patient relationship require an absolute privilege, rather than a qualified one, subject to a judge's balancing the competing interest in confidentiality and disclosure? Is access to "the truth" more important than the protection of confidentiality? Can psychotherapy succeed without patients feeling free to say all to the therapist? How would lack of a privilege affect the way one practices psychotherapy and keeps notes? Let us examine Wigmore's criteria from the viewpoint of psychotherapy:

## 1. Communications to a psychiatrist during the course of treatment are of a confidential and secret nature

Just as claims are made over geographical territory, individuals by natural impulse seek to control information about themselves. Ethologists call the geographical claim a "territorial imperative" and a set of facts, which are of several varieties, a "territorial-like information preserve." This preserve includes the content of one's mind or biographical facts about the individual. There is also, akin to the information preserve, as ethologists put it, a "conversational preserve."[4] One court put it this way, "If there is a quintessential zone of human privacy, it is the mind. Our ability to exclude others from our mental processes is intrinsic to the human personality."[5]

The general public assumes that communications to a psychiatrist are confidential. The very essence of psychotherapy is confidential personal revelations about matters which the patient is normally reluctant to reveal or discuss. Freud placed "a confessional ritual at the very heart of the psychoanalytic movement."[6] Frequently, a patient in analysis or psychotherapy will make disclosures to his psychiatrist which he would not make even to the closest members of his family. In therapy, patients reveal their private personality—they reveal that which they have kept secret from the world, and indeed often from themselves. While much that is said or observed in therapy is known to others, personal secrets—the innermost, the vulnerable, often the shameful—lie at its core.

In this regard, it is interesting to note the etymology of the word "person." It stems from the Latin "persona," meaning the character of a novel or play. "Persona" is the public personality, those aspects which one displays to the world as contrasted with the private personality which exists behind the social facade. It is the mask which is worn by an individual in response to the demands of social convention and tradition. The mask is what we daily see; it conceals the inner nature and conflicts of the individual. The mask is like the outer layer of the Russian wooden doll with successively smaller ones fitted into it. In psychotherapy, for purposes of therapy, the mask or outer doll is removed, but in law the outer layer, by and large, is what is relevant and determinative of the outcome of litigation.

The motives or desires of an individual underlying intent or behavior are usually of no moment in resolving a dispute in litigation. In either a tort or criminal case, in judging whether or not a person should be held responsible for an action, it usually does not matter whether he has a vice, a bad character, or a bad attitude. In sentencing, however, the blame attributed to a person may be lessened on account of his motives or desires, though they do not justify or excuse the person's actions. Pragmatic considerations may suggest that psychiatric treatment would be a better alternative than prison.

The psychotherapeutic situation is unique and unlike any other that the patient or anyone else is likely to encounter. The structure and rules of the psychotherapeutic relationship bear little resemblance to usual social or professional relationships. For example, therapists if they think that it will promote treatment, will not respond to a patient's questions or comments. Social etiquette is abandoned in psychotherapy; it has no place in the interpersonal relationship of psychiatrist and patient. Politeness is dropped. The patient is encouraged to talk in the session without regard to the usual social amenities. Editing of one's thoughts is discouraged in the session. Therapists refer to this aspect of therapy as letting down defenses.

The unconventionality of the relationship is illustrated by the following: a patient who is a minister reveals aggressive attributes; patients at the end of each session leave without saying goodbye; a lady of social position regularly greets her therapist with the rebuke, "Haven't you lost weight yet, you fat little fool?"; a woman talks about mutilating her previous therapist; a preacher's wife talks about fecal matter; a man reveals a fantasy of performing fellatio on his young son. The examples are without limit, but these are sufficient to illustrate that the statements of a person in the psychotherapeutic relationship may be at variance with his daily life. Without question, the patient reveals his private personality expecting strict confidence. Revelation by the therapist of the patient's inner life would likely shame or stigmatize the patient.

One can imagine what lawyers would try to do with the following that occurred in a therapy session:[7]

> *Patient*: My friends were telling each other their dreams, but I felt I couldn't. They are too violent.
> *Therapist*: Can you tell me?
> *Patient*: I had this dream which feels like a flashback of a dream I have had often. I was running from these bad guys who wanted to kill me. I was on a raft in a river with this guy Jack who I wanted to have sex with, but he was paying attention to another woman and I was upset, but then it turns out he was interested in me. We had sex and I felt like I was a whore for wanting it. These same bad guys got one guy and were mutilating his body. My dream is filled with sex being bad and me being a whore, and the world being so dangerous. How can I have a relationship if being with someone just brings up all these horrors. It's too hard to walk out in the world with all that being true.

The psychiatric profession requires that confidentiality be maintained even with respect to the fact that a person is in therapy. Unlike cases involving organic illness, a person in psychotherapy by and large visits his psychiatrist with the same secrecy that a man would go to a bawdy house. Less so now than previously, office design allows the patient to enter by one door and to leave by another, in order to avoid being seen by other patients.

While communications to a therapist are of a confidential nature, there is much about a psychiatric patient that is not of a secret nature. Such matters as sexual impotency is secret, but much about the mentally ill, especially the seriously mentally ill, is apparent to one and all. It is obvious, for example, in the case of the individual who is "mad" (in ordinary lexicon) or who suffers panic attacks. Consider the individual given a diagnosis of "borderline" (a common diagnosis) as described in the *American Journal of Psychiatry*: "These borderline patients see their lives, their interactions, and the world around them as totally polarized. All is love or rejection, hateful or good; there is nothing in between. They are volatile in their lives and in therapy."[8]

And consider the news report of Margot Kidder, the Lois Lane of the Superman movies, who was hospitalized after she was found dazed and cowering by a woodpile in a suburban backyard. It was reported:[9]

> Canadian-born Kidder, 47, who has battled health and financial problems in recent years, had been missing for three days and apparently was living in bushes near where she was discovered.
>
> She appeared "frightened and paranoid" and was in "obvious mental distress," police Sgt. Rick Young said. Kidder was taken to a psychiatric center in Sylmar.

Hence, in most cases that involve litigation, it may not be necessary to have more than lay testimony about the individual in order to resolve the issue in controversy. Lay witnesses are allowed under the law of evidence to give an opinion about sanity.

## 2. The inviolability of this confidence is essential to the achievement of the purpose of the relationship

Realistic or not, the mentally ill person feels that his life has been scored by betrayals. To afford a corrective emotional experience, a therapist must not turn out to be another traitor. Of utmost importance in psychotherapy is honesty with a patient. A therapist must be trustworthy. The American Psychiatric Association's "Principles of Medical Ethics with Annotations Especially Applicable to Psychiatry" puts it in terms of confidentiality. It states: "Confidentiality is essential to psychiatric treatment. This is based in part on the special nature of psychiatric therapy as well as on the traditional ethical relationship between physician and patient."[10]

Dr. Harold Eist, as president-elect of the American Psychiatric Association, put it thus: "One has to understand that American psychiatry has to be the conscience of American medicine. Because while confidentiality is critical to all medical care, it is more critical to psychiatric care, because of the stigma against the mentally ill. Confidentiality is the *sine qua non* of health care delivery. Without it people will be afraid to go to their doctors."[11]

The thesis is oft-repeated. In the recent book *The New Informants*, Christopher Bollas, a British psychoanalyst, and David Sundelson, an American lawyer, argue strongly that psychotherapy depends utterly on the confidence of patients that they can reveal to the therapist the most intimate thoughts and fantasies in a privacy that is inviolate.[12] Dr. Herbert Sacks, as president-elect of the American Psychiatric Association, said, "The centerpiece of psychiatry is the covenant between the doctor and the patient, which insures confidentiality is maintained. Without such assurances, treatment will go no place."[13]

Yet one must ask: is it confidentiality or is it trust, of which confidentiality is an aspect, that is the essential to psychiatric treatment? Dr. W. Walter Menninger, President and Chief Executive Officer of the Menninger Foundation and Clinic, for example, cites trust as essential. He writes: "In the absence of the guaranty of confidentiality, the basic trust in the psychotherapist's relationship with the patient is compromised. This basic trust is essential for the psychotherapeutic process to go forward."[14]

In a study of the psychotherapist-patient privilege, Law Professor Daniel Shuman and Dr. Myron Weiner found that most individuals whom they interviewed were not aware if a privilege did exist, and when questioned, they indicated that the existence or lack thereof would not affect their decision to seek therapy, but when they were told to assume that no privilege existed, they indicated a lesser willingness to disclose. Shuman and Weiner concluded, however, that disclosure by patients would probably not be greatly enhanced by a statutory privilege. The basic reason, they say, why patients hesitate to talk about something or other is because they fear the judgment of their therapist. Nonetheless, they argue, privilege is important, not because relationships will falter in the absence of privilege, but because it is inappropriate for society to intrude in this private sphere.[15]

Professor David Louisell also made a deontological analysis of privilege. He wrote:[16]

> I believe that the historic privileges of confidential communication protect significant human value in the interest of the holders of the privileges, and that the fact that the existence of these guarantees sometimes results in the exclusion from a trial of probative evidence is merely a secondary and incidental feature of the privileges' vitality. These convictions contrast with much recent thinking which regards the privileges chiefly from the viewpoint of their exclusionary function in litigation, and deprecates their social and moral significance and worth.

Just suppose the U.S. Supreme Court had ruled against privilege under federal law in the case it decided in 1996, *Jaffee v. Redmond.*[17] Being of high visibility, as are Supreme Court decisions, it would have created doubt in the public about confidentiality in psychotherapy. The public is unaware that as a practical matter the privilege, even the one pronounced by the Supreme

Court, is a shield with a lot of holes. As a result of the extensive publicity given the *Jaffee* case, the awareness of the public about privilege was increased.[18] But the public remains in the dark about exceptions. Shuman and Weiner's research, carried out before the *Jaffee* case, suggested that the public is unaware of the existence or nonexistence of a psychotherapist-patient privilege, but the public believes that what patients tell a therapist will be held in strictest confidence.[19]

In a dissent in the case (the case is hereinafter discussed), Justice Antonin Scalia derided the majority opinion's emphasis on mental health as provided in psychotherapy, and he said:[20]

> How likely is it that a person will be deterred from seeking psychological counseling, or from being completely truthful in the course of such counseling, because of fear of later disclosure in litigation? And even more pertinent to today's decision, to what extent will the evidentiary privilege reduce that deterrent? The Court does not try to answer the first of these questions; and it cannot possibly have any notion of what the answer is to the second, since that depends entirely upon the scope of the privilege, which the Court amazingly finds it "neither necessary nor feasible to delineate." If, for example, the psychotherapist can give the patient no more assurance than "A court will not be able to make me disclose what you tell me, unless you tell me about a harmful act," I doubt whether there would be much benefit from the privilege at all. That is not a fanciful example, at least with respect to extension of the psychotherapist privilege to social workers.

Sissela Bok set out four premises in justification for confidentiality, three supporting confidentiality in general and the fourth, professional secrecy in particular. The first and fundamental premise is that of individual autonomy over personal information. The second premise, closely linked to the first, presupposes the legitimacy not only of having personal secrets but of sharing them, and assumes respect for relationships among human beings and for intimacy. The third premise holds that a pledge of silence creates an obligation beyond the respect due to persons and to existing relationships. The fourth premise assigns weight beyond ordinary loyalty to professional confidentiality because of its utility to persons and to society. According to this premise, says Bok, individuals benefit from such confidentiality because it allows them to seek help they might otherwise fear to ask for.[21]

Communications are more likely to be inhibited if the patient fears they may be revealed during the course of some future lawsuit. Freud expressed the need for confidentiality thus: "The whole undertaking becomes lost labor if a single concession is made to secrecy." In therapy, or at least in psychoanalysis, the patient is asked to report whatever goes through his mind; saying all is the desideratum. (Actually, this may be accomplished only near the end of therapy, when therapy is successful. According to Freud, the goal of treatment, expressed in almost synonymous terms, is "the making conscious of the unconscious," "the removal of infantile amnesia," or "the overcoming of the resistances.") Speaking freely is difficult, and an essential factor in overcoming the usual resistance and inhibition is trust.·

There has been some judicial recognition of this fact. Judge Edgerton of the Court of Appeals of the District of Columbia pointed out, "Many physical ailments might be treated with some degree of effectiveness by a doctor whom the patient did not trust, but a psychiatrist must have his patient's confidence or he cannot help him."[22] Judge Luther Alverson of the Superior Court of Atlanta extrajudicially remarked, "Psychotherapy by its very nature is worthless unless the patient feels assured from the outset that whatever he may say will be forever kept confidential. Without a promise of secrecy from the therapist, buttressed by a legal privilege, a patient would not be prone to reveal personal data which he fears might evoke social disapproval."[23]

Perhaps without knowing why, a person may feel exceedingly anxious about any probing into his inner self. Denial and repression are principal psychic defenses. Encountering one's self for the first time, learning the irrational side of one's self, can be a very frightening experience. It may be deemed desirable, as H.L. Mencken put it, "to leave your mind alone," when one cannot tolerate learning personally unacceptable reasons for one's behavior. Psychiatric patients are heard to say, "How can I live knowing the reasons for what I do?" "I don't want to get all stirred up." There is an old adage, commonly applied, "let sleeping dogs lie." It is by no means easy for a person to report his feelings. There are conflicts not only within one's self but also with society. Achievements which society rewards are often won at the cost of a diminution of personality. A person does not like to say or reveal what he knows of himself. He wants to protect and keep secret his world of Walter Mitty, his hopes, his fears, his fantasies. Introspective data may be produced only if the therapist will keep the confidence and will not disseminate the information.

It is generally assumed that sexual thoughts or behavior are main areas of exploration in psychotherapy. The psychiatrist, it is said, is "the doctor who has sex on his mind." Where the patient is involved in marital infidelities, he may fear litigation and, consequently, would not speak freely if he suspected that the therapist could be compelled to testify. Laws in nearly all states penalize numerous forms of sex activity, hence almost any clinical details concerning sexual material could conceivably be the basis of criminal action or divorce proceedings against the patient.[24]

The desire to avoid trouble, of some sort or other, is often the reason a person seeks psychotherapy. He is bothered and seeks help in trying to control unconventional activity, or he wants relief from intolerable discomfort.

Admittedly, some people seek or enter psychotherapy although lacking genuine motivation for treatment—some may enter psychotherapy because it is fashionable, or to write an exposé. (Tennessee Williams allegedly went into therapy with a newspaper sensation in mind—he attacked psychiatry in a series of articles in the *New York Post*, but his analysis was unsuccessful.) The treatment regime is short-lived in such cases.

All types of people are in therapy, but an individual who goes to a therapist with the aim of plotting a crime or fraud is indeed rare. The exceptional cases mostly arise out of the situation where the patient is referred by an attorney for treatment (as, for example, women who go to a psychiatrist after they have seen an attorney and then file a sexual harassment claim). It does not fall within the realm of a therapist's professional function to become involved in promoting a crime or fraud. The fear that the privilege would be used to shield nefarious schemes is unwarranted.

Almost without exception, psychiatrists and other psychotherapists maintain that without an assurance of confidentiality, at least about one's private thoughts, a person would hesitate to contact them, much less to enter into a meaningful therapeutic relationship. Confidentiality in court as well as out of court is essential, they say, not only to achieve successful treatment but also to induce a person to consult a psychiatrist. It is vital, they also say, to maintain confidentiality concerning the fact of treatment as well as communications made in treatment.[25] David C. Clark, professor of psychiatry and psychology at Rush Medical College, observed:[26]

> Empirical studies of epidemiological trends in the United States consistently document that most persons with major psychiatric disorders and most persons with problems do *not* choose to see a mental health professional for help—this reluctance is related to social stigma, real and perceived expense, uncertainty about the usefulness of mental health services, fear of disclosure, and an acute sense of privacy. It is clear that even *fewer* people in need of help would seek mental health services if they knew or believed that patient-therapist communications were not privileged.

Would not society be better served if those needing mental health services were encouraged to obtain it, rather than be frightened away? Dr. Clark points to the hazards of placing barriers in the way of mental health treatment:[27]

> The psychopathology that afflicts and impairs so many psychiatric and psychological patients only serves to make them more reserved, withdrawn, distrustful, and suspicious. When a patient can be reassured that his communication with the therapist is protected by law, so that no third party can have access to that information, many (not all) patients will talk frankly with their

therapist about concerns, symptoms, and history. In the absence of confidentiality safeguards, therapists simply cannot assess, diagnose, and treat patients adequately. This is particularly true in the area of suicide risk assessment and treatment, my own area of expertise. Patients will not be frank about their suicidal or homicidal thoughts with the therapist unless that therapist can offer legal reassurance that all communications will be safeguarded as confidential up to the point where a person must be protected from dangerous behavior.

By and large, people in the community, including many who are well informed on other matters, consider a person's treatment by a psychiatrist as evidence of his "queerness" or possible "insanity." Government surveys have concluded that "the public generally fears and dislikes the mentally ill and believes them to be unpredictable and untrustworthy."[28] So strong is the fear of stigma that many people choose to pay their own therapy bills rather than submit them to insurers whose records may be available to an employer or others.

The mental patient, even today in many circles, is rejected as "alien," a second-class citizen; an ex-convict may have an easier time getting a job than an ex-mental patient.[29] The ex-mental patient is often regarded as unreliable. In some cases, the rejection of the mentally ill may arise out of denial or avoidance. Seeing a mentally ill person is a reminder that man's most highly prized possession—his mind—is fragile. It is a threat to one's self-image.

There is also an old belief that mental illness is the product of possession by demons, or that it is self-induced, or that it can be overcome by self-control and will-power. Physical illness evokes a wide variety of helping responses, but in the case of psychiatric illness the patient usually feels shame for being ill and finds himself the object of uncanny dread and aversion to others. Psychiatric hospitalization is equated with being "put away"—and with good reason, psychiatric patients often have no visitors, receive no flowers, or get-well cards. As a result, the most frequent initial manifestation of a psychiatric problem will likely be disguised as a physical complaint.[30]

The traditional medical privilege is often restricted to communications relating to the particular ailment for which the patient sought or was being given treatment. In psychotherapy, however, every statement is a link in the chain. Thus all statements are relevant to treatment, and require confidentiality. All physicians may discuss matters with their patients which have no relevance to the illness, but in psychotherapy, almost all, if not all, statements are pertinent to and essential for treatment.

What about managed care? The argument for the need of confidentiality in the practice of psychoanalysis or psychoanalytic psychotherapy is strong, but quick-fix drug therapies are scanting talking therapies. Managed care providers are opting not only for shorter treatment and for medication over psychotherapy, but they are also actively opposing long-term psychotherapy or psychoanalysis. Managed care along with the explosion in new medications has transformed the practice of psychiatry.

Psychiatrists are now often called "hydraulic doctors"–they raise and lower dosages; they are less and less "the listening and talking doctor." The "P" word is no longer psychoanalysis, but Prozac. Rapidly fading are the days of free association, dream analysis, and an exploration of one's past history.[31] This change in the practice of psychiatry very much undercuts the argument distinguishing psychiatry from medicine in regard to privilege.[32]

### 3. The psychiatrist-patient relationship is one that should be fostered

Is this criterion generally accepted? The anti-psychiatry movement speaks against it. According to Jeanine Grobe, editor of the book *Beyond Bedlam*, "Society blindly regards psychiatry as safe medicine, a position that is very comfortable since people who reject it are likely to wind up with psychiatric labels themselves."[33] Psychiatrists, until recently, were legally and medically called "alienists"–they dealt with persons alienated from self and society and they themselves were alienated from the medical profession.[34] To deal with the image problem, the American Psychiatric Association carried out (and still does) an extensive public relations program. Sigmund Freud regarded Carl Jung's doubts about psychoanalysis as "resistance" that had to be analyzed away.

During the past decade an untold number of people in psychotherapy have come to believe that they suffer from "repressed memories" of incest and sexual abuse allegedly inflicted when they were youngsters and they are urged by their therapists to confront their abuser. In turn, those who have been accused would hail outlawing psychotherapy. Legislation has been introduced and adopted in a number of states restricting "revival of memory" therapy and some professional liability insurance policies exclude coverage of the practice. The most popularly disseminated of recent critiques is a pair of essays by UC Berkeley English professor emeritus Frederick Crews, published in two 1994 issues of the *New York Review of Books* and later released as a book, *The Memory Wars: Freud's Legacy in Dispute*. Crew's primary target is Freud's theory of repression: the notion that infantile sexual desires "disappear" into the psyche and influence later behavior. The currently popular belief that traumatic memories can be repressed by the psyche and later recovered wholesale, Crews says, is but the latest mutation of Freud's "fraudulent theories."[35]

The psychiatrist-patient relationship is frequently the subject of caricature. *The New Yorker*, for example, rarely misses an opportunity to make psychiatry the butt of a joke. The general practitioners of medicine, the nonpsychiatric specialists, and lawyers retain, in varying degrees, a hostile attitude toward psychiatry. Psychoanalysis, the form of psychotherapy that especially calls for confidentiality, is the particular target of criticism. By and large, the public sees psychoanalysis as, at best, an indulgence. Psychoanalytic teaching and therapy have inadvertently fostered a "private club" model and thereby compromised its relevance to society at large.

Numerous tracts have derided psychoanalysis as a treatment modality.[36] It has been called the greatest intellectual con job of the 20th century. The following comment by Vladimir Nabokov of *Lolita* fame is illustrative:[37]

> Our grandsons will no doubt regard today's psychoanalysis with the same amused contempt as we do astrology and phrenology. I cannot conceive how anybody in his right mind should go to a psychoanalyst, but of course if one's mind is deranged one might try anything: after all, quacks and cranks, shamans and holy men, kings and hypnotists have cured people.

Community attitudes toward psychiatry, however, represent the epitome of ambivalence. Psychiatry is both hailed and derided. Explanations of the poor image are various. According to one explanation, a psychiatrist is a person who tries to make people confront themselves–this frightens people and, consequently, psychiatrists are disliked and distrusted. Another explanation is that psychiatrists (and lawyers) deal with disease or conflicts in people or between people; they are often identified with the disruptive forces in ourselves (inner space) or in society (outer space). Psychiatrists are also feared because it is believed that they can read a person's mind and, thus, they can invade privacy without consent. According to another explanation, the critical view toward psychiatry stems from the fetish basic to our culture that one has the responsibility to work out one's own problems. It is a blow to self-esteem, an admission of defeat, to seek assistance. Some of the critical comment is by paranoid hate groups. A distorted mind, as we all know, forms a distorted image.

Attitudes toward mental illness and their healers contributed to the late emergence of psychiatry among the major medical specialties. Yet, for all the hard words said over the years about psychiatry, and especially about psychoanalysis, it gained a position of popularity, respect, and status. Now, however, psychoanalysis, as well as psychiatry generally, is characterized by (1) fewer patient referrals, (2) lower fees per visit (except for those psychiatrists who remain in private practice),(3) shorter inpatient and outpatient time to cure the patient, and (4) alternatives to psychiatrists, including social workers, psychologists, and B.A. level or below. In 1995, the Michigan Psychoanalytic Institute, so bereft of candidates, opened its doors to attorneys to train to become psychoanalysts.

Are the changes reversible? Dr. Peter Kramer, author of *Listening to Prozac*, thinks so. He wrote:[38]

> [A] reporter for a major television network phones to ask whether there is a story to be done on Prozac and prepaid health care. What, I inquire, makes him ask? He says two producers for a news program sought help for depression. Both were HMO subscribers, and each was offered the same remedy, an antidepressant prescribed by an internist, and no referral for further evaluation or psychotherapy. The outraged producers, and the reporter, want to know, is this how depression is treated nowadays?

And he concluded:

> This is my train of thought—we will not end up with such a system so long as the profession argues convincingly that psychotherapy is part of the best care for a variety of ailments. Patients believe as much. In a survey published [in November 1995] in *Consumer Reports*, respondents indicated that psychotherapy was the most valuable part of their mental health treatment.

The in-depth survey of *Consumer Reports* subscribers (4,000 readers responded) reported that psychotherapy alone worked as well as psychotherapy combined with medication, like Prozac or Xanax (few of the people responding had a chronic disabling condition such as schizophrenia or manic depression).[39] Most who took medication did feel it was helpful, but many reported side effects. They were just as satisfied and reported similar progress whether they saw a social worker, psychologist, or psychiatrist. Those who consulted a marriage counselor, however, were somewhat less likely to feel they had been helped. Those who sought help from their family doctor tended to do well, but those who saw a mental-health specialist for more than six months did much better. The longer people stayed in therapy, the more they improved. This suggests that limited mental-health insurance coverage, and the new trend in health plans—emphasizing short-term therapy—is misguided.

It is generally agreed, the ambivalence notwithstanding, that the psychiatrist-patient relationship is one that should be fostered. Even characters in comic strips seek psychiatric care. For 65 years, Dagwood Bumstead found the answers to his problems in an overstuffed sandwich or a snooze on the couch, but in the 1990s he and Blondie went to a marriage counselor, Dr. Marjorie Squabble. The public now expects psychiatric service comparable to other medical service—immediate attention, relief of symptoms, twenty-four hour emergency service, and availability of the psychiatrist, but insurance coverage is not on a parity. This third of Wigmore's four criteria is satisfied.

## 4. The information if revealed would produce far fewer benefits to justice than the consequent injury to the individual and to the entire field of psychiatry

Psychiatrists and others have pointed out the great social harm that may be done to countless numbers of patients, ex-patients and future patients by even a rare subpoena of a psychiatrist to testify. A great deal of time is required before a psychiatrist is able to obtain the necessary confidence of his patient, and if there were any suspicion of revelation in the courtroom or anywhere else, the psychiatrist would not have the benefit of this information either for treatment of his patient or for use in court. The denial of the privilege begets the worst of both worlds.

Consider, for example, suicide and homicide by automobile (which is attempted more frequently than is generally recognized). Dr. John M. MacDonald pointed out that when police officers suspect deliberate suicidal intent, they are often handicapped in their investigation by their natural reluctance to press inquiries in the presence of serious injury and grieving relatives.[40] The great emotional distress of the driver's wife at the scene of the wreck may not be due to injury but rather to awareness of her husband's homicidal and suicidal action. Such awareness may not be shared with police officers, even though they may be solicitous. Also, not wanting to be charged with crime, these drivers may not reveal the true circumstances of the wreck to police officers, but they will often freely reveal this information to physicians. Psychiatric treatment might avoid another suicide or homicide attempt. A fine for careless driving, on the other hand, usually will do little to remove the danger to self or others.

The preservation of human dignity, a value which is transcendent for the *summum bonum*, is involved in preserving the privacy of the therapeutic relationship. Man's dignity is more dependent on the privacy of the unconscious than on freedom from disclosure of any conscious content or overt conduct. Furthermore, unlike the case for other privileges, justice may indeed be served by sealing the psychiatrist's lips. Treatment is directed primarily toward the feelings and attitudes which are unacceptable to the patient and others. Treatment often deals with attitudes considered asocial or antisocial by the community. The unconscious is a storehouse of a lifetime's sinful wishes (and every man in varying degree is a combination of Dr. Jekyll and Mr. Hyde). The patient in psychotherapy has the task of revealing his private personality, the personality which exists behind the social facade. Incongruous attitudes emerge which are completely at variance with the patient's everyday-functioning personality. Their production is necessary in treatment but devastating if revealed to public scrutiny.

Data from free-association, fantasies, or memories are not reliable for use in court as they primarily represent the way the person experienced an event, and not how the event occurred. They are not "facts." Patients talk in ways that may be so utterly at varience with real-world facts that in other situations they would be called lies. Psychic reality (inner reality) is not the same as actual reality (outer reality). Freud's example is classic of the young girl whose imagined sexual traumatic relationship with her father affected her personality, yet in reality, the father had had no sexual contact with her.[41] As the material revealed in psychotherapy does not deal with reality of the outer world, it would make poor, yet prejudicial, evidence. The value of the material is similar to that which is elicited under hypnosis or anaesthesia. It comes out of the unconscious, rather than the conscious, layer of the mind. The material is often of childhood fantasies, and it is not directly germane to current activities of the patient. By and large, it leads to false accusation, and should be excluded as irrelevant and immaterial.

The concepts and language employed by a witness or in a document are extremely important considerations in evaluating the strength of evidence. There is a difference of language between the inner and outer world. There is a higher degree of accuracy in data of the outer world than in introspective data. The language is not in terms of cause and effect. The language does not comply with the laws of logic. Opposites are presented in dreams. The "truth" of the patient's thoughts is not a necessity for diagnosis and treatment; the correspondence theory of truth does not prevail in the treatment situation.

When there is a medical privilege, it applies not only to the physician but also to medical reports and hospital records (of course, the exceptions in the medical privilege, as discussed, apply to the records as well). Conversely, where there is no privilege, the entire medical report, hospital record, and office records are subject to discovery. The psychiatrist in his records uses language having a special and rather abstruse meaning to him, such as "unresolved oedipal difficulties," "castration complex," "*folie à deux*," "inadequate personality," "narcissistic identification," and "latent homosexuality." Introduced in court, the record will unfairly prejudice the patient's case. The words have a different meaning and connotation for the layman. It is not to be expected that the psychiatrist will forego his specialized language and record his professional data for the benefit of the common man. Moreover, the record is of value only if viewed in the context of the total symptomatology and treatment.[42]

Even when reports are especially prepared for the courts, or other agency, there are difficulties in interpretation of language.[43] Thus, in one case, a psychiatrist appointed by the court to examine a juvenile defendant employed the term "homosexual" in his report to denote, in the context of his discipline, a stage in psychosexual development. The judge construed the term colloquially and committed the juvenile because "you can't have 'homosexuals' running around loose."[44]

Interprofessional communication is always difficult, especially so when the terms are words of art, and especially misleading when decisions are made solely on the basis of a label.[45] Labels are handy references to a body of knowledge, not a substitute for understanding. As Lewis Carroll said, the question is whether words are to be the master. Charlie Chaplin, in his autobiography, says that one day he was stopped by some children of the neighborhood—"Your mother's gone insane," said a little girl. The words were like a slap in Chaplin's face. "What do you mean?" he mumbled. "It's true," said the little girl, "she's giving away pieces of coal, saying they are birthday presents for the children."[46]

In criminal cases, a psychiatrist may describe a person as a "sociopathic personality," and then the court will draw conclusions based on what "sociopaths" are like—that is, on the label, rather than on a psychodynamic evaluation of the individual defendant. Judges and juries have been mired in confusion over labels used in cases involving criminal responsibility.[47] Some attorneys and juries, notwithstanding the popularization of psychiatry, have been heard to interpret the term "sociopathic personality" to mean a "sociological person" (whatever that is).[48] Labels mean widely different things to different people.[49]

It is to be remembered that lawyers are advocates and they play at the margins. Quite often, when a lawyer makes a demand for the psychiatric records of a patient, he is really not interested in their contents or their possible use at trial. More likely than not, he recognized that the information would not be probative of any issue in dispute. The demand for the record is designed to frighten the patient about the loss of privacy and many a litigant has caved in and settled or abandoned a lawsuit. Of course, some lawyers can construct an argument why an extramarital affair is relevant to an automobile accident (thinking about it distracted his attention). In child custody disputes, where the issue is "the best interests of the child," everything may be said to be relevant and nothing is dispositive. As some lawyers argue, "You never know what peccadillo will tip the balance." A privilege cannot prevent a demand for information, but it might alleviate concern that disclosure will be required. In this way, by privilege, both justice and therapy are benefitted.

The Group for the Advancement of Psychiatry (GAP), an organization of some 200 psychiatrists, in 1960 published a report (no. 45 in GAP's history) which in sum and substance argued, as we have, that the psychiatrist-patient relationship satisfies Wigmore's criteria, and it concluded thus:[50]

[T]he special character of psychiatric treatment . . . requires confidentiality as a sine qua non for successful therapy . . . [The] confidential relationship needs to be safeguarded . . . [A] psychiatrist best fulfills his professional responsibility to the community by maintaining primary emphasis on problems of treatment . . . Privilege has been challenged on the ground that it substantially obstructs justice by withholding evidence. It is our belief that the social value which effective psychiatric treatment has for the community far outweighs the potential loss of evidence resulting from the withholding of testimony by a psychiatrist about his patient. The absence of privilege, among other results, may obstruct the public need to have unencumbered access to psychiatric treatment resources.

Time and again, therapists complain that whereas the attorney-client relationship is covered by a solid shield, the therapy relationship is not. Is there greater justification for one than the other? Why not a solid shield for both, they ask, given the need for confidentiality and the justification for the privilege? Is it justice, or just us lawyers?[51]

One prominent psychiatrist asks, "Why are lawyers allowed absolute confidentiality? It seems to me that if the issue is justice, honesty, and truth, then lawyers should have no more right to absolute confidentiality than anybody else. At the same time, I realize that those people who write the laws enjoy the benefit of the laws."[52]

Rather than divulge confidences, many psychiatrists, in the spirit of Thoreau's *Walden*, claim that they would risk contempt charges. It is cause for concern, however, whenever people attempt to take the law into their own hands.

## NOTES

1. A.A. Hutschnecker, *The Drive for Power* (New York: Bantam Books, 1976), p. 77.
2. B. Diamond & H. Weihofen, "Privileged Communication and the Clinical Psychologist," *J. Clin. Psychology* 9:388, 1953; D. Louisell, "Confidentiality, Conformity and Confusion: Privileges in Federal Court Today," *Tul. L.Rev.* 31:101, 1956; J. Rappeport, "Psychiatrist-Patient Privilege," *Md. L. Rev.* 23:39, 1963; E. Zenoff, "Confidential and Privileged Communications," *J.A.M.A.* 182:656, 1962; Note, *Nw. U. L. Rev.* 47:384, 1952. The late Charles T. McCormick of the Texas Law School, one of the leading commentators on the law of evidence, supported special protection of privileged communications between psychiatrist and patient though he was critical of the medical privilege. Letter to author (July 10, 1961).
3. J.R. Ewalt & D. Farnsworth, *Textbook of Psychiatry* (New York: McGraw-Hill, 1963), p. 299.
4. Sociologist Erving Goffman has written extensively on this topic. See, *e.g.*, *The Preservation of Self in Everyday Life* (New York: Anchor, 1959).

5. Long Beach City Employees Assn. v. City of Long Beach, 41 Cal.3d 937, 227 Cal. Rptr. 90, 719 P.2d 660 (1986).

6. R. Webster, *Why Freud Was Wrong: Sin, Science, and Psychoanalysis* (New York: Basic Books, 1995).

7. S.D. Perlman, "'Reality' and Countertransference in the Treatment of Sexual Abuse Patients: The False Memory Controversy," *J. Am. Acad. Psychoanal.* 24:115, 1996.

8. J.H. Gold (editorial), "The Intolerance of Aloneness," *Am. J. Psychiatry* 153:749, 1996.

9. AP & Reuter news report, "Actress Kidder undergoing psychiatric test," *Detroit News,* April 25, 1996, p. 4. See also J.D. Reed & D. Morton, "Starting Over," *People* (cover story), Sept. 23, 1996, p. 44.

10. Section 4, Anno. 1 (1995 ed.).

11. Quoted in R. Karel, "Legislation on Medical Record Access Could Hurt Patients," *Psychiatric News,* Dec. 15, 1995, p. 1.

12. C. Bollas & D. Sundelson, *The New Informants* (Northvale, N.J.: Jason Aronson, 1995); reviewed in D.J. Kevles, "The Suspect on the Couch," *New York Times Book Review,* Dec. 31, 1995, p. 9.

13. Quoted in E.J. Pollock, "Mother Fights to Keep Daughter's Records in Rape Case Secret," *Wall Street Journal,* Aug. 22, 1996, p. 1.

14. Statement in Brief of the Menninger Foundation as Amicus Curiae in Jaffee v. Redmond, 116 S.Ct. 1923 (1996).

15. D.W. Shuman & M.F. Weiner, *The Psychotherapist-Patient Privilege/A Critical Examination* (Springfield, IL.: Thomas, 1987).

16. D. Louisell, "Confidentiality, Conformity and Confusion: Privileges in Federal Court Today," *Tul. L. Rev.* 31:101, 1956.

17. 116 S.Ct. 1923 (1996); reported in J. Biskupic, "Therapist-Patient Talks Are Shielded," *Washington Post,* June 14, 1996, p. 1; L. Greenhouse, "Justices Uphold Psychotherapy Privacy Rights," *New York Times,* June 14, 1996, p. 1.

18. B.J. Winick, "The Psychotherapist-Patient Privilege: A Therapeutic Jurisprudence View," *U. Miami L. Rev.* 50:249, 1996.

19. P.S. Appelbaum, G. Kapen, B. Walters, C. Lidz & L.H. Roth, "Confidentiality: An Empirical Test of the Utilitarian Perspective," *Bull. Am. Acad. Psychiatry & Law* 12:109, 1984.

20. 116 S.Ct. 1923 at 1932.

21. S. Bok, "The Limits of Confidentiality," *Hastings Center Report* 13:24, Feb. 1983; adapted from her book *Secrets* (New York: Pantheon Books, 1982).

22. Taylor v. United States, 222 F. 2d 398, 401 (D.C. Cir, 1955).

23. Address delivered at the North Georgia Chapter of the National Association of Social Workers in Atlanta, Ga., Oct. 21, 1958.

24. Even a cursory look at *A Guide to Sex Laws in the United States* (Chicago: University of Chicago Press, 1996) will show that the nation's laws governing what two consenting adults can do with one another are a jungle. That's one reason why Federal Judge Richard Posner and Law Professor Katharine Silbaugh wrote it. "What surprises me most is the sheer complexity and ver-

bal obscurity of these laws," says Judge Posner. "It's extraordinary."

25. P.S. Appelbaum, G. Kapen, B. Walters, C. Lidz & L.H. Roth, "Confidentiality: An Empirical Test of the Utilitarian Perspective," *Bull. Am. Acad. Psychiatry & Law* 12:109, 1984. Though recognizing his need for psychiatric care, Sol Wachtler, chief judge of New York's highest court, feared that it would jeopardize his chances of becoming governor, and he engaged in self-medication to deal with his depression. For the crime of aggravated harassment, he was sentenced to 15 months in prison. He describes his ordeal in *After the Madness* (New York: Random House, 1997). See Part IV, Chapter 3.

26. Statement in amicus brief of the Menninger Foundation in Jaffee v. Redmond, 116 S. Ct. 1923 (1996).

27. *Ibid.*

28. H.E.W., *Public Opinions and Attitudes About Mental Health* (Washington, D.C.: Gov't Ptg. Office, 1963).

29. See Part II, Chapter 5 on identity of a patient.

30. C.W. Wahl, "Physical symptoms as a mask of psychiatric disorders in the hospital," *Hosp. Med.*, Dec. 1964, p. 28.

31. C.S. Austad, *Is Long Term Psychotherapy Unethical?/Toward a Social Ethic in an Era of Managed Care* (San Francisco: Jossey-Bass, 1996); P. Gold & D. Holzman (cover story), "Shrunken Head Shrinkers/Freud is Out, Drugs Are In," *Insight*, Dec. 1, 1986, pp. 8-17. Dr. David Kaiser of Chicago writes, "As a practicing psychiatrist, I have watched with growing dismay and outrage the rise and triumph of the hegemony known as biologic psychiatry. Within the general field of modern psychiatry, biologism now completely dominates the discourse on the causes and treatment of mental illness." D. Kaiser, "Not by Chemicals Alone: A Hard Look at 'Psychiatric Medicine,'" *Psychiatric Times,* Dec. 1996, p. 42.

32. Drs. George Caesar and Joseph Lifschutz, however, say: "In those areas such as medications visits, where the patient reveals few confidences to the clinician, the reason for the privilege is the same as that for the age-old physician-patient privilege: to encourage the patient to seek help while protecting against unnecessary disclosure of matters of great personal embarrassment, such as the symptoms of a psychosis, a history of confinement in a mental hospital and the like." Statement in brief as amicus curiae in Jaffee v. Redmond, 116 S. Ct. 1923 (1996).

33. J. Grobe (ed.), *Beyond Bedlam* (Chicago: Third Side Press, 1995).

34. See H. Davidson, "The Image of the Psychiatrist," *Am. J. Psychiat.* 121:329, 1964.

35. See D.A. Poole, A. Memon, S.D. Lindsay & R. Bull, "Psychotherapy and the Recovery of Memories of Childhood Sexual Abuse: U.S. and British Practitioners' Opinions, Practices, and Experiences," *J. Consulting & Clinical Psychology* 63:426, 1995; J. Jacobs, "False recovered memories almost ruin life," *San Jose (Calif.) Mercury News,* May 22, 1996, p. 7; K. Robinson, "The end of therapy/Freud is out. Prozac is in. Who needs therapists?", *Seattle Weekly* (cover story), Nov. 13, 1996.

36. See, *e.g.,* A. Salter, *The Case Against Psychoanalysis* (New York: Citadel, 1963). The various and sundry criticisms directed against psychiatry are collected in M.H. Miller & S.L. Halleck, "The Critics of Psychiatry: A Review of Contemporary Critical Attitudes," *Am. J. Psychiat.* 119:705, 1963.

37. Quoted in *Life,* Nov. 20, 1964, p. 68.

38. "What's News," *Psychiatric Times,* Jan. 1996, p. 4.

39. "Mental Health/Does Therapy Help?" *Consumer Reports,* Nov. 1995, p. 734.

40. "Suicide and Homicide by Automobile," *Am. J. Psychiat.* 121:366, 1964.

41. See Freud's analysis of a case of hysteria in the well-known "Case of Dora," as it is generally called. See also Freud's paper "A Child Is Being Beaten," which describes a child who produced the fantasy of being beaten although he had never been physically maltreated.

42. See Part V, Chapter 3 on the stigma of psychiatric discourse.

43. In making a report to document a disability claim under an insurance or welfare program, the psychiatrist is advised: "To minimize the potentially unfavorable impact that information in his report may have on a third party (possibly the patient himself), the psychiatrist should report only the clinical and historical data required in assessing functional capacity for work. He should also be selective in his medical phraseology, using euphemistic terms where a third party might consider more commonly used terms objectionable." J. Lerner, "Confidentiality of psychiatric reports used in evaluating Social Security disability claims," *Am. J. Psychiat.* 120:992, 1964.

44. R. Allen, "The Dynamics of Interpersonal Communication and the Law," *Washburn L.J.* 3:135, 1964.

45. In a Task Force Report of the American Psychiatric Association on the use of psychiatric diagnoses in the legal process, it was stated, "When diagnoses are used to infer functional impairments in a global, categorical fashion, a disservice is performed to the courts." S.L. Halleck, S.K. Hoge, R.D. Miller, R.L. Sadoff & N.H. Halleck, "The Use of Psychiatric Diagnoses in the Legal Process: Task Force Report of the American Psychiatric Association," *Bull. Am. Acad. Psychiatry & Law* 20:481, 1992; see United States v. Thigpen, 4 F.3d 1573 (11th Cir. 1993), psychiatrists testified that Thigpen suffered from a schizophrenic disorder and then were asked a series of questions to elicit an opinion as to whether such a condition by necessity implies that a person would be unable to appreciate the nature and quality of his acts. Discussed in R. Slovenko, "On the Revival of the 'Ultimate Issue' Objection," *Newsletter of Am. Acad. Psychiatry & Law* 21(2):70, Sept. 1996.

46. C. Chaplin, *My Autobiography* (New York: Simon & Schuster, 1964).

47. R. Slovenko, "Psychiatry, Criminal Law, and the Role of the Psychiatrist," *Duke L.J.* 1963:395.

48. State v. Prudhomme, Orleans Parish Criminal District Court, Nov. 1964. Lawyers practicing criminal law–defense lawyers and prosecuting attorneys–usually come from the bottom of law classes, hence more gobbledygook may be expected in criminal trials than in civil trials.

49. See Part V, Chapter 3, on the stigma of psychiatric discourse.

50. Report No. 45, Group for the Advancement of Psychiatry (Washington, D.C.: American Psychiatric Association, 1960).

51. The foundation of the attorney-client privilege is succinctly summarized as follows: "It is based on the ground of public policy, and is essential to the proper administration of justice, of the aid of persons having knowledge of the law and skilled in its practice, which assistance can be safely and readily availed of only when free from the consequences or the apprehension of disclosure." 97 Corpus Juris Secundum 280.

52  Communication from Dr. Robert H. Weinstein, chairman of the Department of Psychiatry of the New Hanover Regional Medical Center in North Carolina, to author (Oct. 13, 1996).

# Chapter 5

# MISGUIDED HOPE IN PSYCHOTHERAPIST-PATIENT PRIVILEGE

Psychiatrists as well as other related professionals have been led to believe that a shield statute would protect the communications made to them by their patients or clients against a demand for disclosure by tribunals and agencies of the state. The exceptions that have been carved in the shield, however, make it quite apparent that the proponents for adoption of privilege were false prophets.

Tending to frustrate privilege are concerns about the dangers in secrecy, whether or not it has a lawful basis. There can be no mention of secrecy nowadays without some reference to Watergate, where secrecy laid the cover for dirty tricks. Given that disclosure is salutary in the political arena, to maintain representative or accountable government, it is deemed appropriate to question the justification of a shield in other areas. Justice prevails, this thesis runs, when lanterns blaze on the antics of all. Justice Brandeis once observed, "Sunlight is the best of disinfectants."

Exceptions, purportedly designed to achieve balance, have been carved into the psychotherapy privilege, where it exists, leaving little or no shield cover. These exceptions in the privilege law originated in response to the general feeling that privilege may work an injustice. The privilege appears too available to those who would defraud an adversary or insurance company about the extent of an alleged injury or mislead about character or competence.

Moreover, as far as the legal world is concerned, the assertion by psychiatry that a testimonial privilege is essential for the practice of psychotherapy has never really been substantiated. And while a subpoena or court order for information worries psychiatrists most, the demand that affects them and their patients most frequently comes in the noncourtroom situation, which, as we have noted, is not the concern of privilege–the request for information from an insurance company which pays all or part of the treatment; from the

57

employer, who may be paying for the treatment, and who is responsible for the acts of his employees; from parents or other members of the family who are concerned about the patient; from the state in such areas as drug use and child abuse; and from researchers and investigators, who are concerned with the adequacy and cost of treatment.

At one time, court actions involving psychotherapists were so rare, or so little publicized, that few psychotherapists or their patients ever thought about the need for the legal recognition of "privileged communication." Increasingly, however, evidence has been sought of psychiatrists in personal injury litigation and disability claims under insurance programs. The increase in the number of court actions involving psychiatrists, and the White House-ordered burglary of the office of Daniel Ellsberg's former psychiatrist, turned the subject of psychiatric testimony and records into a matter of public interest.

According to a number of psychiatrists, many patients are asking about confidentiality, inquiring whether the fact of their visit or its content will be revealed. As in any relationship, people interact comfortably only after they begin to trust one another. Confidentiality is said to be an issue that increasingly has to be explored. Many psychiatrists have attempted to reassure patients by advising them, "I keep no records; and I will reveal nothing without your permission."

Until recently, not keeping records or much of a record was very much the norm. Today, however, the demands of peer review, insurance or managed care—not the demands of therapy—call for recordkeeping. But actually, when a psychiatrist is subpoenaed, the attorney does not await his testimony or records with bated breath. The records, if any, are illegible or cryptic; and if called as a witness against the patient, the psychiatrist is not apt to be a friendly one.

The primary purpose of the attorney issuing the subpoena, in effect, is not to investigate but rather to intimidate the patient into foregoing or settling the case. Privilege offers no protection against such blackmail. Generally speaking, since the privilege covers only the content of a communication and not the fact of a relationship, the identity of a treating psychiatrist can be elicited under a discovery demand. Pressure then can be brought to bear which frightens the patient, notwithstanding assurances from his attorney, into thinking that all of his statements made in psychotherapy will be revealed in open court. It is impossible to estimate the number of cases which patients have dropped or feared to initiate because of the apprehension of disclosure.[1] Many persons feel that they will become objects of stigma, censure, and ridicule if even disclosure of seeing a psychiatrist is made.[2]

Two developments have come to pass. One development is the idea that psychiatric testimony or records has special value or relevancy. (In the Old

Testament, Joseph was made the most powerful man in Pharaoh's kingdom because of his ability to interpret dreams.) The other development is the idea that a shield law would protect against a demand for information in court.

Finding that the medical privilege (enacted in approximately 40 states) is so riddled with qualifications and exceptions that it does not adequately shield patients in psychotherapy, psychiatrists lobbied for a special privilege. In 1959, Georgia was the first state to enact a specific "privilege for communication between psychiatrist and patient."[3] That statute did not elaborate; it was more in the nature of a commandment or injunction than a law, and probably would receive a grade of failure if submitted in a law class on legal draftsmanship, yet it was probably respected more than the detailed statutes later enacted in other states–demonstrating that it is not the statute but the attitude about confidentiality in psychotherapy that is determinative. In any event, since then, Georgia has enacted more detailed legislation.[4]

The Group for the Advancement of Psychiatry (GAP) in its report in 1960 urged enactment of legislation granting the same privilege to psychiatrist-patient communications as exists between attorney and client. GAP, following the approach of Georgia in 1959, proposed the following model statute: "The confidential relationship and communication between psychiatrist and patient shall be placed on the same basis as regards privilege, as provided by law between attorney and client." Alabama places "the confidential relations and communications between licensed psychologists and licensed psychiatrists and clients" upon "the same basis as those provided by law between attorney and client."

The GAP proposal was presented as the conclusion of a 24-page report on confidentiality in the practice of psychiatry and was essentially a statement of policy. GAP sought the same kind of protection for psychiatrist-patient communications as provided attorney-client communications. GAP recognized that some provisions of the attorney-client privilege would be inapposite for the psychiatrist-patient privilege, but it did not spell them out. In a footnote to its report, GAP simply stated: "If in some jurisdictions the attorney-client privilege contains provisions not applicable to the psychiatrist-patient privilege, this will have to be considered in the drafting of the specific patient-psychiatrist statute." GAP sought a policy from the law; it wanted the same acceptance of the psychiatrist-patient relationship as existed for the attorney-client relationship.[5]

Shortly thereafter Professor Joseph Goldstein and Dr. Jay Katz of Yale University pointed out the difficulties which would arise from legislation by mere reference to the attorney-client privilege.[6] Thereupon GAP revised its proposal and urged the enactment of a detailed psychotherapist-patient privilege similar to the 1961 Connecticut statute.[7] (Goldstein and Katz were members of the committee that prepared the Connecticut bill.) The

Connecticut law was the model of a number of subsequently enacted statutes.[8] All fifty states have now adopted varying forms of the psychotherapist-patient privilege.[9]

The Federal Rules of Evidence (FRE) of 1975 omitted a medical privilege, but its Advisory Committee recommended a psychotherapist-patient privilege, Rule 504, also modeled on the Connecticut law. This proposed rule, along with several others, evoked considerable criticism. Two committees of the American Bar Association recommended to the A.B.A. House of Delegates "the complete abolition of any and all privilege in the physician-patient area including the proposed 'psychotherapist-patient privilege.'" The Committee on the Judiciary of the House of Representatives, after extensive hearings, recommended and the House approved the scrapping of all the proposed rules on privileges and left federal law of privileges unchanged, to wit, that the federal courts are to apply the state's privilege law in actions founded upon a state-created right or defense, while in other civil cases and in criminal cases, according to Rule 501, the principles of the common law, as interpreted by the federal courts in "the light of reason and experience," would be applied.

Though not adopted by the Congress, Rule 504 influenced various states into enacting a similar rule, and a number of federal courts "in the light of reason and experience" have applied the rule.[10] Given the split among the various federal circuits, the U.S. Supreme Court granted certiorari to decide whether federal evidence rules incorporate a psychotherapist-patient privilege.[11] In 1996, by a vote of 7-2 in *Jaffee v. Redmond*,[12] the Supreme Court held that a psychotherapist-patient privilege falls under the scope of Rule 501. Heretofore, "in the light of reason and experience," federal evidence law included only the attorney-client privilege and the marital privilege.[13]

In recognizing a marital privilege in its 1980 decision in *Trammel v. United States*,[14] the Supreme Court observed: "In rejecting the proposed Rules and enacting Rule 501, Congress manifested an affirmative intention not to freeze the law of privilege. Its purpose rather was to provide the courts with the flexibility to develop rules of privilege on a case-by-case basis, and to leave the door open to change."[15]

In *Jaffee*, the Supreme Court found the adoption of a psychotherapy privilege by all 50 states to be a persuasive factor in meeting "the light of reason and experience test." However, in relying on the existence of state privileges, it glossed over the fact that legislatures—not courts—had established them, and it also evaded sketching out the contours of the privilege.

The proposed Federal Rule 504 (a replica of the Connecticut statute and adopted in the various states) provided:

(a) *Definitions.*
(1) A "patient" is a person who consults or is examined or interviewed by a psychotherapist.

(2) A "psychotherapist" is (A) a person authorized to practice medicine in any state or nation, or reasonably believed by the patient so to be, while engaged in the diagnosis or treatment of a mental or emotional condition, including drug addiction, or (B) a person licensed or certified as a psychologist under the laws of any state or nation, while similarly engaged.

(3) A communication is "confidential" if not intended to be disclosed to third persons other than those present to further the interest of the patient in the consultation, examination, or interview, or persons reasonably necessary for the transmission of the communication, or persons who are participating in the diagnosis and treatment under the direction of the psychotherapist, including members of the patient's family.

(b) *General rule of privilege.* A patient has a privilege to refuse to disclose and to prevent any other person from disclosing confidential communications, made for the purposes of diagnosis or treatment of his mental or emotional condition, including drug addiction, among himself, his psychotherapist, or persons who are participating in the diagnosis or treatment under the direction of the psychotherapist, including members of the patient's family.

(c) *Who may claim the privilege.* The privilege may be claimed by the patient, by his guardian or conservator, or by the personal representative of a deceased patient. The person who was the psychotherapist may claim the privilege but only on behalf of the patient. His authority so to do is presumed in the absence of evidence to the contrary.

(d) *Exceptions.*

(1) *Proceedings for hospitalization.* There is no privilege under this rule for communications relevant to an issue in proceedings to hospitalize the patient for mental illness, if the psychotherapist in the course of diagnosis or treatment has determined that the patient is in need of hospitalization.

(2) *Examination by order of judge.* If the judge orders an examination of the mental or emotional condition of the patient, communications made in the course thereof are not privileged under this rule with respect to the particular purpose for which the examination is ordered unless the judge orders otherwise.

(3) *Condition an element of claim or defense.* There is no privilege under this rule as to communications relevant to an issue of the mental or emotional condition of the patient in any proceeding in which he relies upon the condition as an element of his claim or defense, or, after the patient's death, in any proceeding in which any party relies upon the condition as an element of his claim or defense.

In Congress, the proposed Rule 504 ran into difficulty because it had become enmeshed with related politically hot issues of news media privilege and presidential privilege. Another of the controversial elements entering into the discussion on privilege, other than these claims for privilege, was instigated by Dr. Ernest B. Howard, Executive Vice President of the American Medical Association. Recognizing Rule 504 as being a replacement for the old physician-patient privilege, he argued against it. He decried the absence of a physician-patient privilege although, as carried out in practice, it offered little or no shield.

The observation of Judge Spencer A. Gard (chairman of the special committee of the Commissioners on Uniform State Laws that drafted the Uniform Rules of Evidence) about the physician-patient privilege enacted in 1959 in Illinois is also applicable to the Uniform Rule and the FRE proposals:[16]

> [T]he exceptions contained in the act are so comprehensive that . . . there is scarcely any room left for the privilege to operate.

History repeats. Like the medical privilege, the psychotherapist-patient privilege amounts to a zero-sum game. Like the Roman god Janus, the law on privilege faces in opposite directions at the same time—what it gives with one hand it takes away with the other. Virtually nothing is shielded by the shield. The concerns that prompted the exceptions in the medical privilege also prompted similar ones in the psychotherapy privilege. Santayana would not be surprised by the repeat of history.

In every jurisdiction, the exceptions or waivers are so many and so broad that it is difficult to imagine a case in which the privilege applies. The most common form of forfeiture is the one in which a patient is said to waive the privilege by injecting his condition into litigation, as when his condition is an element of claim or defense.[17]

It has been urged that this exception apply to witnesses as well as to litigants on the theory that, in testifying, an individual puts credibility in issue.[18] In the O.J. Simpson trial, police detective Mark Fuhrman's credibility was attacked by his psychiatric records in which it was recorded that he had "a desire to choke people." In the early 1980s, Fuhrman sought to leave the force and his lawyers asserted that in the course of his work, Fuhrman "sustained seriously disabling psychiatric symptomatology" and as a result should receive a disability pension from the city. The extensive case file documenting his efforts, replete with detailed psychiatric evaluations of him, was made available to the defense.[19]

No-fault automobile insurance legislation eliminates the physician-patient privilege.[20]

In proceedings for hospitalization, the interests of both patient and public are said to call for a departure from confidentiality.

Another exception is made in child-custody cases out of regard for the best interests of the child.[21]

On one ground or another, the privilege has little or no application in criminal cases.[22]

The commentator on privilege is thus in a position analogous to that of the history professor who was invited to give a lecture on the private life of

Catherine of Russia. He began his lecture: "Gentlemen, I am to lecture on the private life of Catherine of Russia. Gentlemen, Catherine of Russia had no private life."

California's psychotherapist-patient privilege, which was a copy of the Connecticut statute and a model for the proposed FRE Rule 504, was tested shortly after its enactment in 1965 in a much publicized case involving Dr. Joseph E. Lifschutz and came to naught.[23] The case was featured in national news weeklies,[24] and was reported at numerous meetings of psychiatric societies and in psychiatric and psychoanalytic bulletins and news letters. The Northern California Psychiatric Society made a nationwide appeal to psychiatrists for contributions to cover legal expenses. The American Psychoanalytic Association and the National Association for Mental Health filed amicus curiae briefs. Although great effort was exerted on behalf of privilege, the case illustrates the irrelevancy of privilege law (as well as the irrelevancy of much psychiatric testimony).

Joseph Housek, a high school teacher, brought a damage suit against John Arabian, a student, alleging an assault which caused "physical injuries, pain, suffering, and severe mental and emotional distress." During a deposition taken by defense counsel, Housek stated that he had received psychiatric treatment ten years earlier from Dr. Lifschutz over a six-month period. The defendant then sought from Dr. Lifschutz Housek's psychiatric records. Dr. Lifschutz refused to produce any of his records, assuming there were any, and also declined to disclose whether or not Housek had consulted him or had been his patient.

Thereupon defendant Arabian sought a court order to compel Dr. Lifschutz to answer questions on deposition and to produce the subpoenaed records. The court determined that the plaintiff had put his mental and emotional condition in issue by instituting the pending litigation, and the statutory psychotherapist-patient privilege did not apply. The privilege belongs to the patient—not to the physician—and is waived by the patient as a consequence of bringing suit as to that which is relevant.

Dr. Lifschutz argued a right of privacy separate from that of any individual patient, a right derived from what he saw as a duty not to Housek alone but to all his patients. He argued that the disclosure of one patient's confidential communications causes damage to all of the therapist's other patients. He also argued that compelling him to testify unconstitutionally impairs the practice of his profession.[25] The court was unpersuaded. It said: "[W]e cannot blind ourselves to the fact that the practice of psychotherapy has grown, indeed flourished, in an environment of a non-absolute privilege."[26]

Statements made by a patient to a physician or a psychiatrist as to the symptoms and effects of his injury or malady are admissible in evidence on his behalf as an exception to the hearsay rule. Under the sporting theory of justice it is deemed only fair that the defendant also have the benefit of these statements when they are favorable to him. Since the privilege is intended as a shield and not a sword, it is considered waived by the patient when he makes a legal issue of his physical or mental condition. Thus, when plaintiff Housek claimed that he had suffered "emotional distress" as a result of the injuries he had suffered, the privileged status of his communications with his psychiatrist was waived, said the trial court. However, on appeal, the California Supreme Court doubted that "the 10-year-old therapeutic treatment sought to be discovered from Dr. Lifschutz would be sufficiently relevant to a typical claim of 'mental distress' to bring it within the exception."

In *Jaffee v. Redmond*,[27] the Supreme Court made the privilege absolute, or so it said, saying anything less would be worthless. "Making the promise of confidentiality contingent upon a trial judge's later evaluation of the relative importance of the patient's interest in privacy and the evidentiary need for disclosure would eviscerate the effectiveness of the privilege," said Justice John Paul Stevens writing for the 7-2 majority. The decision went further than the appellate decision that it affirmed. The Seventh Circuit had created not an absolute privilege but a qualified one, to be balanced in appropriate cases by the "evidentiary need for disclosure." The case, as we shall discuss, grew out of an effort by a licensed clinical social worker and her patient, a police officer who received counseling after killing a man in the line of duty, to protect records of the therapy sessions from being disclosed in a federal civil rights suit. The Court's ruling was more inclusive than proposed Rule 504 and some of the state privileges in extending the rule to cover clinical social workers.[28]

The decision applies to only federal trials and moreover, on constitutional grounds, privileges are delimited in criminal cases. The *Jaffee* case involved tort litigation; it was not a criminal case. Suppose, hypothetically, the police officer had been prosecuted for the killing, and the prosecution sought the records of the therapist. Suppose the police officer claimed insanity. Suppose the police officer claimed the victim was the aggressor and sought the records of the victim to establish the character of the victim. These issues are discussed later on in the chapter on criminal cases.

Kenneth Flaxman, the lawyer for the family of the victim, criticized the opinion as unnecessarily broad and going further to protect the confidentiality of conversations in federal trials than the various states had. "This cries out for congressional correction," he said.[29]

The decision is not as broad, however, as the publicity would indicate. While calling the privilege absolute, Justice Stevens in a footnote to his opinion wrote, "Although it would be premature to speculate about most future developments in the federal psychotherapist privilege, we do not doubt that there are situations in which the privilege must give way, for example, if a serious threat of harm to the patient or to others can be averted only by means of a disclosure by the therapist." Justice Stevens also said, "Because this is the first case in which we have recognized a psychotherapist privilege, it is neither necessary nor feasible to delineate its full contours in a way that would govern all conceivable future questions in this area." In any event, psychotherapists are enthused by the news of the Court's decision–at least it did not deflate the myth in the public mind and in the mind of therapists that the privilege is a solid shield. With it in hand, the American Psychiatric Association urged the military to adopt a psychotherapy privilege.[30] Dr. Leon Hoffman, director of the Parent Child Center of the New York Psychoanalytic Center, wrote (mistakenly) that the Supreme Court in *Jaffee* ruled that "therapist-patient confidentiality is of such paramount importance that in federal cases it cannot be overridden by a trial judge," and thus, he argued, the privilege should be absolute in all situations, including psychological treatment under managed care.[31]

Under prevailing law, with relevancy or materiality as the guideline, the burden rests upon the patient to convince the court that a given communication is not directly related to the issue he had tendered to the court.[32] Only the patient knows both the nature of the injury for which recovery is sought and the general content of the psychotherapeutic communications. He may either have to delimit his assertion of "mental or emotional distress" or explain the object of the psychotherapy in order to convince the court that the psychotherapeutic communications sought are not directly relevant to the mental condition that he has placed in issue.[33] With a bit of luck, from the patient's viewpoint, the court as a matter of course, without any showing, will rule that psychotherapeutic communications are irrelevant and immaterial, or that other, less prejudicial evidence is available.

As a practical matter, the real test in protecting confidentiality in psychotherapy is one of relevancy or materiality (which arises regarding all evidence in every trial), hence it must be asked: "What are the material issues?" and "What is relevant or competent to establish them?" In other words, does the item of evidence tend to prove that contention or fact which is sought to be proved? In every case where the testimony or records of a physician or psychotherapist have been required by a court, it was because the evidence was deemed relevant or material to an issue in the case. As a consequence, in the last analysis, the confidentiality of a physician-patient or psychotherapist-patient communication is protected from disclosure in a courtroom only by a showing that the communication would have no relevance or materiality to the issues in the case.[34]

By and large, psychotherapists are dismayed to learn about exceptions to privilege that they thought inviolate and they consider the concept of relevancy as less than satisfying in protecting confidentiality. They would find it difficult to explain "relevance" to patients or to assure them of confidentiality by that concept. They say that "relevance" allows the judicial system the potential to embark essentially on a fishing expedition into a person's psychiatric records. Just knowing, they say, that one's psychiatric records are being scrutinized by persons not connected with one's treatment carries the potential for harassment of a witness.[35]

To be sure, the primary intent of privilege is to prevent entry of "relevant" information into a legal proceeding, but, by and large, the statutory privilege as a guideline is "much sound and fury signifying nothing." The privilege as a shield is a venture that has accomplished little or nothing. The practice in states where there is no physician-patient privilege or until recently no psychotherapist-patient privilege is the same as in states where there is a privilege. Moreover, the practice in states enacting a privilege is generally found to be the same thereafter as it was before enactment.[36] The harm done, though, by the crusade for privilege is that it gives an undue sense of importance to communications in psychotherapy. The privilege concept tends to invest them with an aura or sense of relevancy and materiality to issues on trial.

Is the relevancy test workable as a shield? Does it offer assurance to therapists and patients? Is it fair to place the burden on the plaintiff, albeit the mover in the case, to establish that the evidence is irrelevant or immaterial? It is to be noted that in pretrial discovery (interrogatories and depositions) relevancy is a looser limitation than at trial since an important role of discovery is to obtain information which will lead to further investigation. An inquiry is permitted even though it is not strictly relevant to the precise issues formulated by the pleadings.[37]

Under the Federal Rules of Evidence (and their counterpart in state rules), the general policy is to increase—not decrease—the flow of information to the fact finder at trial. The Rules define "relevant evidence" as "evidence having *any tendency* to make the existence of any fact that is of consequence to the determination of the action more probable or less probable than it would be without the evidence" (emphasis added).[38] The phrase "any tendency" would seem to open the door wide, but it is not applied that way.

The court in *Lifschutz* conceded that it could not tell whether the 10-year-old therapeutic treatment had any relevance, direct or not, to the mental condition in issue. The court then shifted the burden to the plaintiff-patient to extricate himself from this dilemma by requiring "the patient initially to submit some showing that a given confidential communication was not directly related to the issue he has tended to the court." The patient must thus disclose something of his therapy to his lawyer and to the trial judge (in chambers) as a condition to retaining the confidentiality of the communication.[39]

Out of a sense of pride, a person may fear disclosure of the confidences he makes about his sexual life, his dependency, his insecurity, his struggle in interpersonal relations, all interspersed with fantasy. But these subjects have little or no significance in legal proceedings. The dialectic of one's right of privacy versus the danger that secrecy will allow truth to go undetected is not here the contest. One individual, when in analysis with Dr. Karl Menninger, told about relating one of his dreams to his wife. Dr. Menninger said tersely, "Your unconscious is none of your wife's business." Nor should it be the court's as it can only confuse and complicate matters. The sunlight advocated by Justice Brandeis would not come from disclosure of psychotherapy sessions, even if they were tape recorded.[40]

Time and again, therapists are urged to refrain from being a fact witness or giving expert testimony on behalf of a patient, given the irreconcilable role conflict and inherent bias, and in the case of a current patient, the likely disaster for the treatment. Unlike an examiner, a therapist is bound by the ethic of *primum non nocere*–the time-honored admonition to physicians of the importance of doing no harm.[41]

## NOTES

1.  Communication from Dr. Maurice Grossman, then Chairman of American Psychiatric Association Task Force on Confidentiality.
2.  See A.A. Hutschnecker, "The Stigma of Seeing a Psychiatrist," *New York Times*, Nov. 20, 1973, p. 39.
3.  Ga. Code Ann. § 38-418.
4.  O.C.G.A. § 24-9-21 (patient and psychiatrist); O.C.G.A. §43-39-16 (patient and psychologist).
5.  Psychologists in New York also sought the same kind of privilege as provided attorneys. Lobbyists of the New York State Psychological Association about a quarter of a century ago were able to obtain passage of a law (§4507, Civil Practice Law and Rules) reading: "The confidential relations and communications between a psychologist registered under the provisions of article one hundred fifty-three of the education law and his client are placed on the same basis as those provided by law between attorney and client, and nothing in such article shall be construed to require any such privileged communication to be disclosed." Much to the chagrin of the psychologists, a lower court ruled that this psychologist-patient privilege (CPLR, §4507) is not broader than the physician-patient privilege (CPLR, §4504). The court said, "While CPLR, §4507 places the psychologist-patient privilege on the same basis as the attorney-client privilege, it would be anomalous to hold that a psychologist has a greater privilege than a psychiatrist." Hence, the court held, the defendant by pleading insanity waived the privilege (as is the rule under the physician-patient or psychotherapist-patient privilege). State of Florida v. Axelson, 80 Misc.2d 419, 363 N.Y.S.2d 200 (Sup. Ct., N.Y. Cy. 1974).

6.   J. Goldstein & J. Katz, "Psychiatrist-Patient Privilege: The GAP Proposal and the Connecticut Statute," *Am. J. Psychiat.* 118:733, 1962. They wrote:

> The GAP statute suggests a host of problems which call into question the appropriateness of the attorney-client model. Who is to be classed as a psychiatrist? The attorney-client privilege affords no guidance since attorneys are licensed by the state while psychiatrists are licensed simply as physicians. Are communications from members of the patient's family protected? The law of attorney-client privilege would ordinarily answer in the negative. Yet virtually all psychiatrists would deem it essential to effective treatment that the patient's family be assured its disclosures would be treated as confidential. What of communications to clinical psychologists and social workers, who play so large a part in psychiatric diagnosis and treatment? There is precedent for treating as "privileged" the communications made by a client to the "agent" of an attorney, but the law on the subject is by no means clear. There is little assurance that it will be applied to protect disclosures to non-psychiatrist treatment personnel. When can the privilege be said to be waived or terminated? Does it end, for example, when the patient discloses to his psychiatrist his intention to commit a crime, e.g., that he plans to kill his wife? Under the cases construing the attorney client privilege, there is what is known as the "future crime or fraud" exception, which treats the obligation of confidence as ended when the conversation takes such a turn. If a death results, the psychiatrist could then be subpoenaed to testify regarding his patient's incriminating statement. Yet one of the very things psychiatric treatment strives for is the elicitation of such material, on the assumption that less harm will ensue if it is ventilated than if it remains suppressed. One well-publicized disclosure by a psychiatrist of material of this kind could do incalculable harm to the cause of treatment.

7.   Conn. Stat. Ann. § 52-146d (1974). GAP quickly published an appendix retracting its proposed model statute and in its stead recommended as a model the then recently enacted Connecticut statute. Citing the Goldstein & Katz article, GAP continued: "Since this report has been written it has become increasingly clear that the proposed model statute is inadequate. The recently enacted Connecticut statute may serve as a better model."

8.   The Connecticut statute is discussed by Goldstein & Katz, *op. cit. supra.*

9.   See Appendix. See also "Developments in the Law: Part IV. Medical and Counseling Privileges," *Harv. L. Rev.* 98:1530, 1985 (noting that by 1985, 45 states, not including Alaska, Iowa, Nebraska, South Carolina and West Virginia, had enacted psychotherapist-patient privileges).

10.  The Second, Sixth and Seventh Circuits determined that "reason and experience" compel the recognition of the psychotherapist-patient privilege in both civil and criminal cases. *In re* Doe, 964 F.2d 1325 (2d Cir.1992); *In re* Zuniga, 714 F.2d 632 (6th Cir.), *cert. denied*, 464 U.S. 983 (1983); Jaffee v. Redmond, 51 F.3d 1346 (7th Cir. 1995). In *In re* Doe, where the psychiatric

history of a witness was sought, the 2d Circuit recognized the privilege but said that the need for the evidence outweighed the witness's privacy interests. In *In re* Zuniga, the 6th Circuit recognized privilege but said that it did not cover information as to the identity of the therapist's patients, the dates on which they were treated, and the length of the treatment on each date. In *Jaffee v. Redmond*, the 7th Circuit recognized privilege and protected the police officer's communications to a social worker but it also concluded that the evidence was not needed as it was cumulative. Thus, in all of these cases, privilege though recognized was not determinative of the admissibility of the evidence. See also Cunningham v. Southlake Ctr. for Mental Health, 125 FRD 474 (N.D. Ind. 1989); *In re* Grand Jury Subpoena, 710 F. Supp. 999 (D.N.J. 1989).

The Fifth, Ninth, Tenth and Eleventh Circuits rejected the privilege, each interpreting Rule 501 as limiting the development of privileges to those recognized by the common law. See United States v. Burtrum, 17 F.3d 1299 (10th Cir.1994) (declining to recognize a psychotherapist-patient privilege in criminal child sexual abuse case); *In re* Grand Jury Proceedings, 867 F.2d 562 (9th Cir.), *cert. denied,* 493 U.S. 906 (1989) (rejecting assertion of a psychotherapist-patient privilege by target of grand jury murder investigation); United States v. Corona, 849 F.2d 562 (11th Cir. 1988), *cert. denied,* 489 U.S. 1084 (1989) (refusing to recognize a psychotherapist-patient privilege in criminal firearms case); United States v. Meagher, 531 F.2d 752 (5th Cir.), *cert. denied,* 429 U.S. 853 (1976) (rejecting criminal defendant's assertion of psychiatrist-patient privilege in bank robbery trial).

11. P.M. Barrett, "Justices to Decide if Federal Rules Allow for Psychotherapist Patient 'Privilege,'" *Wall Street Journal,* Oct. 17, 1995, p. 9; L. Greenhouse, "Supreme Court to Rule on Therapist-Client Privilege in Judicial Proceedings," *New York Times,* Oct. 17, 1995, p. 131.

12. 116 S.Ct. 1923 (1996); noted in L. Greenhouse, "Justices Uphold Psychotherapy Privacy Rights," *New York Times,* June 14, 1996, p. 1.

13. The federal courts refused to create a federal physician-patient privilege under Rule 501. See Gilbreath v. Guadalupe Hospital Foundation, 5 F.3d 785 (5th Cir. 1993); Hancock v. Dodson, 958 F.2d 1367 (6th Cir. 1992). For a discussion of Rule 501, see E.J. Imwinkelried, "An Hegelian Approach to Privileges Under Federal Rule of Evidence 501: The Restrictive Thesis, the Expansive Antithesis, and the Contextual Synthesis," *Nebraska L. Rev.* 73:511, 1994.

14. 445 U.S. 40 (1980).

15. 445 U.S. at 47.

16. S.A. Gard, *Illinois Evidence Manual* (Rochester, N.Y.: Lawyers Cooperative, 1963), p. 549. Moreover, the Physician patient privilege as a practical matter is eliminated in diversity cases in federal courts under Rule 35 of the Federal Rules of Civil Procedure, which became effective in 1938. Under that rule, a party physically examined pursuant to court order, by requesting and obtaining a copy of the report or by taking the deposition of

the examiner, waives any privilege regarding the testimony of every other person who has examined him in respect of the same condition. While waiver under Rule 35 may be avoided by neither requesting the report nor taking the examiner's deposition, the price is one which most litigant patients are probably not prepared to pay. Proposed Federal Rules of Evidence, Rule 510, Advisory Committee Note.

17. California's Evidence Code (§999) provides: "There is no privilege under this article as to a communication relevant to an issue concerning the condition of the patient in a proceeding to recover damages on account of the conduct of the patient if good cause for disclosure of the communication is shown." In a number of cases, courts have held that an allegation of "pain and suffering" does not ipso facto place mental condition in issue as an element of a personal-injury claim; the privilege is waived only when "emotional condition" is put in issue. Tylitski v. Triple X Service, 126 Ill. App.2d 144, 261 N.E.2d 533 (1970). In Michigan, the privilege is deemed waived only if the plaintiff brings an action to recover personal injuries or for malpractice and if the plaintiff shall produce in his own behalf any physician as a witness who has treated him for such injury. Eberle v. Savon Food Stores, 30 Mich. App. 496, 186 N.W.2d 837 (1931).

18. In cases where credibility is challenged, as when a witness is psychotic or delusional, a psychiatric examination may be ordered (rather than discovery of therapy records). See R. Slovenko, *Psychiatry and Criminal Culpability* (New York: Wiley, 1995), chap. 14; *Psychiatry and Law* (Boston: Little, Brown, 1973), chap. 3. In criminal cases, in particular situations, the defendant may obtain the psychiatric records of the complaining witness. See the discussion in the chapter on criminal cases, Part II, Chapter 6.

   The Texas Court of Appeals allowed a party in a child custody case to obtain discovery of the mental health records of the court-appointed counselor for the children. The court said, "[It is] a necessary intrusion upon the privacy rights of persons who become prospective expert witnesses in judicial proceedings involving the status, welfare, and interest of children." Cheatham v. Rogers, 824 S.W.2d 231 (Tex. App. 1992). Professor Daniel Shuman of SMU Law School observed, "There is some logic to the decision if what mental health professionals offer is grounded in their own experience and not in research." Communication to author.

19. J. Toobin, *The Run of His Life/The People v. O.J. Simpson* (New York: Random House, 1996), p. 149; also discussed in Mark Fuhrman Interview by Diane Sawyer on ABC's "Prime Time Live", Oct. 8, 1996.

20. See, *e.g.*, Mich. Act 294, Public Act of 1972, § § 3158-59.

21. S.R. Smith, "Medical and Psychotherapy Privileges and Confidentiality/On Giving With One Hand and Removing With the Other," *Ky. L. J.* 75:473, 1987.

22. See Part II, Chapter 6.

23. *In re* Lifschutz, 2 Cal.3d 415, 467 P.2d 577, 85 Cal. Rptr. 829 (1970).

24. *Time*, April 27, 1970, p. 60.

25. Dr. Lifschutz, through his attorney, Kurt W. Merchior of San Francisco, contended that the court order was invalid as unconstitutionally infringing his personal constitutional right of privacy, his right effectively to practice his profession, and the constitutional privacy rights of his patients. He also attacked the order, or more specifically, the statutory provisions which authorize the compulsion of his testimony in these circumstances, as unconstitutionally denying him the equal protection of the laws since, under California law, the clergy cannot be compelled to reveal certain confidential communications under these circumstances.

When all appeals were exhausted, including an appeal to the U.S. Supreme Court, Dr. Lifschutz was ordered to produce the records and when he refused he was ordered confined in jail. On a writ of habeas corpus, Judge Tobriner of the California Supreme Court discussed the contentions in a 14-page opinion, the most extensive ever written on the subject.

Insofar as Dr. Lifschutz's argument rested on the economic loss that psychotherapists may suffer as a result of the disclosure requirement, the court pointed out that this position runs contra to the current trend of constitutional adjudication involving the regulation of economic interests. Legal requirements prescribing mandatory disclosure of confidential business records are regular occurrences. Although all compelled disclosures may interfere to some extent with an individual's performance of his work, such requirements have been upheld so long as the compelled disclosure is reasonable in light of a related and important governmental purpose. Moreover, the court said, the patient-litigant exception at issue evolves only that special instance in which a patient has chosen to forego the confidentiality of the privilege, and therefore the court questioned whether the deterrence of patients and the impairment to the practice of psychotherapy would be as great as Dr. Lifschutz anticipated.

The court acknowledged that the second basis of Dr. Lifschutz's contention raised a more serious problem—namely, his contention that if the state is authorized to compel disclosure of some psychotherapeutic communications, psychotherapy can no longer be practiced successfully. It is a contention by no means unique to psychotherapy. Journalists, accountants, and social workers, among others, have sought the enactment of a privilege and have proclaimed that required revelation of information received in confidence would jeopardize their calling.

Supported with affidavits from psychotherapists, Dr. Lifschutz argued that the unique nature of psychotherapeutic treatment, involving the probing of a patient's thoughts and emotions, requires an environment of total confidentiality and absolute trust. He claimed that unless the psychotherapist can truthfully assure his patient that all revelations will be held in strictest confidence and never disclosed, patients will be inhibited from participating fully and the psychotherapeutic process and proper treatment would be impossible. He urged that the patient-litigant exception conflicts with the preservation of an environment of absolute confidentiality and unconstitutionally constricts the field of medical practice.

Although Dr. Lifschutz submitted affidavits of psychotherapists who concurred in his assertion that total confidentiality is essential to the practice of their profession, the court noted that the practice of psychotherapy has grown, indeed flourished, in an environment of nonabsolute privilege. No state in the country recognizes as broad a privilege as Dr. Lifschutz claims is constitutionally compelled. Whether psychotherapy's development has progressed only because patients or therapists are ignorant of the existing legal environment can only be a matter of speculation.

Dr. Lifschutz's broad assertion, the court said, overlooks the limited nature of the intrusion into psychotherapeutic privacy actually at issue in the case. The patient-litigant exception compels disclosure of only those matters which the patient himself has chosen to reveal by tendering them in litigation. It is unknown, of course, to what extent, if at all, patients are deterred from seeking psychotherapeutic treatment by the knowledge that if, at some future date, they choose to place some aspect of their mental condition in issue in litigation, communications relevant to that issue may be revealed.

Dr. Lifschutz maintained that, given the purpose of the clergy-penitent privilege, the distinction between clergy and psychotherapists cannot stand. Dr. Lifschutz characterized the "modern" purpose of the clergy-penitent privilege as fostering a "sanctuary for the disclosure of emotional distress"; as so characterized, relevant distinctions between the clergy and psychotherapists do diminish. The court said, however, that Dr. Lifschutz's portrayal of the clergy-penitent privilege, while perhaps identifying one of the supporting threads of the statutory provision, does not reflect a complete analysis of the foundation of the privilege.

The Law Revision Commission Comment accompanying the adoption of California's privilege states: "At least one underlying reason seems to be that the law will not compel a clergyman to violate—nor punish him for refusing to violate—the tenets of his church which require him to maintain secrecy as to confidential statements made to him in the course of his religious duties." The court said that, while many psychotherapists are no doubt strongly committed to the "tenets" of their profession, as indeed Dr. Lifschutz exhibited by his determined action, the source of this commitment can be reasonably distinguished from the distinctive religious conviction out of which the penitential privilege flows.

26.  2 Cal.3d at 426.
27.  116 S. Ct.1923 (1996).
28.  Justice Stevens was joined by Justices Sandra Day O'Connor, Anthony Kennedy, David Souter, Clarence Thomas, Ruth Bader Ginsburg and Stephen Breyer. Justices Antonin Scalia and Chief Justice William Rehnquist dissented. Chief Justice Rehnquist joined a portion of Justice Scalia's dissent that took specific issue with extending the privilege to social workers. The Chief Justice's view on the general psychotherapy privilege was unclear, because he did not write separately and joined neither the majority opinion nor the bulk of Justice Scalia's dissent.
29.  Quoted in J. Biskupic, "Therapist-Patient Talks Are Shielded," *Washington Post,* June 14, 1996, p. 1.

30. "Confidentiality Concerns Prompt Meeting Between APA and Pentagon Officials," *Psychiatric News*, Sept. 6, 1996, p. 1.
31. Ltr., "Psychotherapy Privacy at Risk," *Wall Street Journal*, Nov. 6, 1996, p. 21.
32. In some situations the pleadings may clearly demonstrate that the patient is placing his entire mental condition in issue and that history of past psychotherapy will be relevant. This was illustrated when a mental patient in a prison hospital sought release, contending that he was not a dangerous or violent individual as the state mental health officials asserted. When the patient's medical records were offered to substantiate the state's position, he claimed such records were privileged. The court, analogizing the facts before it to those of the patient-litigant exception to the medical privilege, found that "petitioner himself caused his mental condition to be put in issue by his application for habeas corpus and averments of his brief." *In re* Cathey, 55 Cal.2d 679, 361 P.2d 426, 12 Cal. Rptr. 762 (1961).
33. President Nixon argued (unsuccessfully), it may be recalled, that he would give the House Judiciary Committee only such evidence as he, Mr. Nixon, decided relevant to impeachable offenses listed by the committee.
34. A motion to quash a subpoena is in order when other evidence more relevant and material is available, or would be less intrusive to obtain. Such a procedure might even protect a patient from having to state in discovery processes whether or not he ever saw a psychiatrist. Even under the patient litigant exception, the judge ought to determine whether or not there are other available sources from which to obtain the information; and if not, to propound the questions that need clarification to resolve the issue at hand, and limit testimony to those factors. A proposal some years ago to protect newsmen, who have more relevant and material evidence to offer than a treating psychotherapist, would have required disclosure only if the party seeking the information satisfied the court that the information was indispensable to the prosecution or defense of the case and could not be obtained from any other source, and that there was a compelling public interest in disclosure. AP news- release, "News Shield Bill Spurred in House," *New York Times*, Jan. 4, 1974, p. 41.
35. G.B. Leong, J.A. Silva & R.Weinstock (ltr.), "Another Courtroom Assault on the Confidentiality of the Psychotherapist-Patient Relationship," *J. For. Sciences* 41:551, 1996.
36. Dr. Jonas R. Rappeport of Maryland, however, says that in his experience prior to 1965 (when Maryland enacted a privilege) attorneys quite frequently used the lack of privilege as the basis for going on "fishing expeditions" through psychiatrists' records. He states that since the law has been passed there has been a cessation in Maryland of such "fishing trips," although in law the exceptions to privilege would allow the same fishing as would prevail under a situation of no privilege. He observed (in a personal communication):

> While I recognize that the crucial test is one of relevancy and materiality, I still believe that certain patients or at least their psychiatrist

need to feel secure in a privilege statute when asking for or receiving reassurance that communications essentially are privileged. While this may not in itself be as necessary for the type of very intensive relationship that occurs in a psychoanalytic practice, I do believe that in the practice of psychotherapy at lesser levels of intensity when strong transference neuroses do not develop that such reassurances are indicated and, in fact, very necessary for the smooth operation of a treatment program.

37.    Marchard v. Henry Ford Hosp., 247 N.W.2d (Mich. 1976).

38.    Rule 401, Federal Rules of Evidence.

39.    In *In re Lifschutz,* the California Supreme Court said: "Even when the confidential communication is directly relevant to a mental condition tendered by the patient...the codes provide a variety of protections that remain available to aid in safeguarding the privacy of the patient. When inquiry into the confidential relationship takes place before trial during discovery...the patient or psychotherapist may apply to the trial court for a protective order to limit the scope of the inquiry or to regulate the procedure of the inquiry so as to best preserve the rights of the patient. [The] Code of Civil Procedure grants the court broad discretion to issue any...order which justice requires to protect the party or witness from annoyance, embarrassment or oppression. [It] specifically enumerates a number of protective orders that might be particularly helpful to a patient-litigant. For example, [it] provides that, upon good cause shown, the court may direct that at the oral deposition (1) certain matters shall not be inquired into or (2) that the scope of the examination shall be limited to certain matters, books, [or] documents,...or (3) that the examination shall be held with no one present except the parties to the action and their...counsel, or (4) that after being sealed the deposition shall be opened only by order of the court..." This having been said, it must be noted, however, that many judges allow discovery, saying that the opposing attorney has a right to review the record in full in order to see whether useful information can be found.

40.    It is well recognized that certain circumstances call for the exclusion of evidence, even when of unquestioned relevance, if its "probative value is substantially outweighed by the danger of unfair prejudice, confusion of issues, or misleading the jury, or by considerations of undue delay, waste of time, or needless presentation of cumulative evidence." Federal Rules of Evidence, Rule 403. In Kilarjian v. Horwath, 379 F.2d 547 (2d Cir. 1967), an action for personal injuries and property damage sustained in a collision between plaintiff's automobile and defendant's truck, medical experts testified on behalf of the plaintiff that the shock of the collision produced a nerve root irritation which affected plaintiff's left arm. The defendant asserted that the condition was not caused by the accident, and further asserted that plaintiff was actually suffering from a "conversion reaction" stemming from his anxieties about his one and one-half year separation from his wife and children, and his frustrated desire to marry his secretary with whom he had

been living. The trial judge refused to admit into evidence the portions of the psychiatric report of a neurological examination of plaintiff which stated that the plaintiff had been living with his secretary and intended to marry her. In affirming judgement for the plaintiff, the appellate court noted the established principle that it is within the discretion of the trial judge to exclude evidence, though otherwise admissible, when he is convinced that it will create a danger of prejudice which outweighs its probative value.

41.    In a number of recent highly publicized cases, therapists who treated an accused have been called to testify either as a fact or expert witness. In the trial in Colorado or Renee Polreis, charged with the murder of her adopted baby boy, two therapists who treated her testified about the relationship that she had with the boy. K.Q. Seelye, "Women Sentenced to 22 Years in Death of Adopted Son," New York Times, Sept. 23, 1997, p. 7. Staff therapists are usually called upon to testify in the prosecution of a violent psychiatric inpatient. S.Rachlin, "The Prosecution of Violent Psychiatric Inpatients: One Respectable Intervention," Bull. Am. Acad. Psychiat. & Law 22:239, 1994. In a hearing of South Africa's Truth and Reconciliation Commission, Jeffrey Benzien's psychiatrist, Ria Kotze, testified on his behalf and described him as a man who saw himself as a good policeman but now is full of self-loathing and suffers acutely because of the torture he carried out as an apartheid-era policeman. S. Daley, "Apartheid Torturer Testifies, As Evil Shows Its Banal Face," New York Times, Nov. 9, 1997, p. 1.

Forensic psychiatrists who totally distance themselves from a treatment role are usually considered "hired guns." Many law firms will not engage a psychiatrist for forensic purposes if that psychiatrist exclusively confines his practice to indepenent evaluaitons and does not treat patients. The Workers' Compensation Commission in many states will not permit psychiatrists to be listed as assigned evaluators unless they conduct active psychiatric practice, in addition to doing independent evaluation. The controversy arises when a treating psychiatrist is called upon to testify about his patient, past or present.

For discussion on the debate concerning expert forensic psychiatrists versus treating psychiatrists as witnesses, see Part VI. See also S.A. Greenberg & D.W. Shuman, "Irreconcilable Conflict Between Theraputic and Forensic Roles," *Professional Psychology: Research and Practice* 28:50, 1997; L.H. Strasburger, T.G. Gutheil & A. Brodsky, "On Wearing Two Hats: Role Conflict in Serving as Both Psychotherapist and Expert Witness," *Am. J. Psychiatry* 154:448, 1997.

# Part II

# PSYCHOTHERAPY AND PRIVILEGE PROBLEMS

Chapter 1. Therapists Under the Privilege
Chapter 2. Divorce and Alienation of Affections
Chapter 3. Child Custody
Chapter 4. Tort Cases
Chapter 5. Identity of Patient
Chapter 6. Criminal Cases
Chapter 7. Proceedings to Hospitalize
Chapter 8. Hospital and Health Records
Chapter 9. Group Therapy
      Interview of Group Confidentiality

# Chapter 1

# THERAPISTS UNDER THE PRIVILEGE

Given that privilege is a *privata lex*, a special law intended for or restricted to the use of a particular person or class of persons, it is necessary to define the parties protected by the privilege. Currently, some forty states and the District of Columbia have statutes covering physician-patient communications. Within the last three decades, every state has afforded privilege to psychiatrist- or psychotherapist-patient communications.

Congress expressed the need for confidentiality in the treatment of alcohol and drug abuse, both of which are closely related to and often overlap with mental health care, by legislation mandating the confidentiality of patient information pertaining to "substance abuse education, prevention, training, treatment, rehabilitation, or research, which is conducted, regulated, or directly or indirectly assisted by any department or agency of the United States."[1] Congress observed that "the strictest adherence" to such confidentiality provisions "is absolutely essential to the success of all drug abuse prevention programs....Without that assurance, fear of public disclosure of drug abuse or of records that will attach for life will discourage thousands from seeking the treatment they must have if this tragic national problem is to be overcome."[2]

Psychiatrists are included within the statutory medical privilege governing "physicians," but because of the exceptions in that privilege, psychiatrists and mental health associations in various states pushed for a special privilege protecting the confidentiality of the psychiatrist- or psychotherapist-patient relationship.

By and large, privilege statutes envision a one-to-one relationship. That was commonplace in an earlier day, but much less so today, be it medical care generally or psychotherapy. Psychotherapy nowadays may take place in community centers or clinics, where many people may have contact with the patient. Classical psychoanalysis or other one-to-one therapy relationship is not always justified or feasible as the treatment modality. Group therapy is an innovation which casts doubt on a privilege based on a dyadic relationship. Child therapy cannot be a strictly dyadic arrangement. Likewise, the one-to-one relationship alone, analytically oriented or otherwise, does not meet the needs of many of the mentally ill. The family unit and the therapeutic team have vital roles to play.

The courts, however, have traditionally taken the position that disclosure to a person not included within the statute "pollutes" or terminates the privilege. The courts equate disclosure to a third person with a general publication to the world. Hence, the rationale, "The world knows about it, why not the court?"

In arriving at a determination of which therapists should be covered under privilege, GAP sought in its proposal of 1960 to cover the "psychiatrist-patient" relationship. The proposal did not include coverage for psychologists, social workers, counselors, or other psychotherapists. Through lobbying in some states, psychologists and social workers have obtained a privilege as part of the licensing or certification law.

In recent years the various states have enacted, as we have noted, a "psychotherapist-patient" privilege as part of the code of evidence. The proposed, but House-rejected, privilege in the Federal Rules of Evidence, like the laws adopted in the various states, defined a "psychotherapist" as a medical doctor who devotes all or part of his time to the practice of psychiatry, and a licensed or certified psychologist who devotes all or part of his time to the practice of clinical psychology. The definition of "psychotherapist" under the rule is so broad that any medical general practitioner who practices some form of psychotherapy in treating his patients is included.[3] The privilege extends to communications made to pretenders who are reasonably believed by their patients to be medical doctors, as well as general practitioners doing part time counseling whether or not they have special qualifications.[4]

Unlicensed therapists and counselors of all kinds, however, can be required to reveal the confidences of those whom they have counseled. Therapists involved in "revival of memory" of child abuse are often unlicensed. The Advisory Committee on the proposed Federal Rules of Evidence said that the distinction made between unlicensed persons thought to be medical doctors and unlicensed persons doing psychotherapy "is believed to be justified by the number of persons, other than psychiatrists, purporting to render psychotherapeutic aid and the variety of their theories."

Nebraska's "physician-patient privilege" enacted in 1984 defines a "physician" as including a psychologist and it defines a "patient" as one who consults a physician "for purposes of diagnosis or treatment of his physical, mental or emotional condition."[5] Psychologists may be surprised to learn that under this statute they are defined as a physician.

The state of Georgia is a jurisdiction at the forefront in the breadth given its psychiatrist-patient privilege. Georgia does not have a general physician-patient privilege, but the Georgia Supreme Court has interpreted "psychiatrist" in its psychiatrist-patient privilege to include any "person authorized to practice medicine who devotes a substantial portion of his or her time to the diagnosis or treatment of a mental or emotional condition, including alcohol or drug addiction."[6] The court judicially defined psychiatrist in such a way as to shield communications of a patient who seeks treatment for mental disorders from a medical doctor who is not a psychiatrist.

In the case at hand, the Georgia Supreme Court said that it was not necessary to delineate what constitutes a substantial portion of a doctor's time. In this case, the doctor testified that she treats one-third of her patients for mental problems, considers counseling as part of her medical practice, and had treated the patient involved in this case for a mental condition for two years.[7] In a dissent, Chief Justice Willis Hunt said:[8]

> [N]owadays the general practice of medicine almost always involves a consideration of and treatment of a patient's emotional disorders, as well as those of a physical nature. Treatment for anxiety, depression, and related problems are routine matters for internists such as [the doctor in this case]. But that fact does not convert the internist into a psychiatrist any more than the routine treatment of cardiovascular complaints converts the internist into a cardiologist. Rather than voting for the judicial legislation proposed by the majority opinion, I would refer this matter to the General Assembly for its consideration as to whether the statute should be amended so as to protect communications of this sort regardless of the kind of practice engaged in by the person to whom the information is communicated.

In another case in Georgia, a wife was charged with the murder of her husband and she sought to call as a witness a psychiatrist who counseled both her and her husband.[9] The state, on behalf of the deceased husband, asserted the psychotherapist-patient privilege. The wife argued that because their consultation with the psychiatrist was joint counseling, her presence as a third party vitiated the privilege.[10] In rejecting this contention, and applying the privilege even in a criminal case, and even after the death of the patient, the Georgia Supreme Court said:[11]

> While it is true, as defendant suggests, that the presence of a third party will sometimes destroy the privileged nature of communications, we join the weight of authority from other jurisdictions in holding that there is a strong public policy in favor of preserving the confidentiality of psychiatric-patient confidences where a third party is present as a necessary or customary participant in the consultation and treatment....

> It is clear from the defendant's testimony that she and the victim were jointly seeking psychiatric counseling for marital problems. As such we find that the

victim was a necessary participant in the psychiatric sessions and his communications to the psychiatrist were entitled to protection. This privilege survives the death of the communicant. The presence of the victim's spouse, also a necessary participant in the treatment, does not destroy the privilege. The trial court did not err in refusing to allow the psychiatrist to testify to the victim's communications.

Personnel in probation departments, welfare offices, social agencies, and child guidance clinics frequently have access to case files. Can they be trusted with confidential information? Experience generally confirms the trustworthiness of nonclinical employees (career correctional workers and welfare workers) regarding confidential material in the case history when the importance of confidentiality has been fully explained to them. Likewise, experience with teachers confirm that they are, when properly prepared, as respecting of confidential material as are clinicians, lawyers, or other professional people.[12]   The Connecticut psychiatrist-patient privilege includes "such persons who participate, under the supervision of the psychiatrist, in the accomplishment of the objectives of diagnosis or treatment."

Actually, there is no better use for case histories, so costly in their preparation, than that their findings be used by those who are involved responsibly in the care or treatment of the patient. In institutions, basic psychotherapeutic help is furnished by the ordinary staff member who spends many hours with the patient or inmate, rather than by the specialist who sees the patient only occasionally. Moreover, the work of the psychiatrist can be sabotaged unless it is complemented and carried out by nurses, aides, and other attendants. The Connecticut privilege, as noted, covers communications between any persons who participate, under the supervision of the psychiatrist, in the accomplishment of the objectives of diagnosis or treatment. Various statutes or court decisions do not protect disclosures to non-psychiatric treatment personnel.

Professional practitioners of psychotherapy are almost as varied as the range of persons they seek to help. Much thought has been given to defining psychotherapy and attempting to set it apart from such clearly nonmedical processes as advice, conversation, and friendly reassurance.[13] Dr. Thomas Szasz over the years has maintained that no such distinctions can be made, and that the medical group seems to be attempting an institutional definition of a process which can only be understood in instrumental terms.[14] There is involved a struggle for prestige and power among the various professional groups; some arguments are reminiscent of debates over the closed shop in labor-management relations.

Clinical psychologists and psychiatric social workers are members of treatment teams in hospitals and clinics under psychiatric supervision, but they also practice independently in social agencies, family agencies, marriage counseling centers, and so on, and as private practitioners. In addition, a wide variety of counselors and guides (such as marriage counselors, rehabilitation and vocational counselors, parole officers, group workers, and clergy) may use psychotherapeutic principles with their clientele. The different disciplines tend to describe their activities in different terms: for example, medical and quasi-medical practitioners "treat" patients, psychiatric social workers do "case work" with clients, clergymen offer "pastoral counseling" and group workers do "group work."

The general physician-patient medical privilege covers psychiatrists (as they are physicians), but the shield afforded various members of the treatment team, unless specifically provided in the statute, as we have noted, is minimal. The attorney-client privilege covers the attorney's agent,[15] but in many states, the physician's agent, the nurse, is often not included within the medical privilege.[16] Likewise, psychologists, social workers, counselors, and stenographers may not come within the scope of the medical privilege, even when working under the supervision of the psychiatrist. Psychiatrists often rely on such persons in a team approach in evaluation and treatment. The physician or psychiatrist may refer a patient to a psychologist for consultation and testing, and he provides certain necessary information about the patient to the psychologist. Unless covered by an extension of the physician-patient privilege or specially privileged, the psychologist could be called to testify about the patient.

The Connecticut psychotherapist-patient statute included clinical psychologists and social workers working with psychiatrists, but not under other conditions. A number of states have adopted special statutes granting an independent privilege to communications with psychologists, and also with social workers and marriage counselors.[17] The committee on the Connecticut bill discussed extending a special privilege to psychologists who engage in the independent practice of psychotherapy—some members of the committee favored such an extension; others thought it would go too far; yet a third group felt it would make obtaining support for the bill more difficult and therefore urged postponement of a decision on the matter.[18]

Employee assistance programs (EAP) are common in today's workplace, and they are staffed principally by social workers, not psychiatrists or psychologists, mainly due to cost containment efforts. Insurance plans often cover therapy only by a social worker.

In the Protection and Advocacy for Mentally Ill Individuals Act of 1986,[19] Congress broadly recognized the qualified mental health professionals who deliver care under the Act "to include mental health specialists who are licensed or certified by the state, or where no state licensure exists, possess national licensure or certification."[20]

Psychiatric social workers and others were not included in the proposed Rule 504 of the Federal Rules of Evidence nor are they recognized by evidence codes in various states. Can the omission be justified? Social workers, the mainstay of staffs of most public health facilities, are called the "poor man's psychiatrist." Their clients are referred to as "patients."[21] Since it is the therapeutic function, rather than any particular group, that the law on privilege is theoretically designed to protect, there is little justification for extending privileged status to one group and denying it to another that is functionally accomplishing the same thing.[22] What difference, it may be asked, whether a person achieves a "corrective emotional experience" by talking with a psychiatrist, psychologist, social worker, preacher, or a good friend?

**HERB & JAMAAL** By Stephen Bentley

The case that went to the Supreme Court on the question of whether there is a psychotherapist privilege under federal law, *Jaffee v. Redmond,* involved a social worker. In recognizing a federal privilege, Justice Stevens, writing for the majority, said the privilege would apply to clinical social workers as well as to psychiatrists and psychologists because the reasons for having the privilege "apply with equal force" to all the professions. He noted that social workers' clients often "include the poor and those of modest means."[24]

In the course of oral argument, when counsel was urging application of the privilege to social workers, Justice Souter cut in, "But in principle...there's no reason to draw [the line] there, is there? I have had law clerks tell me things in confidence, and I presume they feel better after telling me," he said, eliciting laughter. In a follow-up exchange, Justice Souter referred to this role with his clerks as a "poor man's psychiatrist."

To draw a distinction between various types of therapists is hard to justify since there is no evidence that one type of psychotherapy produces better results than another. The major determinants of outcome in psychotherapy, it seems, are not therapeutic procedures per se, or what is said. Rather, personal qualities of therapist and patient and the concordance between the patient's belief as to his needs and the therapeutic method employed are more apt to affect the result. The source to which the patient attributes his symptoms, which is a function of his education and cultural status, and the views of the therapist he happens to encounter, determine whether the relationship will be successful.

The party to the relationship seeking help is usually called a "patient," for lack of a better term. "Sufferee" sounds like women's liberation; "client" or consumer sounds too commercial; "counselee," "student," or "pupil" are associated with schools. In ordinary conversation the term "patient" has medical connotations: a patient is a sick individual under the care and treatment of a physician or surgeon—a client for medical services. But "patient" as an adjective also refers to one who bears pain or trial calmly or uncomplainingly, one who is not hasty—and considering the traditional length of psychotherapy, it is an apt term. "Patient" was defined in the proposed Federal Rules of Evidence (Rule 504) as "a person who consults or is examined or interviewed by a psychotherapist for purposes of diagnosis or treatment of his mental or emotional condition."

Persons may come to psychotherapy for relief of specific symptoms or disabilities, but the underlying reason for seeking help is demoralization, a state of mind that results from persistent failure to cope with internally or externally induced stresses. As Dr. Jerome D. Frank put it, all psychotherapy is a form of education, a means of restoring morale.[25]

Where or to whom we speak is a factor in the type of script we employ. The manner and content of our conversation is tempered by where we talk. Speech, like clothes, must be appropriate to the occasion. One speaks differently in a church than in a tavern. Funerals require a pale make-up and solemn expression. The temple of justice is traditionally a place of civility. Chief Justice Burger regarded dress and decorum as seriously as he did the complex problems of the law and required lawyers to wear "conservative business dress." In any jurisdiction, with or without privilege, a judge will look askance at the offer of data from psychotherapy sessions. The setting itself forms something of a barrier, and there are certain standards which people impose on themselves not because of any rule but because good taste or other honorable prompting requires it. While there is less reluctance to subpoena a psychiatrist or other therapist than a priest, questions probing into psychotherapy are likely to be regarded as offside, to use football terminology. "Tut, tut," we hear the judge (though minutes earlier having ruled adversely on a claim of privilege) admonishing an attorney asking improprieties, "let's get on with the case."[26]

Every situation has its own scripting. All the world's a stage, said Shakespeare. The script depends not only on the question asked but also on where the answer is made. Even so-called "free association" in psychoanalysis and the "spontaneous" behavior in "encounter groups" can be defined as learning the appropriate script for free association or spontaneous behavior. Those psychiatrists at universities who hold a joint appointment in law and psychiatry invariably see their patients at their medical school office—never at their law school office—recognizing that atmosphere evokes a certain posture and language. And that which takes place in one forum may not be translatable to another.

The law script has its language, and its boundaries, designed to reach a decision that will balance conflicting interests in a way that is theoretically best for all. Proof-making in law is conditioned by the philosophy of jurisprudence, the mechanisms of trial, and the rules of substantive and procedural law current at a given time.[27] A few illustrations will suffice. Most people, practicing humility, avoid the use of any word or expression that imports a fixed opinion, but in the courtroom, where a two-value logic system prevails, a witness is expected to answer yes or no. Quite frequently the very language of testimony is identical from one case to another. The criminal law, moreover, says that the fact that a defendant had committed other crimes is not admissible for the purpose of showing that he is more likely to have perpetrated the crime charged. The criminal law functions without revealing to the fact finder the previous conviction of even murder.

## NOTES

1.	42 U.S.C. §§290dd-2(a), 290ee-3, and 42 C.F.R. §§ 2.3(b)(1),2.13(a),2.63, restricting disclosure of substance abuse patient records, including in any "civil, criminal, administrative, or legislative proceedings conducted by any Federal, State, or local authority." A court order may permit disclosure.

2.	H.R. Rep. 775, 92d Cong., 2d Sess.; see also S. Rep. No. 1206, 94th Cong., 2d Sess. 116 (1976). See W.C. Whitford, "The Physician, the Law, and the Drug Abuser," *U. Pa. L. Rev.* 119:933, 1971.

3.	The Advisory Committee to the proposed Federal Rules of Evidence stated: "The definition of psychotherapist embraces a medical doctor while engaged in the diagnosis or treatment of mental or emotional conditions, including drug addiction, in order not to exclude the general practitioner and to avoid the making of needless refined distinctions concerning what is and what is not the practice of psychiatry. The requirement that the psychologist be in fact licensed, and not merely be believed to be so, is believed to be justified by the number of persons, other than psychiatrists, purporting to render psychotherapeutic aid and the variety of their theories. The clarification of mental or emotional condition as including drug addiction is consistent with current approaches to drug abuse problems." Comment to Proposed Rule 504.

4.  Proposed Federal Rules of Evidence, Rule 504(a)(2) defined a "psychotherapist" as (A) a person authorized to practice medicine in any state or nation, or reasonably believed by the patient so to be, while engaged in the diagnosis or treatment of a mental or emotional condition, including drug addiction, or (B) a person licensed or certified as a psychologist under the laws of any state or nation, while similarly engaged.

5.  The Nebraska statute, § 27-504, provides:

    (a) A patient is a person who consults or is examined or interviewed by a physician for purposes of diagnosis or treatment of his physical, mental or emotional condition;

    (b) A physician is (i) a person authorized to practice medicine in any state or nation, or is reasonably believed by the patient so to be, or (ii) a person licensed or certified as a psychologist under the laws of any state or nation, who devotes all or a part of his time to the practice of clinical psychology; and

    (c) A communication is confidential if not intended to be disclosed to third persons other than those present to further the interest of the patient in the consultation, examination or interview, or persons reasonably necessary for the transmission of the communication, or persons who are participating in the diagnosis and treatment under the direction of the physician, including members of the patient's family.

6.  Wiles v. Wiles, 264 Ga. 594, 448 S.E.2d 681 (1994).

7.  448 S.E.2d at 684.

8.  448 S.E.2d at 685.

9.  Sims v. State, 251 Ga. 877, 311 S.E.2d 161 (1984).

10. The wife claimed that her psychiatrist had instructed her to "obey the absurd demands [the husband] made when he would go into a rage" on the theory that he would see how "stupid" his demands were and "would calm down." Following this advice, at a time when the husband went into a rage at his office, the defendant testified she went home, located the husband's pistol and returned to his office. The husband in a rage had told her to go and get the gun. The defendant testified the gun discharged as she raised her arm to protect herself from her husband, killing him. The couple had quarreled frequently over methods of raising and disciplining their son. 311 S.E.2d at 163.

11. 311 S.E.2d at 165-166

12. N. Fenton, *Group Counseling–A Preface to Its Use in Correctional and Welfare Agencies* (Institute for Study of Crime and Delinquency, Sacramento, Calif., undated).

13. A. Fischer, "Nonmedical Psychotherapists," *Arch. Gen. Psychiat.* 5:7, 1961.

14. T.S. Szasz, *The Myth of Mental Illness* (Harper & Row, rev. ed. 1974); "Psychiatry, Psychotherapy and Psychology," *Arch. Gen. Psychiat.* 5:455, 1959; "Psychoanalytic Treatment as Education," *Arch. Gen. Psychiat.* 9:46, 1963. The issue is oft-debated: who makes a good therapist? Anna Freud was a teacher of mathematics; August Aichhorn too was a teacher. Pastoral

counseling at times may be the treatment of choice. Freud was so much in favor of lay analysis that he donated $2,200 to the establishment of an association of lay persons interested in psychoanalysis. S. Freud, *The Question of Lay Analysis* (New York: Norton, 1926); E. Jones, *The Life and Work of Sigmund Freud* (New York: Basic Books, 1957), vol. 3, p. 287.

15.  Lindsay v. Lipson, 116 N.W.2d 60 (Mich. 1962); City & County of San Francisco v. Superior Court, 321 P.2d 26 (Cal. 1951); Comment, *Yale L.J.* 71:1226, 1962.

16.  First Trust Co. of St. Paul v. Kansas City Life Ins. Co., 79 F.2d 48 (8th Cir. 1935); Leusink v. O'Donnell, 255 Wis. 627, 39 N.W. 675 (1949); Ostrowski v. Mockridge, 242 Minn. 265, 65 N.W.2d 185 (1954).

17.  The District of Columbia and at least 46 states expressly include a privilege for confidential communications to a social worker: Ala., Alaska, Ariz., Ark., Calif., Colo., Conn., D.C., Del., Fla., Ga., Hawaii, Idaho, Ind., Iowa, Kan., Ky., La., Maine, Md., Mass., Mich., Minn., Miss., Mo., Mont., Neb., Nev., N.H., N.J., N. Mex., N.Y., N. Car., N. Dak., Ohio, Okla., Ore., Pa., S. Dak., Tenn., Utah, Vt., Va., Wash., W. Va., Wis., and Wyo.

Social workers in medical settings may also possibly be covered by whatever medical privilege exists, on the theory of agency. The so-called executive privilege on Veterans Administrative records protects, to some extent, information entrusted to social workers employed by the Veterans Administration. 38 U.S.C. § 520.

In State v. Locke, 502 N.W.2d 891 (Wis. App. 1993), the Wisconsin Court of Appeals held that the trial court erroneously admitted testimony of a social worker that the defendant told her that he had uncontrollable sex drive and problem with pedophilia. In People v. Wood, 447 Mich. 80 (1994), the Michigan Supreme Court held that Michigan law requires a social worker to seek the assistance of and cooperate with law enforcement officials "if law enforcement intervention is necessary for the child's protection."

See generally J.T. Alves, *Confidentiality in Social Work* (Washington, D.C.: Catholic University of America Press, 1959); S.J. Wilson, *Confidentiality in Social Work* (New York: Free Press, 1978); R.C. Turkington, "Legal Protection for the Confidentiality of Health Care Information in Pennsylvania," *Villanova L. Rev.* 32:259, 1987.

18.  J. Goldstein & J. Katz, "Psychiatrist-Patient Privilege: The GAP Proposal and the Connecticut Statute," *Am. J. Psychiat.* 113:733, 1962. See generally B. Diamond & H. Weihofen, "Privileged Communication and the Clinical Psychologist," *J. Clin. Psychol.* 9:388, 1953; D. Louisell, "The Psychologist in Today's Legal World," *Minn L. Rev.* 39:235, 1955; Part II, "Confidential Communications," *Minn. L. Rev.* 41:731, 1957.

19.  Publ. L. No. 99-319, 100 Stat. 478, codified as amended at 42 U.S.C. §§ 10801-10851.

20.  S. Rep. No. 109.

21.  In a number of writings, Ivan Illich argued that most curable sickness can be diagnosed and treated by laymen. He wrote:

People find it so difficult to accept this statement because the complexity of medical ritual has hidden from them the simplicity of its basic procedures. It took the example of the barefoot doctor in China to show how modern practice by simple workers in their spare time could, in three years, catapult health care in China to previously unparalleled levels. In most other countries health care by laymen is considered a crime.

I. Illich, "The Professions as a Form of Imperialism," *New Society*, Sept. 13, 1973, p. 634, in *Tools for Conviviality* (New York: Harper & Row, 1973).

22. See Comment, "Underprivileged Communications: Extension of the Psychotherapist-Patient Privilege to Patients of Psychiatric Social Workers," *Calif. L Rev.* 61:1050, 1973. Should a patrolman or parole officer have some measure of privilege when he is acting in the role of counselor? Only a small percentage of citizens' requests for service from the police department relate to crime. The Police Department of Kansas City, Mo., for example, receives about 1,300 calls per day, and of these calls only 91, or 7 percent relate to crime in any way. Ninety-three percent of the calls relate to emergency service, conflict resolution, and miscellaneous requests. Letter from James R. Newman, Assistant Chief of Police, Kansas City, Mo., to author (Nov. 20, 1973). A parole officer likewise has the task of being both law enforcement officer and social worker. T. Wicker, "The Lessons of Parole," *New York Times*, March 8, 1974, p. 33. The hairdresser is often regarded as the closest confidant of women. See J. Steinbeck, *Travels with Charley: In Search of America* (New York: Viking, 1962). While it may be argued that talking is not the essence of hairdressing, as it is of psychoanalysis, women may really let their hair down while at the hairdresser. N. Loupos, *The Happy Hairdresser* (New York: Simon & Schuster, 1973).

23. 51 F.3d 1346 (7th Cir. 1995).

24. 116 S. Ct. 1923 (1996).

25. See J. Frank, "Psychotherapy: The Restoration of Morale," *Am. J. Psychiat.* 131:271, 1974.

26. The Code of Professional Responsibility of the American Bar Association provides: "The duty of a lawyer to represent his client with zeal does not militate against his concurrent obligation to treat with consideration all persons involved in the legal process and to avoid the infliction of needless harm." EC 7-10. "Judicial hearings ought to be conducted through dignified and orderly procedures designed to protect the rights of all parties. Although a lawyer has the duty to represent his client zealously, he should not engage in any conduct that offends the dignity and decorum of preceedings." EC 7-36.

In People v. Whalen, 390 Mich. 672, 213 N.W.2d 116 (1973), the prosecutor was not allowed to impeach the defendant's alibi witnesses by questions implying a lesbian relationship between the alibi witnesses. The court cited the State Code of Professional Responsibility, which provides that a lawyer shall not "ask any question that he had no reasonable basis to believe is relevant to the case and that is intended to degrade a witness or other person."

27. See I. Illich, *Tools for Conviviality* (New York: Harper & Row, 1973), p. 95; R. Slovenko, *Psychiatry and Law* (Boston: Little, Brown, 1973), p. 3. Jack Weinstein, then professor of law and later judge, described the script in a law court thus:

> That the parameters of the law mark out an artificial world is not nec-essarily a valid basis for objection, for somewhat the same reason that it is not a telling criticism of the artistic quality of a painting by Chagall that it distorts a scene; nor is it a proper objection to Sandburg's biog-raphy of Lincoln that not everything then known about Lincoln is in the book. The writer's as well as the artist's success in re-creating a world must be tested within the frame of reference being used. The law is not interested in the "whole truth" but only in the evidence on the propositions of fact it deems material . . . . Even were it theoreti-cally possible to ascertain truth with a fair degree of certainty, it is doubtful whether the judicial system and rules of evidence would be designed to do so. Trials in our judicial system are intended to do more than merely determine what happened. Adjudication is a practical enterprise serving a variety of functions. Among the goals, in addition to truth finding, which the rules of procedure and evidence in this country have sought to satisfy are economizing of resources, inspiring confidence, supporting independent social policies, permitting ease in prediction and application, adding to the efficiency of the entire legal system, and tranquilizing disputants.

J.B. Weinstein, "Some Difficulties in Devising Rules for Determining Truth in Judicial Trials," *Colum. L. Rev.* 66:223, at 240-41, 1966. See also J.F. McCarthy, "On Playing the Game of Expert Witness in a Two-Value Logic System," *J. For. Sci.* 19:130, 1974.

# Chapter 2

# DIVORCE AND ALIENATION OF AFFECTIONS

This chapter discusses divorce and also alienation of affections. (Divorce is called in many states "dissolution of marriage.") In divorce or alienation of affections, by and large, communications to therapists or marriage counselors have been shielded by privilege.

## DIVORCE

In the tale of Adam and Eve, Eve was defined by what Adam lacked and was to satisfy Adam's loneliness. Leon Panetta and Robert Reich resigned their positions with the Clinton administration because, they said, they wanted to spend more time with their family. They felt lonely away from them.[1]

Yet countless others seek escape from their marriage—or a particular marriage—that they have entered into. Woody Allen's film "Annie Hall"—about two people who cannot decide if they need each other more than their freedom—struck a responsive chord with a very large audience.

There's an old Russian folk saying: "If you want to go to war, think once; if you want to go to sea, think twice; if you want to get married, think three times." That attitude is reflected in a Jules Feiffer cartoon: "I thought school was a jail...until I got a job. Boy, was that a jail! Then I got married. Even more of a jail! Until I got drafted into the army. The worst jail yet! Until I got in trouble and went to jail...and learned that jail is even more of a jail than school, a job, marriage, or the army. So finally I know what freedom's all about: the right to choose which jail."

For untold numbers of people, the opposite of marriage is freedom. "Give me liberty or give me death," shouted Patrick Henry in 1775 at a time when he had his disturbed and disturbing wife confined in a basement room.

91

There is now an organization of divorced men in the United States called the "National Coalition of Free Men." The Italian Interior Ministry not long ago decreed that identity cards will no longer reveal why someone is single, so instead of divorce, widowed, bachelor or spinster, the cards will simply say "libero," or free.[2] Ironically, at the same time, homosexuals seek commitment in marriage.

The statistics on divorce are daunting. Marry today (if at all), divorce tomorrow. Given the change in relationships, untying the marital knot is not as onerous as it once was (even in Ireland, where in 1995 its constitutional ban on divorce was lifted). In Jules Feiffer's *Little Murders*, the clergyman performing the marriage ceremony says, "Let me state frankly to you, Alfred, and to you, Patricia, that of the two hundred marriages I have performed, all but seven have failed. So the odds are not good. We don't like to admit it, especially at the wedding ceremony, but it's in the back of all our minds, isn't it?"[3]

The extended family became outmoded with changes in the economic system. To be sure, family ties are determined not just by the economic system, but the ties, whatever they may be, have to be consistent with economic reality–the traditional family ties have become less and less compatible with the economic reality. As a result, almost worldwide, the traditional family is disappearing or has disappeared, and as a consequence, the restrictions on divorce or other restrictions keeping a family together have fallen by the wayside.

In times long ago, the family had to join and work together as a unit for survival. Later, the husband went out to the factory or office and the wife remained at home. Divorce would result in the abandonment of a wife unable to manage in commerce. Today, husband and wife can look outside the family for food and services (including sex) and they often work in different cities and meet on weekends. Women today are in commerce and even in the military. Now, even the nuclear family is in peril. Writing about the collapse of marriage, Maggie Gallagher advises, "To be financially secure, a woman had best remain single and childless." A 1994 New York Times/CBS poll of American teenagers revealed that only 26 percent of teenage girls and 38 percent of teenage boys deemed marriage as essential to their happiness.[4]

With the repeal of fault as the basis for divorce, there is no need for psychiatric or other testimony (child custody is another matter). Traditionally, the law resolved matrimonial questions, like many other questions, in terms of fault or wrongdoing. In order to obtain a divorce, incompatibility had to be couched in terms of fault.

The film about a half-century ago, "Divorce Italian Style," depicted how to break up a marriage in then divorceless Italy: the unwanted wife is shed in the only way the law seemed to allow–the husband provides her with a lover, catches them together, and shoots her dead. Some American states at the time granted a divorce following a period of living separate and apart (quarreling spouses were advised to have no contact with each other; a one-night reconciliation, if proven, interrupted the period), but the divorce laws of most states were based entirely on the doctrine of the matrimonial offense, and as a result often led to tactics reminiscent of "Divorce Italian Style."

In other words, where law on divorce is strict, the parties will try to obtain one by "hook or crook." Couples will practice flagrant fraud to obtain a divorce, by contriving evidence of adultery attested to by paid witnesses and hired detectives. A spouse, it was said, must fornicate for freedom. Adultery was contrived; "cruelty" was invented. The courts generally recognized that the evidence was often fraudulent or collusive (judges are not naive), but judges are usually sympathetic to pleas for dissolution of a marriage, and when the parties have technically made out a case, especially when calendars are overburdened, the courts readily granted a divorce.

A movement is now afoot, led by conservative Christian groups, to repeal the no-fault divorce statutes adopted by nearly every state over the last two or three decades. Serious efforts to change or repeal no-fault divorce have taken place recently in Georgia, Idaho, Illinois, Michigan, Minnesota, Pennsylvania, Virginia, and Washington. The movement rests on the conviction that government can help children and save families by setting up barriers to divorce. The proposal to repeal the no-fault law in Michigan would require a finding of fault (desertion, an extramarital affair, physical or mental abuse) in all contested divorce cases, and in uncontested cases, couples with minor children would be required to undergo counseling.[5] As of this writing, no important changes have been enacted in any of the states, except for "covenant marriage" which has been adopted in Louisiana and pending before numerous other state legislatures.

By choosing to contract into a "covenant marriage," the parties undergo premarital counseling by a trained clergyman or secular marriage counselor of their choice. They commit to marital counseling and other "reasonable steps" to preserve their union "if difficulties arise during the marriage." Under covenant marriage, divorce would be permitted only on the grounds of adultery, physical or sexual abuse of a spouse or child, abandoning the other spouse for one year, or a mutually agreed-upon two-year separation. Only the offended spouse who kept the marriage promises is permitted to seek an immediate end to a convenant marriage. Critics of covenant marriage predict that it will bring back the days of "fault" divorce where the parties got mired in accusations and repudiations. Thus far in Louisiana few have opted to enter into a covenant marriage.

**THE LOCKHORNS** By Hoest & Reiner

"Send in Bosnia and Serbia."

Reprinted with special permission of King Features Syndicate.

The law governing family relationships in the United States is state law; the states retain the right under the Constitution to make their own laws in this field. In criminal matters, federal law (*e.g.*, the Mann Act on prostitution) may be concurrent with state law, but in matters of marriage and family relationships, state law alone governs. Uniformity in laws is achieved by a preemption by federal laws or by agreement between the states; a national marriage and divorce law would apparently require a constitutional amendment. At one time Senator Arthur Capper of Kansas proposed an amendment, which he unsuccessfully promoted for some 25 years, providing: "The Congress shall have power to make laws, which shall be uniform throughout the United States, on marriage and divorce, the legitimation of children, and the care and custody of children affected by annulment of marriage or by divorce."

Congress, implementing the full faith and credit clause of the Constitution, could only prescribe the minimum standards which would *entitle* a decree to full faith and credit in every other state, and could not *deny* to any state the right to grant full faith and credit to decrees from sister states when those decrees failed to meet the minimum congressional standards. The lack of uniformity among the several states was criticized more in matters of family relationships than in criminal matters (this criticism usually came from people who were obliged to travel to states where divorce laws were lax, and from lawyers who lost their business).

The various jurisdictions make minimal effort to prevent quick marriages or the marriage of persons suffering from serious physical or mental illness.

It is easier to obtain a marriage license than a driver's license, for in the latter case the applicants must know the rules of the road. The most common premarital test is, of course, for venereal disease. A few states consider habitual criminals, drug addicts, and chronic alcoholics unsuited for marriage and reproduction. There is (properly) no restriction on intermarriage of diabetics (there is, however, a high incidence of fetal mortality and congenital abnormalities among children born to diabetics; as a precaution, they take resort to contraception, sterilization, or abortion; the difficulty in having children gives rise to marital discord). Some states forbid epileptics to marry, and a few states prohibit the marriage of people with advanced or infectious tuberculosis. Approximately a dozen states prohibit the marriage of the "insane" and mentally defective people. There is, however, apparently, no solid scientific basis for the prohibition of marriage of the mentally ill. Hereditary factors are apparently unproven except possibly in bipolar disorders, depression, and schizophrenia and the course of a mental illness is not easily predicted.

The limitations on marriage are designed essentially to prevent the propagation of defective children, but mental defectives and mentally ill persons who have little control over what they do usually breed without the sanction of formal marriage. The problem is related as a practical matter to another issue, of sterilization. Eugenic considerations led some states (*e.g.*, Conn., Kan., N.D., N.H., Va., Wash.) to permit marriage of "mentally ill persons" only with women over forty-five or without age limit if such persons are sterilized or otherwise incapable of procreation (*e.g.*, Neb., N.C., S.D.). In mental hospitals, attendants are on the alert to prevent sexual intercourse among patients; consider, for example, the following hospital directive, motivated in part by political and community pressures: "Male and female patients are not allowed to sit and hold hands, or engage in any form of 'courting.'"

By today's standards, some marriages are not worth saving, and should be terminated for the welfare of all concerned. Sometimes a divorce is better than a bad marriage. Where this is indicated, the task of a marriage counselor or therapist as well as the lawyer is one of education for divorce and perhaps future marriage. The cooperative efforts of marriage counselor and lawyer can help the counselee in recognizing the problems and making decisions with understanding.

The movement to repeal no-fault divorce laws has also spawned a campaign to encourage–or even compel–premarital counseling. The leading crusader for compulsory counseling is Christian syndicated columnist Michael McManus, author of "Marriage Savers."[6] A proposal in Maryland would make couples wait 60 days to get a marriage license unless they have premarital counseling; the Michigan proposal would require couples who decline premarital counseling to pay a substantially higher fee and wait longer for a marriage license; and proposals in Minnesota and Mississippi would require counseling before granting licenses. Premarital counseling has been required in Catholic churches in the United States for about 25 years, but apparently it has not been studied whether counseling has affected Catholic divorce rates.[7] The movement brought about the adoption of the "covenant marriage" law in Louisiana.

An ironic joke states that marriage itself is the cause of the high divorce rates—that is to say, it is the immature character of many marital partners which creates the high divorce rates, and which leads to protracted battles. One time or another, "marital fitness" tests by psychologists have been suggested, but no one recommends that they should become obligatory for marriage. It is one thing to determine whether a person has venereal disease, or is mentally defective, but it is quite another matter to determine whether a person is "emotionally mature" for marriage.[8] The factors involved in marital choice and later harmony are much too complex for psychological testing. Marriage counselors, however, have commented that persons who voluntarily seek premarital counseling usually should not get married. They are, according to these counselors, generally immature and burdened with psychological problems, for which they need therapy. They usually want quick, simple, magical advice.

On a TV program, popular for a considerable period of time, couples were selected as proper mates for marriage by computer. The machine, fed objective data on thousands of people, ground out names or pairs "ideally" suited to each other. Each week the couple appeared on TV to report publicly on the progress of their courtship. It was left to the couple themselves, and not to the machine, to decide whether or not they would marry, and for this, philosopher William Barrett laconically stated, "let us at least be thankful for small favors." He added, commenting on the craze for "objectivity": "What was most appalling in this whole performance was the great spirit of cheerfulness and good fun with which both audience and lucky couple accepted this submission of the human to the mechanical. After all, the machine is objective, and therefore should know better than our mere subjective feelings whom we should or should not take in marriage."[9]

"If there are any among us who know of some reason why Todd and Janet should not be joined in marriage, let them speak now or..."

CLOSE TO HOME © by John McPherson. Reprinted by permission of Universal Press Syndicate. All rights reserved.

If a marriage does take place despite a legal prohibition, it will nonetheless usually be accorded full recognition as a valid marriage. The laws on marriage (age of parties, waiting period, license) are essentially desiderata, of persuasive quality. As regards competency, it is considered that the obligations implicit in the "marriage contract" are simple and within the grasp of a small child: daily work (husband earns the money) in return for daily work (wife cleans the house, bears children and cooks the meals). Of course, those are no longer considered obligations. Under the traditional marriage ceremony, the minister in most religious denominations would say, "Who gives this woman in marriage?" It was assumed that the woman must be given in marriage by father or some male representative of the father since she herself was assumed not to be capable of entering into marriage on her own account (in early times, a woman was regarded as an object or possession).[10] A marriage would be set aside only when the evidence was overwhelming that the husband or wife was utterly deteriorated and confused.[11] The courts are more willing to annul an unconsummated marriage than a consummated one (intercourse before marriage does not count); the theory of the courts, one might say, is that the bride is still in the "original package." In fact, though, a "marriage contract," while called that in law, actually creates a status rather than a contract. (Furthermore, engagements to marry are not usually understood to be legally binding.)

Even when a divorce action had to be couched in terms of fault, most marital controversies yielded to the noncontest approach, but when a case was contested, hate often erupted in the courtroom. It took on scandalous proportions in a drag-out fight. New York attorney Louis Nizer wrote that "litigations between husbands and wives exceed in bitterness and hatred those of any other relationships." No litigation, even in their most aggravated form, Nizer wrote, could equal the sheer, unadulterated venom of a matrimonial contest.[12] As a rule, therapists do not attempt to "fix the blame," but they were summoned to testify.[13]

The acrimony associated with divorce prior to the enactment of no-fault divorce laws has been transferred under no-fault to the arena of child custody battles. Divorce and its effects on children have come under study as a specific mental health issue. In her book *Second Chances,* Judith Wallerstein found that about half of all the couples she studied were still locked in bitter conflict five years after divorcing.[14]

While various states in the United States now have very lax divorce laws, making unnecessary any allegations of fault, fault is still considered, and increasingly so, in alimony, property settlement, or child custody. In proof of fault, the testimony of the psychiatrist who had treated one of the spouses would be highly pertinent. In negotiations on property settlements, therapists are known to attend the hearings and the lawyer-client conferences and they set out what they consider to be in their patient's long-term interest.[15]

Various countries have enacted rules of procedure which authorize judges to order physical or mental examinations in cases where an individual's condition is in controversy. A litigant who refuses to be examined cannot be compelled to do so, although the court may dismiss the claim of the disobedient party or rule appropriately against the party. The U.S. Supreme Court has held it is constitutional for a court to enter judgment against a defendant who fails to comply with a court-ordered medical examination.[16] A court-examination may do away with any need for the testimony of a psychiatrist who may have seen both spouses as patients, either separately or jointly.

In recent years, the conjoint family therapy approach has commanded increasing attention in psychiatry and, in such cases, the legal question arises whether or not the psychiatrist can testify on behalf of the spouse who may want him to testify. The opponent spouse can apparently claim privilege as to communications obtained from him and observations made of him by the psychiatrist. Yet, by seeing the opponent spouse in therapy, the psychiatrist will naturally be affected in his evaluation and testimony on behalf of the proponent spouse. No medical statute expressly covers the problem.[17]

Various states have provided that whenever the parties to a separation or divorce proceeding effect a reconciliation prior to rendition of judgment, all pleadings and testimony can be separated from other court records and maintained in a confidential status. The legislation applies only to cases of reconciliation effected prior to judgment.[18]

Some years ago Victor Schwartz, a leading authority on tort law, pointed out that total nonfault marital dissolution left two unfortunate consequences in its wake. First, he said, "the serious marital offender," a spouse who has without cause substantially abused his or her marital partner physically or mentally, may be able to escape any criminal or civil law sanction. Conversely, a spouse who has suffered abuse from a serious marital offender may be unable to obtain any compensation from the damage he or she has endured. Schwartz therefore recommended that tort law should perform compensatory, deterrent and admonitory functions by allowing the injured spouse to pursue a claim after the marriage has been dissolved.[19]

With the demise of interspousal immunity, a tort action along with divorce has become an emerging trend.[20] In the tort action, under a theory of waiver, disclosure of records of psychotherapy is allowed to explore whether the complainant's psychological condition attributed to the acts of cruelty existed prior to their alleged commission.[21]

Depending upon the jurisdiction, interspousal tort claims and divorce actions may be subject to require joinder, permissive joinder, or prohibited joinder rules.[22] Reasons of procedure, jurisdiction, and policy are cited in support of prohibiting joinder. In any event, there is no bar to a predivorce interspousal tort action.[23]

For years, New Jersey case law followed the minority rule that tort claims that occur during marriage must be joined to dissolution proceedings pending in family court under the state's "entire controversy" doctrine, but in 1996, the state supreme court ruled that a spouse may as in the majority of states present a tort claim to a jury. To grant marital tort claimants the right to a jury trial reflected New Jersey's "profound interest" in curbing domestic violence, the court said. It also said that "there is no such thing as an act of domestic violence that is not serious."[24]

The noted writer Philip Roth, who suffered mental breakdowns, demanded the return of everything he had given Claire Bloom, his estranged wife, including a portable heater, and he sought $62 billion from her–a billion dollars for every year of her life–for her refusal to honor their prenuptial agreement. Bloom escaped to Ireland to film a television role, only to be followed by a telephone call from his psychiatrist urging her to vacate their New York apartment for six months so that Roth, out of the hospital by then and fearful of living alone in his country home, could be nearer his therapist and friends.

## ALIENATION OF AFFECTIONS

Most states at one time allowed an action against a third party for "alienation of affections" of a spouse. A few states continue to allow the action. What can the alleged damages be based upon? A member of the Louisiana Supreme Court quipped that the spouse has not lost anything but rather learned something.[26] In a 1987 case in Louisville, a jury of eight women and four men put a price tag on a wife's stolen affections, for the future "Christmases and good times" the husband will miss. The wife claimed her love for her husband diminished five years before their marriage ended because of her husband's inability to communicate.[27]

Unless there is a privilege, a psychiatrist involved in the treatment of one of the parties could be called upon to testify whether a third person, who is sued, alienated the patient-spouse's affection from the other spouse, the complainant. Very often, the plaintiff in these cases is pathologically jealous or paranoid. A common delusion, especially to be found in a psychotic spouse, is infidelity.

One of the best known cases on the issue of confidentiality and privileged communication involving a suit for alienation of affections occurred in Illinois.[28] The attorney for Mr. X sought to question Mrs. X's psychiatrist concerning information she had revealed during psychiatric consultations. Judge Harry Fisher of the trial court excused the psychiatrist–Dr. Roy Grinker of Michael Reese Hospital–from testifying. Grinker was prepared to stand in contempt rather than testify, but that was not necessary. Judge Fisher wished to establish new law. In the course of his opinion, written in 1952, Judge Fisher pointed out that psychiatry is just now beginning to gain recognition and understanding in the courts, and he said:

> I am persuaded that the courts will guard the secrets which come to the psychiatrist and will not permit him to disclose them. I am persuaded that it is just one of those cases where the privilege ought to be granted and protected. And the social significance of it is probably even greater than that which comes from the protection of the communications between lawyer and client.

The decision attracted a great deal of attention. Illinois had no medical privilege statute, and consequently, the decision was generally considered to be without solid justification in law. Rules of evidence in part are formulated by the judiciary, but privilege has long been accepted as being within the domain of the legislature. Judge Fisher, although a lower court judge, was willing to reach out so as to create a privilege, and to leave it to the appellate court to affirm or reverse. In legal circles, it is generally believed that had the case been appealed to a higher court, the psychiatrist would have been instructed to testify or would have faced punitive action for contempt.

In matters of breakdown of marriage, some judges are known to shield communications to therapists or marriage counselors by applying the rule of evidence banning admission of statements made during the course of compromise negotiations. That rule is grounded on the policy of encouraging the settlement of disputes without resort to litigation, but that purpose was intended to cover issues of liability or damages, not marital disputes.[29]

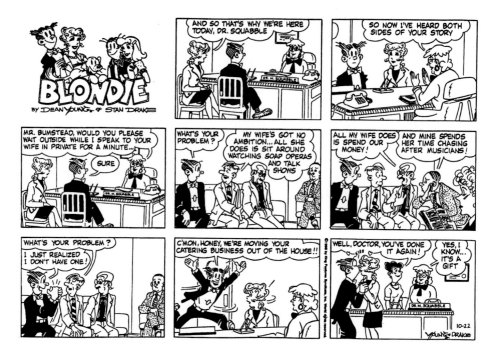

Figure 4. Reprinted with permission of King Features Syndicate.

## NOTES

1.  R. B. Reich, "My Family Leave Act," *New York Times*, Nov. 8, 1996, p. 15; "White House Shuffle," *Detroit Free Press*, Nov. 9, 1996, p. 1. At the wedding of Mimi Lister and Sheldon Toney (Chester, N.J., Aug. 15, 1992), a friend gave the bridegroom a bowling ball with a chain attached and the message "You are no longer a free man" written on it. The bridegroom said, "I'm real happy about the ball-and-chain aspect of marriage. I have nothing bad to say about it."

2.  AP news-release, "Are you married or free?", *Detroit News*, Sept. 29, 1996, p. 5.

3.  New York: Random House, 1968, p. 64.

4.  M. Gallagher, *The Abolition of Marriage* (Washington, D.C.: Regnery, 1996).

5.  D. Johnson, "No-Fault Divorce Is Under Attack," *New York Times*, Feb. 12, 1996, p. 8; K. Cole, "Bills would make divorce harder," *Detroit News*, Feb. 13, 1996, p. D-1.

6.  McManus advocates use of a questionnaire called PREPARE that helps couples identify areas where they are in agreement—or not. M. McManus,

*Marriage Savers: Helping Your Friends and Family Avoid Divorce* (Grand Rapids: Zondervan, 1993). See Cover Story, "The Promise Keepers," Time, Oct. 6, 1997, p. 34.

7.  M. Puente, "Lawmakers counsel against divorce," *USA Today*, Feb. 21, 1996, p. 6; see also C. Spratling, "Stop in the name of love," *Detroit Free Press*, Feb. 25, 1966, p. J-1.

8.  H. Pilpel & T. Zavin, *Your Marriage and the Law* (New York: Collier, 1964).

9.  Quoted in R. Slovenko (ed.), *Sexual Behavior and the Law* (Springfield, Ill.: Thomas, 1965), p. 18.

10. Petruchio in Shakespeare's "Taming of the Shrew" (Act III, Scene 2) said of his wife: "She is my goods, she is my house, my household stuff, my field, my barn, my horse, my ox, my ass, my anything."

11. L. Frank, *The Conduct of Sex* (New York: Morrow, 1961), p. 95; H. Davidson, "Marriage, Divorce and Mental Disorder," Va. Med. Monthly 82:108, 1955.

12. *My Life in Court* (New York: Doubleday, 1961).

13. See, in general, M.C. Phillips, "Spousal Exception to California's Statutory Prohibition Against Disclosure of Confidential Medical Information?" *Sw. U. L. Rev. 25:75, 1995.*

14. J. Wallerstein, *Second Chances* (New York: Ticknor & Fields, 1989). See also B.D. Whitehead, *The Divorce Culture* (New York: Knopf, 1997); M. Gallagher, "Why Make Divorce Easy?" *New York Times*, Feb. 20, 1996, p. 15; L.R. Kass, "The end of courtship," *Public Interest*, Winter 1997, p. 39.

15. See A. Sarat & W.L.F. Felstiner, *Divorce Lawyers and Their Clients* (New York: Oxford University Press, 1995); see also J.M. Suarez, N.L. Weston & N.B. Hartstein, "Mental Health Interventions In Divorce Proceedings," *Am. J. Orthopsychiat.* 48:273, 1978.

16. Schlagenhauf v. Holder, 379 U.S. 104 (1964); discussed in Chapter 4. In 1974 the Rabbinical High Court of Israel ruled that a court, on a show of good cause, has the power to compel a litigant in a divorce action suit to undergo a psychiatric examination. The Rabbis dismissed the defendant's claim that such an order constituted a violation of her right to privacy, but they split on the question whether "good cause" was indeed demonstrated, with the minority believing it had not. The minority, however, concurred that on a clearly valid show of good cause a court would have the authority to compel a medical examination. D.I. Frimer, "Medical Examinations by Order of the Court and the Right to Privacy: Common Law and Jewish Law Experiences," *Israel L. Rev.* 17:96, 1982

17. See Renzi v. Morrison, 249 Ill. App. 3d 5, 188 Ill. Dec. 224, 618 N.E.2d 794 (1993); discussed in Chapter 3.

18. See, *e.g.*, La. R.S. 13:4687.

19. V.E. Schwartz, "The Serious Marital Offender: Tort Law as a Solution," *Family L.Q.* 6:219, 1972.

20. R.B. Siegel, "'The Rule of Love': Wife Beating as Prerogative and Privacy," *Yale L.J.* 105:2117, 1996. There is also a possible cause of action under the "Violence Against Women Act," passed as part of the 1994 Crime Bill, which allows victims of "gender-motivated violence" to sue their attackers in federal court. This statute was struck down by Judge Jackson Kiser in Brzonkala v. Virginia Polytechnic Institute, 1996 U.S. Dist. LEXIS 11436, when he dismissed VPI student Christy Brzonkala's federal suit based on alleged sexual assault by two members of the college's football team. Judge Kiser found that Congress had exceeded its authority in passing the "Violence Against Women Act," on the ground that there is no basis for the federal judiciary to have jurisdiction over sexual assault and spousal abuse, crimes that properly belong in the state courts. A few weeks earlier, Judge Janet Arterton came to the opposite conclusion in Jane Doe v. John Doe, 929 F. Supp. 608 (D. Conn. 1996), where the plaintiff claimed that her husband, whom she was divorcing, beat her and treated her like a slave throughout their 17 years of marriage. C. Young, "Crime, the Constitution and the 'Weaker' Sex," *Wall Street Journal*, Aug. 21, 1996, p. 15.

21. Kinsella v. Kinsella, 287 N.J. Super. 305, 671 A. 2d 130 (1996).

22. In Nash v. Overholser, 757 P.2d 1180 (Idaho 1988) and Stuart v. Stuart, 410 N.W.2d 632 (Wis.App. 1987), the courts permitted plaintiffs to bring a tort suit after their divorces, refusing to require such actions be brought in the divorce itself. In both cases, the former husbands interposed a res judicata defense to the post-divorce lawsuit. Both courts termed mandatory joinder of tort claims with divorce actions to be undesirable as well as unfair.

23. C.L. Chaimp & A. Argiroff, "Tort Remedies for Domestic Abuse: An Underused Avenue of Relief," Mich. Bar J., Sept. 1994, p. 930; B.G. Fines, "Joinder of Tort Claims in Divorce Actions," *J. Acad. Matrimonial Lawyers* 12:285, 1994.

24. Brennan v. Orban, 1996 WL 393681 (N.J. July 16, 1996).

25. P.J. Smith, "Marrying Portnoy," *New York*, Oct. 21, 1996, p. 26.

26. Moulin v. Monteleone, 165 La. 169, 115 So. 447 (1928).

27. 1987 UPI news-release, reported in P.N. Swisher, H.A. Miller & W.I. Weston, *Family Law: Cases, Materials and Problems* (New York: Matthew Bender, 1990), p. 84. Recently Dorothy Hutelmyer, a 40-year-old mother of three and PTA president, in Burlington, N.C., successfully sued her husband's lover for "wrecking" their marriage. The verdict was $1 million. Some see the verdict—believed to be the largest of its kind—as a stern warning on extramarital affairs. Others see it as one more sign of the growing backlash against no-fault divorce. Some lawyers compare alienation of affections to a business arrangement gone sour: If one executive interferes with a contract made between two others, then he is subject to a lawsuit for interference with business relations. N. Gibbs, "An Antique Law Sends Tremors Through Many a Heart," *Time*, Aug. 18, 1997, p. 50.

28. Binder v. Ruvell, Civil Docket 52C2535, Circuit Court of Cook County, Illinois, June 24, 1952, reported in *J.A.M.A.* 150:1241, 1952, and discussed in *Nw. U.L. Rev.* 47:384, 1952.
29. Rule 408, Federal Rules of Evidence.

# Chapter 3

# CHILD CUSTODY

In a dispute between parents over the custody of a child, the "best interest of the child" sets the standard for decision-making. It is a rubric that can mean whatever one wants it to mean. It opens the door to a wide range of evidence pertaining not only to the fitness of the parents but also to the environment in which the child will be raised. As a general principle, the "best interest" standard overrides any psychotherapist-patient privilege, thereby allowing access to therapy records and to compelling the testimony of the therapist. The statutory law mandates that the court consider, among other factors, the mental and physical health of the parties.[1]

In contentious proceedings, attorneys search for data that will support their case. The case law reveals that the privilege provides some but uncertain protection of confidentiality. The majority of courts say, under the mandate of the statutory law, or otherwise, that the privilege yields automatically in child custody or related matters.[2] Other courts order disclosure only when health is in issue or when the circumstances indicate abuse or neglect. According to these decisions, the question is whether there is a compelling need to have past psychiatric records to evaluate the capacity of the parent with respect to current parenting abilities.[3]

"In every custody proceeding and in every proceeding for the modification of a custody decree," as one court put it, "the mental and physical health of not only the parents but of the child is of great concern and importance to the court." The court went on to say, "Whenever custody of infants is in dispute, the parties seeking custodial authority subject themselves to extensive and acute investigation of all factors relevant to the permanent and, hopefully, proper award of custody. Of major importance is the mental and physical health of all of the parties and whether the child is in an environment likely to endanger his physical, mental, moral or emotional health." As another court put it, "The paramount consideration in a child custody matter is the child's best interest...A court cannot determine the best interests of the child without considering whether [the parent] is physically, financially, or mentally able to care for the child."[5]

Quite often, the testimony as well as the records of the treating therapist are demanded. To quote an attorney, who has been involved in considerable child custody litigation, in an address to a law group: "The more I know about a parent the better. I would depose the treating doctor. The record standing alone is not sufficient."[6]

As a matter of routine, court-appointed or lawyer-appointed evaluators ask for the psychiatric records of the parents or child, and they usually get them. An evaluator would be remiss in not obtaining these records, for on cross-examination, the evaluator would likely be asked about matters revealed there, and legitimately so. Typical questions: "Didn't you know that she (or he) was diagnosed as schizophrenic?" "Didn't you know that she (or he) threatened the life of the child?"

Even if the expert may not need the records to carry out an evaluation, the expert will want them to defuse a cross-examination, and also to confirm the evaluation, thereby enhancing the probative value of the report. This is all the more true where a party resists production of the records. When a party refuses a request, suspicion arises that the party is hiding something, and the records gain even more importance. Moreover, refusing to disclose psychiatric records is usually an expensive and time-consuming exercise in futility as the trial judge will likely order disclosure, but disclosure without court order may result in liability for breach of confidentiality.

There may be circumstances when the confidentiality of reports will be protected, particularly if it can be shown that the "best interest of the child" is advanced by confidentiality rather than disclosure. In some cases, disclosure of statements of the parents or the child could harm the parent-child relationship. In the process of evaluation, children may make statements that may result in a vendetta against the child. The evaluator is in a dilemma— how to inform the court and at the same time protect the child? A youngster says, "I hate my father." The data, put in a report in raw form, will expose the child negatively. In this type of situation, the trial judge might very well shield these communications. Disclosure may then be limited to communications relevant to fitness, or to the interaction and interrelationship of the child with the parent.[7]

One argument claims that the "best interest of the child" is enhanced by confidentiality of parental psychotherapy records, by encouraging parents to obtain treatment that might otherwise not be sought. Discouraging people from consulting a psychotherapist, out of fear that confidences will be used against them in later court appearances, does not inure to the welfare of the child. The protection of confidentiality, with its attendant encouragement to seek help, may better serve the child. As one Florida Court of Appeal observed, successful therapy can be dependent upon the psychiatrist's ability to assure confidentiality.[8]

Records of treatment of a parent or child occurring years ago might be protected on relevancy grounds. In a Florida case, the husband, claiming a substantial change in circumstances warranting a change of custody, alleged, among other things, that the wife was psychologically unstable and suffered from migraine headaches which prevented her from providing a stable home for the child. The wife admitted that she had brief psychiatric counseling some seven years ago, following the divorce, and stated that the counseling "enabled her to provide an even more stable, nurturing, and healthy home" for the child. The trial court ordered the wife and husband to undergo psychological evaluations; the wife expressed her willingness to comply with that order. The husband, however, sought to depose the psychiatrist who had treated the wife seven years ago. The trial court denied her motion for a protective order, but the appellate court ruled in her favor. The appellate court said:[9]

> At issue...in custody modification proceedings are the parents' present circumstances....Testimony from a psychiatrist who briefly treated the wife seven years ago can be of no relevance to the wife's present ability to care for the child. Because the wife has agreed to submit to a psychological examination, the husband and the court will be adequately apprised of her present psychological condition.

In a similar scenario, a Michigan Court of Appeal said:[10]

> [W]e do not find relevant to a party's present condition the testimony of a physician who has not treated the party for years....Moreover, the...court was able, with the [party's] participation, to gather information with regard to her mental condition....We also reject as meritless defendant's argument that by virtue of submitting to a court appointed psychological examination and introduction of the psychologist's testimony, plaintiff waived her medical privilege.

Privilege claims aside, judges must decide the relevancy of all proffered evidence, and must also consider whether there is less intrusive but equally probative evidence available. In any kind of case, when the psychotherapist-patient privilege is raised, the guideline on the admissibility of evidence is relevancy, not privilege. Thus, in tort cases, where health is at issue, a litigant is said to waive the privilege but lack of relevancy may keep out the evidence.

The fact that one parent has been seen in outpatient psychotherapy and given a diagnosis, while the other parent has not, should not be taken as presumptive of a difference in the mental health of the parties. In addition, written records of outpatient psychotherapy are often not helpful or are even actively damaging for several reasons. First, introducing such written material into litigation without appropriate restrictive protections runs the risk of making such matters accessible to the community at large. Second, parenting issues are seldom discussed in detail in such records. Third, therapists vary widely in their experience. Fourth, therapists tend to advocate for their own patients. Fifth, therapists usually are unable to provide comparative data on both parents, because they have not seen both. Hence, it may be argued, therapy records may be more prejudicial than probative on the issues involved.[11]

Health issues are significant in a child custody proceeding to the extent that they impact on parenting; to the extent that health problems exist which do not adversely affect parenting, they are not relevant. Usually reports of mental health professionals are significant only if they document severe emotional problems or hospitalizations. Therefore, records of inpatient psychiatric hospitalizations are likely to be of more use than records of outpatient treatment. A history of inpatient treatment, however, needs to be investigated to see how the psychiatric difficulties actually affected parenting. Compare these two records:[12]

(A) Mr. X has a long, documented history of manic-depressive illness. Records from the hospital were reviewed which indicate that he has had four hospitalizations in the previous three years. The records indicate that the hospitalizations were preceded by a period of several weeks in which he gradually became increasingly delusional and showed little insight into the approaching breakdown. In order to hospitalize him, involuntary commitment was necessary. During these periods, his ability to parent the children was severely compromised.

Record (A) conveys a very different picture than this record (B):

(B) Mrs. X has a long, documented history of manic-depressive illness which has required hospitalization. However, the records from her psychiatrist and statements of her husband indicate that she is aware of the episodic nature of her illness, and is aware when she begins to decompensate. At those times, she alerts her psychiatrist and has had her mother come stay with her to help out with the children. While the illness has caused a number of separations from her children, she has been able to provide for adequate parenting during those times.

Records will likely be deemed relevant in the case of a patient who is hospitalized during the course of the litigation,[13] or is suicidal,[14] or is using illegal drugs, or is surreptitiously engaged in homosexual activity,[15] or is abusing the child. Indeed, reporting laws mandate that a therapist report child abuse to the authorities. Increasingly, in child custody disputes, one spouse alleges that the other has been abusing the child, sexually or otherwise.

In recent years, sexual abuse allegations in the context of divorce or child custody disputes have occurred with some frequency. A rather high proportion of such allegations are either false or unverifiable.[16] Such a case is sometimes approached simultaneously through divorce litigation, a child protection action, and a criminal case against the alleged perpetrator, approaches which often conflict. For instance, the extent to which evaluations of these cases are made by the Friend of the Court, rather than by Protective Services or the police, is something which varies widely from county to county. Too, there is often acrimony between experts, such as mental health professionals and pediatricians, as they argue over appropriate standards, techniques, and conclusions.[17]

Disclosure of mental health records is frequently contended for on grounds that there has been a waiver of confidentiality. Under the rules of evidence, communications relevant to an issue of health–including a mental or emotional condition–are not privileged if the patient relies upon the condition to prove or assist in his or her claim or defense. This concept was developed in personal injury cases, and in criminal cases where the defendant pleads not guilty by reason of insanity. In these cases, a party has put his physical or mental condition into issue, and cannot then preclude an opposing party's inquiry into that condition by asserting a privilege.

What about in child custody cases? Is health put in issue in every custody case, simply because the health of the parties is a consideration in determining fitness? The courts say that whenever custody is disputed, as we noted at the outset, the persons involved subject themselves to "extensive and acute investigation."[18] Likewise, in actions to terminate parental rights, the courts say that one who resists action by the State to terminate his or her parental rights over a child places his or her mental health in issue and thereby waives the physician-patient privilege.[19] In several states, by statute, the mental condition of the parties is made a determinant and thus, theoretically, an issue. For example, Delaware's statute provides that in determining the best interests of the child, the court *shall* (that is, mandatorily) consider the mental and physical health of all the individuals involved.[20] A Massachusetts statute states that the mental condition of the child or the proposed custodian *may* (that is, permissively) be issues in the child placement decision. It provides that the trial judge, in the exercise of discretion, should determine whether the psychotherapist has evidence bearing on ability to provide suitable custody.[21]

A minority of courts, notably in Florida and Georgia, have resisted the trend toward waiver of the privilege. For example, a Florida Court of Appeal said, "The psychiatrist-patient privilege would be seriously compromised if a treating psychiatrist could be required to testify against his patient in any divorce proceeding where the issue of child custody [is] raised." The court stated that although the mental condition of a parent is relevant in determining the best interest of the child, a party seeking custody does not thereby waive the psychiatrist-patient privilege. An alternative to breaching the privilege, the court said, is a court-ordered examination.[22] Likewise, a Missouri court said that ordering a mental examination of a party is to be utilized when a question is raised as to the mental condition of a parent seeking custody.[23]

In another opinion by a Florida Court of Appeal, a court-appointed psychologist informed the trial court that it would be helpful for him to review the records of the wife's psychiatrist in making his evaluation. The trial court thereupon overruled the wife's claim of privilege. On appeal, the appellate court held that unless there is a radical change in condition, such as commitment for mental treatment during the custody dispute, the alternative of a court-appointed expert should eliminate any need to breach the privilege.[24]

In yet another opinion by a Florida Court of Appeal, it was stated: "Mere allegations that the custodial parent is mentally unstable are not sufficient to place the custodial parent's mental health at issue and overcome the privilege....Likewise, the custodial parent's denial of allegations of mental instability does not operate as a waiver of the patient-psychotherapist privilege. To hold otherwise would eviscerate the privilege; a party seeking privileged information would obtain it simply by alleging mental infirmity."[25] Quoting an earlier opinion, the court said: "If such were the law, no psychiatrist could ever assure his patient of confidentiality."[26]

Should a court deem the psychotherapist-patient privilege waived only when the health of the party is "clearly in controversy"? Or is it necessary to depose the doctor or see the records in order to determine whether health ought to be a serious consideration? While arguments are available on both sides, usually other evidence than the records themselves is available to justify discovery when health is an issue. Mental disorder of a serious nature is not hidden—it's apparent in demeanor and behavior. An Alabama Court of Appeal spoke to "clearly in controversy." It wrote: "We recognize that the psychologist-patient privilege is an important one, not to be easily disregarded. We do not seek to discourage troubled parents from obtaining professional help. However, we are convinced that where the issue of the mental state of a party to a custody suit is *clearly in controversy*, and a proper resolution of the custody issue requires disclosure of privileged medical records, the psychologist-patient privilege must yield" (emphasis added).[27]

The prevailing rule in a child custody dispute is that the psychotherapist-patient privilege does not shield testimony or records of a psychotherapist.

Usually the statutory or common law of the state provides that a parent's mental or physical health is an important factor in deciding whether he or she will be able to tend to the child's needs. The relevance of the issue is held to "waive" the privilege. Given the absence of juries in most custody decisions, an attempt to counter this waiver, by protective order or otherwise, may prove counterproductive even if successful. The more the attorney emphasizes the degree of embarrassment and humiliation disclosure would produce for the client, the more the argument suggests to the judge–the ultimate decision-maker–that there is real cause for concern. Suppressed evidence gives rise to an adverse inference that it is unfavorable to the party.

A legal practitioner is better advised to assume that disclosure will be required, and to undertake prompt measures for "damage control." These may include early personal review of the client's records *before* they are requested by the opponent or the court; meetings with the expert to explore ways to control or minimize the impact the patient's difficulties have on the children; and retention of an independent expert in the face of an unreasonably adverse opinion by the treating psychotherapist. Indeed, many informed, mature lawyers will refuse to advocate custody for a client whose mental health problems truly make the other party a more appropriate custodial parent–but such decisions and counseling can only be provided by an informed lawyer, not one who at every turn reflexively shouts "privilege!" or one who sees his duty as absolute to serve the expressed wishes of his client. As with many legal matters, sober reflection and mature judgment produce better advice than a mindless dedication to total war.[28]

## NOTES

1. See, *e.g.*, Ala. Code § 26-18-7 (a)(2); Ky. Rev. Stat. 403.270; Mich. Comp. Laws Ann. 722.21. The best interest standard is not used to award custody to a nonparent over a natural parent absent dependency or abuse and neglect. In cases where a nonparent seeks custody, the main focus is on the fitness of the parent or parents. *In re* A.R.A., 919 P.2d 388 (Mont. 1996).
2. See, *e.g.*, Matter of A.J.S., 630 P.2d 217 (Mont. 1981); In re Norwood, 194 Neb. 595, 234 N.W.2d 601 (1975); D. v. D., 108 N.J. Super. 149, 260 A.2d 255 (1969); Perry v. Fiumano, 61 A.D. 512, 403 N.Y.S.2d 382 (N.Y. App. Div. 1978); People *ex rel.* Chitty v. Fitzgerald, 40 Misc.2d 966, 244 N.Y.S.2d 441 (Sup. Ct. 1963). Pending Maryland SB 51 would specifically exclude from privilege: (1) Any administrative or judicial nondelinquent juvenile proceeding; (2) Any guardianship and adoption proceeding initiated by a child placement service; (3) Any guardianship and protective services proceeding concerning disabled persons; and (4) Any criminal or delinquency

proceeding in which there is a charge of child abuse or neglect or which aries out of an investigation of suspected child abuse or neglect.

3. See C.P. Malmquist, "Psychiatric Confidentiality in Child Custody Disputes," *J. Am. Acad. Child Adolesc. Psychiat.* 33:158, 1994.
4. Atwood v. Atwood, 550 S.W.2d 465, at 467 (Ky. 1976).
5. Matter of von Goyt, 461 So.2d 821, at 823 (Ala. Civ. App. 1984).
6. Address by Marianne Battani on April 30, 1991, at Michigan's Institute of Continuing Legal Education.
7. Critchlow v. Critchlow, 347 So.2d 453 (Fla. App. 3d Dist. 1977).
8. Roper v. Roper, 336 So.2d 654 at 656 (Fla. App. 4th Dist. 1976).
9. Peisach v. Antuna, 539 So.2d 544 (Fla. App. 3d Dist. 1989).
10. Navarre v. Navarre, 191 Mich. App. 395, 479 N.W.2d 357 (1991).
11. Michigan Custody Investigation Model (Lansing, MI.: State Court Administrative Office, 1990).
12. *Ibid.*
13. In Critchlow v. Critchlow, 347 So.2d 453 (Fla. App. 3d Dist. 1977), in the course of a divorce proceeding, the mother voluntarily admitted herself to a mental hospital. The husband sought disclosure of her hospital records. The trial court granted a protective order but was reversed on appeal. The appellate court said that the mother's health was "a highly relevant issue." 347 So.2d at 455. In Wilson v. Upell, 119 Mich. App. 16 (1982), the plaintiff's weaker physical and mental health was evidenced by two periods of hospitalization, one for overuse of prescription drugs.
14. In Miragliv v. Miragliv, 462 So.2d 507 (Fla. App. 4th Dist. 1984), the court held that the mother's attempted suicide during the child custody proceeding put her mental capacity at issue. In Feldman v. Feldman, 55 Mich. App. 147 (1974), evidence of the father's attempted suicide by drinking Bowlene was damaging to his claim.
15. Homosexuality has been a factor in the determination of moral fitness. Hall v. Hall, 95 Mich. App. 614 (1980).
16. In a highly publicized child custody case in Michigan that went on for years, Linda Orley told therapists that her two daughters were molested not only by her husband but also by the paternal grandparents and the family dog. She subjected the girls to (unnecessary) physical examinations and therapy for sexual abuse. In a five-part series that ran in March 1996, the *Detroit Free Press* chronicled the father's efforts to have a relationship with his daughters despite what psychologists said was their mother's attempts to sabotage it. Nonetheless, the trial judge ruled that sexual abuse had occurred and gave the mother full custody, but finally, after a long battle, the state court of appeals gave custody to the father, calling the allegations of sexual abuse ludicrous. "I can hardly believe it," said the father, after being awarded full custody of the daughters. "We're going to Disneyland," he said, if he could somehow get the money after spending a fortune on legal fees. J. Kresnak, "Dad wins custody after 8-year battle," *Detroit Free Press*, Aug. 2, 1996, p.1.
17. *Child Custody: Nuts and Bolts for the Active Practitioner* (Ann Arbor, MI.: Institute of Continuing Legal Education, 1991).

18. Atwood v. Atwood, 550 S.W.2d 465, at 467 (Ky. 1976).

19. *In re* M.M., 153 Vt. 102, 569 A.2d 463 (1989); *In re* M.C., 391 N.W.2d 674 (S.D. 1986).

20. Del. Code Ann. tit. 13, § 722(a)(5)(Supp. 1980) (emphasis added). In Betty J.B. v. Division of Social Services, 460 A.2d 528 (Del. 1983), where the testimony of the mother's psychotherapist was entered in a termination of parental rights proceeding, the court said, "When otherwise inaccessible and privileged information becomes pertinent to an issue vital to the future well-being of the child, the parent's right to privacy and confidentiality must yield." 460 A.2d at 531.

21. Mass. Gen. Laws Ann. ch. 233, § 22B(e) (Supp. 1981)(emphasis added).

22. Roper v. Roper, 336 So.2d 654 (Fla. App. 4th Dist. 1976), noted in T.F. Guernsey, "The Psychotherapist-Patient Privilege in Child Placement: A Relevancy Analysis," *Villanova L. Rev.* 26:955, 1981.

23. Griggs v. Griggs, 707 S.W.2d 488 (Mo. App. 1986); see also State *ex rel.* Husgen v. Stussie, 617 S.W.2d 414 (Mo. App. 1981).

24. McIntyre v. McIntyre, 404 So.2d 208 (Fla. App. 2d Dist. 1981).

25. Peisach v. Antuna, 539 So.2d 544, at 546 (Fla. App. 3d Dist. 1989).

26. 539 So.2d at 546, quoting Roper v. Roper, 336 So.2d 654 (Fla. App. 4th Dist. 1976).

27. Matter of Von Goyt, 461 So.2d 821, at 823 (Ala. App. 1984), noted in M.F. Knowles & C.C. McCarthy, "Parents, Psychologists and Child Custody Disputes: Protecting the Privilege and the Children," *Ala. L. Rev.* 37:391, 1986.

28. See M.G. Goldzband, "Confidentiality in Disputes Over Custody and Visitation," in R.I. Simon (ed.), *Review of Clinical Psychiatry and the Law* (Washington, D.C.: American Psychiatric Press, 1990), vol. 1, p. 133; M.G. Goldzband, "Dual Loyalties in Custody Cases and Elsewhere in Child and Adolescent Psychiatry," in R.I. Simon (ed.), *Review of Clinical Psychiatry and the Law* (Washington, D.C.: American Psychiatric Press, 1991), vol. 3, p. 201; see also A.M. Fazzio, "The Use of Medical Records in Child Custody Cases," *La. Bar J.* 40:178, 1992; P.J. Mastrangel, "The Psychologist-Patient Privilege in the Child Custody Hearing," *Mich. Bar J.*, Oct. 1989, p. 980; K.A. Schwarzberg, "Privileges in Custody Cases: Uses, Non-Uses and Alternatives," *Mich. Bar J.*, March 1992, p. 290.

# Chapter 4

# TORT CASES

The medical privilege was of comparatively little importance in tort law when New York and other states enacted a privilege. That is because tort law itself was then of little importance. "The law of torts was totally insignificant before 1900," writes Professor Lawrence Friedman, "a twig on the great tree of law."[1] Data from the New York City trial court indicates that as late as 1870, torts comprised only one percent of the cases filed, increasing to 11.3 percent by 1910; of contested cases, torts accounted for 4.2 percent in 1870, 40.9 percent in 1910.[2]

The increase in the number of tort suits at the turn of the 20th century along with the development of life and accident insurance and workers' compensation rapidly expanded the role of the medical privilege. Today personal injury litigation represents approximately 90 percent of all litigated cases, and the medical privilege permeates many of these cases.

The patient as litigant is said to waive the privilege because, in bringing suit, he has chosen to make his health a matter of public record. Furthermore, it is said, a claimant acting in good faith would not object to the testimony of any physician who examined or treated him, but rather would want the physician to testify. The patient as plaintiff, as the saying goes, may not turn a shield into a sword.[3] A plaintiff in personal injury litigation who refuses to release his medical records can just as well forget about his lawsuit–the defendant is entitled to procure evidence that would show that the injuries claimed by the plaintiff actually predated the time of the alleged harm.[4]

Moreover, there is no privilege as to communications relevant to an issue of the mental or emotional condition of the patient in any proceeding in which he relies on that condition as an element of defense. The waiver occurs not in every case where the patient is a defendant but usually only when the patient relies on that condition as an element of defense. A ready example (in criminal cases) would be a plea of not guilty by reason of insanity. Some jurisdictions hold that the exception terminates the privilege whenever any party relies on the condition of a patient as part of that party's claim or defense, even when the patient does not personally place the condition at issue or is not a party to the suit.[5]

There is also no privilege in a wrongful death action in which a party relies on the deceased's condition as an element of his claim or defense. In this type of action, the patient is not a party litigant, but rather the subject of the litigation. The defendant is entitled to discover evidence, including the testimony of a treating psychiatrist, to establish that the patient died, not as a result of any wrongful act on the part of the defendant but, on the contrary, as a suicide.[6]

The typical psychotherapist-patient privilege includes the following exception:

> There is no privilege under this rule as to communications relevant to an issue of the mental or emotional condition of the patient in any proceeding in which he relies upon the condition as an element of his claim or defense, or, after the patient's death, in any proceeding in which any party relies upon the condition as an element of his claim or defense.

The Advisory Committee's Note to proposed Rule 504 of the Federal Rules of Evidence states: "By injecting his condition into litigation, the patient must be said to waive the privilege, in fairness and to avoid abuses. Similar considerations prevail after the patient's death." A statutory exception to privilege is also set out for claims under workers' compensation.[7]

The issue of condition as an element of claim or defense has led to a substantial number of appellate court rulings. For example, in *Britt v. Superior Court*,[8] the California Supreme Court reaffirmed the proposition set out in the *Lifschutz* case, discussed earlier, that plaintiffs may not "withhold information which relates to any physical or mental condition which they put in issue by bringing this lawsuit" but that plaintiffs can retain the confidentiality of all "unrelated medical or psychotherapeutic treatment they may have undergone in the past."[9]

In a New York case, *Prink v. Rockefeller Center*,[10] the plaintiff's husband was killed in a fall from an office building and brought a wrongful death action against the owners and architects of the building, alleging that their negligence in the installation of a desk and maintenance of a window caused the decedent to fall. The death was unwitnessed. The defendants contended that the death was suicide. At issue was whether the decedent's communications with his psychiatrist were privileged. The court held that they were not. Had the decedent survived and brought suit, he would not have been permitted to claim that the communications were privileged since the suit in effect put his mental condition in issue, and thus constituted a waiver of the privilege.

The court said, "[Because of] the unfairness of mulcting a defendant in damages without affording him an opportunity to prove his lack of culpability, [the decedent] as plaintiff could not assert the physician-patient privilege to foreclose inquiry concerning whether his injury was the result of an attempt at suicide."

The exception tends to be narrowly construed in cases where the insurer attempts to establish suicide. Typically, a life insurance policy includes a limitation that in the event of suicide within the first two or three years of coverage, benefits are limited to the return of premiums paid. Is the insurer entitled to invade a deceased's confidential communications to, and diagnosis by, a psychotherapist, in order to establish suicide? Does the beneficiary, by the executing and filing the proof of death form, waive the privilege under the patient-litigant exception? The courts say that invasion of the privilege is limited to cases in which something more than "mere speculation" supports the invasion, but something more than "mere speculation" is rarely, if ever, found, thus making it difficult for an insurer to establish suicide.[11] In this spirit, the courts also tend to rule that as a result of insanity, the deceased did not have the requisite intent to commit suicide.

On the other hand, psychiatric testimony about a defendant (in contrast to that about a plaintiff or a plaintiff's decedent) in a tort case usually faces an objection of privilege or relevancy. In *City of Alhambra v. Superior Court*,[13] a tort action against police officers, the plaintiffs sought information as to whether the police officers had ever received psychiatric treatment. The court denied the request, holding that the defendants had not raised the issue of their mental and emotional condition merely by denying liability for the alleged offenses.

In a civil rights case, one that went to the U.S. Supreme Court, *Jaffee v. Redmond*,[14] surviving family members of a man who was shot and killed by a police officer sought the therapy records of the officer. The Seventh Circuit upheld privilege under Rule 501 of the Federal Rules of Evidence because "key to successful treatment lies in the ability of patients to communicate freely without fear of public disclosure." As we have noted, the case went on certiorari to the U.S. Supreme Court to decide whether federal evidence rules incorporate a psychotherapist-patient privilege.[15]

The Seventh Circuit had ruled that the privilege was not absolute and should be determined by balancing the interests protected by shielding the evidence sought with those advanced by disclosure. In this case, the court found in favor of applying the privilege noting the strong interest in encouraging officers who are frequently forced to experience traumatic events by the nature of their work to seek qualified professional help. At the same time, the court noted that there were many witnesses to the shooting, and the plaintiffs' need for the officer's personal innermost thoughts about the shooting were cumulative at best, compared to the substantial nature of the officer's privacy interest. So, once again, privilege or no privilege, the outcome depended essentially on relevancy or materiality.

The Supreme Court went further than the Seventh Circuit and created an absolute privilege, or so it said, not a qualified one to be balanced by the evidentiary need for disclosure. Anything less than an absolute privilege, the Court said, would be worthless, but in a footnote, the Court allowed exceptions. Although the ruling applies generally to federal litigation, the Court found the law-enforcement context of the case to be particularly persuasive. "The entire community may suffer if police officers are not able to receive effective counseling and treatment after traumatic incidents," Justice Stevens said, "either because trained officers leave the profession prematurely or because those in need of treatment remain on the job."

Two law enforcement organizations, the International Union of Police Associations and the National Association of Police Organizations, joined numerous organizations of mental health professionals in urging the Court to adopt the privilege. Dr. Joseph Lifschutz and Dr. George Caesar of California, psychiatrists who long strived to protect confidentiality by privilege, also filed an amicus brief.

Justice Scalia along with Chief Justice Rehnquist dissented. Judge Scalia made the following argument:

> Even where it is certain that absence of the psychotherapist privilege will inhibit disclosure of the information, it is not clear to me that that is an unacceptable state of affairs. Let us assume the very worst in the circumstances of the present case: that to be truthful about what was troubling her, the police officer who sought counseling would have to confess that she shot without reason, and wounded an innocent man. If (again to assume the worst) such an act constituted the crime of negligent wounding under Illinois law, the officer would of course have the absolute right not to admit that she shot without reason in criminal court. But I see no reason why she should be enabled both not to admit it in criminal court (as a good citizen should), and to get the benefits of psychotherapy by admitting it to a therapist who cannot tell anyone else. And even less reason why she should be enabled to deny her guilt in the criminal trial— or in a civil trial for negligence—while yet obtaining the benefits of psychotherapy by confessing guilt to a social worker who cannot testify. It seems to me entirely fair to say that if she wishes the benefits of telling the truth she must also accept the adverse consequences. To be sure, in most cases the statements to the psychotherapist will be only marginally relevant, and one of the purposes of the privilege (though not one relied upon by the Court) may be simply to spare patients needless intrusion upon their privacy, and to spare psychotherapists needless expenditure of their time in deposition and trial. But surely this can be achieved by means short of excluding even evidence that is of the most direct and conclusive effect.

An individual who harms another may feel guilty about it whether or not it was done in lawful self-defense or defense of others. Expressing such feelings in the course of therapy, however, may appear as a confession of wrongdoing when it is used in a legal proceeding. An examination by an appointed examiner would be less tinged by these feelings.

Under the Federal Rules of Civil Procedure and in those states that have adopted similar rules, the trial court may order examination by a physician of a person whose mental or physical condition is in controversy.[16] The rule does not invade the confidentiality of communication for when a psychiatrist is hired solely for evaluation purposes, there is no therapeutic relationship between the reporting psychiatrist and the person examined, hence there is no psychotherapeutic relationship to be disrupted. As a matter of ethics, the person examined is advised, or should be advised, that he is not in a confidential relationship with the examiner. The promise of confidentiality is important for therapy, but less so for diagnosis. It is true that cooperation with the examining psychiatrist will lead to a more reliable report. However, the party usually cooperates with the examiner, but if not, this will come out at the trial and work to his prejudice. The psychiatrist's report will include the fact of noncooperation. The testimony of the treating physician might be valuable, but in considerable measure the second-best evidence of the appointed examining physician is usually adequate.[17]

Information provided to a psychotherapist by the patient's immediate family has been held to fall under the privilege for confidential communications. In a California case, *Grosslight v. Superior Court*,[18] the plaintiff sued the parents of a young girl for injuries inflicted by the girl. The plaintiff's theory was that the parents were liable for the injuries because they were aware of the girl's dangerous propensities and had failed to control her behavior. To prove the parents' knowledge, the plaintiff sought to inspect the girl's psychiatric records. In one of the rare decisions upholding confidentiality on the ground of privilege, the court held that the parents' statements to the girl's therapists were privileged because they were made for the purpose of facilitating her diagnosis and treatment.

Under federal or state rules of procedure, judges are authorized to order physical or mental examinations in cases where such condition is in controversy. Initially, this power came under attack as, among other things, a violation of the right to privacy. In *Sibbach v. Wilson & Co.*,[19] the U.S. Supreme Court in 1940, by a narrow majority, upheld the validity of these rules. Such rules merely regulate procedure, the majority maintained, while the individual's substantive right to privacy remains intact. Accordingly, a litigant who refuses to be examined cannot be compelled to do so, although the court may dismiss the claim of the disobedient party or rule appropriately against him.[20]

On an issue of first impression, in 1964 in *Schlagenhauf v. Holder*,[21] the U.S. Supreme Court held that Rule 35(a) of the Federal Rules of Civil Procedure applies to defendants as well as plaintiffs, so that the former may be required to submit to an examination. In this case, however, it was not shown that the proposed examinee's condition was "in controversy" nor had "good cause" been shown. It was claimed that a bus driver was not "mentally or physically capable" of driving a bus at the time of the accident. The plaintiffs petitioned for an order directing the bus driver to submit to both a physical and mental examination. Justice Douglas, dissenting in part, would deny all relief asked under Rule 35 for an examination of a defendant in a tort case, saying that it would result in a "fishing expedition" in search of anything which will tend to prove that the defendant was unfit to perform the acts which resulted in the plaintiff's injury.[22]

Not long ago a British woman claimed her lover, a Cypriot fisherman, knew he had HIV and had been warned by his physician of the risks yet nonetheless had sex with her. He denied knowingly and negligentaly infecting her. To prove her case (or to establish a criminal case against him), disclosure of the physician's notes was allowed, as his condition was "in controversy" and "good cause" had been shown. It was not a fishing expedition, so to speak.

In *Brewster v. Martin Marietta Aluminum Sales*,[23] a Michigan case, a dismissed employee, Joy Brewster, brought an action against the employer alleging sex discrimination. She sought a psychiatric examination of the supervisor, alleging that he "possessed attitudes concerning women in the workplace which were sexist in that he could not react to the actions and activities of a woman employee the same as a man employee." The Michigan Court of Appeals noted that the trial court did not reach a decision on whether the supervisor's mental condition was actually placed in controversy or whether good cause existed for granting the requested examination. Citing *Schlagenhauf,* the court remanded the matter to the trial court for determination of whether the plaintiff has established that the supervisor's mental condition is in controversy and whether good cause existed for granting the mental examination.

What about proof in cases of sexual harassment? Under Title VII of the Civil Rights Act, the U.S. Supreme Court in 1993 in *Harris v. Forklift Systems*[24] held that the standard for determining whether conduct is actionable as an "abusive work environment" harassment requires an objectively hostile or abusive environment—one that a reasonable person would find hostile or abusive (some states under its civil rights law use a "reasonable woman" standard)—as well as the victim's subjective perception that the environment is abusive.[25]

In resolving a split of authority in the circuits, the Supreme Court ruled that while the victim must also subjectively perceive the environment to be abusive, it need not seriously affect the employee's psychological well-being. Certainly, the Court said, Title VII bars conduct that would seriously affect a reasonable person's psychological well-being, but the statute is not limited to such conduct. The Court said that so long as the environment would reasonably be perceived, and is perceived as hostile or abusive, there is no need for it also to be psychologically injurious.

In *Harris*, the Supreme Court rejected an "actual injury" test, holding that a sexual harassment victim need not suffer psychological injury in order to prevail in a Title VII action. Psychological harm is but one factor but not a necessary one in determining whether an environment is hostile or abusive; others include frequency and severity of conduct and whether the work environment unreasonably interferes with the employee's work.[26]

In theory, tort law might provide redress to sexual harassment victims– they are, after all, victims of intentionally or negligently inflicted harm, and they frequently suffer loss of job status as well as emotional or physical harm. In practice, however, the tort remedy was unsatisfying. First, some states bar claims of emotional distress in the absence of demonstrable physical harm. Second, workers' compensation statutes bar many claims for employment-related torts.

Spurred by the Equal Employment Opportunity Commission's 1980 Guidelines on Discrimination Because of Sex, the courts began to find Title VII violations where employers created or condoned sexually hostile work environments. The law came to recognize and proscribe two types of sexual harassment under Title VII: (1) *quid pro quo* or "this for that" (a demand or request for sex in exchange for some job-related benefit), and (2) hostile environment. It is the second type of harassment that has evoked criticism and debate because, unlike *quid pro quo* harassment, it is often difficult to identify.[27] Psychologists and sociologists have been called as expert witnesses to testify on the "reasonable person" or under the law of some states, the "reasonable woman" standard.

Liability and damage issues have to be distinguished. For liability, as we have noted, the Supreme Court adopted objective and subjective standards to determine whether the alleged conduct rose to the level of unlawful sexual harassment. A court, first of all, must inquire whether a reasonable person would objectively think the conduct created a hostile environment. Then, the court must inquire whether the person bringing the action subjectively found the environment hostile or abusive.

For damages, in the absence of an emotional damage claim, what is the injury and what is the measure of damages? The damages may be for "constructive discharge," or for annoyance, insult to dignity and interference with work, or to punish the offender (some state laws do not allow punitive damages). In a concurring opinion, Justice Scalia suggested that interference with work performance should be the most heavily weighed factor.

Congress intended the Civil Rights Act to encourage victims to act as "private attorneys general" in the effort to eradicate workplace discrimination. In these actions, the complainant places her work environment–not her mental condition–in controversy. However, while not necessary for the cause of action, evidence of emotional damage, supported by expert testimony, would make out a case for enhanced or punitive damages. Jury verdict research estimates that the median compensatory damage award in sexual harassment cases in 1995 was $120,000; one-third of these cases also resulted in punitive damages.

How are defendants protected from deluded or vindictive complainants? For one, it can be shown that there was no objectively hostile or abusive environment.[28] For another, that the complainant did not subjectively perceive the environment to be abusive. Or for another, that the complainant incited the conduct complained about.[29]

Apart from the issue of damages, Dr. Sara Feldman-Schorrig has suggested that experts can assist in assessing credibility or identifying psychodynamics that could be crucial in the clarification of legal questions such as "welcomeness" (that is, "soliciting or inciting" the conduct). In the Latin maxim: *Volenti non fit injuria* (to one willing there is no injury). Dr. Schorrig cites the example of a complainant who was inspired by a talk show to file for sexual harassment so as to be able to leave her job and ensure a continuing source of income. She cites examples of factitious sexual harassment (*i.e.* prompted by the lure of victim status).[30]

In contrast to therapist-patient sex allegations, the recognition of false sexual harassment claims is more difficult because less information about the plaintiff's past history is readily accessible. Dr. Schorrig argues that to deny access to medical records is justifiable in rape cases but not in sexual harassment cases in which plaintiffs have placed their mental state at issue.[31] In her writings, she describes cases of factitious sexual harassment that could only have been recognized with access to medical records to show that an alleged event was fabricated.[32] Women who file factitious sexual harassment claims usually voice their allegations in a very convincing manner and present a diagnostic challenge. Jurors are expected to make credibility decisions based on their common sense, or intuition or experience, but a number of courts have permitted expert witnesses to testify about a witness's credibility.[33]

The issue of the mental health of the complainant became critical in 1991 when the Civil Rights Act was amended to allow punitive damages and damages for emotional distress. It put pressure on companies who were sued to use any means available to illustrate that the complainant was "damaged goods" upon hiring. It gave rise to the so-called "nuts or sluts" defense: Prove the woman is crazy, or demonstrate that she sleeps around. Many employees are compelled to use industry-run arbitration—and there's no judge to assure that defense lawyers do not go too far.[34]

And what about disputes between the parties covered by the privilege? As a general principle, in the case of any privilege, it is waived as to relevant information. Thus, for a tort action by the therapist against a patient or a criminal prosecution of a patient for an assault on the therapist, information may be provided in order to pursue a lawsuit or prosecution. Likewise, the therapist-patient privilege is waived when the patient brings a malpractice action against the therapist.[35]

Malpractice insurance policies usually require that the insured notify the insurer as soon as the insured becomes aware "of any act or omission which would reasonably be expected to be the basis of a claim or suit" covered by the policy, even if a claim has not been made against the insured. Under "claims made" policies, the failure to give required notice during the policy period is fatal to coverage, even without a showing of prejudice to the insurer.

Therapists are usually asked by their insurance carriers to report untoward events such as suicide that may lead to a lawsuit, but actual release of the entire record prior to initiation of suit is not necessary. A New York appellate court held that a physician's disclosure of records to his insurer and the insurer's solicitation of the disclosure were justified in response to the patient's authorization to release the records to his own attorney. The court indicated that, when the physician has a "reasonable belief that a claim for medical malpractice will be made against him," disclosure may be made. The fact that the patient hired an attorney to investigate the claim and authorized release of records to that attorney justified disclosure, the court said.[36]

In *Psychiatric Times*, Dr. Victor Bloom suggested:[37]

> It is useful to prevent a suit, when one is threatened, by warning the patient in advance that he or she waives confidentiality. The psychiatrist can then recount items in the history which would be damaging to the patient if publicly revealed, which in most cases would deter the patient.

Dr. Abraham L. Halpern, past president of the American Academy of Psychiatry and Law, and Dr. Alfred Freedman, past president of the American Psychiatric Association, deplored the advice. They responded in a joint communication:[38]

> Such intimidating conduct, nothing short of blackmail, would in our opinion, be a violation of the code of ethics, which states, "The psychiatrist should diligently guard against exploiting information furnished by the patient and should not use the unique position of power afforded him/her by the psychotherapeutic situation to influence the patient in any way not directly relevant to the treatment goals."[39]
>
> Furthermore, it would give the potential plaintiff a substantial reason to sue the psychiatrist for malpractice, on a charge far more serious than what might otherwise be a baseless or frivolous complaint.

In another response, Dr. Edmund F. Kal of the University of California at Fresno wrote to say that while Dr. Bloom's suggestion may work well as a legal ploy, it would be unethical, if not illegal, and would certainly destroy the therapeutic relationship.[40]

In the case of a patient claiming sexual exploitation by a therapist ("undue familiarity"), the notes of a subsequent treating therapist will be discoverable by the defendant's lawyer even though, for treatment purposes, the subsequent treating therapist relies on the patient's psychic reality as opposed to focusing on establishing the objective elements of the complaint. Linda Jorgenson, who specializes in cases of undue familiarity, advises subsequent treating therapists to keep in mind that the patient's expert will rely on the therapist's notes to formulate his testimony concerning the patient's damages.[41] A perpetrator's defense might focus on the subsequent treating therapist's role in causing or increasing the patient's harm. The perpetrator may also argue that the subsequent treating therapist convinced the patient to file a complaint, thus worsening the patient's condition.[42] A few states mandate reporting.[43]

Unlike when a patient sues a therapist, a third party suing a therapist on account of harm inflicted by the patient faces obstacles in obtaining information as to what went on in therapy. There may have been a duty to warn or protect and in that event the dangerous patient exception to the therapist-patient privilege would come into play. The privilege is not applicable when the therapist has reasonable cause to believe that the patient was dangerous.[44]

That situation aside, a third party faces a claim of confidentiality when seeking information about the competency of the therapy. As noted, a number of jurisdictions hold that the privilege is terminated whenever any party relies on the condition of a patient even when the patient does not personally place the condition at issue or is not a party to the suit.[45] In any event, in many cases, therapists keep no records, especially about matters that may be relevant in litigation, and so discovery is frustrated.

In what is called a landmark case, Gary Ramona in California sued a medical center and a pair of psychotherapists who he claimed created false memories in his daughter of his sexually abusing her as a child. He was given standing to sue. He was awarded damages for emotional suffering from the breakup of his family, and for harm to his career and reputation.[46] The daughter was satisfied with the therapy, she testified against her father, and she filed a lawsuit against him. Confidentiality, as a result, was waived.[47] Quite often in cases of "revival of memory" of child abuse the therapist is unlicensed and as a consequence the therapist-patient privilege would be inapplicable.

Certainly, a therapist's duty to third parties would have little meaning if third-party plaintiffs were not able to procure the information needed to vindicate their claims. Moreover, out of self-defense, a therapist would have to be allowed to make reference to his records or recollection. The Illinois statute expressly excludes from privilege "actions, civil or criminal, against the physician for malpractice"[48]–as commonly understood "malpractice" means an action by a patient against a physician for treatment in a manner contrary to accepted standards and with injurious results to the patient, but the term has also included actions of a third party against the physician arising out of his practice, as when a third party is injured by a patient in a case where the physician should have given warning of a danger posed by the patient (and any judgment against the physician is covered by the professional liability policy).[49]

Clearly, as soon as an alleged abuse survivor files a lawsuit against her alleged abuser, as in *Ramona*, the records of the therapy lose the protection of privilege. In the usual case when a third party sues a therapist in the case of "revival of memory," the patient has retracted and joins the parents in a lawsuit against the therapist, or when the patient sues her parents, the parents implead the therapist. In these situations, by filing a lawsuit, the patient waives the privilege.[50]

In a Michigan case, Joseph Landelius was severely and permanently injured when Peter Rafko lost control of his car and ran him over. Rafko blamed the mishap on an epileptic seizure. Upon being sued, Rafko gave Landelius access to his hospital records. The case was settled, and thereupon Landelius sued the physician and the hospital, claiming there had been negligence in diagnosing and treating Rafko's epilepsy and that he should have been prevented from driving. The defendants objected to the use of the records against them, claiming that Rafko had consented to their use only in the suit against him. The Michigan Supreme Court ruled that the physician-patient privilege could not be recaptured after the earlier disclosure of records.[51]

In a case in Maryland involving a lawsuit against a state hospital and two staff psychiatrists, the question was whether the estate of a murdered boy could discover the killer's medical records, absent his express consent to disclosure. The records were in the possession of the state hospital. In answering the question affirmatively, the Maryland Supreme Court noted that the convicted man previously had released his records in similar litigation brought by the estate of another boy he had murdered. As the court said, the defendant may not selectively waive his privilege relating to the medical information by arbitrarily picking and choosing among similarly situated parties, at least when it is the same information requested by each party and for the same purpose. Accordingly, by the authorizing of the first plaintiff to obtain the medical records, the privilege was waived with respect to discovery by the second plaintiff.[52]

In a variation of the theme where the record of a patient may be relevant to a resolution of a lawsuit yet is not a party to the litigation are cases where third parties file a lawsuit against a pharmaceutical company claiming that its product had a disinhibiting effect on the patient and resulted in injury or death to third parties. In a much-publicized case, Joseph Wesbacker in 1989 entered the Standard Gravure printing plant in Louisville, and armed with an AK-47 assault rifle, he killed or wounded 20 people, then turned the gun on himself. He had been on disability leave from Standard Gravure for a year, reeling from setbacks in his personal life and on the job. Suffering from severe depression, he was given Prozac, the popular antidepressant. The survivors and victims' families sued its maker, Eli Lilly and Company. Both sides to the litigation had an interest in disclosing Wesbecker's psychiatric history, so no objection to disclosure of records was made. In the defense of Prozac, it was argued, "Joseph Wesbecker's attack on Standard Gravure on September 14, 1989 was not the act of a man suddenly turned mad by Prozac....It was the final chapter in a very complex life, filled with hostility, fueled by job stress. It grew out of a life twisted by insidious mental illness. It was generated out of a lifetime of estrangements and isolation, and hostile withdrawals from spouses, parents, children, friends, co-workers and bosses." In any event, Wesbecker's family brought a wrongful death action against his psychiatrist, Dr. Lee Coleman, and as a consequence, privilege was waived.[53]

The question has arisen as to a waiver of the privilege shielding the health records of the plaintiff's family in a lawsuit involving a condition that is arguably genetic. Since the privilege belongs to the patient and is waivable only by the patient, as by filing a lawsuit, the privilege is not waived as to the records of other members of the family. Upholding the privilege as to other members of the plaintiff's family may make it impossible for the defendant to explore the cause of the condition. The issue thus becomes under what circumstances, if any, the defendant may gain access to the medical records of the plaintiff's family members in order to show genetic causation.[54]

In *Jones v. Superior Court*,[55] an adult plaintiff instituted a products liability action for injuries allegedly sustained due to her mother's ingestion of a drug while pregnant with the plaintiff. The defendants sought to secure records of the mother's ingestion of the drug and of her physical condition during her pregnancy. The court held that although the mother may still have had the right to assert the privilege to protect that information after the plaintiff instituted the action, she waived the right by her subsequent deposition disclosures, which revealed the circumstances of her drug ingestion and the related communications with her physician.

Over the past decade, courts in various jurisdictions have dealt with the issues of whether an attorney who represents a defendant in a personal injury action may privately (*ex parte*) interview the plaintiff's treating physician, who is not a party to the litigation, in order to prepare the case.[56] While a physician is not compelled to speak to the attorney in the ex *parte* situation, the issue is whether he may do so in view of the fact that the patient has filed a lawsuit and thereby waives the physician-patient privilege.[57]

The jurisdictions are split. In Pennsylvania, in *Alexander v. Knight*,[58] the court sharply rebuked a physician for giving a medical report on a patient, without consent, to another physician employed by attorneys who represented an opponent in the litigation. The court said:

> We are of the opinion that members of a profession, especially the medical profession, stand in a confidential or fiduciary capacity as to their patients. They owe their patients more than just medical care for which payment is exacted; there is a duty to total care; that includes the comprehensive duty to aid the patient in litigation, to render reports when necessary and to attend court when needed. That further includes a duty to refuse affirmative assistance to a patient's antagonist in litigation. The doctor, of course, owes a duty to conscience to speak the truth; he need, however, speak only at the proper time.

Other courts reason that once the privilege is waived, informal methods of discovery, such as *ex parte* interviews, are as appropriate as the formal methods set out in court rules. In fact, said the Michigan Supreme Court, "prohibition of all *ex parte* interviews would be inconsistent with the purpose of providing equal access to relevant evidence and efficient, cost-effective litigation."[59] The court put to rest the argument that the waiver of privilege by filing a lawsuit applies only to formal discovery, that is, those discovery measures explicitly identified in court rules.

## NOTES

1.  L.M. Friedman, *A History of American Law* (New York: Simon & Schuster, 2d ed. 1985).
2.  R.E. Bergstrom, *Courting Danger: Injury and Law in New York City, 1870-1910* (Ithaca, N.Y.: Cornell University Press, 1992).
3.  Dr. Jack Gorman of Columbia University gives an example from his practice of a case justifying discovery of records: "Once I received a request from a patient's attorney to produce my office notes about [a patient]. She was apparently suing a driver following an automobile accident in which she claimed she had injured her back. The problem was that when I first saw the patient she had told me that she had suffered from back trouble for many years preceding the car accident. I had written that down. My records would obviously reveal that the patient was lying about the car accident; in fact, it hadn't hurt her back at all. When I told her what was in my records she was forced to amend her lawsuit." J.M. Gorman, *The New Psychiatry* (New York: St. Martin's Press, 1996), p. 353.

4.   Z. Chafee, "Privileged Communications: Is Justice Served or Obstructed by Closing the Doctor's Mouth on the Witness Stand?", *Yale L.J.* 52:607, 1943.
5.   Such a case is Easter v. McDonald, 903 S.W.2d 887 (Tex. App. 1995). In this personal injury action brought against the defendant by his stepdaughter for allegedly sexually assaulting her, the Texas Court of Appeals held that the defendant was not entitled to psychotherapist-patient privilege to protect his treatment records. The court's order to turn over the mental health records was based on the exception to privilege for disclosure of records when "relevant to an issue of the physical, mental or emotional condition of a patient in any proceeding in which any party relies upon the condition as a part of the party's claim or defense." The court rejected the defendant's argument that his right against self-incrimination precluded discovery of the records (on the ground that he would not lose any privilege against self-incrimination he may have because the disclosure would not be voluntary).
6.   Annot., 25 A.L.R. 3d 1401.
7.   Alabama's code (§25-5-77), *e.g.*, contains the following language: "A physician whose services are furnished or paid for by the employer, or a physician of the injured employee who treats or makes or is present at any examination of an injured employee may be required to testify as to any knowledge obtained by him or her in the course of the treatment or examination as related to the injury or disability arising therefrom." See pp. 75, 526.
8.   20 Cal.3d 844, 143 Cal. Rptr. 695, 574 P.2d 766 (1978).
9.   *In re* Lifschutz, 2 Cal.3d 415, 85 Cal. Rptr. 829, 467 P.2d 557 (1970).
10.   48 N.Y.2d 309, 422 N.Y.S.2d 911, 398 N.E.2d 517 (1979).
11.   See, *e.g.*, Grey v. Los Angeles Superior Court, 62 Cal. App.3d 702, 133 Cal. Rptr. 318 (1976).
12.   See, *e.g.*, von Dameck v. St. Paul Fire & Marine Ins., 361 So.2d 283 (La. App. 1978); Comment, *Loy. L. Rev.* 23:122 at 131, 1977.
13.   110 Cal. App.3d 513, 168 Cal. Rptr. 49 (1980).
14.   51 F.3d 1346 (7th Cir. 1995), *aff'd*, 116 S.Ct. 1923 (1966).
15.   P.M. Barrett, "Justices Do Decide if Federal Rules Allow For Psychotherapist-Patient 'Privilege,'" *Wall Street Journal*, Oct. 17, 1985, p. 9; L. Greenhouse, "Supreme Court to Rule on Therapist-Client Privilege in Judicial Proceedings," *New York Times*, Oct. 17, 1995, p. 13.
16.   *See* Fed. R. Civ. P. 35. *See also* A. Hare, "Medical Testimony: Doctors and Lawyers Cooperate," *J. Am. Jud. Soc.* 41:78, 1957; Note, "The New York Medical Expert Project: An Experiment in Securing Impartial Testimony," *Yale L.J.* 63:1023 (1954).
17.   The courts, however, will usually rule that if the testimony of both the treating and examining physicians are presented, the opinion of a treating physician who has been in close contact with a patient over a long period of time is entitled to greater weight than the opinion of an equally qualified expert who has not had the benefit of close and frequent contact and examination. The rule is well established that the testimony of specialists as to matters falling within their fields is entitled to greater weight than that of general

practitioners, but it is equally well established that the opinion of the treating physician who has been in close contact with the patient over a long period of time is entitled to greater weight. These issues usually arise in workers' compensation cases. See, *e.g.*, Nixon v. Pittsburgh Plate Glass Co., 161 So.2d 361 (La. App. 1964). See also Part VI.

The examining physician is financially rewarded for his testimony whereas the treating physician may not be. An attending physician rates only the fee of witness, not that of an expert. A physician who merely testifies to facts relating to course of treatment is not entitled to an expert-witness fee, even though expert opinions are elicited from him. Rizzuto v. Employer Liability Assurance Corp., 152 So.2d 857 (La. App. 1963). "A physician whose medical talents are desired in court—either as a fact witness or as an expert witness, or both—should be adequately compensated for his work and time," says Howard Hassard, executive director and general counsel of the California Medical Association. *AMA News*, April 5, 1965, p. 10.

18.   72 Cal. App.3d 502, 140 Cal. Rptr. 278 (1977).
19.   312 U.S. 1 (1940).
20.   See D.I. Frimer, "Medical Examinations by Order of the Court and the Right to Privacy: Common Law and Jewish Law Experiences," *Israel L. Rev.* 17:96, 1982.
21.   379 U.S. 104 (1964).
22.   Justice Douglas wrote (379 U.S. at 125-126):

I do not suppose there is any licensed driver of a car or a truck who does not suffer from some ailment, whether it be ulcers, bad eyesight, abnormal blood pressure, deafness, liver malfunction, bursitis, rheumatism, or what not. If he or she is turned over to the plaintiff's doctors and psychoanalysts to discover the cause of the mishap, the door will be opened for grave miscarriages of justice. When the defendant's doctors examine plaintiff, they are normally interested only in answering a single question: did plaintiff in fact sustain the specific injuries claimed? But plaintiff's doctors will naturally be inclined to go on a fishing expedition in search of *anything* which will tend to prove that the defendant was unfit to perform the acts which resulted in the plaintiff's injury. And a doctor for a fee can easily discover something wrong with any patient—a condition that in prejudiced medical eyes might have caused the accident. Once defendants are turned over to medical or psychiatric clinics for an analysis of their physical wellbeing and the condition of their psyche, the effective trial will be held there and not before the jury. There are no lawyers in those clinics to stop the doctor from probing this organ or that one, to halt a further inquiry, to object to a line of questioning. And there is no judge to sit as arbiter. The doctor or the psychiatrist has a holiday in the privacy of his office. The defendant is at the doctor's (or psychiatrist's) mercy; and his report may either overawe or confuse the jury and prevent a fair trial....[W]hen a *plaintiff* claims damages his "mental or physical condition" is "in controversy," within the meaning of Rule 35, governs the present case. The *plaintiff* by suing puts those issues "in controversy." Thus it may be only fair to provide that he may not be permitted to recover his judgment unless he permits an inquiry into the true nature of his condition.

A defendant's physical and mental condition is not, however, immediately and directly "in controversy" in a negligence suit. The issue is whether he was negligent. His physical or mental condition may of course be relevant to that issue; and he may be questioned concerning it and various methods of discovery can be used. But I balk at saying those issues are "in controversy" within the meaning of Rule 35 in every negligence suit or that they may be put "in controversy" by the addition of a few words in the complaint.

Neither the Court nor Congress up to today has determined that any person whose physical or mental condition is brought into question during some lawsuit must surrender his right to keep his person inviolate....[B]efore today it has not been thought that any other "party" had lost this historic immunity. Congress and this Court can authorize such a rule. But a rule suited to purposes of discovery against defendants must be carefully drawn in light of the great potential of blackmail (emphasis by J. Douglas).

23. 309 N.W.2d 687 (Mich. App. 1981).
24. 510 U.S. 17 (1993).
25. The U.S. Supreme Court in *Harris* stated that illegal harassment occurs when the conduct is "severe or pervasive enough to create an objectively hostile or abusive working environment–an environment that a *reasonable person* would find hostile or abusive" (emphasis added). In rejecting a "reasonable woman" standard, the Michigan Supreme Court in Radtke v. Everett, 442 Mich. 368, 501 N.W.2d 155 (1993), asserted:

> [A] gender-conscious standard is clearly contrary to the gender-neutral principles underpinning the Michigan Civil Rights Act. Although well intended, a gender-conscious standard could reintrench the very sexist attitudes it is attempting to counter. The belief that women are entitled to a separate legal standard merely reinforces, and perhaps originates from, the stereotypic notion that first justified subordinating women in the workplace. Courts utilizing the reasonable woman standard pour into the standard stereotypic assumptions of women which [imply that] women are sensitive, fragile, and in need of a more protective standard. Such paternalism degrades women and is repugnant to the very ideals of equality that the act is intended to protect.

Paradoxically, at the same time, the Michigan Supreme Court noted that the reasonable person standard is sufficiently flexible to "incorporate gender as one factor." 501 N.W.2d at 167. The Fifth Circuit in DeAngelis v. El Paso Mun. Police Off. Assn., 51 F.3d 591 (5th Cir.), *cert. denied,* 116 S. Ct. 473 (1995), warned that the harassment standard must be set at a level high enough that it not "insulate women from everyday insults as if they remained models of Victorian reticence." In a humorous statement on standard of care in tort law, A.P. Herbert wrote in a 1935 classic, *Uncommon Law* (London: Methuen): "In all that mass of authorities which bears upon this branch of the law there is no single mention of a reasonable woman." He suggested that "reasonable woman" would be a contradiction in terms.

26. See K.D. Streseman, "Headshrinkers, Manmunchers, Moneygrubbers, Nuts & Sluts: Reexamining Compelled Mental Examinations in Sexual Harassment Actions Under the Civil Rights Act of 1991," *Cornell L. Rev.* 80:1268, 1995; L.T. Zappert, "Psychological Aspects of Sexual Harassment in the Academic Workplace: Considerations for Forensic Psychologists," *Am. J. For. Psychology* 14:5, 1996.

27. The courts have held that the intent of the actor is not relevant, so ignorance of the harmful consequences of the conduct is not a defense. See Ellison v. Brady, 924 F.2d 872 (9th Cir. 1991); Harris v. International Paper Co., 765 F. Supp. 1509 (D. Me. 1991); Lynch v. Des Moines, 454 N.W.2d 827 (Iowa 1990). In *quid pro quo* cases, the employer is held responsible simply by virtue of the fact of employment but the employer is generally not liable for a hostile environment unless it knew or should have known of the harassment and failed to take reasonable steps to stop it. See Meritor Savings Bank v. Vinson, 477 U.S. 57 (1985); Nichols v. Frank, 42 F.3d 503 (3d Cir. 1994); Carr v. Allison Gas Turbine Div., 32 F.3d 1007 (7th Cir. 1994).

   The subject of foul language and free speech is discussed in R. Dooling, *Blue Streak/Swearing, Free Speech and Sexual Harassment* (New York: Random House, 1996); K.R. Browne, "Title VII as Censorship: Hostile Environment Harassment and the First Amendment," *Ohio State L.J.* 52:481, 1991; J.B. Gerard, "The First Amendment in a Hostile Environment: A Primer on Free Speech and Sexual Harassment," *Notre Dame L.Rev.* 68: 1003, 1993; E. Volokh, "Freedom of Speech and Workplace Harassment," *U.C.L.A. L. Rev.* 39:1791, 1992.

28. Personality disorders often can be the cause of emotional distress that may be disattributed to workplace events that occur in temporal proximity with those events. In Sudtelgte v. Reno, 63 FEP Cases 1257 (W.D. Mo. 1994), the court found that while the complainant may have subjectively felt harassed, on account of her abnormal sensitivity, the objective "reasonable person" prong of the test was not satisfied. See J.J. McDonald & P.R. Lees-Haley, "Personality Disorders in the Workplace: How They May Contribute to Claims of Employment Law Violations," *Employee Relations L.J.* 22:57, 1996. Mae West, playing the role of a bitter working-class prostitute in the play "Sex," says angrily, "Why, ever since I've been old enough to know about sex, I've looked at men as hustlers....I began to hate everyone of them, used them for what I could get out of them, and then laughed at them." C.R. Pierpont, "The Strong Woman," *New Yorker*, Nov. 11, 1996, p. 106.

29. In a California case, the complainant announced one morning at work that she was not wearing underwear. During the day employees were talking about it, mostly to her. It was deemed that she incited the conduct. Reported

by James J. McDonald, Jr., an attorney in California, at the 1996 annual meeting of the American Academy of Psychiatry and Law.

30.  S. Feldman-Schorrig, "Need for Expansion of Forensic Psychiatrists' Role in Sexual Harassment Cases," *Bull. Am. Acad. Psychiatry & Law* 23:513, 1995. See also S.P. Feldman-Schorrig & J.J. MacDonald, "The Role of Forensic Psychiatry in the Defense of Sexual Harassment Cases," *J. Psychiatry & Law* 20:5, 1992. At a meeting (April 14, 1996) of the Michigan Society for Psychoanalytic Psychology, Betty Glickfield, Ph.D., presented the case of a patient who, feeling guilty about her sexual thoughts, became aggressive and made false accusations of sexual harassment.

31.  Of her experiences as an expert in obtaining medical records of the complainant in sexual harassment cases, Dr. Feldman-Schorrig said (personal communication, March 14, 1996):

> Redaction of records is unfortunately very commonly allowed by judges who do not understand the importance of providing the records in their complete form. In one case, enough was known about the plaintiff (whose sexual harassment accusations were believed to be highly exaggerated, if not fabricated) from what she had told "friends" to suggest that she had been severely sexually abused by at least one male relative and had led a very chaotic sexual life. When her medical records were obtained, they were heavily redacted. Despite all kinds of legal maneuvers, the defense attorney was unable to convince the judge to overturn the redaction. I did not fully understand what took place legally, but I was left with the impression that civil judges are intimidated by the political climate, and are most reluctant to allow the defense to obtain a full psychosexual history of the plaintiff. That case was settled with a high figure.
>
> It is true that a history of childhood sexual abuse or some other past sexual experiences does not necessarily mean that the plaintiff's case is invalid. However, I strongly believe that such evidence may at times play a significant role and that, when it exists, the jury should be able to take it into consideration before reaching a decision. How do you explain to judges that the probative value of objective information outweighs the danger of harm to any "victim"? Should not the jury or trier of fact have access to all pertinent information and be allowed to make the determination of what evidence supports the validity of a claim and what doesn't?

Under the rape shield law in the Federal Rules of Evidence and their counterpart in state laws, evidence offered in *civil cases* to prove the sexual behavior or sexual predisposition of any alleged victim is admissible if it is otherwise admissible under the rules and its probative value substantially outweighs the danger of harm to any victim and of unfair prejudice to any party (emphasis added). Rule 412, Federal Rules of Evidence. The right of an individual in criminal cases to obtain discovery of clinical records is discussed in Part II, chapter 6.

32.     "Factitious Sexual Harassment," *Bull. Am. Acad. Psychiatry & Law* 24:387, 1996. Factitious disorders are characterized by the intentional production or feigning of signs or symptoms solely in order to assume the sick or victim role. M.D. Feldman & C.V. Ford, *Patient or Pretender: Inside the Strange World of Factitious Disorders* (New York: Wiley, 1996); H.K. Gediman & J.S. Lieberman, *The Many Faces of Deceit/Omissions, Lies, and Disguise in Psychotherapy* (Northvale, N.J.: Jason Aronson, 1996); M.H. Stone, "Factitious Illness: Psychological Findings and Treatment Recommendations," *Bull. Menninger Clin.* 41:239, 1977.

33.     The California Court of Appeals wrote, "A witness may be cross-examined about her mental condition or emotional stability to the extent it may affect her powers of perception, memory or recollection, or communication. Expert psychiatric testimony may be admissible to impeach the credibility of a ... witness where the witness' mental or emotional condition may affect the ability of the witness to tell the truth." People v. Herring, 20 Cal. App.4th 1066, 25 Cal Rptr.2d 213 (1993). Generally, however, attempts to impeach a witness by expert psychiatric testimony has been rejected except in certain sex offense cases. See R. Slovenko, *Psychiatry and Criminal Culpability* (New York: Wiley, 1995); S.I. Friedland, "On Common Sense and the Evaluation of Witness Credibility," *Case W. Res. L. Rev.* 40:165, 1989-90.

34.     S. Antilla, "White-Collar Sexual Harassment: Digging–or Rigging–Dirt," *New York Observer,* June 24, 1996, p. 24.

35.     Haney v. Mizell Memorial Hosp., 744 F.2d 1467 (11th Cir. 1984). Under Michigan law, within 56 days of giving notice of a malpractice claim the plaintiff must allow the health professional/entity access to all of the plaintiff's relevant medical records that are in the plaintiff's control and must provide releases for any records not in the plaintiff's control of which plaintiff has knowledge. Likewise, within 56 days the defendant health professional/entity must allow the plaintiff access to all records which are in the professional/entity's control and which are related to the claim. Mich. Compiled Laws 333.2912b.

36.     Rea v. Pardo, 522 N.Y.S.2d 393 (App. Div. 1987).

37.     Ltr., "Confidentiality," *Psychiatric Times,* Oct. 1995, p. 5.

38.     Ltr., "Confidentiality on Trial," *Psychiatric Times,* Dec. 1995, p. 6.

39.     Principles of Medical Ethics with Annotations Especially Applicable to Psychiatry, Sec. 2, Annot. 2.

40.     Dr. Kal wrote (ltr., *Psychiatric Times,* Dec. 1995, p. 6):

> In any human relationship, the mutual duties of the parties are governed by the nature of their relationship–in this case, the doctor-patient relationship. This imposes [upon the doctor] the fundamental duty of "beneficence," further elaborations of which are the precepts of "doing no harm," keeping of confidences and respecting boundaries. This [should be] the situation prior to the threat of lawsuit.
>
> If a patient threatens to sue, the psychiatrist needs to determine if that threat is such that it abrogates the previous therapeutic relation-

ship, creating an attacker-versus-attacked relationship. Or is the threat due to a legitimate unremedied complaint of the patient? If the doctor determines that the threat does not create a situation where the need for self-protection becomes paramount, then all is not lost.

If the patient's threat is due to a legitimate, unremedied complaint, the psychiatrist should try to make appropriate amends. If the complaint is the result of misunderstanding, ignorance of the patient's mental illness (transference or parataxic distortion) the problem can be discussed in therapy—it becomes grist for the therapeutic mill.

In any case, if the doctor instead offers a counterthreat (even for the "beneficent" purpose of saving the patient from potential embarrassment, but certainly if done in "self-defense"), the patient will experience this as blackmail, pure and simple. I would consider it so, whether sitting on a jury or on an ethics committee. The doctor would be taking advantage of information received in trust for the patient's benefit only. (Note: I do not claim it is unethical to use the material if it is necessary to exonerate the doctor in an actual lawsuit; I do claim it to be so for the purpose of interfering with the patient's right to sue.)

Even if the doctor's counterthreat did prevent a lawsuit, the therapeutic relationship would have been destroyed forever, the patient would always feel at the mercy of the doctor, and would, at best, be able to maintain nothing better than a hostile dependent relationship—hardly the ideal situation for any kind of therapy. Albeit physically different, [the doctor's counterthreat] would be psychologically the same as seducing or raping a patient.

Even if the patient's threat and its accompanying situation has abrogated the doctor-patient relationship, warning the patient against potential embarrassment should then become the duty of the patient's own lawyer. But for the doctor to point this out to the patient personally would, I suspect, amount to intimidation of a witness. Whether the doctor's lawyer should use it when talking with the patient's lawyer is a matter of legal ethics and savvy; I won't go into it.

This is why I conclude that attempting to deter a lawsuit by pointing out to the patient the potential for embarrassment is not only clinically destructive, but also unethical and, very likely illegal.

Dr. Bloom responded (ltr., *Psychiatric Times,* Jan. 1996, p. 6):

I am happy that Drs. Halpern, Freedman and Kal took so great an interest in my comments about the legal aspects of confidentiality....It is a subject worthy of interest, but unfortunately my brief letter on the subject failed to indicate that my suggestion about warding off a potential malpractice suit in this case referred to a former patient, no longer in therapy....[A] therapist is .... a living, breathing, functioning human being, one who has the right to defend himself or herself against the slings and arrows. It is a fact that bringing suit for malpractice waives confidentiality, and the former patient needs to be reminded of it. If the knowledge of this reality serves to deter a frivolous and rancorous suit that would be damaging to both parties, mostly the former patient, then this knowledge would be ethically applied and serve a beneficent purpose.

41. L.M. Jorgenson, "Countertransference and Special Concerns of Subsequent Treating Therapists of Patients Sexually Exploited by a Previous Therapist," *Psychiatric Annals*, Sept. 1995, p. 525. For a comprehensive book-length coverage of the legal issues surrounding sexual misconduct cases, see S.B. Bisbing, L.M. Jorgenson & P.K. Sutherland, *Sexual Abuse by Professionals: A Legal Guide* (Charlottesville: Michie, 1995).

42. J. Edelwich & A.M. Brodsky, *Sexual Dilemmas for the Helping Professional* (New York: Brunner/Mazel, 1991).

43. L.H. Strasburger, L.M. Jorgenson & R.M. Randles, "Mandatory Reporting of Sexually Exploitative Psychotherapists," *Bull. Am. Acad. Psychiatry & Law* 18:379, 1990.

44. People v. Hopkins, 119 Cal. Rptr. 61 (Cal. App. 1975). See discussion in Part IV, Chapter 2.

45. See, *e.g.*, Easter v. McDonald, 903 S.W.2d 887 (Tex. App. 1995).

46. Illinois generally does not allow anyone but the patient to sue over negligent malpractice, even when that malpractice causes physical injury to others, as occurs when infectious disease is improperly treated and is passed on to family members, but an exception is made for the wrongful death of a patient, and also when the negligent treatment constitutes acts "intentionally and directly interfering with the parent-child relationship." Sullivan v. Chesier, 846 F. Supp. 654 (N.D. Ill. 1994). In some jurisdictions, there is a cause of action arising out of negligence only when there has been physical impact or injury; an intentional tort does not require physical impact or injury. A Georgia circus case reduced the matter to an absurdity by finding "impact" where the defendant's horse "evacuated his bowels" onto the plaintiff's lap. Christy Bros. Circus v. Turnage, 38 Ga. App. 581, 144 S.E. 680 (1928).

47. Ramona v. Isabella, Rose & Western Medical Center, case no. C618989 (1994); discussed in M. Johnston, Spectral Evidence (New York: Houghton Mifflin 1997); K. Butler, "Clashing Memories, Mixed Messages," *Los Angeles Times Magazine,* June 26, 1994, p. 12. See E.F. Loftus, J.R. Paddock & T.F. Guernsey, "Patient-psychotherapist Privilege: Access to Clinical Records in the Tangled Web of Repressed Memory Litigation," *U. Richmond L. Rev.* 30:109, 1996.

48. Ill. Comp. Stat. Ch 735, §5/8-802; M.H. Graham, *Handbook of Illinois Evidence* (Boston: Little, Brown, 6th ed. 1994), pp. 279-90.

49. See Part III, Chapter 2 on the self-defense exception to privilege.

50. See P.S. Appelbaum & R. Zolteck-Jick, "Psychotherapists' Duties to Third Parties: *Ramona* and Beyond," *Am. J. Psychiat.* 153:457, 1996; C.G. Bowman & E. Mertz, "A Dangerous Direction: Legal Intervention in Sexual Abuse Survivor Therapy," *Harv. L. Rev.* 109:549, 1996; R. Slovenko, "The Duty of

Therapists to Third Parties," *J. Psychiatry & Law* 23:383, 1995; S. Taub, "The Legal Treatment of Recovered Memories of Child Sexual Abuse," *J. Legal Med.* 17:183, 1996; see also J. Johnson, "A Proposal to Adopt a Professional Judgment Standard of Care in Determining the Duty of a Psychiatrist to Third Persons," U. *Colo. L. Rev.* 62:237, 1991; S.F. Rock, "A Claim For Third Party Standing in Malpractice Cases Involving Repressed Memory Syndrome," *Wm. & Mary L. Rev.* 37:337, 1995.

51. Landelius v. Sackellares, Landelius v. University of Michigan, and Landelius v. Rafko, 453 Mich. 470, 556 N.W.2d 472 (1996).

52. Hamilton v. Verdow, 287 Md. 544, 414 A.2d 914 (1980). See also Conn. Tit. 52, Ch. 899, §52-146f (7), allowing disclosure.

53. See J. Cornwall, *The Power to Harm* (New York: Viking, 1996).

54. A California appeals court held that a mother's records relating to her pre-natal care were discoverable and not protected by physician-patient privilege in a medical malpractice case she brought on behalf of her 16-month old son. Palay v. Superior Court, 22 Cal. Rptr.2d 839 (Cal. App. 1993). See L.B. Wright, "Genetic Causation and the Physician-Patient Privilege in Michigan: Shield or Sword?" *Wayne L. Rev.* 36:189, 1989; see also L.O. Gostin, "Genetic Privacy," *J. of Law, Medicine & Ethics* 23:320, 1995.

55. 119 Cal. App.3d 534, 174 Cal. Rptr. 148 (1981).

56. See Seltrecht v. Bremer, 536 N.W.2d 727 (Wis. App. 1995); J.A. Kelly, R.A. Glaser & B.H. Erard, "Ex Parte Interviews with Plaintiff's Treating Physicians: The Offensive Use of the Physician-Patient Privilege," *U. Detroit L. Rev.* 67:502, 1990; reprinted in *Defense L.J.* 4:321, 1991; J. Ropiequet, "*Ex Parte* Communication with Defense Counsel: Hidden Dangers of the Physician-Patient Privilege," *For the Defense,* June 1995, p. 16.

57. The arguments in favor of ex parte interviews are summarized as follows:
• The physician-patient privilege has been waived by filing suit and cannot be reasserted, so the method by which the information comes to defense counsel is not important.
• Pretrial discovery is not limited to the forms prescribed in the rules, and informal interviews are therefore permissible.
• Informal interviews are less expensive and time-consuming than depositions and can obviate the need to take some depositions.
• Off-the-record interviews promote candor and spontaneity in the witness and allow defense counsel to test theories without divulging work product to the opponent.
• Since the plaintiff does not "own" the physician or the physician's testimony, permitting interviews treats plaintiff and defendant fairly and equally.
• Both attorneys and physicians should be trusted to stay within ethical bounds generally and to avoid disclosing irrelevant and harmful information. Adequate sanctions are available to deal with transgressions.
• The scope of the interviews can be properly circumscribed with a notice and authorization procedure or by protective orders.

The arguments against *ex parte* interviews are summarized as follows:
- Physicians owe patients a duty of "total care" which is fiduciary in nature and includes an affirmative duty to assist the patient in court.
- The patient's trust and confidence in his or her physician would be chilled if the patient's attorney is not present.
- Active supervision by plaintiff's counsel and the court is necessary to prevent disclosure of irrelevant and harmful information.
- All relevant information can be obtained by ordinary means of discovery, such as subpoenas for records and depositions.
- The physician risks suit for breach of confidentiality or disciplinary action by revealing confidential information; it is unfair to place such a risk on the physician.
- Defense counsel can exert unfair pressure on a physician, especially if counsel represents the physician's insurance carrier.
- Defense counsel may have to testify in court in order to use the *ex parte* interviews.

J.L. Ropiequet, "Ex Parte Communications with Defense Counsel: Hidden Dangers of the Physician-Patient Privilege," *For the Defense*, June 1995, p. 16.
58. 197 Pa. Super. 79, 177 A.2d 142 (1962).
59. Domako v. Rowe, 438 Mich. 347, 476 N.W.2d 30 (1991).

# Chapter 5

# IDENTITY OF PATIENT

Whether the identity of a patient is discoverable is an issue that has divided the courts. In its formulation, a testimonial privilege covers only the content of communications and not the fact of a relationship. For a person to seek to invoke the privilege, there must be an initial showing, by affidavit or otherwise, that the person is one covered by the privilege. It is necessary to set out the existence of a therapist-patient relationship—the privilege does not cover communications between social guests.[1]

While sometimes acknowledging that the identity of a psychiatric patient must be protected to maintain the purpose of the privilege, many courts nonetheless adhere to the formula and hold that the identity of patients, the dates on which they were treated, and the length of treatment on each date do not fall within the scope of the privilege.[2] Other courts, however, say that when disclosure of the fact of consultation also of necessity discloses the nature of the condition for which the patient sought treatment, then the fact of disclosure also becomes privileged.[3]

"Clearly," it is argued, "the idea of confidential communication must encompass the identity of the patient as well."[4] Illinois expressly includes the fact of psychotherapeutic treatment within the privilege.[5] Federal law prohibits the use or disclosure of "patient identifying information" concerning anyone diagnosed or treated for substance abuse at facilities receiving federal funds.[6] The principles of ethics of the profession declare that "The identification of a person as a patient must be protected with extreme care."[7]

Under a discovery demand, in which the information is not protected, individuals might be asked whether they have ever been in treatment and, if so, where, when, and by whom. In an assault case, the fact of psychiatric care might suggest that the patient was the aggressor in the fray. However, there is no justification in asking the question unless there is some basis in fact that would raise a legitimate question concerning the individual's sanity.

In a Wisconsin case, a man later determined to be Roger Allen had been coming to the hospital for treatment using two different names. At that time, certain of Allen's hospital bills were being paid under medical assistance, and, at the same time, under the name of "Roger Roz," he was also receiving treatment paid by a workers' compensation carrier. Investigators interviewed the hospital's patient services representative who provided the investigators with information from the billing records. The investigators did not receive any detailed medical treatment information. They learned that Roger Allen and Roger Roz were one and the same person. Allen was charged with felony welfare fraud, and he filed a motion to suppress information directly or indirectly procured from the hospital on the grounds that his billing records were confidential and privileged information. The Wisconsin Court of Appeals ruled against him. First, it said, under legislation, the department of health and social services may request from any person any information it determines appropriate and necessary for the administration of the medical assistance program. Second, the court said, the information obtained under that legislation may be admitted as evidence in a criminal proceeding.[8]

In a malpractice action, a plaintiff may attempt to discover the names and addresses and, sometimes, the case histories of other people who have been treated by the defendant-physician. The attorney for the complainant wants the opportunity to talk to other patients of the physician in order to establish a pattern that would give credence to the complaint.[9] For example, a claim that the physician sexually exploited the plaintiff is more credible when supported by testimony of similar incidents with other patients. As a rule, discovery is disallowed on the ground of privilege or relevancy.[10]

In an article in *Trial*,[11] Linda Jorgenson, Pamela Sutherland, and Steven Bisbing cite research suggesting that "up to 80 percent of therapists who have had sexual contact with one patient, had sexual contact with other patients" (a debatable statistic), and they recommend the admission of evidence of these other acts to prove a case against an alleged abusing therapist. But how is evidence of these other acts to be obtained? Linda Jorgenson is a lightning rod for these types of cases so she may have been consulted by several women who have been involved sexually with the same therapist. But usually an attorney does not have more than one complaint against a single therapist. Newspaper publicity of a lawsuit against a therapist for undue familiarity may bring forth other patients who have been violated, as occurred in *Roy v. Hartogs.*[12]

But in lieu of that, is an attorney to be allowed to discover the names of all the therapist's patients, and then is the attorney to be allowed to contact the patients and ask them whether they have been sexually involved with their therapist? What will these patients think of the invasion of their privacy? What will they think of their therapist? What will it do to the therapeutic relationship with their therapist?[13] The authors respond:[14]

The kinds of evidence we envision as potentially admissible in proving prior acts of misconduct include complaints to disciplinary boards, the existence of civil or criminal actions against the therapist, information in public court documents, and testimony provided by victims referred through self-help organizations.

Former or current patients identified through these sources would have already made some public disclosure about their abuse and, at least in that context, confidentiality would have already been waived.

In a California case,[15] a physician and a hospital who were defendants in a malpractice action asked that a discovery order for information about other patients be set aside on the ground that it violated the physician-patient privilege. The physician could claim the privilege on behalf of the patients because they were not privy to the action. In this lawsuit, the plaintiff was seeking to recover damages from the defendants for injuries allegedly arising out of various tests performed on him. The plaintiff sought disclosure of the names and addresses of other patients to whom the defendants had given the same (angiographic) tests. The purposes of giving the plaintiff this information was to enable investigators to seek out and interrogate these patients and attempt to persuade them to discuss their experiences regarding the tests. The court barred discovery—it concluded that disclosure of identity of patients receiving such tests would necessarily be revealing confidential information.[16]

In a 1996 Michigan case, *Dorris v. Detroit Osteopathic Hosp.*,[17] the plaintiff, Deborah Dorris, claimed that she was given the medication Compazine intravenously even though she tried to refuse that medication and asked for another. The medication allegedly triggered an abrupt drop in her blood pressure. The doctor who treated her denied giving her the medication against her wishes, but she insisted a patient who shared her room heard the dispute and she sought a court order requiring the hospital to disclose the patient's name. Reluctantly, the Michigan Court of Appeals declined to order disclosure of the patient's name, feeling bound by the precedent of a 32-year-old ruling of the Michigan Supreme Court in *Schechet v. Kesten*,[18] where it was held that the privilege "prohibits the physician from disclosing, in the course of any action wherein his patient or patients are not involved and do not consent, even the names of such noninvolved patients." In Schechet, a physician brought suit to recover damages resulting from an alleged defamatory report made by the defendant, the then chairman of the department of surgery of a hospital, to the "credentials and executive committee" of the hospital. That report was, to say the least, critical of the plaintiff's surgical competence and it concluded with the recommendation that the plaintiff "should be permanently suspended from the staff." The plaintiff sought discovery of the sources of information conveyed by the defendant to the hospital. The state supreme court held that the identity of the third parties was privileged. However, in 1988, in *Porter v. Michigan Osteopathic Hosp. Assn.*,[19] the Michigan Court of Appeals, over a strong dissent, allowed discovery in a case where the plaintiff was allegedly raped in a hospital of the names and addresses and the room assignments of any and all suspected assailants and also the name of a patient who may, or may not have overheard a conversation between the plaintiff and medical personnel. Distinguishing *Porter*, the Michigan Court of Appeals in *Dorris* said that *Porter* presented stronger policy reasons than in *Dorris* for disclosure.

Picketing the offices of therapists and thereby seeing the individuals who enter for therapy is a recent matter of concern. It arises out of the controversy about therapists, among whom are psychiatrists, who are promulgating memory return therapy as well as several fringe therapies including space alien abduction therapy, satanic cult therapy and past life therapy. These therapists encourage patients to sever ties with their families. Angered by allegations of decade-delayed memories of sexual abuse, parents have brought suit against these therapists and they have picketed their offices. In one publicized case, the ACLU represented Chuck Noah, who picketed his daughter's therapist in Seattle, for his right to picket. One therapist who has been picketed said in anguish in a communication to the ACLU:

> Should the ACLU defend a group whose members carried signs like 'Toxic Legal Advice' and 'Voodoo Law' outside the offices of attorneys whose clientele are people worried about undocumented alien status and possible deportation? Would this action affect the rights of those who want legal counsel but fear public identification? Would those living in fear risk letting a picketer observe them entering offices providing specialized legal services. Would they know whether picketers would take and circulate their pictures, take down their license numbers, or follow them home?

Picketing, as is well known, has occurred outside the offices of physicians performing abortions. The legality of picketing (as a form of freedom of speech) is measured by considerations of time, place, and manner. The courts have held that protesters who display names of women receiving abortions may be held liable for invasion of privacy and infliction of emotional distress. The Michigan Court of Appeals held that although the subject of abortion is one of public interest, matters concerning medical treatment and sexual relations are considered private. The identities of the patients are not a matter of public interest or public record, said the court. Finding that the defendant protesters had unreasonably given publicity to purely private matters, the court said that their conduct was sufficiently outrageous to support the claim for infliction of emotional distress as well as for invasion of privacy.[20]

It is often recalled that, through the centuries, stigma has been attached to mental illness. In early times the mentally ill were regarded as possessed by demons—hence the expression "to beat the devil out of a person." Exorcism was another cure. In the New Testament, Matthew tells of Jesus curing a "lunatic" by rebuking a devil which then departed from him that very hour. The terms "devil's sickness" and "witch disease" were frequently used. During the reign of George III, the king against whom the English colonies in America revolted, the two houses of Parliament passed a bill authorizing court physicians to beat the devil out of the lunatic king, and the physicians whipped him. In Shakespeare's "Macbeth," a "nervous breakdown" is depicted as morally merited punishment for evil deeds. Families hid a demented member to hide what was considered evidence of sin; they were kept in attics or cellars. Mental illness was bound up in dark suspicion and shame.

Many people would rather be labeled bad than mad. It is defamatory (truth is a defense) to say of a person that he is insane, an idiot, mentally deranged, or the like, or to impute any other form of mental defect, so a statement in the presence of others, "Do me a favor and see a psychiatrist" may give rise to a cause of action.[21] When the National Basketball Association ordered the erratic Dennis Rodman to see a league psychiatrist, Jesse Jackson intervened, "It's one thing to punish a man. It's another thing to take away his dignity." Jackson said he would take on the job of counseling Rodman.[22]

The stigma associated with mental hospitalization is so great that the U.S. Supreme Court has held that prisoners are entitled to an administrative hearing to determine the need for a transfer to a psychiatric facility before they can be so transferred.[23] The Supreme Court pointed to "the stigmatizing consequences of a transfer to a mental hospital."[24] In *Lessard v. Schmidt*,[25] a federal district court quoted Bruce Ennis, then of the ACLU, that "former mental patients do not get jobs" and "in the job market, it is better to be an ex-felon than ex-patient," and it wrote:[26]

> In addition to the statutory disabilities associated with an adjudication of mental illness, and just as serious, are the difficulties that the committed individual will face in attempting to adjust to life outside the institution following release. The stigma which accompanies any hospitalization for mental illness has been brought to public attention in the news stories surrounding the recent resignation of a vice-presidential aspirant from further candidacy. Evidence is plentiful that a former mental patient will encounter serious obstacles in attempting to find a job, sign a lease or buy a house.

To counter the stigma, an increasing number of celebrities and others in recent years have at podiums or in writings revealed and discussed their treatment for mental illness or addiction. Kitty Dukakis, wife of Massachusetts Governor and Presidential candidate Michael Dukakis, opened her William C. Menninger Memorial Lecture at the 1989 annual meeting of the American Psychiatric Association with these words, "My name is Kitty. I'm an alcoholic and a drug addict."[27] In other annual meetings of the APA, Art Buchwald, Betty Ford, and William Styron, among others, related their history of mental illness and treatment. Tipper Gore, the wife of Vice President Al Gore, speaks publicly about her mother's depression. There are countless others who have spoken publicly or written about their psychiatric care. Judge David Bazelon of the D.C. Court of Appeals made no secret of his analysis. Barbra Streisand admitted to spending $300,000 on 2,700 hours on the couch before she could with conviction sing "On a Clear Day."

Marlon Brando confessed that the principal benefit acting afforded him was the money to pay his psychiatrists. Truddi Chase wrote about her treatment as a multiple personality and her psychiatrist writes the introduction and epilogue.[28] A book edited by Lucy Freeman contains a collection of accounts by famous people of the problems that sent them into analysis and of the progress and results of their treatment, including Sid Caesar, Jayne Meadows, Tennessee Williams, Jim Brosman, Bud Freeman, Ken Heyman, Patty Duke, Dr. Sandor Lorand, Graham Greene, Josh Logan, and Dr. Harold Greenwald.[29]

In a unique program, patients at the Borda Psychiatric Hospital in Buenos Aires every Saturday afternoon gather around portable radios. "Good afternoon, you crazy people, Loony Radio is on the air!" the announcer yells, to the excitement and applause of patients. "Today, we will hear reflections from Garces, the Emperor of Paranoia, and next we'll have a report from correspondent on Mars!" Loony Radio–Radio La Colifata, in Spanish slang– has become one of Argentina's most popular radio programs, broadcast to millions of listeners. Although it may sound like mockery or unsavory humor, Loony Radio is produced by Borda patients who serve as its hosts and correspondents as part of their therapy. The program is intended as a bridge between the psychiatric hospital and the outside world, giving patients contact with society, and society a window into the mentally ill.[30]

Writing about one's illness is often therapeutic as occurred in the case of Amber Pollina, a 17-year-old student at Berkley High School in Michigan. She suffered from depression and she wrote a play about it, and it won the 1995 Very Special Arts Young Playwright Award. It was performed that year at the Kennedy Center in Washington and thereafter in numerous places in Michigan. In it, she questioned the label society gives to what is normal and what is not normal. It all, she said, was a positive experience for her; she received the cheers of former classmates, teachers and friends.[31]

In its confessional talk shows, television has also contributed to breaking down many of the boundaries between public and private. On "Larry King Live," Art Buchwald, Dr. Kay Jamison, Naomi Judd, and Mike Wallace openly and freely discussed their bouts with depression. Mike Wallace insisted, "It's a good idea to go public"; he named his psychiatrist and spelled out his treatment.[32]

During the 1960s, it was especially fashionable to be in analysis and to talk about it at gatherings. In many of these cases, the individuals did not consider themselves "mentally ill" but sought analysis to understand themselves, to resolve problems of living, or to campaign against the stigma of mental illness. The journal *Psychiatric Services* of the American Psychiatric Association publishes first-person accounts of experiences with mental illness and treatment in a "Personal Accounts" column.

In all of these cases, the individuals came forward on their own and revealed their identities—it was not against their will. However, certain gay activists and others are publicly revealing the sexual orientation of certain persons without their consent, a process known as "outing." Outing advocates contend that the benefits for all concerned outweigh the injury to the individual. They claim that the target will become a more fully integrated person, and society will become more tolerant of gay persons. Others conclude that outing is not morally defensible. As Professor Susan Becker put it, the overriding moral choice must be one that allows individuals to make the decision to come out in their own time and in their own fashion.[34]

Apart from the matter of confidentiality, an ethical question arises when mental health professionals encourage patients to act as advocates or as fundraisers on behalf of mental health programs.[35] On occasion there is joint physician-patient advocacy in meeting with legislators or in actions against managed care.[36] Patients picket when hospitals are closed and they are shown on television.

And patients upon their discharge sometimes protest their treatment (protests are often organized by Scientology). Quite often, at meetings of the American Psychiatric Association, former patients walk the sidewalks carrying signs protesting their treatment. In any event, in all of these situations, it was the wish of these individuals to bare themselves publicly.

For many, however, the fear of disclosure is not misplaced. Dr. Jack Gorman put it thus: "[Psychiatrists] are rightfully pleased when famous individuals like Betty Ford, Governor Chiles of Florida, and Mike Wallace acknowledge that they have psychiatric problems and have sought treatment. Nevertheless, it can be harmful to some people's standing in the community if it is known that they are seeing a psychiatrist."[37] A study by the

National Institute of Mental Health in 1993 found that even ex-convicts rank above former mental patients in societal acceptance.

The doctrine of breach of confidentiality or invasion of privacy is applicable to the extrajudicial disclosure identifying a person as a psychiatric patient whereas the law on privilege applies to disclosure in a judicial process.[38] For further discussion, see Part V, Chapter 2, on "Accountability and Abuse of Confidentiality" and Chapter 3 on "The Stigma of Psychiatric Discourse."

## NOTES

1. State *ex rel.* Green Bay Newspaper Co. v. Circuit Court, 113 Wis.2d 411, 335 N.W.2d 367 at 372 (1983).

2. *In re* Zuniga, 714 F.2d 632 at 640 (6th Cir. 1983); *In re* Grand Jury Subpoena Duces Tecum, 638 F. Supp. 794 (D. Me. 1986); Sweeney v. Green, 116 Pa. Super. 190, 176 A. 849 (1935). "The privilege applies to 'confidential communications,' not names and addresses." Ley v. Dall, 150 Vt. 383, 553 A.2d 562 (1988). Under the attorney client privilege, the general rule is that the fee arrangement is not protected by the privilege. See *In Re* Michaelson, 511 F.2d 882 (9th Cir. 1975); M.L. Proctor, "Privilege and Fee Arrangements," *Mich. Bar J.*, Aug. 1996, p. 822.

3. City of Alhambra v. Superior Court, 110 Cal. App.3d 513, 168 Cal. Rptr. 49 (1980); Rudnick v. Superior Court of Kern County, 11 Cal.3d 924, 114 Cal. Rptr. 603, 523 P.2d 643 (1974).

4. D. Louisell & C. Mueller, *Federal Evidence* (Rochester, N.Y.: Lawyer's Co-operative, rev. ed. 1985), vol. 2, § 216, p. 857. See also E.S. Soffin, "The Case for a Federal Psychotherapist-Patient Privilege that Protects Patient Identity," *Duke L.J.* 1985:1217.

5. 740 Ill. Comp. Stat. Ann. 110/2 (Supp. 1995).

6. 42 C.F.R. §§ 2.11, 2.12.

7. "The Principles of Medical Ethics with Annotations Especially Applicable to Psychiatry" (1995 ed.); P.B. Gruenberg, "Some Thoughts on Confidentiality," Newsletter, *So. Calif. Psychiatrist*, Sept. 1996, p. 4.

8. State v. Allen, 546 N.W.2d 517 (Wis. App. 1996).

9. Anno., "Discovery in Medical Malpractice Action, of Names of Other Patients to Whom Defendant Has Given Treatment Similar to that Allegedly Injuring Plaintiff," 74 A.L.R.3d 1055.

10. *Ex parte* Abell, 613 S.W.2d 255 (Tex. 1981); see also Ltrs., "Ethics of Contacting Past Patients of Alleged Molester," *Clinical Psychiatry News*, Feb. 1989, p. 9.

11. "Evidence of Multiple Victims in Therapist Sexual Misconduct Cases," *Trial*, May 1995, p. 30.

12. 381 N.Y.S.2d 587 (1976).

13. R. Slovenko (ltr.), "Evidence of Multiple Victims," *Trial*, July 1995, p. 11. In Weisbeck v. Hess, 524 N.W.2d 363 (S.D. 1994), the South Dakota Supreme Court said, "[O]ne may assume the potential damage to [a] woman should one day a stranger come to her door to interrogate her about possible sexual liaisons between her and her mental health counselor." In this case a husband sued a psychologist for professional negligence arising out of the psychologist's affair with the husband's wife. The South Dakota Supreme Court held that the trial court abused its discretion by ordering the defendant psychologist to divulge his list of clients and by allowing the plaintiff to depose the defendant's therapist. The South Dakota Supreme Court, in a split decision, said "[T]his discovery fishing expedition does not provide the facts or rationale necessary to violate the privacy of uninterested parties. Releasing the names of these clients would directly discourage uninhibited communication, due to [the husband's] *mere* suspicion that such information *may possibly* contain relevant information. This plan is not reasonably calculated to lead to the discovery of admissible evidence." (Emphasis by court). The Court also held that the defendant's communications with his therapist were shielded as privileged communications. The decision is criticized in M.E. Slaughter, "Misuse of the Psychotherapist-Patient Privilege in *Weisbeck v. Hess*: A Step Backward in the Prohibition of Sexual Exploitation of a Patient by a Psychotherapist," *So. Dak. L. Rev.* 41:574, 1996.

14. Ltr., *Trial*, July 1995, p. 11.

15. Marcus v. Superior Court of Los Angeles County, 18 Cal. App.3d 22, 95 Cal. Rptr. 545 (1971).

16. See also Smith v. Superior Court, 118 Cal. App.3d 173 Cal. Rptr. 145 (1981) (action for spousal support); Costa v. Regents of the University of California, 116 Cal. App.2d 445, 254 P.2d 85 (1953); Boddy v. Parker, 45 App. Div.2d 1000, 358 N.Y.S. 218 (1974).

17. 220 Mich. App. 248, 559 N.W.2d 76 (1996).

18. 372 Mich. 346, 126 N.W.2d 718 (1964).

19. 170 Mich. App. 619, 429 N.W.2d 719 (1988).

20. Doe v. Mills, 1995 WL 411883 (Mich. App. 1995).

21. See Iverson v. Frandsen, 237 F.2d 897 (10th Cir. 1956); O'Barr v. Feist, 296 So.2d 152 (Ala. 1974); Modla v. Parker, 17 Ariz. App. 54, 495 P.2d 494 (1972). For further discussion, see Chapter 7 on proceedings to hospitalize where statements to a court may be justified.

22. D. Wickham, "Rodman Needs Help, But Not Jackson's," *Detroit News*, Feb. 6, 1997, p. 11.

23. Vitek v. Jones, 445 U.S. 480 (1980).

24. 445 U.S. at 494.

25. 349 F. Supp. 1078 (E.D. Wis. 1972).

26. 349 F. Supp. at 1089.
27. "Kitty Dukakis Shares Hard-Won Insights on Treatment, Recovery, Stigma," *Psychiatric News,* June 2, 1989, p. 2.
28. *When Rabbit Howls* (New York: Dutton, 1987).
29. *Celebrities on the Couch/Personal Adventures of Famous People in Psychoanalysis,* (Los Angeles: Ravenna Books (no date)). Patty Duke joined with medical reporter Gloria Hochman to write about her manic depression in *A Brilliant Madness* (New York: Bantam, 1992). Personal accounts by less famous people who have suffered the pain of depression are collected in K. Cronkite, *On the Edge/Conversations About Conquering Depression* (New York: Dell, 1994).
30. C. Sims, "Loony Radio's Not So Crazy. It's Great Therapy," *New York Times,* May 14, 1996, p. 4.
31. W. Wendland, "Teen puts her depression on stage," *Detroit Free Press,* Sept. 9, 1996, p. 1.
32. CNN, April 22, 1996; replayed May 16, 1996. Julie Solomon in "Breaking the Silence," *Newsweek,* May 20, 1996, p. 20, writes about prominent Americans trying to erase the lingering shame of mental illness.
33. The column is edited by Dr. Jeffrey L. Geller, professor of psychiatry at the University of Massachusetts Medical School and a member of the journal's editorial board.
34. S.J. Becker, "the Immorality of Publicly Outing Private People," *Oregon L. Rev.* 73:159, 1994.
35. Panel discussion, "The Psychiatrist as Double-Agent: Is It Ethical?", annual meeting of the American Psychiatric Association on May 6, 1996 in New York.
36. The American Psychiatric Association's Division of Government Relations advises: "Treating psychiatrists have an obligation to discuss denials of coverage with their patients. Depending on the clinical circumstances, treating psychiatrists may choose to enlist patients' assistance early, prior to the initiation of the appeal process. Patients and their families may be able to bring additional pressures to bear on the reviewers. Alternatively, psychiatrists may appeal adverse coverage decisions and involve patients only after appeals are denied." "State Update," Oct. 1995, p. 7. See also M.J. Mehlman, "Medical Advocates: A Call for a New Profession," *Widener L. Symposium J.* 1:299, 1996; E. Felsenthal, "When HMOs Say No to Health Coverage, More Patients Are Taking Them to Court," *Wall Street Journal,* May 17, 1996, p. B-1; E. Schine, "In California, It's 'Hell No, HMO!'/A Protest Against Managed Care's Excesses Gains Momentum," *Business Week,* May 20, 1996, p. 38.
37. J.M. Gorman, *The New Psychiatry* (New York: St. Martin's Press, 1996), p. 325.
38. There is a long list of cases on breach of confidentiality, or invasion of privacy, by a disclosure of an individual as a patient. See, *e.g.,* Feeney v. Young, 181 N.Y.S. 481 (1920) (unauthorized publication of

the filming of patient's operation); Clayman v. Bernstein, 38 Pa. D. & C. 543 (1940) (unauthorized photograph taken of semiconscious patient for medical education purposes); Barber v. Time, 348 Mo. 1199, 159 S.W.2d 291 (1942) (unauthorized publication of photograph and description of medical condition of patient in magazine); Commonwealth v. Wiseman, 249 N.E.2d 610 (Mass. 1969) (intrusive invasion of privacy in unauthorized filming of Bridgewater psychiatric patients); Doe v. Roe, 400 N.Y.S.2d 668 (1977) (unauthorized publication of a commercial book of a case history of a psychiatric patient's therapy), Anderson v. Strong Memorial Hospital, 140 Misc. 2d 770, 531 N.Y.S.2d 735 (1988), *aff'd,* 151 App. Div. 2d 1033, 542 N.Y.S.2d 96 (1989) (photo of patient in a waiting room at hospital's infectious disease unit).

# Chapter 6

# CRIMINAL CASES

Criminal cases, as other cases, may involve a treating or examining psychiatrist. The shield law is applicable, at best, only to a treating psychiatrist and not to an examining one. In the examining situation, the relationship is likely to be one entered into at arm's length (the person examined is called an examinee or evaluee, not a patient). In criminal cases, however, even in the treating situation, there is in many jurisdictions no medical or psychotherapist privilege whatsoever.

The medical privilege, as we have previously noted, is not applicable in most states in serious criminal cases.[1] In the District of Columbia, there is no medical privilege in criminal cases where "the accused is charged with causing the death, or causing injuries upon, a human being, and the disclosure is required in the interests of public justice."[2] In all states, by statute or caselaw, the medical privilege or the psychotherapist-patient privilege is inoperative when a defendant raises an insanity defense or a mental disability defense.[3]

The Illinois psychiatrist-patient privilege (enacted in 1963, four years after its passage of a physician-patient privilege) expressly states that it does not apply in criminal proceedings in which the mental condition of the patient is introduced by him as an element of defense.[4] Indiana and Wisconsin have similar statutory provisions.[5] Nebraska states that "[t]here is no privilege...in any judicial proceedings...regarding injuries to children, incompetents, or disabled persons or in any criminal prosecution involving injury to any such person or the willful failure to report any such injuries.[6] New Jersey's privilege does not cover cases of driving while under the influence of alcohol.[7] And as a general rule, the privilege is inapplicable when the "services of the therapist were sought, obtained, or used to enable or aid anyone to commit or plan a crime or fraud or to escape detection or apprehension after the commission of a crime or fraud."[8]

The privilege, moreover, does not cover communications involving fraud in receiving Social Security benefits.[9] Various states exclude the privilege in any judicial proceeding involving narcotics or to communications made to procure narcotics unlawfully.[10] And therapists have a duty to reveal information about the contemplation of a crime or harmful act.[11]

The various rules that have been developed to restrict the role of an examining psychiatrist in criminal cases are rooted in constitutional principles against self-incrimination and coerced confession, not the shield law. It is well established that a psychiatric examination does not violate the constitutional rights of the accused.[12] As one court put it, "Even a cat can look at a queen."[13] However, the psychiatrist may testify only as to his evaluation of the defendant (although in reaching this evaluation inferences are made from the facts of the crime or other crimes). Under the law of the various states, he may not reveal admissions made to him by the defendant in the instant proceeding or in another proceeding.[14]

A disclosure cleared up for CBS anchor Dan Rather, after being baffled for a decade, that the man who had beat him in a bizarre New York incident was William Tager, the same man who in 1994 fatally shot an NBC technician on the street outside the "Today" show studio. Rather had been ribbed and ridiculed over it; the rock group R.E.M. even turned it into a hit song. The incident was lumped together with a subsequent incident in which Rather stomped off the set, leaving the network with dead air time, as signs that he was losing his cool. Even CBS's Andy Rooney said he was "suspicious" about Rather's version of the alleged attack.

In 1996, according to news reports, Rather was informed by the forensic examiner, who at the request of prosecutors examined Tager, that he was certain Tager had attacked him. The media was also informed that Tager, serving a 12-to-25 year sentence for manslaughter, believed that the networks were out to get him."[15] Properly speaking, a psychiatric report may include other offenses to establish state of mind in the case at hand but not to establish the offense or other offenses, and a disclosure could also be made under the *Tarasoff* duty to warn about a danger. That was not the scenario in this case, but it served to bolster Rather's reputation, and in the words of CBS News president Andrew Heywood, "I'm particularly pleased that the person who could be a danger to others is behind bars." In any event, given the prosecution for a homicide resulting in a long sentence, another prosecution for a battery would be of little moment. In that event, the testimony of the forensic examiner or evidence flowing out of his disclosure would be inadmissible to establish the battery.[16]

Statements to an examining psychiatrist made by a defendant claiming insanity may be introduced, however, to challenge the defendant's claim of insanity or lack of mental capacity and is not deemed to violate the defendant's Fifth Amendment privilege against self-incrimination. The question of Fifth Amendment protection in criminal psychiatric evaluation was raised in a District of Columbia case that evoked a strong dissent by Judge David Bazelon.[17] In this case, Billy Byers, charged with the murder of his lover of 15 years, was evaluated at St. Elizabeths Hospital and found to have been insane at the time of the offense. He repeatedly said he did not know why he had killed the woman. At some point, his wife suggested that he had acted under the influence of a magic spell. For reasons not articulated in the record, he was transferred to a hospital in Springfield, Missouri, for an additional eight-week observation. He again said that he did not know why he committed the offense, but when "pressed" by a psychiatrist at the hospital, he said that his wife suggested magic spells.

The statement was used as the basis for the prosecution's argument that he was malingering in order to take advantage of an insanity defense. The statement was taken to be an admission that he and his wife concocted the idea of claiming magic spells several weeks after the murder. The trial judge described the statement as "devastating" to the insanity defense. His conviction was upheld on appeal, but in a 38-page dissent, Judge Bazelon cast doubt on the reliability of the evidence, which was critical to the judgment in the case, by the absence of any "reference whatsoever to malingering or to the defendant's statement" in the written report by the psychiatrist. He urged that, at a minimum, compulsory psychiatric examinations be audiotaped to protect against potential miscarriages of justice.[18]

Surreptitious psychiatric interrogation is prohibited. Confessions elicited with the aid of hypnosis, narcosis, or other forms of removal of inhibitions, especially when induced by the administration of drugs, have uniformly been struck down.[19] It is contrary to medical ethics, as well as against the law, for the police or the prosecutor to resort to the relationship of physician and patient to obtain a confession from the accused.[20] In *United States v. D.F.*,[21] the court noted the close relationship that the staff at a mental health facility had with law-enforcement officials and so it held that they were "state actors" and therefore the law applicable to law-enforcement officials on the obtaining of evidence was applicable to them. The appellate court said that "if it can be reasonably concluded that the caregiver goes beyond accepted medical roles and affirmatively takes on the role of delivering someone who is in his care and custody to the prosecutor, the district court is entitled to determine that the caregiver has changed his role substantially."

In *People v. Sanders*,[22] the defendant, after being advised of his *Miranda* warnings and declining to make a statement to the police, voluntarily spoke to a psychiatrist and admitted that he shot his wife. The statement was overheard by the police; there was no evidence that the psychiatrist was acting as an agent of the police. The police transported the defendant to the hospital for a psychiatric evaluation, and they did not give him an option of conversing with the psychiatrist in private. The court held that the communication came under the doctor-patient privilege. The court said, "[W]here the presence of the third party who overheard the statements was required by law and was absolute, the privilege cannot be said to have been waived by the officer's presence." To rule otherwise, the court said, would force a prisoner to abandon the right against self-incrimination in order to obtain medical evaluation and treatment.

As a matter of practice, psychiatrists who carry out an examination on court order point out to the accused that communications are not privileged, but this is not a legal requirement. For one reason, the examiner is not a law-enforcement official and thus is not required to give a *Miranda* warning that "you do not have to say anything and anything you say may be used as evidence against you." Another reason no warning is required is that the accused has an attorney.[23] And by pleading insanity, the accused invites an examination. However, a Miranda-type warning is advisable so as to overcome any claim of a surreptitious interrogation. But despite any disclaimer, the uneducated accused, just by seeing a doctor, not to mention his manner, may be seduced into believing that the examination is for his benefit.[24] The examinee's attorney, whose presence might be allowed, would likely impart an adversarial tone that would chill the examination.[25]

Jeffrey Dahmer, the Milwaukee anthropophagite, when examined by Dr. Park Dietz, one of the prosecutor's experts, believed that he was seeing someone who would help him notwithstanding the warning given by Dr. Dietz: "I'm not here as your doctor. You have to know that everything you tell me can all come out in court. It's not like when you see a doctor. I'm not here to help you. I'm not your doctor." (Of course, Dr. Dietz did not say, "I'm here to get you!")[26]

Whatever the warning, there is what is known as the "therapeutic seduction."[27] An examiner tends to utilize an empathetic relationship-building technique, and as a consequence the examinee may interpret the relationship as therapeutic. Under the various statutes on privilege, a "physician" or "psychotherapist" is a person "reasonably believed" so to be, and so, without adequate warning, there is the possibility of the application of a privilege.[28]

For the testimony or records of a treating psychiatrist, it is necessary to distinguish: (1) cases involving a plea of insanity (NGRI); (2) cases where law enforcement officials seek information about the defendant; and (3) cases where the defendant seeks information about the complainant or witnesses. Of course, it is clear that in jurisdictions where there is no medical or psychotherapist privilege in criminal cases, the treating psychiatrist can be called upon for his records or testimony when deemed relevant. The following is a discussion of these three areas and post-trial issues.

## 1. PLEA OF INSANITY

In the case of a defendant who asserts a defense of insanity (or other diminished capacity defense), the prevailing law is that he cannot claim possible self-incrimination with respect to psychiatric evidence, be it by a treating or examining psychiatrist. If the defendant does not cooperate with the court's or prosecutor's psychiatrist, he is deemed to have waived his insanity defense, or is denied the right to employ expert testimony on his own behalf.[29] In the *Byers* case, then D.C. Judge Antonin Scalia discussed the multitude of federal cases holding that a defendant who pleads insanity may not invoke the Fifth Amendment's self-incrimination clause to quash psychiatric testimony resulting from a court-ordered examination.[30]

By pleading and offering evidence of insanity, the accused puts his mental state in issue, and thus waives any psychotherapist-patient privilege; his medical or psychiatric history is open to the prosecution, as occurred for example in the trial of John Hinckley Jr., the would-be assassin of President Reagan.[31] The very nature of an insanity defense is premised on a broad inquiry into every aspect of the defendant's life. As a matter of practice, the fact of treatment is often brought up by defense counsel in plea bargaining to demonstrate an interest in rehabilitation.

Until there is some testimonial support for a defendant's claim of insanity, the defendant is presumed sane and conceivably, even though notice of a defense of insanity is entered, he may decide not to offer such testimonial support. Proper procedure requires the prosecution to withhold evidence of sanity until the defendant has placed in issue the question of his insanity by offering supporting testimony. Under a plea of insanity, the defendant has the burden of going forward with evidence of insanity and then the state in rebuttal is obliged then to come forward with evidence of sanity.[32]

John Wigmore, the leading authority on the law of evidence, went so far as to say that when insanity is made an issue, "any and all conduct of the person is admissible in evidence."[33] Thus, once the defendant has raised the insanity defense, the prosecution may offer evidence of prior arrests, convictions, and assaultive and antisocial conduct. Ordinarily, such evidence is not permitted because it could unfairly prejudice the jury as to whether the defendant is guilty in a specific instance, but it is material and admissible on the issue of sanity.[34] As a consequence, a defendant with a criminal record rarely raises the defense for fear that his history will be brought to the attention of the jury and will tend to guarantee conviction rather than acquittal.[35]

In the usual case of a plea of not guilty by reason of insanity (NGRI), the commission of the crime is admitted and the only issue is the accused's state of mind. It is rare for an accused to contend, in effect, "I didn't do it but if I

did, I must have been crazy." The accused, following a psychiatric examination, may withdraw his NGRI plea and enter a not guilty plea.

If and when the state's expert takes the stand and testifies, he will probably reveal incriminating information disclosed by the defendant, even if the
testimony is limited to a discussion of the defendant's mental condition.
Clinical testimony about the defendant's sanity, for instance, will usually
reveal admissions by the defendant with respect to the act associated with the
crime in question or about other criminal acts committed by the defendant
that are pertinent to establishing a guilty mind.

In an instruction of dubious effect, but as he must, the judge cautions the
jury that "the psychiatrist's testimony is only to be used in determining
defendant's sanity and not his guilt." The psychiatrist, who has testified or
made an evaluation of the accused's insanity at the time of the offense or as
to competency to stand trial, may not testify, for example, on the validity of
an alibi.[36] A defendant retains his privilege against self-incrimination even
after calling psychiatrists to testify in support of an insanity defense, and if
cross-examination of the defense psychiatrists elicits statements made by the
defendant, a jury may use these statements only on the insanity issue, not to
determine guilt or innocence. A bifurcated proceeding—one to determine
state of mind, another to determine commission of the act—is not constitutionally required.[37]

As we have noted, the Fifth Amendment places restrictions on trial use of
disclosure made during an evaluation of insanity or competency to stand
trial. To this effect, the Model Penal Code formulation, which has been
adopted in several states, provides, "A statement made by a person subjected to a psychiatric examination or treatment...shall not be admissible in evidence against him in any criminal proceeding on any issue other than that of
his mental condition."[38] The more recent Federal Rules of Criminal
Procedure sets out more comprehensive protection: "No statement made by
the defendant in the course of any [psychiatric] examination...whether the
examination be with or without the consent of the defendant, no testimony
by the expert based upon such statement, and no other fruits of the statement
shall be admitted in evidence against the defendant in any criminal proceeding except on an issue respecting mental condition on which the defendant has introduced testimony."[39]

Thus, the Federal Rules not only prohibit direct use of the defendant's
evaluation statements on issues other than those he has raised, but also forbid use of the defendant's disclosures for investigative purposes. Laws to that
effect have been adopted in various states.[40] In *Estelle v. Smith*,[41] the prosecutor used information which the prosecution-retained psychiatrist gathered
in a competence to stand trial evaluation of the defendant at a capital-penal-
ty phase of a murder trial. The U.S. Supreme Court ruled that this violated
the defendant's privilege against self-incrimination.

As earlier noted, statements made by the defendant to a psychiatrist engaged by an attorney to examine the defendant would be privileged under the attorney-client privilege. In such cases, the psychiatrist is considered as acting as an agent of the attorney.[42]

## 2. DISCOVERY BY LAW-ENFORCEMENT OFFICIALS

In jurisdictions where the privilege covers criminal cases, it shields a patient who is charged with a crime against prosecutorial discovery (except when insanity is pleaded).[43] Here's a law school examination question:

> At the Superbowl, Roseanne Arnold was shot dead while singing the national anthem. Forensic experts place the origin of the shot at seat 6, row 3 in section 201–the seat occupied by Tom Arnold. In the murder trial, the defendant Tom Arnold takes the stand and testifies that he was away from his seat during the singing of the national anthem. He states that he was buying and consuming his lunch: ten hotdogs and a beer. A year before Roseanne's murder, Tom's personal physician recorded in his medical records that Tom told him that he was severely allergic to hotdogs. Can the prosecution have testimony from the physician regarding Tom's statement admitted in evidence?

The answer depends on whether the jurisdiction has a privilege covering criminal cases. Yet a word of caution: In murder or other serious crimes, law enforcement agencies may try to get psychiatric records from psychiatrists not based on any evidence linking the crime to that psychiatrist's caseload. Fishing expeditions are part of law-enforcement investigation. A psychiatrist ought not respond to such a request. If served with a subpoena, the psychiatrist should follow the procedure of notifying the specific patient, and advising the patient to seek legal advice. The psychiatrist should also challenge a search warrant lacking specificity as necessary to protect the confidentiality of his caseload.

Law-enforcement officials obtained audiotapes and records made by Leon Jerome Oziel, a clinical psychologist, during treatment of Lyle and Erik Menendez, accused of murdering their parents. They obtained the tapes pursuant to a warrant authorizing a search of Oziel's office and residence. At issue was whether alleged threats made by the brothers during the therapy sessions endangered Oziel, his wife, and his lover, thereby justifying the disclosure of the communications.[44] Oziel warned his wife and girlfriend that the Menendez brothers might be dangerous to them. Oziel asked the girlfriend to eavesdrop on a therapy session with the brothers and to call the police if the conversation turned dangerous. She heard the brothers describe how they murdered their parents. With a tip from the girlfriend, the police searched Oziel's office, seizing the tapes and records of his sessions with the brothers.[45]

It is held that a duty to report such as a duty to report a patient who poses a danger to others undercuts any privilege.[46] Thus, in the Menendez trial, Oziel was obliged to provide testimony and the tapes that he had made in the course of therapy.[47] Once the patient gives the psychiatrist good cause to warn a potential victim of a dangerous patient, the privilege is lost as to the communications that provide the cause for warning.[48] The obvious question is why the duty to warn should be construed to do more than authorize disclosure to the potential victim.

It is to be noted that the privilege disappears even if the therapist does not give a warning. The court in *Menendez* said, "[T]he exception [is] not keyed to disclosure or warning, but to the existence of the specified factual predicate, *viz.*, reasonable cause for belief in the dangerousness of the patient and the necessity of disclosure."

Most damaging to the defense was the audiotape of the therapy session, which the defense struggled for three years to suppress, in which Lyle said he and his brother killed their mother to put her "out of her misery" over her loveless marriage, and making a joint decision that the father "should be killed" because of "what he's doing to my mother."[49] There was no question at the trial that they killed their parents, but rather why they killed them. They claimed that they had been terrorized all their lives by their parents, and eventually killed them out of terror, believing at the moment of the killings that their lives were in imminent danger. The prosecution claimed that they killed their parents for their inheritance, estimated at $14 million.

What about Fifth Amendment protection in cases where a privilege is wanting? "It frightens me to think that the private thoughts, hopes, dreams and despairs of all our citizens can now be seized by the government," said Senator Bob Packwood over enforcement of an Ethics Committee subpoena for his personal diaries.[50] The Fifth Amendment reads, in relevant part, "nor shall [any person] be compelled in any criminal case to be a witness against himself."[51] In 1886, in *Boyd v. United States*,[52] the U.S. Supreme Court held that the Fifth Amendment protected individuals from compelled production of private books and papers, but in 1976, in *Fisher v. United States*,[53] the Court held that it provided no protection for private, non-compelled, self-incriminating information, such as voluntarily-prepared documents. According to the Court, a subpoena requiring a person to produce voluntarily prepared written records compels neither oral testimony nor a restatement or affirmation of the truth of the contents of the documents sought. The Court stressed that only compelled incriminating testimony receives Fifth Amendment protection.[54]

The ethical position of the psychiatrist must be considered if indeed a specific patient is known to have committed a crime during the course of therapy. The actual fact of the crime demonstrates that therapy has not afforded society necessary protection. In the view of many, the obligation to protect society has priority over the purposes for confidentiality. Although such a confession may be based on the psychodynamics of a truly innocent patient, it would be prudent to discuss it with the authorities.

A distinction is to be made between a crime with an ongoing investigation or a threatened crime and a crime committed in the relatively distant past. "I killed a man 20 years ago," says a patient. Reporting a past crime, as a rule, does not avert an imminent danger or protect society. There is no ethical basis for reporting such a disclosure unless an innocent individual is serving time for that crime.[55]

One of the most frequently asked questions at law and psychiatry seminars is whether therapists have an obligation to report a past crime. Simply hearing of a patient's past felony and not reporting it is not sufficient to convict the therapist of misprision of a felony. Conversely, reporting a patient to legal authorities could constitute a breach of confidentiality, but a lawsuit for breach of confidentiality would be unlikely, and even more unlikely to result in an adverse judgment. The therapist could more likely justify disclosure and testify under the exception to privilege that the past crime is an indication of future potential for violence.[56] The issue here is actually less one of privilege but one more of confidentiality and the duty to report.[57]

As a matter of practice, unless there are records, a prosecutor is not likely to call a therapist as a witness against his patient. It would likely boomerang. Usually, the fact that a defendant has been seeing a psychiatrist is not advanced by the prosecutor; in the event of trial, a prosecutor would establish the commission of the act or *mens rea* independently of the treating psychiatrist. The fact of treatment is, instead, brought up by defense counsel, as a show of rehabilitation, in plea bargaining or obtaining a dismissal of the charge.

As far as privilege is concerned, the furtherance of a criminal or fraudulent plot cannot be part of the physician's function. If he knowingly takes part in preparing a crime, he ceases to act as a physician and becomes a criminal.[58] The "future crime or fraud" exception applies to all of the testimonial privileges, Thus, under the cases construing the attorney-client privilege, conversations to facilitate crime or fraud, when established by extrinsic evidence, vitiates the privilege.[59]

Quite frequently a physician is called upon for advice about sexual behavior. Health and morality are not always one and the same (*e.g.*, it may be healthy to eat someone else's food, but it would not be moral or legal to steal it), but without making a value judgment on a nonmarital coitus, the fact remains that fornication may be a healty milestone in the life of some people.[60] There are also problems in giving advice to married couples, *e.g.*, on birth control. A patient in psychotherapy may have committed or may be planning adultery or evasion of taxes. In such cases, the therapist will be in possession of highly incriminating evidence.

The majority of patients in office psychotherapy try to adapt to the rules of society. If a patient "acts out" his feelings, he will not derive much benefit from therapy. A man who ponders, "I don't know why I keep beating my wife," or, "I wonder why I hang around homosexuals," will never know as long as he keeps it up. Therapy requires that a person refrain from acting out his impulses or feelings; only in that way will he be able to deal with his problems effectively.[61]

In general, individuals in mental hospitals as well as in outpatient therapy are not characterized by antisocial activity or by a striking inability to pursue lawful goals. Usually, the patient in psychotherapy suffers from an overly strict conscience. The criminal, on the other hand, has a conscience (if it can be called that) which sets few limits on his behavior. He makes others suffer. When the exceptional case of a criminal in therapy arises, psychotherapy might provide the best possibility of having the individual return to lawful and gainful pursuits. As Professor Joseph Goldstein and Dr. Jay Katz put it:[62]

> As a class, patients willing to express to psychiatrists their intention to commit crime are not ordinarily likely to carry out that intention. Instead, they are making a plea for help. The very making of such pleas affords the psychiatrist his unique opportunity to work with patients in an attempt to resolve their problems. Such resolutions would be impeded if patients were unable to speak freely for fear of possible disclosure at later date in a legal proceeding.

Dr. Victor Sidel observed:[63]

> Except under very special circumstances such as the prevention of the spread of communicable disease or prevention of a specific criminal act, the physician may best serve his patient by the strictest protection of his confidences, even if that patient is a criminal, a social, religious or sexual deviant or a defector. By thus strengthening his ability to communicate with the individuals who form his community, and preserving his ability to help them, the physician best serves his nation and humanity.

Moreover, as a general proposition, patients who are dangerous to themselves or to others are hospitalized. They are not treated on an outpatient basis. Dr. Karl Menninger said:[64]

> I personally will not accept for outpatient psychotherapy a man subject to homosexual tendencies who will not agree to eschew homosexual activities

during the treatment period. Many normal people in the world, for one reason or another, manage to remain continent in spite of temptation, and I see nothing unjust in expecting a person afflicted with a temptation toward an illegal type of gratification to control his behavior and remain continent during the period of treatment in which we attempt to relieve him of his pathological propensities. I am willing to try to help him with his temptations; but not with his crimes. I am willing to try to help a man who is tempted to commit murder or arson, but I am not willing to treat a man—as an outpatient—who can't resist doing so. I grant that homosexual seductions, etc. are less serious than arson or murder, but the principle is the same.

The Connecticut statute on the psychiatrist-patient relationship, expressly made applicable to both civil and criminal cases, does not include a "future crime or fraud" exception, thus adopting the view that there is less danger of such acts being carried out if patients are allowed the freedom to vent their angers and discuss their criminal intentions with a psychotherapist.[65] The proposed Federal Rule of Evidence 504 also does not contain a future crime or fraud exception. In the psychotherapist-patient context, there is no need for a "crime or fraud" exception *per se*, because an individual cannot use communications with a psychotherapist, as he might use communications with a lawyer, "for the purpose of getting advice for the commission of a fraud or crime."[66] However, the duty to warn or protect when a patient poses a danger overrides the privilege, as discussed in Part IV, Chapter 2.

What about when a patient is a victim of a crime? In this situation, law-enforcement officials may seek information from the therapist in the hope of identifying the assailant. Was the patient threatened? Did the patient fear someone? A Michigan case is illustrative. Every Thursday morning for several years Dr. Deborah Iverson, a 38-year-old ophthalmologist, would drive to see a psychiatrist, Dr. Lionel Finkelstein, and would park in an adjoining area. One Thursday morning she disappeared after leaving Dr. Finkelstein's office and was found strangled a distance away in the backseat of her car. As the media reported, law-enforcement officials questioned Dr. Finkelstein for possible clues, but apparently unsatisfied with their interview, they obtained a search warrant and seized the patient's file.[67] (Members of the Alliance for Mental Health Services protested the newspaper publicity of the fact that the victim, Dr. Iverson, was a psychiatric patient.[68]) Whatever testimonial privilege there may be, it is no bar to a properly executed search warrant.[69] And for the admission of evidence at trial, the privilege, in jurisdictions where there is a privilege in criminal cases, would likely be waived. In an investigation or prosecution in the case where a patient has been killed, the therapist's testimony as to statements of the patient as to whether or by whom threats were made would be helpful.[70]

That absolute confidentiality is not acceptable to common sense is illustrated by cases like the Iverson slaying. Actually, in all cases, trust—not absolute confidentiality–has to be the measure in confidentiality. Assuredly, the patient or the patient's family would want law-enforcement officials to be informed about any fear that the patient may have had of an attack. Confidentiality cannot be turned into a holy grail without concern for good judgment in these matters. As the investigation in the Iverson slaying proceeded, it was learned from the psychiatric records that she had been having problems with hospital coworkers and also "troubles or conflicts" with some relatives. Using that information, detectives focused much of their probe on relatives and coworkers, but it shed no light on the killing.[71] Then, months later, two young adults were arrested on the basis of a tip and they confessed to the crime–a random act of violence.[72]

Some years ago, in California, following a triple murder in a drugstore, a search warrant was issued on a San Francisco drug abuse clinic. The support for the warrant was an anonymous phone call that an unnamed acquaintance of the caller had had a conversation with unnamed men in that clinic planning the drugstore robbery. They seized the records of all patients in the clinic to get photos and recorded fingerprints in the files. The police obtained the identity, photos, and fingerprints of all the narcotic users going to the clinic.

And suppose a homicide charge against a defendant whose defense is that the victim had not been murdered but had committed suicide. Just as in a wrongful death action, the victim's therapist, if any, can be called to establish whether or not the victim was of a suicidal state of mind. The hearsay exception, however, would not allow a declaration to prove a past fact or event, such as "My husband has poisoned me."[73]

## 3. DEFENDANT SEEKS DISCOVERY

A defendant in a criminal case is entitled under the Constitution to summon witnesses and to obtain evidence to establish his innocence. The U.S. Supreme Court has recognized on a number of occasions that a state's interest as expressed in its evidentiary laws are secondary to the constitutional considerations of fully confronting witnesses who testify against the defendant and of fairness to a defendant seeking to defend against criminal charges.[74] It is prevailing law that a criminal defendant is entitled to review the psychiatric records of a prosecuting witness but only after a judge has determined there is good cause for disclosure and that the material will in some way be relevant to the defense.[75]

In *United States v. Lindstrom*,[76] the Eleventh Circuit held that the right of cross-examination was unconstitutionally curtailed by denying defendant access to medical records relating to the psychiatric treatment of the government's chief witness. The owners of a therapy clinic were on trial for mail fraud in charging clinic patients for treatments that they did not need or did not receive. The defense contended that the witness was conducting a personal vendetta against them. The witness's records indicated a diagnosis of hysterical personality, paranoia, delusions, hallucinations, and chronic misinterpretation of the words and conduct of others. Because the witness provided key testimony for the government's case and the line of inquiry sought by the defense was relevant to the witness's perceptions and motives in testifying, the court concluded that the constitutional right of confrontation dictated access to the records.

In *People v. Webb*,[77] involving a defendant charged with murder, robbery, and burglary, the prosecution relied on the testimony of the defendant's girlfriend. Shortly after the criminal complaint was filed, the defendant subpoenaed a private psychiatrist and a county mental health center for the girlfriend's psychiatric records with regard to the time period prior to the girlfriend's contacting the police and becoming a prosecution witness. The defendant argued that assuming the records showed that she suffered from "delusions" or other mental disorders affecting her competence or credibility as a witness, his right to "fairly cross-examine" her under the due process and confrontation clauses of the Constitution prevails over any privilege or privacy interest she might otherwise claim. The California Supreme Court held, as in other cases, that the trial court must examine *in camera* to determine whether the records contained evidence relevant to guilt or innocence.[78]

The same principle applies when an accused seeks evidence from a victim treatment or rape crisis center.[79] An individual who claims to have been raped, for example, and having identified the defendant as the rapist, may confess in therapy that she had in fact consented to the sexual activity. This behavior ought to be regarded as criminal as crimes committed by a patient in the course of therapy. The psychiatrist's response should give precedential concern to the protection of society. The victim treatment center or rape crisis center may or may not have evidence that would be important in a criminal proceeding.[80] Alan Dershowitz posed the legal and ethical issues in his novel *The Advocate's Devil*.[81]

In an Alaska case, a young woman whose records in a rape counseling center were sought by the defense protested strenuously, "[The defense] thinks there's something big in the records, but there's not. That's the funny thing. There's stuff in there I haven't even told my parents. There's stuff in there I don't want to review. There's stuff I just wanted to get off my chest and never think about again...[T]here written down [are] all my humiliating moments, my happy moments and my sad moments. They might as well strip me naked and make me walk in front of everybody naked. I'll tell you, it would be easier."[82]

In dealing with any privilege, the courts have recognized that before a judge can determine whether communications are to be protected, the judge should conduct an *in camera* inspection in order to know whether the requirements of the privilege are met.[83] Accordingly, when a psychotherapist-patient or sexual assault counselor-victim privilege is asserted, the trial judge under proper circumstances should conduct an *in camera* inspection. The court should determine whether there are statements of the victim that may relate to important issues, such as identity of the assailant or consent. Due process and confrontation does not require disclosure of all the victim's statements; only those that are relevant to the preparation and presentation of the defense.[84]

A refusal by the alleged victim to release her psychological records for *in camera* review will result in the exclusion of her testimony at trial.[85] An *in camera* review is not granted based solely on a defendant's request. There must be a threshold showing by the defendant that the records may reasonably be expected to provide information material to the defense. A general assertion that inspection of the records is needed for a possible attack on the victim's credibility is insufficient to meet this threshold showing.[86]

In a prosecution in California for forcible sex offenses,[87] the defendant sought to cross-examine the victim, his minor daughter, regarding persons in her therapy group at a state hospital to whom she had revealed details of the offenses allegedly perpetrated against her. The victim declined to provide the names of the persons in her therapy group on the ground of confidentiality. After a hearing in chambers in which the victim's counselor at the state hospital testified, the trial court refused to allow defense counsel such line of cross-examination on the basis that it fell within the psychotherapist-patient privilege. The California Court of Appeals denied the petition. It held that the identification of persons in the victim's group counseling could only have been relevant in a subsequent attempt to impeach her testimony at trial and that the exclusion of the cross-examination did not deny the defendant a fair hearing.[88]

To avoid involvement in the criminal justice system, some counseling centers announce that they do not keep records, and make no evaluation or diagnosis. Failure to keep records, however, has generally lost its immunizing value. The fact that most psychiatrists or other therapists give reports to third parties for various purposes tends to cast doubt on not keeping records. In the current malpractice climate, the best defenses are records that detail the clinical factors that determine the judgment of the therapist to hospitalize or not to hospitalize in situations where hospitalization might be considered, or not to report behavior patterns that might be questioned in the future, where an infinite number of ambivalent situations requiring hairline judgments might be made. Certainly, one must be circumspect about what is included in a record since the current vogue of getting search warrants easily is a threat to every record. Now our attention turns to the posttrial or post-guilty plea stage in regard evaluation for sentencing, therapy in correctional institutions and community-based programs, and parole.

## EVALUATION FOR SENTENCING

From 1924 until the trial of O.J. Simpson, the crime of the century was generally thought to be the brutal murder of little Bobby Franks by two brilliant University of Chicago students, Nathan Leopold and Richard Loeb, who were represented by the famed Clarence Darrow. The biggest difference between the two cases was that Darrow pled his clients guilty. In doing so, he kept the case out of the hands of the jury, and then during the sentencing stage, he brought psychopathology into his arguments. The sentencing hearing took three months, during which the prosector called 102 witnesses, and Darrow put on psychiatrists who helped him argue that these boys were "irresponsible, weak, diseased" and that to hang them would be as savage an act as their own. (He sought to bring Sigmund Freud from Europe to testify, but Freud was too ill to make the voyage.) The boys were not executed.

A presentence investigation report of a probation department, diagnostic center, or court probation clinic plays a role in sentencing and its confidentiality is a matter which has received increased attention. While these reports may play an influential role in sentencing, little guidance typically is provided mental health professionals on the type and purpose of information being sought.[89] There is controversy over the extent to which there should be disclosure of the contents of the report to the defendant.[90]

When the District Court of Appeal of Florida had the opportunity to indicate, for the first time in the jurisdiction, the status of a presentence investigation report, it concluded that the report should be treated as a confidential compilation of information for the use of the sentencing judge, and not as a public document, hence the defendant is not entitled to access thereto.[91] Counsel for the defendant, as might be expected, argued that the right to see a presentence report is basic and fundamental and that to deny him this right is to allow hearsay evidence to stand against him, depriving him of cross-examination and confrontation of witnesses. "To strip a presentence investigation report of its confidentiality," the court observed, "would be to divest it also of its importance and value to the sentencing judge, because there might be lacking the frankness and completeness of disclosures made in confidence." The rules of evidence do not apply to sentencing.[92]

Most judges feel that strict adherence to confidentiality in the use of the presentence report has made it possible for the probation officer to obtain for the court a much more accurate picture of the defendant than could be obtained if it were known that the contents of the report were going to be divulged to others.

There is, however, a sizeable body of opinion which feels very strongly that no presentence report should be so confidential that the defendant should not be given an opportunity to reply to any information entered in it. Making the report available to defense counsel provides certain safeguards to the defendant's rights. It gives the defendant an opportunity to explain some matters which may not have been explained in the report as fully as the defendant feels they should have been.[93] In 1944, an advisory committee of the United States Supreme Court recommended full disclosure of a presentence report. The recommendation, however, was rejected. More recently it has been suggested that a "summary" of the presentence report be made available to the defendant.

The vast majority of judges, however, have found routine disclosure (mandatory upon request) an unwarranted practice. They are opposed to either full disclosure or "summary" disclosure. A mandatory requirement that upon request a summary of information from the presentence investigation report must be disclosed, inevitably will lead to difficulties relating to sources and content of information contained in the report. The presentence report would no longer be a "meaningful, professional document."[94] It is believed that the Federal Rules of Criminal Procedure as now stated are adequate to protect the defendant's rights. They give the court full discretion to disclose information in the presentence report when the court believes it is necessary to do so.[95]

With the development of probation and diagnostic services, the issue of the extent to which the presentence investigation report ought to be preserved as a confidential document has assumed increased importance. Probation and diagnostic services have long sought to have this problem of confidentiality thoroughly considered in an effort to reach some sort of agreement on criteria.[96] Perhaps the federal practice giving the court discretion to disclose contents of the report affords the best compromise. There are other situations where the defendant in criminal procedure does not have an absolute right to participate in the proceeding (the accused, for example, has no absolute right to present his side of the case to the grand jury when it is considering an indictment against him).[97]

The Sentencing Reform Act, which revolutionized federal sentencing and introduced guideline sentencing in the federal courts, does not address evidentiary matters, but Congress did continue to prohibit any "limitation on the [kind] of information" a sentencing court may consider about the "background, character, and conduct" of the convicted defendant before it.[98] In addition, the Sentencing Commission Guidelines states that "the court may consider relevant information without regard to its admissibility under the rules of evidence applicable at trial, provided that the information has sufficient indicia of reliability to support its probable accuracy."[99] The rules of evidence with respect to testimonial privileges apply, however, although the other rules of evidence do not apply to sentencing proceedings.[100]

## THERAPY IN CORRECTIONAL INSTITUTIONS AND COMMUNITY-BASED PROGRAMS

And what about therapy in correctional institutions? Because of the dismal failure of the so-called community care concept, an increasing number of individuals with severe mental illness are not in a state mental health system but in the criminal justice system. Throughout the nation, state mental health systems have been dismantled. As a consequence, individuals with severe psychotic disorders are jailed for minor offenses. Correctional officers are now the primary mental health workers, and the county jail is the new mental health facility.

With the closing of mental hospitals, some states have increased the number of psychiatrists working in penal institutions, but still, to date, 43 state prison systems have been sued over medical and mental health services. More often than not, the behaviors of prisoners are interpreted not as symptoms of mental disorder, but as disruptive breaking of rules, leading to solitary confinement, psychological or physical abuse by guards, and prolonged use of physical restraints.

For the most part, the practice of psychiatry in penal institutions (as it has become in the outside world) is mainly chemotherapy rather than psychotherapy or behavioral therapy. In any event, for psychotherapy, confidentiality or trust is especially important in a penal institution inasmuch as prisoners tend to be distrusting. Like adolescents, they have difficulty knowing whom to trust, if anyone, and how much to trust them, and at the same time they are ready to explode at minimal provocation. More so than in the outside world, a prison psychiatrist is duty bound to report knowledge of new crimes being planned by the patient.[101] As a rule, a prison psychiatrist will advise "keep an eye on him" without divulging information, say, about a weapon or a plan to escape.

Some prison psychiatrists, however, complain about reporting. As one put it, "It is my personal conviction that it is not the role of the psychiatrist to uncover such information under the guise of therapy, if he expects to expose it to the warden. I cannot help feeling that disclosure under these circumstances is a sort of 'psychic entrapment.' The physician ought either to warn his patient beforehand of the reservations he has concerning confidentiality or, having committed himself to secrecy, he should maintain it."[102] Norman Fenton, who has had extensive experience in group counseling in institutions, observed:[103]

> The practice of reporting nothing more than attendance should be carried out steadfastly. If any genuine changes for the better or the worse occur in inmates they will be made evident by their behavior in other situations and noted and reported in the customary ways by teachers, shop foremen, dormitory supervisors or others. Such changes offer a better and more realistic measure than what the group leader might observe and report. It is obvious that if the group leader reported unfavorably on an inmate, the feelings that would arise among others in the group, even though they agreed with the appraisal, might undermine the group counseling program. The spontaneity of the procedure would be lost after a report of any kind from the group leader. The inmates would carry into the counseling group the contrivances they use elsewhere in the prison to impress the staff favorably. This has been confirmed by studies which described the manipulative behavior of inmates in groups where the group leader reported to the parole board on the attitudes and other characteristics of the members of the group.

Increasingly, in recent years, group therapy or counseling has been carried on in correctional institutions. In particular, the increasing alarm over sex offenses has fueled sex-offender treatment programs. Therapy for sex offenders, in or out of an institution, has emerged as a popular, though controversial solution. In group sessions, offenders are often encouraged to confront each other about their crimes. To help offenders develop "victim empathy," some therapists ask the offenders to write letters of apology to victims. Some therapists use a device known as a penile plethysmograph to measure arousal to sexual images and situations.

In community-based therapy programs, therapists are discouraged from guaranteeing confidentiality, partly to help parole and probation officers determine if an offender has violated the terms of his release. Not surprisingly, parole officers tend to steer offenders to programs that cooperate with law enforcement.[104]

In a Montana case, a man was convicted of sexually assaulting a 7-year-old girl over his assertion of innocence, but the sentence, five years in prison, was suspended on the condition that he take part in an outpatient sexual therapy program. After four months, the therapist refused to treat the man, Donald Imlay, because he was still denying that any sexual contact had occurred. The therapist said no progress could take place in light of the continued denial. After a hearing, the trial court revoked his probation and ordered him to serve the rest of his sentence in the state prison. The Montana Supreme Court set aside the sentence on the ground that the Fifth Amendment prohibits increasing a defendant's sentence as a penalty for refusing to confess to a crime.[105] In appealing that ruling to the U.S. Supreme Court, the State of Montana argued that the decision "effectively eviscerates sex offender programs and other similar therapy programs" that require participants to accept responsibility for their behavior. The Supreme Court agreed to hear the case but then decided to dismiss the petition. The State's "concession"–that a defendant would have immunity from prosecution based upon incriminating statements made to a therapist–rendered the matter moot.[106]

## Parole

As a general practice, the office of the prosecutor has the responsibility to review the record to determine whether a parole board's decision complies with statutes governing parole, and in order to determine whether to appeal a particular parole, the prosecutor's office must have access to the complete record that went before the parole board. In a Michigan case, the Department of Corrections agreed to provide the prosecutor's office all of the records *except* "information or records subject to...psychologist-patient privilege" and "clinician's packet and psychological information," asserting the psychological records of prisoners were privileged under the Freedom of Information Act. The Michigan Court of Appeals ruled that the psychological records of prisoners do not constitute privileged information under the FOIA and must be turned over at the request of the prosecutor's office. The decision came in the case of three prisoners–Jerome Allen, Mickey Hicks and Todd Sparks–who were granted parole by the Michigan Parole Board. The appellate court said that, by seeking parole, a prisoner places his mental health in issue and gives implicit consent that such information be furnished to the parole board. Once otherwise privileged information is disclosed to a third party (the parole board) by a person who holds the privilege, the privilege disappears. The appellate court acknowledged that a prisoner's psychological records contain information that is personal, intimate and likely embarrassing, but the court said, even though the information is of a personal nature–which is mentioned in one of the FOIA exceptions–the invasion of privacy is warranted in such instances as parole proceedings to ensure that a person who might pose as a menace to society is not paroled.[107]

## NOTES

1.  The medical privilege may be inapplicable in serious or in any criminal case. See, *e.g.*, Cal. Evid. Code §998 (physician-patient privilege inapplicable in criminal proceedings); Ill. Comp. Stat. ch. 735, ¶5/8-802 (physician patient privilege inapplicable "in trials for homicide when the disclosure relates directly to the fact or immediate circumstances of the homicide"); Kan. Stat. Ann. §60-427(b) (physician-patient privilege applicable "in a civil action or in a prosecution for a misdemeanor"); Mo. Ann. Stat. § 337.636 (privilege does not apply to information pertaining to a criminal act); Pa. Stat. Ann. §5929 (physician-patient privilege applicable only to civil matters); Blunt v. State, 724 S.W.2d 79 (Tex. Crim. App. 1987) (physician-patient privilege inapplicable in any criminal case where the patient is "a victim, witness or defendant"). See also People v. Dutton, 62 Cal. App. 2d 862, 145 P.2d 676 (1944); State v. Bounds, 74 Idaho 136, 258 P.2d 751 (1953); State v. Dean, 69 Utah 268, 254 Pac. 142 (1927).

    See, on the other hand, Conn. Gen. Stat. §52-146c (privilege applicable to civil, criminal, juvenile, probate, commitment, and arbitration proceedings); La. Code. Evid. Art. 510(c)(1)(1993) (privilege applicable in criminal proceedings); Md. Code. Ann. Cts. & Judic. Proc. §9-109(b) (psychotherapist-patient privilege applies in "all judicial legislative or administrative proceedings").
2.  D.C. Code Ann. § 14-307.
3.  See, *e.g.*, Ariz. Rev. Stat. Ann. §13-3993; D.C. Code Ann. §14-307; Free v. State, 455 So.2d 137 (Ala. Crim. App. 1984).
4.  Ill. Stat. Ann. ch. 740, § 110/10.
5.  Ind. Code Ann. §25-33-1-17; Wis. Stat. Ann. §905.04(4)(d).
6.  Neb. Rev. Stat. §27-504 (1984).
7.  State v. Schreiber, 122 N.J. 579, 585 A.2d 945 (1991).
8.  See, *e.g.*, Alaska R. Evid. 504(d)(2); La. Code Evid. Art. 510. In United States v. Witt, 542 F. Supp. 696 (S.D. N.Y.), *aff'd*, 697 F.2d 301 (2d Cir. 1982), a doctor working at a "stress center" claimed to be a psychotherapist and raised the psychotherapist-patient privilege in response to a subpoena duces tecum. The Court assumed that the privilege might be applicable (under federal law), but found that where a grand jury had found probable cause to believe that the center was used as part of a conspiracy to evade taxes and distribute controlled substances, the privilege would not be recognized. In *In re* Grand Jury Subpoena (Psychological Treatment Records), 710 F. Supp. 999 (D. N.J. 1989), the district judge concluded that a strong policy supported a psychotherapist-patient privilege (in federal law), but that "[i]n a situation where the psychotherapist-patient relationship itself is potentially criminal in nature, this Court believes that the privilege must give way to the federal government's interest in probing the true nature of the relationship." The patient's billing and treatment records were requested in a federal grand jury investigation of the patient's alleged fraudulent insurance claims for medical and psychological services.

9. D.C. Code Ann. 4-307(b)(4).

10. See, *e.g.*, Neb. Rev. Stat. § 27-504; Nev. Rev. Stat. § 49.254; R.I. Gen. Laws §5-37.3-3,4.

11. See, *e.g.*, Alaska Stat. §08.86.200(3); Ill. Stat. Ann. ch. 740, § 110/10.

12. Under the Constitution, the defendant in a criminal case has the right to refrain from giving evidence or testifying against himself. In a criminal case, the State must prove guilt beyond a reasonable doubt, and in attempting to do so, it has no right to summon the accused as a witness. The accused, in effect, may be a bystander at his trial.

13. In McDonough v. Director of Patuxent Institution, 183 A.2d 368 (Md. 1962), the defendant, a delinquent, refused a psychological examination on the basis of the Fifth Amendment, but the court found no violation of his constitutional rights. The following question was put to the Committee on Ethics of the American Academy of Psychiatry and the Law: "A psychiatrist who was asked to evaluate a defendant found him sleeping and testified that the defendant could not be schizophrenic since schizophrenics do not sleep so soundly. Is that ethical?" *Answer*: "Since there is no evidence for such a statement, it would contradict AAPL's requirements for honesty and striving for objectivity and the APA requirement for competent medical service, and is therefore unethical. AAPL does not forbid testimony expressing minority points of view, but there needs to be some evidence for an opinion and unusual opinions need to be honestly labeled as such." R. Weinstock, "AAPL's Committee on Ethics–Additional Opinion," *Newsletter of Am. Acad. of Psychiatry & Law* 20(2):49 at 51, Aug. 1995.

14. "[T]here exists an inherent right to order psychiatric examinations under appropriate circumstances [but] limits are placed upon the latitude of the examination as well as the resulting expert testimony in order to avoid clear violation of the right against self-incrimination. If the accused is ordered to submit to an interview conducted by court appointed psychiatrists, it is incumbent upon the court to insure that the resulting testimony be limited to the expression of an opinion of the accused's sanity. *Any inculpatory statements made by the defendant during the interview are not competent as admissions on the issue of his guilt* (emphasis by court). However, in the course of the psychiatric examination, questions relating to the commission of the crime are not improper, if in the opinion of the expert such questions and the related answers are necessary in the formulation of an opinion regarding the accused's mental condition....[N]o statement made by an accused in the course of a court ordered examination shall be admitted in evidence on the issue of guilt at the accused's trial. We hold that the trial court committed reversible error in allowing [the examiner] to testify that defendant admitted the crime in question." People v. Stevens, 386 Mich. 579, 194 N.W.2d 370 (1972).

15. F. Bruni, "Belatedly, the Riddle of an Attack on Rather is Solved," *New York Times*, Jan. 30, 1997, p. 16; "So Dan wasn't batty after all...," *Detroit Free Press*, Jan. 30, 1997, p. D-16.

16. It may be surmised, however, that as a result of the disclosure of the attack on Dan Rather, William Tager will serve closer to the maximum of the 12-to-25 year sentence imposed on him for the killing of the NBC technician. The issue is discussed further in the next section on the plea of insanity.

17. United States v. Byers, 740 F.2d 1104 (D.C. 1984).

18. Symposium, "Law and Psychiatry/The Constitutional Contours of the Forensic Evaluation," *Emory L.J.* 31:71, 1982.

19. However, in one case, a conviction was upheld where a drug administered to an addict in custody, to alleviate narcotic addiction withdrawal pains, rendered the arrested person talkative enough for production of a confession. G. Mueller, "The Law Relating to Police Interrogation: Privileges and Limitations," in C. Sowle (ed.), *Police Power and Individual Freedom*, 1962, p. 131; C.E. Sheedy, Narcointerrogation of a Criminal Suspect," *J. Crim. L., C.&P.S.* 50:118, 1958.

20. In Leyra v. Denno, 347 U.S. 556 (1954), the defendant, after being questioned by the state police for the greater part of four days, concerning the murder of his aged parents, complained of an acutely painful attack of sinusitis. The police promised to get a doctor. They got a psychiatrist with a considerable knowledge of hypnosis. Instead of administering medical aid, the psychiatrist, working in a room which was wired, "by subtle and suggestive questions simply continued the police effort" to get the accused to admit guilt. The procedure was tantamount to a form of mental coercion. The United States Supreme Court threw out the evidence.

In Oaks v. People, 371 P.2d 443 (Colo. 1962), it was held that a psychiatrist could not testify to what he had been told about the defendant, whom he examined for the state (before charges had been brought) on the basis that under the guise of a psychiatric examination, the psychiatrist had obtained information on guilt.

The police deception in these cases exploited the trust inherent in the physician-patient relationship and it is to be distinguished from the police use of jail plants and other informants to gain information from defendants. The Constitution does not forbid "strategic deception by taking advantage of a suspect's misplaced trust in one he supposes to be a fellow prisoner," said the Supreme Court in Illinois v. Perkins, 496 U.S. 292 (1990).

21. 63 F.3d 671 (7th Cir. 1995).

22. 646 N.Y.S.2d 955 (N.Y. Sup. Ct. 1996).

23. In Estelle v. Smith, 451 U.S. 454 (1981), where testimony by a psychiatrist who conducted a court-ordered pretrial competency examination was admitted at the penalty phase of a capital murder trial and was held to violate the defendant's privilege against self-incrimination, Justice William Rehnquist, concurring in the opinion, wrote, "Even if there are Fifth Amendment rights involved in this case, respondent never invoked these rights when confronted with Dr. Grigson's questions. The Fifth Amendment privilege against compulsory self-incrimination is not self-executing. 'Although Miranda's requirement of specific warnings creates a limited

exception to the rule that the privilege must be claimed, the exception does not apply outside the context of the inherently coercive custodial interrogations for which it was designed.' [citation] The *Miranda* requirements were certainly not designed by this Court with psychiatric examinations in mind. Respondent was simply not in the inherently coercive situation considered in *Miranda.* He had already been indicted, and counsel had been appointed to represent him. No claim is raised that respondent's answers to Dr. Grigson's questions were 'involuntary' in the normal sense of the word. Unlike the police officers in *Miranda*, Dr. Grigson was not questioning respondent in order to ascertain his guilt or innocence. Particularly since it is not necessary to decide this case, I would not extend the *Miranda* requirements to cover psychiatric examinations such as the one involved here." 451 U.S. at 475-6.

The Michigan Mental Health Code (applicable to the public sector and agencies or clinics under contract with the state to provide services), however, calls for notice in the case of civil commitment or guardianship. MCL 330.1750(b). Psychiatrists are taken aback by these provisions, written by civil libertarian lawyers. Can it be expected that psychiatrists or other therapists will discuss these matters at the outset of therapy? See Part II, Chapter 7 on proceedings to hospitalize.

24. See K.E. Meister, "*Miranda* on the Couch: An Approach to Problems of Self-Incrimination, Right to Counsel, and *Miranda* Warnings in Pre-Trial Psychiatric Examinations of Criminal Defendants," *Colum. J. of Law & Social Problems* 11:403, 1975.

25. The Michigan Supreme Court has said: "Counsel for defendant need not be permitted to be present [at the examination of defendant] if, in the opinion of the psychiatrist counsel's presence would tend to thwart or interfere with the examination. This is not to say that in a particular case the judge may not order that counsel for a defendant be present or require that a recording be made of any interviews with a psychiatrist. These are matters better left to the sound discretion of the trial judge. Basically, it is assumed that, in the search for truth, a psychiatrist should be able to pursue his methodology unfettered and that the traditional methods of cross-examination will enable the judge or jury critically to scrutinize all results obtained." People v. Martin, 386 Mich. 407, 192 N.W.2d 215 (1971); see R.I. Simon, "'Three's a crowd': the presence of third parties during the forensic psychiatric examination," *J. Psychiatry & Law* 24:3, 1996.

26. "It would appear proper," says one commentator, "for the attorney for the defendant to request the court to instruct the psychiatrist before he makes his examination that he will not be called upon to reveal admissions of the defendant, on the issue of guilt, without the consent of the defendant. If such a ruling is not granted, the psychiatrist should carefully avoid permitting the defendant to make admissions to him regarding the crime with which he is charged." H. Hassard, "Privileged Communications," *California Med.* 90:411, 1959. The right to such an instruction is apparently implicit in the defendant's right against self-incrimination.

27. Annual meeting, American Academy of Psychiatry & Law, Oct. 19, 1995, in Seattle.

28. D.W. Shuman, "The Use of Empathy in Forensic Examinations," *Ethics & Behavior* 3:289, 1993.

29. Fed. R. Crim. P. 12.2(c) provides in pertinent part that "[i]n an appropriate case the court may, upon motion of the attorney for the government, order the defendant to submit to an examination pursuant to 18 U.S.C. 4241 or 4242." Sections 4241 or 4242 pertain to the court's authority to require a defendant to submit to an examination to determine mental competency to stand trial or insanity at the time of the offense. While the interplay between Rule 12.2(c) and these sections is not clear upon a literal reading of them, some courts have held Rule 12.2(c) applies to cases in which a defendant intends to rely on a mental incapacity defense other than insanity, such as diminished capacity. See United States v. Banks, 137 F.R.D. 20 (C.D.Ill. 1991); United States v. Vega-Penarete, 137 F.R.D. 233 (E.D. N.C. 1991); People v. Al-Kanani, 33 N.Y.2d 260, 351 N.Y.S. 969, 307 N.E.2d 43, *cert. denied,* 417 U.S. 916 (1973); Lee v. County Court of Erie County, 27 N.Y.2d 432 (1969), *cert. denied,* 404 U.S. 823 (1971).

30. United State v. Byers, 740 F.2d 1104, 1109-15 (D.C. Cir. 1984).

31. United States v. Hinckley, 525 F. Supp. 1342 (D.C. 1981); see also Collins v. Augur, 577 F.2d 1107 (8th Cir. 1978); Magwood v. State, 426 So.2d 918 (Ala. Crim. App.), *aff'd,* 426 So.2d 929 (Ala. 1982), *cert. denied,* 426 U.S. 1124 (1983); Lukaszewicz v. Ortho Pharmaceutical Corp., 90 FRD 708 (E.D. Wis. 1981); see M.E. Phelan, "The Pitfalls of Presenting a Diminished Capacity Defense," *Criminal Justice* 5:8, 1990.

32. People v. Plummer, 37 Mich. App. 657, 195 N.W.2d 328 (1972).

33. J. Wigmore, *Evidence* (Boston: Little, Brown, 1940), vol. 2, §228. "Where insanity is relied upon as a defense to a criminal act, the whole previous career of the accused may be relevant to his mental condition at the time of the alleged offense." E.L. Fisch, *New York Evidence* (New York: Lond, 1959), p. 133. The insanity defense, opening the door to the history of the defendant, shifts the focus of attention from the act to the actor, and is criticized as a perversion of justice. W. Gaylin, *The Killing of Bonnie Garland/A Question of Justice* (New York: Empire Books, 1980); reviewed by H.H.A. Copper, *J. Psychiatry & Law* 10:373, 1982.

34. Thus, in United States v. Madred, 673 F.2d 1114 (10th Cir. 1982), where the defense of insanity was urged, the state's psychiatrist was allowed to testify that the defendant was sane, an opinion based, in part, on the fact that the accused "had committed armed robberies of stores prior to the offense in question in order to support a heroin addiction." *See also* People v. Woody, 380 Mich. 332, 157 N.W.2d 201 (1968).

35. See R. Slovenko, *Psychiatry and Criminal Culpability* (New York: Wiley, 1995). For a contrary opinion, see P.S. Appelbaum, Book Review, *Am. J. Psychiat.* 153:284, 1996.

36. Thus, admissions to the crime cannot be considered in determining whether the defendant committed the acts constituting the crime charged. Lee v.

County Court of Erie County, 27 N.Y.2d 432, 267 N.E.2d 452 (1969), *cert. denied,* 404 U.S. 823 (1971). It is to be noted that what is not achieved directly is often achieved indirectly. As no opinion is value-free, a confession to the psychiatrist by a person charged with, say, public drunkenness, that he recently cut a person's throat will color the psychiatrist's report on competency to stand trial or on criminal responsibility.

37.  Noggle v. Marshall, 706 F.2d 1408 (6th Cir.), *cert. denied,* 104 S. Ct. 530 (1983).

38.  See American Law Institute, Model Penal Code; W.T. Fryer (ed.), *Selected Writings on the Law of Evidence and Trial* (St. Paul: West, 1957), p. 259.

39.  Fed. R. Crim. P. 12.2.

40.  Massachusetts provides: "In the trial of an indictment or complaint for any crime, no statement made by a defendant therein subjected to psychiatric examination . . . shall be admissible in evidence against him on any issue other than that of his mental condition, nor shall it be admissible in evidence against him on that issue if such statement constitutes a confession of guilt of the crime charged." Chap. 233, Sec. 23B.

In State v. Mulrine, 183 A.2d 831 (Del. 1962), the defendant, indicted for murder, resisted the state's motion for an order that he submit to a mental examination by the State psychiatrist, maintaining that such an examination, if required by court order, would be in violation of his constitutional rights. The Delaware court noted that although the Delaware statutes and decisions impose no requirement that an accused submit to a mental examination, at common law the court could in its discretion inquire into the mental state of an accused and could call upon professional assistance. The Court said: "Defendant's constitutional rights may be protected by limiting the scope of the examination and the use to be made of the findings.... An examination by the state psychiatrist will be permitted in order to assist the Court and jury to pass upon any defense of mental illness that may be raised but not to assist the state in the prosecution of the case-in-chief." To the same effect, see Mich. Complied Laws §767.27a4; People v. Martin, 386 Mich. 407, 192 N.W.2d 215 (1972); People v. Garland, 44 Mich. App. 243, 205 N.W.2d 195 (1972); see also State v. Fontana, 152 N.W.2d 503 (Minn. 1967).

41.  451 U.S. 454 (1981).

42.  City and County of San Francisco v. Superior Court, 37 Cal.2d 227, 231 P.2d 26 (1951); noted in Part I, Chapter 2. Courts disagree, however, whether a defendant who offers psychiatric testimony waives the attorney psychotherapist-client privilege as to all examiners who have evaluated the defendant, or only to the examiner actually called by the defendant to testify. See Noggle v. Marshall, 706 F.2d 1408 (6th Cir.), *cert. denied,* 104 S. Ct. 530 (1983); United States v. Talley, 790 F.2d 1468 (9th Cir. 1986); noted in Part I, Chapter 2.

43.  See, *e.g.,* State v. Miller, 300 Or. 203, 709 P.2d 225 (1985); State v. Andring, 342 N.W.2d 128 (Minn. 1984). In State of Wisconsin v. Locke, 502 N.W.2d 891 (Wis. App. 1993), involving a defendant charged with sexual assault of

minors, the court held that the trial court was in error in admitting the testimony of a therapist that the defendant admitted that he had an uncontrollable sex drive and a problem with pedophilia, and it reversed the conviction.

44. D. Dunne, "Nightmare on Elm Drive," *Vanity Fair*, Oct. 1990, p. 198; R. Reinhold, "Case of Two Brothers Accused of Killing Parents May Test Secrecy Limit in Patient-Therapist Tie," *New York Times*, Sept. 7, 1990, p. B 9; "Therapist's Audiotapes Will Play at Murder Trial," *Psychiatric Times*, Oct. 1992, p. 14.

45. Erik, the younger and weaker brother, confessed the crime to Dr. Oziel, the therapist. When Lyle found out what Erik had done, he became very angry and threatened Dr. Oziel. Dr. Oziel told the story to his girlfriend, Judalon Smyth, to protect himself. She directed the police to look at gun purchase records in San Diego, which resulted in the arrest of the Menendez brothers. She feared the Menendez brothers. In a book about the case, Hazel Thornton, one of the jurors, describes the therapist as "unprofessional," a "slime ball," a liar, and as "Dr. Weasel." H. Thornton, *Hung Jury/The Diary of a Menendez Juror* (Philadelphia: Temple University Press, 1995). About the case see also D.J. DeBenedictis, "Privileged Confession?" *ABAJ*, Dec. 1990, p. 37; D. Dunne, "Menendez Justice," *Vanity Fair*, March 1994, p. 108; N. Giffs, "The Hottest Show in Town," *Time*, Oct. 1, 1990, p. 46.

46. The "dangerous patient" exception in the California Evidence Code, section 1024, provides: "There is no privilege...if the psychotherapist has reasonable cause to believe that the patient is in such mental or emotional condition as to be dangerous to himself or to the person or property of another and that disclosure of the communication is necessary to prevent the threatened danger." In People v. Wharton, 53 Cal.3d 522, 280 Cal. Rptr. 631, 809 P.2d 290 (1991), the California Supreme Court said that once the "dangerous patient" exception applies, the prosecutor can compel the therapist to testify concerning (1) the substance of the warning given to the victim, and (2) the defendant's statements given in therapy that "triggered" the warning.

47. Menendez v. Superior Court, 3 Cal.4th 435, 11 Cal. Rptr.2d 92, 834 P.2d 786 (1992). See G.B. Leong, S. Eth & J.A. Silva, "The Psychotherapist as Witness for the Prosecution: The Criminalization of *Tarasoff*," *Am. J. Psychiat.* 149:1011, 1992.

48. In People v. Clark, 50 Cal 3d. 583, 268 Cal. Rptr. 399, 789 P.2d 127 (1990), the California Supreme Court held that therapy records lose their privilege by virtue of the *Tarasoff* disclosure duty. See J. Baumoel, "The Beginning of the End for the Psychotherapist-Patient Privilege," *U. Cin. L. Rev.* 60:797, 1992.

49. J. Willwerth, "Waiting for the Verdicts," *Newsweek*, Dec. 20, 1993, p. 48.

50. K. Seelye, "Packwood Gives Up, Agreeing to Deliver Diary to Committee," *New York Times*, March 15, 1994, p. 21.

51. U.S. Const. amend. V, cl. 3.

52. 116 U.S. 616 (1886).

53. 425 U.S. 391 (1976).

54. See D.E. Will, "'Dear Diary–Can You Be Used Against Me?': The Fifth Amendment and Diaries," *Bost. College L. Rev.* 35:965, 1994.

55. In a symposium in the Loyola of Los Angeles Law Review, a hypothetical is discussed about disclosing a patient's confession to a capital offense for which someone else is to be put to death. In an interview, one therapist said, "There are probably a couple of psychoanalysts on the Upper East Side of New York City who'd say they wouldn't divulge this information, but those guys would never treat a street criminal in the first place." That aside, the psychiatrist must ponder: Is the patient delusional, fantasizing, or deliberately lying? Therapists or others can tell when an individual is angry by the tone of his voice, his gestures, *et cetera*, but it is more difficult to know when a person is feeling guilty of whatever. The authors in the symposium argue that by analogy to *Tarasoff* (hereinafter discussed), a public peril exists in that an individual would be executed for a crime he did not commit and therefore the therapist should take whatever steps necessary to protect the condemned man from being executed. *Tarasoff* focused on harm that would be caused directly by a patient's violent actions, but the principle of the decision is that confidentiality must yield in situations of peril. But no court would stop an execution based on this evidence or admit it as evidence at trial. Under the hearsay exception for statements against interest, it is provided, "A statement tending to expose the declarant to criminal liability and offered to exculpate the accused is not admissible unless corroborating circumstances clearly indicate the trustworthiness of the statement," Rule 804 (3), Federal Rules of Evidence. See Symposium, "Executing the Wrong Person: The Professionals' Ethical Dilemmas," *Loyola of Los Angeles L. Rev.* 29:1543-1798, 1996.

56. See M.L. Commons, P. Lee, T.G. Gutheil, E. Rubin, M. Goldman & P.S. Appelbaum, "Moral State of Reasoning and the Misperceived 'Duty' to Report Past Crimes (Misprision)," *Int'l J. of Law & Psychiatry* 18:415, 1995.

57. See the discussion in Part IV, Chapter 2.

58. The privilege against self-incrimination of crime is available to the physician as well as to the patient.

59. "I don't want to hear anything about it. There's no confidentiality between us with that kind of information," says the lawyer to the client in T. Alibrandi & F.H. Armani, *Privileged Information* (New York: Harper, 1984), a true story of an attorney who risked protecting his client's secrets. See United States v. Crews, 781 F.2d 826 (10th Cir. 1986) (no privilege where the patient told a nurse that he was going to kill the president).

60. Heterosexual activity may be a sign of health where a person has been treated for inhibition, frigidity or homosexuality and is beginning to free himself of these deterrents to heterosexual activity. R. Slovenko (ed.), *Sexual Behavior and the Law* (Springfield, Ill.: Thomas, 1965).

61. K. Eissler, "Some Problems of Delinquency," in K. Eissler (ed.), *Searchlights on Delinquency* (New York: International Universities Press, 1949), p. 3.

62. J. Goldstein & J. Katz, "Psychiatrist-Patient Privilege: The GAP Proposal and The Connecticut Statute," *Am. J. Psychiat.* 118:733, 1962.

63. V. Sidel, "Confidential Information and The Physician" *New England J. of Med.* 264:1133, 1961.

64. J. Hall & K.A. Menninger, "'Psychiatry and the Law'–A Dual Review," *Iowa L. Rev.* 38:687, 703, 1953.

65. C.B. Mueller & L.C. Kirkpatrick, *Evidence* (Boston: Little, Brown, 1995), p. 496.

66. See United States v. Zolin, 491 U.S. 554 (1989).

67. The victim's husband, Dr. Robert Iverson, director of critical care at Detroit's Hutzel Hospital, signed a waiver for the law-enforcement officials to see his file. He was not a suspect but again it was thought that the file might provide a clue to the killing. He was treated together with his wife, then she alone, by Dr. Finkelstein. J. DeHaven, "Police seek clues to Bloomfield Hills doctor's death," *Detroit News,* May 20, 1996, p. C-3; "Murder pits press, police in love-hate relationship," *Detroit News,* May 26, 1996, p. 1; "Cops seize Iverson's files along with wife's" *Detroit News,* June 5, 1996, p. C-1. In a way, the situation resembles that of the exception to privilege for "any proceeding [involving a patient's death] in which any party relies upon the condition as an element of his claim or defense." Proposed Rule 504(d)(3), Federal Rules of Evidence.

68. Conference of Alliance for Mental Health Services, "Ethical Dilemmas in Mental Health Practice," Detroit, Oct. 4, 1996.

69. A search warrant must be able to withstand the command of the Fourth Amendment, which states: "The right of the people to be secure in their persons, houses, papers, and effects, against unreasonable searches and seizure, shall not be violated, and no warrants shall issue, but upon probable cause, supported by oath or affirmation, and particularly describing the place to be searched and the persons or things to be seized." Hence, before a search begins, a warrant must be issued by a neutral and detached magistrate, finding probable cause, and specifically describing what is to be seized and from where. U.S. Const. amend. IV; Horton v. California, 496 U.S. 128 (1990) (warrantless searches are presumptively unreasonable). In Linch v. Thomas Davis Medical Centers, 925 P.2d 686 (Ariz. App. 1996), where patient records were seized in response to a search warrant served on a medical center in a criminal investigation of a patient, the Arizona Court of Appeals stated, "In the face of a search warrant, an individual has no choice but to comply with the warrant, even if it is later found to be illegal....By definition, a search warrant is a court order....This is true, despite the privileged nature of the property to be seized. Because of the immediacy of a search warrant, the party being served has no choice but to comply with the warrant at the time of service, there being no mechanism to contest the seizure before compliance."

Some jurisdictions have enacted legislation protecting offices of lawyers and others from a search. The California Legislature in 1979 amended its

Penal code to prohibit a magistrate from issuing a warrant to search for documentary evidence in the possession of an attorney, physician, psychotherapist, or clergyman not reasonably suspected of criminal conduct unless special protective procedures are employed, such as appointing a special master to conduct the search, permitting the subject of the search to be present and to tender the evidence voluntarily, ensuring that purportedly privileged material will be placed under seal for transmission to the court for *in camera* review, and requiring that an expedited adversary hearing will be available following the search. L.H. Bloom, "The Law Office Search: An Emerging Problem and Some Suggested Solutions," *Georgetown L.J.* 69:1, 1980; M.G. Weinberg & K. Homan, "Challenging the Law Office Search," *Champion*, Aug. 1996, p. 10.

70. There is an exception to the hearsay rule for statements made for purposes of medical diagnosis or treatment that are "reasonably pertinent" to diagnosis or treatment. Rule 803(4), Federal Rules of Evidence. The identity of an abuser has been held to be reasonably pertinent to proper diagnosis and treatment. See, *e.g.*, United States v. Renville, 779 F.2d. 430 (8th Cir. 1985); People v. Meeboer, 484 N.W.2d 621 (Mich. 1992); State v. Robinson, 153 Ariz. 191, 735 P.2d 801 (1997).

71. J. Martin, "Slain doctor talked of conflicts," *Detroit Free Press*, June 20, 1996, p. B-1.

72. "With Charges, Shock at Act Said to Have Been Random," *New York Times*, Jan. 2, 1997, p. 8.

73. Shepard v. United States, 290 U.S. 96 (1933). Statements of an accused to a therapist, on the other hand, are admissible as admissions.

74. In State of Pennsylvania v. Ritchie, 480 U.S. 39 (1987), the U.S. Supreme Court held that a defendant accused of child abuse has a right to have the trial judge review, *in camera*, the confidential files of the state agency regarding their investigation of the child abuse allegations. See also Davis v. Alaska, 415 U.S. 308 (1974); Chambers v. Mississippi, 410 U.S. 284 (1973); Smith v. Illinois, 390 U.S. 129 (1968).

75. In a California prosecution charging Kevin Keables with sexual battery, the defense attorney served a subpoena duces tecum for the mental health records of the prosecuting witness, Susan Shartzer, from The Harbour mental health treatment facility. Harbour mistakenly sent the records to the defense attorney rather than to the court for an *in camera* review. The defense attorney read the records, transmitted them to the defense psychiatrist and used them in cross-examining Shartzer. In a subsequent tort action, Shartzer sued the defense attorney for invasion of privacy. Allowing the lawsuit, the California Court of Appeal analogized the opening and reading of the medical records to eavesdropping on a private telephone conversation. Shartzer v. Israels, 51 Cal. App.4th 641, 59 Cal. Rptr.2d 296 (1996).

76. 698 F.2d 1154 (11th Cir. 1983).

77. 6 Cal.4th 494, 24 Cal. Rptr.2d 779, 862 P.2d 779 (1993).

78. The case is discussed in G.B. Leong, J.A. Silva & R. Weinstock, "Another Courtroom Assault on the Confidentiality of the Psychotherapist-Patient Relationship," *J. For. Sci.* 40:862, 1995. See also United States v. Hansen, 955 F. Supp. 1225 (D. Mont. 1997).

79. A number of states have enacted legislation to specifically cover communications made to a sexual or domestic assault counselor. Michigan's legislation, for example, provides that the communications "shall not be admissible as evidence in any civil or criminal proceeding without the prior written consent of the victim." MCL 600.2157. But an absolute privilege cannot be sustained. See, *e.g.*, State v. Davis, 546 N.W.2d 30 (Minn. App. 1996); State v. Crims, 540 N.W.2d 860, 865-66 (Minn. App. 1995) (noting a constitutional defendant's right to present evidence that is material and favorable to the theory of defense); *see also* Sandoval v. Acevedo, 996 F.2d 145, 149-50 (7th Cir.) (recognizing the constitutional right of a rape defendant to introduce vital evidence favorable to his defense), *cert. denied,* 114 S. Ct. 307 (1993); *accord,* Wood v. Alaska, 957 F.2d 1544 (9th Cir.1992); United States v. Saunders, 736 F.Supp. 698 (E.D.Va. 1990), *aff'd,* 943 F.2d 388 (4th Cir. 1991), *cert. denied,* 502 U.S. 1105 (1992); Government of Virgin Islands v. Jacobs, 634 F.Supp. 933 (D.Vi.1986); Matter of Pittsburgh Action Against Rape, 428 A.2d 126 (Pa. 1981); State v. Vaughn, 448 So.2d 1260 (La. 1983); State v. Patnaude, 140 Vt. 361, 438 A.2d 402 (1981); State v. Hudlow, 99 Wash.2d 1, 659 P.2d 514 (1983); M.B. Hogan, "The Constitutionality of an Absolute Privilege for Rape Crisis Counseling: A Criminal Defendant's Sixth Amendment Rights Versus a Rape Victim's Right to Confidential Therapeutic Counseling," *Bost. College L. Rev.* 30:411, 1989; A. Meisel, "Confidentiality and Rape Counseling," *Hastings Center Report* 11:5, 1981; C.J. Scarmeas, "Rape Victim-Rape Crisis Counselor Communications: A New Testimonial Privilege," *Dick. L. Rev.* 86:539, 1982.

80. J.R. Evrard, "Rape: The Medical, Social, and Legal Complications." *Am. J. Obstet. Gynecol* 111:197, 1971; A. Meisel, "Confidentiality and rape counseling," *Hastings Center Report,* 11:5, 1981.

81. In Dershowitz's novel (New York: Warner Books, 1994) a basketball star, Joe Campbell, is accused of rape by Jennifer Dowling. Here is a bit of the dialogue (Abe Ringel is the defense attorney and Cheryl Puccio is the prosecutor):

   "Your Honor," Abe rebutted, "what if she admitted to the psychologist that she had made up the entire story of the alleged sexual harassment episode in order to cover up her own inadequacies at work?"

   "Do you have any evidence of that, Mr. Ringel?" Judge Gambi shot back.

   "No. That's why I want to *question* her about it– to develop evidence."

   "It's a goddamned fishing expedition," Puccio objected. "He's just fishing for dirt. He's got no basis."

   "Do you have any basis, Mr. Ringel?"

   "Yes, I do. My client tells me that Ms. Dowling told him that she had gone to a psychologist after an unpleasant episode several months earlier. It is fair to infer that she was referring to the events that led up to her firing."

82. Quoted in E.J. Pollock, "Mother Fights to Keep Daughter's Records in Rape Case Secret," *Wall Street Journal,* Aug. 22, 1996, p. 1.
83. See United States v. Nixon, 418 U.S. 683 (1974); Donner v. Edelstein, 415 So.2d 830 (Fla. App. 1982).
84. West Virginia v. Roy, 460 S.E.2d 277 (W. Va. 1995).
85. State v. Solberg, 553 N.W.2d 842 (Wis. App. 1996).
86. In State v. Cisneros, 535 N.W.2d 703 (Neb. 1995), the defendant, charged with tampering with a witness, sought the alleged victim's confidential juvenile medical records gathered during juvenile court proceedings. For impeachment purposes, the defendant requested the results and reports of physical or mental examinations made within the prior last three years. The defendant did not state why the discovery was essential to his defense. The court held that the motion lacked specific facts to create any reasonable grounds to believe that the failure to produce the information would impair his right to confront the alleged victim.

 In People v. Stanaway, 521 N.W.2d 557 at 562 (Mich. 1994), a case involving a sexual assault counselor, the Michigan Supreme Court set out the following test for disclosing information to the defense:

> We hold that where a defendant can establish a reasonable probability that the privileged records are likely to contain material information necessary to his defense, an *in camera* review of those records must be conducted to ascertain whether they contain evidence that is reasonably necessary, and therefore essential, to the defense. Only when the trial court finds such evidence, should it be provided to the defendant.

The court accorded a great deal of discretion to the judge conducting the *in camera* hearing, holding that the information will be disclosed to the defense only if the records reveal information material and necessary to the defense. The court said, "We are confident that trial judges will be able to recognize such evidence. The presence of defense counsel at such an inspection is not essential to protect the defendant's constitutional rights and would undermine the privilege unnecessarily." 521 N.W.2d at 575 and n. 40.

 Following its decision in *Stanaway,* the Michigan Supreme Court set out a court rule requiring trial judges to privately inspect privilege-protected records when the defense shows "a good-faith belief" based on "articulable fact" that there is a "reasonable probability" the records are likely to contain information the defendant needs. The rule closely follows the court's decision in *Stanaway.* C. Parks, "Rule proposed on access to counseling records," *Detroit Legal News,* Nov. 30, 1995, p. 1.

 In State of Wisconsin v. Shiffra, 175 Wis.2d 600, 499 N.W.2d 719 (Wis. App. 1993), the defendant encountered the complaining witness, Pamela P., at a bar. After having a drink, the two went to the defendant's apartment where, she alleged, he sexually assaulted her. The defendant claimed that the sexual contact was consensual. Shortly before trial, the state revealed that the complaining witness had a history of psychiatric problems. The defendant then sought an order requiring Pamela "to reveal to the defendant her psychiatric history, psychiatric records and to execute an authorization from any doctors, hospitals or counselors seen by Pamela [P.] with respect to her mental condition." The state maintained that such records were absolutely privileged and that the defendant was just on a "fishing expedition." The trial court found that defendant had made an adequate showing that Pamela's psychiatric condition might affect her ability to accurately perceive events and ordered the records to be produced for *in camera* judicial review. When Pamela refused to waive her privilege, the district court issued an order barring her from testifying. The Wisconsin Court of Appeals recognized that suppressing testimony from a complaining witness who refuses to obey appropriate discovery orders is an appropriate sanction.

In another Wisconsin case, State of Wisconsin v. Munoz, 546 N.W.2d 570 (Wis. App. 1996), Samuel Munoz was convicted of sexually assaulting R.S. after R.S. decided to end their relationship. The jury based its verdict on the credibility of Munoz and R.S. On appeal, Munoz argued that he was entitled to an *in camera* inspection of R.S.'s mental health records because R.S. had received psychiatric counseling for prior, unrelated sexual assaults. In *Shiffra*, the earlier case, the defendant asserted the sexual contact was consensual and presented proof that the victim had post-traumatic stress disorder stemming from repeated sexual attacks by her step-father and might have flashbacks to the assaults, which might cause her to view consensual sex as nonconsensual. In this case, however, the court said, Munoz did not allege that R.S. had a psychological condition that would impact her ability to accurately relate events. The *Shiffra* standard, the court reiterated, requires a defendant to show more than a mere possibility that the privileged records may be helpful to the defense. The fact that R.S. received psychiatric counseling for prior sexual assaults, without more, was not relevant and could not counter the confidentiality granted under Wis. Stat. §905.04(2). Munoz did not allege that R.S. had not been sexually assaulted in the past, or that her experiences or counseling compromised her credibility.

In yet another Wisconsin case, State v. Behnke, 553 N.W.2d 265 (Wis. App. 1996), the trial court reasoned that even if the medical history of the complainant confirmed self-abuse, as the defense contended, the evidence would not be material to the charges that the defendant hit the complainant in the eye, face and chest because those kinds of wounds could not be self-inflicted. A medical history describing the complainant cutting or bruising herself on the arm would not be relevant to the physical evidence alleged to exist in this case—namely, a black eye and bruises on the chest.

In a New York case, People v. Pena, 127 Misc.2d 1057 (N.Y. Sup. Ct. 1985), the judge denied access to statements made and records kept in a rape crisis center because the defendant made no specific showing that the records contained information bearing on "guilt or innocence, unreliability of witnesses or exculpatory material."

In Love v. Johnson, 57 F.3d 1305 (4th Cir. 1995), the Fourth Circuit U.S. Court of Appeals held that the defendant's due process rights were violated when the trial court quashed various subpoenas without having conducted any in chambers inspection. The defendant "at least made some plausible showing" that the records would be favorable to the defense.

A criminal defendant is entitled to cross-examine the state's prosecuting witness as to what information was communicated to the prosecution. That issue arose in State of New Mexico v. Gonzales, 912 P.2d 297 (New Mex. App. 1996), where the victim authorized her medical records to be released to the Albuquerque police department and gave prosecutors access to her psychologist's records. The state refused to release the records to the court arguing the records were privileged. The appeals court, affirming the trial court, found that the victim waived any right to privilege by authorizing her records to be released to the state. When medical or psychotherapy records are disclosed, though otherwise they may be protected by privilege, waiver occurs. In addition to the psychotherapist privilege, the state argued that the medical and mental health records regarding the victim's history or problems with alcohol were not relevant. Records previously released to the court showed that the victim had blackouts from alcohol and she had been drinking the evening she allegedly was assaulted. The court sought an *in camera* review of her medical and mental health records for evidence relevant to whether she had cognitive difficulties that would affect her credibility at trial. Because the state refused to release her records for the court to review, the court refused to permit the victim to testify. The court dismissed the charges when the state informed the court that it had no case without the victim's testimony. See R.M. Capoccia, "Piercing the Veil of Tears: The Admission of Rape Crisis Counselor Records in Acquaintance Rape Trials," *So. Calif. L. Rev.* 68:1335, 1995

87.  Farrell L. v. Superior Court, 203 Cal. App. 3d 521, 250 Cal. Rptr. 25 (1988); discussed in Part II, Chapter 9.

88.  The court said (203 Cal. App.3d at 528):

Denial of cross-examination concerning events which were part of the actual criminal transaction itself denies the defense a substantial right. By contrast, a trial judge or a magistrate conducting a preliminary hearing is within his discretion in denying cross-examination of a prosecution witness as to matters not relating to the criminal event itself and which only affect the weight of the direct testimony. In the instant case, the identification of persons in [the] group counseling could only have been relevant in a subsequent attempt to impeach her testimony. Thus the excluded evidence could only have been relevant, if at all, to the ultimate weight of the direct evidence. "Exclusion of cross-examination which 'only go[es] to the weight of the direct evidence' does not deny the defendant a fair hearing (citations)." Moreover, defense counsel failed to establish good cause justifying the discovery of the sought-after, privileged information. Indeed, counsel indicated he did not intend to pursue the questioning once he had the names of the persons she had spoken to regarding the alleged atrocities committed against her. Defense counsel represented to the court that he had "no idea" as to whether he would subpena any of the people whose identity might be revealed. Therefore, good cause was not shown for overriding the psychotherapist-patient privilege in the instant case.

89. In sentencing a trial judge is not required to consider results of psychological testing. In People v. Dulger, No. 180864 (unpublished opinion, Jan. 31, 1997), the Michigan Court of Appeals ruled that the trial judge did not err in failing to take into account test results that purportedly indicated a very low probablity of recidivism.

90. M. Guttmacher, *The Mind of the Murderer* (New York: Farrar, Straus, 1960), chap. 19.

91. Morgan v. State, 142 So.2d 308 (Fla. App. 1962).

92. Rule 1101(3), Federal Rules of Evidence.

93. R.C. Thomsen, "Confidentiality of the Presentence Report: A Middle Position," *Fed. Probation* 28:8, 1964. "The late Professor George Dession was greatly interested in this problem . . . Professor Dession agreed that it might frequently be quite destructive to the individual to have him read his psychiatric report. He believed, however, that the defendant's counsel should have access to the report to afford the opportunity to determine, as far as possible, the accuracy of the factual data on which the psychiatric opinion was based." M. Guttmacher, *op cit. supra*, at p. 172.

94. J.B. Parsons, "The Presentence Investigation Report Must Be Preserved as a Confidential Document," *Fed. Probation* 28:3, 1964.

95. Rule 32(c), Federal Rules of Criminal Procedure. The rule provides that a presentence report shall not be submitted to the court, or its contents disclosed to anyone else, unless the defendant has pleaded guilty or has been found guilty. The policy behind the rule is to avoid prejudice on the part of the court. Smith v. United States, 360 U.S. 1 (1959); United States v. Chrisos, 291 F.2d 535 (7th Cir. 1961). If the purpose of the report is not for sentencing but is to provide the court with information to assist it in passing upon the advisability of reducing bail, the report is permissible even though it contains certain "pre-sentence factors." E.N. Barkin, "Looking at the Law," *Fed. Probation* 28:61, 1964.

96. The above observation was made by Louis J. Sharp, Chief, Division of Probation, Administrative Office of the United States Courts, at the Sentencing Institute and Joint Council for the Fifth Circuit, May 1961. See 30 F.R.D. 185 (1962). Justice Black's opinion in Williams v. New York, 337 U.S. 241 (1948), seems to be authority for confidential treatment, although as noted there is controversy about the point. L.J. Sharp, "The Confidential Nature of Presentence Reports," *Catholic U. L. Rev.* 5:127, 1955.

97. Under New York's Criminal Procedure Law (§190.50), a defendant is given the right to be a witness "to present his side of the case to the grand jury" under certain circumstances, for example, "upon...signing...a waiver of

immunity...such person must be permitted to testify before the grand jury and to give any relevant and competent evidence concerning the case under consideration. Upon giving such evidence, he is subject to examination by the people."

98. 18 U.S.C. §§ 3551-3586.

99. U.S. Sentencing Comm'n, Federal Sentencing Guidelines Manual § 6A1.3(a)(1992); see E.R. Becker & A. Orenstein, "The Federal Rules of Evidence After Sixteen Years–The Effect of 'Plain Meaning' Jurisprudence, the Need for an Advisory Committee on the Rules of Evidence, and Suggestions for Selective Revision of the Rules," *Geo. Wash. L. Rev.* 60:857, 1992; S.J. Schulhofer, "Due Process of Sentencing," *U. Pa. L. Rev.* 128:733, 1980.

100. Rule 1101(d)(3), Federal Rules of Evidence and counterpart in various state rules of evidence.

101. A. MacCormick, "A Criminologist Looks at Privilege," *Am. J. Psychiat.* 115:1079, 1959.

102. Dr. Jonas Rappeport, one of the founders of the American Academy of Psychiatry and the Law and chief medical officer for many years for the circuit court for Baltimore, had this to say about prison psychiatry:

> Difficult problems arise when psychiatrists work in prisons, particularly if they lack a clear contractual relationship with the institution, and do not make their position clear to the patient (inmate). It might be tempting for such psychiatrists to align themselves with the administration, and to feel out possible riots, smuggling of contraband, or other illegal acts. Perverting the role of therapist in this manner is certainly improper. On the other hand, some psychiatrists tend to identify with the prisoner, align themselves not with, but against, the administration, and offer inmates a level of confidentiality which they cannot guarantee. In one such situation the warden, following a murder within his institution, attempted to obtain the psychiatrist's records so that he could get more information about the suspect. The psychiatrist believed, incorrectly, that he had a confidential relationship with the inmate, and that the records were in his control. However, no psychiatrist employed in that institution had ever established such a contract with the warden, and the psychiatrist's records were turned over. Was the doctor irresponsible in not gaining a prior clarification of this issue, and in believing that he could walk into a public institution and set his own ground rules? For instance, what should one do when an inmate in individual therapy reveals that he is currently involved in an escape plan? Is it ethical to report this to the prison authorities? The answer might depend on the psychiatrist's contract with the patient and with the administration. At the very least, it would be a difficult problem, particularly if the incipient escape or riot plan could cause injury to others.

J. Rappeport, "Ethics and forensic psychiatry," in S. Bloch & P. Chodoff (eds.), *Psychiatric Ethics* (New York: Oxford University Press, 2d ed. 1991), chap. 18.

103. N. Fenton, "Group Counseling: A Method for the Treatment of Prisoners and for a New Staff Orientation in the Correctional Institution," in R. Slovenko (ed.), *Crime, Law and Corrections* (Springfield, Ill.: Thomas, 1966).

104. S.N. Mehta, "Treating Sex Offenders Becomes an Industry, But Does It Work?" *Wall Street Journal*, May 24, 1996, p. 1; see, in general, B.K. Schwartz & H.R. Cellini (eds.), *The Sex Offender/Corrections, Treatment and Legal Practice* (Kingston, N.J.: Civic Research Institute, 1996).

105. State of Montana v. Imlay, 249 Mont. 82, 813 P.2d 979 (1991).

106. Montana v. Imlay, 113 S. Ct. 444 (1992). The Michigan Court of Appeals ruled that a rapist who maintains his innocence can be denied admission to a group therapy program required in order to obtain parole. Spikes v. Michigan Parole Board, No. 189740 (Jan. 21, 1997, unpublished opinion). In State ex rel. Warren v. Schwarz, 566 N.W.2d 173 (Wis. App. 1997), the Wisconsin Court of Appeals upheld a revocation of probation because of the offender's failure to carry out a sexual offender treatment program required as a condition of probation in that he failed to acknowledge responsibility for the sexual assault for which he was convicted. the court noted that due process and the privilege against self-incrimination were not violated as he had already been sentenced for the offense.

   In North Carolina v. Alford, 400 U.S. 25 (1970), the U.S. Supreme Court held that an express admission of guilt is not a constitutional prerequisite to the imposition of a criminal sentence upon a plea of guilty. An Alford plea has come to mean the profer and acceptance of a guilty plea even though the defendant refuses to concede factual guilt or even denies it. After judicial acceptance of an Alford plea and the imposition of sentence, the offender does not have a Fifth Amendment claim that would bar his being required to admit in treatment to the offense underlying the plea. The offender is not in jeopardy of another prosecution for the offense related to the Alford plea.

107. Oakland County Prosecutor v. Department of Corrections, 222 Mich. App. 654, 564 N.W.2d 922 (1997). Therapy secrets of sex offenders were held dis coverable in Beaver v. Alaska, 933 P.2d 1178 (Alaska App. 1997); People v. Elsbach, 934 P.2d 877 (Colo. App. 1997).

# Chapter 7

# PROCEEDINGS TO HOSPITALIZE

In proceedings to involuntarily hospitalize a patient, there is no privilege for communications relevant to the issue when the doctor has determined during the course of diagnosis or treatment that the patient is in need of such care. The Advisory Committee to the Federal Rules of Evidence commented, "The interests of both patient and public call for a departure from confidentiality in commitment proceedings. Since disclosure is authorized only when the doctor determines that hospitalization is needed, control over disclosure is placed largely in the hands of a person in whom the patient has already manifested confidence."[1] And as one court put it, "The evidence is not used against the individual but to aid the court in evaluating alternate treatment plans. Involuntary commitment proceedings are not penal in nature but humanitarian."[2]

The hospitalization exception does not mention guardianship but the justification for the exception would seem to apply as well to guardianship. Under the law, there are provisions for appointment of a guardian of one's person (*e.g.*, with authority over health care decisions) and a guardian of one's estate (*e.g.*, with authority over the making of contracts to sell one's property). In some jurisdictions, a guardian might be appointed for the specific purpose of consent to psychiatric hospitalization.[3] In a number of states, guardianship and civil commitment as a "gravely disabled person takes place through a conservatorship proceeding (a guardian of one's estate is often called a "conservator" or "committee").[4] In most cases where a psychiatrist is involved in giving testimony in a guardianship proceeding, it is as an examining rather than as a treating psychiatrist.[5]

The intent of the hospitalization exception in the typical psychotherapist-patient privilege is for the treating psychiatrist to play a key role in commitment proceedings (and presumably in guardianship proceedings). In nearly all jurisdictions, as a matter of law, no warning as to privilege against self-incrimination or right to silence need be given prior to examination or treatment.[6] Michigan is apparently exceptional.[7]

A patient opposed to hospitalization, however, may be angered by the breach of confidentiality. The issue of whether disclosures by a therapist to a court-appointed examiner are reasonably necessary to protect the interests of the patient or others is one for the jury, said the Michigan Court of Appeals; hence the therapist is not entitled to summary disposition.[8] This ruling came out of a case where the patient's estranged wife (later divorced) petitioned for the patient's commitment. The patient and his wife quarreled over finances and he contended that she wanted to "put him away." The psychiatrist who was appointed to undertake an examination consulted with the treating psychiatrist.

In a lawsuit called unprecedented, the patient sued the treating psychiatrist for breach of confidentiality. The trial court held that the defendant was entitled to judgment on motion for summary disposition, but the Michigan Court of Appeals held that the issue of whether the disclosures were reasonably necessary to protect the interests of the patient or others was one for the jury, since the facts of the case were such that reasonable minds could differ. The appellate court rendered that decision though the psychiatrist was in private practice and hence not governed by the Michigan Mental Health Code which provides that a patient must be informed that communication may be used in a hospitalization (or guardianship) proceeding.[9] In Australia, among other countries, the treating psychiatrist must have the consent of the patient as a requisite for discussions with an examiner.

In a comment on the hospitalization exception in the Connecticut statute that was included in the federal proposed rule, Goldstein and Katz had this to say:[10]

> [It] authorizes a psychiatrist to end the privilege to a limited extent when he determines that his patient needs hospitalization. To that end, it incorporates by reference the language of the Connecticut commitment statute. But it is important to note that the privilege is to be terminated only for the purpose of securing hospitalization or instituting commitment proceedings. It remains in force after the patient is hospitalized, so long as he is communicating with psychiatrists and other hospital personnel for the purpose of diagnosis or treatment. Such an exception is essential if the psychiatrist is to perform his role which will, in some instances, require that he use the material supplied by the patient as a basis for hospitalization. There is, however, a restriction on the exemption. Only those communications may be disclosed which are relevant to the commitment proceeding in which he is asked to testify.

In an oft-cited New Zealand case, *Furniss v. Fitchett*,[11] the defendant physician had been the physician for both the plaintiff and her husband. Several times the plaintiff had told the physician that her husband was doping her and that he was insane. These accusations were unfounded but they "engendered a certain amount of domestic discord," which had a serious effect on the husband's health. He asked the physician whether he could have the plaintiff certified to a mental institution, and at one time he came to the physician "almost desperate" and demanded, "You must do something for me, doctor—give me a report for my lawyer." The physician gave him a letter summarizing his observations of the plaintiff, and concluding, "I consider she exhibits symptoms of paranoia and should be given treatment for same if possible. An examination by a psychiatrist would be needed to fully diagnose her case and its requirements."[12] About a year later, the plaintiff brought a separation and maintenance action against her husband. During cross-examination of the plaintiff, her husband's attorney disclosed the physician's letter for the first time, and the plaintiff thereupon sued the physician for mental distress caused by the breach of his duty of confidentiality. The court overruled the defendant's motion for judgment, holding that the doctor did not take precautions in the expression of his opinion.[13]

In a California case, *In re Cathey*,[14] a mental patient confined in a prison hospital sought release contending that he was not a "dangerous" or "violent" individual as the state mental health officials asserted; when the officials offered his medical records to substantiate their position, he claimed the records were privileged. The court analogized the facts before it to those of the patient-litigant exception and found that "petitioner himself caused his mental condition to be put in issue by his applications for habeas corpus."

The judicial record on commitment is traditionally and generally considered a matter of public record and, in the absence of express legislation, the hearing and the resulting records are open. Various states have provided for maintaining the secrecy of judicial commitment records.[15] A number of states by statute provide that, so long as the patient consents, the court may exclude all persons not having a legitimate interest in the proceedings.[16] Quite often, the published opinion of the court, if any, uses a pseudonym or only the initials of the individual (*e.g.*, *In re* D.W.H.). In those states which join hospitalization (commitment) and incompetency proceedings, further difficulties arise as, for example, when a patient or ex-patient proposes to buy or sell property. Those who deal with him have a legitimate interest in inquiring as to his status; the transfer of title might be voidable due to the incompetency.

On the basis of a physician's certificate (or otherwise), the police may take a person into civil custody and bring him to a treatment facility. The American Bar Association's Criminal Justice Mental Health Standards recommend that police records of taking a mentally ill (or mentally retarded) person into civil custody should not be identified as, or commingled with, arrest records, except where an arrest for a felony and other serious crime is involved. The Standards provide that records of contacts with mentally ill persons should receive a high degree of confidentiality, at least equivalent to that which governs the dissemination of arrest records. Dissemination of these materials is allowed for the furtherance of police purposes, and given to attorneys for prehearing review and examination. Access is also granted to authorized personnel in order to assist in the diagnosis and treatment of mentally ill persons and in pursuit of appropriate service of process in connection with litigation.[17] With all this exposure, it is necessary for the psychiatrist to be circumspect about the details reported in the process. Generalities may suffice, but may also lead a court to reject a petition.

## NOTES

1. Federal Rules of Evidence, Rule 504.
2. *In re* Winstead, 67 Ohio App.2d 111, 425 N.E.2d 943 (1980).
3. Some 20 states have statutory provisions that allow commitment by guardians (Arizona, Arkansas, California, Colorado, Connecticut, Florida, Georgia, Idaho, Kansas, Maine, Massachusetts, Minnesota, Mississippi, Missouri, Montana, New Hampshire, North Dakota, Ohio, South Dakota, Wyoming). Ten states and the District of Columbia specifically prohibit commitment by guardians (Alaska, District of Columbia, Illinois, Maryland, New York, Oklahoma, Pennsylvania, Texas, Vermont, Washington, Wisconsin). In the absence of an express statute, it is generally held that a guardian does not have a right to commit an adult ward. The use of guardianship for commitment is, in effect, an end-run around commitment statutes. See D.M. English, "The Authority of a Guardian to Commit an Adult Ward," *Mental & Physical Disability Law Reporter* 20:584, 1996.
4. Cal. Welf. Inst. Code §§5350-5371.
5. Michigan's Mental Health Code (applicable to the public sector and agencies or clinics under contract with the state to provide services) sets out a requirement of notice. It states that privileged communications shall be disclosed "[w]hen the privileged communication is relevant to a matter under consideration in a proceeding to determine the legal competence of the patient or the patient's need for a guardian but only if the patient was informed that any communications made could be used in such a proceeding." MCL 330.1750.
6. Matter of Farrow, 41 N.C. App. 680, 255 S.E.2d 777 (1979).
7. See notes 5 and 9.
8. Saur v. Probes, 190 Mich. App. 636 (1991).
9. MCL 330.1750. This and the aforementioned requirement of notice as a condition for testifying in a guardianship proceeding (note 5) are subject to constitutional challenge, given that in Michigan under its constitution the state supreme court is given the function of adopting rules of practice and procedure including the rules of evidence. Hence, any rule of evidence

adopted by the legislature at odds with rules adopted by the court is subject to constitutional challenge. The Michigan rules of evidence adopted by the court do not require notice to a patient. See Mich. Const. 1963, art. 6, §5; Perin v. Peuler, 373 Mich. 531, 130 N.W.2d 4 (1964); McDougall v. Schanz, 1996 Mich. App. LEXIS 266.

10. J. Goldstein & J. Katz, "Psychiatrist-Patient Privilege: The GAP Proposal and the Connecticut Statute," *Am. J. Psychiat.* 118:733, 1962.
11. [1958] N.Z.L.R. 396 (Sup. Ct.).
12. Id. at 398.
13. Id. at 404.
14. 55 Cal.2d 679, 12 Cal. Rptr. 762, 361 P.2d 426 (1961).
15. See Chapter 8 for discussion on hospital and health records.
16. Ohio Rev. Code Ann. § 5122.15(A)(5)(6); Tex. Rev. Civ. Stat. Ann. art. 5547-49(e).
17. American Bar Association Criminal Justice Mental Health Standards, Part II, 7-2.9 (Washington, DC.: American Bar Association, 1989).

# Chapter 8

# HOSPITAL AND OFFICE RECORDS

Until the latter part of the nineteenth century, medical records were used almost exclusively for purposes of treatment, teaching, and research. In the twentieth century, a new use developed for them—as evidence in personal injury litigation and as documentation of disability claims under various insurance and welfare programs.[1]

Mental illness, especially hospitalization in a mental institution, carries a stigma, the extent of which is dependent on the individual case. Once a person has a record of having been in a mental hospital the public at large, both formally in terms of employment and other restrictions, and informally in terms of day-to-day social treatment, considers him, to some degree, to be set apart. Public disclosure of hospitalization does not allow the patient an easy return to the community.[2]

Does the testimonial privilege cover hospital records, given that the hospital setting is a situation where a one-to-one relationship is impossible? Hospital records are inevitably passed into the hands of nurses, social workers, and clerks. Furthermore, treatment in a hospital requires an organized effort on the part of all members as a therapeutic team, and they must be given such information as will make their efforts meaningful and helpful. Since so many people know about the patient and have the information, courts in many states have taken the position that the medical privilege does not protect the record. It was that type of holding that prompted the push for a special psychotherapist privilege.

When called to court, physicians and other staff members have often found themselves trying to justify or excuse an awkward or inadequate recording in the hospital record, on which the legal profession perhaps unduly places great value.[3] Impressions derived from reading case summaries or test reports, especially those of state mental hospitals, are often misleading. Undue value is placed on them. Consider the following court opinion: "There is good reason to treat a hospital record entry as trustworthy. Human life will often depend on the accuracy of the entry, and it is reasonable to presume that a hospital is staffed with personnel who competently perform their day-to-day tasks. To this extent at least, hospital records are deserving of a presumption of accuracy even more than other types of business entries."[4]

Health agencies and others complain, when information is withheld as confidential, that they cannot obtain necessary information to institute preventive health or disease control measures. Newspapermen, while they seek a privilege to protect from disclosure their sources of information, protest secrecy of hospital and health department records. In a report to the American Society of Newspaper Editors, it was said:[5]

> A multitude of statutes exist under which public and press inspection of many records is barred except for bare statistical data without identification of individuals. These statutes cover, for example, reports of numerous diseases ranging from sufferers from venereal disease through epileptics to "typhoid Marys." Secrecy is tight. It provides a wide field for official revelry in statistical activity. Opportunity for checking official activity is scant. Opportunities for citizens in an increasingly dangerous age to ascertain through their usual purveyors of information the conditions of those who serve their food, drive their locomotives, or pilot their planes are practically nil.

However, such statements are not wholly accurate. Even in those states which have legislation barring the inspection of hospital and health records, they are usually made available to those with a legitimate ground for inquiry.[6]

The necessity for certain research and administrative personnel to have access to the records of patients is clear, but this can usually be done in a way to protect the patient's confidentiality. In much research, identification of the patient is unnecessary (for example, number of cases of hepatitis), but some research cannot be accomplished without names of patients and other information (for example, follow-up studies of children seen in guidance clinics). In general, statutes on the subject provide that all information used in the course of medical study shall be confidential; that such information shall not be admissible as evidence; and that the furnishing of such information shall not subject any person or institution to damages.[7] In effect the statutes provide that disclosures made for scientific studies are not to be considered a public disclosure which would terminate the privilege.[8]

While the hospital record and the records of physicians or health officers are generally kept confidential, the judicial record on commitment, however, is traditionally considered a public record and in the absence of express legislation the hearing and the resulting records are available to one and all. It is to be noted that in the United States, at least until recently, court commitment has been the procedure most commonly used in the admission of patients to mental hospitals.[9] In various states, the law on obtaining care or treatment for mentally ill persons provides that the committing court, hospital, or medical records of any patient (or former patient) are privileged and may not be disclosed except as specifically provided in the law.[10] A great deal of confidential information in a psychiatric record comes from many sources beside the patient; hence, selectivity of disclosure could protect the patient's family, friends, and others from whom the confidential information has been obtained. Most important, when disclosure is selective and related to the questions at hand, all of the patient's private life, fantasies, and disturbed thinking would not automatically be made available to the inquirer. Disclosure would not go beyond what would be needed in the special circumstances.

In some states, the decision on disclosure is made by the head of the hospital, while in other states, the judge "weighs the contrary needs of the individual and the community" and prevents any unnecessary disclosure of confidential information. The specific circumstances usually set out in the law allowing disclosure of records include: (1) consent of the patient (or former patient); (2) disclosure necessary for the medical care or treatment of the patient (or former patient); (3) disclosure of certain information to appropriate persons and agencies for purposes of accreditation, statistical analysis, administrative supervision and scholarly research (provided such disclosure shall not be made in such a way as to reveal the identity of the patient); and (4) disclosure necessary for the conduct of court proceedings and the record is otherwise admissible in evidence.[11]

Difficulties arise when hospitalization (commitment) and incompetency (interdiction) proceedings are joined. For example, as we have noted, when a patient, even when discharged, proposes to sell property, prospective purchasers and title companies would have a legitimate interest in inquiring as to the patient's status (that is, whether he is on conditional release and whether the incompetency has been judicially removed).

Today, hospitalization is no longer long-term; hence, mental health codes now provide for separation of hospitalization and incompetency proceedings. It provides in effect that a person is not deprived of his right to sell or buy property, execute documents, or enter into contracts because he has been hospitalized as mentally ill.

Problems may arise, however, where a person is not adjudicated incompetent at the time of commitment. During the course of hospitalization, or afterwards, it may be essential to institute incompetency proceedings for the appointment of a guardian (curator). In doing so, attorneys often communicate with the hospital, seeking evidence to justify the proceeding. More often than not, the proceeding is in the interest of the patient or ex-patient. It seeks to appoint someone to manage the patient's affairs, which the patient may be unable to do while hospitalized or afterwards. Not all incompetency proceedings, as the myth would have it, are maliciously instituted by members of the family to rob the patient. However, the patient on occasion does not consent to release of information; he does not want to be tagged an incompetent. The result is a begging of the question: incompetency proceedings are instituted because it is felt that the patient does not have the legal capacity to consent, yet hospital cooperation is refused because the patient declines to consent.[12]

There is considerable discussion in the literature on the duty of a physician to tell the "truth" to a patient about his illness. Hospitals encounter requests by patients for a copy of their record, purely for their own information. There are circumstances, however, when the hospital or doctor cannot, for the patient's own good, tell him the "whole truth." The paranoid is the type of psychiatric patient that most frequently requests a copy of his record; compliance with the request may further aggravate his condition. To avoid doing a patient harm, there is a "therapeutic privilege" to withhold information from a patient but the physician has the burden of justifying it; otherwise it may be said that there is not "informed consent" for treatment.[13]

Medical records are considered the property of the hospital or of the physician in the case of private practice, but they are subject in most states, by legislation or court decision, to a "limited property right" on the part of the patient with respect to the information which they contain.[14] Some courts recognize a patient right to records based on the fiduciary duty of the physician to the patient.[15] The patient can therefore demand disclosure, not only for himself, but also, for example, for disclosure to an insurance company.

By and large, psychiatrists argue that a different principle is needed for psychiatric patients given the nature of its contents. Psychiatric records are different from records of physical disorders, they point out. Dr. Steven Hoge, as chairman of the American Psychiatric Association's Council on Psychiatry and Law, suggested at a hearing of the Subcommittee of the House of Representatives on medical records privacy that mental well-being be accepted as a reason for denying access to medical records. He testified, "One of the arts of psychotherapy is timing, and to impose a requirement on the psychiatrists to share with the patient understandings, interpretations and thoughts of the practitioner, when the patient is not ready to receive this information, may not reach the 'endangerment to life or safety' exception standard outline in the bill, and could very well endanger the therapy."[16] Yet other psychiatrists willingly go over records with their patients. Apparently it depends on how records are written.

In a study of individuals committed to a security unit as not competent to stand trial or as not guilty by reason of insanity, Dr. Robert Miller and colleagues found that they wanted access to their records in order to see how the staff really viewed them, to check for accuracy of their records, to increase communications and trust with staff members, and to see how their treatment was progressing. It is interesting to note that only eight of thirty-two individuals in the unit actually requested to see their record once access was granted. Those who did review their records felt access had been useful and that they were better informed about treatment and staff opinions about them. There was no evidence that their conditions became worse. The staff expressed discomfort with patient access before it was granted, but most reported positive attitudes by the end of the study.[17]

In a study at a teaching hospital of the University of Pittsburgh, Dr. Loren Roth and colleagues found similar results from patient access of records. They concluded that the benefits of psychiatric patients having access to their records outweighed any detriments. The study, as Miller's forensic study, noted the importance of patients being accompanied by staff persons to answer any questions or to clear up any misconceptions.[18]

In a Canadian study, the staff reported benefits from patient access to records including enhanced trust between patient and staff, a greater awareness by the patients of behavior and behavioral objectives, and a greater sensitivity by the staff of the need for accuracy or discretion in recording.[19]

The ownership of records of patients seen in clinics or guidance centers presents a special problem as to whether they belong to the physician or to the clinic. On the termination of the psychiatrist's employment with the clinic or center, the question arises as to the proper custodian of the records developed during the term of employment.[20] It has been urged that psychiatric records are the property of the psychiatrist preparing them and are not subject to "transfer" to another psychiatrist coming to the center, or to a court or social agency, unless the records were prepared in the first instance by the request of such other person or body. In a controversy in Rock County, Wisconsin (which did not go to litigation but instead was compromised), the psychiatrist claimed records and files relating to patients who availed themselves of psychiatric services offered at the Rock County Guidance Clinic upon a public basis. The psychiatrist, and social workers and psychologists under her direction and control, compiled the records. Upon the termination of employment with Rock County, the psychiatrist claimed the records, alleging: a proprietary interest in the records as constituting her work product, and a right to the records as being privileged confidential communications.

This argument presupposes that the clinic and the replacing psychiatrist will not maintain the confidentiality of the records. Nowadays in the operation of guidance clinics, physicians go and come—they are transient employees, but the records remain; otherwise the clinic would be very much damaged by the departure of a physician. The records remain where they have always been; they are not "transferred." Patients usually return to a clinic irrespective of the presence of a particular physician. Also, taking a page from the law on self-incrimination, we might note that it has been many times held that "quasi public records" as well as "public records" are deemed to belong to the government, and the record keeper therefore may not object to their introduction as evidence.[21]

Records of a deceased physician cannot be sold because the information they contain is confidential (and therefore they are not inventoried as property of the estate of the physician). It is recommended that records of a deceased physician which might be pertinent to any litigation in which a patient may be involved should not be destroyed without prior notice to the patient.[21]

For further discussion of confidentiality in hospital care, consultation, and recordkeeping, see Part IV, Chapters 6 and 7, and Part V, Chapter 1.

## NOTES

1. E. Hayt, *Medicolegal Aspects of Hospital Records* (Berwyn, Ill.: Physicians' Record, 2d ed. 1977); see also C. McCormick, "The Use of Hospital Records as Evidence," *Tul. L. Rev.* 26:371 1952.

2. How often are job opportunities closed off for such persons? Under what circumstances is a former mental patient able to resume normal roles? Sociologist John Clausen points out the realistic basis for negative responses when one must deal with unreasonable behavior, whether or not the individual has a history of hospitalization. J.A. Clausen, "Stigma and Mental Disorder: Phenomena and Terminology," *Psychiatry* 44:287, 1981. See Part V, Chapter 3 on the stigma of psychiatric discourse.

3. Dr. Thomas Gutheil suggests that health care professionals employ paranoia as a motivating force to stimulate themselves to make their records effective for forensic purposes, utilization review, and sound treatment planning. T.G. Gutheil, "Paranoia and Progress Notes: A Guide to Forensically Informed Psychiatric Recordkeeping," *Hosp. & Community Psychiatry* 31:479, 1980.

4. Thomas v. Hogan, 308 F.2d 355 (4th Cir. 1962); see B. Radauskas, A.A. Kurland & S. Goldin, "A Neglected Document–The Medical Record of the State Psychiatric Hospital Patient," *Am. J. Psychiat.* 118:709, 1962.

5. H.L. Cross, *The People's Right to Know* (New York: Columbia University Press, 1953), p. 87.

6. Special laws usually govern records of health departments. Reports as to some diseases are kept secret. The New York Public Health Law has provided since 1909 that a report of tuberculosis "shall not be divulged or made public"; similar reports as to other communicable diseases (*e.g.*, typhoid) are not kept secret. Hence, the record of the health commissioner with respect to a typhoid carrier is amenable to court subpoena. In a case occurring in

New York, the information in the health commissioner's file, said the court, was not acquired by the health commissioner in attending a patient in a professional capacity nor was the information necessary to enable him to act in that capacity. Although the information may have come to the commissioner from a physician in private practice, the transmittal from that physician to the public officer was in obedience to the express command of the Public Health Law. Accordingly, the court ordered the production in trial of the records asked by the administrator. Thomas v. Morris, 36 N.E.2d 141 (N.Y. 1941). Serious transgressions of medical ethics occur "frequently" during clinical trials and experimental, surgery some with fatal consequences, others producing severe and often life-long impairment. "Unethical Testing Under Fire," *Medical World News*, April 19, 1965, p.43.

In Hyman v. Jewish Chronic Disease Hospital of Brooklyn, 21 A.D. 495, 251 N.Y.S.2d 818 (1964), the Court of Appeals of New York upheld the right and responsibility of directors of hospitals to know the nature and fate of experiments conducted in the hospital. In this case, the plaintiff, a director of the hospital, filed suit to obtain hospital records after three physicians on the hospital staff resigned in protest against a set of experiments. Live cancer cells had been injected into twenty-two elderly patients who did not have cancer at the time of the injections. The plaintiff charged that the patients' informed consent had not been obtained. The hospital, on the other hand, contended that the plaintiff had no right to examine the records of the experiments because these were records of confidential relationship between physician and patient. The court stated: "The petitioner, being a director of a hospital corporation, is entitled as a matter of law to an inspection of the records of the hospital to investigate into the facts as to alleged illegal and improper experimentation on patients."

7.  A number of states have passed laws protecting members of committees and hospital groups engaged in special studies of morbidity and mortality.

8.  Louisiana's statute provided: "The governing authority of each public hospital, public mental health center or public state school for the mentally deficient may make and enforce rules under which . . . charts records, documents or other memoranda may be exhibited or copied by or for persons legitimately and properly interested in the disease, physical or mental, or in the condition of patients. La. R.S. 44:7(B). Regulations of the Food & Drug Administration, concerning investigational stage of new drugs, require complete records of the disposition of the drug and case histories of the patients, and that adequate reports be furnished to the sponsor, and that these records be open to inspection by the Food & Drug Administration on request. The records must include "characteristics of patients by age, sex and condition."

9.  H.A. Ross, "Commitment of the Mentally Ill: Problems of Law and Policy," *Mich. L. Rev.* 57:945, 1959; R. Slovenko & W. Super, "Commitment Procedure in Louisiana," *Tul. L. Rev.* 35:705, 1961; *J. of La. State Med. Soc.* 113:463, 1961. The Ohio Mental Health Law provides that patient records,

including hospital and court records, shall be kept confidential except under certain circumstances. An exception is made for court journal entries and docket entries, apparently for the benefit of those concerned with property and contract problems of patients since judicial hospitalization in Ohio still results in incompetency. Records may be disclosed upon consent of the patient and approval of the request by the hospital or court; when necessary in court proceedings; and when necessary to carry out the provisions of the mental health law. R.A. Haines & W. Meyers, "Hospitalization and Treatment of the Mentally Ill: Ohio's New Mental Health Law," *Ohio State L.J.* 22:659, 1961.

10.    U.S. Public Health Service, Publication No. 51 (rev. ed. 1952). A brief summary of the model "Draft Act Governing Hospitalization of the Mentally Ill," by one of its authors, appears in R. Felix, "Hospitalization of the Mentally Ill," *Am. J. Psychiat.* 107:712, 1951.

11.    See, *e.g.*, La. R.S. 44:7(A).

12.    "Confidential medical information about a patient should not be released without the consent of the patient, if he is competent, or someone authorized to consent for him, if he is not competent, unless the disclosure is required by law or is vitally necessary for protection of the public interest. Where a court commits a patient to a mental hospital, authority to act for the patient will be granted either to a guardian appointed for that purpose or to a public official. This guardian or public official is subjected to the control of the court. He is required to act in the best interest of the patient in all matters, including the release of information." *AMA News*, Sept. 17, 1962. Illinois and New York established a "Mental Health Information Service" (Mental Health Review Service), as part of the judicial system and designed to inform hospitalized patients of their rights under the law.

13.    C.C. Lund, "The Doctor, The Patient and the Truth," *Tenn. L. Rev.* 19:344 (1946); H.W. Smith, "Therapeutic Privilege to Withhold Specific Diagnosis from Patient Sick with Serious or Fatal Illness," *Tenn. L. Rev.* 19:349 (1946).

14.    In some states, patients have no legal right to review or copy their medical records, but when a patient sues a physician or hospital for malpractice, the patient has a clear right of discovery. See B.L. Kaiser, "Patient's Rights of Access to His Hospital and Medical Records," *Buffalo L. Rev.* 24:317, 1975; N.A. Jeffrey, "Getting Access to Your Medical Records May be Limited, Costly—Or Impossible," *Wall Street Journal,* July 31, 1996, p. B-1. The Judicial Council of the AMA stated, "Whether the contents of the medical report are to be given to the patient rests with the decision of the doctor who knows all the circumstances involved in the situation." The Judicial Council also pointed out, "The records are medical and technical, personal and often informal. Standing alone they are meaningless to the patient but of value to the physician and perhaps to a succeeding physician. The patient, however, or one responsible for him, is entitled to know the nature of the illness and the general course or regimen of therapy employed by his physician. The extent to which the physician must advise his patient may be limited by the

nature of the illness and the character of the patient. The physician in advising his patient must always act as he would wish to be treated were he in a like situation." *AMA News*, April 30, 1962.

See Greyhound v. Superior Court of Merced County, 56 Cal. 355, 15 Cal. Rptr. 90, 364 P.2d 266 (1962); McGarry v. Mercier Co., 72 Mich. 501, 262 N.W. 296 (1935); Wallace v. University Hospitals of Cleveland, 171 Ohio St. 487, 172 N.E.2d 459 (1961).

In Pierce v. Penman, 357 Pa. Super. 225, 515 A.2d 948 (1986), the patient brought suit against her physicians seeking damage for severe emotional distress suffered when the physicians repeatedly refused to turn over copies of her medical records. The court noted that the patient had a history of emotional problems known to the physicians and the physicians conceded that the patient was legally entitled to receive promptly copies of her medical records. The Pennsylvania Supreme Court upheld an award of compensatory and punitive damages.

15. Emmett v. Eastern Dispensary & Cas. Hosp., 396 F.2d 931 (D.C. Cir.1967).
16. S. Barlas, "The Washington Report/Confidentiality Focus of Medical Records Bill," *Psychiatric Times*, Aug. 1996, p. 10.
17. R. Miller, B. Morrow, M. Kaye & G.J. Maier, "Patient Access to Medical Records in a Forensic Center: A Controlled Study," *Hosp. & Comm. Psychiat.* 38:1081, 1987.
18. L. Roth, J. Wolford & A. Meisel, "Patient Access to Records: Tonic or Toxin?", *Am. J. Psychiat.* 137:592, 1980.
19. W.J.G. McFarlane, R.G. Bowman & M. MacInnes, "Patient Access to Hospital Records/A Pilot Project," *Can. J. Psychiat.* 25:497, 1980.
20. Hospital records are exclusively the hospital's property. A few states apparently hold that clinical records are the property of the hospital and also the physician's property. K.A. Menninger, *A Manual for Psychiatric Case Study* (New York: Grune & Stratton, 2d ed. 1962), p. 35. In the Veterans Administration, the clinical records belong not to the hospital but to the Veterans Administration.
21. See Amato v. Porter, 157 F.2d 719 (10th Cir. 1946); Comment, "Constitutional Limits on the Admissibility in the Federal Courts of Evidence Obtained From Required Records," *Harv. L. Rev.* 68:340, 1954.
22. *AMA News*, Dec. 11, 1961, p. 14.

# Chapter 9

# GROUP THERAPY

With the increasing number of psychotherapy groups, questions have frequently arisen (mainly in nonlegal circles) regarding privileged communication and confidentiality. While there has been some litigation involving confidentiality of joint marital counseling and family therapy, there is scant little involving group therapy, notwithstanding its wide use. Is, then, the prevailing concern warranted?

Various medical and psychiatric societies have sought to organize therapy or support groups for members who are facing a malpractice lawsuit. During this time, while these individuals may have the support of an attorney, they feel under stress and they feel isolated during the years awaiting the outcome of the litigation. In general, lawyers advise their clients not to talk to anyone about the litigation and this increases their sense of isolation. Many hesitate to enter a therapy or support group, it is said, out of concerns about confidentiality.

Bar associations in various states have sponsored therapy groups for its members who have a problem with alcoholism. While their competency to practice may be questionable, they usually are not facing a malpractice suit as are the members of medical and psychiatric societies who have been sued and enter a therapy group.

Across the country, group therapists express different views about the concern of group members about confidentiality. Sponsored by ProMutual Medical Professional Insurance Company of Boston, Dr. Miguel Leibovich, a Cambridge, Massachusetts, private practitioner, as of 1994 has conducted a monthly support group for defendant physicians and dentists involved in liability suits. "What an incredible emotional trauma it is for a physician to be sued," says Dr. Leibovich. "Rage, sadness, and shame are the common emotions that doctors bring to the group."[1] Dr. Leibovich says that concerns about confidentiality are dispelled by a promise of members of the group to maintain confidentiality. What members of the group talk about is their emotional reactions to being sued, he says, not about details of the lawsuit. In his experience, concerns about confidentiality have not come up very much.[2]

In a recent article in the *American Journal of Psychiatry*, Dr. Howard Roback and colleagues surveyed 51 therapists who led psychotherapy for physicians recovering from substance abuse and they report that concern about confidentiality was a significant factor in the group members' willingness to share secrets. Of those group therapists surveyed, 49 percent rated physician group members as exhibiting a moderate amount or a great deal of concern over potential confidentiality infractions. Moreover, they report, 27 percent of group therapists who treat impaired physicians have been subpoenaed at some time in the past to testify about physician members. Some states require physicians to report impairment of other physicians. They suggest that group therapy would provide a safer milieu for patients to share highly personal information if the members themselves could be held liable for violating confidentiality. They recommend legislation making group members liable for violating confidentiality.[3]

In an article years ago in the *International Journal of Group Psychotherapy* provocatively titled "Group Psychotherapy: A Pool of Legal Witnesses?", Dr. Leila Foster presented the problem of an apparently hypothetical divorce proceeding which involved two group members. A third member of the group was named in the suit as "the other woman." All members of the group received notices to appear at a deposition. As a consequence, they all called to terminate therapy. A nightmare situation, said Foster.[4]

I was prompted to survey the situation. I interviewed several group therapists and members of a group. In my survey, I discovered that therapists are far more concerned about confidentiality than members of the group.[5] Some group therapists say that a person involved in litigation should not be in group therapy for his or her own protection. I am told by group therapists, novice and veteran alike, that while they have many times discussed the problem of confidentiality with colleagues and students, they know of no actual instance where there has been any serious problem in connection with lack of confidentiality. For example, Dr. Joseph J. Geller, who had been doing group therapy for many years, said:[6]

> Over all the years, with many people becoming privy to a wealth of personal details about others, there seems to have been very little harmful use of the material. This is true of my own practice as well as the experiences of others. Each of us, having this rather uneventful experience, assumed it was unusual, but without comparing notes with others, we learned that it is fairly generally true.

The executive director of the National Commission on Confidentiality of Health Records, Natalie D. Spingarn, advised that no incidents of group therapy breaches of confidentiality have been reported to the Commission.[7]

On the face of it, with so many people involved, such secrecy is remarkable. Perfection is not ordinarily expected in this world, but only in the Kingdom to come.[8] All things considered, should confidentiality in the group therapy situation be realistically expected? Is a secret really possible when spread among so many people? One member may develop an "intense negative transference" with another, and may seek to do him in.

One might say a person should turn to transcendental meditation or prayer if he really wants to preserve a secret. Benjamin Franklin, in his *Poor Richard's Almanac,* dispersed homespun wisdom and casual philosophy during much of the 18th century, creating in the process a number of aphorisms so well known as to become fixtures in the language, and he advised: "Three may keep a secret, if two of them are dead."[9]

In the group as well as dyadic therapy situation, the participants are engaged in a therapeutic alliance in which it is assumed nothing will be spread abroad. Usually, group leaders make explicit the expectation of confidentiality, and they repeat it during the course of therapy. The late Dr. Jacob L. Moreno, pioneer in group therapy, put it this way:[10]

> In group psychotherapy the Hippocratic Oath is extended to all patients and binds each with equal strength not to reveal to outsiders the confidences of other patients entrusted to them. . . . Every patient is expected to divulge freely whatever he thinks, perceives or feels, to every other in the course of the treatment sessions. He should know that he is protected by the "pledge" and that no disadvantage will occur to him because of his honest revelations of crimes committed, or psychological deviations from sexual or social norms, secret plans and activities.

He suggested the formal taking of a group oath swearing the members to secrecy, as follows:[11]

> Just as we trust the physician in individual treatment, we should trust each other. Whatever happens in the course of a session of group therapy and psychodrama, we should not keep anything secret. We should divulge freely whatever we think, perceive or feel for each other; we should act out the fears and hopes we have in common and purge ourselves of them.
>
> But like the physician who is bound by the Hippocratic Oath, we are bound as participants in this group, not to reveal to outsiders the confidences of other patients. Like the physicians, each of us is entrusted to protect the welfare of every other patient in the group.

Others have suggested that this pledge of secrecy, while better than nothing, is inadequate to protect confidentiality. Dr. Alexander Wolf, group therapist, observed, "It seems to me that, while certainly a patient is entitled to the security that the privacy of his communications will be kept in trust, no reliable guarantees against the danger of betrayal is secured by subjecting the therapeutic group membership to a 'pledge' of secrecy."[12]

Since there is no clear legal remedy when group members discuss with outsiders matters revealed in a group, Dr. James K. Morrison and colleagues suggested a written contract, including a "liquidated damages clause."[13] In event of breach of this contract, it was their belief that therapy clients would more clearly be able to proceed in a lawsuit against the offending party (when the disclosure is not compelled by law). As precedent in other areas, it may be noted that when joining the Central Intelligence Agency and various federal agencies, one signs a contract pledging secrecy as to what is learned. In the nongovernmental domain, employees promise confidentiality as to trade secrets, and the courts provide relief by injunction or damages in the event of a breach.[14] The wording of the agreement formulated by Morrison is as follows:

> We, the undersigned, in consideration of and return for receiving group psychotherapy and its possible benefits, and in consideration of and return for similar promises by other members of the psychotherapy group, consciously and willingly promise never to reveal the identity of any group member (listed below) to anyone who is not in group therapy, other than staff of the psychiatric agency from which we receive services. We realize that to relate specific problems of a group member to a nongroup member, even though the name of the group member may not be directly revealed, may at times lead to the eventual disclosure of the group member's identity. Therefore, we promise to avoid speaking of any group member's problems in any manner which would even remotely risk revealing the identity of that group member. We fully realize and strongly agree that in the event of a lawsuit for breach of contract, we give the offended party the right to recover for damage to his/her reputation the minimum amount of $—. Also, such party may recover for any other damages which can be proved.

Using this contract, Morrison reported that his clients are significantly more able to be self-disclosing, presumably because they now have more trust in the group.[15] Despite his concern for secrecy, however, Morrison, like others interviewed, knew of no instance in which a group member has divulged information revealed in the group to any outsider, and, he added, no one has sought to compel a group member to reveal such information.[16] This is also the case apparently when group members do not expressly agree to confidentiality in writing.

In another study, a graduate psychology student at Georgia State University sent a questionnaire to 70 psychologists, 16 psychiatrists, and six psychiatric residents in Atlanta, a total of 92 therapists, all reputed to be doing group work. Completed questionnaires were received from 33. None of the respondents believed that any of their patients had been "seriously damaged" by a breach of confidentiality during the previous year (no illustrations were given). Thirty-nine percent made confidentiality an explicit part of the contractual agreement with the group, 72 percent replied that they remind the group of its responsibility to honor confidentiality at group formation, when new members join, or at regular intervals. Twelve percent (four respondents) replied that they do not remind the group of any responsibility regarding confidentiality. Fifteen percent (five respondents) prohibit people who know each other from joining the same group. Some groups participate on a first-name-only basis to protect confidentiality. One respondent makes the stipulation in the contractual agreement that group members have the right to decide what they will choose to discuss in the group.[17]

As a shield against a demand for disclosure in legal proceedings, the enactment of a legal privilege which will excuse testimony from a group member or therapist was often suggested. The American Group Psychotherapy Association, desiring greater protection for group therapy, recommended the enactment of a specific privilege to cover group therapy. The history of privilege, however, as pointed out, reveals that it has not been very much of a shield. When push has come to shove, the privilege has ended up not shielding very much, if anything. It is like the warranty where the bold print giveth, and the fine print taketh away.[18]

A rule of privilege law which is of particular significance in group therapy is that a communication loses any privileged status it may have had if it takes place in the presence of a "third party." The privileges are formulated with the dyadic relationship in mind (attorney-client, physician-patient, accountant-client), and the presence of a third party is said to "pollute" confidentiality. The law equates disclosure to a third person with a general publication to the world. The rationale is: "The world knows about it, why not the court?" Will group members (and the insurance company) be considered a third party, polluting privilege, or will they be considered as agents taking part in the therapy process?[19] It has been noted that a number of courts have said that a nurse does not come under the umbrella of the medical privilege, and because of this, some statutes dealing with medical privilege specifically include nurses and other attendants within the scope of privilege (for whatever the privilege may be worth).

The prominent legal commentator Charles McCormick discussed the issue of whether the presence of third parties renders a statement to a physician nonprivileged, and he argued that the court should analyze the problem in terms of whether the third persons are necessary and customary participants in the consultation or treatment and whether the communications were confidential for the purpose of aiding in diagnosis and treatment.[20] In a

Minnesota case,[21] where the defendant was charged with criminal sexual conduct, the prosecutor sought the records of group psychotherapy sessions in which the defendant participated. The Minnesota Supreme Court applied McCormick's approach and upheld privilege:[22]

> Under [McCormick's] approach, we conclude that the medical privilege must be construed to encompass statements made in group psychotherapy. The participants in group psychotherapy sessions are not casual third persons who are strangers to the psychiatrist/psychologist/nurse-patient relationship. Rather, every participant has such a relationship with the attending professional, and, in the group therapy setting, the participants actually become part of the diagnostic and therapeutic process for co-participants.

Likewise, an appellate court in California held that disclosing information in the presence of members of a therapy group does not defeat the privilege.[23] The court said:[24]

> [C]ommunications made by patients to persons who are present to further the interests of the patient comes within the privilege. "Group therapy" is designed to provide comfort and revelation to the patient who shares similar experiences and/or difficulties with other like persons within the group. The presence of each person is for the benefit of the others, including the witness/patient, and is designed to facilitate the patient's treatment. Communications such as these, when made in confidence, should not operate to destroy the privilege.

Of course, there may be an exception to privilege, which is usually the case, and at best, the privilege deals with the situation when an outsider has a dispute with, and seeks information about the party whose confidential communication is protected. It does not deal with disputes which may arise between the members themselves of the covered relationship, as when one member of the group sues another member of the group, or when a member of the group sues the therapist. Likewise, when two or more persons consult an attorney with regard to a matter of common interest, nothing that is said by the parties or the attorney is deemed confidential in an action arising subsequently thereto between these parties.[25] Thus, by analogy, a New York court in a paternity proceeding found that no privilege existed as to the testimony by a social worker of a social agency (Jewish Family Service) who during the time of pregnancy of the petitioner, had interviewed her and the alleged father together. The court reasoned: "By analogy and on the same theory, where two or more persons consult a social worker in regard to a matter of common interest to them, nothing that is said by the parties or the social worker is deemed confidential in an action arising subsequently thereto between the parties."[26]

A New York trial court parted company with this line of reasoning, calling the comparison an indiscriminate one. The decision was featured as "judicial highlight" of the law reports. In this case parties to a divorce proceeding and custody of children had several years earlier sought the help, advice and guidance of the Jewish Family Service. The parties were interviewed together on a number of occasions by staff personnel of that agency, including social workers and at least one psychiatrist. At that time they did not have litigation in mind. They sought the help of the agency in an attempt to deal with their marital problems.

In this case, Justice Arthur Blyn refused to permit the husband to subpoena the records and reports of the parties' consultations or to permit the husband to produce in court the agency personnel who had interviewed the parties. He held that the totality of the agency functions fell within the ambit of protection provided by the state's statutes granting a privilege with respect to certified social worker-client relationships, psychologist-client relationships, or physician (psychiatrist)-patient relationships. The court stated:[27]

> If parties who are in need of help face the danger that some court will at some later date balance the privilege, which the clients believe they have every right to rely on, with some other so-called interest, what happens to the necessary "baring of the souls", the necessary "self revelation," the necessary honesty required to provide the basis for such aid?
>
> Who would wish to be subjected to such self revelation faced with the possibility that at some later time a court will do a balancing act and declare that the privilege relied upon was a myth?
>
> When the courts begin to destroy this privilege on the grounds, amongst others, that when custody or paternity, or some other so-called community interest is involved, then privilege is not the right it should be but a feeble pretense of privilege at the mercy of some balancing act by some court.
>
> Privilege granted by the legislature was not meant to be a myth. It was meant to cure the evil which had resulted from social workers either voluntarily or by court direction being forced to disclose communications given to them of the most intimate nature by people desperately in need of help. People were, and are, told that in order to be helped they must reveal the innermost parts of their emotional being–their most dreadful fantasies, their fears, their angers and desires. How can such persons have faith in this process if they become aware that some court can subsequently find that the confidence in which such feelings were revealed can be betrayed? This court takes he position that any communication which is privileged when made remains privileged forever unless the privilege is waived by the client.

A few years earlier, a similar precedent-making decision was rendered on appeal of a divorce case in another jurisdiction. The Tennessee Court of Appeals had before it the question of admissibility of testimony of a psychiatrist with respect to communications made by one of the spouses in the presence of the other. The court stated:[28]

> We are of the opinion that communications made to psychiatrists, when the confidential relationship of psychiatrist and patient exists, even though made in the presence of a spouse, are privileged, including any diagnosis therefrom. This is not to say that the parties themselves, in a divorce action, cannot testify as to statements made by the other spouse under such circumstances, but we do hold that the psychiatrist cannot divulge the privileged communications, whether it be the actual conversations or diagnosis drawn therefrom, unless the patient waives the privilege or it falls within the exceptions.

Thus, present-day privilege laws offer a modicum of assurance in litigation of family matters that communications in psychotherapy are shielded from disclosure, but they offer no assurance whatever in personal injury litigation where a group member makes his health a matter of issue. Likewise, should one group member assault another in the course of therapy, and suit ensue, the occurrence would not be shielded.

The law is more Procrustean that Promethean—it puts things in boxes, so it is necessary to define the type of group that would be covered under a group therapy statute, just as the parties in the dyadic relationship must be defined under its privilege statute. An amendment to the Colorado privilege statute specifically covered the group therapy situation; it is limited to group therapy conducted "under the supervision of a person authorized by law to conduct such therapy."[29] The question remains: Who should be "authorized by law"?

Group processes oriented toward personal change are expanding in many directions. What are the boundaries of group psychotherapy? Nowadays, there are theme-oriented groups, category-oriented groups, action-oriented groups, and talking groups, and they are mushrooming. It is not really surprising for, after all, from the dawn of human history, people have organized into groups for aid and support of one kind or another. The current fashion in groups stems from the dwindling sense of community in our times. As Leslie H. Farber put it, "As community fellowship disappears, a variety of arbitrary, even makeshift, communities are devised, in which we join together for reasons of therapy, drugs, alcohol, schizophrenia, old age, youth, integration, urban violence and urban renewal."[30]

Concerned by developments in insurance and licensing, the American Group Psychotherapy Association appointed a "Defining Boundaries Task Force" to define "group psychotherapy." Surveying approximately 200 experts, it came up with the following tentative definition:[31]

Group psychotherapy is a small, carefully planned treatment system composed of the interactions of a clinically trained therapist and other group members who are clinically assessed for their suitability to the group. The therapist utilizes his or her own, and each group member's emotional, intellectual and non-verbal communications to effect personality change and greater mental health. All group members contract to participate in the group process, which they believe and feel is consistent with their personal goals and their emotional difficulties.

Like any definition, it raises many questions, *e.g.*, what is "small"?, what is "carefully planned"?, what is "treatment system"?, what is "mental health"? In short, will the definition hold up? Will it influence the law? In some groups, such as Alcoholics Anonymous, the professional psychiatrist is often looked upon with disfavor, and at the same time, AA is reputedly the most successful agency in helping those with drinking problems. The comfort and therapy comes, say the members, from the knowledge "that you are not alone." "You get serenity from talk with like-minded people."

At a Westchester, New York, murder trial, seven members of Alcoholics Anonymous testified under subpoena that another member, Paul Cox, had told them about his emerging memories of one terrible, drunken New Year's Eve, when he thought he had killed a Larchmont couple as they slept in their home. As news of the trial spread, members of self-help groups, who rely on a cooperative sense of confidentiality and anonymity, flooded the National Self-Help Clearinghouse in New York, a center with a referral list of hundreds of groups, with calls of protest. Its director said most people were outraged that the court allowed a breach of confidence, but in fact, they were alarmed about losing a legal protection that recovery groups like AA never had in the first place.[32]

Is there more to be said on behalf of one modality than another? What are the strengths and limitations of each type of group, the success or failure of various techniques? How significant is the modality? Actually one might say that there is as much difference among groups of the same modality, depending on the leader and members, as there are among groups of different modalities, but the law of privilege does not test them ad hoc. Group therapy has an ancient history, but it is now more or less commercialized, and certified, but there is no evidence warranting privilege for one type of group and not another.[33] Politics aside, in seeking privilege, it may be sink or swim together. Like the Three Musketeers, "one for all, and all for one."

As everyone knows, in *Tarasoff v. Regents of the University of California*,[34] the California Supreme Court mandated a reporting duty when a patient presents a serious danger of violence to another. But when an individual who causes harm to another is discovered to have been in therapy, as a practical matter how will it be discerned that he announced threats in the course of therapy or was considered lethal? From the therapist's records or by evidence that the therapist should have known? In *Tarasoff,* the therapist actually announced (to campus police) that threats were made. Theoretically, *Tarasoff* has greater potential in the group therapy situation, in which one or another group member might support an allegation that indeed threats were made by one of the members in the course of therapy. In the dyadic physician-patient situation, there would not be this verification unless it were put in a record that the patient made threats and is dangerous, a not very likely entry. In group therapy, my interviews seem to indicate, it appears that the group would look to the leader to defuse or handle the situation.

Maintaining a secret is a burden. Sometimes, though the secret may be interesting, we may not wish to hear it because of that burden. There are some things with which one person has no moral right to burden another, and the latter must decide for himself when the former has gone over the borderline and cannot expect the right of confidentiality. Consider one of James Thurber's cartoons where a women says to her new beau, "If you can keep a secret, I'll tell you how my husband died."

None of the testimonial privileges (including the attorney-client privilege) shield communications relating to planned or future criminal conduct. At best, they cover past history. By analogy, there are some out-of-courtroom situations in which one is not justified in holding a confidence. It is not possible to draw a line, and it may be misleading to give specific examples, but it seems that one can accept in confidence a communication from another that he has a history of child molesting, but on the other hand, if he confides that he is going to kill someone and he has obtained a gun for that purpose, then it would seem to be a tenable position for any therapist or group member to make a divulgence in a proper manner. Such decisions seem to be dictated by common sense, a strong conscience, as well as standards of professional ethics.[35]

"Mum's the word," we often say. The word "mum" is a British variant of "mom." In early life, one expects mother not to divulge secrets confided in her (and one hopes to keep things from her). The mummy (of ancient Egyptians) is all taped up. The deodorant, Mum, keeps odor from spreading; other deodorants are named "Secret," "Ban," "Right Guard." But secrets are not just about the odorous. "Mummy, don't tell daddy what I got him for Xmas." Because of the relationship, the obligation of secrecy is maintained, but using good judgment, mummy will do something if the youngster says he is going to kill his father or his siblings and he has the means to accomplish it.

In the law there is no testimonial privilege shielding the parent-child relationship, but as a practical matter there is no need for one. A disclosure could not be compelled, as a practical matter. Similarly, the employer-secretary relationship is such that notwithstanding the fact that there is no privilege covering it, there is little or no effort to subpoena one's secretary. The word "secretary," after all, has its root in *secretum*, a secret; a dictionary definition of "secretary" is "one entrusted with the secrets or confidences of a superior." Without statutory privilege, confidentiality of the relationship has remained inviolate. The much publicized subpoena of Rose Mary Woods, President Nixon's secretary, was extraordinary, but of no avail. The confidential nature of the employer-secretary relationship has maintained itself on (unexpressed) custom and tradition. One might speculate, paradoxically, that if a statutory employer-secretary privilege were enacted, it would soon be punctured with exceptions and limitations. Legislation often results in the very opposite of what it ordains.

For the most part, a member of a profession feels constrained by its code of ethics. One who breaches that ethical duty is subject to the censure of his colleagues. The professional person has his code of ethics to remind him of the need to maintain confidentiality. The average citizen sometimes, though, may need a reminder, or the threat of reprisal to help him safeguard the confidences entrusted to him. The contractual form used by some group therapists may serve that purpose, at least in certain socioeconomic groups. Others rely on periodic reminders.

What protects confidentiality among group members, more than anything else, is that each group member has something on the other, and that is a deterrent against disclosure. Group members in a way are like certain lovers. She wishes he would talk more; that he would confide in her. "Confide what?" he asks. "You pretend that you have no thoughts. Why does there have to be so much silence? I tell you what I think." "But," he says, "do I have to spend every minute talking?" Thus pressured, he talks, he confides in her, more or less. She has something on him, and he has something on her. They keep their secrets.[36]

Group therapy is something like the gambling trade (and politics) in that both operations depend essentially not on law, but on one's word. While legal protection is fragile, they operate successfully, and they do so because of trust or reliability that prevails in both systems. The conflict of authority as to the legal enforceability of gambling transactions, it may be noted, does not disturb the participants.[37]

Very often, it is not a member of the group but an outsider who is concerned about divulgences made about him in the group. In the "World at War" television series there is a report of a mother in Nazi Germany who told her younger daughter of her opposition to the regime. The little girl tells her classmates at school, and her mother is in trouble. In his book, *The Spaniard and the Seven Deadly Sins*, Fernando Diaz-Plaja says that however Catholic the Spaniard may be, he has a dislike of confession. He explains:[38]

The Spaniard always disliked permitting another what he most appreciates, the intimacy of his home. Many violent and serious bedroom quarrels are due to the disgust with which the husband sees his conjugal life regulated, or at least advised, by his wife's confessor. From this, the extreme suspicion of the psychiatrist follows logically.

Likewise, one may be indignant that he is being talked about by his spouse in the group therapy situation. He feels his privacy is being invaded. One illustration, given by a group therapist, is the wife who seeks help and reveals in group therapy the embarrassing fact that her husband is having sex relations with the family dog and is looking at porno films. Another illustration, given by another group therapist, is an executive, a married man, who is having an affair with his secretary. She enters group therapy, where she divulges all and the wife is informed by a group member.

Should the executive join a group, and talk about the secretary? Should the husband come in with his dog? Good practice may dictate that he too should be in therapy. It bodes ill for a marriage for only one spouse to go into therapy.

An individual who is in combined individual and group therapy may state that the material discussed in the individual setting should not be brought to the group. This is, of course, a defensive mechanism on the part of the patient and a denial of the group process. Nonetheless, it might be suggested that a breach of confidence would invade his right of privacy. As a matter of law, such a holding is unlikely. It might be said that the patient cannot complain when he voluntarily takes part in combined therapy.

The American Psychiatric Association's *Guidelines on Confidentiality* provide in regard group and family therapy:

> Although all group therapy participants should be expected to respect the confidences shared with them by other group members, the psychiatrist generally has no way of enforcing this. Some jurisdictions do, however, have legal requirements for group therapy participants regarding confidentiality. All new group members should be apprised of their responsibility to keep confidential matters that are discussed in the group and about the inherent limitations associated with this process. Because of these limitations, issues of trust and distrust can be expected to surface in the group and may be explored by it in a productive manner. In keeping records of group therapy, no reference to other patients in a manner that would identify them should be included in any individual chart. In order to keep a separate record of group interactions, the psychiatrist may make notes about the group that are not included in the individual charts.

In family therapy, although it may be preferable to keep records on a family basis, it is usually more practical to keep them in one of the participants's individual charts, as most facilities maintain records in this manner. Since authorization from the patient named in the chart is generally sufficient for the release of information, care must be taken about information included about other family members. Whether or not the record is kept on an individual or a family basis, it may be wise to have all of the involved family members sign a statement at the beginning of therapy acknowledging that it will contain information about all of them and specifying which signatures or combination thereof will be required to authorize access to the chart or release information from it. In the event of substantial family change, such as through divorce or a child reaching majority, particular care should be exercised not to release information inappropriately.

By and large, it appears that group therapists are more concerned than members of the group about confidentiality issues and testimonial privilege. In or out of court, group members assume confidentiality, though increasingly the assumption is being made explicit, sometimes in a contractual agreement. Be that as it may, therapists fear that one celebrated case, should it arise, would create a great deal of anxiety about group therapy. One is reminded of the divulgence regarding Thomas Eagleton, the vice-presidential candidate. At that time individuals, particularly those having political aspirations, developed second thoughts about psychiatric care.

Mental health therapists seem to be overcome with fears about *THE LAW*. In fact, though, the likelihood of assault by subpoena is slight, but should it come, there is no need to run scared. In or out of court, there are circumstances and pressures, as discussed, that tilt toward the maintenance of confidentiality. Greta Garbo told John Barrymore to go avay, she wanted to be alone. Group therapists and group members, in effect, can respond much the same to demands for information. But if group therapists have doubts, and spread doubt, can the group members long be without doubt themselves?

## NOTES

1.  "Giving Support to Sued Physicians," *Psychiatric News*, May 3, 1996, p. 1.
2.  Personal communication.
3.  H.B. Roback, R.F. Moore, G.J. Waterhouse & P.R. Martin, "Confidentiality Dilemmas in Group Psychotherapy With Substance-Dependent Physicians," *Am. J. Psychiat.* 153:10, 1996; summarized in "Impaired Physicians In Group Therapy Could Benefit From Proposed Confidentiality Law," *Psychiatric News*, Nov. 1, 1996, p. 30. See also H.B. Roback, R.F. Moore, F. Bloch & M. Shelton, "Confidentiality in Group Psychotherapy: Empirical Findings and the Law," *Int. J. Group Psychotherapy* 46:117, 1996; see P.J. Flores, "Group Psychotherapy With Alcoholics, Substance Abusers,

and Adult Children of Alcoholics," in H.I. Kaplan & B.J. Sadock (eds.), *Comprehensive Group Psychotherapy* (Baltimore: Williams & Wilkins, 3d ed. 1993), pp.429-443.

4.   L.M. Foster, "Group Psychotherapy: A Pool of Legal Witnesses," *Int. J. Group Psychotherapy* 25:50, 1975. That scenario is also presented in the novel by Jeremiah Healy, *So Like Sheep* (New York: Bantam, 1989).

     In New York, Paul Cox, a White Plains carpenter and AA member, was indicted for murdering two physicians. The indictment was based in part upon a report made by a fellow AA mamber to the White Plains Police Department. Six AA members were called as witnesses in Cox's trial to testify under compulsion to confidential communications Cox made to them. He was convicted of first degree manslaughter. J. Berger, "Alcoholic Said He Killed, Colleagues Testify," *New York Times,* June 7, 1994, p. B-1; J. Hoffman, "Faith in Confidentiality of Therapy Is Shaken," *New York Times,* June 15, 1994, p. A-1; "Retrial Begins in Murder Case Tied to Confession to A.A. Group," *New York Times,* Nov. 3, 1994, p. B-7. See also State v. Boobar, 637 A.2d 1162 (Me. 1994); see T.J. Reed, "The Futile Fifth Step: Compulsory Disclosure of Confidential Communications Among Alcoholics Anonymous Members," *St. John's L. Rev.* 70:693, 1996.

5.   I am especially grateful to Dr. Shirley Dobie of Grosse Point Park, Michigan, for suggesting and making it possible to interview one of her groups. Interviewing also a number of trial attorneys and district attorneys, I was left with the impression that they had never thought of therapy groups as a pool of information. However, an unconfirmed report related that in a number of divorce, child custody, and child abuse cases in Lafayette, Louisiana, all members of groups, where a party is involved, have been subpoenaed, frightening everyone. Whether it had gone beyond subpoena is not known. Rumor also had it that in a bank robbery investigation in another jurisdiction, it was suggested that all members of a group in which the suspect's girlfriend is a member would be subpoenaed.

6.    Personal communication.

7.    Personal communication.

8.   "The dinner is out of this world," we say, when it is perfect.

9.   B. Franklin, *Poor Richard's Almanac* (July 1735), quoted in L. M. Foster, "Confidentiality of Group and Family Psychotherapy Records," in *Confidentiality of Health Social Service Records* (Chicago: University of Illinois at Chicago Circle, 1976), p. 121.

10.  J. Moreno, Code of Ethics for Group Psychotherapy in Psychodrama: Relationship to the Hippocratic Oath (Psychodrama and Group Psychotherapy Monograph No. 31, 1962), p. 5; quoted in W. Cross, "Privileged Communications between Participants in Group Psychotherapy," *L. & Social Order* 1970:191.

11.  *Id.* at p. 3.

12.  Comment by A. Wolf to J. Moreno, *supra* note 10, at p. 8.

13.  J. Morrison, M. Frederico & H.J. Rosenthal, "Contracting Confidentiality in Group Psychotherapy," *Forensic Psychology* 7:4-5, 1975.

14. Public safety and health concerns, however, have allowed confidentiality pledges to be broken. Astra USA was not allowed to use confidentiality agreements to keep current and former employees from cooperating with the Equal Employment Opportunity Commission's sexual-harassment probe of the company. A. Choi, "Court Rules Astra Employees Can Talk to EEOC Despite Confidentiality Pacts," *Wall Street Journal,* July 1, 1996, p. B-2. Jeffrey Wigand, a cigarette executive at Brown & Williamson Tobacco Corp., was accused of making devastating allegations about his former employer to CBS's "60 Minutes." He had signed a confidentiality agreement with his employer. He faced a Brown & Williamson lawsuit charging breach of his confidentiality agreement as well as fraud and theft. S.L. Hwang, "The Executive Who Told Tobacco's Secrets," *Wall Street Journal,* Nov. 28, 1995, p. B-1.

15. Morrison sent a brief anonymous questionnaire composed of five questions to each of eight clients who regularly attended a group during 12 months of its existence. In response to Question 1: "How seriously or lightly did you take the contract at the time you signed it?" the mean group rating was 3.24 (using a four-point rating scale), indicating that the group as a whole took the contract seriously. In answering Q.2: "Do you think the contract at any time influenced you not to talk about the problems of group members to non-group members?" five clients responded affirmatively, and three negatively. Responding to Q.3: "Can you remember any occasion on which you revealed to a non-group member the name of a group member along with some confidential information about that person?" six clients replied "no," one "not sure" and one "yes." In response to Q.4: "Did you approve of engaging in a legal contract to ensure confidentiality of group information?" seven of the eight clients responded affirmatively, one was unsure. In answering Q.5: "Would you have been less likely to reveal confidential information about yourself in group had there not been a contract?" five group members replied "yes," two "no," and one "not sure."

16. Personal communication. A lawsuit alleging breach of confidentiality in group therapy followed the publication of a novel by Gwen Davis Mitchell, entitled *Touching,* in which she allegedly described a nude marathon which she attended. A jury in a California superior court returned a verdict of $50,000 for libel in favor of the psychotherapist, Paul Bindrim, against the publisher, Doubleday, and the author. The book was called a novel, and the name of the therapist and all the participants were changed, but the jury apparently felt that the main character was identifiable as Bindrim, and that the novelist had painted a distorted picture of what had transpired in the therapy session. The judgment was affirmed on appeal.

The therapist in this case had asked all of the group participants, including the author of the book, to sign a contract in which they agreed not to discuss or write about what transpired in the session nor talk about who was present. He then openly and with the knowledge of the participants recorded all group sessions and kept these tapes on file. In the litigation that followed the publication of *Touching*, it was shown that the author's description of the nude marathon group reflected what had transpired as recorded on the tape, but that she had distorted events in a libelous manner. Apparently, proving the allegation of libel would have been much more difficult without the tape recordings. (Truth is a defense to a defamation action.) Three members of the group who joined the therapist in the suit dropped their cases, apparently because of the potential difficulty of proving that their identities had been disclosed to others or that the facts revealed about them were false. The therapist's case was stronger in that he was the only person nationally known to conduct nude marathons at the time the novel was published, and he was depicted as a charlatan. Bindrim v. Mitchell, 92 Cal. App.3d 61, 155 Cal. Rptr. 29, hearing denied by California Supreme Court, 1979; *cert. denied*, 444 U.S. 984, *reh. denied*, 444 U.S. 1040 (1980).

17. N. Mykel, "The Application of Ethical Standards to Group Psychotherapy in a Community," *Int. J. Group Psychotherapy* 21:248, 1971.

18. The privilege has protected communication in marriage counseling in matrimonial actions (but usually not in child custody disputes). See Wichansky v. Wichansky, 126 N.J. Super. 156 (1973).

19. In a California case the complainant, who was enrolled in a prepaid health care plan operated by Blue Cross, brought suit against Blue Cross, charging it with wrongful refusal to pay medical expenses incurred for psoriasis treatment. As a means of pretrial discovery, the complainant propounded interrogatories, one of which sought the names, addresses and telephone numbers of other Blue Cross subscribers who had filed claims for psoriasis treatment. Blue Cross objected to the interrogatory, claiming over breadth and privilege. The California Evidence Code (§992) provides that confidentiality is lost by disclosure to a third person but retained if the third person is one "to whom disclosure is reasonably necessary for . . . the accomplishment of the purpose for which the physician is consulted." It being agreed that the patients' names and ailments were disclosed to Blue Cross for the purpose of paying the doctor's fees, the court held that confidentiality was not lost and the privilege not waived. Blue Cross v. Superior Court and Blair, Super. Ct. No. 32612 (Sept. 10, 1976). See also Whalen v. Roe, 97 S.Ct. 869 (1977) (reporting of prescription for certain drugs).

20. *McCormick's Handbook of the Law of Evidence* (St. Paul, MN.: West, E. Cleary 2d ed. 1972), §101. This point is more fully developed in W. Cross, "Privileged Communications Between Participants in Group Psychotherapy, *L. & Soc. Order* 1970: 191, 196-98, 200-01.

21. State v. Andring, 342 N.W.2d 128 (Minn. 1984); see P.S. Appelbaum & A. Greer, "Confidentiality in Group Therapy," *Hosp. & Community Psychiatry* 44:311, 1993.

22. 342 N.W.2d at 133.

23. Farrell L. v. Superior Court, 203 Cal. App.3d 521, 250 Cal. Rptr. 25 (1988); discussed in Part II, Chapter. 6.

24. 203 Cal. App.3d at 527.

25. When two or more clients retain or consult the same lawyer, the communications are not privileged unless they have expressly agreed otherwise. *The Restatement of the Law Governing Lawyers* (Tentative Draft No. 2, 1989) § 125, states that unless co-clients "have expressly agreed otherwise" their communications with lawyer or other privileged person "are not privileged as between co-clients in subsequent litigation between them." The rationale for this exception is that joint clients do not intend their communications to be confidential from each other, and typically their communications are made in each other's presence. It is said that there is no basis for favoring a joint client who seeks to assert the privilege as against the other who seeks to waive it in subsequent litigation between themselves. C.B. Mueller & L.C. Kirkpatrick, *Evidence* (Boston: Little, Brown, 1995), pp. 385-387. There may be an ethical obligation to advise joint clients of this exception to privilege. ABA Model Rules of Professional Conduct, Rule 1.7(b)(2); ABA Model Code of Professional Responsibility, EC 5-16. See Hurlburt v. Hurlburt, 127 N.Y. 420, 28 N.E. 651 (1891); Wallace v. Hurlburt, 216 N.Y. 28, 109 N.E. 872 (1915); Lawless v. Schoenaker, 147 Misc. 626, 264 N.Y.S. 280 (1933). See also Weatherford v. Bursey, 97 S.Ct. 837, at 848 (1977); "The Attorney-Client Privilege in Multiple Party Situations," *Colum. J. Law & Soc. Problems* 8:179, 1972.

26. In the Matter of Humphrey, 79 Misc.2d 192, 359 N.Y.S.2d 733 (1974).

27. Yaron v. Yaron, 83 Misc.2d 276, 372 N.Y.S.2d 518 (1975).

28. Ellis v. Ellis, 472 S.W.2d 741 (Tenn. App. 1971), noted in *Tenn. L. Rev.* 40:110, 1972. The court relied on a Michigan case, Bassil v. Ford Motor Co., 278 Mich. 173, 270 N.W. 258 (1936), where the patient was accompanied to the physician by his wife. The doctor's diagnosis was sought to be introduced in evidence. The Michigan court, holding that the wife did not constitute a third party, excluded it on the ground that it was a confidential communication.

29. It provides: "[N]or shall any person who has participated in any psychological therapy, conducted under the supervision of a person authorized by law to conduct such therapy, including but not limited to group therapy sessions, be examined concerning any knowledge gained during the course of such therapy without the consent of the person to whom the testimony sought relates." Colo. Stat. § 13-90-107 (1963).

30. L.H. Farber, *Lying, Despair, Jealousy, Envy, Sex, Suicide, Drugs and the Good Life* (New York: Basic Books, 1976), p. 4. There are in this day of specialization psychotherapy groups for married couples, homosexuals, alcoholics, narcotic addicts, gamblers, businessmen, delinquent cab drivers, released juvenile offenders, parents of all descriptions (lesbian mothers, bisexual fathers, child-beaters), and apparently any other category of humanity which shares something in common. The theme-oriented groups deal with such specific topics as creativity, sexual dysfunction, and weight reduction. Some of the newer groups are known by their theoretical underpinning, such as gestalt groups, bioenergetic groups, psychodrama groups, sensitivity groups, con-

sciousness raising groups, and marathon groups. J.Perlez, "Three's a Group," *New York Post*, Feb. 3, 1973, p. 25.

31. Presented for discussion at the 1977 annual meeting of the American Group Psychotherapy Association.

32. J. Hoffman, "Faith in Confidentiality of Therapy is Shaken," *New York Times*, June 15, 1994, p. 1.

33. The early Christian Passion Plays can be considered as group therapy, with catharsis occurring through identification with participants. Among the various cults and religions, one of the foremost techniques in relieving symptoms is confession. Among certain American Indian tribes, dreams are reported every morning, and the members of the group all associate to it.

Dr. E. Fuller Torrey in his study of psychotherapy practices around the world suggests that confession is probably more effective in relieving symptoms when done in a group setting. Confession, role-playing, and abreaction, the reliving of an emotional experience, which are all integral parts of psychodrama, are found in ceremonials in various cultures. E.F. Torrey, *The Mind Game/Witch Doctors and Psychiatrists* (New York: Emerson Hall, 1972).

Dr. Ross Speck, originator of "network therapy" (which includes the patient's family and also neighbors and friends) points to its similarity to tribal healing rituals in which the extended family, and usually other members of the tribe, join to heal a sick member by participating with him in rites that stress mutual confession and mutual aid. R.V. Speck & U. Rueveni, "Network Therapy–A Developing Concept," *Family Process* 8:182, 1969. See also J. H. Masserman, "Faith and Delusion in Psychotherapy," *Am. J. Psychiatry* 110:324, 1953.

34. 118 Cal. Rept. 129, 529 P.2d 553 (1974), on rehearing, 551 P.2d 334 (1976).

35. A. MacCormick, "A Criminologist Looks at Privilege," *Am. J. Psychiat.* 155:1068, 1969.

36. Replacing seclusion, repose, a jug of wine and thou, a weekend activity that has evolved over the past decade is the "marathon." When one goes into it, he is told something like this: "It's a form of nonstop therapy in which a dozen or so strangers shut themselves up in a room with a couple of trained therapists and try to practice total honesty 30 or 40 hours at a stretch. Privacy, save in the bathroom, is nonexistent. Meals are eaten on laps; naps, if necessary, take place right on the floor; alcohol is forbidden. This type of get-together forces out buried emotions which otherwise would take months of couch time to surface." Columnist Shana Alexander tried it, and writing for Life magazine, she had this to say: "I don't know that it was the greatest weekend of my life, but the Marathon did confirm some things that most great weekends only hint at: it can be a marvelous feeling to trust a stranger." S. Alexander, "The 300-Year Weekend," *Life*, Sept. 24, 1965, p. 29.

37. English law humorist Henry Cecil once observed: "Racing men rightly say that, whereas in ordinary transactions everything is normally written down, and often long and (to the laymen) unintelligible contracts are signed in

transactions involving only quite small amounts, in the racing world many thousands of pounds are staked by word of mouth only, and the parties are entirely dependent upon one another's honesty....The reason for it is simply that betting could not otherwise exist in this country. There are, of course, some defaulters and fraud is sometimes practiced. But the average book-maker and punter, though not in the rest of their lives necessarily conspicuous for their reliability, are completely honest in their betting transactions." H. Cecil, *Daughters-in-Law* (Middlesex: Penguin, 1963).

38. F. Diaz-Plaja, *The Spaniard and the Seven Deadly Sins* (New York: Scribner's, 1970).

# INTERVIEW OF GROUP ON
# CONFIDENTIALITY

In the course of discussing confidentiality in group psychotherapy with Dr. Shirley Dobie of Grosse Pointe Park, Michigan, Dr. Dobie made the suggestion, "Why not interview one of my groups?" It was a wonderful idea. With the permission of the group, one evening, following the group's weekly 7-9 p.m. meeting, I appeared with tape recorder. I am grateful to Dr. Dobie and members of the group for the following interview.

*Ralph Slovenko (RS)*: I am Professor of Law and Psychiatry at Wayne State University. I am grateful to have this opportunity to explore confidentiality as related to group therapy. Is confidentiality a matter of concern to you? Is it something that you think about? But first, let me ask—I understand that this group has been meeting now for some five years, is that correct?

*Man (M)-1*: Some of the group.

*M-2*: I've been here about 14 months.

*Woman (W)* 1: I've been here 2 1/2 years.

*M-3*: I'm a lifer! I think you also might want to have on tape that the composition of the group is four men, three women and a woman therapist.

*M-2*: Four women!

*M-3*: I said three women and a woman therapist.

*RS*: May we return to our initial question? Have you been concerned about the protection of privacy of what goes on here? Are you concerned about whether some member might talk about you outside the group? Has that been a matter of concern?

*W-1*: No, not to me. I assume no one would say anything.

*RS*: I understand that in some groups a formal oath to that is taken.

*Dr. Shirley Dobie, Group Therapist (GT)*: You mean the members of the group or the therapist?

*RS*: All the members of the group take an oath. I brought along a contract used by one group therapist. Everyone in the group signs, agreeing to preserve confidentiality. I can read it. [The contract is read.]

*W-3*: If anyone in the group would say anything about me, I'd talk about them. I mean, it's worked since I was in grade school. You shut up about me, I shut up about you.

*W-1*: It's kind of like an unspoken agreement.

*W-2*: Well, it isn't merely an unspoken agreement. [The group therapist] has implored us not to talk among ourselves outside the group.

*GT*: That's to say, outside the group, the other people.

*W-3*: A lot of us are in the same profession, and we run into each other outside of here.

*M-4*: Socially.

*W-3*: Yes, we run into each other socially.

*RS*: Is that a cause of embarrassment?

*W-3*: No, I enjoy running into them.

*M-4*: (speaking to W-3): I think there was a time when I went to your apartment and we were going to ride here together. I was up tight because I thought you told your roommate that I was in group therapy with you. Remember that, is was 10 years ago? I was very conscious of the fact at that time. I'm not any more.

*W-2*: I'm reminded of something. When the Aetna Life Insurance Company came to interview us for policies he asked us about psychiatric treatment. I, of course, denied that I was under psychiatric care. But one of my coworkers said he was in a group. So they put a rider on his disability insurance. I would not put it on any application form—job application form or insurance application form.

*W-3* I couldn't get insurance from several companies because I was in therapy. Blue Cross was the only one who would give it to me.

*RS*: So you would be asked whether you were in therapy and if you would reveal it, you would lose out. So you kept it a secret?

*W-3*: No, I didn't keep it a secret.

*RS*: What did you say?

*W-3*: Blue Cross just gave it to me. They didn't even ask. Prudential asked. They asked specifically whether I had had any psychiatric treatment in the last 5 years. I said yes.

*M-2*: Was that under an individual policy or group policy?

*M-3*: Individual. In a group policy I don't think they ask. But Blue Cross will give anybody insurance.

*RS*: Is your therapy here covered by insurance?

*GT*: Yes.

*M-1*: Some, but not others. Mine is not. I think I'm the only one here not covered.

*W-2*: Mine's covered.

*M-3*: General Motors has the biggest contract in the world with Blue Cross-Blue Shield. This particular GM executive, I know, wanted some information about an employee and he called Blue Cross-Blue Shield, and he got a rundown on the guy.

*M-4*: That's pretty scary.

*M-3*: Because of the fact they spend so much money there's no way the insurance company is going to refuse them that information. That was kind of alarming.

*M-4*: Who did they go to for the rundown?

*M-3*: I don't know who the guy called.

*M-4*: Where did they get the rundown?

*M-3*: Well, I don't know.

*M-4*: You mean it would be as though someone would call [the group therapist] and say–

*W-3*: No, they call Blue Cross.

*M-3*: They then found out he was taking therapy, they didn't find out the nature of it.

*W-2*: They got the name of the doctor, and everything?

*M-4*: Is there a diagnosis on the form?

*M-3*: A top executive at GM talked to a top executive at Blue Cross. There's no way they will turn that kind of information down. GM's so powerful.

*M-1*: The same way with law enforcement.

*W-1*: Let's not go into that one. I run groups. No one with a legal problem is ever in my groups. We would be waiting for the long arm of the law. I don't do group therapy with them, they're always taken individually. You open your big mouth and say "I have 400 lbs. of such-and-such in my basement" or whatever. You know it can come out. You're under stress in therapy.

*W-2*: Don't you think we should be protected legally?

*RS*: Suppose somebody just voluntarily reveals?

*M-1*: What is the answer to the question as to protection? What if I'm asked to testify?

*RS*: There are two types of problems. One, where you are called for testimony, and the other, the out-of-court situation, such as where an insurance company might ask for information, or where someone here voluntarily talks about a member of the group.

With regard to the problem of being called to testify, under prevailing law, you have no right to keep secret. But how is an attorney going to know what you are going to say? Because he doesn't know, he's not likely to call you. It's liable to boomerang against him. But strictly speaking, there is no right to remain silent when subpoenaed.

Suppose a member of this group here admits to a crime. What compulsion do you feel as a member of the group about reporting? We all know that it is a burden to have placed on us, a secret such as that. Say, a member of the group admits he killed somebody, or he plans to kill somebody. Those are two different situations.

*W-2*: I would think the responsibility would be for the therapist to do what she thought was necessary. I wouldn't feel that I was responsible.

*RS*: You would leave it to the therapist to report or not to report?

*W-2*: Or provide the treatment, or whatever she felt was appropriate.

*RS*: Would you distinguish cases where a member of the group reports a past crime for example, fondling school children—from a future act like that which happened recently in California where a man in therapy said he was going to kill a girl who had spurned him?  Would you distinguish those two situations?

*M-1*: In the first case I would feel as with anything else brought up here, that it is confidential within the group. The main thing for us is to feel free to express ourselves and have confidence in each other to do that. So if that was brought up I would respect and keep the confidence, I am sure.  With respect to a future event I think I would look to the guidance of the therapist whether she thought that could be handled by treatment or not.

*RS*: Have there been any cases that you feel you can talk about here where you feel that confidence has been breached?

*M-3*: I had an incident where I related an incident in the group. One person was absent and another member of the group met that absent person outside the group and related what I had said. But it was all within the group.

*GT*: Nonetheless, you had some strong feelings about that at the time.

*M-3*: Yeah, I felt very angered about it although in a sense it was within the group.  What we talk about here we relate to each other on a level on other than what you might on the outside.  So I felt betrayed.

*RS*: Can secrecy be realistically expected? This is an interesting activity, you hear and experience intriguing matters. How can you separate this part of your life from the rest of your life? How is it possible not to talk about what you talk about here with, say, your spouse or a close friend?  How is that possible?

*M-1*: Well, I relate bits and pieces to friends. First of all, I never mention their name.  Secondly, I don't necessarily say where I had the experience. I never mention two pieces of information that can be linked up. Naturally, sure, some days I leave here very keyed up and the first friend I run into is going to know that I'm keyed up.

*M-4*: Sure, you know it's not enough sometimes to say "I had a bad night."

*W-2*: I can, you know, pretty much show feelings after I've come out of here. If I'm feeling something I can express it to someone. I never try to relate an experience. They'll never understand, so I don't even bother. I wouldn't even want to tell anyone, it would take away the meaning of it to me.

*W-1*: The internal process—

*W-2*: But it isn't always for me. I discuss what goes on in group with my husband because some of the things that happen here give me valuable feedback in my relationship with him. He knows that it occurs in group and I do talk about it. Now he's the only one because I wouldn't discuss it with the lady I stand behind at A&P or whatever. Hell, that's why I'm here.

*M-1*: We don't get into last names and whatever.

*W-2*: We don't even know last names.

*W-3*: With a couple of exceptions.

*RS*: You don't know each other's last names?

*M-1*; *W-2*: No.

*W-3*: I know a few.

*RS*: You never use last names here?

*M-1*: No. As a matter of fact we've never named our professions.

*R.S.*: You've never revealed your professions?

*W-3*: Yeah. We all know because–

*W-2*: Because we discuss work problems here. But when I came into this group, I had no idea who was what and there were no rules whatsoever.

*RS*: I had thought that it was just in the one- or two-time group encounters where last names were not revealed. You have been meeting here for several years, and you don't know each other's last names!

*M-2*: I know the last names of two women in this group, that's it.

*M-1*: I know the people I meet professionally. And it's pretty rough when you walk up to them. "Oh, you know each other."

*RS*: Why not know a person's last name?

*W-2*: It's against the rules.

*RS*: For the purpose of keeping confidentiality?

*W-3*: I like to know last names and I think I know just about everybody's last name here. I don't call them up ever–but if I want to, I can.

*M-1*: I think it's interesting that I don't recall it ever having been a rule, but I've never asked anybody's last name.

*RS*: You think it's unconsciously a way to maintain distance?

*M-1*: A kind of cloak in here, too.

*W-2*: I think probably, you don't use last names with people you're meeting regularly, like you don't call your wife by her last name.

*W-3*: The other groups I've been in, we may even go around in a circle but most of us only use our first names. There are a few people who say "John Jones."

*W-1*: At workshops, somewhere else, I meet people and I don't know their last names.

*W-3*: There are some groups though that socialize. This group doesn't. If we did, we'd probably know last names, what size underwear they wore and everything.

*M-2*: We do our therapy here.

*RS*: What's the justification for that?

*W-3*: Very little.

*M-2*: It's a different philosophy of therapy. I'll let the people who know answer that.

*M-3*: There's one transactional analysis group I know about. They are divided into two groups, you can go to either one of them. If you miss the Monday night one you can go to the other. The group therapist encourages the members to socialize. In fact, two of them went on vacation together. In another group I know about, the group therapist encourages sexual relations. That was a very, very sticky thing because this one guy was having a relationship with a woman in the group and the husband found out about it and he was going to sue the other member in the group and subpoena all the members in the group to testify.

*M-4*: What became of it?

*M-3*: I think it's still going on.

*RS*: Is this a pending suit?

*M-3*: Threatened. I don't know what happened.

*RS*: How did the husband know about it?

*M-3*: I don't know.

*W-3*: The wife probably told him.

*RS*: Did she say it was for the purpose of therapy?

*M-3*: No, the therapist encourages this type of activity when a person really feels the need, when they are inhibited. He encouraged it especially for himself. He would be very glad to be the source for breaking down the defense barriers for the female patient. But she had a relationship with another member of the group besides the relationship she had with her therapist. The husband found out–he caught them in a motel–but he wanted to sue the third party.

*RS*: How do you describe the therapy here?

*W-1*: Much more restrained.

*W-2*: More of an analytical type of group therapy. We work on the transference. Relating on the outside–that messes up the transference we want to bring here to work on.

*W-1*: You're supposed to be more honest here than with anyone else. If you live with someone day-to-day you don't get really angry at them. You try not to get really mad at them because they remind you of your mother or your father. But here, you're supposed to do that.

*RS*: Do you feel that you're closer to the group than to people on the outside?

*W-1*: Yes.

*M-3*: In some ways. You could certainly go a lot further here than you could with a friend, very often.

*M-1*: It's really a testing ground, you know, for feelings you're not sure of. Here you can express them and see how they sound and feel and not have to act out with other people.

*W-2*: What this is really is a recapitulation of the primary family.

*RS*: Do you think you reveal more of your inmost thoughts here than you would, say, in a one-to-one therapy situation?

*W-2*: No.

*W-1*: Yes, for me. Here I get pushed into it. I'll say something and clam up and somebody will notice what's going on or they get to know me well after a few years and then more comes out.

*RS*: You say more comes out in a group than in individual psychotherapy?

*W-1*: It did for me–that's why [the therapist] put me in the group. Yes, these fellows know me when I start talking about a problem with a man they all [say] "hey, we know this, look what you're doing, etc." Yes, I think we are more revealing here.

*M-1*: There are more personalities to interact with here than just the therapist.

*M-3*: I wouldn't agree. Maybe after a while but things of a sexual nature...it took me ages before I would talk about it.

*RS*: Suppose one of you were called to testify against another; say, one of you is involved in a divorce proceeding, or child custody dispute and the attorney finds out that the litigant is in group therapy and now subpoenas you members of the group to testify regarding her fitness as a parent or whatever? Or, take another type situation. In a wrongful death action it is important to know how the deceased related to members of his family. Suppose the deceased had been a member of the group; and he had said he was planning a divorce. If you were called, how do you think you would approach this?

*M-1*: For any group to function they must do so with trust and confidence in what the members say. Therefore I would not say anything. I would try not to answer any questions.

*RS*: Suppose there were a suit between two of you. Suppose a dispute between husband and wife?

*W-2*: That doesn't exist.

*M-2*: I would say I was not competent. Whatever someone might say to me here–

*RS*: All you have to do is say what is told to you.

*M-1*: Would it not be hearsay?

*RS*: There is an exception to the hearsay rule for "admissions" of a party litigant. You're just reporting what the party has admitted. He can't complain that he was not under oath or subject to cross-examination when he made his statement.

*M-1*: Don't I have a fifth amendment right to my own mind?

*RS*: The fifth amendment applies when you are asked a question the answer to which might tend to incriminate you of crime.

*M-1*: Am I not involved? My involvement with that person in therapy might be very deep. I wouldn't be competent to testify if I had a deep, deep emotional attachment for that person.

*RS*: You feel that you would be so biased or prejudiced that anything you would say would be–

*W-1*: As a witness aren't you supposed to be objective?

*RS*: All you have to do is simply state what was said to you.

*M-4*: I might be closer to W-3 than to my own wife. In some ways. Here it is possible for me to go very, very deep and have a very deep attachment and relationship with this woman who is not my wife, more so than with my wife. I'm sure it's happened. I therefore wouldn't be competent to testify against her.

*RS*: You feel that a member here is like an extension of yourself and–

*M-1*: What goes on between us happens inside of my head, that's my fifth amendment right to keep that private and–

*W-1*: It would be very dangerous to ask me to testify either for or against a man I was perceiving as my father who had molested me as a child. It would be very dangerous for an attorney to call me as a witness, I would think.

*RS*: But here you've talked about it. You've broadcast it in a way. Suppose you had written it down in a diary. Though private, a diary may be taken from you.

*M-1*: I feel that when there is a strong, intense emotional interaction taking place, plenty of time I have misinterpreted in my own perception what was said. It was not what was said at all. I would have to say I would be incompetent as a witness because of my emotional involvement.

*RS*: But are you incompetent to repeat what was said?

*M-1*: Yes. We block.

*RS*: Why is it less reliable what you hear in the group than what you hear outside in a conversation?

*W-1*: There's more emotional involvement here.

*W-3*: Can a man competently testify against his wife? He can't.

*RS*: There is a marital privilege which bars calling one spouse as a witness against the other. But group members, in law, have no equivalent privilege.

*W-3*: I would tell them to go to hell. I would not testify against anyone in here. I wouldn't care if I was mad at them or not. I just wouldn't do it.

*RS*: But would you on his or her behalf?

*W-3*: No. I don't know if I could serve that way.

*RS*: Not even on behalf of a group member, you say? Suppose a member here asked you to testify on his behalf, let us say, in a custody dispute? His fitness as a parent may be in issue.

*M-3*: I wouldn't.

*RS*: On what grounds?

*M-3*: That what is said in here is between us and not to be disclosed in any way to anybody.

*RS*: Even though that person requests you to do so?

*M-3*: I would have conflicting views about it if I thought somebody here was being unjustly accused of an immoral act.

*RS*: Regarding a sexual crime or regarding fitness as a parent?

*GT*: It depends on the circumstances and how bad that person would need you for the testimony. If anybody in this room would need one of us to come and testify whether or not they should have custody of a child, there would be something wrong with that person. If they couldn't win custody without the group as witnesses, that would be looked at as a problem.

*M-4*: Well, what about somebody being accused of something immoral and they needed a character witness?

*W-1*: Tell them to get it from [the group therapist].

*M-4*: I'm just saying—

*W-1*: They could get somebody who would be more qualified, that would be my thought.

*M-3*: I wouldn't hesitate to do it.

*RS*: Suppose a case like one litigated in California. A young lady is in an automobile accident. Shortly thereafter she goes into therapy, and she brings suit claiming emotional and physical injury as a result of that accident. The defendant contends that this emotional condition existed prior to the accident. To establish that, he wants to depose her therapist. The therapist refuses, claiming privilege. Well, suppose one member of the group is involved in an accident and brings suit. The defense attorney seeks evidence from the other members of the group to establish that what the plaintiff complains about actually predated the accident. Members of the group could verify that what the plaintiff is complaining about was long ago revealed in the group and talked about—insomnia, nightmares, etc.

*W-2*: And the group members could verify this?

*RS*: Yes, we're assuming the plaintiff disclosed these complaints in the group, predating the accident.

*W-2*: It is scary. What would happen if we didn't testify?

*RS*: A litigant who does not allow her therapist to testify could be thrown out of court on the ground that she in effect is concealing evidence. As the argument goes, she can't use a testimonial privilege (even if one existed) as a sword. At best, it's a shield.

*M-2*: That sort of comes down to what [the group therapist] said earlier. If a person needed someone from this group to come to their defense, it's likely that something's wrong.

*RS*: Here the defense counsel wants a member of the group to establish that the plaintiff was having all these symptoms before. The defense, in effect, is claiming that the plaintiff is lying.

*M-3*: I think the key is in what M-1 said earliei about trust. Use the example of "being a fit parent" in a custody dispute. If a member of the group is sort of operating with litigation in the background, then it seems to me he might be inclined to try to create a favorable impression within the group.

*M-1*: It would change the tenor of the group. It would make it less effective if we knew in the background that there was always the possibility that somebody might have to testify as a character witness or whatever. Under those circumstances I think I would try to create a favorable impression in here and be less open or candid.

*RS*: Is that assuming that you knew that litigation was pending?

*M-1*: Just with that thought in the background–the possibility. You wouldn't be fair if you acted that way.

*M-3*: You never know what's going to happen. It's in the process of change.

*W-1*: I can't imagine [the group therapist] being able to run a group with all of us wondering who was going to testify next year should I get divorced, or something.

*RS*: The interesting thing is that while in the dyadic, one-to-one situation, there have been many subpoenas of therapists, it is rather remarkable that notwithstanding the large number of people in group therapy, there apparently has been no subpoena of any member of a group anywhere in the country.

*W-2*: Until now?

*GT*: Not now either.

*RS*: One type of problem that has arisen is very similar to the situation that you've presented with regard to a husband complaining about his wife having a sexual affair with a member of the group. It often seems that the person who complains is one outside the group. This person does not want to be talked about in the group. For example, an executive is having an affair with his secretary. The secretary goes into a group. The executive, a married man, doesn't want the secretary talking about him. He may be concerned it will get to his wife. It may be or may not be a realistic fear. More often than not it is a person outside the group, a husband or a person someone is having an affair with–complaining about what goes on in the group. Maybe your spouse complains about being talked about in the group?

*M-4*: We had this happen to us. W-3 and I worked for the same company and she related something in here about one of her employees that she was having problems with. Being a director in the particular agency, I was concerned about it and I went to the executive director and pressured him to fire the guy. Not just for what she said, but it tipped it off. I had known the guy was psychotic for years and there were a lot of things coming to a head. I didn't ask her for permission to do that, I did it on my own. W-3's internal problems are her own, but she did reveal to him that we were in a group together.

*W-3*: Right, I did. I think the thing that he was concerned about was his name. He was saying "what about the confidentiality of the agency?"

*RS*: An agency?

*W-3*:Yes, I brought the name of the agency into the group because I was having problems with a particular employee, someone who worked for me. So I talked about my job and what was going on. There are a lot of different segments of the agency and he works for a different branch, so he talked to the executive director about this and the executive director came to me. He was angry that I had told him about it.

*RS:* In a way then, you're carrying outside something that was told inside, in the group.

*M-4*: This man had made threats against her. I got a little concerned and so—but again, it was a breach, in a way, that she mentioned it to him so he told her not to mention anything more about this in group. Of course, he has no jurisdiction to do it but it could have resulted in a firing possibility.

*GT*: That's the same issue which you're taking about—somebody outside is complaining about being talked about, the privacy of the outside person.

*RS*: Yes, he feels his privacy is being invaded. You may have a husband or wife who is not a member of the group and is being talked about here.

*M-4*: It's going to happen.

*RS*: Why is the group a particular factor here? Might not you talk about this on the street? Why is this something that would only be revealed in a group? What's so secret about it?

*W-3*: Feelings are involved in here. OK, when I was upset about something that happened in my agency it had just happened and I came here and felt comfortable enough and felt the support of the group that I could tell them about it.

*RS*: You wouldn't say it—

*W-3*: On the outside? Well, I can't say I wouldn't say it to people on the outside too. Yeah, I would talk about it on the outside.

*RS*: So what is secret about that information?

*GT*: That's a good point, you don't have a confidentiality agreement with him.

*M-4*: You may very well have discussed it at lunch.

*RS*: Agency people—that's a bit different from a situation where there's something private outside and one of the people to that private relationship divulges it in a group.

*M-4*: But outside I try to flavor everything. I won't tell the whole thing unless it's to my wife, but in here I can let it all hang out and I might be kind of jaundiced that day in the view of the whole thing. But say M-3 heard me say these particular things about my agency or my particular program or the director—say somebody came to him and wanted to know if they could get a job at my place—you know, he could very well be influenced into saying "now they're all scattered, or they're all mixed up." You know.

*RS*: Well, how do you justify using information that you've learned in a group to act on outside?

*M-4*: Well, you shouldn't. You don't. I did in this instance, but I shouldn't.

*W-2*: W-3 was very mad at M-4 for it.

*W-3*: I was concerned about the confidentiality about this and he broke it when he went outside. But I understood that he was doing it for my best interest. He was doing it because he felt protective of me.

*W-2*: I think this is an example that confidentiality does get broken. So you know, those fancy contracts you were talking about—people act out unconsciously.

*RS*: This contract that some group therapists recommended is based on the idea everybody needs some kind of restraint. The fact that you have this contract with a stipulation about a certain amount of money damages may make you think twice about talking or acting outside the group on information learned here.

*M-2*: There is no restraint.

*RS*: On using it outside?

*M-2*: I don't see how we could do therapy if we were restrained.

*RS*: It would be a strong reminder not to talk about it outside. Maybe you just forgot about privacy. Maybe you might feel it's not important—

*M-2*: See, it's two different questions. The legal thing I wasn't worried about naturally. I don't care anymore if anybody knows if I'm in therapy. I used to. So I'll mention it to—well the secretary, she's in group therapy, we'll talk about it and I forget after a while who told me who was in group, there are so many people in therapy. So I'll mention it. You also may say you're in group with me.

*RS*: Maybe now on voir dire examination any attorney ought to ask prospective jurors whether they are in group therapy with any party, witness, or member of the court!

*M-4*: I was wondering, for instance, M-3 and I work for competing companies, and I were to take an unfair advantage over his firm from something I learned here. Conceivably I might learn the weak points of his company, and vice versa. I might steal business from him.

*RS*: One group therapist in New York tells me of a situation he had in his group in which one woman in the group was complaining bitterly (among other things) of great poverty and privation in her life. Others in the group felt she was exaggerating and needlessly "poor mouthing" her life, to arouse sympathy. One of the group members finally undertook a door-to-door can-vass, in the complaining woman's neighborhood, collecting several bags of old clothes, and some money for her, then bringing these into the group. In a sense, she had publicized that the women in question was talking about being poor, but had hardly revealed anything very great. As far as the reac-tion back in the therapy group was concerned, there was chagrin on the part of the complaining woman, some indignation from other group members about "taking group matters outside the group" but generally, I'm told, the matter was of little consequence. It was the only situation that this group ther-apist in his long experience was able to report where members of the group had acted out outside the group.

*GT*: The only situation that I can think of where that might be acceptable to me would be, for example, if a group member were accused of a murder which everybody in here was absolutely sure she hadn't had anything to do with and she brought it up and said: "look the court date is Wednesday and I don't think I have enough witnesses. Could you, would you consider testi-fying for me?" I think it would be something we could discuss you know—

*RS*: To what would you testify?

*GT*: To whether we would be willing to testify.

*RS*: As to what?

*GT*: For her.

*W-2*: As to whether I was there at the time of the murder—yeah, I'd pull [the group therapist] in.

*W-1*: That we think that you didn't do it.

*RS*: What would you testify to, how would you know?

*W-1*: I would testify that she didn't do it.

*W-3*: How do you know?

*W-1*: Well, maybe she was in the group that night, at the time of the mur-der.

*W-2*: If I was here that night I would pull [the group therapist] in, I would-n't have to use the group.

*W-1*: Or that you told us all that you did something else. Or as character witnesses, or some reason.

*W-3*: I can see agreeing as a group that it would be a good idea that we should do it and thus agreeing we would be willing to do it?

*W-3*: What are the implications of all these malpractice suits?

*RS*: Group therapy or what?

*M-1*: Surprisingly, suits involving group therapy are so infrequent that it's almost something not even thought about.

*RS*: What is your concern about malpractice?

*M-3*: We run groups also and we run individual therapy, and we're wor-ried about malpractice.

*RS*: Where a member of the group would sue the group therapist?

*M-3*: Hmmm. In the process of referring one person to another there would be a number of people who would have access to information about that person. You would have to give his records to so-and-so and maybe that person would have to transfer them to another agency, they have a waiting list or whatever, and the implications of having insurance in case the client sued you because somebody got the wrong information.

*M-4*: They sign a release of information, I hope, if you're transferring records.

*M-1*: The point is that there are very few suits in the field.

*RS*: Do you keep records?

*GT*: Hmmm.

*RS*: After each meeting you make a record on each member?

*GT*: Primarily I keep record of who was there and maybe a couple of sentences about the mood of the group. I used to keep very elaborate notes. I used to tape. I stopped that because of legal things. I don't want to have a lot of records.

*RS*: Do you write down and report things that have been said or just the mood of the group?

*GT*: The mood.

*RS*: Could you give an example.

*GT*: I probably would write tonight that all the members of the group had some kind of break-through and got into some intense feeling that was new.

*W-2*: Do you keep group notes? Do you write down under each of our records what happens or do you just keep group notes?

*GT*: Group notes.

*M-3*: [The therapist] once said she might look up the fact whether or not somebody had a beard or mustache at a certain point in time. That interested me.

*GT*: I used to keep much more elaborate notes.

*W-2*: For what?

*RS*: Why did you stop?

*GT*: Legally. I didn't want to have–

*RS*: Why did you keep them before, for what purpose?

*GT*: I thought it would be helpful to go back over my notes.

*RS*: What made you stop–what did you fear in the law?

*GT*: A subpoena. I started doing more court work.

*RS*: What do you mean?

*GT*: Lawyers–don't trust them so I stopped taking notes.

*RS*: In what way don't you trust them?

*GT*: A little bit like what you're doing now. They push. You don't have the freedom to talk about things the way you want to talk about them.

*RS*: I'm trying to get answers to questions that have come up and that's why—

*GT*: I'm in the mood of ducking you.

*M-3*: The psychiatrist that works at my clinic keeps no records.

*W-3*: You've got to for Blue Cross, though.

*M-4*: Uhuh. Not in private practice, though.

*RS*: In an agency you have to keep records.

*W-3*: Even in private practice you have to.

*M-4*: You do not.

*GT*: You have to keep attendance records.

*M-4*: Attendance records only.

*W-3*: Every time you charge someone you have to have something written down for the date that you charged them.

*M-4*: Just by saying they were there.

*W-3*: I thought it had to be a little more than that.

*W-1*: Agencies have more on the record.

*M-4*: It depends on the agency. In some you have to have an explanation of the diagnosis.

*GT*: I don't keep any records and we don't mention any criminal activities. I don't care if they told me blah-blah-blah.

*M-1*: If a guy's on heroin, it's a criminal activity.

*GT*: That's right.

*M-3*: We have groups, we run groups. Blue Cross-Blue Shield will be coming in pretty soon to look at our notes. We just became aware of all of this stuff and have to go back through all those notes and change a lot of stuff in there.

*GT*: They never read my notes. I never let them. I hold the record and she would say, "Do you have a note on 6/16/96?" and I'd say, "Yes, the patient was in and was seen by the therapist and did blah-blah."

*M-2*: But can they get the record?

*GT*: They never demanded.

*M-3*: You can say I will stand here with the record and I will show you that there was an entry on this date.

*GT*: Yes, they do not have to go through the record.

*M-4*: They have a right to that information. We're changing our dictation to make it so general that if they do look they're not going to see anything, but some of the older records have all kinds of material collected.

*W-1*: I don't know what [the therapist] does to try to protect confidentiality.

*W-3*: When I had my job interview for where I'm working now, we talked about therapy. I mentioned I was in.

*W-2*: Well, you're in the mental health field.

**R.S.**: Are you covered by insurance?

**W-3**: Yeah.

**RS**: How do you go about getting it paid?

**W-3**: I dropped Blue Cross-Blue Shield because I was having a big hassle with them getting the money. Their computer broke down and they said I owed them money for which I had not reimbursed them. I have new insurance.

**RS**: And what does this insurance cover? Is it an individual or group policy?

**W-3**: It's through work.

**RS**: Does the employer then get to know about your therapy?

**W-3**: No, he doesn't know, but it could happen that he could find out if he wanted to. He could check probably and find out. But he hasn't.

**RS**: The insurance company doesn't advise the employer that its employees are—

**W-3**: No.

**M-3**: I once worked in a personnel department with people who handle those records. They are my personal friends. I went to therapy every week or every two weeks and claimed it on my Blue Shield. The Blue Shield clerk was a good friend of mine and I never had any indication from those people that they knew.

**W-3**: Now bills are sent directly to Blue Cross.

**RS**: How does the insurer know that you're an employee covered by the group policy?

**M-3**: By your number.

**W-3**: Yes, you have a number and a card. You fill out all these papers—reams of papers. They have all this garbage on you.

**M-3**: Your group number indicates what kind of coverage you're receiving.

**RS**: But it never gets back from the insurer to your employer?

**W-2**: In a way it is logical to say that your employer owns that information since it pays for your policy. I think it's immoral but the employer could think that way.

**W-1**: They don't own the information—

**W-2**: If the employer wanted to fire me they'd probably dig up that information.

**M-1**: They don't have the legal right to do it, I don't think.

**W-1**: Well, do they or not?

**M-3**: They don't have the legal right.

**M-2**: To go back—what if I'm called to testify, and I say I don't want to. What would be the consequence?

**RS**: On the one hand it's a theoretical problem; on the other a practical one. An attorney is not likely to put you on the stand unless he knows what you're going to say or unless he can get hold of a record. Unless he had this handle over you—

*M-2*: Wait a minute. It would seem to me that a lawyer, if he wanted to peruse this, would say that there are sanctions if I don't testify.

*RS*: Consider, if you will, the Tarasoff case that occurred in California. A young immigrant student was in individual therapy at the university clinic. He felt spurned by a girl at the school. He told the therapist that he was going to kill her when she returned from vacation. The clinic felt that confidentiality precluded revealing these threats. When the girl returned to school, he did indeed carry out the threat. It was known that he had made these threats because the therapist, a psychologist, had told the campus police (who had no arrest authority) about it; they found him rational and simply cautioned him about making threats. The clinic did nothing further on the grounds of confidentiality. As a practical matter in the dyadic situation nobody would ever know that the patient made threats unless records were kept. Now that possibility is greater in a group because if one of you—hypothetically speaking—commits an offense and then it is found out that you were a member of a group, and then—this is all theoretical but possible—the members of the group are asked, "Did this member of the group make threats that he was going to kill or injure someone?" The California Supreme Court in the Tarasoff case imposed a duty on the therapist to divulge. Now when you have the group situation, does that mean that there is a duty not only for the therapist but on each member of the group? You are all something of a therapist to other members of the group, are you not?

*W-2*: So we would all have to divulge, in other words?

*RS*: That might be required.

*W-2*: Now this psychiatrist with the girl in the accident—he said he wouldn't testify?

*RS*: Apparently he's taking contempt.

*W-2*: Well that's what I think we'd have to do.

*W-1*: Did the therapist adequately serve his client? If I was that therapist, having a client who said he was going to kill someone, I would take steps to protect my client. If he kills someone, he's going to jail. That's not protecting my client.

*RS*: How would the therapist act?

*GT*: You could talk about hospitalization. You could talk about the ramifications that if you do this you may end up dead.

*RS*: It may be difficult to have him committed. However, good sense and good conscience would dictate doing something about a member making serious threats, and who has a gun.

*W-1*: In that case I think you would have an obligation to notify the police as well as the girl who was being threatened.

*M-1*: You mean the therapist doing that?

*W-1*: Yes, I think that's one time, to protect others, you violate confidentiality.

*W-2*: The therapist did.

*RS*: The campus police in the Tarasoff situation did not have police power. The California court said that the therapist had a duty to tell the girl or her parents or the police. What about the case that was presented where there is a sexual affair going on between two members of the group and one of them is married? Do you feel any responsibility there?

*W-1*: To testify?

*RS*: To testify or to inform.

*W-1*: Oh no. No way.

*RS*: How about child abuse? Assume you know that one member of the group is battering his child.

*W-1*: I would turn that over to the therapist. I think if the therapist didn't do something, I would have some strong feelings about the therapist. What was she doing, anyhow?

*W-2*: Yes, she would have to do something about it on her own initiative.

*M-1*: Is there a legislative remedy for all this? Can we march on Lansing?

*RS*: Actually, when I was invited to present on group therapy and confidentiality at the meeting of the American Group Psychotherapy Association, I said, "You know there apparently haven't been any legal problems involving group therapy. Will discussing it open a Pandora's box?"

*M-3*: I think Dr. Johnson from Masters and Johnson already did that at the convention in San Francisco when she addressed the sex therapists' association. She said the "lawyers are getting hungry." There's a Pandora's box if you want to go for suits.

*M-1*: Suppose someone in this group is involved in the way you mentioned where we might all be subpoenaed. Some of us, do we not have a right, not to have it published that we're in therapy? Suppose the case is covered in the newspaper. Don't I have a right to my own privacy? I come here voluntarily; it's a very private matter. It involves my right to privacy.

*RS*: You feel that on the basis of this right to privacy that the very fact that you're here ought to be kept secret, and even more, what you say here?

*M-1*: Right. Just the fact that I'm in this process I would not want my employer to know.

*RS*: Is privacy the greatest value?

*M-2*: No.

*M-1*: Is testifying the greater value?

*RS*: That is the question

*M-1*: What if it distorted me? What if I'm really hung up?

*RS*: I see that we must now bring this to a close. It has been very interesting. Thank you very much.

# Part III

# TERMINATION OF PRIVILEGE

Chapter 1. Waiver of Privilege
Chapter 2. The Self-defense Exception

# Chapter 1

# WAIVER OF PRIVILEGE

The essence of any privilege is that it may be waived or terminated by the person who enjoys it. Thus, for testimonial privileges, a confidential communication is protected from disclosure at the instance of the person who owns the privilege (or one acting on his behalf). The medical or psychotherapy privilege belongs to the patient, not to the physician. It is for the benefit of the patient. The patient has the option to require either silence or testimony from his physician (under ordinary process of summoning witnesses) on any communication made on the basis of the professional relationship which existed between them.

Likewise, the attorney-client privilege belongs to the client and not to the attorney. In Roman law, however, the attorney had both the privilege and the duty to refuse to give testimony. The conventional word of honor of a gentleman seems to have accounted for the attorney's obligation under Roman law and later. In the age of gallantry, there was legal recognition of a gentleman's instinctive revulsion at violating a confidence. Therefore, it was expected that an attorney, being an officer of the court, as well as the representative of his client, should not be forced to violate the accepted code of a gentleman. The privilege was in the beginning strictly the attorney's.[1]

From the eighteenth century on, however, the duty of loyalty, conceived in terms of the attorney's duty to his client (his employer), overtook the notion of the gentleman-attorney's honor.[2] The attorney was no longer "immune" from a waiver. Professor Max Radin stated:[3]

> At common law the case has been different ever since the eighteenth century....
> It was not the lawyer's dignity but the client's interest that forbade disclosure
> of anything communicated between the two, and the inevitable inference was
> that since the client was the best judge of his interest, he might permit such a
> disclosure.

From the beginning of the eighteenth century, following the French Revolution, all personal rights were cast in law in terms of property rights. Dr. Thomas Szasz, describing the patient's ownership of the medical privilege, wrote:[4]

> [T]he patient's secret and potentially self-damaging communications are regarded as if they were his possession, like material things that can be owned (for example, money). Thus, his "property-right" is protected by tradition and law. By the same token, since the "secrets" are the patient's, he may give them away, should he wish to.

Since the privilege is the patient's, the physician or psychiatrist can be compelled to testify when the patient or ex-patient so desires. The patient is given legal control over his destiny, irrespective of other factors. The patient may believe, quite unrealistically, that testimony by his psychotherapist may aid his legal position. A patient's waiver of the privilege may conceivably be a self-destructive technique; it may be an expression of hostility toward the psychiatrist; or it may be an attempted repetition of an early power struggle. Even an attempt to clarify to a patient why it would be inadvisable to call upon the therapist to testify can be markedly prejudicial to effective therapy, especially when it comes at an inappropriate stage in treatment.

It has been urged that privilege in the psychiatrist-patient relationship should belong to the psychiatrist as well as, or rather than, to the patient. When an individual waives a privilege such as the attorney-client privilege, or the privilege against self-incrimination, the decision is made with awareness of the material which will be disclosed. However, in psychotherapy it may be detrimental for the patient to see, for example, the report of projective tests which he has taken. When the patient waives the psychotherapy privilege, he does not know what he is waiving. It may be harmful to reveal to the patient that he has been labeled schizophrenic (whatever that might mean).

Should the law allow an individual to make an irrational or irresponsible decision? Should the privilege be waivable? Privacy of the unconscious or of one's fantasy life is a requisite of man's dignity; no one can remain dignified when the contents of his unconscious are disclosed. The philosopher Immanuel Kant contended that man must assert his own dignity so far as it is the general dignity of man represented in him. Under such a view, such general human dignity is not waivable.[5] Moreover, it is generally considered in the law that a person may not waive a right if he is a minor or incompetent (mentally ill or senile).

As discussed earlier, Dr. Lifschutz argued a right of privacy separate from that of any individual patient, a right derived from what he saw as a duty not to a particular patient alone but to all patients. He argued that the disclosure of one patient's confidential communications causes damage to all of the therapist's other patients. That argument is echoed in the book *The New Informants* by Christopher Bollas and David Sundelson.[6]

It is to be noted that an Episcopalian priest (and other clergy) must keep absolutely secret anything told to him in a confession, even when the penitent (confessor) requests that the priest divulge what was communicated.[7] The Episcopal Church's *Reconciliation* states: "The secrecy of a confession is morally absolute for the confessor, and must under no circumstances be broken."[8] The opinion expressed by Rev. Percy Rex in regard to waiver of the priest-penitent privilege is noteworthy. When asked to testify upon waiver of the penitential privilege, he stated publicly:[9]

> It is impossible to see how anyone could or would waive his privilege of confidence in a clergyman unless he is under some kind of pressure and falls into the trap of "selling his soul for a mess of pottage" .... I refused to answer questions about information given me in confidence, because (a) as a priest in the church of God I must hold inviolate information, given me in confidence, for the protection and welfare of those who seek my godly counsel, and for the protection of my function as a pastor in the community where I serve; (b) as a priest in the Church of God I consider that information given me in any pastoral counseling situation is in the nature of a confession under religious sanction, no matter how informal the counseling situation may be; (c) as a priest in the Church of God any action by a person in waiving his privilege of confidence does not free me to give amy information I may have about him or his trouble, even under subpoena, for public record or for any use he may wish to make of such testimony at the moment.... The attempt to waive the privilege of confidence by a person who comes to me does not free me from my obligation as a priest to hold in confidence information given me in the counseling situation. I fail to see what useful purpose would be served by my revealing what was said. He knows what he said to me and if he chooses he can say the same things in his own testimony in court.

Does a patient's consent to a therapist to write an article or book about the patient constitute a waiver of the privilege? Does it constitute a waiver as to other communications related to those actually revealed in the publication? The issue arose in the context of the attorney-client privilege involving a book about a sensational case. After a Rhode Island jury acquitted Claus von Bulow in 1984 on charges of assault with intent to murder his wife, she brought through next friends a federal civil action against him alleging common law assault, negligence, fraud and RICO violations arising out of the same circumstances as the state criminal prosecution. In May 1986, Random House published defense counsel Professor Alan Dershowitz's book *Reversal of Fortune - Inside the von Bulow Case.* The plaintiff's attorney notified von Bulow in April 1986 that publication of the book amounted to waiver of the attorney-client privilege and later sought discovery of various other attorney-client discussions relating to communications referred to in the book. Agreeing that a waiver had taken place, the district court ordered discovery.[10]

Disagreeing with both, Von Bulow petitioned the Second Circuit for a writ of mandamus directing the lower court to vacate its discovery order. Reasoning that the discovery issue is one of first impression and important to the administration of justice, the Second Circuit, in an opinion by Judge Richard Cardamone, spoke to the merits of the case and ordered the discovery ruling set aside as overly broad.[11] Conceding that waiver extends to those communications the client had authorized Dershowitz to include in the book, Judge Cardamone nevertheless concluded that the lower court erred in extending the doctrine of "implied waiver" based on fairness considerations to include all communications between Von Bulow and Dershowitz relating to these published conversations as well as all communications between Von Bulow and any defense counsel relating to the published conversations. Distinguishing those instances where a client makes "selective" and self-serving disclosures of privileged material in a litigation setting, Judge Cardamone declared:

> But where, as here, disclosures of privileged information are made extrajudicially and without prejudice to the opposing party, there exists no reason in logic or equity to broaden the waiver beyond those matters actually revealed. Matters actually disclosed in public lose their privileged status because they obviously are no longer confidential. The cat is let out of the bag, so to speak. But related matters not so disclosed remain confidential. Although it is true that disclosures in the public arena may be "one-sided" or "misleading," so long as such disclosures are and remain extrajudicial, there is no *legal* prejudice that warrants a broad court-imposed subject matter waiver. The reason is that disclosures made in public rather than in court—even if selective—create no risk of legal prejudice until put at issue in the litigation by the privilege-holder.

After the death of the patient, many of the modern privilege laws, unlike the original privilege laws, enumerate the persons who may waive the privilege (*e.g.*, Ohio, Wisconsin). The various statutes provide that the bringing of certain types of action (such as personal injury, will contest, or malpractice) will waive the privilege.[12] Properly speaking, the latter situations might be called "termination of privilege" rather than "waiver." Although a waiver results in the termination of privilege, the term "waiver" ought to apply only to the situation where the patient voluntarily gives up his privilege and requires the physician to testify, and not to other cases where the privilege is terminated.

It is not uncommon for therapists to receive requests after the death of a patient for disclosure of confidential information. Such requests may be by relatives contesting the patient's will, police or life insurance companies investigating the cause of death, or bereaved family members attempting to deal with their own guilt or emotional distress.[13] The therapist is bound, both ethically and legally, to maintain confidentiality to the same extent after death of the patient as before, unless the law otherwise authorizes disclosure. The great weight of authority is that the right to waive the privilege extends to the patient's legal representatives after the patient's death.[14] (The writing of articles or books about a deceased patient occurs in an extrajudicial context and therefore raises issues of confidentiality, not privilege.)

In will contest cases, where the testamentary capacity of the testator is often under inquiry, there may be an attempt to overthrow a will through proof of the mental capacity of the testator at the time of the making of the will.[15] As a general rule, the courts say that those who stand in the place of the patient (the owner of the privilege) may waive the privilege. This is generally held to include the heirs of the deceased as well as the executor or administrator of the estate. The reason given is that the heir or personal representative will be as concerned with the preservation of the decedent's reputation and estate as was the decedent.

The majority of courts hold that a person having the right of waiver may exercise it as either a proponent or contestant of the will. The purpose of contesting the will is to determine whether the purported testament is, in fact, that of the decedent, or whether it is void as a result of the decedent's mental incapacity at the time of its making. Thus, in a Minnesota case, the court decided that the beneficiary of an insurance policy, the husband of the deceased, could waive the privilege, and implied that any personal representative or heir claiming an interest would be allowed to do the same.[16] A New York statute limits the right of waiver of the deceased patient's representative to those communications which are not confidential and which do not tend to disgrace the memory of the decedent. In a case that generated considerable critical comment in the law reviews, the physician was not allowed to answer questions concerning the effect of arteriosclerosis on the individual's mental capacity in writing a will.[17] The heir's waiver of the privilege permitted the doctor to testify only as to matters a layman could notice and describe, namely, that the patient had arteriosclerosis. The physician could not testify, however, as to information derived by reason of treating the patient. There is, however, no restriction in most other states in a waiver provision excluding confidential communications. A few courts suggest that disclosures which would tend to disgrace the decedent's memory should be barred. The Connecticut statute on the psychiatrist-patient privilege provides that when a deceased patient's mental condition is introduced by any party claiming or defending through or as a beneficiary of the patient, there is no privilege if the judge finds "that it is more important to the interests of justice that the communication be disclosed than that the relationship between patient and psychiatrist be protected."[18]

Some law firms, at the time of preparation of a will, assemble proof that might be needed in the event of a will contest. Statements are taken from lay witnesses who can establish, if any issue is later raised, that the testator was of sound mind. However, if a psychiatrist is called in to examine the testator, and a will contest should later occur, the argument would inevitably then be made that there must have been serious misgivings about the testator's mental competency, otherwise a psychiatrist would not have been called.[19] To avoid suspicion, law firms can make it a matter of ordinary routine by regularly resorting to psychiatric evaluation even though the testator clearly has capacity to make a valid will. This procedure, however, would be inordinately costly for the small law firm.

Like many therapists, Susan Forward, a clinical social worker in Los Angeles, wrongly believed patient confidentiality rules do not prevail after death of the patient. She had treated Nicole Brown Simpson and she told reporters, when O.J. Simpson was charged with killing her and Ron Goldman, that Simpson had beaten her during their seven-year marriage and stalked her after their divorce. The California Board of Behavioral Science Examiners brought charges and the California attorney general's office, in a seven-page accusation, accused her of "soliciting media exposure" and thereafter disclosing "unauthorized confidential communications."[20] The American Psychiatric Association's *Guidelines on Confidentiality* state:[21]

> Psychiatrists should remember that their ethical and legal responsibilities regarding confidentiality continue after their patients' deaths . . . In cases in which the release of information would be injurious to the deceased patient's interests or reputation, care must be exercised to limit the released data to that which is necessary for the purpose stated in the request for information.

The various state statutes on the psychiatrist-patient privilege, as noted, provide three general situations in which the privilege is to be treated as terminated: The first authorizes a psychiatrist to end the privilege to a limited extent when he determines that his patient needs hospitalization; the second deals with the situation in civil or criminal cases in which a person is ordered by court to submit to an examination; the third applies in civil cases where the patient sues for compensation for a psychiatric disability.[22] There is also the situation that we shall discuss where the patient has declared his intention to commit a violent crime and does so and the therapist is obliged to testify.[23]

Under the majority rule, the privilege is waived whenever the patient makes an issue of his medical condition.[24] It is usually held that not only does the filing of a lawsuit that places the plaintiff's medical condition at issue constitute waiver of the plaintiff's privilege, but that it also allows for *ex parte* interviews of the plaintiff's treating physician by defense counsel.[25] Two minority views, however, hold that there is no automatic waiver upon the filing of a lawsuit. Under one view, there is no waiver until the patient testifies or proffers the physician's testimony at trial. Under a second minority view, the filing of a lawsuit creates a limited waiver of the privilege for discovery purposes, but prohibits any use of the privileged matter until the plaintiff testifies at trial.[26]

As a general principle, a privilege must be timely asserted in order to prevent discovery.[27] The privilege is waived when records are released to the opposing attorney or a witness list is filed naming the treating physician.[28] Once the privilege has been waived, the physician is like any other witness.[29]

Upon a claim of privilege, the judge (not jury) decides whether the privilege applies. The judge decides whether the appropriate relationship existed, whether the communication was confidential, whether there is an exception, or whether it has been waived or terminated. In making this decision, the judge puts the burden of persuasion on the claimant to show that the privilege applies, but puts the burden on the party seeking information or offering evidence to prove an exception applies. While litigants are not obliged to seek an advance ruling by a "motion in limine" ("at the threshold"), the judge will usually rule in advance on an evidence objection.

The therapist has an obligation to assert the privilege on the patient's behalf unless the patient has indicated an intention that it be waived. One asserting waiver has the burden of proving that waiver occurred. The exceptions to privilege do not *ipso facto* warrant a voluntary disclosure by the therapist. Thus, a therapist who makes disclosures to a court-appointed examiner for purposes of commitment or to a Friend of the Court in child custody cases must justify that the disclosures were reasonably necessary to protect the interests of the patient or others.[30]

A voluntary disclosure of information even in a judicial proceeding may result in liability for breach of confidentiality. In *Renzi v. Morrison*,[31] Dr. Helen Morrison saw Neil and Diane Renzi, separately, for marriage counseling. After the husband filed for divorce and temporary custody of their daughter, the wife learned that Dr. Morrison had discussed her tests and evaluations with him. She informed Dr. Morrison that she intended to exercise her right to keep her communications privileged pursuant to Illinois' Mental Health and Developmental Disabilities Confidentiality Act.[32] At the custody hearing, the court overruled the wife's objection and allowed Dr. Morrison to testify about her communications, her psychological test results, and to give an opinion of her emotional health. Based on Dr. Morrison's testimony, the court awarded temporary custody of the child to the husband. The wife brought suit for damages, claiming that Dr. Morrison's testimony violated her right to keep the communications privileged pursuant to the Illinois legislation. The appellate court, finding that Dr. Morrison could be held liable for damages, noted that Illinois law allows a therapist to reveal a patient's confidences only after a court examines the testimony in camera and determines that it is relevant, admissible, and more important to the interest of justice than a patient's right to confidentiality. Furthermore, the party seeking to disclose confidential communication must establish a compelling need for its production. The court pointed out, "In this case the court did not appoint Morrison to evaluate Renzi. The court did not subpoena Morrison to appear or order her to testify. She appeared voluntarily and offered to testify for Renzi's husband. Morrison's function was to treat Renzi, not to advise the court."[33] The court rejected Dr. Morrison's argument that Illinois common law grants witness immunity for testimony given at a judicial proceeding, because the state's Confidentiality Act specifically grants to anyone aggrieved by the Act's violation the right to sue for damages.[34]

While the patient is the owner of the privilege, the therapist as a fiduciary has an obligation to exercise it on behalf of the patient. Though there may be an exception to privilege, the trial judge may find otherwise or may rule that the evidence is cumulative or not relevant. Disclosure of protected information that is made voluntarily, without prior resort to judicial evaluation, is not given immunity by virtue of the fact that the disclosure is made in the course of a judicial proceeding.[35] There is divided opinion, as discussed in another chapter, about an attorney for the defense communicating *ex parte* with the patient's physician when the patient has filed a lawsuit alleging injury and thereby has waived the privilege under the patient-litigant exception.[36]

Unless the patient signs forms allowing for the release of records or the court orders disclosure, the treating doctor is well advised to maintain confidentiality. It is a safeguard against a disciplinary action or a lawsuit for malpractice or breach of confidentiality.[37] While a court would likely order disclosure, when push comes to shove, one cannot say with certainty, given that the law on privileged communication has a number of slippery concepts—"relevancy" and "prejudice." Without the patient's consent to disclose, the prudent course is to stonewall.

When a subpoena is received, a therapist tends to think that it is an order of the court, and willy-nilly releases treatment records. Subpoenas are issued by the attorney without court review. The therapist has the right—nay, obligation—to assert the therapist-patient privilege on behalf of the patient, at least until such time as the patient has had the opportunity to be notified and involved in the legal proceeding.[38] The therapist should alert the patient's attorney, who may file a motion to quash the subpoena or to obtain a protective order limiting disclosure to that which is necessary and relevant.[39]

## NOTES

1. The common law attorney-client privilege originated in England in Elizabethan times (there had been no compulsory process for witnesses earlier). See M. Guttmacher, *The Mind of the Murderer* (New York: Farrar, Straus, 1960), p. 162; E. Morgan, "Suggested Remedy for Obstructions to Expert Testimony by Rules of Evidence," *U. Chi. L. Rev.* 10:285, 1942.

2. An attorney who is asked to testify for his client would turn the case over to another attorney, so that the court (judge or jury) would not confuse what he says as a witness and what he advocates as an attorney, and there is also the element of prejudice to be avoided. Should the attorney-client relationship come to an end, there are two possibilities: (1) If the ex-attorney attempts to testify for the adversary, the client would assert the privilege. (2) If the ex-attorney testifies for the client, the hearsay objection (unless there is an exception) can be urged to bar the production of the client's statements.

3. M. Radin, "The Privilege of Confidential Communication Between Lawyer and Client," *Calif. L. Rev.* 16:487, 1928.

4. T.S. Szasz, "The Problem of Privacy in Training Analysis," *Psychiatry* 25:195, 1962.

5. H. Silving, "Manipulation of the Unconscious in Criminal Cases," in L. Bear (ed.), *Law, Medicine, Science—And Justice* (Springfield, IL.: Thomas, 1964),p. 247.

6. Northvale, N.J.: Jason Aronson, 1995.

7. Dr. Abraham L. Halpern reports (in a personal communication) a criminal case in which he testified on behalf of the defendant that an Episcopal priest who had had conversations with the defendant and who was privy to information that would have been very helpful to him, and who indeed had affection and respect for the defendant and believed in his innocence, nevertheless felt duty-bound to reveal nothing of what had been communicated to him though the defendant pleaded with him to do so. In any event, the evidence would not likely be admissible at trial. Statements of a party may be used against him as an admission but statements offered on his behalf require some other exception to the hearsay rule.

8. *Reconciliation,* p. 446.

9. In the Van Sant alienation-of-affections suit in Delaware, where at the time there was not a priest-penitent privilege, counsel made a motion asking that the Rev. Percy Rex be compelled to answer any and every question put to him. Rev. Rex asked the court that he be excused. Answer to Motion to Compel Answer, Civil Action No. 154, Superior Court, Wilmington, Del. The suit was finally settled out of court, and the Delaware Legislature shortly thereafter passed a privileged communication statute for clergymen.

10. Von Bulow by Auersperq v. Von Bulow, 114 FRD 71 (S.D. N.Y. 1987).

11. *In re* Claus Von Bulow, 828 F.2d 94 (2d Cir. 1987).

12. See, respectively, statutes in Michigan, California and Nevada. The California statute expressly withholds the privilege from actions for personal injury or for wrongful death, and it provides that either before or after probate, upon the contest of any will, the attending physician may testify to the mental condition of the deceased patient and may disclose information acquired by him in his professional capacity. Cal. Proc. Code § 1881.4 (1941); H. Hassard, "Privileged Communications: Physician-Patient Confidences in California," *Calif. Med.* 90:411, 1959.

13. R.L. Goldstein, "Psychiatric Poetic License? Post-Mortem Disclosure of Confidential Information in the Anne Sexton Case," *Psychiatric Annals* 22:341, 1992; J.N. Onek, "Legal Issues in the Orne/Sexton Case," *J. Am. Acad. of Psychoanal.* 20:655, 1992.

14. The son of a decedent requested to see his father's hospital records in Emmett v. Eastern Dispensary & Cas. Hosp., 396 F.2d 931 (D.C. Cir. 1967). The court recognized the duty of physicians to protect the interests of their patients under the privilege, but it also said there was a duty to reveal what the patient should know. "This duty of disclosure," the court said, "extends after the patient's death to the next of kin."

15. G.L. Usdin, "The Psychiatrist and Testamentary Capacity," *Tul. L. Rev.* 32:89, 1957; see generally H. Weihofen, "Guardianship and Other Protective Services for the Mentally Incompetent," *Am. J. Psychiat.* 121:970, 1965.

16. Olson v. Court of Honor, 100 Minn. 117, 110 N.W. 734 (1907).

17. Matter of Coddington, 307 N.Y. 181, 120 N.E.2d 777 (1954); noted in *Cornell L.Q.* 40:148, 1954; *Minn. L. Rev.* 39:800, 1955; *N.Y.U.L.Rev.* 30:202, 1955; *Syr. L.Rev.* 6:213, 1954.

18. Conn. Gen. Stat. §17-183; § 17-206d.

19. Proceedings of the Institute on Law and the Mind (U. of Wis. Extension Law Dept., 1961), p. 28.

20. M.J. Grinfeld, "The Furor Over OJ: A Tale of Two Therapists," *Psychiatric Times*, April 1995, p. 17; F. Weinstein, "Death not a reason to tattle, say therapists," *Detroit News*, June 18, 1994, p. C-1.

21. APA Committee on Confidentiality, "Guidelines on Confidentiality," *Am. J. Psychiatry* 144:1552, 1987.

22. Some courts have held that an allegation of "pain and suffering" does not *ipso facto* place mental condition in issue as an element of a personal injury claim and that the privilege is waived only when "emotional condition" is put in issue. Tylitski v. Triple X Service, 126 Ill. App.2d 144, 261 N.E.2d 533 (1970); M.W. Hogan, "Waiver of Physician-Patient Privilege in Personal Injury Litigation," *Marq. L. Rev.* 52:75, 1968; Annot., 25 A.L.R.3d 1401.

23. See Part IV, Chapter 2.

24. As previously noted, some jurisdictions hold that the privilege is terminated whenever any party relies on the condition of a patient even when the patient does not personally place the condition at issue or is not a party to the suit. See, *e.g.*, Easter v. McDonald, 903 S.W.2d 887 (Tex. App. 1995), noted in Part II, Chapter 4.

25. Thomsen v. Mayo Foundation, No. 4-84-1239 (D. Minn. 1986)(WL 9159). See Part II, Chapter 4 for discussion.

26. Noggle v. Marshall, 706 F.2d 1408 (6th Cir.), *cert. denied,* 464 U.S. 1010 (1983); Urseth v. City of Dayton, 653 F. Supp. 1057 (S.D. Ohio 1986).

27. Court rules set out the procedure for obtaining medical records of a party whose physical or mental condition is in issue. See, *e.g.,* Michigan Court Rule 2.314, which states, in pertinent part: "A party who has a valid privilege may assert the privilege and prevent discovery of medical information relating to his or her mental or physical condition. The privilege must be asserted in the party's written response... A privilege not timely asserted is waived in that action, but is not waived for the purposes of any other action."

28. Domake v. Rowe, 184 Mich. App. 137 (1990); Schuler v. United States, 113 F.R.D. 518 (W.D. Mich. 1986). In State of New Mexico v. Gonzales, 912 P.2d 297 (N. Mex. App. 1996), the victim of an alleged rape authorized her records to be released to the local police department and gave prosecutors access to her psychiatrist's records. In doing so, though the prosecutor was not the opposing attorney, the court said that the victim waived any right to privilege, and therefore the defendant had a right to see the records. The case is discussed in the chapter on criminal cases.

29. Lawrence v. Bay Osteopathic Hosp., 175 Mich. App. 61 (1989).

30. Saur v. Probes, 190 Mich. App. 636 (1991).

31. 249 Ill. App.3d 5, 188 Ill. Dec. 224, 618 N.E.2d 794 (1993), *appeal denied,* 622 N.E.2d 1226 (Ill. 1993).

32. Ill. Rev. Stat. ch. 91 1/2.

33. 618 N.E.2d at 797.

34. Ill. Rev. Stat. ch. 91 1/2, 815.

35. Cutter v. Brownbridge, 183 Cal. App. 3d 836, 228 Cal. Rptr. 545 (1986); Schaffer v. Soucerm 215 N.W.2d 134 (S.D. 1974); Smith v. Driscoll, 94 Wash. 441, 162 P. 572 (1917).

36. See Part II, Chapter 4.

37. In Mississippi State Board of Psychological Examiners v. Hosford, 508 So.2d 1049 (Miss. 1987), a psychologist sought review of an order of the State Board of Psychological Examiners, which suspended his license for revealing confidential information in an affidavit entered in a divorce proceeding involving temporary custody. The State Board of Examiners ruled that he had violated Principle 5 on confidentiality of the American Psychological Association's Ethical Principles of Psychologists and Code of Conduct. Under Principle 5, the only exceptions allowing a breach of confidentiality are consent by a patient, and in those unusual circumstances in which not to do so would result in a clear danger to the person or to others. The psychologist claimed that the welfare and best interests of the child outweighed the confidentiality principle. The psychologist argued that the "clear danger" exception allowed him to break the privilege in the best interest of the child. The Mississippi Supreme Court stated: "The Board

construes the exception narrowly to apply only to cases where 'life and limb' were in danger. [The psychologist] would have us read it more broadly, to cover situations where the best interests of the child are at stake. In the context of this case, the danger at issue is that without the disclosure temporary custody of the child may not be placed with the parent better suited to exercise such custody in the child's best interest. The Board has considered this danger as one not within the scope of the ethical principle." 508 So.2d at 1056. The court went on to say, "[W]e are not prepared to say that the psychologist's lips will be forever sealed by the privilege." 508 So.2d at 1056.

38. Rost v. State Bd. of Psychology, 659 A.2d 626 (Pa. Comm. Ct., 1995). For further discussion, see Part IV, Chapter. 1.

39. R. Slovenko & M. Grossman, "Confidentiality and Testimonial Privilege," in R. Michels (ed.), *Psychiatry* (Philadelphia: Lippincott, 1986), vol. 3, chap. 31, at p. 9; M. Grossman, "The Psychiatrist and the Subpoena," *Bull. Am. Acad. Psychiatry & Law* 1:245, 1973.

# Chapter 2

# THE SELF-DEFENSE EXCEPTION

The media, in 1992, carried numerous articles describing the alleged misconduct of Harvard psychiatrist Margaret Bean-Bayog, whose patient, Paul Lozano, a medical student at Harvard, had committed suicide after being treated by her. These accounts were based on 3,000 pages of documents filed in court by the lawyer for the deceased patient's family. They included allegations that the psychiatrist had fallen in love with her patient, had seduced him into a sexual relationship, and had regressed him to a stage where he believed she was his mother. Lozano killed himself about a year after Bean-Bayog stopped treating him.

The patient's family settled out of court for $1-million, but with the stipulation that the settlement contain no admission of liability on the part of the psychiatrist. Bean-Bayog also resigned her license rather than face a televised hearing before the Massachusetts Board of Registration in Medicine, which alleged that she provided substandard care, causing harm to her patient.

Then came a report from the Committee on Therapy of the Group for the Advancement of Psychiatry (GAP) that said:[1]

> An immediate consequence that emerges from the Bean-Bayog case is that since a practitioner must adhere to the rules of confidentiality he or she cannot respond, without risk of a lawsuit, against charges of a patient or patient's family, regardless of how unfounded those charges may be. If a celebrity such as Michael Jackson or Woody Allen is accused of misconduct, he or she is free to call a press conference and openly refute the charges, revealing any information to strengthen his or her defense. This is not the case for physicians or other mental health therapists, who are required to keep the details of their patients' treatment confidential.

In a press interview, Bean-Bayog stated, "It is important for a psychiatric audience to understand that if anything like this ever happened to them, they will not be able to say anything because of patient-therapist confidentiality."

"As the law now stands," the GAP committee said, "any accused therapist must bear all such accusations in silence."

Is it so? While the privilege of confidentiality belongs to the patient (or the representatives of the patient in the event of the death of the patient), it is waived when the patient charges the practitioner with misconduct or malpractice.

Any professional who is bound by confidentiality has the right of "self-defense." The self-defense exception is justified on the well-established theory that a patient or client impliedly "waives" the privilege by making allegations against the professional. As the Advisory Committee to the Federal Rules of Evidence put it: "The exception is required by considerations of fairness and policy when questions arise out of dealings between attorney and client, as in cases of controversy over attorney's fees, claims of inadequacy of representation, or charges of professional misconduct." Wigmore in his classic treatise on evidence likewise stated, "When the client alleges a breach of duty to him by the attorney, the privilege is waived as to all communications relevant to that issue." This applies to other professionals as well as attorneys; hence, a therapist may disclose privileged information to defend against a malpractice action.[2]

For waiver, it is not necessary for the client or patient to bring formal charges or proceedings against the professional. The self-defense exception in the attorney-client privilege arises most frequently in the context of post-trial assertions of a convicted defendant that put in issue the legitimacy of advice provided by the attorney, the effectiveness of the attorney's representation, or the attorney's competence.

Thus, as one court said, "It is well established that if a client assails his attorney's conduct of the case, or if a patient attacks his physician's treatment, the privilege as to confidential communications is waived, since the attorney or physician has a right to defend himself under the circumstances."[3] And in another case, the court said, "While the rule with respect to privileged communication between attorney and client should be zealously guarded, yet this privilege may be destroyed by the acts of the client in attacking the attorney on a charge of dereliction of duty."[4]

James Earl Ray, the assassin of Rev. Martin Luther King Jr., claimed that he was "coerced" by his attorney, Percy Foreman, into a plea of guilty so as to avoid a trial that might have implicated high-level accomplices. In response, Foreman said that he never recommended that Ray plead guilty to the murder of King, but advised Ray that "there is a little more than a 99 percent chance of your receiving a death penalty" if the case went to trial. Foreman displayed a letter he wrote to Ray. Foreman also disclosed that interviews with Ray convinced him that Ray alone assassinated King in the hope of becoming a white hero.[5]

In another high-profile case, F. Lee Bailey reacted to claims about his defense of heiress Patricia Hearst for bank robbery. All over the United States it was being said, "Lee Bailey fouled up the case." Bailey threatened to open up "a whole new bucket of worms" if she did not shut up about his defense of her; she did. She claimed that Bailey "pursued his own interest in publication rights rather than her interest in acquittal."[6]

The American Law Institute's Model Rule 1.6, adopted by the various states, permits disclosure "to the extent the lawyer reasonably believes necessary" to defend himself regarding (1) a "controversy between the lawyer and the client," (2) a criminal or civil case against the lawyer based on conduct in which the client was involved, or (3) "allegations in any proceeding." "Controversy" would be surplusage if it did not mean a dispute outside of a case or proceeding actually filed. The cases make clear that a lawyer may respond to allegations in proceedings even though the lawyer is not a party and such allegations are not directed at seeking to prove the lawyer's civil or criminal liability.

The test of whether a lawyer, or psychiatrist, has complied with his or her ethical duty is the reasonableness of the response to the client's or former client's statements. For example, Bailey probably acted reasonably in warning Hearst, but would not have been justified in responding immediately by disclosing confidences. For one thing, the client is presumably not expert in ethical requirements (beyond a general understanding that statements to a professional are privileged) and should be advised if necessary that statements derogating the professional may waive the privilege and related duties of confidentiality. The Model Rule also implies that any disclosure must be germane to the issue raised by the client. For example, Bailey could not reasonably have disclosed (nor threatened to disclose) embarrassing facts about Hearst not relevant to her charges about him.

Traditionally, the waiver theory did not apply where allegations against the professional are made by someone other than the client or patient or their representative. Increasingly, however, in a significant departure from traditional privilege jurisprudence, the courts permit a professional to disclose otherwise protected confidences to protect his own interests when he is charged with misconduct by a third party.

Thus, it has been held that where a lawyer has been charged with misconduct by a person or entity other than the client, the lawyer has the right to disclose without the client's consent otherwise privileged communication to the extent reasonably necessary to the attorney's defense of that charge. In an oft-cited case,[7] a lawyer was allowed to invoke the self-defense exception and reveal client communications to exonerate himself from liability to third parties for securities violations. The courts, for the most part, have adopted this expanded exception during the last two decades.

Under the self-defense exception, there is the concern that claims will be made against the client's lawyer, as well as the client, in order to obtain discovery from the lawyer that otherwise would not be permitted. Law Professor Paul Rice suggests that "These potential abuses can only be effectively addressed if courts require that disclosure be made under judicial supervision, that the party making the claim against the attorney establish a *prima facie* case before disclosure is permitted, and that the disclosure be strictly limited to matters reasonably necessary to provide significant assistance to the attorney's defense."[8] To this end, Professor Rice recommends that "Where the breach is asserted by a third party, privileged communications may only be revealed under judicial supervision after the court has determined that the party making the allegations has made a *prima facie* showing that the breach occurred."

To sum up, professionals may in self-defense make disclosures to defend their competency or integrity. They may (or should) make disclosures, and may (or should) file an action for defamation.

Quite often, when professionals decline to make a disclosure or other defense on the ground that the confidences of a client or patient must be protected, they are acting to cover up their misconduct. At least, that's the common inference. A federal district court encouraged self-defense disclosures, saying: "[T]o keep silent would justify inferences being drawn that some act or deed was committed on [the professional's] part that was not legal or in accordance with the direction of his [or her] client."[9] Maybe that applies to Bean-Bayog.

## NOTES

1. For the GAP report, see "Aftermath: Repercussions of the Bean Bayog Case," *Psychiatric Times*, Feb. 1995, p. 7.
2. Ill. Comp. Stat. Ch 735, § 5/8-802; M. Graham, *Handbook of Illinois Evidence* (St. Paul: West, 6th ed. 1994), pp. 279-80.
3. Pruitt v. Payton, 243 F. Supp. 907, 909 (E.D. Va. 1965).
4. United States v. Butler, 167 F. Supp. 102 (E.D. Va. 1957).
5. AP news-release, "Lawyer denies he advised Ray to admit killing King," *Detroit Free Press*, Nov. 14, 1978, p. D-3.
6. "Hearst Attorney Prepared to Talk," *Washington Post*, Aug. 9, 1978, p. A-7.
7. Meyerhofer v. Empire Fire & Marine Ins. Co., 497 F.2d 1190, 1194 1195 (2d Cir. 1974).

8. *Attorney-Client Privilege in the United States* (New York: Lawyers Cooperative, 1993), § 9:56; see First Federal Sav. & Loan Assn. v. Oppenheim, Appel, Dixon & Co., 110 F.R.D. 557 (S.D. N.Y. 1986).

9. Popovitch v. Kasperlik, 70 F. Supp. 376 at 381 (W.D. Pa. 1947). In California a group of schizophrenia researchers have been accused of disgraceful behavior, apparently quite incorrectly. The researchers stated they were bound by their school to make no comments whatsoever because of confidentiality. It would be of substantial importance to both research and practice if self-defense were better understood.

Virginia's recently enacted legislation expressly provides for disclosure "reasonably necessary to establish or collect a fee or to defend a provided or the provider's employees or staff against any accusation of wrongful conduct; also as required in the course of an investigation, audit, review or proceedings regarding a provider's conduct by a duly authorized law-enforcement, licensure, accreditation, or professional review entity." 1997 Va. Ch. 682.

## Part IV

# PSYCHOTHERAPY AND CONFIDENTIALITY

Chapter 1. Introduction
Chapter 2. Jeopardy to Patient or Others
Chapter 3. "Very Important Persons"
Chapter 4. Teaching and Writing
Chapter 5. Treatment of Minors and Young Adults
Chapter 6. Hospital Care, Consultation, Supervision
      and Research
Chapter 7. Communications to Non-Medical
      Persons in Respose to Inquires
Chapter 8. Fee Collection
Chapter 9. Consent to Release of Information

# Chapter 1

# INTRODUCTION

Before a physician releases information about a patient, including the fact that a person was even a patient, the patient must give his authorization (except when the information is required as under the exceptions to testimonial privilege). Most of the cases involving a breach of confidence discuss more than one theory of liability, or fail to indicate which of the bases is relied upon.[1] Clearly, a breach of the physician's duty to maintain the confidentiality or privacy of his patient may give rise to tort actions for infliction of mental distress, invasion of privacy or defamation. In a tort action, the familiar classifications are intent and negligence (negligence is also known as "malpractice" or "professional negligence" when a professional is involved). A tort of "malpractice" calls into play liability insurance coverage, a special statute of limitations, and the need for expert testimony.[2]

In many cases of breach of confidence, multiple bases of liability will be appropriate because it involves elements of both a harmful disclosure and a broken relation. Some courts call it a "breach of the fiduciary duty of confidentiality."[3] A "fiduciary relationship" is defined as a situation "where one person reposes special confidence in another, or where a special duty exists on the part of one person to protect the interests of another, or when there is a reposing of faith, confidence, and trust, and the placing of reliance by one person on the judgment and advise of the other."[4]

Breach of confidence may also give rise to an action for breach of contract. One court put it thus: "[A] physician, who enters into an agreement with a patient to provide medical attention, impliedly covenants to keep in confidence all disclosures made by the patient concerning the patient's physical or mental condition as well as all matters discovered by the physician in the course of examination or treatment."[5]

Irrespective of any privilege to withhold testimony in a legal proceeding, there is a legal duty arising out of the professional relationship to maintain confidentiality. To that effect, two opinions, one by the New Jersey Supreme

259

Court and the other by the Alabama Supreme Court are oft-quoted. In *Hague v. Williams*,[6] the New Jersey Supreme Court found a confidential relationship between doctor and patient gave rise to a general duty not to make non-testimonial disclosures of information obtained through the relationship. The court said:

> The benefits which inure to the relationship of physician-patient from the denial to a physician of any right to promiscuously disclose such information are self-evident. On the other hand, it is impossible to conceive of any countervailing benefits which would arise by according a physician the right to gossip about a patient's health.
>
> A patient should be entitled to freely disclose his symptoms and condition to his doctor in order to receive proper treatment without fear that those facts may become public property. Only thus can the purpose of the relationship be fulfilled. This is not to say that the patient enjoys an absolute right, but rather that he possesses a limited right against such disclosure, subject to exceptions prompted by the supervening interest of society. We conclude, therefore, that ordinarily a physician receives information relating to a patient's health in a confidential capacity and should not disclose such information without the patient's consent, except where the public interest or the private interest of the patient so demands. Without delineating the precise outer contours of the exceptions, it may generally be said that disclosure may, under such compelling circumstances, be made to a person with a legitimate interest in the patient's health.

In *Horne v. Patton*,[7] the Alabama Supreme Court said:

> [I]t must be concluded that a medical doctor is under a general duty not to make extra-judicial disclosures of information acquired in the course of the doctor-patient relationship and that a breach of that duty will give rise to a cause of action. It is, of course, recognized that this duty is subject to exceptions prompted by the supervening interests of society, as well as the private interests of the patient himself.

The exceptions must be considered. One exception is when the doctor is ordered by a court to disclose information. This does not necessarily mean that he is privileged to make a disclosure or turn over records merely on receiving a subpoena. As we have noted, the mere issuance of a subpoena does not mean authority or justification for the demand. An attorney may issue a subpoena and demand information even though there is no legal right to command disclosure. The issuance of a subpoena is a perfunctory matter; it is done without any review by a judge. The individual served has a right, if not a duty, to contest the subpoena.

In an appeal of a reprimand issued by a state board of psychology, a Pennsylvania court held that a psychologist breached her confidentiality duty by releasing a client's records pursuant to a subpoena without seeking the client's consent or challenging the propriety of the subpoena before a judge.[8] In this case the psychologist treated a young woman for recurring headaches allegedly caused by a fall at a community center. A suit was filed against the center alleging that the center's negligence caused the injuries. The center's attorney subpoenaed the psychologist requesting the treatment records, which the psychologist provided. Although the hearing examiner of the state board of psychology concluded that the psychologist-client privilege is waived by a claim for emotional damages, the board issued the psychologist a formal reprimand. In upholding the reprimand, the court said:[9]

> Whenever a professional in possession of confidential information is served with a subpoena, a conflict naturally arises between one's duty to the courts and one's duty of confidentiality towards one's client. In this respect, [the appellant] is no different from the numerous other psychologists, doctors, lawyers, and clergymen who receive subpoenas in this Commonwealth each year. The value of a psychologist's, or other professional's duty of confidentiality would be illusory if it could be overridden anytime a conflicting duty arose which was thought to be more important. Although [the appellant] may have been placed in an unfavorable position, she is not excused from following the ethical guidelines of her profession which plainly forbid her from disclosing a client's records without her consent.
>
> [The appellant] argues that it is unreasonable to expect a psychologist, lacking formal legal training, to know the proper procedure to follow after receiving a subpoena. [The appellant] apparently believes that she was in an untenable position in which she would have had to either violate the rules of professional conduct or disregard a subpoena. However, this argument is flawed. [The appellant] could have challenged the subpoena in court or obtained permission from her client before releasing the information. If [the appellant] was uncertain about her legal rights and responsibilities, she should have at least obtained advice from an attorney instead of unilaterally releasing her client's records. As a licensed psychologist, she had an obligation to be aware of the ethical duties which govern her profession. Having received the benefits of being licensed by the state, [the appellant] cannot now argue that she is a "layman" who lacks the knowledge and training necessary to understand and comply with the Board's regulations.

A subpoena of itself compels a person to appear, not to testify or turn over documents. Clearly, unless the subpoena is accompanied by a court order or a signed release from a competent patient, records should not be released. A subpoena ought to be tested (on a motion to quash) to ascertain whether there is privilege, relevancy or materiality.[10] An insurer, however, will not step in to help quash a subpoena unless a claim has been made against the insured. Usually, in cases where a demand for records is made on a therapist, the patient has an attorney and the matter can be referred to him.

In a number of situations, reporting by a physician is specifically required under the law. The classic example of mandated reporting is of a patient having epilepsy who operates a motor vehicle. Another example of mandated reporting involves child abuse (some jurisdictions exempt the doctor who is trying to deal in treatment with the child abuse) and elderly or disabled abuse. Other notable examples of mandated reporting include dangerous or contagious disease, firearm and knife wounds, and the reporting of patients in drug abuse treatment programs. And, as much publicized, the duty to warn or protect in the case of a patient who presents harm to others.

In the famous decision in *Tarasoff v. Regents of University of California,*[11] the California Supreme Court ruled that a psychotherapist who has a reason to believe that a patient may injure or kill another must notify either the potential victim, his relatives, his friends, or the authorities. In the absence of a specific statute or judicial decision mandating reporting, the doctor who makes a disclosure has the burden of establishing that it was justified in order to safeguard the patient or others.

In certain situations where the doctor may not have a duty to report, he may nonetheless have a "qualified privilege" (sometimes called "conditional privilege") to make a disclosure. The duty to maintain confidentiality may be outweighed by a more compelling consideration. This qualified privilege has limitations, all of which the doctor has the burden of establishing: the information must protect some other sufficiently important interest; it must be done in good faith and reasonable care must be exercised as to its truth; the information must be reported fairly; only such information should be conveyed and only to such persons as is necessary to the purpose. In an Oklahoma case, a convicted rapist brought an action for breach of confidentiality against a physician who treated him for a serious bite wound to the penis and who thereafter reported the condition and the patient's identity to the police. The court held that the physician's communication to the police was justified on the basis of public policy.[12]

In the case of an incompetent patient, it is necessary to talk about the patient with the legal guardian or a family member. It is they who have the authority to give consent to the treatment of an incompetent patient. This being the case, it is necessary to have a discussion about the patient. As a general proposition, only a legal guardian has the authority to give consent on behalf of an incompetent patient, but it is the custom in the medical community to ask for the consent of the next of kin (though not appointed as legal guardian), and some judicial decisions imply that there is some authority vested in the next of kin.[13]

There are relatively few reported cases (only appellate court decisions are reported) involving medical breaches of confidentiality. This can mean that such breaches seldom occur, that patients do not know of breaches that do occur, that patients do not sue for uncertain damages and possible further publicity of the confidential information, or that almost all such cases are settled before reaching the appellate level. Those cases that are reported have usually involved a breach of confidentiality in one of the following situations: disclosure to a spouse (involving either a disease or illness related to the marriage or a condition relevant in a divorce, alimony, or custody action); disclosure to an insurance company; or disclosure to an employer.

There are apparently more lawsuits against therapists for failure to disclose information than there are for breach of confidentiality. In any event, the judgments are larger in the failure-to-disclose cases. They involve lawsuits by third parties who have been injured by patients wherein it is claimed that disclosure could have prevented the harm. In lawsuits by patients alleging a breach of confidentiality, the claimed harm is emotional rather than physical. Judgments for emotional distress are smaller than for physical injury.

It is the unjustified or promiscuous disclosure of information which leads to liability. The outcome of lawsuits involving disclosure by a physician or psychiatrist to a patient's spouse is marked by variation, as are other cases of disclosure, and attests to the Polish philosopher Leszek Kolakowski's "Law of the Infinite Cornucopia" which states that there is never a shortage of arguments to support whatever you want to believe in for whatever reasons.[14] In *McDonald v. Clinger*,[15] a New York appellate court summarized:[16]

> Although the disclosure of medical information to a spouse may be justified under some circumstances, a more stringent standard should apply with respect to psychiatric information. One spouse often seeks counseling concerning personal problems that may affect the marital relationship. To permit disclosure to the other spouse in the absence of an overriding concern would deter the one in need from obtaining the help required. Disclosure of confidential information by a psychiatrist to a spouse will be justified whenever there is a danger to the patient, the spouse, or another person; otherwise information should not be disclosed without authorization. Justification or excuse will depend upon a showing of circumstances and competing interests which support the need to disclose ....Because such showing is a matter of affirmative defense, defendant is not entitled to dismissal of the action.

Invasion of privacy or breach of confidentiality by unwarranted disclosure of information to an employer or insurance company has been recognized and given redress. The key term is "unwarranted disclosure."[17] In *Horne v. Patton*,[18] the aforementioned oft-cited Alabama case, the complaint charged that the defendant, the plaintiff's physician, wrongfully disclosed to the plaintiff's employer that the plaintiff suffered from a longstanding nervous condition with feelings of anxiety and insecurity. The verity of the medical opinion was not denied. The Alabama Supreme Court held that the release of this

information constituted an invasion of the plaintiff's privacy and a breach of
the physician's implied contractual obligation to keep confidential all personal information given him by the patient. Justice Daniel McCall dissented,
saying: "In my opinion the overriding competing interest and responsibility
of an employer for the welfare of all of his employees, to the public who
come to his establishment and who buy his merchandize, and to the furtherance of his own business venture, should entitle him to be free from the
shackles of secrecy that would prevent a physician from disclosing to the
employer critical information concerning the physical or mental condition of
his employees."[19]

In a New York case, *Clark v. Geraci*,[20] also oft-cited, a civilian employee of
the Air Force, an accountant, asked his physician to make an incomplete disclosure to the Air Force to explain absences, but the physician made a complete disclosure including the patient's alcoholism. The employee sued the
physician for allegedly causing the Air Force to discharge him. The court
commented, "It is...the doctor's claim that he had an overriding duty to make
a disclosure of the underlying cause of plaintiff's illnesses and absences when
required by a military unit of the United States Government so to do, especially since he had previously supplied incomplete information. The delicate
balance of conflicting duties must thus be weighed...to determine the doctor's
paramount duty. Was the duty to divulge the employee's weakness which,
conceivably could be used to rid the government of a worthless servant and
thereby save public funds, greater than the duty to maintain a confidential
professional communication?"[21] The court said, "Certainly the doctor's act
was justified by reason of his concept of duty to his government."[22] In any
event, the patient, by asking for and permitting the physician to make an
incomplete disclosure, was estopped from preventing the physician from
making a full disclosure.[23]

Defamation, be it about the patient or others, must also be a concern when
making a disclosure. In the trial of Claus von Bulow on charges of trying to
kill his wife on two occasions, the defense lawyer on cross-examination asked
the wife's physician why he did not tell her of his suspicions that he suspected on the first time she fell into a coma that her husband might have secretly injected her with insulin. Pressed for an answer, the doctor said, "I can't
go to a spouse and say, 'I suspect your mate is trying to harm you.' There are
libel laws in this country."[24]

It will be remembered that the privilege of confidentiality is not the doctor's but the patient's, and therefore it cannot be asserted against the patient.
Hence, the doctor cannot claim a right of privacy to deny the patient access
to the medical records. There is a narrowly defined "therapeutic privilege"
which allows a doctor to keep from a patient information that may have "a
significant negative impact" upon the patient, but when it comes to push

against shove–the patient suing the doctor in malpractice–the patient is entitled to all of the records. In the case of a patient who is a minor, the parent is generally the consenting party, and in order for the parent to be able to give informed consent, the parent is entitled to essential information. However, in the case of a "mature minor" or in cases of treatment for venereal disease or drug addiction or in some cases of psychiatric hospitalization, many jurisdictions allow the minor to consent to his own care and in such cases the parents would not need the information for consent purposes.[25]

For some, ethics must be justified on a pragmatic basis. Perhaps some psychotherapists preserve confidentiality out of fear of a damage suit for defamation or for invasion of privacy. And psychotherapists recognize that the very practice of psychotherapy, their livelihood, vitally depends upon the reputation in the community that the therapist will not divulge a confidence.

Ethics, though, call for something more than a pragmatic basis. As a matter of integrity, a person (especially a professional person) does not reveal a confidence. Ethics and integrity ought to be more powerful than laws. Hence, confidentiality demanded by the ethical code exceeds the requirements of the law. The manner in which psychotherapists maintain out-of-courtroom confidentiality would attest to the fulfillment of Wigmore's criteria that "the communications originate in a confidence that they will not be disclosed" and "this element of confidentiality is essential to the full and satisfactory maintenance of the relation between the parties," thereby justifying a privilege to maintain confidentiality in the courtroom.

To what extent is out-of-courtroom confidentiality maintained by psychotherapists? Psychiatrists and other psychotherapists say that the patient may assume that their communications will not be revealed to others except possibly for the purpose of rendering necessary help. Do they make good on their word? Is confidentiality a professional fact?

The First Amendment of the Constitution, protecting free speech, ordains that we are a "public opinion" state. We talk freely about politics, and also about our activities, and we love to gossip. Work constitutes a major part of our life, and many of us find little else to talk about. It is not surprising then to find a tendency among psychotherapists to discuss their patients outside the office, at home, at the club, and at cocktail parties.[26] Sometimes, patients' names are used, and oft-times the discussion degenerates into mere chatter. Some serious difficulties, for example, have arisen in the treatment of patients in clinics as a result of open discussion of patients in hallways. As a result, patients overhearing the discussion become quite upset and threaten to terminate therapy.[27]

Psychiatrists are cautioned to avoid the tendency to talk freely about work activities. In large measure, revelation of treatment material is the result of the psychiatrist's own need for attention or feelings of importance. It may be a cover-up of insecurity and a form of exhibitionism. In addition, treatment material is often discussed to obtain free or nonstructured supervision and support. Psychiatrists get anxious about their patients, but the solution, obviously, does not lie in cocktail party discussion. There is, as pointed out, a violation of the patient's right of privacy when treatment material is not kept confidential.

Does the psychiatrist talk too much? Does the modern practice of psychiatry threaten confidentiality? Whatever disagreement may exist regarding the methods used by a therapist in the course of psychotherapy, there is a near unanimity of opinion among therapists that nothing about a patient should be divulged to third parties. Allegedly, the patient's full participation, essential to psychotherapy, cannot be obtained without an assurance of absolute confidentiality.

Some years ago, a book review in a professional journal quoted several remarks made by Dr. Sandor Rado to a group of students about his analysand, Dr. Otto Fenichel. Rado stated that Fenichel was one of the most obsessional individuals he had ever attempted to psychoanalyze, and that he considered the analysis a failure. This quote prompted much criticism. In response to the criticism, the reviewer replied, "But what was it that was really revealed in my review?"[28] Dr. Marvin Drellich, in a letter to the editor, responded by pointing out that such a question "betrays his failure to comprehend that confidentiality must be complete and absolute."[29]

Central to a discussion on confidentiality is an examination of whether therapists are concealing what should be told and revealing what ought to be kept confidential. When may the therapist divulge, when should he divulge, and when must he divulge? Although adopting the stance of protecting the patient's privacy and creating a "safe atmosphere" for all potential patients, it is possible that the therapist is equally concerned with his own privacy and method of practice. At times it may be that the therapist's self-gratification prompts divulgences. These concerns of the therapist are legitimate, to be sure, but may do little to further the best interests of the patient.

The traditional confidentiality between the physician/psychiatrist and his patient is said to be threatened by the growing complexity of health care and the utilization of computers. The number of page-one articles in *Psychiatric News*, the biweekly newspaper of the American Psychiatric Association, indicates that privileged communication and confidentiality are high-priority issues among psychiatrists. At the invitation of Dr. Alfred M. Freedman, then president of the American Psychiatric Association, representatives of various psychiatric, psychological, medical, hospital, legal, and insurance associations met to consider alternative methods to cope with the growing threat to the confidentiality of health records. These meetings had the benefit of numerous state society conferences and task force investigations. In addition, local hospitals and psychiatric societies in various states had been formulating protocol on preserving confidentiality. The meetings resulted in the recommendation that a national commission on the preservation of confidentiality of health records be established, but it is not clear what such a commission would do to preserve confidentiality.[30]

The APA Task Force on Confidentiality confirmed that a court demand for information worries psychiatrists most, but apart from statutory disclosure requirements and judicial compulsion, there is no legal obligation to furnish information—even to law enforcement officials. It is the individual himself who makes the disclosures or authorizes his psychiatrist to make them in order to receive benefits such as employment, a driver's license, charge accounts, welfare benefits, or insurance.

## NOTES

1.  A.B. Vickery, "Breach of Confidence: An Emerging Tort," *Colum. L. Rev.* 82:1426, 1982.
2.  As a general rule, the need for expert testimony is excused when "the thing speaks for itself" (in the Latin phrase, res ipsa loquitur). However, as part of medical malpractice litigation, a number of states have codified the res ipsa loquitur doctrine, limiting its application to specific types of medical mishaps. One statute allows a "rebuttable inference of negligence" only for foreign bodies unintentionally left in the body following surgery, an explosion or fire originating in a substance used for treatment, or a surgical procedure on the wrong patient or the wrong part of the body. 18 Del. Code Ann. tit. 18, § 6853 (1992). See also Lacy v. G.D. Searle & Co., 484 A.2d 527 (Del. Super. 1984).
3.  McDonald v. Clinger, 446 N.Y.S.2d 801 (N.Y. A.D. 4th Dept. 1982) (psychiatrist's disclosure of confidential information to patient's wife constituted "a breach of the physician's fiduciary duty to his patient").
4.  Lank v. Steiner, 213 A.2d 848 (Del. Ch. 1965). In Omer v. Edhren, 38 Wash. App. 376, 685 P.2d 635 (1984), a sexual exploitation case, the court characterized the relationship between physician and patient as fiduciary.
5.  Doe v. Roe, 93 Misc.2d 201, 210, 400 N.Y.S.2d 668, 674 (Sup. Ct. 1977).
6.  37 N.J. 328, 181 A.2d 345 (1962).
7.  291 Ala. 701, 287 So.2d 824 (1973).
8.  Rost v. State Bd. of Psychology, 659 A.2d 626 (Pa. Comm. Ct. 1995); see also discussion in Part III, chap. 1.
9.  *Id.* at 630-631.
10. M. Grossman, "The Psychiatrist and the Subpoena," *Bull. Am. Acad. Psychiatry & Law* 1:245, 1975; M.K. Goin, "You and the law-problem areas," *Psychiatry News*, April 2, 1982, p. 12.
11. 17 Cal.3d 425, 551 P.2d 334, 131 Cal. Rptr. 14 (1976).

12. Bryson v. Tillinghast, 749 P.2d 110 (Okla. 1988).

13. G.J. Annas, L.H. Glantz, & B.F. Katz, *The Rights of Doctors, Nurses and Allied Health Professionals* (New York: Avon, 1981), p. 79.

14. In Curry v. Corn, 277 N.Y.S.2d 470 (1966), a physician was held not liable on account of revealing to the patient's husband information obtained in the course of treating the patient. The court said, "[A] prospective husband or wife is entitled to know before marriage whether his or her future spouse is suffering from a diseased condition [and likewise] during marriage each has the right to know the existence of any disease which may have bearing on the marital relation....[A] physician who reveals the nature of the condition of the patient to the patient's husband may hardly be charged with reprehensible conduct." 277 N.Y.S.2d at 471-472. In Schaffer v. Spicer, 215 N.W.2d 134 (S.D. 1974), where the wife's physician disclosed information to the husband's attorney to aid him in a child custody case, the court held that the issue of the truth or falsity of the statement in an action for defamation is for the trier of fact. See also Furness v. Fitchett, [1958] N.A.L.R. 396.

15. 446 N.Y.S.2d 801 (N.Y.A.D. 4th Dept. 1982),

16. 446 N.Y.S.2d at 805.

17. In Beatty v. Baston, 13 Ohio L. Abs. 481 (1932), the physician revealed to a patient's employer during a workers' compensation action that the patient had venereal disease. In Hague v. Williams, 181 A.2d 345 (N.J. 1962), the pediatrician of an infant informed a life insurance company of a congenital heart defect that he had not informed the child's parents of and recovery on the policy was denied; disclosure held proper. In Hammonds v. Aetna Cas. & Sur. Co., 243 F. Supp. 793 (N.D. Ohio 1965), the physician revealed information to an insurance company when the insurance company falsely represented to him that his patient was suing him for malpractice. See also Gesiberger v. Willuhn, 72 Ill. App.3d 435, 390 N.W.2d 945 (1979); Carr v. Watkins, 227 Md. 578, 177 A.2d 841 (1962).

18. 287 So.2d 824 (Ala. 1973).

19. 287 So.2d at 835.

20. 208 N.Y.S.2d 564 (N.Y.S. Ct. 1960).

21. 208 N.Y.S.2d at 567.

22. 208 N.Y.S.2d at 569.

23. *Ibid.*

24. "Physician for Mrs. von Bulow tells jury of his suspicions," *New York Times,* Feb. 20, 1982, p. 7.

25. The right to hospitalize a minor psychiatrically no longer resides totally within parental prerogatives—a judicial hearing is required in the case of minors over the age of 14 who object to hospitalization—so it has been held that the minor enjoys the right of confidentiality of records. M. Weinapple & I.N. Perr, "The Right of a Minor to Confidentiality: An Aftermath of *Bartley v. Kremens,*" *Bull. Am. Acad. of Psychiatry & Law* 9:247, 1981.

26. In a talk on "Ethics for Doctors' Wives," Dr. G. Overton Himmelwright observed that a physician's wife is "quite a part of the medical profession" and "must observe rules which add stability to the life of her husband." This

means, he urged, that "the physician's Hippocratic oath becomes a part of his wife's philosophy."

27. Consider the following memorandum posted on the bulletin board for the attention of residents training in psychiatry: "Some serious difficulties have arisen in the treatment of some of the patients here in the Clinic as a result of open discussions of patients in the hallway. The discussions were between residents; personal information was being revealed and comments were being made. As a result, the patients who heard the discussion became upset and, in one case, there was a threat of terminating therapy since there was obvious evidence that the treatment material and situation were not always confidential. While the above incidents were surely unintentional, they nevertheless have effected a most undesirable situation. Thus, it is requested that if you do wish to discuss or make comments to anyone in the Department concerning your patients or their treatment, etc., that you do so only in reasonable privacy such as in one of the offices. But above all, not in the hallway!"

28. *The Academy* (American Academy of Psychoanalysis), Sept. 1974, p. 5.

29. *The Academy*, Feb. 1975, p. 5.

30. American Psychiatric Assn., *Confidentiality: A Report of the Conference on Confidentiality of Health Records* (Washington, D.C. 1975). See also W. Barton, "Should a National Commission for the Preservation of Confidentiality of Health Records Be Formed?," *Psychiat. Opinion*, 12:15, 1975; Special Issue, "Is Privacy Obsolete? The Challenge to Medicine & Society," *Prism*, June 1974.

# Chapter 2

# JEOPARDY TO PATIENT OR OTHERS

Sometimes the keeping of a confidence may jeopardize the patient or society. There may be danger of the patient committing suicide. There may be danger in an epileptic driving a bus. There may be an airplane pilot who should be grounded because of severe mental illness, but, fearful of losing his job, he does not tell his employer. There may be a patient who is dissipating, without the family's knowledge, all of the family's funds and property.

There are times when revelation may be necessary for the protection of society. In 1960, this thorny problem received wide publicity when two National Security Agency employees, Vernon F. Mitchell and William H. Martin, defected to the Soviet Union. The psychiatrist, who had seen Mitchell, turned over his records and testified before a secret session of the House Un-American Committee. He stated: "I believe a man loses his right to privileged communication if he defects. Furthermore, if the national security is threatened, I believe the rights of the Government far exceed the rights of individuals." The psychiatrist disclosed problems of family, religion, and sex. For this, he was taken to task by a number of general practitioners and psychiatrists.[1]

It is always debatable whether a disclosure can be construed as benefiting the patient or the community. However, revelation of information which is of no benefit to the patient or the community though demanded by subpoena, may be subject to criticism, but more subject to criticism is disclosure of information without legal compulsion (as apparently happened in the Mitchell situation).[2] Arguably, the State can ferret out its evidence, and make its proof, without impinging on confidential relationships.[3]

FBI Director J. Edgar Hoover at one time urged all physicians to report to the Bureau any facts relating to espionage, sabotage, or subversive activity coming to their attention. Psychiatrists generally criticized the American Medical Association for cooperating with the federal police, and for going even further by urging its members to help catch even the petty thief. Dr. Manfred Guttmacher attacked this suggestion with wry humor: "It is not too

270

fantastic to predict that before long the physician's inner examining room may resemble a rural post office with its walls plastered with the mugs of wanted felons."[4]

Under the law, there is no duty to come to the aid of third parties, but the psychiatrist may act in emergencies. He may reveal a confidence when it becomes necessary in order to protect the welfare of the patient or the community. In such situations, the revelation is made to avert a catastrophe. As the revelation is with just cause, the psychiatrist if that can be established would not be liable in damages for invasion of privacy. Thus, a physician who revealed to a patient's spouse that the patient was suffering from a venereal disease was held not liable (but was put to the burden of a trial).[5] Likewise, no liability was imposed on a physician who, after warning the patient to vacate a hotel, reported to the owner that his "guest" probably was afflicted with a "contagious disease."[6] However, there is redress for wrongful invasion of privacy by "unwarranted disclosure" of information which results in the patient's loss of employment.[7]

In a Utah case in mid-1950, Robert Berry sued Dr. Louis Moench for publishing in a letter allegedly false and derogatory information acquired in connection with treating him as a patient. The letter was written in response to one in which Dr. J.S. Hellewell had requested information, asking for "your impression of the man," for the stated purpose of passing it on to a Mr. and Mrs. Williams, parents of Mary Boothe who was then keeping company with Berry. In significant portion, Dr. Moench wrote to Dr. Hellewell:

> Since I do not have his authorization, the patient you mentioned in your last letter will remain nameless, He was treated here in 1949 as an emergency. Our diagnosis was Manic depressive depression in a psychopathic personality...He had one brother as a manic, and his father committed suicide...The patient was attempting to go through school on the G.I. bill...Instead of attending class he would spend most of the days and nights playing cards for money. Because of family circumstances, we treated him for a mere token charge (and I notice even that has never been paid). During his care here, he purchased a brand new Packard, without even money to buy gasoline. He was in constant trouble with the authorities during the war, ... did not do well in school, and never did really support his wife and children. Since he was here, we have repeated requests for his record indicating repeated trouble. My suggestion to the infatuated girl would be to run as fast and as far as she possibly could in any direction away from him. Of course, if he doesn't marry her, he will marry someone else and make life hell for that person. The usual story is repeated unsuccessful marriages and a trail of tragedy behind.

In justification of writing the letter, Dr. Moench relied on these defenses: That the statements were true; that he had a reasonable basis for believing them to be true; that he made them under conditional privilege; and that they were not defamatory. The Utah Supreme Court, in an opinion rendered in 1958, said the evidence was sufficient to present a jury issue as to whether Dr. Moench exercised proper discretion in passing on the information. The court said, "[The girl's] concern for her well-being and happiness was a sufficient interest to protect, and...it was within the generally accepted standards of decent conduct for the doctor to reveal the information which might have an important bearing thereon."[8] It is unknown whether the case was settled or went to trial.[9] Quite likely, the courts today would say that the disclosure was indiscreet.

The physician is bound by loyalty to his patient and a responsibility for treating the professional relationship with respect and honor, but he also has other responsibilities. In this regard, Dr. Karl Menninger, the acclaimed dean of American psychiatry, observed:[10]

> [The physician] has a responsibility to society, to the hospital, to the rest of the medical profession, and to science. No patient has a right to exploit the confidential relationship offered by the physician a *particeps criminis*. The physician cannot condone moral and legal irresponsibility on the part of the patient and to do so may be actually harmful to the patient. For example, a patient comes to a VA hospital with certain psychiatric symptoms and in the course of his history he confesses that he has been receiving compensation for self-inflicted gunshot wounds, which he had claimed were received in combat. The psychiatrist who receives this information has no right to withhold from the (hospital) clinical record the fact that the patient has been defrauding the government, even though this confession was made in confidence. Another instance that recently came to my knowledge was one in which a patient was accepted in a VA hospital for treatment for which he was completely ineligible. Because certain individuals were sympathetic and felt that he needed the hospitalization (and considered that the information concerning his ineligibility was given to them in confidence and could not be betrayed), they joined in concealing this information from the Register over a period of nearly two years. In effect, this was conspiracy to defraud the government and did irreparable harm to the patient even though those in charge of him really felt that they were doing the best thing. If a patient tells a doctor in confidence that he has brought a time bomb into the hospital and hidden it under the bed of one of the other patients, it is a strange doctor indeed who would feel that this professional confidence should not be violated.

The general public or prospective patients as well as patients in therapy do not lose faith in the psychiatrist as a keeper of secrets when, in cases of emergency, he acts contrary to strict and absolute confidentiality. Sooner or later, the patient usually realizes that the psychiatrist has acted in his best interest (which is just the contrary when an opposing party in litigation compels the psychiatrist to testify). However, situations of real emergencies necessitating disclosure are rare.

Trust in the physician or psychiatrist is fundamental. The guiding principle that governs the therapeutic efforts of the physician is: "To help, or at least to do no harm." Otherwise put: *Primum non nocere*--above all do no harm.[11] Arguably, that principle includes dissuading or protecting a patient from hurting himself directly (by suicide) or indirectly (by acts of violence against others). To what extent, if at all, should responsibility toward a patient translate into a responsibility, legal as well as ethical, toward third parties? Does the establishment of a doctor-patient relationship present sufficient involvement by a therapist to impose on him an obligation of care not only of the patient but also of the public?

The version of the Hippocratic oath which states that "what should not be published abroad" should not be divulged, implies that divulgence may at times be proper. There are different wordings in published excerpts: "Whatsoever things I see or hear concerning the life of men, in my attendance on the sick, or even apart therefrom, which ought not to be noised abroad, I will keep silence thereon, counting such things to be as sacred secrets." "That whatsoever I shall see or hear of the lives of men which is not fitting to be spoken, I will keep inviolably secret." "Whatsoever in the course of practice I see or hear [or even outside my practice in social intercourse] that ought never to be published abroad, I will not divulge, but will consider such things to be holy secrets."

Yet another wording is found in the study of the oath by Ludwig Edelstein which makes no exception to silence: "What I may see or hear in the course of the treatment or even outside of the treatment in regard to the life of men, which on no account one must spread abroad, I will keep to myself holding such things shameful to be spoken about."[12] Edelstein had this to say about this promise of silence:[13]

> The physician accepts the obligation to keep to himself all that he sees or hears during the treatment; he also swears not to divulge whatever comes to his knowledge outside of his medical activity in the life of men. The latter phrase in particular has always seemed strange. It is so far-reaching in scope that it can hardly be explained by professional considerations alone. To be sure, other medical writings also advise the physician to be reticent. The motive in doing so is the concern for the physician's renommée which might suffer if he is a prattler. But the Oath demands silence in regard to that "which on no account one must spread abroad." It insists on secrecy not as a precaution but as a duty. In the same way silence about things which are not to be communicated to others was considered a moral obligation by the Pythagoreans.
>
> O. Korner states that this clause means that the physician should keep to himself everything except that which it is his duty to bring to public

attention. In other words, Korner finds in the Oath a distinction between that which the physician owes to his patient and that which he owes to the community. Apart from the fact that the physician's obligations towards the state are nowhere mentioned in the document, such an interpretation is not warranted by the words.... Moreover, the text gives no indication as to what the physician should say, but only as to what he should keep to himself.

In the Code of Ethics of the Royal Australian and New Zealand College of Psychiatrists, an annotation to the principle that "psychiatrists shall hold information about the patient in confidence" includes the following provisions for allowing disclosure of confidential information:[14]

Confidentiality cannot always be absolute. A careful balance must be maintained between preserving confidentiality as a fundamental aspect of clinical practice and the need to breach it on rare occasions in order to promote the patient's optimal interests and care, and/or the safety or other significant interests of third parties.

Whilst upholding the principle of confidentiality, psychiatrists must do so within the constraints of the law and with regard to statutory requirements... Disclosure is... mandatory under legal compulsion and psychiatrists, as well as their clinical records, are compellable witnesses...

Psychiatrists may be released from their duty to maintain confidentiality if they become aware of, and are unable to influence, their patient's intention to seriously harm an identified person or group of persons. In these circumstances, psychiatrists may have an overriding duty to the public interest by informing either the intended victim(s), the relevant authorities, or both, about the threat.

As every psychiatrist by now knows, the California Supreme Court imposed a legal duty on a psychotherapist to protect a third party from the hazard of physical harm posed by a patient. The name of the case is now a household word in the psychiatric community: *Tarasoff v. Regents of the University of California.*

Actually, there were two cases, known as *Tarasoff I* and *Tarasoff II*.[15] The court in *Tarasoff I*, in 1974, held the duty was only "to use reasonable care to give threatened persons such warnings as are essential to avert foreseeable danger."[16] The decision was vacated following a petition for rehearing. In *Tarasoff II*, decided in 1976, the court modified its holding and imposed a duty "to exercise reasonable care to protect the foreseeable victim."[17] The duty to warn became a duty to protect.

The *Tarasoff* case also gets much attention in legal education. Law students, the lawyers of tomorrow, are alerted, to say the least, to the therapist's potential liability. The decision appears in a number of casebooks used in various courses, including evidence, jurisprudence, law and medicine, and torts. Law journal articles delve into it. Few other cases get that kind of attention. It fascinates, and it will continue to fascinate for years to come.[18]

The case has been discussed with unending frequency in publications by psychiatrists and psychologists as well as at their meetings.[19] Yet surveys reveal that the vast majority of psychiatrists have a skewed view of the decision. The surveys report that more than 75 percent of psychiatrists believe incorrectly that the one and only way to discharge the legal duty imposed in *Tarasoff* is to warn the potential victim.[20] Dr. Mark J. Mills, a psychiatrist holding a law degree, observed, "No doctrine in forensic psychiatry is as universally misunderstood as the so-called duty to warn."[21] Psychologists Leon VandeCreek and Samuel Knapp noted that the *Tarasoff* decision has "led to much commentary but little understanding."[22]

The case has been clouded by the fog of rhetoric and misinformation. Heavy alarms were sounded; unfounded fears spread. Therapists are heard to say, time beyond count: "The decision makes us incredibly vulnerable— we can be sued by the injured party for failure to warn and we can be sued by the patient for breach of confidentiality if warning turns out to be unnecessary." While the crucial question is whether a complaint is subject to summary disposition, and not whether a suit can be filed (anyone can file a suit against anyone for anything), therapists report that the decision has given them bad dreams, and they go astray in their practice.

How did the misinformation come about? Was the American Psychiatric Association, through its various committees and publications, less than helpful in educating the membership? Does the fault lie in understanding the nature of the legal process, or in understanding what the court is saying, or both? An axiom states that no learning is preferable to a little learning, so one might say, the best advice at the time would have been to just carry on with good clinical practice, have some malpractice insurance (which would cover legal representation), and do not worry about the law.

Surely, one cannot expect therapists to read the opinions of the courts, but even if they do, they may not be any wiser. The observations of W. Ray Forrester, the highly esteemed professor of constitutional law, about the opinions of the U.S. Supreme Court are applicable, if not more so, to the opinions of other courts. He said:[23]

> The typical opinion of the Supreme Court is so long and verbose, so filled with legalese synonyms, so encrusted with substantive footnotes, so totally unclear and inconsistent in the use of legal terms of art that only the devoted professional can hope to follow and understand what is going on. In fact, it has been said that Supreme Court opinions are so long and obscure that by the time the reader wades through the river of words he doesn't care how the case turns out.

The result is that the American people are separated by this wall of words from any real understanding of what the court is doing.

What the California Supreme Court did on rehearing in *Tarasoff* was to set out various options for therapists who treat potentially dangerous patients: to warn the intended victim or others likely to apprise the victim of danger, to notify the police, or take whatever other steps are reasonably necessary under the circumstances.[24] The protective action might include, but is not limited to, directly warning the intended victim. *Tarasoff II* is a mandate not simply to warn but to exercise reasonable care. The court declared that "the discharge of this duty of due care will necessarily vary with the facts of each case."[25] Thus, the means of fulfilling the duty may include informing the police, initiating commitment, conducting anger-release therapeutic encounters, or warning foreseeable victims or people likely to relay the warning. These options, one might say, exhaust the range of possibilities under the circumstances and are dictated as well by the demands of good patient care.[26]

Not faced by the court in *Tarasoff* is the question of whether the patient himself could have a claim against the therapist on the ground that the therapist should have prevented the harm.

Dr. Emanuel Tanay took his colleagues in psychiatry to task for their criticism of *Tarasoff*. He wrote in *Psychiatric News*, the biweekly of the American Psychiatric Association, as follows:[27]

> A patient in treatment has the right to expect from his therapist a rescue intervention in the face of realistic danger. To be the perpetrator of a homicide is one of the most self-destructive actions one can take. The therapist as a human being also has an obligation to an innocent victim and, last but not least, he has a duty to his own human dignity....There are many areas where the law has intervened unnecessarily into the practice of mental health professionals. [The *Tarasoff* case] is not such a situation. The decision does not require a therapist to report a fantasy....It simply means that when he is realistically convinced that a homicide is in the making, it is his duty to act like a human being and not like a robot.

One might imagine the public outcry had the court ruled differently, that is, that a therapist has no legal responsibility whatever to third parties in the face of danger posed by a patient. One might also consider litigation involving the care of patients even in a general hospital. In one case, to take an illustration, a nurse's aide at a general hospital discovered a patient assaulting another patient, and she attempted to render assistance to the victimized patient, and she was injured by the assaultive patient. Her complaint alleged that the physician "knew or should have known of the patient's violent traits or propensities, and that [he] was negligent in failing to order quieting medication, segregation, restraint, or attention in a ward or hospital environment consistent with his condition and for the protection of those patients near him." The court held that she stated a cause of action.[28]

The *Tarasoff* case involved outpatient psychotherapy, but how far, if at all, does the command of the case depart from traditional law or sound clinical practice? Long before *Tarasoff*, the courts ruled that mental hospitals must exercise reasonable care in preventing escapes and in deciding on releases. In numerous cases, hospitals or staff members have been held liable for breach of this duty of reasonable care. Thus, in 1943, in *Jones v. State of New York*,[29] the court held that where a state mental hospital fails to exercise reasonable care in preventing a patient's escape, the state is liable for injuries resulting from the escapee's assault and battery. The court said that the state "has a duty to protect the community from acts of insane persons under its care."[30] In this case, the state breached its duty of care by failing to provide adequate security in light of the patient's known violent tendencies.

To take another illustration, in 1956, in *Fair v. United States*,[31] doctors at a government hospital, after an allegedly superficial psychiatric examination, released a patient without warning to a foreseeable victim, despite knowledge of the patient's previous threats against that victim. The Fifth Circuit Court of Appeals held that the complaint sufficiently made out a cause of action in negligence which could go to the jury for trial on the merits. The court said that hospital treatment of mental patients induces the public to rely on and to expect an exercise of reasonable care. The "obligation of due care extends to the public," the court said.[32]

In 1967, in *Merchants National Bank & Trust Co. of Fargo v. United States*,[33] a mental patient at a Veterans' Administration hospital was allowed a leave of absence, during which he killed his wife. Failing to run over her with a car, he shot and killed her. In a lawsuit on behalf of the three minor children, it was alleged that the hospital staff had ignored indications of the seriousness of the patient's illness. The court agreed that the patient had been negligently given a leave of absence, without sufficient precautions, and awarded $200,000 as compensatory damages.

In 1974, in *Homere v. State*,[34] the New York Court of Claims held that while a state hospital is not liable under the state's tort claims act for "an honest error of professional judgment," it is liable for injuries inflicted by a psychiatric patient whose release was due to the negligent failure of the hospital to reconvene, in the special circumstances of the case, including a history of hospitalization and many acts of assault, a three-psychiatrist commission to reevaluate the patient's condition before his release. The court noted, "The assailant had been discharged and readmitted some fifteen times in the 'revolving door' of our state's mental health institutions. The patient's records contain innumerable entries relating to acts of aggression, clearly evincing that he was an extremely violent, assaultive man, who attacked females without reason, cause or justification." And the court noted, "The circumstances of his discharge were also ignoble. The patient apparently was simply dropped off at a subway station with instructions to go to the Social Services Office to obtain quarters. The assailant was an uneducated, borderline mental retardate."

Thus, in cases where the action was not barred by charitable or governmental immunity, the courts have placed on mental hospitals a duty to exercise reasonable care in escape prevention or release decisions. This is a duty extending to the general public. The courts, for the most part, did not distinguish between foreseeable and unforeseeable victims. The cases, for the most part, involved rather obvious administrative or communication errors.

Social changes have increased the likelihood that therapists will care for potentially dangerous patients who are not under custodial control. *Tarasoff* was a pleading case, that is, it resolved the question whether there exists in the law a duty owing to third parties as a result of a danger posed by a patient in an outpatient setting.[35] By holding in the affirmative, the court makes the therapist a proper party defendant whenever a patient causes injury to another. The trial court had sustained a demurrer to the complaint.[36] In jurisdictions following *Tarasoff*, it no longer is possible for the therapist to get out of the case by summary disposition on the ground that he owed no duty in law to the injured party. Under *Tarasoff*, it is now a matter for the jury to decide on the basis of the facts of the particular case whether reasonable care was exercised. The outcome then becomes, many say, a lottery.[37]

"It must be borne in mind," the Supreme Court once observed, "negligence cannot be established by direct, precise evidence such as can be used to show that a piece of ground is or is not an acre. Surveyors can measure an acre. But measuring negligence is different."[38] The *Tarasoff* litigation did not reach the merits, that is, there was no trial on the basis of the facts involved.

In this case, Prosenjit Poddar, a 25-year-old graduate student from India at the University of California, had met weekly with Dr. Lawrence Moore, a 34-year-old clinical psychologist at the outpatient department of the university hospital, for a total of eight sessions. He revealed his fantasies of harming, even killing, a young woman, who had rejected him. He came to distrust Dr. Moore, for he believed that Dr. Moore might betray him. A friend of Poddar's, concerned about him, reported to Dr. Moore that Poddar planned to purchase a gun. As it turned out Poddar purchased a BB gun.[39]

Poddar is described as an Indian untouchable, so low as to fall outside the country's caste system, who had risen light-years beyond his wildest imaginings from a tiny primitive village to a place in Berkeley's Masters in Naval Engineering program, where he meets Tatiana (Tanya), a lovely but insecure local junior college student from a disturbed home. What was for her an ego-satisfying casual flirtation became for him an obsession.

Dr. Moore pondered, we are informed, "He's gone behind my back and bought a gun. I'm going to have to confront him about it. I'm going to take that gun away." "You'll lose him for sure," responded Dr. Stuart Gold of the clinic, with whom he consulted. "I guarantee you. He'll be out the door faster than you can blink an eye." "The number one rule," advised another colleague, "is to keep the patient coming back for treatment. As long as you have him in tow, you have some control over his acting out." "Just don't do anything rash," advised Dr. Gold. "Just remember, you're under no obligation to act." And Dr. Gold suggested, "You may not have enough experience to handle this case."[40]

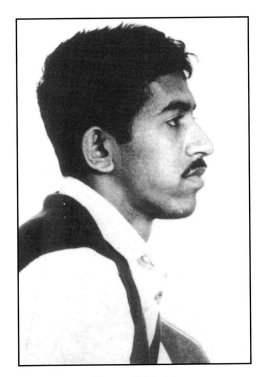

Prosenjit Podder

Tatiana Tarasoff

Dr. Moore confronted Poddar about the gun he had bought, but Poddar refused to turn it over to him. In India, Poddar's friends had called him a *gabhir jaler mach*, "deep water fish," because so little of him met the eye. Dr. Moore, with the concurrence of a colleague at the clinic, concluded that Poddar should be committed for observation under a 72-hour emergency psychiatric detention provision of the California commitment law. He did not seek longer detention. He notified the campus police both orally and in writing that Poddar was dangerous and should be committed. He wrote:

At times he appears to be quite rational, at other times he appears quite psychotic...[C]urrently the appropriate diagnosis for him is paranoid schizophrenic reaction, acute and severe. He is at this point a danger to the welfare of other people and himself. That is, he has been threatening to kill an unnamed girl who he feels has betrayed him and has violated his honor. He has told a friend of his...that he intends to go to San Francisco to buy a gun and that he plans to kill the girl. He has been somewhat more cryptic with me, but he has alluded strongly to the compulsion to "get even with," and "hurt" the girl.

The campus police went to his apartment, brought him to the station for questioning, and they also talked to other people familiar with Poddar. They gave him a warning to stay away from the girl. They concluded that commitment was not necessary. Poddar did not return to the clinic. Two months later, when Tatiana returned from vacation, he stabbed her to death. She was 19, but immature, unaware of what her sexuality was doing to Poddar.

Dr. Harvey Powelson, chief of the clinic, was outraged that Dr. Moore would break confidentiality and report Poddar to the police. He scolded Dr. Moore, "You realize, don't you, that by betraying his trust, you destroyed whatever chance you had of helping him?" "It was past that point," replied Dr. Moore. "And besides, I think he wanted me to break confidentiality. His telling me of his intentions was his way of saying, 'Look, I'm out of control. I'm going to kill this girl unless you stop me. Won't you please stop me.'"[41]

What if the *Tarasoff* case had gone to trial? What would the plaintiff have had to prove at trial? How should the warning have been made and to whom should it have been made? It may have been held that the therapist in fact discharged the duty mandated by the court, as he had notified the campus police, and the victim's brother, Alex Tarasoff, also had notice of the threat. Alex was Poddar's roommate and close friend. The police spoke to Poddar in Alex's presence. Alex did not take the threats seriously and did not report them to his family. Given these facts, could it not be said that the therapist discharged his duty of care as outlined by the court?

However, one might ask, was the therapy below standard of care? The *Tarasoff* case might have been litigated, purely and simply, as one of mal-psychotherapy, like mal-chemotherapy, resulting in the patient harming others. Dr. Gold had suggested that the treatment of Poddar may have been beyond the ability of Dr. Moore. Was he sufficiently experienced to handle the case? Not long before, events in Dr. Moore's life—a suicide attempt by his wife and her attempted murder of their child—had traumatized him. Following the death of Tatiana, he was dismissed from the clinic.[42] Could not the case have been litigated or decided on the basis of negligent treatment rather than on the formulation of a special duty to third persons?[43] Was that approach not taken because of the difficulty in establishing standard of care in psychotherapy?

When do therapists owe a duty to persons other than their patients? The threshold question in a negligence action is whether the defendant owed the plaintiff a legal duty. As a general principle, the risk that may result from one's behavior, as reasonably perceived, determines the duty of care as well as to whom the duty is owed. A "special relationship" between the parties may also created a duty of care. And legislation may impose a reporting duty (as in the case of child abuse).[44]

It is an axiom that good medical care involves consideration not only of the patient but also of others. The duty to others finds expression in legislation imposing various reporting obligations on physicians. However, in determining to whom a duty of care is owed, the courts are mindful of the extent of liability insurance coverage.[45] The courts not only consider the foreseeability of harm, but they also assess the competing public policy considerations for or against imposing a duty. One way or another, as the courts say, liability must be controlled by workable and just limits.[46] Summary disposition—judgment without the necessity of going to trial—is the appropriate remedy when the court determines the defendant did not owe the plaintiff a duty of care.

The issue of duty was highlighted in the most discussed of all torts cases, *Palsgraf v. Long Island R.R. Co.*[47] A passenger, rushing to catch the defendant's train, was pushed by a train porter as he was about to board and a package was dislodged from his grasp, falling upon the rails. It contained fireworks, it exploded, and the concussion overturned a weight scale, a distance away on the platform, injuring Mrs. Palsgraf, the plaintiff. Judge Cardozo, for the majority, ruled against liability because there was no negligence toward the plaintiff. Negligence, he said, must be founded upon the foreseeability of harm to the person in fact injured. The defendant's conduct was not a wrong toward the plaintiff merely because there was negligence toward someone else. The plaintiff must "sue in her own right for a wrong personal to her, and not as the vicarious beneficiary of a breach of duty to another." The law on negligence does not include a concept of "transfer of negligence." The train porter's behavior was reasonably foreseeable to cause injury to the passenger but not to Mrs. Palsgraf standing a distance away on the platform.

As a matter of law, can therapy or care of a patient result in a foreseeable risk of harm to a third person? The answer is a problematical yes. One result of mal-psychotherapy may be a patient's acting out in an unlawful manner. Clearly, to take an extreme example, a therapist who hypnotizes a patient and suggests the commission of a crime is a wrongdoer.[48] Mental hospitals are obliged to exercise reasonable care in preventing escapes or approving releases; they have a duty to protect third parties.[49] For the most part, the courts in these cases have not distinguished between foreseeable and unforeseeable victims.[50]

Policy lines, to some extent arbitrary, are drawn to narrow the scope of duty and also actionable causation. A number of states do not allow anyone but the patient to sue over negligent treatment even when that malpractice causes physical injury to others, as occurs when an infectious disease is improperly treated and is passed on to family members. In Illinois, in a case of this sort, the defendant physician raised the specter of a potentially unlimited liability to all those infected by his patient as well as all those whom they infect, and he also asserted that allowing the patient's immediate family to sue would constitute an artificial distinction between family members and all others whom his patient or they might infect. The majority of an intermediate appellate court agreed.[51] Justice Freedman, dissenting, would have extended the duty to the patient's immediate family. He said, "I cannot agree that limiting the right to sue...to a patient's immediate family members, *i.e.*, to those with whom he has special relationships, is an artificial and arbitrary distinction."[52]

In this type of situation, other states have not limited a cause of action only to patients. In a case decided by the Pennsylvania Supreme Court,[53] a physician negligently advised a patient exposed to hepatitis that if she remained symptom-free for six weeks, she had not contracted the disease and was not contagious. The advice should have been six months rather than six weeks. The patient refrained from sexual intercourse for eight weeks after the exposure and then resumed sexual intercourse with the plaintiff. Both patient and plaintiff were diagnosed with hepatitis. The court held that the plaintiff had a cause of action against the physician.[54]

In various jurisdictions, the courts have held a physician liable to members of a patient's family who contracted tuberculosis as a result of negligent failure of the physician to warn of danger of contagion.[55] A physician's liability has also been held to run to unidentifiable third persons in cases where the physician failed to warn the patient not to drive because of an uncontrollable diabetic condition.[56] In products litigation, liability has been extended at times to foreseeable victims of a defective product.[57] A spouse has a cause of action against a therapist who has an affair with his wife.[58]

In a 1980 California case, *Molien v. Kaiser Foundation Hospital*,[59] a physician incorrectly and negligently diagnosed his patient's illness as syphilis and directed her to inform her husband and have him tested for the disease. The court allowed the husband to bring an action against the physician for the emotional distress he suffered as a result of the misdiagnosis. Although the husband did not have any direct relationship or contact with the physician, the court held the husband could seek emotional distress damages as a "direct victim" of the physician's conduct. In *Molien,* the court drew a distinction between "direct victims" and "indirect victims," or bystanders.[60] In *Molien,* the physician directed his tortious conduct (misdiagnosing a disease) at the husband because the physician told his patient to convey the misdiagnosis to her husband and have him tested.[61]

In another California case, in 1995, *Reisner v. Regents of the University of California,*[62] a day after a 12-year-old patient received a transfusion, her doctor discovered that the blood had been contaminated with HIV antibodies. Although the same doctor continued treating the patient, he never told her about the situation. Three years later, she became intimate with the plaintiff. Two years after that, the doctor told the patient, who died a month later. Shortly thereafter, the plaintiff was tested and learned that he was HIV seropositive. The court, relying largely on *Tarasoff,* held that the defendant doctor owed a duty to the plaintiff despite the lack of a physician-patient relationship. According to the theory of the case, if the patient had been told when she should have been told, she would have warned the plaintiff and he would not have been infected.

The distinction is to be drawn between harm to third parties from negligent psychotherapy versus the independent duty to warn and protect potential victims irrespective of the standard of care. *Tarasoff* might have been litigated and decided on the basis of negligent treatment, with the third person regarded as a direct victim, rather than on the formulation of a special duty or relationship to third persons. A "special relationship" to a third party need not be found in cases where the treatment of the patient is negligent and results in "direct injury" to the third person. The negligent-treatment approach was not taken because of the difficulty in establishing standard of care in psychotherapy.[63]

The California Supreme Court during the 1970, was "a progressive court" that wanted to expand theories of law and did so in this case and others. The California Supreme Court held that by virtue of the "special relationship" that a therapist has with a patient, there results a duty of care to third parties who might be injured by the patient. It is immaterial whether or not the treatment of the patient falls below standard of care, or whether or not there is a causal nexus between the treatment and the injury to the third person. The court said:

> Although under the common law, as a general rule, one person owed no duty to control the conduct of another, nor to warn those endangered by such conduct, the courts have carved out an exception to this rule in cases in which the defendant stands in some special relationship *to either the person whose conduct needs to be controlled or in a relationship to the foreseeable victim of that conduct* (emphasis added).

Innovating, the court ruled that the special relationship with the patient also creates a special relationship with a victim of the patient.[64] Under this innovation, a special relation between *A* and *B* creates a special relation between *A* and *C* who is threatened by *B*. Thus, *A* is liable for the injury *B* causes to *C* even though *A* is not directly negligent toward *C*. Because of the special relation to *B*, a duty is imposed on *A* to safeguard *C* from harm by *B*. *Tarasoff* and its progeny represents an evolution of the law from no duty, to a duty to those in a special relation, and now to those who might be harmed by one to whom a duty is owed. Again, in the words of the court:

> Although plaintiffs' pleadings assert no special relation between [the victim] and defendant therapists, they establish as between [the patient] and defendant therapists the special relation that arises between a patient and his doctor or psychotherapist. Such a relationship may support affirmative duties for the benefit of third persons .... Although the California decisions that recognize this duty have involved cases in which the defendant stood in a special relationship *both* to the victim and to the person whose conduct created the danger, we do not think that the duty should logically be constricted to such situations (emphasis by court).

Under this ruling, a third party victim may bring a claim against a therapist regardless of whether or not the therapist's care and treatment of the patient constituted malpractice. Indeed, it could have been the best of therapy. One might imagine a situation where an individual comes to a therapist and confides a plan to harm a third party but departs immediately thus depriving the therapist of any therapeutic opportunity. The *Tarasoff* ruling would require the therapist to protect the potential third party victim. Under *Tarasoff*, the focus of concern is the foreseeable risk to a third party.[65]

The court in *Tarasoff* rationalized its holding in part by citing earlier decisions holding physicians liable for failing to warn third parties who contracted contagious diseases from their patients, but these are "direct victim" cases based on negligence.[66] What care to protect potential victims is reasonably necessary, the court said in *Tarasoff*, can be determined only on a case-by-case basis.[67]

Psychotherapists feel that they are between a rock and a hard place in deciding between confidentiality and reporting. On the one hand, psychotherapy is dependent on an atmosphere of trust and patients expect confidentiality. On the other hand, psychotherapists are expected to protect third parties who may be harmed by a patient. Following the much publicized decision in *Tarasoff*, the courts or legislatures of various states have imposed a legal duty to report when a patient poses a serious danger of violence to another. Americans have thought of California as a place apart, but what happens there soon spreads elsewhere.

While the majority of jurisdictions have limited the duty to warn or protect to circumstances of a specific threat to a reasonably identifiable victim, others have held that neither a specific threat nor an identifiable victim is needed for this duty to arise. Therapists are confused about how best to respond.[68]

Under the American Psychiatric Association's (APA) code of ethics, the psychiatrist is charged with the responsibility to "safeguard patient confidences within the constraints of law." In effect, the profession's ethics have accommodated society's interest in obtaining otherwise private information. Even before *Tarasoff,* the APA's code of ethics indicated that "psychiatrists at times may find it necessary in order to protect the patient or the community from imminent danger to reveal confidential information disclosed by the patient." The California Supreme Court in *Tarasoff* referred to the APA's code allowing breach of confidentiality in the face of "imminent danger."

And long before *Tarasoff,* in his 1952 book, *A Manual for Psychiatric Case Study,* Dr. Menninger wrote of breaking confidence when a patient presents imminent, severe, and certain danger to another person. He said, as earlier quoted, "If a patient tells a doctor in confidence that he has brought a time bomb into the hospital and hidden it under the bed of one of the other patients, it is a strange doctor indeed who would feel that his professional confidence should not be violated." And also years before *Tarasoff,* Neil Chayet, an attorney and a frequent commentator on issues of law and medicine, wrote, "No patient has the moral right to convince his psychiatrist that he is going to commit a crime and then expect him to do nothing because of the principle of confidentiality."[69]

In a Louisiana case decided in 1994, *Viviano v. Stewart,*[70] the patient, Billy Viviano, sued his psychiatrist, Dr. Dudley Stewart, for breach of confidentiality in notifying Federal Judge Veronica Wicker that Viviano threatened to kill her. The plaintiff argued that the danger, if any, was not "imminent" and therefore the breach of confidentiality was not justified. The jury decided in favor of the defendant following four weeks of trial. The decision was finally upheld by the Louisiana Supreme Court, after nine years of legal wrangling.[71]

Following the *Viviano* litigation, in December 1994, the word "imminent" was removed from the APA ethics guidelines, thereby allowing a disclosure in less than imminent circumstances. The qualification "imminent" was originally included in order to narrow the situation calling for a breach of confidentiality but, as illustrated by the *Viviano* case, it put a difficult burden on the therapist to establish an "imminent" danger.

The APA in an *amicus* brief in the *Tarasoff* case argued against the imposition of any legal duty to warn or protect because, it said, there is no professional standard for the prediction of violence, and such predictions are unreliable. That viewpoint has receded. From time out of memory, when certifying an individual for commitment to a hospital, psychiatrists attest to danger to self or others. In doing so, the future is forecast by referring back to previous behavior. In any event, by court decision or legislation, a duty has been imposed on therapists to warn or protect others.

In many states, by statute, physicians are permitted or required to report to the state Department of Motor Vehicles those patients whose physical or mental conditions (*e.g.*, visual impairment, loss of consciousness) impair their driving.[72] Usually, immunity is provided in the reporting statutes (thus relieving the physician if sued for breach of confidentiality of the burden of justifying the report).[73] Some therapists urge the patient to self-report as a condition of continued treatment. Reporting of mental disorders to the DMV does not automatically result in the loss of a license. Actually, one might say, the automobile way of life is itself a form of insanity.[74]

In a position statement, the American Psychiatric Association states that the presence of mental disorder does not, by itself, imply an impaired capacity to operate a motor vehicle. It advises:[75]

> Accurate assessment of the impact of symptoms on functional abilities usually is not possible in an office or hospital setting because such an assessment typically requires specialized equipment or observation of actual driving, which goes well beyond the scope of ordinary psychiatric care. Moreover, psychiatrists have no special expertise in assessing the ability of their patients to drive.

As the population of the United States ages, problems associated with dementia will increase. California requires physicians to report to the Department of Motor Vehicles individuals diagnosed with chronic confusional states caused by Alzheimer's disease and related disorders.[76] Approximately 33 states and the District of Columbia require more frequent or rigorous testing for older drivers.[77]

Physicians are required to report to public health agencies certain conditions such as gunshot wounds, occupational diseases, child abuse, infectious diseases, including AIDS, and, in some states, that a person is HIV-positive.[78] Also, under legislation regulating the purchase and sale of firearms, mental health facilities must report to the state Department of Justice those: (a) persons taken into custody as a danger to themselves or others, admitted to a facility, and evaluated and treated under state law; (b) persons admitted for "certified intensive treatment care." Those individuals covered by the requirements are prohibited from "owning, possessing, controlling, receiving or purchasing any firearm" for five years after they are released from the facility. The facility is required to inform the admitted person of this prohibition as well as the right to petition a court for permission to have a firearm.

Reports by the mental health facilities will be confidential except for "purposes of court proceedings" and determining "firearms eligibility."

So what is a therapist to do when a patient does not make a threat of violence but poses a danger? Christopher Alar, a senior high school student, was appointed to the U.S. Air Force Academy. His girlfriend told him that since they would be going to separate universities, she wanted to date other men. He attempted suicide and was taken to Mercy Memorial Hospital where he was seen by Dr. Gayle Godsell-Stytz, an ER specialist, and later transferred to the psychiatric unit of the hospital. She felt that the Air Force Academy needed to be informed of Alar's condition and she notified the Academy. The Academy, after a review of the medical records, revoked his admission. Applicants to the Academy are required "to disclose any new illness or injury since completing the final qualifying medical examination and failure to so comply may cause the applicant to be refused admission."

Alar brought suit against Dr. Godsell-Stytz and the hospital for breach of the physician-patient privilege and intentional interference with a business relationship. Following an 8-day trial, a jury returned a verdict in favor of the plaintiff, but the Michigan Court of Appeals reversed it.[79] Judge Mark Cavanagh, writing for the majority, said that what the doctor did made no difference—that her conduct was not a proximate cause of Alar's loss—because he had an obligation to report his hospitalization to the Academy. Judge Cavanagh wrote, "The integrity of the legal process demands that the courts assume that persons with such an obligation will honor it. It would corrode the integrity and effectiveness of the legal system to do otherwise."

In a dissent, Judge Kathleen Jansen said that she could not agree that the doctor's conduct was not a proximate cause of the injury. Alar, she wrote, could have presented his admission to the hospital in a different light. Judge Jansen concluded, "I cannot agree that the doctor's conduct made no difference."

The case attracted the attention of the media and Dr. Godsell-Stytz explained, as she had at trial, why she notified the Academy. Her husband was a graduate of the Academy and she was familiar with its rigors. In the previous year, there had been several suicides there. She believed that Alar could present a risk of harm to himself or others as a result of the stresses at the Academy. Alar was scheduled to be there in a couple of weeks. She believed the danger was imminent. She also claimed that Alar gave oral consent for the divulgence, which he denied. She found herself, as she put it, in a medical-legal-moral dilemma. She agonized over it. To be sure, what is entailed in confidentiality in the therapeutic relationship is uncertain.

Apart from fault, under tort theory, a causal nexus must be established between the fault and the harm. Thus, for example, one is at fault in driving without a driver's license, but it may have nothing to do with an accident, which may have been caused by the road condition. Negligence in the air, so to speak, is not sufficient. There must be what the law calls "proximate cause," which is often a policy question. Could it be said that the failure to certify Poddar for commitment, or treat him differently, was the proximate cause of the death, inasmuch as he could have done the same thing irrespective of hospitalization or other treatment?

*Tarasoff* was settled for a figure rumored at $50,000, a nominal sum in a wrongful death action. Insurance companies, we know, do not relish being placed at the peril of the jury. In this case the cost of litigating probably would have exceeded the settlement. It is a pity, in a way, that the case was not tried as it is more likely than not it would have been decided in favor of the defendant and thus would not have caused such a stir in the psychiatric community. In this sense, settling was penny wise and pound foolish.[80]

Since a medical malpractice case is expensive to litigate, a lawyer (on the customary contingency fee) is not likely to pursue a case, whatever the malpractice of the doctor, if injury is minimal. However, if a death (suicide or homicide) is involved, the lawyer is likely to take the case even when malpractice is barely discernible since the potential award is substantial. This is why litigation involving breach of confidentiality rarely occurs or is inconsequential as compared to cases involving physical injury or death. In tort theory, fault is the cornerstone of liability and then questions of causation and damages are raised, but in practice it is the reverse. The tail wags the dog—the greater the injury, the greater the chance of an adverse judgment.[81]

Insurance, as every lawyer knows, underlies verdicts. Of course, this is not expressed in judicial opinions, but the California Supreme Court has been especially candid about viewing tort law fundamentally as a vehicle for compensating injured victims.[82] In a society permeated by violence, the psychiatrist under *Tarasoff* is the unarmed policeman with a deep pocket; malpractice insurance becomes a victim's compensation fund.[83] But this is not to say that the concept of fault is wholly abandoned. Quite often, in the litany of cases following *Tarasoff*, the judge or jury when imposing liability is expressing dissatisfaction with the quality of care.

What about the duty of others? Why therapists, they ask, and not others? If a warning is earnestly believed to be of protective value to victims, why not extend the duty to guardians of public safety (the police and correctional facilities) or to lawyers? The court in *Tarasoff I* said that police officers, jail and prison officials may also be liable for failing to warn of potential violence whenever a prisoner is released pursuant to bail order, parole, or completion of sentence. They raised a hue and cry, and on rehearing, in *Tarasoff II*, they were dropped. Under that decision, therapists, but not law-enforcement officials, have the duty since they have "a special relationship with the potentially dangerous person." In recent years, most states have enacted some kind of law requiring officials to notify victims of violent crimes or sex offenses when the suspect or inmate is about to be released from custody.[84]

Duties in the law of tort are imposed, as we have noted, when there is what is known as a special relationship.[85] Arguably, researchers and evaluators have the same duty as therapists.[86] What about a patient advocate in the hospital? A patient advocate faces an ethical dilemma when, after conversations with the patient, he is led to believe that the patient poses a threat of serious harm to another.[87] Arguably, the patient advocate will be regarded like a lawyer, who, under the American Bar Association's *Model Rules of Professional Conduct*, may reveal a client's criminal intentions but is not obligated to do so.[88]

To gauge by the volume of literature, the following issues are of most concern: breach of confidentiality; the foreseeability of the victim; the prediction or assessment of dangerousness; and the methods of discharging the duty to protect. The United States is a litigious society, but even so, the number of lawsuits against a therapist for harm done by a patient to a third party are few, and only a small number of those result in an adverse judgment, but all of them get a lot of publicity. Yet, of all medical malpractice claims, psychiatry accounts for substantially less than 2 percent of all paid claims. Only a tiny percentage of cases proceed to trial.

Courts are routinely asked to balance two important yet conflicting claims. As the court in *Tarasoff* recognized, the conflict exists between the patient's claim to privacy and society's need for security.[89] The confidential character of the relationship must end "where the public peril begins," said the court, analogizing violence to contagious diseases where reporting is required. Even then, the court said, disclosure must be discreet, and accomplished in a way that protects privacy to the "fullest extent compatible with the prevention of...danger."[90] In a dissent, Justice William Clark would maintain confidentiality in order to safeguard psychotherapy.

The majority opinion in *Tarasoff* was written by Chief Justice Mathew O. Tobriner. He was steeped in the Talmud which gives primacy to the safeguarding of life. On numerous occasions, LEXIS informs us, he kept valuable interests from being sacrificed on "false altars." During his tenure on the bench, he gave a great deal of thought to the function of the courts in our increasingly industrialized and impersonal society.[91] In *Tarasoff*, he wrote, "A patient with severe mental illness and dangerous proclivities may, in a given case, present a danger as serious and as foreseeable as does the carrier of a contagious disease or the driver whose condition or medication affects his ability to drive safely." He added, "Our current crowded and computerized society compels the interdependence of its members. In this risk-infested society we can hardly tolerate the further exposure to danger that would result from concealed knowledge of the therapist that his patient was lethal."

In the same year, the California Supreme Court held a physician and hospital liable for failure to report suspected child abuse.[92] It was the first appellate decision holding a physician or hospital liable in tort to the victim of the abuse for failure to comply with the reporting statute. All states have child abuse reporting laws, but at least three states exempt physicians from reporting when, through counseling, they are trying to deal with the abuse.[93]

In view of the statistics of 5 to 12 percent of physicians in the United States are so impaired that their condition affects their practice, a number of states have enacted laws requiring physicians to report their impaired colleagues to the medical board.[94] The American Psychiatric Association's *Principles of Medical Ethics* directs its members to "strive to expose those physicians deficient in character and competence," but at the same time they are to "safeguard patient confidence within the constraints of the law." There is a very real problem when a treating psychiatrist recognizes a threat to society posed by any of his physician-patients.[95]

Apparently most psychiatrists try to persuade the physician-patient to take a leave from practice to avoid having to notify the medical board. Legally, the psychiatrist may be held liable for not having reported the physician-patient if anyone suffers as a result. It may also be noted that the California physician-patient testimonial privilege, among others, provides that there is no privilege to remain silent in a proceeding brought by a public entity to determine whether a right, authority, or license should be revoked, suspended, or limited.[96]

A number of states require a subsequent treating therapist who is informed by a patient that a prior therapist was involved sexually with the patient to the appropriate licensing authority, or to inform and enable the patient to report.[97] Unless the reporting is mandated by statute, a therapist may not reveal a patient's communications during therapy to any other person except with the patient's express permission, or under very restricted circumstances. In general, the decision about whether to report the abuse ultimately rests with the patient.[98] A number of states have also made it a crime for a psychotherapist to engage in sexual relations with a patient.[99] Apparently, criminalizing psychotherapist-patient relations may make it less likely that therapists will report offending colleagues or admit their own behavior given the threat of prosecution. It also shifts control of the offending therapist away from licensing boards, which may provide rehabilitation, to the prosecutor. Apparently there have been no prosecutions notwithstanding the number of civil suits brought against therapists for engaging in sexual relations with a patient. Patients are more interested in a civil award than in prosecution.

There is increasing pressure to disregard confidentiality when a patient tests positive for the virus that causes AIDS, the human immunodeficiency virus, or HIV. Should a physician be allowed, or required, to report a positive test result to a spouse, family member, or known sexual partner of the carrier?[100] Should legislation be adopted allowing, or requiring, the disclosure of a positive test result to institutions with which the carrier is or may become involved, *e.g.*, hospitals, funeral directors, employers, schools? Various state legislatures have been considering these questions. Most states now require physicians to report cases in which they diagnose AIDS to a public health agency; only a few require the reporting of cases of individuals who test positive for HIV.[101] Most states have legislation, enacted in response to the danger of tuberculosis, that permits public health officials to quarantine persons who threaten to spread a disease to others. While the likelihood of transmission is still open to question, it may be said that there is a *Tarasoff*-like duty to warn or protect.[102]

In *Tarasoff*, the American Psychiatric Association in a friend-of-the-court brief, argued that a revelation of confidential communications by therapists would significantly deter persons from seeking therapy and those already in therapy would be inhibited in making disclosures. These feared results, the court said, however, were entirely too speculative. The court commented that the forecast of harm was as "equally dubious" as in the earlier case of *In re Lifschutz*, where it was argued that any exception to a testimonial privilege covering physician-patient communications would inhibit patient disclosures.[103] The California Supreme Court in *Lifschutz* stated, "Although petitioner has submitted affidavits of psychotherapists who concur in his assertion that total confidentiality is essential to the practice of their profession, we cannot blind ourselves to the fact that the practice of psychotherapy has grown, indeed, flourished, in an environment of non-absolute privilege."[104]

Absolute privacy may be found only in the grave. Privacy or confidentiality is a protection often assumed by patients to be total, but known by therapists to be severely limited. In 1978, a survey of psychotherapists in California indicated that approximately 632 of 1,272 psychologists and psychiatrists surveyed, or 49 percent, had breached confidentiality and warned at least one potential victim or member of a potential victim's family, or the police, sometime during their average of 14 years of practice prior to *Tarasoff*.[105] As a matter of ethics, many urge the therapist to obtain an informed consent at the outset of therapy. This "Miranda"-type warning, they say, would protect the unwary patient from dangerous self-disclosure, and would aid in the assessment of dangerousness since any revelation made after such a warning ought to be taken seriously.[106] This warning, they suggest, would also serve to protect the therapist against suits for breach of confidentiality.[107]

Although not legally required, many therapists nowadays give a "Miranda"-type warning. The discussion is on-the-one-hand and on-the-other-hand. Should they warn, or should they inquire about dangerousness?

Dr. Paul Appelbaum suggests that two questions be routinely asked: "Have you ever seriously injured another person?" and "Do you ever think about harming someone else?"[108] Actually, what type of therapy would it be if destructive urges were not explored? Anger prompts a lot of people to enter therapy; good therapy gets people in touch with their anger. Apparently, most therapists, though they do not inform their patients of the limits of confidentiality at the inception of treatment, will seek consent or at least advise the patient before disclosing any information to a potential victim or others. Psychiatrists have discreetly advised employers to make a shift at work because of a conflict that a patient has with a co-employee or supervisor. It's called "environmental manipulation." A trust relationship is impeded by a collusive communication between the therapist and others.

We may say: Trust–not confidentiality–is the cornerstone of psychotherapy. Disclosing information about a patient without knowledge or consent would be a breach of trust.[109] A warning actually discussed with the patient, Dr. James Beck concludes in an empirical study, strengthens the therapeutic relationship. Only where the patient "experienced the warning as unexpected and felt betrayed" did negative results occur.[110]

A number of therapists treat potentially dangerous individuals on a contractual-type basis. At the inception of the relationship, the doctor sets certain limitations, among them the agreement that if the patient finds himself in a position where he might hurt himself or others he will go into the hospital. When learning that a patient is stepping outside the agreement, he advises the patient that he has broken the principles of the treatment relationship and therefore must enter the hospital immediately. If he refuses to do so, the therapist terminates treatment. (Arguably, the therapist cannot legally terminate the relationship under these circumstances.) Once treatment is terminated, and someone is in danger, the therapist feeling a responsibility to help the patient will seek hospitalization, or notify the next of kin or the intended victim. If the primary goal is to aid the patient, then the therapist is not making a legal or political decision, but is making a decision which is therapeutic.

The very fact that the patient is communicating the threat to the therapist implies that the patient wants help and does not want to carry out the threat. He is reaching out for help, therapists say. More often than not, the fact of communication of these threats to the therapist usually means that a patient will not act upon them.

## FORESEEABILITY OF THE VICTIM

Is the identity of the victim a matter of consequence? Legally, should it be? Should it matter whether danger is to person or property? Logically, what difference should the identity of the victim or type of harm make? Logically, the test must be: Is the threat serious, and is the potential harm imminent and serious?[111] The patient says he plans to poison the water supply, blow up a building, or kill the first person that crosses his path. Is there not a *prima facie* absurdity to limiting the duty of care to the situation when the victim is identifiable? The scope of harm is potentially greater when the general populace is threatened. The answer, of course, lies not in logic but in law–the legal consequences of the distinction are enormous. If the therapist's duty is to protect society, every victim can sue, but if his duty is only to an identifiable victim, only that victim has a cause of action. Under a duty to protect society, one and all in a crowd of people harmed by the patient could maintain a suit against the therapist. The potential of liability could be withering (save the practice of limiting liability to insurance limits).[112]

In the years since *Tarasoff*, the courts in various states have responded either by narrowing its range of applicability to a specific individual or by broadening it to include unidentifiable individuals.[113] In *Tarasoff*, the plaintiffs alleged that two months prior to their daughter's death, the patient, Prosenjit Poddar, informed his therapist that he intended to kill a young woman fitting Tatiana Tarasoff's description. Although Poddar did not specifically name Tatiana as his intended victim, the complaint alleged that the therapist could have readily identified the endangered person as Tatiana. The court stated that, while it would be unreasonable to require the therapist to conduct an investigation, a "moment's reflection" is required.[114]

Four years later, in 1980, the California Supreme Court, in *Thompson v. County of Alameda*,[115] stated that "for policy reasons, the duty to warn depends upon and arises from the existence of a prior threat to a specific identifiable victim." The court observed, "The *Tarasoff* decedent was known and specifically foreseeable and an identifiable victim of the patient's threats. We concluded that under such circumstances it was appropriate to impose liability on those defendants for failing to take reasonable steps to protect her." In this case, a juvenile had indicated that he would, if released from custody, take the life of a young child residing in the neighborhood. No identifiable child was named. According to the complaint, county mental health professionals "knew that [the juvenile] had latent, extremely dangerous and violent propensities regarding young children" and he had "indicated that he would, if released, take the life of a young [neighborhood] child." Within 24 hours of his temporary leave to his mother's home, the juvenile attacked and killed the plaintiff's five-year-old son.

The court rejected the imposition of liability for the county's failure to provide a blanket warning in the community. That would flood airwaves, phone lines, or mailboxes. The county, at great cost, would have to assign police or others to knock on doors, stuff mailboxes, or phone residents. Should the warning be written across the skies? Indeed, the court said, "the sheer volume of warnings" would dilute their impact; they would be impractical and they would negate rehabilitative efforts. Therefore, the majority in *Thompson* declined to impose a duty to warn when there was not a specific, identifiable victim; and of course, by so doing, it limited the scope of liability, of which courts must be mindful.[116] Limiting the scope of liability to identifiable victims as a matter of policy may seem to go hand in glove with the idea of warnings as a safeguard but warnings are the least helpful way to deal with a danger. Two justices, Justices Tobriner and Mosk, dissented, charging that the majority missed the point of *Tarasoff*, namely, that for identifiable victims, a warning may fulfill the duty, but for unidentifiable but foreseeable victims, "reasonable care may require other actions."[117]

In 1983, in *Brady v. Hopper*,[118] the individuals injured as a result of John Hinckley Jr.'s unsuccessful assassination attempt on President Reagan sued the would-be assassin's therapist. They argued that, although Hinckley had voiced no actual threats, the therapist should have known that he posed a serious danger to others. The federal district court in Colorado rejected the argument, and held that the scope of the duty to protect was limited to those instances where there were "specific threats to specific victims." The court said, this rule offers a "workable, reasonable and fair boundary" on the scope of a therapist's liability.[119]

Discerning a "readily identifiable" victim is not as difficult, of course, as finding a needle in the haystack. Where there is the will, there is the way. In a result-oriented decision, the Michigan Court of Appeals that same year, 1983, in *Davis v. Lhim*,[120] found a victim "identifiable" on the basis of what critics have said to be very questionable evidence.[121] Davis, the victim's son, shot and killed his mother two months after he was discharged from voluntary hospitalization. The evidence that the victim was "readily identifiable" was contained in a single entry in an emergency room record documented two years before the violent act. The note indicated that the patient's aunt had told the treating physician that the patient had been pacing the floor and threatening his mother for money. The court reasoned that since the threats were directed at a specific person, and since the condition that gave rise to the threat (lack of money) continued, the mother was a readily identifiable victim. The court found the information "sufficient."[122]

While the finding in *Davis v. Lhim* that the victim was "readily identifiable" is open to question, the decision of the jury may be justified by the number of early cases holding mental hospitals responsible for the care and discharge of patients. This case involved a patient who had been in and out of hospitals over the years. In posttrial interviews, the jury expressed its dissatisfaction with the policy of deinstitutionalization. By returning a verdict in the amount of $500,000 for a victim's sister, who is usually not considered a strong claimant in a wrongful death action, the jury was sending a message to the state to change social policy. At trial, the treating doctor justified his discharge of the patient on the basis of the policy of deinstitutionalization. He cited President Kennedy's program establishing community mental health centers. It was an "I had to do it" defense. The jurors were dismayed too by the practice of psychiatry where the psychiatrist's mastery of the English language is less than understandable. In any event, the expert testimony on behalf of the defendant actually made out a strong case for the plaintiff and at a conference following the case, the plaintiff's attorney thanked the defendant's expert for his testimony! Why was the expert put on the stand? All too often, the staff members of the Attorney General's office, who defend physicians employed at state hospitals, are no match for the seasoned trial lawyers representing the plaintiff.

In the 1850s, Charles Dickens satirized the sluggishness of England's civil justice. Lo and behold, the Michigan Court of Appeals' decision in *Davis v. Lhim* was overturned some five years later, in 1988, by the State's Supreme Court, under the state's governmental immunity law in effect at the time of the filing of the lawsuit. The court ruled that the decision to discharge a patient is a discretionary act (as distinguished from a ministerial act) for which a state hospital doctor enjoys immunity.[123] The court said that because the doctor was immune from liability for discretionary acts, there was no need to determine whether he was under a duty to protect third persons from harm. In a footnote, the court distinguished the case from *Tarasoff*, which occurred in California, where state employees are not given governmental immunity.[124]

In Michigan, for cases filed after the "tort reform legislation" enacted in 1986, a governmental employee is liable, without regard to the discretionary or ministerial nature of the conduct in question, when his conduct amounts to "gross negligence that is the proximate cause of the injury or damage."[125] "Gross negligence" means "conduct so reckless that it demonstrates a substantial lack of concern for whether an injury results."[126] Why not the usual standard of negligence? Given the public's negative feelings about immunity, "gross negligence" will likely be interpreted in such a way as to put mental health professionals in public agencies on the same footing as those in the private sector. Indeed, from the viewpoint of the victim, why should there be a distinction?

King George III said he was not accountable—"The King can do no wrong." Americans did not like that, and made a revolution. The concept of sovereign immunity is mocked in the ditty:

I am the King of England
I like to sing and dance
And if you don't like what I do
I'll punch you in the pants
I am the King of England
I like to sing and dance.

In 1987, in *Jackson v. New Center Community Mental Health Service*,[127] the Michigan Court of Appeals said that when a psychiatrist finds that a patient poses a serious danger of violence to a readily identifiable person, he has a duty to use reasonable care to protect that person, but he owed no duty to the plaintiffs in this case, the court said, because they were the victims of a random shooting spree. They were not readily identifiable potential victims. Again, in 1988, in *Adams v. Ludorf*,[128] the Michigan Court of Appeals ruled that no duty is owed to unidentified third parties. In this case, an alcohol and drug abuse treatment center treated a patient who killed the plaintiff's decedent. There was no allegation of a threatened identifiable victim. The court reiterated that a duty is owed only to third parties readily identifiable as foreseeably endangered by the patient. The treatment center was granted summary disposition because the plaintiff failed to plead that the decedent was readily identifiable. As in the 1987 case, the decedent was a member of the general public who became the victim of the patient's random violence.

In 1983, in a federal case, *Jablonski v. United States*,[129] involving a V.A. hospital, the court imposed liability for failure to protect even though the patient had made no threats, either verbal or written, against any individual. The patient had, however, assaulted and attempted to rape his girlfriend's mother. The court relied heavily on the conduct of the patient and information contained in an old record, which the defendant doctor had failed to review. The courts consider that an accurate assessment cannot be made without a review of records. The prior records, the court concluded, documented a profile indicating violence toward women close to the patient. The records of the patient's prior hospitalization documented "homicidal ideation toward his wife" that had on several occasions resulted in attempts on her life. Furthermore, the record noted a "distinct" possibility of future violence. The patient's girlfriend, the court reasoned, became "readily identifiable" by virtue of her relationship with him.[130] The district judge's findings of malpractice included failure to record and communicate a police warning, to obtain medical records, and to warn the girlfriend.

The court in *Jablonski* said that these acts or omissions were not a "discretionary function" giving immunity within the meaning of the Federal Tort Claims Act. The distinction generally made in the application of the discretionary function exemption is between those decisions which are made on a policy or planning level, as opposed to those made on an operational level. To the defense argument that the doctor's failure to warn was not the proximate cause of the death, the court said that the information about the patient "if properly used, would have prevented the murder in question...The record adequately supports the finding that preventative actions would have been taken but for these failures."

In 1983, in *Hedlund v. Superior Court of Orange County*,[131] the California Supreme Court extended the therapist's duty to protect beyond the readily identifiable victim to include those in "close relationships with the object of a patient's threat." LaNita Wilson and Stephen Wilson were both outpatients at the defendant hospital. During the course of treatment, Stephen expressed his intent to injure LaNita. LaNita was not warned. Subsequently, Stephen shot and severely wounded LaNita as she sat in her car, her young son Darryl beside her. The young child suffered emotional trauma as the result of the assault on his mother. The court held that the child was a "foreseeable and readily identifiable" victim. The court reasoned: Where the mother is, her child "will not be far distant."[132]

In a 1979 New Jersey case, *McIntosh v. Milano*,[133] a young woman was killed by the defendant's patient who had been in outpatient therapy for two years. During that time, the patient expressed intense feelings of jealousy, anger, and violence, and had, on at least one occasion, fired a BB gun at the car of either the victim or her boyfriend. The plaintiffs, the parents of the victim, alleged that the defendant should have known of the danger to their daughter. Likening dangerousness to a disease, the court held that, apart from the special relationship between psychiatrist and patient, the duty to protect could be predicated on a more broadly-based obligation as a practitioner to protect the general welfare of the community.[134]

In 1980, in another case based on a motion to dismiss, *Lipari v. Sears, Roebuck*,[135] an outpatient at a Veterans' Administration hospital, Ulysses Cribbs, threatened to harm others but did not specify whom he would attack or when. After less than a month of outpatient care, he terminated treatment, evidently disgruntled with it. Previously he had been committed to a mental institution. He bought a shotgun at Sears, went into a crowded dining room in Omaha and randomly fired into the crowd, killing plaintiff's husband and blinding her. The plaintiff filed suit against Sears in federal court, under diversity of citizenship jurisdiction, and Sears filed a third-party complaint against the United States, alleging that the V.A. was negligent in failing to detain Cribbs or to initiate civil commitment proceedings against him. In a criminal prosecution, Cribbs was found not guilty by reason of insanity. In the civil case, Sears urged by way of defense that the hospital's treatment was negligent because the professionals knew or should have known that the patient was dangerous to himself and others and that measures should have been initiated to prevent the acts of violence. The complaint alleged that Sears was negligent in selling a shotgun to a mentally ill individual. The court ruled that the hospital decision concerning the patient's detention would not be considered a discretionary function, which would have given immunity, and it also retained Sears as a party defendant.

Absent Nebraska precedent on the duty to protect third parties, the federal district court in *Lipari* framed the issue as follows: "This court must therefore determine whether Nebraska law would impose a duty on a psychotherapist to take reasonable precautions to protect potential victims of his patient, when the psychotherapist knows or should know that his patient presents a danger to others." In finding the therapist potentially liable, the court specifically rejected the notion that the duty to protect arose only when the victim is readily identifiable. The duty arose, said the court, when the therapist knew or should have known that his patient's dangerous propensities presented an "unreasonable risk of harm" to others.[136] The court rejected the contention that the duty exists only when the victim is known (as in *Tarasoff*) or reasonably identifiable (as in *McIntosh*). The case, like *Tarasoff*, was thereupon settled out of court. Sears and the V.A., not wanting to risk placing a blind widow with six children before a jury, settled for some $200,000.

In the California progeny to *Tarasoff*, Justice Tobriner in *Thompson v. County of Alameda*, in 1980, urged in a dissent that "the principles underlying the *Tarasoff* decision indicate that ...the existence of an identifiable victim is not essential to the cause of action." The focus was public safety. "The absence of an identifiable victim," he said, "does not postulate the absence of a duty of reasonable care."[137]

In a 1983 Washington case, *Peterson v. State*,[138] the plaintiff was injured when her car was struck by a vehicle driven by defendant's patient who had been discharged five days prior to the accident. The plaintiff argued that the defendant knew of his patient's dangerous propensities and should have acted to protect her. The patient's history, of which defendant was aware, revealed acts of self-mutilation while under the influence of drugs. In addition, the day before his discharge while out on a day pass, the patient was apprehended while driving his car recklessly in the hospital parking lot. The court agreed with the plaintiff, and held that a therapist has a duty to protect "anyone who might be foreseeably endangered by [the patient's] mental problems."

In a Delaware case, *Naidu v. Laird*,[139] Hilton Putney apparently drove his automobile deliberately into a vehicle driven by George Laird, killing him. Putney had a long history of mental illness, and at the time of the accident was in a psychotic state. He was charged with manslaughter but found not guilty by reason of insanity. Some five months prior to the fatal accident, Putney had been treated for a seventh time at Delaware State Hospital. In a wrongful death action, Laird's widow alleged that the defendant, Dr. Venkataramana Naidu, was grossly negligent in the care, treatment, and discharge of Putney and that such gross negligence was a proximate cause of her husband's death. The jury returned a verdict in favor of Mrs. Laird, awarding her damages in the amount of $1.4 million. The appellate court affirmed. The court rejected the doctor's contention that "no duty required him to prevent a former patient from causing injury to members of the public at large." He had argued that Putney posed no present danger to himself or others at the time of his discharge, and that, as a matter of law, he had no choice but to release him. He argued that the court should reject imposition of liability on state-employed psychiatrists for the harm inflicted by patients whom the psychiatrists were obligated to release. However, the court found that the evidence showed that Putney was a present danger to himself and was eligible for involuntary commitment at the time of his release. It therefore affirmed the jury verdict. As in the Michigan case of *Davis v. Lhim,*[140] the patient in this case had an extensive history of mental illness involving numerous mental health institutions and psychiatrists. He was "a well-known patient with many admissions." Following the sixth of his seven admissions, his community residence caseworker wrote in the medical record: "How could a physician discharge such a sick patient ten days after he made a suicide attempt?....The consequences of off-hand, careless, indifferent medical malpractice in this case can be very tragic."

This extension of liability from a specific identifiable victim to any foreseeable victim means the prediction of "dangerousness in general terms." In any event, the limitation of a readily identifiable victim does not apply in cases where a patient is potentially dangerous because of medication given to him. The physician may be held responsible, even if the victim cannot be specifically identifiable in advance, if within the "scope of foreseeable risk."

There are numerous cases in the context of medication-related automobile accidents. In *Welke v. Kuzilla,*[141] the plaintiff's wife was killed in a car collision with the defendant Kuzilla. Kuzilla was a patient of Dr. Capper, who had prescribed medication for her, including an unknown substance on the evening prior to the accident. Dr. Capper was joined as a defendant on a malpractice theory. In *Watkins v. United States,*[142] the plaintiff was injured in a collision with a patient of the defendant doctor. The doctor had prescribed a 50-day supply of Valium® without checking the patient's psychiatric history and the patient proceeded to drink alcohol and take the pills. He then tried to kill himself by deliberately driving his car into the plaintiff's car. The doctor was held negligent as to anyone who would be endangered by the patient's predictably irresponsible behavior.[143]

## PREDICTION OF VIOLENCE

The most controversial issue emerging out of *Tarasoff* is that of prediction of violence. Dangerousness is not an inherent quality but the result of a number of variables. The parameters controlled, one can predict that a switch will turn on a light. That is not the case in human affairs. Will the patient take medication? Will the patient turn again to the use of alcohol or drugs, which may make him dangerous? Will the patient get a gun? Who knows?

In the limpid light of North Africa, Paul Klee discovered the sense of color and felt for the first time that he was a painter. The sculptor Henry Moore observed, "Every day is a new day. I don't know what I'll do tomorrow." What can be predicted? Early research suggested that therapists were "vastly overrated" as predictors of violence.[144] More recent literature, however, maintains that a therapist's predictive abilities may be better than originally suspected.[145] The therapist in *Tarasoff* was very much concerned that Poddar would kill.

In that pleading case, the court ruled that the duty to protect arose when the therapist "determines" or "should determine" that his patient presents a serious danger of violence. The court in *Tarasoff* said that "once a therapist does in fact determine, or under applicable professional standards reasonably should have determined, that a patient poses a serious danger of violence to others, he bears a duty to exercise reasonable care to protect the foreseeable victim of that danger." On predicating liability of therapists upon the prediction of violent acts, the court observed:[146]

> The role of the psychiatrist, who is indeed a practitioner of medicine, and that of the psychologist who performs an allied function, are like that of the physician who must conform to the standards of the profession and who must often make diagnoses and predictions based upon such evaluations. Thus the judgment of the therapist in diagnosing emotional disorders and in predicting whether a patient presents a serious danger of violence is comparable to the judgment which doctors and professionals must regularly render under accepted rules of responsibility.
>
> We recognize the difficulty that a therapist encounters in attempting to forecast whether a patient presents a serious danger of violence. Obviously we do not require that the therapist, in making that determination, render a perfect performance; the therapist need only exercise "that reasonable degree of skill, knowledge, and care ordinarily possessed and exercised by members of [that professional specialty] under similar circumstances."
>
> Within the broad range of reasonable practice and treatment in which professional opinion and judgment may differ the therapist is free to exercise his or her own best judgment without liability; proof, aided by hindsight, that he or she judged wrongly is insufficient to establish negligence.

The assessment, at trial, of the threat is thus made on the basis of expert testimony.[147] Psychiatrists, in the wake of *Tarasoff*, say that there are no professional standards for evaluating dangerousness but, for years, they have had little or no hesitation in certifying individuals for commitment to a hospital because of danger posed by a patient to self or others. There are phrases in civil commitment statutes such as "reasonable expectation that there is a substantial risk of physical harm" and "can reasonably be expected within the near future to intentionally or unintentionally seriously physically injure himself or another."[148]

In *Barefoot v. Estelle*,[149] a death penalty case where evidence of future dangerousness is a consideration in the imposition of the death penalty, the American Psychiatric Association urged the U.S. Supreme Court to bar expert testimony by psychiatrists on the prediction of violence on the ground that therapists are unable to predict violent behavior over the long term.[150] The Court said that the suggestion was "somewhat like asking us to disinvent the wheel."[151] In the *Tarasoff*-progeny case, *Lipari v. Sears, Roebuck*,[152] the federal district court stated that "the standard of care for health professionals adequately takes into account the difficult nature of [prediction]."

Predict the therapist must. His failure to do so can result in liability if other practitioners "pursuant to the standards of the profession" would have done so. The question is, by what standard should his conduct be judged?

## STANDARD OF CARE IN ASSESSING DANGER

Foreseeability determines duty, breach of which subjects the individual to liability.[153] In *Tarasoff*, the court adopted a two-step process of assessment, each step having its own distinct standard of care.[154] In determining whether the patient is a danger to others, as we have noted, the judgment of the therapist is to be measured by a "professional" standard of care, requiring the therapist to exercise the "reasonable degree of skill, knowledge and care ordinarily possessed and exercised by members of 'his professional specialty.'"[155] That, of course, is a malpractice standard. To establish what the defendant "should have known," expert testimony regarding the standards of the profession is required, but what can be said when professional guidelines are ill-defined or nonexistent?

The *Tarasoff* court itself was not unanimous in its adoption of a "professional" standard of care. Justice Mosk, in a concurring and dissenting opinion, would impose a duty only if the therapist had, in fact, determined his patient was dangerous.[156] In practice, however, this is a standard that would insulate the psychiatrist from liability.[157] What evidence could a plaintiff possibly have? The psychiatrist would be able to avoid liability by merely refusing to formulate a prediction.[158] Another approach is a "substantial departure" (or "gross negligence") standard.[159]

In assessing danger, the therapist must gather information relevant to the determination of dangerousness. Sources of such data include patient interviews and mental status evaluations, a review of past medical records, communications from other professionals involved in treatment, and information provided by other reliable sources such as family or police.[160] Liability can and has been mostly predicated on inadequate performance of this step. As Appelbaum concluded, "Many *Tarasoff*-like cases to date have not faulted therapists for inaccurate prediction but rather for failing to gather the data that most clinicians would believe relevant to an evaluation of a person's dangerousness."[161] In *Jablonski v. United States*,[162] as we may recall, the court found that the defendant's failure to obtain old records for review, as well as failing to record and transmit information to the treating physician, resulted in an inaccurate assessment of dangerousness. The courts opine: an accurate assessment cannot be made without history.[163]

All too often, it is quite difficult if not impossible to obtain old records, especially of records in other states. Can the doctor get it all, and examine it all? Our civilization, after all, is being engulfed in a rising tide of paper. In the *Jablonski* case, the victim's mother contacted the police after being attacked by Jablonski. Prior to his being transported to the V.A. Hospital for evaluation, the police called the hospital. The admitting physician was not available, so they gave the information concerning Jablonski's actions to another doctor, who assured them he would relay it on. This he failed to do. The court came to the conclusion that if the evaluating psychiatrist had the information available from these sources, he would have determined that the patient indeed posed a serious threat to the victim. The evaluating psychiatrist testified that if he had received the information related by the police, he would have sought involuntary hospitalization. The requirement that doctors obtain and communicate relevant information was, the court indicated, based on medical practice not overly burdensome.

In the second stage of assessment, the therapist must make a determination of dangerousness on the basis of the data collected. Liability on this account is problematic—ascertaining dangerousness is not like ascertaining who is the best man at a nudist wedding; the latter is readily done. In assessing dangerousness, it is advisable to document in a record why the therapist considers that there is no imminent danger since juries tend to be persuaded against liability when there is evidence to show that the therapist reflected over the issue, and consulted with colleagues. It is a plaintiff lawyer's dream when the doctor after the fact writes this into the record. From time to time, out of anxiety, doctors have done this to their detriment.

Studies indicate that where an individual has exhibited a history, even if somewhat distant, of serious violence, he is likely to act violently again unless there has been a significant change in the attitudes and circumstances that originally led to the violence. Factors considered important in the assessment of dangerousness include: the abuse of drugs or alcohol; past or current assaultive behavior or threats of such; availability of lethal weapons; and the presence of command hallucinations. Assessment and documentation of variables associated with violence may prevent allegations of negligent assessment.[164] In *McIntosh v. Milano*,[165] the defendant knew of his patient's use of drugs, his previous minor assaults on the victim with a BB gun, and his recent purchase of a knife with which to scare people who frightened him. The plaintiff's expert testified that based on such knowledge the defendant "should have" known his patient was dangerous.

Even experts who believe prediction of assaultive behavior is possible under certain circumstances caution that therapists function within a limited time frame. Will the patient act out before the next therapy session? In *Soutear v. United States*,[166] Dr. Herbert Modlin of the Menninger Foundation testified that the outside time limit beyond which prediction becomes meaningless is two to four weeks. Dr. Elliot Luby, my colleague at Wayne State University, who apparently regards himself as less clairvoyant, gave a time frame of approximately a week, but why not 24 hours? These time limits seem to be pulled out of thin air. In general, while estimates vary, therapists question the validity of a prediction going beyond a month.[167] The California Supreme Court said, in a case following *Tarasoff*, that the necessity of disclosure that gives rise to the duty must take into account not only the seriousness but also the imminence of the danger posed by the patient.[168] In the cases coming before it, the Michigan Courts of Appeals appear to have largely ignored the circumstance of imminence. In these cases the violent act complained of occurred more than two months after the discharge of the patient or termination of treatment.[169] (The issue has not come before the State's Supreme Court.) It may be said that the longer the time frame, the weaker the causal connection between any fault on the part of the therapist and the harm done.[170]

Once the therapist determines or should determine that his patient presents a danger to others, the second stage of the *Tarasoff* analysis begins, namely, the manner of the discharge of the duty to protect.

# STANDARD OF CARE IN DISCHARGING
## THE DUTY TO PROTECT

With danger known or knowable, the therapist is obliged to use "reasonable care" to protect the potential victim. The adequacy of the therapist's conduct in dealing with the danger, the court held in *Tarasoff*, is to be measured according to the traditional negligence standard of "reasonable care under the circumstances," that is, without expert testimony, just like negligence is measured in ordinary automobile accident cases.[171] Influenced by a law review article written during the course of the litigation by John G. Fleming (prominent law professor and author on torts) and Bruce Maximov (then law review editor),[172] the court would not require a professional standard in measuring the adequacy of the therapist's conduct. The issue of adequacy of the therapist's conduct is a "matter of social conduct, not a matter of professional expertise."[173]

What was reasonable, the court ruled in *Tarasoff II*, was not, as in *Tarasoff I*, limited to the issuance of a warning. As we have mentioned, for what is "reasonable," the court offered various courses of action: warning the victim or someone likely to tell the victim of the danger; notifying the police; or taking other steps reasonably necessary under the circumstances. What is "reasonable," the court said, could only be determined on a case-by-case basis.[174] The court commented in a footnote: "The giving of a warning....would in many cases represent a far lesser inroad upon the patient's privacy than would involuntary commitment."

Fleming and Maximov stressed, in their law review article, that the solution to the dangerous patient problem lay in the selection of a means of intervention that provides sufficient safeguards to the potential victim while at the same time offers the greatest protection of the patient's rights.[175] Warning, they suggested, was only one option among many possible interventions, not the only acceptable solution.[176] While the California Supreme Court in *Tarasoff II* referred to the use of "other steps reasonably necessary," the various judicial opinions following *Tarasoff* have made no mention of clinically-oriented interventions such as maintaining the patient in outpatient status combined with adequate medication or increased frequency of visits. Dr. Maurice Grossman, my esteemed friend, for long strongly felt that the soundest practice is to try to defuse a person's homicidal urges through therapy. The minute you report the patient, he noted, the patient drops out of

treatment. Warning, he said, is superfluous or counterproductive. If Poddar's therapist had not reported him, would he have remained in psychotherapy and the life of Tatiana saved? In nearly all of the reported cases, where harm has occurred, psychiatric care had been terminated.[177] More often than not, the fault lay in the termination of treatment. In litigation, however, given the harm done, the therapist may be hard put to justify outpatient psychotherapy over civil commitment.

Law professor David B. Wexler suggests involving the potential victim in therapy. He wrote:[178]

> Whatever may be the case with respect to schools of psychiatric thought regarding the treatment of other problems, the literature regarding violence directed at specifically identified victims suggests overwhelmingly that the treatment of that particular "condition" should transcend an "intrapsychic" individual pathology approach. Ideally, the treatment should in many cases involve not only the self-referred violence-prone patient, but also the targeted victim–typically a family member–who may well contribute to a violence-prone ongoing pathological relationship with the potentially violent patient. In essence, then, when a patient in therapy speaks seriously of hostile acts or hostile urges directed at another, the patient and the potential victim should both be considered prime candidates for a type of "couple" or "family" therapy.

Following up on Wexler's suggestion, Appelbaum and Gutheil said:[179]

> [T]he threat of harm often involves members of the patient's immediate family who, by virtue of the duty to warn, may be brought into the therapeutic purview. Thus it might even be said that the *Tarasoff* decision forces a family systems approach on the clinician. Clinical experience confirms that attention to the possibilities of forming (or repairing) an alliance with family members through the "warning" itself may yield valuable therapeutic advantages for the patient; a liability threat is thus transformed into potential clinical leverage.

"Couple" or "family" therapy, drawing the intended victim into the therapy, sounds idyllic, but is usually unrealistic, other therapists say. When a situation has developed to the point that the patient wants to kill the victim, the victim has "worked damned hard" to make the patient that angry. In that situation, the victim is not likely to cooperate in the patient's conflict resolution.

The high degree of clinical variability in the practice of psychiatry offers the courts little by way of guidance.[180] This, coupled with the relatively few instances the court has had to discuss what is "reasonable," has resulted in an apparent focus on the formalism of warnings. The majority of the *Tarasoff* progeny cases have actually been judicial resolution of a demurrer plea, that is, an allegation that facts as stated in the pleadings, even if admitted, are not legally sufficient for the case to proceed any further.

In selecting a response to danger posed by a patient, the therapist must consider both its appropriateness and effectiveness.[181] The court's advocacy of public protection, however, is inconsistent with reforms that have affected the mental health field, especially the area of civil commitment, where criminal justice standards have been introduced. The question is posed: Is the doctor expected to monitor the efficacy of his chosen response? Physicians, by custom, have patients return to them for follow-up; they do not go out and monitor. To what extent must medical practice resemble police practice? If medication is prescribed, must the therapist ensure that it is being taken and is proving effective? Under *Tarasoff,* the answer seems to be, yes.[182] Some endeavors in carrying out the duty of care seem like a page out of a tragi-comedy. In Florida, a psychiatrist instructed his patient, who was making threats, to go himself to the police station and tell the police about the threats. He didn't, but instead carried out the threat. The incident was the talk of the town. Speculation about a lawsuit abounded.

Of course, if hospitalization is agreed upon, the therapist must ensure that the new treating physician is aware of the conduct that prompted admission. Policies on hospital admission, however, skew the data. To get a person admitted into a hospital, be it a private or state facility, the physician not infrequently exaggerates the individual's condition, which makes it more difficult for the hospital doctor to justify discharge.

Of the various options set out by the court in *Tarasoff,* hospitalization of the patient is the best assurance against liability. In the emergency setting, the obligation to warn the potential victim or the police will most commonly arise when the individual under evaluation leaves or escapes before hospitalization can be accomplished. In Michigan and other states, alcoholism or drug addiction is not a basis for commitment. In any event, should the court decline to commit, the responsibility is the court's.[183] Of course, with good reason, the psychiatrist will question this recommendation when the patient is not psychotic. The clinical questions are: Is the hospital a useful therapeutic tool? Can the patient be better treated in a hospital or out? Will the responsibility of treating troublesome patients be foisted on the public sector, where there may be immunity? Notifying the police or the victim may be an empty gesture, and may prompt the patient either to leave treatment or sue for breach of confidentiality, which the doctor must defend as a qualified privilege.[184] The police department more likely than not will respond with the terse comment, "Don't bother us with people who make threats. We have enough dead bodies to investigate."[185]

As a threat is not a crime, California Republican Rep. Ed Royce, when a state senator, sought passage of a stalking law. His interest in victims' rights, specifically stalking, began when four women were murdered in Orange County within six weeks of each other in 1990. All of them had sought police protection from their stalkers but were turned down because they had yet to be physically attacked. Royce's efforts in California prompted all 50 states to adopt some form of antistalking law.[186]

May a claim against a therapist be based on failure to seek civil commitment? Yes, the courts have said.[187] Psychiatrists, by profession, are expected to help excommunicate the mad from human society. In 1986, the U.S. District Court in North Carolina ruled that "a psychotherapist judgment rule" would be appropriate, under which the "good faith, independence and thoroughness" of a decision not to seek commitment should be examined. The court indicated that liability would not be imposed for "simple errors of judgment." In this case, *Currie v. United States*,[188] an IBM employee, Leonard Avery, was being seen irregularly on an outpatient basis at the Veterans Administration Hospital in Durham. He had originally consulted the V.A. staff due to "rage attacks" he had been increasingly experiencing, including one incident in which he left work because he feared "losing control" due to anger at a fellow employee and another incident when he became angry at a neighbor and started shooting a gun. He was diagnosed as suffering from posttraumatic stress disorder. A doctor at the hospital advised IBM to take Avery's threats seriously and urged them to contact the appropriate law enforcement authorities. He had also threatened the staff at the V.A. At a staff meeting at the hospital, attended by 15 psychiatrists, it was unanimously concluded that Avery could not be committed under North Carolina law. (More often than not, psychiatrists prejudge who is committable and do not certify, without really knowing whether the court would have actually committed the patient.) They discussed any obligation they might have under *Tarasoff* and concluded that because law enforcement officials, as well as IBM, had been notified and given the necessary data on Avery and his threats, those obligations had been fulfilled. A few hours later, Avery entered the IBM building dressed in army fatigues and carrying a semiautomatic rifle and homemade bombs, shot and killed one person and wounded several others. He was subsequently convicted of first degree murder. In the civil action, the court said: "What society in general desires and expects psychotherapists to do when considering whether a patient should be involuntarily committed is to actively consider the public interest and to use their professional judgment in light of that interest." In this case, the court said, the doctors performed this duty. Given that threats were also made against them, the court said, indicates that they acted in good faith in limiting their action to warning IBM and not seeking a commitment of the patient.[189]

The adequacy of the discharge of the duty is, as noted, one of "reasonable care under the circumstances," ascertained without expert testimony. The lawyers will argue that when a therapist feels obliged to warn the victim, the family, or the police, he ought to do something more, like seeking hospitalization of the patient. If the therapist in the *Tarasoff* case had not given a warning about Poddar, he probably could have denied the assessment of dangerousness and been excused of the duty to protect.

The ex-husband of Laurie Wasserman Dann, who opened fire on a class of second-graders in Winnetka (a North Shore suburb of Chicago), desperately sought help from various law-enforcement officials, to no avail.[190] Early in their marriage, which lasted from 1982 to 1987, she stabbed her husband, Russell Dann, the son of a wealthy Highland Park family, in his sleep, with an ice pick. Some of his relatives sensed something "eerie" about Laurie, who, according to relatives, seemed to hide fearfully inside her new $230,000 home. In the latest episode, in 1988, she attempted to burn down a day-care center, then she delivered poisoned foods and drinks to dozens of people, and days later she entered a grade school where she shot six children, one of whom died, then taking her own life in a besieged neighborhood home, after she shot a young man there. A few years earlier, she had been in psychiatric treatment in Madison, Wisconsin, where she was a student, and later in Chicago.[191] In her apartment building in Madison, she became known as a loner and the "psycho elevator lady." Her history indicates a paranoid in possession of guns, and prone to violence. A Cook County grand jury has subpoenaed the records of her therapists; the Madison therapist has told police she never related to him thoughts of violence.[192] Not long before the shooting police, had interviewed her after receiving a report she had been acting erratically but had decided she posed no danger to herself or others and could not legally be committed to a mental hospital.[193]

Notwithstanding a long history of bizarre, sometimes violent behavior, she was considered a responsible baby-sitter by many parents on the North Shore. One trained social worker, who had engaged her several times, recommended her to friends, to their regret, discovering that she would slash their furniture and rugs. Her parents would pay for the damage. She was the daughter of a well-to-do accountant. Questions are posed: "If Dann had been identified as a human time bomb, why hadn't she been institutionalized? With police files in three states and a record of psychiatric illness, how had she managed to obtain a permit for three handguns?"[194] After the event, law-enforcement officials said that "she clearly should have been committed."[195] When her former in-laws, who had been receiving threatening phone calls from her ever since the couple's separation, approached her parents and begged them to institutionalize their daughter, they resisted. Says one former in-law: "She was crying out for help, and her parents should have realized it."[196]

A therapist's simply issuing a warning is not an adequate approach to managing the violent patient, though it is listed as one of the options in *Tarasoff.*

Assuredly, sending a letter is the road to mockery; it's legal formalism. Should the potential victim leave for parts unknown? The warning may cause him, for an indefinite period, to live under extreme anxiety. He might attack the patient, in a peremptory strike, in order to avoid being harmed.[197]

A warning, however, can be most helpful in safeguarding a known partner or hospital staff in the case of an AIDS patient, but some states have enacted statutes forbidding the disclosure of HIV test results without a patient's consent. Because AIDS is a disease that impacts most heavily on male homosexuals and because gay-rights organizations have acquired considerable political influence in some jurisdictions, the issue of confidentiality has been politicized. In the 13th century, prostitutes were forced to wear a knotted cord from one shoulder, which marked them, along with lepers, for social exclusion.[198]

In general, given the ineffectiveness of warning a victim, the identity of the intended victim ought to be considered an irrelevancy. As a legal matter, the identity limitation is designed to limit liability. By and large, clinicians say, the great majority of dangerous patients can be managed through good clinical practice.[199] Under that view, *Tarasoff* is a codification of clinical practice. In fact, once the rhetorical smoke is cleared away, it is seen that nothing in *Tarasoff* commands therapists to forsake their clinical judgment in treating potentially violent patients. The duty to protect is invoked only when the danger is imminent and other therapeutic interventions do not have a reasonable chance to circumvent it. Put into law, however, the doctor feels belegaled, as Dr. Jonas Rappeport once put it. "It is an infringement on my right to practice medicine," doctors say, and they ask: "Why can't there be a return to the pre-*Tarasoff* days when psychiatrists were not sued for harm done by their patients?"[200]

In actual fact, as we have noted, psychiatrists have long been held responsible in cases of inpatient care arising out of negligent discharge and in other cases. When poor care of a patient, or untimely discharge, results in harm to a third person, the therapist has been held responsible, and the Tarasoff case might have been framed that way, as negligent treatment, without any need to formulate a special theory about duty to third persons. In 1984, the American Psychiatric Association indicated that it is quite proper to hold a psychiatrist liable for "flagrantly negligent" failures to protect others from harm.[201]

## THE LEGISLATIVE RESPONSE

As a consequence of lobbying efforts, a number of states in the United States have passed legislation delimiting the responsibility of the therapist and making it possible for the therapist to get out of the lawsuit by summary disposition. These states include California, Colorado, Florida, Indiana, Kentucky, Louisiana, Michigan, Minnesota, Montana, New Hampshire, and Washington.[202] More or less, the legislative response has been to backtrack from *Tarasoff II* to *Tarasoff I*. The statutes are more helpful to therapists, legally speaking, than for the protection of patients or potential victims.

A number of these states have adopted a "serious threat" or "actual threat" standard. California's legislation provides that a psychotherapist is subject to liability only "where the patient has communicated to the psychotherapist a serious threat of physical violence against a reasonably identifiable victim or victims."[203] What is a "serious threat"? Kentucky, Montana, and Washington use the term "actual threat." Indiana's legislation retains the language of *Tarasoff*, "should have determined."

*Tarasoff II* established the duty to protect "intended" or "foreseeable" victims and as we have noted, some courts in various jurisdictions extended the duty to protect society generally. The legislative response has been to narrow the scope of the duty to identifiable victims. Colorado has adopted the most restrictive statute, adopting the decision by the federal district court in that state in *Brady v. Hopper*.[204] It provides that liability only arises where there is a threat of violence "against a specific person or persons." The other states have adopted broader language extending liability to the "clearly identifiable" victim, the "reasonably identifiable" victim, or both. Louisiana and Minnesota have a "clearly identifiable" requirement. Louisiana's statute limits liability to cases where "a patient has communicated an immediate threat of physical violence against a clearly identifiable victim or victims, coupled with the apparent intent and ability to carry out that threat." The legislation in California, Indiana, and Washington have a "reasonably identifiable" requirement, while Kentucky, Montana, and New Hampshire have adopted both "clearly identifiable" and "reasonably identifiable" language. The goal in *Tarasoff* was the protection against danger in "this risk-infested world" posed by a patient who is "lethal." Imposing liability on the basis of whether or not a victim is identifiable misses that goal, though it may affect the scope of liability. Should it matter whether a patient tells his therapist he is going to "kill everybody with blue eyes" or is going "to kill my girlfriend"? In addition to killing his girlfriend, he also kills her mother, who was present at the time. How different are the situations? Equally important is the question whether action by the therapist could have prevented the harm. Could the therapist prevent the death of blue-eyed persons? Could he have prevented the death of his patient's girlfriend or her mother?[205] In one of the cases earlier cited, *Hedlund v. Superior Court of Orange County*,[206] a patient said, "I'm going to kill my girlfriend." The therapist took no action and subsequently the woman was shot, and the child accompanying her, injured. Is the child a "specific" person identified by the patient or a "clearly" or "reasonably" identifiable victim? Should liability extend to the child as a person within a "foreseeable zone of danger"? Could the therapist have prevented the harm?

The Washington statute is typical—the duty to warn or protect is discharged if "reasonable efforts are made to communicate...to the victim or victims and to law enforcement personnel." Kentucky's statute provides that when there is an "actual threat of some specific violent act and no particular victim is identifiable," the therapist is nonetheless required to act. Under the Kentucky statute, the duty of the therapist is only to inform the police. California's statute states that the duty to warn and protect shall be discharged by "reasonable efforts to communicate the threat to the victim or victims and to a law enforcement agency." What are "reasonable efforts"? Minnesota's statute states, "reasonable efforts means communicating the ... threat to the...victim and if unable to make contact with the victim communicating the...threat to the law enforcement agency closest to the...victim or the patient." Louisiana's statute provides that "a psychologist's or psychiatrist's duty to warn or to take reasonable precautions to provide protection from violent behavior...shall be discharged by the psychologist or psychiatrist if he makes a reasonable effort to communicate the immediate threat to the potential victim or victims and to notify law enforcement authorities in the vicinity of the patient's or potential victim's residence."

Questions continue to be asked: How should the warning be delivered? Should the warning be accompanied with a bottle of tranquilizers? What if the potential victim is out of the country or away on vacation? May the family be informed? Will it be expected that the police will notify the potential victim upon his return?

Under legislation providing summary discharge by giving a warning, therapists are likely to take that route, though it is formalistic, and not likely to be helpful. These statutes do not exclude other options, but under these statutes warning is the easy way to discharge the duty. Alexander Solzhenitsyn said in an address at Harvard, "A society with no other scale but the legal one is less than worthy of man" (but a society without the measure of law is a lawless society).

In 1976, Dr. Alan A. Stone, then president-elect of the American Psychiatric Association, warned in an oft-cited article "that the imposition of a duty to protect, which may take the form of a duty to warn threatened third parties, will imperil the therapeutic alliance and destroy the patient's expectation of confidentiality, thereby thwarting effective treatment and ultimately reducing public safety."[207] In 1975, Slovenko, on the other hand, wrote, "It may be predicted that *Tarasoff*, modified or unmodified, will not bring in a parade of horribles."[208] In 1984, Stone reconsidered and concluded that "the duty to warn is not as unmitigated a disaster for the enterprise of psychotherapy as it once seemed to critics like myself."[209] Dr. Kathleen M. Quinn reports that while warnings to potential victims and their families and other limit-seeking actions appear to have been done voluntarily by responsible therapists for years before *Tarasoff*, there has been one obvious change in the therapist's warning behavior since *Tarasoff*-a greater percentage are now including the potential victim among those they warned.[210]

The primacy established in *Tarasoff* of societal protection over the patient's right to confidentiality was seen by many as putting psychiatrists on the horns of a dilemma. Suits for breach of confidentiality were feared. The legislative response is to provide a broad grant of immunity. The New Hampshire statute is typical. It provides that no liability or cause of action will result from "information disclosed to third parties in an effort to discharge the duty" to protect or warn. Louisiana's statute states that there shall be no liability "for a breach of confidentiality for warning of such threat or taking precautions to provide protection from the patient's violent behavior." The statutes do not require that the therapist's actions be reasonable. They also do not require a "Miranda" warning.

Under the common law, a breach of confidentiality was allowed under a qualified privilege, depending on the manner and purpose of the disclosure. Patients will suffer, however, if therapists are permitted to respond in rote fashion with warnings that they know are ineffective. Consider the situation of the patient who, during therapy, reveals that he intends to kill his supervisor. Although the therapist does not believe the patient will act, he safeguards himself by mailing a letter to the personnel office of the patient's employer, revealing the threat. The patient is fired.[211] Under a literal reading of the statute, the patient has no recourse against the therapist.

The statutes, or a majority of them, have the potential of causing violence rather than preventing it. Under the Washington statute, or others like it, can the therapist discharge his duty by following the language of the statute, notifying the victim or a law-enforcement agency, without a real risk of causing violence? If the therapist notifies the police, as was done in *Tarasoff*, the police might visit the home, an act likely to provoke a violent confrontation between the patient and the potential victim; and if he notifies the potential victim, violence is still a likely outcome. Under Colorado's statute, an echo of *Tarasoff II*, discharge of the duty to protect (an identifiable victim) can be accomplished by "taking other appropriate action including, but not limited to, hospitalizing the patient."

Unless formalism is to be the rule of the day, states enacting legislation would do better to provide a duty to protect that is dischargeable either by: making reasonable efforts to communicate with the intended victim or victims; making reasonable efforts to communicate with a close member of the victim's family likely to apprise him of the danger or the local law enforcement agency nearest the victim; or taking other appropriate action including, but not limited to, hospitalization of the patient. Given a scenario of imminent danger, and unavailing psychotherapy, what other options are open to the therapist? The appropriateness or adequacy of the action should be measured by the standard of an ordinary practitioner in that professional specialty.

## CONCLUSION

The basic question is whether one person ought to be held responsible for the conduct of another. On this score, opinions differ. The *Tarasoff* case has sharpened the consciousness of psychotherapists about dangerousness. As a result of the decision, a number of suits have been filed against therapists, but actual liability is exceptional. Nonetheless, many therapists say the mere possibility of having to defend a suit is itself a major concern. The publicity, if not the expense of protracted litigation, can be devastating. Even more serious is the belief that therapists should not be cast in the role of policeman and should not be responsible for societal breakdown in law-enforcement. The legislation recently enacted in a number of jurisdictions, however, does not mandate responsible action to avoid a tragedy, which was the gist of *Tarasoff II*.

In a parallel development, the courts during the past decade have imposed a duty on business owners and landlords to protect people on the premises from criminal acts of third parties. Thus, in 1975, in a Michigan case where an outpatient at a mental health clinic leasing space in an office building knifed and robbed a secretary in the elevator, the State's Supreme Court, in a ruling now common around the country, imposed a duty on owners of buildings to take precautionary measures in light of possible dangerous conditions in the building.[212] In 1982, the New Jersey appellate court, imposing liability on a supermarket for a parking lot attack, said: "In the modern context of merchandising, our placement of these costs is consistent with the principles of the common law....It is fair that the costs of negligent failure to protect against crime be...borne by the operators and indirectly patrons of such shopping facilities."[213] In 1980, the New York Court of Appeals held a building owner liable to an invitee shot on the premises by an unknown attacker, even though the attack seemed personal to the invitee.[214]

In these cases the court transmutes the obligation of society to provide police protection into a personal duty of an individual defendant. In effect, it exacts a kind of tax from a certain class of defendants, since a requirement of guards will be both costly and will provide the kind of service normally provided by the public through police officers. As a consequence of these decisions, merchants and owners of buildings have provided armed, visible security guards.

What measures will discharge the duty? It is an easy matter to know whether a stairway is defective and what repairs will put it in order. Again, it is fairly simple to decide how many ushers or guards suffice at a skating rink, to deal with the crush of a crowd and the risk of unintentional injury which the nature of the business creates, but how can one know what measures will protect against the thug, the narcotic addict, the degenerate, the psychopath and the psychotic? Must the owner prevent all crime? The police force in the friendliest community does not achieve that end. In 1988, the Michigan Supreme Court backtracked, saying that imposing this duty on merchants is against the public interest. The court said, "The inability of government and law enforcement officials to prevent criminal attacks does not justify transferring the responsibility to a business owner...To shift the duty of police protection from the government to the private sector would amount to advocating that members of the public resort to self-help. Such a proposition contravenes public policy."[215]

As noted by Oliver Wendell Holmes in his lecture on the theory of negligence, "Any legal standard must, in theory, be capable of being known. When a man has to pay damages, he is supposed to have broken the law, and he is further supposed to have known what the law was."[216] Furthermore, shifting the financial loss caused by crime from an innocent victim to another innocent person is without warrant.[217] So, in 1988, as noted, the Michigan Supreme Court reversed the trend on premises liability. "The merchant is not an insurer of the safety of his invitees," the court said, and for reasons of public policy he does not have the responsibility for providing police protection on his premises.[218]

With lethal weapons, private fantasies readily become historical reality. "Guns don't kill people; people kill people," say gun advocates, but people are not so dangerous without guns. We would not have to worry so much about the dangerous individual were it not for the availability of lethal weapons. The handgun is so ubiquitous, so readily available in the United States, that almost anyone who wants one can get one. A handgun is about as common as an ordinary household appliance. That state of affairs has prompted commentators around the world to quip that the term "American civilization" is oxymoronic. True, there are a lot of ways to inflict harm and death: knives, poison, fire, cars—yet, of the cases, how many were by any of those means? And how many by the gun? Tatiana Tarasoff was stabbed to death, but in nearly all of the other cases, death was by gun.[219]

Be that as it may, the therapist in jurisdictions where a duty of care is owed only to readily identifiable third parties may think about putting a sign in the office, "Please don't identify people you are threatening." In these jurisdictions the therapist would have incentive for the patient to withhold information, since it would produce no duty. It is no wonder that the formula "Two and two make five" has its attractions.

## NOTES

1. In a page-one article, "Psychiatrist of Defector Maintains Welfare of Nation Took Precedence," *Washington Post*, Sept. 22, 1960, Eve Edstrom wrote:

   Should a psychiatrist reveal the confidence of a patient who becomes involved in a major controversy affecting national security? "Yes," says Dr. Clarence Schilt who stoutly defended his position . . . in revealing information obtained from defector Beron F. Mitchell.

   "No," say numerous area general practitioners and psychiatrists, including forty who . . . signed a petition, declaring divulgence of such information should not be permitted unless there exists "well-defined criminal circumstances."

   In between these two views are those physicians who believe the question boils down to one of judgment, that it is up to the individual psychiatrist to determine whether the circumstances are serious enough to warrant a violation of confidence. Dr. Schilt said he agrees with his critics when they stated, in their petition, "that information given to a physician within the doctor-patient relationship must be considered confidential and must not be disclosed except with the permission of the patient or under certain well-defined criminal circumstances." But, Dr. Schilt continued, he did not agree with them that the disclosure of the contents of interviews between Mitchell and himself "does not fall under the criterion of criminal content."

2. The report of the House Committee on Un-American Activities said Martin was "sexually abnormal: in fact, a masochist." It said Mitchell had "posed for nude color slides perched on a velvet-covered stool." AP News-Release, Aug. 14, 1962.

3. The image of the physician *qua* physician is little enhanced by divulgence of information. Dr. Victor Sidel commented: "The doctor's professional role, simply stated, is the healing of the sick....The doctor's duty to heal the sick. . . includes a duty to keep others from getting sick [and]. . . to keep others from getting injured. When a patient, therefore, tells a physician that he plans to commit a crime of violence—for example, 'I'm going to murder the mayor at noon tomorrow'—the physician takes steps to see that the mayor is protected. Furthermore, such a patient is almost always really saying, 'I have a terrible urge (or very vivid fantasies involving the urge) to kill the mayor. Please protect me from my urge.' This is usually true also of the patient who tells the doctor that he plans to commit suicide. The doctor will not hesitate

to make appropriate revelations to prevent violence, either self-inflicted or inflicted on others, because in so doing he is furthering his professional goals for his patient and for his community....I believe...that except under very special circumstances such as the prevention of the spread of communicable disease or prevention of a specific criminal act, the physician may best serve his patient by the strictest protection of his confidences, even if that patient is a criminal, a social, religious or sexual deviant or...a defector. By thus strengthening his ability to communicate with the individuals who form his community, and preserving his ability to help them, the physician best serves his nation and humanity." V. Sidel "Confidential Information and the Physician," *New England J. Med.* 264:1133, 1961; see also V. Sidel, "Medical Ethics and the Cold War," *The Nation* 19:325, 1960.

4.  M. Guttmacher, *The Mind of the Murderer* (New York: Farrar, Straus, 1960), p. 215.
5.  A.B. v. C.D., 7 F. (Scott) 72 (1905).
6.  Simonsen v. Swenson, 104 Neb. 224, 177 N.W. 831 (1920)
7.  Carr v. Watkins, 227 Md. 578, 177 A.2d 841 (1962); see R.B. Little & E.A. Strecker, "Moot Questions in Psychiatric Ethics," *Am. J. Psychiat.* 113:455, 1956.
8.  331 P.2d at 818.
9.  Berry v. Moench, 8 Utah 2d 191, 331 P.2d 814 (1958).
10. K. Menninger, *A Manual for Psychiatric Case Study* (New York: Grune & Stratton, 2d ed. 1962), pp. 36-37.
11. The oath of Hippocrates states: "I will follow that system of regimen which, according to my ability and judgment, I consider for the benefit of my patients, and abstain from whatever is deleterious and mischievous." Various medical schools have revised the oath. Of some of the revised versions, Dr. Paul R. McHugh, director of the Department of Psychiatry and Behavioral Sciences at Johns Hopkins, argues that they tend to be more "self-centered" than patient centered and are ridden with "vague precept." He is particularly displeased with a provision in the 1989 Harvard oath stating, "To serve others most effectively, I must maintain my own well-being." That's a "sentiment suitable for a bodybuilder, rather than a physician," he says. He notes that the 1994 Harvard oath "carried this impulse further, saying, 'I ask that my colleagues be attentive to my well-being, as I will be to theirs.'" P.R. McHugh, "Hippocrates · la mode," *Nature Medicine*, May 1996; discussed in J. Price, "Hippocratic oath gives way to 'ethics á la mode,'" *Washington Times*, May 22, 1996, p. 1.
12. L. Edelstein, *The Hippocratic Oath/Text, Translation and Interpretation* (Baltimore: Johns Hopkins Press, 1943), pp. 36-37.
13. *Id.* at pp. 36-37.
14. RANZAP Code of Ethics, annotations to Principle 3 (1992); discussed in M. Coady & S. Bloch, *Codes of Ethics and the Professions* (Melbourne: Melbourne University Press, 1996).
15. Tarasoff I, 118 Cal. Rptr. 129, 529 P.2d 553 (1974), *vacated*, Tarasoff II, 17 Cal.3d 425, 131 Cal. Rptr. 14, 551 P.2d 334 (1976).

16. "We conclude that a doctor or a psychotherapist treating a mentally ill patient, just as a doctor treating physical illness, bears a duty to use reasonable care to give threatened persons such warnings as are essential to avert foreseeable danger arising from his patient's condition or treatment." 118 Cal. Rptr. at 135, 529 P.2d at 559.

17. 17 Cal.3d 439, 131 Cal. Rptr. 25, 551 P.2d 345.

18. For commentary by members of the legal profession, see E.M. Crocker, "Judicial Expansion of the *Tarasoff* Doctrine: Doctors' Dilemma," *J. Psychiatry & Law* 13:83, 1985; M.J. Dykstra, "Duty to Warn of Potentially Dangerous Patients," *Res Gestae* 29:461, 1986; C.W. Laughran & G.M. Bakken, "The Psychotherapist's Responsibility Toward Third Parties Under Current California Law," *Western State U. L. Rev.* 12:1, 1984.

19. See J.C. Beck (ed.), *The Potentially Violent Patient* and the Tarasoff *Decision in Psychiatric Practice* (Washington, D.C.: American Psychiatric Press, 1985); Symposium, "Duty to Warn Third Parties," *Behav. Sci. & Law* 2:235, 1984; A. R. Felthous, *The Psychotherapist's Duty to Warn or Protect* (Springfield, Ill.: Thomas, 1988); T.A. Goodman, "From *Tarasoff* to *Hopper*: The Evolution of the Therapist's Duty to Protect Third Parties," *Behav. Sci. & Law* 3:195, 1985; C.J. Meyers, "The Legal Perils of Psychotherapeutic Practice: Coping with *Hedlund* and *Jablonski*," *J. Psychiatry & Law* 12:39, 1984; R.F. Schopp & M.R. Quattrocchi, "*Tarasoff,* the Doctrine of Special Relationships, and the Psychotherapist's Duty to Warn," *J. Psychiatry & Law* 12:13, 1984. Dr. Joseph T. Smith devotes 100 pages of his 600-page book, *Medical Malpractice/Psychiatric Care* (Colorado Springs: Shepard's/McGraw Hill, 1986), to *Tarasoff* and its progeny.

20. D. Givelber, W.J. Bowers & C.L. Blitch, "Tarasoff, Myth and Reality: An Empirical Study of Private Law in Action," *Wis. L. Rev.* 1984:443. See also D.J. Givelber, W.J. Bowers & C.L. Blitch, "The *Tarasoff* Controversy: A Summary of Findings From an Empirical Study of Legal, Ethical, and Clinical Issues," in J.C. Beck (ed.), *The Potentially Violent Patient and the* Tarasoff *Decision in Psychiatric Practice* (Washington, D.C.: American Psychiatric Press, 1985), p. 35. Dr. Allen R. Dyer in one of the American Psychiatric Press's best-selling books cites *Tarasoff II* but says that the California Supreme Court concluded that therapists have a duty to warn a potential victim. Other options are not mentioned. See A.R. Dyer, *Ethics and Psychiatry: Toward Professional Definition* (Washington, D.C.: American Psychiatric Press, 1988), p. 61. Dr. Irwin N. Perr, who also holds a law degree, writes that "the Tarasoff case in California has promulgated the principle that therapists must warn potential victims of violence," and he cites *Tarasoff I* and *Tarasoff II* as authority. I.N. Perr, "Privacy, Privileged Communications, and Confidentiality," in R. Rosner (ed.), *Critical Issues in American Psychiatry and the Law* (Springfield, Ill.: Thomas, 1982), at p. 285. A multiauthored volume in one place sets out the duty of the therapist as one of warning the threatened individual (p. 278) but in another place sets out other options (p. 48). G.B. Melton, J. Petrila, N.G. Poythress & C. Slobogin,

*Psychological Evaluation for the Courts* (New York: Guilford Press, 1987). Lawyers, too, more often than not, describe *Tarasoff* as mandating a duty to warn, nothing more nor less. Jeffrey D. Robertson, a New York attorney and author of *Psychiatric Malpractice* (New York: Wiley, 1988) writes that *Tarasoff* renders "mental health professionals responsible for warning third-party victims of danger from patients." *Trial,* June 1988, p. 95.

21. M.J. Mills, "The So-Called Duty to Warn: The Psychotherapeutic Duty to Protect Third Parties from Patients' Violent Acts," *Behav. Sci. & Law* 2:237, 1984.

22. L. VandeCreek & S. Knapp, "Counselors, Confidentiality, and Life-endangering Clients," *Counselor Education and Supervision* 24:51, 1984.

23. W.R. Forrester (ltr.), "Reversing the Footnote Fetish," *Wall Street Journal,* June 23, 1988, p. 33.

24. 551 P.2d 340.

25. 551 P.2d 345.

26. Dr. Kutaiba Chaleby of Saudi Arabia says that in his country the psychiatrist has the right to exercise his judgment in weighing the advantage to protect a third party versus the disadvantage of the breach of confidentiality, and he is not second-guessed. Communication to author. For other comparisons, see M.A. Menlowe & A.M. Smith (ed.), *The Duty to Rescue* (Aldershot, England: Dartmouth, 1993), where it is stated: "The imposition on psychiatrists of a duty to prevent their patients causing harm to others is a new and disturbing development which, fortunately, has been largely confined to the United States" (p. 84).

27. Ltr., *Psychiatric. News,* April 16, 1975, p. 2.

28. Jones v. Shek, 48 Mich. App. 530, 210 N.W.2d 843 (1973).

29. 267 App. Div. 254, 45 N.Y.S.2d 404 (1943).

30. 267 App. Div. at 257, 45 N.Y.S.2d at 406..

31. 234 F.2d 288 (5th Cir. 1956).

32. 234 F.2d at 294.

33. 272 F. Supp. 409 (D. N.D. 1967).

34. 79 Misc.2d 972, 361 N.Y.S.2d 820 (1974).

35. Duty is essentially a question of whether the law will impose a legal obligation on one party for the benefit of another. While foreseeability of the harm is an important consideration in determining whether a duty exists, courts must also assess the competing public policy considerations for and against recognizing the asserted duty in any individual case. Where a court determines that no duty exists, then summary disposition for failure to state a claim is an appropriate remedy. Marr v. Yousif, 167 Mich. App. 358, 422 N.W.2d 4 (1988).

36. A demurrer declares that even if everything stated in the complaint were true, it does not state facts sufficient to constitute a cause of action. It is, in effect, a legal shrugging of the shoulders: "so what?" In modern procedure a "motion to dismiss" or summary judgment replaces the demurrer, but if denied the case simply proceeds to trial on the merits.

Not understanding *Tarasoff* as a pleading case, Dr. Martin Lakin writes, "Therapists, like other citizens, turn to the police when violence threatens. Thus, the function of the therapist might be to consult with police in given instances. But such consultation did not excuse the therapist in the Tarasoff case." M. Lakin, *Ethical Issues in the Psychotherapies* (New York: Oxford University Press, 1988), p. 135. Dr. David L. Shapiro points out the wide misinterpretation of the case and then himself misinterprets it. He writes: "[A] number of people have misinterpreted the Tarasoff case as one in which liability was imposed because of a failure to predict dangerousness. This is not the case at all. Here, the determination was already made that the patient was dangerous, and the liability resided in the fact that the subsequent actions were not deemed to be sufficient to protect the intended victim." D.L. Shapiro, *Psychological Evaluation and Expert Testimony* (New York: Van Nostrand Reinhold, 1984), pp. 149-150. Such inaccuracies abound in the literature on *Tarasoff.* The case, as we have noted, was not tried on the merits; it was settled.

37.  What count considerably are the talents of the lawyer, the tenacity of the insurance company, the right sort of witnesses, and the musings of the jury. "Unlike the official lotteries that many states now run, the tort lottery is one for which we all are forced to pay." S.D. Sugarman, "Serious Tort Law Reform," *San Diego L. Rev.* 24:795 at 796, 1987. "Imagine, for example, that you are a responsible homeowner who carefully maintains your property. But a person falls on your front steps and, lying there, announces that he has injured his back. At that moment, just how much money would you be willing to pay in return for a promise that the person lying on your sidewalk won't sue you? Knowing yourself to be morally blameless, do you really want your day in court in the American legal system that exists in 1988?" C. Murray, *In Pursuit of Happiness and Good Government* (New York: Simon & Schuster, 1988).

38.  Schulz v. Pennsylvania Railroad Co., 350 U.S. 523, 525 (1956).

39.  A thorough account of the facts of the *Tarasoff* case are set out in W.J. Winslade & J.W. Ross, *The Insanity Plea/The Uses and Abuses of the Insanity Defense* (New York: Scribner's, 1983), pp. 52-73. The chapter is entitled "A Kiss of Death." The authors discuss the companion criminal prosecution of the patient, Prosenjit Poddar. Poddar's conviction for second-degree murder was reversed, because the judge had failed to give adequate instruction to the jury on "diminished capacity." He pleaded guilty to voluntary manslaughter, and was confined in the Vacaville Medical Facility in California, but shortly thereafter he was released, on condition he return to India, where by his account, he is "happily married." See People v. Poddar, 10 Cal.3d 750, 111 Cal. Rptr. 910, 518 P.2d 342 (1974).

Deborah Blum, a sophomore at Berkeley when the slaying of Tatiana Tarasoff occurred, became fascinated by the case and began an investigation that was to last seven years and take her twice to India. She has written an interesting account of Poddar's involvement with Tatiana. What happened to Tatiana, she says, might just as easily have happened to her. D. Blum, *Bad Karma: A True Story of Obsession and Murder* (New York: Atheneum, 1986).

40. Quoted in D. Blum, *supra* at p. 246.

41. Quoted in D. Blum, *supra* at p. 261.

42. Evidence of subsequent remedial measures is not admissible to prove negligence or culpable conduct in connection with the event. Federal Rules of Evidence, Rule 407.

43. If *A* causes *B* to lose control of himself (as, for example, by improper administration of drugs), *A* may be held responsible to one and all injured by *B*, but if *B*'s condition was not caused by *A*, *A* is responsible to others only if there is a special relationship between *A* and *B*. See, *e.g.*, Schuster v. Altenberg. 424 N.W.2d 159 (Wis. 1988), discussed hereinafter. Negligence, it must be repeated, is conduct falling below the standard demanded for the protection of others against unreasonable risk of harm. Because the behavior of individuals is so incalculable in its variety, it has been found undesirable, if not impossible, to formulate precise rules of conduct for all conceivable situations. In general, it is said of a person that he or she is negligent when they act without due care and attention in regard to harmful consequences of their actions. The concept of negligence thus assumes the notion of risk, and the notion of risk entails the idea of foreseeable harm. *Restatement of Law of Torts Second*, §282; J.G. Fleming, *The Law of Torts* (Toronto: Carswell, 6th ed. 1983); J.C. Smith, *Liability in Negligence* (Toronto: Carswell, 1984). The complaint in *Tarasoff* predicated liability on two grounds: defendants' failure to warn plaintiff of the impending danger and their failure to use reasonable care to bring about Poddar's confinement pursuant to the state's commitment law. 118 Cal. Rptr. at 131.

44. In K.L. Steinberg, M. Levine & H.J. Douecek, "Effects of Legally Mandated Child-Abuse Reports on the Therapeutic Relationship: A Survey of Psychotherapists," *Am. J. Orthopsychiatry* 67:112, 1997, it is concluded: "For clients in therapy, there appear to be both positive and negative attributes of mandatory reporting of suspected child abuse." The child-abuse reporting laws cover physical abuse, sexual abuse, emotional maltreatment, and physical neglect, and the range of mandated reporters include mental health professionals, police, teachers, nurses, dentists, and child-care workers, among others. S.C. Kalichman, "Practicing Psychologists' Interpretations of and Compliance with Child Abuse Reporting Laws," *Law & Human Behavior* 17:83, 1993. Under the duty to report child abuse, there is no duty imposed on a resident manager to report suspected abuse of children, and there is no "special relationship" between the manager and the children creating a duty of care. In H.B. *ex rel.* Clarke v. Whittemore, 1196 WL 490748 (1996), four girls, between the ages of four and seven, had reported to the resident manager of a trailer park that one of the residents was sexually abusing them. The manager told the children to tell their parents, but the children did not do so until three weeks later. The Minnesota Supreme Court concluded that a special relationship, which has traditionally been

limited to the relationship between an innkeeper and a guest, a common carrier and a passenger, and a hospital and a patient, was not created from these facts. The children were not in the manager's custody, and the manager exercised no control over their daily welfare, the court added. The court noted the general common law rule that one owes no duty to warn those endangered by the conduct of a third party.

45. Ryan v. New York Central R.R. Co., 35 N.Y. 210, 91 Am. Dec. 49 (1866); A.E. Smith, "The Miscegenetic Union of Liability Insurance and the Tort Process in the Personal Injury Claims System," *Cornell L. Rev.* 54:645, 1969; E.J. Weinreb, "Causation and Wrongdoing," *Chi.-Kent L. Rev.* 63:407, 1987.

46. Stadler v. Cross, 295 N.W.2d 552 (Minn. 1980); quoted in Iacona v. Schrupp, 521 N.W.2d 70 (Minn. App. 1994). "To limit the otherwise potentially infinite liability which would follow every negligent act, the law of torts holds defendant amenable only for injuries to others which to defendant at the time were reasonably foreseeable....Thus, while...foreseeability of the injury [is] to be the primary consideration in finding duty....policy considerations [mandate] that infinite liability be avoided by restrictions that would somehow narrow the class of potential plaintiffs." Thing v. LaChusa, 48 Cal.3d 644, 771 P.2d 814, 257 Cal. Rptr. 865 (1989). *See* R. Slovenko, "Blaming a Book," *J. Psychiatry & Law* 22:437, 1994.

47. 248 N.Y. 339, 162 N.E. 99 (1928).

48. Under the influence of Jim Jones, members of the People's Temple in Jonestown murdered Congressman Leo J. Ryan and then committed suicide en masse. United States v. Layton, 549 F.2d 903 (N.D. Cal. 1982).

49. Jones v. State of New York, 267 App. Div. 254, 45 N.Y.S.2d 404 (1943).

50. See Fair v. United States, 234 F.2d 288 (5th Cir. 1956); Merchants National Bank & Trust Co. of Fargo v. United States, 272 F.Supp. 409 (D.N.D. 1967); Homere v. State, 79 Misc.2d 972, 361 N.Y.S.2d 820 (1974).

51. Britton v. Soltes, 205 Ill. App. 3d 943, 150 Ill. Dec. 783, 563 N.E.2d 910 (1990). See also Renslow v. Mennonite Hosp., 67 Ill.2d 348, 10 Ill. Dec. 484, 367 N.E.2d 1250 (1977).

52. Justice Charles Freeman, dissenting, 563 N.E.2d at 916.

53. DiMarco v. Lynch Homes, 525 Pa. 558, 583 A.2d 422 (1990).

54. The court said (583 A.2d at 424-425):

> Physicians are the first line of defense against the spread of communicable diseases, because physicians know what measures must be taken to prevent the infection of others. The patient must be advised to take certain sanitary measures, or to remain quarantined for a period of time, or to practice sexual abstinence of what is commonly referred to as "safe sex."
>
> Such precautions are taken not to protect the health of the patient, whose well being has already been compromised, rather *such precautions are taken to safeguard the health of others.* Thus, the duty of a physician in such circumstances extends to those "within the foreseeable orbit of risk of harm." If a third person is in that class of persons whose

health is likely to be threatened by the patient, and if erroneous advice is given to that patient to the ultimate detriment of the third person, the third person has a cause of action against the physician, because the physician should recognize that the services rendered to the patient are necessary for the protection of the third person.... We further hold that the class of persons whose health is likely to be threatened by the patient includes *any* one who is physically intimate with the patient. Those, like the trial court, who insist that we cannot predict, or foresee, that a patient will engage in sexual activity outside of the marital relationship and that thus, we need not protect those who engage in "casual" sex, are exalting an unheeded morality over reality. (Emphasis by court.)

55. *See, e.g.*, Hoffman v. Blackmon, 241 So.2d 752 (Fla. App. 1970); Skillings v. Allen, 173 N.W. 663 (Minn. 1919); Anno., "Liability of Doctor or Other Health Practitioner to Third Party Contracting Contagious Disease from Doctor's Patient," 3 ALR5th 370.

56. *See, e.g.*, Myers v. Quesenberry, 193 Cal. Rptr. 733 (Cal. App. 1983). In Reisner v. Regents of University of California, 1995 WL 29397 (Cal. App. 2 Dist.), a physician who discovered after a patient's surgery that blood used for a transfusion was contaminated with HIV antibodies was held to owe to the patient's future boyfriend a duty to warn the patient or her parents of the danger, even though the physician did not know the boyfriend's identity or even that he existed. Three years after the surgery, the patient started dating the boyfriend and they became intimate. Two years later the physician told the patient that she had AIDS. The patient died one month later and, shortly thereafter, the boyfriend discovered he was HIV positive. It appeared that a timely warning to the patient would have prevented the boyfriend's infection. The court held that the physician knew or reasonably should have known that, as the patient matured, she was likely to enter into an intimate relationship.

57. W.H. Hardie, "Confronting Foreseeability in Products Litigation," *For the Defense*, Oct. 1994, p. 4. In Enright v. Eli Lilly, 77 N.Y.2d 377, 570 N.E.2d 198, 568 N.Y.S.2d 550 (1991), the New York Court of Appeals held that a brain-damaged girl had no legal standing to sue the manufacturer of the drug DES (diethylstilbestrol), which her grandmother took during pregnancy. The suit claimed that DES taken by the grandmother caused the plaintiff's mother to be born with a malformed uterus, which in turn caused her premature birth and resulting cerebral palsy. In a 5-1 decision, the court ruled that the third generation had no right to sue because there was no "contact with the substance" and liability should be limited to "those who ingested the drug or were exposed to it in utero." The court said, "For all we know, the rippling effects of DES exposure may extend for generations. It is our duty to confine liability within manageable limits. Limiting liability to those who ingested the drug or were exposed to it in utero serves this purpose."

The concept of "proximate" or "legal cause" is another way that courts limit liability. As a matter of public policy, the court may find there is no "proximate cause" between the harm claimed by the plaintiff and the defendant's negligence. In such an instance, the damages are called "remote." "It is not easy at all times to determine what are proximate and what are remote damages." Ryan v. New York Central R.R. Co., 35 N.Y. 210, 91 Am. Dec. 49 (1866). Usually, foreseeability is considered an element of negligence, not cause. Unlike the question of duty, the proximate cause issue is more within the province of the jury. Stewart v. Wulf, 271 N.W.2d 79 (Wis. 1978).

The duty and proximate cause issues bring to mind Lord Demming's dicta in Spartan Steel ([1973] Q.B. 27 (C.A.)), where he said: "The more I think about these cases, the more difficult I find it to put each into its proper pigeon-hole. Sometimes I say: 'There was no duty.' In others I say: 'The damage was too remote.' So much so that I think the time has come to discard those tests which have proved so elusive. It seems to me better to consider the particular relationship in hand, and see whether or not, as a matter of policy,...loss should be recovered or not." See also Petition of Kinsman Transit Co., 388 F.2d 821 (2d Cir. 1968).

58.   See Weisbeck v. Hess, 524 N.W.2d 363 (S.D. 1994).

59.   27 Cal.3d 916, 616 P.2d 813, 167 Cal. Rptr. 831 (1980).

60.   The California Supreme Court in Thing v. La Chusa, 48 Cal.3d 644, 771 P.2d 814, 257 Cal. Rptr. 865 (1989), traces the distinction, albeit disapprovingly, between direct victim cases and bystander cases. The subtleties in the distinction between the right to recover as a "direct victim" and as a "bystander" has created what is described as an "amorphous nether realm." A "direct victim" is not bound by the strictures governing an action by a bystander: closely related to the injury victim; present at the scene of the injury-producing event at the time it occurs and is then aware that it is causing injury to the victim; and as a result suffers serious emotional distress. J.A. Greenberg, "Negligent Infliction of Emotional Distress: A Proposal for a Consistent Theory of Tort Recovery for Bystanders and Direct Victims," *Pepperdine L. Rev.* 19:1283, 1992.

61.   The court said (27 Cal.3d at 923, 167 Cal. Rptr. at 835):

[T]he risk of harm to plaintiff was reasonably foreseeable to defendants. It is easily predictable that an erroneous diagnosis of syphilis and its probable source would produce marital discord and resultant emotional distress to a married patient's spouse; [the doctor's] advice to Mrs. Molien to have her husband examined for the disease confirms that plaintiff was a foreseeable victim of the negligent diagnosis. Because the disease is normally transmitted only by sexual relations, it is rational to anticipate that both husband and wife would experience anxiety, suspicion, and hostility when confronted with what they had every reason to believe was reliable medical evidence of a particularly noxious infidelity.

> We thus agree with plaintiff that the alleged tortious conduct of defendant was directed to him as well as to his wife. Because the risk of harm to him was reasonably foreseeable we hold, in negligence parlance, that under these circumstances defendants owed plaintiff a duty to exercise due care in diagnosing the physical condition of his wife.

62. 31 Cal. App.4th 1195, 37 Cal. Rptr.2d 518 (1995).

63. Communication with Tarasoff's attorney (July 4, 1988).

64. The common law did not impose an obligation to aid or protect another, even if the other is in danger of losing his life. In a classic example, an accomplished swimmer with a boat and rope at hand, who sees another drowning, but did not put him in that peril, is not required to do anything at all about it. The common law imposed a duty on a person to render aid only when that person created the peril or when there is a special relation between the parties. For example, because of a special relation, a carrier is required to take reasonable affirmative steps to aid a passenger in peril, an innkeeper to aid a guest, or a physician to aid a patient. Unless there is a special relation between the parties, a duty arises only by virtue of misfeasance that forseeably will cause injury to the plaintiff. Osterlind v. Hill, 263 Mass. 73, 160 N.E. 301 (1928).

65. P.C. Cartensen, "The Evolving Duty of Mental Health Professionals to Third Parties: A Doctrinal and Institutional Examination," *Int'l J. Law & Psychiatry* 17:1, 1994.

66. "[T]he single relationship of a doctor to his patient is sufficient to support the duty to exercise reasonable care to protect others against dangers emanating from the patient's illness. The courts hold that a doctor is liable to persons infected by his patient if he negligently fails to diagnose a contagious disease or, having diagnosed the illness, fails to warn members of the patient's family." 551 P.2d at 354.

67. To safeguard themselves and to make sure of their legal duty, psychiatrists in various states have lobbied for legislation to provide that issuance of a warning alone discharges their duty. R. Slovenko, "The Tarasoff Progeny," in R.I. Simon (ed.), *Review of Clinical Psychiatry and the Law* (Washington, D.C.: American Psychiatric Press, 1990), vol. 1, ch. 8, p. 177.

68. A.R. Felthous, *The Psychotherapist's Duty to Warn or Protect* (Springfield, Ill.: Thomas, 1989). In Nasser v. Parker, 249 Va. 172, 455 S.E.2d 502 (1995), the Virginia Supreme Court rejected *Tarasoff.*

69. N.L. Chayet, "Confidentiality and Privileged Communication," *New Eng. J. Med.* 275:1009, 1966.

70. 645 So.2d 1301 (La. App. 1994).

71. In this much publicized case, Dr. Dudley M. Stewart by letter notified U.S. District Judge Veronica D. Wicker that his patient was threatening her life because she had overturned a $1.3 million jury award in his favor. Dr. Stewart believed the patient was capable of carrying out the threat. The patient apparently had bought an automatic rifle and a sub-machine gun. The FBI quickly appeared on the scene. The patient was charged with threatening the life of Judge Wicker. The prosecution, however, ended in a

mistrial. The patient thereupon sued Dr. Stewart alleging breach of confidentiality. "By talking to the doctor about his angry feelings toward Wicker, he was venting frustration in the proper way," said his lawyer. See S. B-12; F.F. Marcus, "Case Underlines Psychiatric Issue: To Keep Confidences or Report Them," *New York Times*, May 23, 1986, sec. 1, p. 8.

72. The Connecticut Motor Vehicles Law, § 14-46, requires the physician to report, in writing, "the name, age and address of each person known to him to be subject to recurrent attacks of epilepsy in any of its forms or to recurrent periods of unconsciousness uncontrolled by medical treatment." The Regulations of the Michigan Department of Mental Health (R 330.7131) provide: "Department hospitals for the mentally ill shall establish procedures for prompt and thorough psychiatric and medical evaluations soon after admission of a patient who possesses a valid driver's license and is admitted as mentally ill to determine whether or not a report to the secretary of state of driving ability is warranted." The New Jersey Motor Vehicle Code provides that: "Each physician treating any person 16 years of age or older for recurrent convulsive seizures or for recurrent periods of unconsciousness or for impairment or loss of motor coordination due to conditions such as, but not limited to, epilepsy in any of its forms, when such conditions persist or recur despite medical treatments, shall, within 24 hours after his determination of such fact, report the same to the Director of the Division of Motor Vehicles." N.J. Stat. Ann. § 39:3-10:4. Pennsylvania requires reporting of certain conditions if, "in the opinion of the provider, the condition is likely to impair the ability to control and safely perform motor functions necessary to drive a vehicle." 67 Pa. Code §§ 83.6, 83.5(b). The reportable conditions include "mental or emotional disorder," "periodic episodes of loss of attention or awareness which are of unknown etiology," and "chronic abuse of alcohol" or other substances known to impair motor skills.

    See T.C. Doege & A.L. Engelberg (eds.), *Medical Conditions Affecting Drivers* (Chicago: American Medical Association, 1986); J. Gunn & P.J. Taylor, *Forensic Psychiatry* (Oxford: Butterworth-Heinemann, 1993), pp. 112-115; J.E. Macbeth, A.M. Wheeler, J.W. Sither & J.N. Onek, *Legal and Risk Management Issues in the Practice of Psychiatry* (Washington, D.C.: American Psychiatric Press, 1994); P.A.B. Raffle, *Medical Aspects of Fitness to Drive* (London: Medical Commission on Accident Prevention, 4th ed. 1985); S.L. Godard & J.D. Bloom, "Driving, Mental Illness, and the Duty to Protect," in J.C. Beck (ed.), *Confidentiality Versus the Duty to Protect: Foreseeable Harm in the Practice of Psychiatry* (Washington, D.C.: American Psychiatric Press, 1990), pp. 191-204; A. Crancer & D.L. Quiring, "The Mentally Ill as Motor Vehicle Operators," *Am. J. Psychiat.* 126:807, 1969; W.A. Tillman & G.E. Hobbs, "The Accident Prone Automobile Driver," *Am. J. Psychiat.* 106:321, 1949; "Position Statement on the Role of Psychiatrists in Assessing Driving Ability," *Am. J. Psychiat.* 152:819, 1995.

73. While these provide immunity in reporting, they give no protection against a lawsuit to those who, in a good-faith exercise of judgment, decide not to

report. This combination of immunity and penalty encourages the overre-porting of questionable situations. D.J. Besharov & L.A. Laumann, "Child Abuse Reporting," *Society*, May/June 1996, p. 40.

74. See R. Slovenko, "Mobilopathy," *J. Psychiatry & Law* 12:293, 1984; see also "MADD or MAD?" *id.* 16:691, 1988.

75. See J.E. Macbeth, A.M. Wheeler, J. W. Sither & J.N. Onek, *Legal and Risk Management Issues in the Practice of Psychiatry* (Washington, D.C.: Psychiatrists' Purchasing Group, 1994).

76. Calif. A.B. 497 (1990); K.W. Kizer, *Reporting Alzheimer's Disease and Related Disorders* (Sacramento, CA.: State of California Dept. of Health, 1990).

77. G. Adler, S.J. Rottunda & M.W. Dysken, "The Driver With Dementia," *Am. J. Geriatric Psychiat.* 4:110, 1996.

78. According to an AIDS policy report approved by the American Medical Association House of Delegates, the physician of an HIV-infected patient who refuses to notify persons with whom he has had sex or shared needles that they may have been exposed to the AIDS virus, should, as a last resort, alert the unsuspecting third parties. The AMA called for "special legislation" that would grant immunity to physicians who find they must either notify public health officials or unsuspecting third parties, or who choose to take no action because the risk to the third party is not deemed substantial. The AMA's stance closely resembles the APA's guidelines on confidentiality and disclosure. "AMA Takes Stand on AIDS-Related Issues," *Psychiatric News*, Aug. 5, 1988, p. 1.

The American Psychiatric Association's Position Statement and Guidelines on AIDS and HIV Disease provide: "The confidentiality of information regarding HIV testing or status should be protected." In many states, the law requires that all marriage license applicants obtain a written certification from a physician that they are free of venereal disease in a com-municable stage, but this provision does not apply to examination of HIV infection. E. Tanay, "Psychiatric Reflections on AIDS Education," *Psychiatric Annals*, Oct. 1988, p. 594.

It is deemed a violation of the constitutional right of privacy for jail employees to disclose to other inmates that an inmate is HIV-positive. Hillman v. Columbia County, 474 N.W.2d 913 (Wis. App. 1991).

See B.M. Dickens, "Legal Limits of AIDS Confidentiality," *JAMA* 259:3449, June 17, 1988; J.D. Piorkowski, "Between a Rock and a Hard Place: AIDS and the Conflicting Physician's Duties of Preventing Disease Transmission and Safeguarding Confidentiality," *Geo. L.J.* 76:169 (1987); see also S. Sesser, "Hidden Death," *New Yorker*, Nov. 14, 1994, p. 62.

79. Alar v. Mercy Memorial Hospital, 529 N.W.2d 318 (Mich. App. 1995).

80. The case was settled because of "problems," says George A. McKray of San Francisco, attorney for the Tarasoff family. Telephone interview (July 4, 1988).

81. To minimize the tail (damages) wagging the dog (liability), a number of judg-es strongly support bifurcating, or splitting, issues of liability from issues of

damages and trying them separately. If the issue of liability is heard alone, and no liability is found, none of the evidence relating to the extent and value of the damages need be presented. The norm for trials, however, is for the jury to hear in one unified process all the issues pertinent to the liability of the defendant and the value of the damages. S.B. Middlebrook, "Liability v. Damages: A Fair Trial Often Means a Split Trial," *Wall Street Journal*, June 13, 1988, p. 12.

82. See, *e.g.*, Jess v. Herman, 26 Cal.3d 131, 161 Cal. Rptr. 87, 604 P.2d 108 (1979); American Motorcycle Assn. v. Superior Court, 20 Cal.3d 578, 146 Cal. Rptr. 182, 578 P.2d 899 (1978); Rowland v. Christian, 69 Cal.2d 108, 70 Cal. Rptr. 97, 443 P.2d 561 (1968).

83. Comment, "The *Tarasoff* Progeny: Creating a Weaponless Policeman with a 'Deep Pocket,'" *Capital U.L. Rev.* 15:699, 1986.

84. Report, National Victim Center, National Clearinghouse on Child Abuse and Neglect Information; discussed in R. Davis, "Computer technology comes to aid of crime victims," *USA Today*, Sept. 15, 1995, p. 9.

85. It is hornbook law that in the absence of a "special relationship" between the parties, there is no duty to control the conduct of another so as to prevent him or her from causing harm to others. *Restatement of Law of Torts Second*, §315. A familiar example of a special relationship that gives rise to a duty is the duty parents have to control their children from posing an unreasonable risk of injury to the public. The court in Ellis v. D'Angelo, 116 Cal. App.2d 310, 253 P.2d 675 (1953), upheld a cause of action against parents who failed to warn a babysitter of the violent proclivities of their child. Another illustration is the liability of a carrier whose employees have failed to exercise reasonable care to control the conduct of its passengers so as to prevent either an intentional harm to other passengers or other conduct which may constitute an unreasonable risk of harm to them. Another illustration is the responsibility of a penal institution for harm to others committed by a dangerous convict whom it had negligently allowed to escape. F.V. Harper & P.M. Kime, "The Duty to Control the Conduct of Another," *Yale L.J.* 43:886, 1934.

86. The reasoning of *Tarasoff* was applied to evaluations in Hicks v. United States, 511 F.2d 407 (D.C. Cir. 1975). Given the minimal degree of confidentiality associated with evaluations, there is even less reason to refrain from disclosure than there is in the therapy context. G.B. Melton, J. Petrila, N.G. Poythress & C. Slobogin, *Psychological Evaluations for the Courts* (New York: Guilford Press, 2d ed. 1997), p77. Hawaii has granted court-ordered psychiatrists immunity from *Tarasoff*-type claims. Seibel v. Kembel, 631 P.2d 173 (Haw. 1981).

87. The issue is raised in G.H. Morris, "Civil Commitment Decisionmaking: A Report on One Decisionmaker's Experience," *So. Cal. L. Rev.* 61:291, at 330, 1988.

88. Rule 1.6(b)(1).

89. 17 Cal.3d at 440, 131 Cal. Rptr. at 26, 551 P.2d at 346.

90. 17 Cal.3d at 441, 131 Cal. Rptr. at 27, 551 P.2d at 347. It would be a justified breach of confidentiality, for example, to report to the health department that a patient, a food handler, has a communicable disease. Ops. Calif. Atty. Gen. 58:904, 1975.

91. R.E. Bird, "Justice Mathew O. Tobriner–The Heart of a Lion, The Soul of a Dove," *Calif. L. Rev.* 70:871, 1982.

92. Landeros v. Flood, 131 Cal. Rptr. 69, 551 P.2d 389 (1976); see D.J. Besharov (ed.), *Protecting Children from Abuse and Neglect* (Springfield, Ill.: Thomas, 1988).

93. Maine Human Services 22:4011(c); Maryland Op. Atty. Gen. 62:157 (1977); Oregon Child Welfare Services 418.750, Rev. Stat. 40.225, 40.295. Maine's exemption is conditioned on "when there is little threat of serious harm to the child."

94. See discussion in Part V, Chapter 2.

95. Michigan law provides that the duty of a physician to report an impaired physician does not apply to a physician who is in a "bona fide health professional-patient relationship" with the impaired physician. MCL 333.16223. For further discussion, see Part V, Chapter 2.

96. California Evidence Code §1007. The Louisiana legislature in 1987 passed House Bill 1712 which gives the State Board of Medical Examiners power to obtain "any and all medical information" of any physician it has under investigation. The Louisiana Psychiatric Association opposed the bill during the legislative session. Since passage of the bill, LPA members actively involved in the Louisiana State Medical Society lobbied within that organization to make their concerns known to the other physicians of the state. As a result, the LSMS, affirming "its commitment to the fundamental principle of confidentiality as a basic tenet of the doctor-patient relationship," resolved that it would work with the State Board of Medical Examiners to develop rules that would define the type of information available to the State Board under HB 1712 with the goal to limit the information to that which is reasonably related to the physician's ability to practice medicine, with the removal of open ended release of information which is contained in HB 1712. Newsletter, Louisiana Psychiatric Association, Spring 1988, p. 22.

97. See S.B. Bisbing, L.M. Jorgenson & P.K. Sutherland, *Sexual Abuse by Professionals: A Legal Guide* (Charlottesville: Michie, 1995); K.S. Pope & J. Bouhoutos, *Sexual Intimacy Between Therapists and Patients* (New York: Praeger, 1986); K.C. Bemmann & J. Goodwin, "New Laws About Sexual Misconduct by Therapists: Knowledge and Attitudes Among Wisconsin Psychiatrists," *Wis. Med. J.*, May 1989, p. 11; L.H. Strasburger, L. Jorgenson & R. Randles, "Mandatory Reporting of Sexually Exploitative Psychotherapists," *Bull. Am. Acad. Psychiatry & Law* 18:379, 1990.

98. See R.I. Simon, *Clinical Psychiatry and the Law* (Washington, D.C.: American Psychiatric Press, 2d ed. 1992), pp. 80-90; L.M. Jorgenson, "Countertransference and Special Concerns of Subsequent Treating

Therapists of Patients Sexually Exploited by a Previous Therapist," *Psychiatric Annals* 25:525, Sept. 1995.

99. Statutes making psychotherapist-patient sexual activity a crime have been enacted in California, Colorado, Florida, Maine, Minnesota, North Dakota, and Wisconsin.

100. California, by Cal. Health & Safety Code § 199.14(c), has provided: "No physician has a duty to notify any person of the fact that a patient is reasonably believed to be infected by the probable causative agent of acquired immune deficiency syndrome." Subsections (a) and (b) provide that, subject to some limitations, no physician shall be held liable for "disclosing to a person reasonably believed to be the [spouse, sexual partner, hypodermic needle sharer, or county health officer] that the patient has tested positive on a test to detect infection by the probable causative agent of" AIDS. The physician must first discuss the matter with the patient and attempt to obtain "voluntary consent for notification of his or her contacts." All persons so notified are to be referred for "appropriate care, counseling, and follow up." See G. Rotello, "AIDS Is Still an Exceptional Disease," New York Times, Aug. 22, 1997, p. 19.

101. J. Barron, "A Debate Over Disclosure to Partners of AIDS Patients," *New York Times*, May 8, 1988, p. E-8. Admiral James D. Watkins, chairman of the President's AIDS Commission, on June 2, 1988, urged that states establish partner notification programs to alert people who might have been infected by their sexual partners and that states adopt laws making it a criminal offense to knowingly transmit the AIDS virus. He also recommended that the names of all people who test positive for infection with the AIDS virus be reported to state health authorities on a confidential basis as an aid to tracking the spread of the virus. *Health Lawyers News Report,* June 1988, p. 5. The American Medical Association has strongly urged physicians to warn the sexual partners of patients found to carry the AIDS virus if there was no other way to alert them to the danger. The House of Delegates, at its 1988 annual meeting, adopted the following:

> Ideally, a physician should attempt to persuade the infected party to cease endangering the third party; if persuasion fails, the authorities should be notified; and if the authorities take no action, the physician should notify and counsel the endangered third party.
>
> In some states, strict confidentiality laws may limit the exercise of this duty by reason of severe penalties for any breach of confidentiality, especially HIV-related information. Special legislation is needed in these states in order to grant a physician legal immunity to act in the following ways: the legal right to notify directly; or the option of notifying public authorities, or the choice of not acting at all if, in the physician's judgment, the danger to the third party is seen to fall short of substantial risk.

I. Wilkerson, "A.M.A. Urges Breach of Privacy to Warn Potential AIDS Victims," *New York Times,* July 1, 1988, p. 1.

102. M. Roth, "HIV Confidentiality Puts MDs in Hot Seat," *Medical Tribune*, June 9, 1988, p. 1. Once a patient has been hospitalized and responsibility for the patient's care has been assumed, the APA's policy guidelines advise the responsible physician to disclose the information to the appropriate staff only after discussions with the patient, if the physician determines that appropriate treatment of the patient requires such disclosure. The guidelines also provide that if the patient engages in behavior likely to transmit the virus and there is a significant risk that such behavior cannot be controlled by other measures, then disclosure of a patient's infectious condition to other patients at risk is permissible. When discharge is otherwise clinically appropriate, if the patient represents a substantial risk to others by virtue of behavior known to transmit the virus but this danger is not related to a specific mental condition, the guidelines state that it is inappropriate to retain the person in the hospital solely for quarantine or preventive detention. "AIDS Policy: Guidelines for Inpatient Psychiatric Units," *Am. J. Psychiat.* 145:542, 1988.

103. 2 Cal.3d 415, 85 Cal. Rptr. 829, 467 P.2d 557 (1970). The *Lifschutz* case dealt with the "patient litigant" exception to testimonial privilege, that is, communications with a therapist lose their privileged status when the patient files a personal injury action claiming damages for mental and emotional distress. See S. Knapp & L. VandeCreek, *Privileged Communications in the Mental Health Professions* (New York: Van Nostrand Reinhold, 1987).

104. 467 P.2d at 562. In a survey conducted not long after the *Tarasoff* decision, 80 percent of 1,093 psychiatrists thought that their patients would be less likely to divulge certain sensitive information to them if they knew that their therapist might divulge it to a third person, and about one-fourth of the therapists observed that their patients were somewhat more reluctant to discuss their violent tendencies when they learned that the therapist might have to breach confidentiality in some circumstances. T.B. Wise "Where the Public Peril Begins: A Survey of Psychotherapists to Determine the Effects of *Tarasoff*," *Stan. L. Rev.* 31:165, 1978.

105. T.B. Wise, "Where the Public Peril Begins: A Survey of Psychotherapists to Determine the Effects of Tarasoff," *Stan. L. Rev.* 31:165, 1978. "[M]ost therapists would probably compromise confidentiality in the likely event of imminent physical danger." A.R. Dyer, *Ethics and Psychiatry* (Washington, D.C.: American Psychiatric Press, 1988), p. 61.

106. The Supreme Court in Miranda v. Arizona, 384 U.S. 436 (1966), ruled that before a confession obtained through custodial interrogation could be used at trial, the government first had to prove that the defendant had been advised of, and waived, certain specified rights. The required warnings before interrogation are: (1) The accused has the right to remain silent; (2) anything he says may be used against him; (3) he has a right to consult with a lawyer before or during questioning; and (4) if he cannot afford an attorney, one will be provided without cost. The *Miranda* decision applies to law-enforcement officials, or those acting at their behest, not to others. Therapists are misled by the advice that it applies to them. Patients need not

be "mirandized," to use police officer slang. See Grand Rapids v. Impens, 414 Mich. 667, 327 N.W.2d 278 (1982) (store security personnel not required to give *Miranda* warnings prior to interrogation); People v. Porterfield, 420 N.W.2d 853 (Mich. App. 1988) (protective services worker not required to give warnings prior to questioning in course of child neglect proceedings).

107.  J.G. Fleming & B. Maximov, "The Patient or His Victim: The Therapist's Dilemma," *Calif. L. Rev.* 62:1025 at 1058 and 1066, 1975.

108.  P.S. Appelbaum, "Implications of *Tarasoff* for Clinical Practice," in J.C. Beck (ed.), *The Potentially Violent Patient and the* Tarasoff *Decision in Psychiatric Practice* (Washington, D.C.: American Psychiatric Press, 1985).

109.  R. Slovenko, "Psychotherapy and Confidentiality," *Clev. State L. Rev.* 24:375 at 395, 1975.

110.  J. Beck, "When the Patient Threatens Violence: An Empirical Study of Clinical Practice after *Tarasoff*," *Bull. Am. Acad. Psychiat. & Law* 3:189, 1982.

111.  In a Vermont case, the court held the duty to protect included a situation where the patient, age 29, son of the plaintiffs, set fire to their barn, located 130 feet from their home. At the time the son was a voluntary outpatient under the care of a counselor in a community mental health clinic. He told the counselor that he "wanted to get back at his father." Peck v. Counseling Service of Addison County, 146 Vt. 61, 499 A.2d 422 (1985).

112.  See the comments on scope of liability in Welke v. Kuzilla, 144 Mich. App. 245, 375 N.W.2d 403 (1985).

113.  Comment, "Psychotherapists' Duty to Warn: Ten Years after *Tarasoff*," *Golden Gate U. L. Rev.* 15:271, 1985.

114.  551 P.2d at 345 n. 11.

115.  152 Cal. Rptr. 226 (1979), *vacated*, 27 Cal.3d 741, 167 Cal. Rptr. 70, 614 P.2d 728 (1980).

116.  See the discussion in Sizemore v. Smock, 422 N.W.2d 666 (Mich. 1988).

117.  614 P.2d at 736. In Cansler v. State, 234 Kan. 554, 675 P.2d 57 (1984), a state prison negligently permitted convicts to escape and then failed to warn nearby law enforcement officers. The plaintiff was an officer who, ignorant of the escape, attempted to confront several men who had apparently stolen a car. They turned out to be the escapees and shot him three times with a high-powered rifle. The court held that the state had a duty both to confine securely and to warn of any escape. This latter duty was to all "area residents," and might be satisfied by a prearranged signal such as a siren. It had further duty to warn law enforcement officials through police communication channels.

118.  570 F. Supp. 1333 (D. Colo. 1983), *aff'd*, 751 F.2d 329 (10th Cir. 1984).

119.  See T.A. Goodman, "From Tarasoff to Hopper: The Evolution of the Therapist's Duty to Protect Third Parties," *Behav. Sci. & Law* 3:195, 1985.

120.  124 Mich. App. 291, 335 N.W.2d 481 (1983), *remanded for reh'g*, 422 Mich. 875, 366 N.W.2d 7 (1985), *aff'd on reh'g*, 147 Mich. App. 8, 382 N.W.2d 195 (1985), *leave to appeal granted*, 425 Mich. 851 (1986).

121.  See, *e.g.*, the criticism in E.J. Kermani & S.L. Drob, "Tarasoff decision: A Decade Later Dilemma Still Faces Psychotherapist," *Am. J. Psychotherapy* 41:271, 1987.

122. In Jackson v. New Center Community Mental Health Service, 404 N.W.2d 688 (Mich. App. 1987), there was no claim that the victims were readily identifiable potential victims of the patient's violence. The record showed that they were the hapless victims of the patient's random shooting spree. As there was no readily identifiable victim, the Michigan Court of Appeals held that the defendants, the health center and the doctor, were entitled to summary disposition.

123. 430 Mich. 326, 422 N.W.2d 688 (1988). See also Brown v. Northville Regional Psychiatric Hospital, 153 Mich. App. 300, 395 N.W.2d 18 (1986), where it was stated: [D]ecisions... concerning diagnosis, course of treatment, and discharge or transfer of a patient are discretionary and protected by governmental immunity. So too...the decision of how best to carry out the discharge, either by outright discharge or transfer to another hospital and with or without medication, is discretionary. However, the execution of those decisions is a ministerial act. Once a decision to discharge a patient and the best method to carry it out is made, the decision must be properly executed. For example, if the decision is made to discharge a patient with medication, a subsequent discharge without medication is a ministerial act which is not protected by governmental immunity.

124. D. Gruber, "Court Clarifies Mental Health Immunity Rules," *Mich. L.W.* 2:677, May 9, 1988.

125. MCLA 691.1407 (2).

126. MCLA 691.1407(2)(c).

127. 158 Mich. App. 25, 404 N.W.2d 688 (1987).

128. 2 Mich. L.W. 793 (June 6, 1988).

129. 712 F.2d 391 (9th Cir. 1983).

130. 712 F.2d at 398.

131. 34 Cal.3d 695, 194 Cal. Rptr. 805, 669 P.2d 41 (1983).

132. 669 P.2d at 46. Prior to 1968, case law authority was virtually unanimous in rejecting recovery by bystanders who suffered emotional harm on the basis of observing an injury that had been inflicted upon another. Annot., 29 A.L.R.3d 1337 (1970). A change came about with the decision of Dillon v. Legg, 68 Cal.2d 728, 69 Cal. Rptr. 72, 441 P.2d 912 (1968). It is eminently foreseeable that an injury to one party will result in adverse consequences that affect others to one degree or another, but foreseeability of injury alone does not mandate recognition of a cause of action. The determination of where to draw the line of liability is essentially a question of policy. As stated by Judge Breitel of New York, "Every injury has ramifying consequences, like the ripplings of the waters, without end. The problem for the law is to limit the legal consequences of wrongs to a controllable degree." Tobin v. Grossman, 24 N.Y.2d 609, 301 N.Y.S.2d 554, 249 N.E.2d 419 (1969).

133. 168 N.J. Super. 466, 403 A.2d 500 (1979).

134. The New Jersey court said: "[A] psychiatrist or therapist may have duty to take whatever steps are reasonably necessary to protect an intended or potential victim of his patient when he determines, or should determine, in

the appropriate factual setting and in accordance with the standards of his profession established at trial, that the patient is or may present a probability of danger to that person. The relationship giving rise to that duty may be found either in that existing between the therapist and the patient, as was alluded to in *Tarasoff II*, or in the more broadly-based obligation a practitioner may have to protect the welfare of the community, which is analogous to the obligation a physician has to warn third persons of infectious or contagious disease." 168 N.J. Super. at 489, 403 A.2d at 511.

135. 497 F. Supp. 185 (D. Neb. 1980).
136. 497 F. Supp. at 193.
137. 27 Cal.3d at 760, 167 Cal. Rptr. at 81, 614 P.2d at 739.
138. 100 Wash.2d 421, 671 P.2d 230 (1983).
139. 539 A.2d 1064 (Del. 1988).
140. *Supra* note 120.
141. 144 Mich. App. 245, 375 N.W.2d 403 (1985).
142. 589 F.2d 214 (5th Cir. 1979).
143. In Schuster v. Altenberg, 424 N.W.2d 159 (Wis. 1988), a patient, who was diagnosed as a manic-depressive and was taking medication, within an hour of seeing her therapist drove into a tree at 60 mph, killing herself and leaving her 17-year-old daughter a paraplegic. The complaint alleged that the therapist, a psychiatrist, was negligent in his management and care of the patient "in failing to recognize or take appropriate actions in the face of her psychotic condition, including failing to seek her commitment, to modify her medication, to alert and warn the patient or her family of her condition or its dangerous implications." The patient was taking Xanax and Nardil, drugs that carry warnings not to drive while under their influence. For the purposes of addressing the legal sufficiency of the complaint, the court categorized the allegations as follows: (1) negligent diagnosis and treatment, (2) failure to warn the patient's family of her condition and its dangerous implications, and (3) failure to seek the commitment of the patient. Generally, once a court determines that a claim has been stated as to one particular theory, it will not proceed to determine what additional theories are valid, but in this case the Wisconsin Supreme Court, upon the request of both parties and in the interest of judicial economy, ruled on all three theories, finding them all legally sufficient. For one, the court said, a therapist may be held liable in negligence for failure to warn of the side effects of a medication if the side effects were such that a patient should have been cautioned against driving, because it was foreseeable that an accident could result, causing harm to the patient or third parties if the patient drove while using the medication. For another, the court said, if it is ultimately proven that it would have been foreseeable to a psychiatrist, exercising due care, that by failing to warn a third person or by failing to take action to institute detention or commitment proceedings someone would be harmed, negligence will be established. The pleadings established grounds upon which a jury could find negligence and could further find such negligence to have constituted the

cause in-fact of the injury. See also Freese v. Lemmon, 210 N.W.2d 576 (Iowa-1973); Duvall v. Goldin, 139 Mich. App. 342, 362 N.W.2d 275 (1984); Kaiser v. Suburban Transportation System, 65 Wn.2d 461, 401 P.2d 350 (1965); Anno., 43 A.L.R.4th 153 (1986). Query: Could not the *Tarasoff* have been litigated or decided on the ground of negligent treatment? See D. Blum, *Bad Karma: A True Story of Obsession and Murder* (New York: Atheneum, 1986).

144. J. Monahan, *Predicting Violent Behavior: An Assessment of Clinical Techniques* (Beverly Hills, CA.: Sage, 1981); H. Steadman, "The Right Not to Be a False Positive: Problems in the Application of the Dangerousness Standard," 52 *Psychiatric Q.* 84 (1980); J.J. Cocozza & H. Steadman, "The Failure of Psychiatric Predictions of Dangerousness: Clear and Convincing Evidence," *Rutgers L. Rev.* 29:1084, 1975; B.J. Ennis & T.R. Litwack, "Psychiatry and the Presumption of Expertise: Flipping Coins in the Courtroom," *Calif. L. Rev.* 62:693, 1974; J.L. Hedlund *et al.*, "Prediction of Patients Who Are Dangerous to Others," *J. Clin. Psychol.* 29:443, 1973.

145. J. Monahan, "The Prediction of Violent Behavior: Toward a Second Generation of Theory and Policy," *Am. J. Psychiat* 141:10, 1984; T.R. Litwack, "The Prediction of Violence," *Clinical Psychologist,* Fall 1985, p. 85; R.M. Wettstein, "The Prediction of Violent Behavior and the Duty to Protect Third Parties," *Behav. Sci. & Law* 2:291, 1984.

146. 551 P.2d at 340.

147. See C. Slobogin, "Dangerousness and Expertise," *U. Pa. L. Rev.* 133:97, 1984.

148. "Dangerousness" is a pervasive concept in law and psychiatry. See S.A. Shah, "Dangerousness: A Paradigm for Exploring Some Issues in Law and Psychology," *Am. Psychologist* 33:224, 1978.

149. 463 U.S. 880 (1983).

150. As a rule, psychiatrists are opposed to the death penalty, and they tend to be critical of psychiatrists who testify on behalf of the prosecution in these cases. Dr. James P. Grigson, who is often a witness for the prosecution, is labeled "Dr. Death." He says: "I agree with the APA and other members of my profession that you can't take a guy off the street and predict what he is going to do tomorrow. But if a guy rapes one woman, is he dangerous? If he rapes two women, is he dangerous now? If he rapes two more women and kills them, can he be considered dangerous in the future? If he rapes six women and hacks them up and he shows no shame, no remorse, he just tells you how much fun it was, can you predict he will be dangerous in the future? Of course you can." Quoted in L. Belkin, "Expert Witness Is Unfazed by 'Dr. Death' Label," *New York Times,* June 10, 1988, p. 23.

151. 463 U.S. at 886.

152. 497 F. Supp. at 192.

153. Palsgraf v. Long Island RR, 248 N.Y. 339, 162 N.E. 99 (1928).

154. 17 Cal.3d at 431, 131 Cal. Rptr. at 20, 551 P.2d at 340.

155. 17 Cal.3d at 438, 131 Cal. Rptr. at 25, 551 P.2d at 345.

156. 17 Cal.3d at 451, 131 Cal. Rptr. at 33, 551 P.2d at 353.
157. This "standard" is supported by Dr. Alan Stone, a psychiatrist, in "The Tarasoff Decision: Suing Psychotherapists to Safeguard Society," *Harv. L. Rev.* 90:358, 1976.
158. R. Reisner & C. Slobogin, *Law and the Mental Health System* (St. Paul, MN.: West, 2d ed. 1990).
159. A "substantial departure" (or "gross negligence") rule finds support in the United States Supreme Court's decision in Youngberg v. Romeo, 457 U.S. 307 (1982). In this case, the Supreme Court dealt with a claim brought by the mother of a severely retarded young man residing in a state facility. Unlike *Tarasoff*, this was not personal injury litigation; she claimed that her son was constitutionally entitled to "training and habilitation." The Court agreed that "minimal efforts" to habilitate were required, but how that habilitation was accomplished, the Court said, was a matter of professional judgment to which the courts should defer. Under that decision, professional decisions are presumptively valid, and liability imposed only when the professional's decision is a "substantial departure from the accepted professional judgments, practice and standards...[and demonstrates] that the person...did not base the decision on such judgments." The substantial departure rule would still require expert testimony, but the plaintiff would have to allege more than the fact that the "ordinary practitioner" would have been more vigorous. The plaintiff would need to show that the defendant acted in a "cavalier or irresponsible fashion."
160. Signed into law in New York in July 1995, S.B. 5441A authorizes state psychiatric facilities to have computer access to patients' criminal records. The legislation was prompted by violent acts of court-committed patients.
161. P. Appelbaum, "*Tarasoff* and the Clinician: Problems in Fulfilling the Duty to Protect," *Am. J. Psychiat.* 142:425 at 426, 1985.
162. 712 F.2d 391 (9th Cir. 1983).
163. In Peck v. Counseling Service of Addison County, 146 Vt. 61, 499 A.2d 422 (1985), the defendant argued that the therapist, acting as a reasonably prudent counselor, "concluded in good faith that (the patient) would not burn his parents' barn." The court found, however, that the therapist was negligent, and did not act as a reasonably prudent counselor, because her good faith belief was based on inadequate information and consultation.
164. See C.J. Frederick (ed.), *Dangerous Behavior: A Problem in Law and Mental Health* (Rockville, Md.: National Institute of Mental Health, 1978); J.R. Lion, *Evaluation and Management of the Violent Patient* (Springfield, Ill.: Thomas, 1972); A.M. Rossi *et al.*, "Characteristics of Psychiatric Patients Who Engage in Assaultive or Other Fear-Inducing Behaviors," *J. Nervous & Mental Disease* 174:154, 1986.
165. 168 N.J. Super. 466, 403 A.2d 500 (1979).
166. 646 F. Supp. 524 (E.D. Mich. 1986).
167. 646 F. Supp. at 535.
168. Mavroudis v. Superior Court for County of San Mateo, 102 Cal.3d 594 at 400, 162 Cal. Rptr. 724 at 730 (1980).

169. Davis v. Lhim, 124 Mich. App. at 294, 335 N.W.2d at 484; Kim v. Bardoni, 151 Mich. App. 169, 390 N.W.2d 218 (1986).
170. In Novak v. Rathman, 505 N.E.2d 773 (Ill. App. 1987), the court found no causal connection between the patient's release and the harm, about a year and a half later, because "the events were too far removed in time to establish the requisite causal connection."
171. 17 Cal.3d at 439, 131 Cal. Rptr. at 25, 551 P.2d at 345.
172. "The Patient or His Victim? The Therapist's Dilemma," *Calif. L. Rev.* 62:1025, 1975.
173. 17 Cal.3d at 439, 131 Cal. Rptr. at 25, 551 P.2d at 345.
174. 17 Cal.3d at 431, 131 Cal. Rptr. at 20, 551 P.2d at 340.
175. *Calif. L. Rev.* 62:1025 at 1065.
176. *Id.* at 1066.
177. Apparently the only exception is Peck v. Counseling Service of Addison County, 146 Vt. 61, 499 A.2d 422 (1985), involving a counselor.
178. D.B. Wexler, "Patients, Therapists, and Third Parties: The Victimological Virtues of Tarasoff," *Int'l J. of Law & Psychiatry* 2:1, 1979.
179. P.S. Appelbaum & T.G. Gutheil, *Clinical Handbook of Psychiatry and the Law* (New York: McGraw-Hill, 1982), p. 195.
180. See D.J. Madden & J.R. Lion (eds.), *Rage, Hate, Assault and Other Forms of Violence* (New York: Spectrum, 1976); J.R. Lion & W.H. Reid (eds.), *Assaults Within Psychiatry Facilities* (New York: Grune & Stratton, 1983); K. Tardiff (ed.), *The Psychiatric Uses of Seclusion and Restraint* (Washington, D.C.: American Psychiatric Press, 1984).
181. P. Appelbaum, "*Tarasoff* and the Clinician: Problems in Fulfilling the Duty to Protect," *Am. J. Psychiat.* 142:425, at 426, 1985.
182. *Id.* at 426-427.
183. Dr. Seymour L. Halleck advised: "Although warnings may be useless, there are ways of providing them without imposing a threat of liability upon doctors. A law could be written which would require the psychiatrist to report serious threats of violence in patients who are unlikely to be civilly committed directly to a magistrate. The court would then have the opportunity to weigh the psychiatrist's report and make a legal decision as to whether the threat was serious enough to warrant violating the patient's confidentiality. It would seem that decisions to warn in this kind of setting would be more rational since they would have the input of legal as well as psychiatric wisdom. Liability would not be an issue since the decision-making power would rest with the magistrate, who could not be sued." S.L. Halleck, *Law in the Practice of Psychiatry* (New York: Plenum, 1980), p. 82. In South Africa it was provided: "If a medical practitioner is of the opinion that any person examined or treated by him is mentally ill to such a degree that he is a danger to others, he shall forthwith in writing report his opinion to the magistrate of the district in which such person is, or if the magistrate is not readily available, to a police official who shall forthwith lay the said report before the magistrate concerned." Mental Health Act of South Africa, Act No. 18 of 1973, sec. 13.

184. In general, see M.B. Lewis, "Duty to Warn Versus Duty to Maintain Confidentiality: Conflicting Demands on Mental Health Professionals," *Suffolk U.L. Rev.* 20:579, 1986.

185. That is the response made over the telephone but in writing police departments advise that they investigate all threats. Some say they do not receive reports from psychiatrists. For example: "The Detroit Police Department is firmly committed to investigating all threats of physical violence regardless of the source of information. However, regarding your inquiry, an investigation failed to confirm any referrals from any psychiatrists regarding the 'Mental Health Practitioners, Duty to Warn Third Parties' statute." Letter (Nov. 8, 1994) from Micah Smith of the Records and Identification Section of the Detroit Police Department.

186. L. Leiter, "The Struggle to Stretch the Long Arm of the Law," *Insight,* July 15, 1996, p. 18. See also D.W. Shuman, "The Duty of the State to Rescue the Vulnerable in the United States," in M.A. Menlowe & A. McCall Smith (ed.), *The Duty to Rescue* (Brookfield, Vt.: Dartmouth, 1993).

187. Schuster v. Altenberg, 424 N.W.2d 159 (Wis. 1988); discussed *supra* at p. 334.

188. 644 F. Supp. 1074 (M.D. N.C. 1986)

189. As perceptive a giant as Sigmund Freud apparently did not anticipate the Hitler invasion or, at least, did not take appropriate, clearly indicated steps, assuming such anticipation. H. Silving, *Memoirs* (New York: Vantage Press, 1988), p. 108.

190. "Nightline," ABC, May 23, 1988.

191. On and off Laurie Dann would continue therapy. A letter from her psychiatrist in Madison pleaded with her to continue psychotherapy. "I am genuinely concerned about your ability to cope with the problems you have been struggling with," the doctor wrote in trying to persuade her to continue therapy. "I think it is important for you to realize, if you don't already, that the nature of your problems go back long before you married your husband, and it relates to your childhood upbringing." The letter also warned her that she could not rely on medication to cure her problems. "The use of medication can only result in a symptomatic improvement and not in a definitive cure for the kinds of difficulties that you are experiencing," the doctor wrote. Quoted in G. Papajohn & J. Kaplan, "The many faces of Laurie Dann," *Chicago Tribune,* June 5, 1988, p. 1.

192. It is reported that Dann was taking an experimental drug that can cause suicidal depression and is not approved for U.S. sale. She is believed to have obtained it from a Canadian pharmacy with her Chicago doctor's prescription. A. Rauma, "Should mental health workers protect patients or the public?" *Detroit News,* June 13, 1988, p. 3.

193. K. Wysocky, "Rites held as officials retrace Dann's path," *Milwaukee Sentinel,* May 24, 1988, p. 1.

194. M. Brower, "Mad Enough to Kill," *People,* June 6, 1988, p. 42.

195. Quoted in J. Kass & J.R. Tybor, "Laurie Dann case: a legal quandary," *Chicago Tribune,* May 29, 1988, p. 1.

196. Quoted in M. Brower, *op. cit. supra.*
197. In his book *Law in the Practice of Psychiatry* (New York: Plenum, 1980), Dr. Seymour L. Halleck tells of his feelings about a warning:

> In the course of studying the *Tarasoff* decision I have had personal experiences which lead me to question its implied rationale that the potential victim is in a substantially better position if warned. About a year after the *Tarasoff* court reaffirmed its decision I received a note from a colleague telling me that a patient had made statements to her that seemed to indicate that he was planning to kill me. My colleague, apparently responding to her perception of the *Tarasoff* ruling, felt that it was her duty to warn me even though there has been no such ruling in my state. I received the information as to the possible threat against my life with some consternation and much confusion. In pondering what I could do about the threat, I realized that there were few possibilities. I could leave town, but I knew that the patient, who was a student, would be in town for several years. I could have bought a gun and kept it at home or in my office, but I found this alternative distasteful and in conflict with my values. I finally did the only thing that seemed to make sense--I called the police. They agreed to drive by my house every now and then, and advised me to change my habits so that I would not be predictably in the same place all the time. They asked my opinion as to whether I thought they should talk to the patient and tell him to stay away from me. I thought this was a good idea and they complied. Nothing more came of the matter, but I must admit that I was overly anxious, hyperalert, and much more aggressive than I usually am during the ensuing few months. The emotional trauma I experienced by being warned, while not overwhelming, was in no way worth the very doubtful benefits I accrued by having been warned. I now fear that if we ever do get to the point of warning all people who are threatened, we will probably not save many lives but we will certainly cause a great deal of mental anguish.

*Query*: What would have been the outcome if Dr. Halleck had not been warned? We can only speculate. If he had not been warned, he would not have contacted the police. The police went to talk with the patient and they may have dissuaded him from hostile action. Dr. Halleck may have been made anxious, but he was not harmed. He may be guessing when he says the warning had doubtful effects.

In a study of two decades of experience with the Tarasoff decision psychiatrist Renee Binder and psychologist Dale McNiel of the University of California, San Francisco, found that reporting did little serious damage to the therapeutic relationship, and that in only four of the 27 cases in their study was the target unaware of the patient's threats of violence against him or her. Of 11 targets who were already aware of the potential danger, there were mixed responses–four said they were glad the patient was hospitalized and wanted to know when he or she would be released so they could avoid the patient, two said they had already taken steps to avoid the patient, and five were convinced the patient would never follow through on the threat. In only two of the 27 cases did the potential victims not seem thankful for the warning. "People usually want to know about potential danger they are in," said Dr. Binder. "This knowledge gives them at least some chance of protecting themselves and gives them more control over their fate." To help build and strengthen a therapeutic alliance, she suggested that it is preferable for therapists to inform patients about a *Tarasoff* warning before rather than after that warning is delivered. The study was reported at the 1996 annual meeting of the American Academy of Psychiatry and Law and reported in "Fallout From *Tarasoff* Decision Not as Dire and Predicted," *Psychiatric News*, Nov. 15, 1996, p. 7.

198. J. Rossiaud, *Medieval Prostitution* (London: Blackwell, 1988).
199. R.I. Simon, *Concise Guide to Clinical Psychiatry and the Law* (Washington, D.C.: American Psychiatric Press, 1988), p. 109.
200. Such a feeling runs through Dr. Howard Gurevitz's comments on the decision in *Tarasoff*:

> It is with a sense of despair that one reads the opinion and recognizes that the increasing manifest violence in our world today has persuaded one of our nation's most distinguished courts to create standards of practice and procedures that ally the psychotherapist more with the goal of protecting society than with that of healing patients. It is not that psychiatrists reject the need to counterbalance these functions; in fact, most psychiatrists attempt to fulfill both responsibilities. However, we have done so with procedures that have not mandated us to routinely perform a duty that is counter to our powers of prescience.

H. Gurevitz, "Tarasoff: Protective Privilege Versus Public Peril," *Am. J. Psychiat.* 134:289 at 292, 1977.
201. Official actions, Council on Psychiatry and Law, *Am. J. Psychiat.* 41:487, 1984.
202. Cal. Civ. Code §43.92 (1987); Colo. Rev. Stat. §13-21-117 (1986); Fla. Sess. Law Serv. Ch. 87-252 (1987); Ind. Code Ann. §34-4-12.4-2 (1987); Ky. Rev. Stat. Ann. §202A.400 (1986); La. R.S. 9:2800.1 (1986); Minn. Stat. Ann. §148.975 (1987); Mont. Code Ann. §27-1-1102 (1987); N.H. Rev. Stat. Ann. §329.31 (1986); Wash. Rev. Code Ann. §71-34-270(2).
203. The California legislation is discussed in M.J. Mills, G. Sullivan & S. Eth, "Protecting Third Parties: A Decade after *Tarasoff*," *Am. J. Psychiat.* 144:68, at 73, 1987.
204. *Supra* note 118.
205. P. Appelbaum "*Tarasoff* and the Clinician: Problems in Fulfilling the Duty to Protect," *Am. J. Psychiat.* 142:425 at 428 (1985).
206. Discussed *supra*.
207. A.A. Stone, "The Tarasoff Decision: Suing Psychotherapists to Safeguard Society," *Harv. L. Rev.* 90:358 1976; reprinted in revised form in A.A. Stone,

*Law, Psychiatry, and Morality* (Washington, D.C. American Psychiatric Press, 1984), pp. 161 190.

208. R. Slovenko, "Psychotherapy and Confidentiality," *Clev. State L. Rev.* 24:375 at 392, 1975.

209. A.A. Stone, *Law, Psychiatry and Morality* (Washington, D.C.: American Psychiatric Press, 1984); quoted in M.J. Mills, G. Sullivan & S. Eth, "Protecting Third Parties: A Decade After *Tarasoff,*" *Am. J. Psychiat.* 144:68, 1987.

210. K.M. Quinn, "The Impact of *Tarasoff* on Clinical Practice," *Behav. Sci. & Law* 2:319, 1984.

211. See P. Appelbaum, "*Tarasoff* and the Clinician: Problems in Fulfilling the Duty to Protect," *Am. J. Psychiat.* 142:425 at 428 (1985); M.J. Mills, G. Sullivan & S. Eth, "Protecting Third Parties: A Decade after *Tarasoff,*" *Am. J. Psychiat.* 144:68, at 73 (1987).

212. Samson v. Saginaw Professional Bldg., 393 Mich. 393, 224 N.W.2d 843 (1975).

213. Butler v. Acme Markets, 89 N.J. 270, 445 A.2d 1141 (1982).

214. Nallan v. Helmsley-Spear, 50 N.Y.2d 507, 429 N.Y.S.2d 606, 407 N.E.2d 451 (1980).

215. Williams v. Cunningham Drug Stores, 418 N.W.2d 381 (Mich. 1988).

216. O.W. Holmes, *The Common Law* (Boston: Little, Brown, 1923), p. 111.

217. In Davis v. Allied Supermarkets, 547 P.2d 963 (Okla. 1976), the plaintiff alleged injury and loss of property by an unknown assailant occurring at night on the defendant's grocery parking lot. The alleged negligence consisted of failure to provide adequate lighting and personnel at its place of business in a high crime area. The Oklahoma Supreme Court, sustaining a demurrer to the petition, held that the defendant was not primarily negligent, but aside from that, the court said, "we think the consideration of proximate cause confirms the conclusion we reach."

218. Williams v. Cunningham Drug Stores, *supra* note 215.

219. In the aftermath of the tragic shootings at the Winnetka elementary school, the Illinois House resoundingly defeated an attempt by some lawmakers to revive stringent gun-control legislation. T. Franklin & S. Johnson, "Gun-control push defeated," *Chicago Tribune,* May 25, 1988, p. 3.

# Chapter 3

# "VERY IMPORTANT PERSONS"

Major problems encountered in the evaluation or treatment of "Very Important Persons" (VIPs) are the reluctance of close advisors to question the capabilities of their leaders, the stigma attached to those in powerful positions who seek psychiatric treatment, the unavailability of objective evaluators, and the legal impotence of those attempting to treat those who are sometimes above the law or able to manipulate it.

"Grave, perhaps insuperable, problems beset the process of making psychiatric evaluation and treatment available to a VIP whose mental functions have become impaired," stated a report *The VIP with Psychiatric Impairment* by the Group for the Advancement of Psychiatry that was formulated with the help of professional and military consultants.[1] The major recommendation of the report called for the establishment of a panel of qualified psychiatrists designated by the American Psychiatric Association, who would be "available to any requesting governmental agency" to provide examination, consultation, and psychiatric recommendation for VIPs. Members of such a panel should be "professionally highly competent, free of political and administrative involvement, and objective and immune to pressure." All aspects of the VIP's life situation would be weighed; the social, political, and economic considerations; and the probable effects of disturbing the equilibrium of the VIP, the members of the group surrounding him, and society at large. Nothing came of the report, though its recommendations arise time and again.

Does the public have a right to know the intimate details of the health of its political leaders or candidates for public office? "It is true to say that if you know a person's history of health problems, then you know more about that person than you would with any other data," said Law Professor Lawrence O. Gostin, as chairman of a national privacy project, but then again, given Professor Gostin's interest, the statement might be discounted.[2]

It is relevant to ask: On what basis do people choose their leaders? How much does a candidate's character or personality determine the votes he gets? There are two contradictory points of view widely held and, frequently, by the same people at different times. Some say that decisions are based on objective evidence. Others say that politics resembles religion where allegiance is often the product of emotion or passion, not reason. Some people said they would not vote for Steve Forbes because "he looks funny." Dr. Hans Eysenck observed:[3]

> Some believe that a person's political opinions are the results of objective experiences, of thought, and of definite decision; they are consciously arrived at after a thorough weighing of the evidence and are modifiable by logical argument and factual proof. The opposite view is that political opinions are the reflections of personality, determined largely by irrational motives of one kind or another, not amenable to logical argument or factual disproof, and altogether an expression of personality rather than a reaction to external reality. Many people feel that the former of these two views adequately characterizes the voting behavior of themselves and their friends; the second type of motivation may be recognized more easily in those voting for the opposite camp.

Presidential character has become very much a part of the political landscape. It is considered so important that candidates in political campaigns resort to character assassination.[4] A political axiom suggests that on election day, it all comes down to "character."[5] Roger Stone, a Republican strategist who worked for Presidents Nixon, Reagan, and Bush, said, "A race for President is principally about character."[6] A national poll conducted in 1996 showed that overall, 56 percent of registered voters believe a president's moral and ethical character is more important than his views on issues.[7] Hardly a month went by without yet another reminder of President Bill Clinton's checkered past.[8] Of the 1996 presidential race, an editorial in the *Wall Street Journal* expressed the opinion:[9]

> The real issue of the day is manifestly an issue of character. This is not a matter of one aberrant personality. Lyndon Johnson was hounded from office over something called the "credibility gap," and Richard Nixon resigned not because of the Watergate break-in but because of the lies in its aftermath. George Bush was cashiered essentially for breaking his "read my lips" pledge.

The book edited by Robert Wilson, *Character Above All,*[10] focused attention on the character of those seeking the nation's highest elective office. In the book, Richard Reeves writes that John F. Kennedy "didn't think that the rules applied to him and he did whatever he could get away with." He says that Kennedy was careless, deceitful, and relished controlling people while setting them against each other for his own amusement. Still, Reeves credits Kennedy with mostly exercising power wisely and appealing to our better instincts.[11]

Richard Dallek cites Lyndon Johnson's "compulsion to be the best, to outdo everybody, to eclipse all his predecessors in the White House and become the greatest president in American history." This compulsion, coupled with the Vietnam war, Dallek says, brought out the worst in him.[12] Like Johnson, Tom Wicker writes, Richard Nixon came to office "mistrusted by a large segment of the American people." As a consequence, both men suffered a credibility problem that neither was able to overcome.[13]

Peggy Noonan's essay on Ronald Reagan cites his courage, decency, and strong moral sense, which, she says, restored pride in America.[14] Hendrick Hertzberg, Jimmy Carter's speech writer, confers sainthood on his former boss, but fails to explain why saints are unsuited for the Oval Office.[15] James Cannon's Gerald Ford is the right man in the right place at the right time to replace the president who had dishonored himself and the office.[16] And Michael Beschloss' George Bush comes across as a man whose moderate character was out of sync with the political conservatism of the 1980s.[17] Bob Dole, of course seemed dull.

Reprinted by permission of Sean Delonas of the *New York Post*

What ought the public to know about a candidate for public office? A democracy is based on public opinion; the United States under the Constitution is a "public opinion" state. Should a candidate for public office be asked to submit to psychological testing or to reveal his medical record? Years ago, in a number of writings, Dr. Leopold Bellak, a clinical professor of psychiatry at Albert Einstein College of Medicine and the developer of a method of testing a child's perception that is still used today, suggested like the GAP report that candidates for president and vice president should be given psychological tests and tested for organic brain problems such as lesions and tumors that could interfere with memory, problem-solving, attention span, and the ability to think abstractly. He repeated the proposal when President Reagan, in advanced age, was running for reelection.[18]

Dr. Abraham Halpern, then director of psychiatry at United Hospital and clinical professor of psychiatry at New York Medical College, took issue with the proposal. He responded:[19]

> I can see much harm and no good that can come from routine psychological testing of candidates for president and vice president. Dr. Bellak obviously disagrees, but the fact remains that such testing is not likely to uncover significant mental impairments or characterological deficits not already discernible by the public.
>
> If Dr. Bellak has such great faith in psychological testing as a necessary means of identifying "organic brain problems such as lesions and tumors that could interfere with memory, problem-solving, attention span and the ability to think abstractly," why doesn't he try to persuade his colleagues who run training programs in psychology and psychiatry to require applicants for admission to undergo such tests?
>
> I trust the American people would prefer to continue with the selection of candidates for president and vice president by way of our democratic process untainted by professional psychological screening, performed even by psychologists who themselves have undergone psychological testing.

In 1995, Russia's Duma, the lower house of Parliament, proposed that psychiatrists be consulted on the competency of political leaders. The country's president, Boris Yeltsin, was a known alcoholic and in ill health. The profession declined, saying that "psychiatry is about patients, not power."

Does or should an individual who is a candidate or holder of public office lose all right of privacy about his health? Dr. Richard Epstein, past president of the Washington Psychiatric Society, says, "Even if one assumes that the public always has a right to know when an elected official suffers from a condition that might impair his or her ability to function in office, that should not justify wholesale inspection of entire medical records. There are many medical and psychiatric conditions that cause no impairment in functioning that nevertheless, if revealed, would stigmatize the individual concerned." But that proposition begs the question of who should decide whether an impairment is serious enough to justify disclosure and who should make the disclosure or whether medical records are needed as the evidence.[20]

Shortly before the Russian 1996 presidential election, Boris Yeltsin suffered a heart attack, but it was kept secret; his physician said after the elec-

tion, "Can you imagine what would have happened if he had told everyone
he's had a heart attack and he's unable to work?"[21] It was, however, common
knowledge among the public that Yeltsin was in poor health.

A few U.S. presidents have opted for complete disclosure of their medical
records. Presidents Eisenhower, Johnson, Nixon, Carter, Reagan, and Bush
allowed their physicians to comment publicly. During President Reagan's
cancer treatment, reporters were given free rein to question his surgeon, and
the same was true when he was treated for bullet wounds after an assassination attempt. During the 1996 presidential campaign, President Clinton and
Vice President Al Gore and opponents Bob Dole and Jack Kemp authorized
their physicians to disclose information about their medical records.[22] Paul
Tsongas, a presidential candidate in the 1992 campaign, presented himself as
a recovered cancer patient and forthrightly told his doctors to lay out the full
details to medical reporters, but they did not. William Safire commented:[23]

> Privacy is a value: the public need not pry into any psychological consulta-
> tions, none of which should be an impediment to public service. But good
> health is a qualification for office. We do have the right not to be misled about
> the life expectancy of the person we make the most powerful leader in the
> world.

The health problems of a number of U.S. presidents were not made public until years afterward. Woodrow Wilson suffered a stroke in 1919 that
made it difficult for him to concentrate on policy matters for more than ten
minutes at a time, and there is some evidence also publicly unknown then
that he may have had several small strokes before he was first elected in
1912. During Franklin D. Roosevelt's fourth term, his failing health was kept
from the public. John F. Kennedy was diagnosed as early as 1947 with
Addison's disease, but he, his doctors, and his family concealed the diagnosis throughout his career (even when asked specifically about the Addison's
diagnosis during the 1960 campaign, Kennedy's physician denied it).
Historians and political scholars debate whether disclosure of these health
conditions would have changed history.[24]

What about the psychological makeup of a candidate for public office?[25]
What about how the individual stands up under pressure?[26] In a bit of self-
examination, Colin Powell said that he did not have "the fire in the belly"
that one needs to be president. Unlocking the head and heart of Thomas
Jefferson, historian Andrew Burstein argued that "the man most renowned in
American history for the pursuit of happiness could not pursue happiness
without feeling stress."[27]

And what about the candidate's wife, as she impacts on her husband?
Insiders say that Nancy Reagan calmed her husband's bellicosity. When it

was thought that Colin Powell would run for the presidency, there were news reports that his wife was taking medication for depression. Was it of any moment?[28]

The motivations of a candidate are often called into question. Of what consequence? Politicians, like other people, may do the right thing for the wrong reasons (and vice versa). In ordinary affairs, we regard a person's actions differently when we are aware of the motivations behind the action. Thus, a man who buys an air-conditioning unit for his father-in-law, on the face of it, has performed a noble deed, but we would think differently about the act if we were advised that he bought it to appease his wife. A politician may act solely out of a narcissistic need for publicity. Police and other law-enforcement officials may be attracted to their work as a psychic defense against their own criminal impulses—knowing this, we may look askance at their work.

Personality testing raises numerous questions. Shall we judge a person by his deeds or by his thoughts? Shall we predict his future actions by his past deeds or by his motivations? Is it one or the other, or are both factors important? Can potential leaders be scientifically evaluated? Who tests the testers? Can the public fairly evaluate psychological data? Do social values outweigh the use of such evidence? In the course of the 1996 presidential campaign, Democrat Senator Christopher Dodd of Connecticut urged a distinction between "political character" and "personal character."[29]

Personality tests, which have been used for all sorts of purposes, have evoked outrage. Martin L. Gross's book *The Brain Watchers* received wide attention at the time of its publication. Gross's major theme was that all personality testing is without value and should be abandoned. He attacked personality tests on two grounds: first, that the "brain-watching" system is a violation of human rights.[30] Second, that it fails to isolate the qualities which its practitioners (quite wrongly) suppose to be the best.[31] The *Economist* suggests that psychological testing can show in pertinent part only that which is already commonly known, to wit, that political candidates or office holders are power hungry or crave adulation.[32]

During the 1964 presidential campaign, *Fact* magazine polled psychiatrists for their opinion about Barry Goldwater: "Is Barry Goldwater psychologically fit to be President of the United States?" Heart surgeons were asked to comment whether President Lyndon Johnson would die in office if elected in 1964. Is any helpful information provided by such polls? Did the public know any more about the candidates after the polls?

The *Fact* magazine poll was an embarrassment to the American Psychiatric Association. A consensus in the profession felt that the signers of the statement were ethically wrong, irrelevant, and inept clinically to think they could say what they did with no clinical data. It led to a provision in the

Association's ethics code that psychiatrists should not render professional opinions or make clinical judgments without having "conducted an examination" of that individual and "been granted proper authorization."[33] Taken literally, the provision would preclude psychohistories or discussions about a criminal or other person without an examination.[34]

Among the reasons given for the expulsion of Dr. James P. Grigson of Dallas was that he arrived at psychiatric diagnoses without first having examined the individuals in question and that the hypothetical questions on which he based his diagnosis were "grossly inadequate to elucidate a competent medical, psychiatric differential diagnostic understanding adequate for diagnosing mental illness according to current standards."[35] In law, the opinion of an expert witness is admissible though based on hypothetical data alone. Lack of personal examination by the expert bears on weight, not on admissibility.[36]

The APA Ethics Committee revisited its ethical principle in 1995 and amended the blanket prohibition against offering a professional opinion about an individual in public attention by adding the language: "In such circumstances, a psychiatrist may share with the public his/her expertise about psychiatric issues in general." Dr. Jerrold Post, a noted figure in psychohistory studies, was perplexed by the amendment and annoyed by the basic principle. He wrote, "What does it mean? Asked about Ross Perot, should I respond, 'Let me tell you about paranoia, but you will have to draw your own conclusions as to whether or not this is applicable to Perot'?"

To address the hazards of injudicious opinions by psychiatrists and yet permit useful contributions, Dr. Post suggested that the prohibition be replaced with guidelines to the effect that such professional opinions should be based on research consistent with psychiatric principles and knowledge; be conveyed in a responsible manner that is mindful of the responsibility to society; and treats the subject with respect. The profiles he offers, he said, are not a psychiatric expert opinion but a "political psychology profile," informed by his education as a psychiatrist, but concerned with such matters as leadership style, crisis reactions, negotiating style, relationship with leadership circle, et cetera.[37]

Would disclosure of a personal examination of Goldwater have added to the public's knowledge of the candidate? Psychiatrists are hired, for example, to screen out Peace Corps applicants who are emotionally unstable. Senator Wayne Morse, in the course of his fight against the confirmation of Clare Boothe Luce as Ambassador to Brazil, asked Mrs. Luce's doctor if she ever had been under psychiatric treatment. Was it an attempt to smear or to obtain pertinent information otherwise unavailable?

Watergate added to the call for candor. Jimmy Carter was praised by many for his openness in revealing even his sex fantasies to *Playboy*. Bill

Clinton as a presidential candidate was asked about marital infidelity. The lasting influence of the Eagleton affair was demonstrated when Gerald Ford released the results of his physical examination to the press. George McGovern, candidate for President in 1972, again recently acknowledged, "The confusion over my selection of Senator Tom Eagleton as my running mate disrupted the campaign when it was revealed that, unknown to me or my other Senate colleagues, Senator Eagleton had long suffered from a serious clinical emotional illness."38

The question, does the public have a legitimate interest in a political candidate's personal or family life?, is not a new one, but it has a special immediacy now at this time when the public is demanding greater frankness and integrity from political leaders. Of course, we want persons of honor, competency, probity, and self-restraint at the head of government, but is there wisdom in "letting it all hang out"? It may be helpful to consider basic principles from the law of evidence: relevancy, and prejudice.

The evidentiary principle of relevancy essentially says: "Keep your eye on the ball." Apply this to a politician's sexual proclivities. Does the relevance lie in whether he can keep his eye on the needs of his constituency, or whether he is distracted by erotic fantasies? Carrying on an affair during a campaign, Gary Hart showed immaturity and arrogance.

Is there a connection or correlation between a person's private life and his ability to serve or govern the public? When President Abraham Lincoln was told of General Grant's fondness for strong drink, he gave instructions to find out what Grant was drinking and to send a bottle of it to his other generals. Will a man who cheats on his wife also cheat on his country? History teaches that good governance and mainstream morality need not go hand-in-hand. Biographers now tell us details about past leaders which might well end their public service if they were active today. President Clinton opined that Lincoln, whom he described as one of our greatest presidents, would not get elected today if his bouts of depression were made a matter of public knowledge.39

It was said that Clinton's alleged past life-style would send a wrong message to the public. In the film "The American President," a snarly Republican senator calls into question the "family values" of the President (played by Michael Douglas). The public looks to its political leaders for purity for the same reason children need to desexualize their parents. It is a defense against the incestuous atmosphere of the family, and the public are children at bottom, with parental transferences to political leaders. We know our parents are sexual, but we try to deny it.

Politicians hug babies at every stop. They pose with their family. They deliver speeches written by others. Even reading George Bush's lips did not reveal his agenda. So, to get behind the facade, the personal has become the political. Indeed, how else to really know anything truthful about the candidate? Image makers, as campaign workers are known, are essentially falsifiers.

What in assessment of character is connected to a person's ability to carry out a job? Public life and private life or early life, Freud said, are all of a piece. Adulation by the public may be sought to make up for lack of adulation in childhood. The measure of a person, however, is by his accomplishments, not by what drives him. The quality of surgery, for example, is measured by its standards and not by the motivations of the surgeon.

Joe Klein in an article in *New York* magazine wrote that there's a question of what's at the "core" of Bill Clinton. Does it matter? Genesis is important in psychoanalysis, but that is for the purpose of treatment. Jackson Pollock, a hero of abstract expressionism, drew inspiration for his "drip" painting by watching—in childhood—his father urinate on a rock.

Turn then to the concept of prejudice. The value of evidence, even relevant probative evidence, may be outweighed by the danger of prejudice. It clouds the real issues, and unduly colors our attitudes. The demand for films of Errol Flynn and Charles Laughton was dropped when their homosexuality was revealed.

News of sexual proclivities and behavior is of small (if any) relevance, yet its prejudicial power is enormous. It not only crucifies competent candidates, but it is a distraction from real issues. There is only so much time to take in information about candidates. Telling too much can cloud the real differences between them by replacing arguments over substantive issues, like that of the state of the economy, with petty gossip. The consequence is a kind of "Gresham's Law of Information"—too much trivia drowns out vital information.

Politicians use smear tactics against each other in their campaign. Rivals impugn each other's motives, or in common parlance, mud-sling. Over the years, the United States Supreme Court has ruled that the Constitution accords citizens and press an almost unconditional freedom to criticize or comment on public officials.[40]

What is to be concluded? On what basis shall we judge a person? The American Psychiatric Association called to task those psychiatrists who responded to the poll conducted by *Fact* magazine.[41] Some say that no individual, irrespective of whether he is a candidate for public office or an applicant for private employment or school admission, should be asked to submit to psychological testing. Suppose, among other things, that the individual refuses to submit to examination? "Mind tapping" without consent and cooperation would be a clear violation of constitutional rights.[42] But even assuming that the individual willingly consents, there may arguably still be a violation of constitutional rights.[43]

Should all personality testing be abandoned, as Gross suggested? That viewpoint was a reaction to an overemphasis in past years of the value of psychological testing. Psychological testing may leave something to be desired in measuring an individual's coping mechanisms, therefore the difficulty in predicting performance. The fact remains, however, that psychological testing can tell us a great deal about an individual's pathological conflicts. Projective and other psychological tests have their value, though they may be subject to criticism.[44] The study of man improves: Rorschach ink blots are an improvement over General Bullmoose's personality test ("the cut of his jib"). Psychological test results, when considered along with other information, can be helpful—when properly used—in making an evaluation, especially when little is known of the person from his past behavior. The principal value of psychological testing, however, lies in evaluation for the selection of the best type of treatment and in the course of treatment.

But in the political arena, social values apparently outweigh probative value of evidence that might be obtained from psychological testing. Psychiatrists and psychologists would be placed in an omniscient and anti-democratic role. Psychiatrists are already accused of presumptuous interference in political, social, and cultural matters which are not directly pertinent to their province, the relief of individual suffering. A political or judicial decision, moreover, does not rest solely on empirical evidence. Should computers replace judges? The paternity suit against Charlie Chaplin illustrates that the aims of science and law are not identical (the court ruled that Chaplin was the father of Miss Berry's child, notwithstanding the findings of blood-grouping tests—Chaplin out of societal considerations was held to bear a responsibility to the girl).

In any event, virtue no longer seems to be a requirement for public office. The political question asked most often these days is why, given that Americans have historically placed honesty and integrity high on the list of personal characteristics they most value, so many people today seem not to care at all about what the mainstream media has come to describe delicately as "the character issue." With the rise of the nanny state, said political commentator M.L. Melcher, what matters to many voters in a president is simply that he be on their side in the great redistribution battle. His personal actions, even if egregious by the standards of several decades ago, are of little interest to these voters.[45] In the same vein, P.A. Gigot, another political commentator, suggested that presidential "character" does not seem to matter any more because voters think all politicians are corrupt and the voters themselves are as corrupt as their politicians.[46]

TOLES © *The Buffalo News.* Reprinted with permission of
Universal Press Syndicate. All rights reserved.

## NOTES

1. Group for the Advancement of Psychiatry, *The VIP with Psychiatric Impairment* (Washington, D.C.: American Psychiatric Assn., 1973) see S. Wachtler, After the Madness (New York: Random House, 1997).

2. Professor Gostin is quoted in G. Kolata, "When Patients' Records Are Commodities for Sale," *New York Times*, Nov. 15, 1995, p. 1.

3. H. Eysenck, *Sense and Nonsense in Psychology* (Baltimore: Penguin, 1958), p. 265.

4. At the 1996 Republican convention Elizabeth Dole told of the character of the man she loved. Would psychological testing have been more probative? See R.L. Berke, "G.O.P. Unleashes An Attack on Clinton Over Character and His Economic Policies," *New York Times*, Aug. 14, 1996, p. 1.

5.    T.J. Bray, "Dole and the politics of 'character,'" *Detroit News*, Aug. 4, 1996, p. B-6; see also Interviews, "Does Character Count?," *Wall Street Journal*, Aug. 20, 1996, p. 10; M. Dowd, "The Politics of Me," *New York Times*, Aug. 18, 1996, p. E-15; J. Lawrence, "Candidates and character: What really matters?", *USA Today*, Oct. 14, 1996, p. 1; T. Sowell (syndicated column), "Character does count in the election," *Detroit News*, Aug. 21, 1996, p. 13.

6.    R. Stone, "Positively Negative," *New York Times*, Feb. 26, 1996, p. 11.

7.    S. Thomma, "President's character is voters' priority," *Detroit Free Press*, Feb. 3, 1996, p. 6; see also E.C. Ladd, "To Voters Picking a President, Character *Does* Matter," *Christian Science Monitor*, July 23, 1996, p. 18.

8.    The best selling novel "Primary Colors" by Joe Klein (no longer anonymous) portrayed an ethically bereft Southern governor running for president–a not-so-thinly veiled view of Clinton's quest for the Oval Office. M. Lawson, "Great Man Lowered By His Trousers," *Spectator*, Feb. 10, 1996, p. 11.

9.    Editorial, "Character Questions," *Wall Street Journal*, Oct. 4, 1996, p. 6.

10.   New York: Simon & Schuster, 1996; reviewed in A. Miller, "Does character determine the presidency?" *Detroit News*, Feb. 21, 1996, p. 9.

11.   *Ibid.*

12.   *Ibid.*

13.   *Ibid.*

14.   *Ibid.*

15.   *Ibid.*

16.   *Ibid.*

17.   *Ibid.*

18.   T. Anderson, "Psychiatrist wants brain tests for presidential candidates," *Gannett Westchester Newspapers*, Aug. 30, 1984, p. 3. The testing of judges is discussed in J. Frank, *Courts on Trial* (Princeton: Princeton University Press, 1949), p. 250; L. Forer, "Psychiatric Evidence in the Recusation of Judges," *Harv. L. Rev.* 73:1325, 1960; see also R.S. Redmount, "Psychological Tests for Selecting Jurors," *U. Kan. L. Rev.* 5:391, 1957.

19.   Ltr., "Democracy beats mental tests," *Gannett Westchester Newspapers*, Sept. 7, 1984, p. 13.

20.   R.S. Epstein (ltr.), "Big Brother Wants to See Your X-Rays," *Wall Street Journal*, Sept. 26, 1996, p. 13.

21.   *Ibid.*

22.   See L.K. Altman, "Clinton's Doctors Answer Opponent," *New York Times*, Sept. 15, 1996, p. 18; Editorial, "Will Anyone Believe?", *Wall Street Journal*, Sept. 16, 1996, p. 16; "Dueling Diagnostics," *Newsweek*, Sept. 23, 1996, p. 6. White House spokesman Mike McCurry said to reporters who persisted in questioning him about President Clinton's health records, "We reported to you that the President had an ingrown pimple." "Perspectives," *Newsweek*, Sept. 23, 1996, p. 27.

23. W. Safire, "Candidates' Health," *New York Times*, April 23, 1992, p. 15; see also L.K. Altman, "Tsongas's Health: Privacy and the Public Rights," *New York Times*, Jan. 17, 1993, p. 16.

24. Historians assembled the health records of political leaders for an exhibition, October 1996, at the College of Physicians of Philadelphia. D. Levy, "Health and executive privilege," *USA Today*, Sept. 13, 1996, p. 6.

25. The book edited by Gordon J. DiRenzo, *Personality and Politics* (New York: Anchor Books, 1974), focuses on dimensions of the relationship of personality to politics: (1) psychological motivation in recruitment to political roles and careers, (2) personality types among politically active people, (3) the relationship of personality to particular political ideologies, (4) the interaction of personality and various political dynamics, (5) the functional interrelations of personality and different kinds of political systems, and (6) methodological and theoretical issues that currently characterize this field of behavioral inquiry. The classic works on these topics are by Harold D. Lasswell, notably *Psychopathology and Politics* (Chicago: University of Chicago Press, 1930); *Power and Personality* (New York: W.W. Norton, 1948).

26. J. DeParle, "Portrait of a White House Aide Ensnared by His Perfectionism," *New York Times*, Aug. 22, 1993, p. 1; J.M. Post, "Suicide and the Pressures of High Office," *Psychiatric Times*, Oct. 1993, p. 1.

27. A. Burstein, *The Inner Jefferson: Portrait of a Grieving Optimist* (Charlottesville: University Press of Virginia, 1995).

28. A.M. Rosenthal, "Two Enemies of the Press," *New York Times*, Nov. 14, 1995, p. 11. See also P. Hay, *All the President's Ladies* (New York: Penguin, 1988).

29. Comment on David Brinkley program, TV-ABC, Aug. 18, 1996.

30. In personality testing, however, the person under examination is aware of the purpose of testing. Therefore, the examiner does not violate confidentiality in making a report; when testing is done for the purpose of treatment, that is another matter. The Supreme Court heard a constitutional challenge to a Georgia law that requires candidates for many state offices, including those of governor, state legislator and justice of the state supreme court, to pass a drug test as a condition of appearing on the ballot. The Justices questioned whether the law could be justified in light of the Fourth Amendment, which bars "unreasonable searches and seizures" by government of "persons, houses, papers and effects." "If you rely on the public's right to know everything about a candidate," Justice John Paul Stevens said, "it seems to me you can justify a search of a whole house for private papers" that might reveal evidence of wrongdoing." L. Greenhouse, "Justices Question Georgia Law Requiring Drug Tests for State Candidates," *New York Times*, Jan. 15, 1997, p. 10.

31. New York: Random House, 1962.

32. "Campaign issues: Character," *Economist*, Sept. 28, 1996, p. 33.

33. The provision appears in Section 10 of the 1973 edition, third paragraph, of *The Principles of Medical Ethics With Annotations Especially Applicable to*

*Psychiatry.* The 1978 edition has the provision in Section 10, Annotation 3. The 1981 edition, streamlining the code of conform with the AMA's *Principles of Medical Ethics*, has the provision in Section 7, Annotation, as do the 1993 edition and the 1995 edition.

34.  See. *e.g.*, T. Omestad, "Psychology and the CIA: Leaders on the Couch," *Foreign Policy*, Summer 1994, p. 105.

35.  "Expulsion," *Psychiatric News*, Aug. 4, 1995, p. 18.

36.  See, *e.g.*, State Farm Fire & Cas. Co. v. Wicka, 474 N.W.2d 324 (Minn. 1991).

37.  J. M. Post, "Profiling Political Leaders: an Ethical Quandary," *Psychiatric Times*, Sept. 1996, p. 27.

38.  G. McGovern (ltr.), "A Painful Distortion of History," *Wall Street Journal*, Feb. 26, 1996, p. 13.

39.  Interview with Barbara Walters, ABC's "20/20", Sept. 20, 1996.

40.  In a suit by a Montgomery city official against the *New York Times*, the Supreme Court in 1964 ruled that a public official must prove actual malice in an action seeking damages for defamatory falsehoods relating to his official conduct. Later in that year, in a case involving New Orleans District Attorney Jim Garrison, the Supreme Court held that the rule set out in the *New York Times* case is not rendered inapplicable because an official's private reputation as well as public reputation is harmed. Garrison had stated that the eight judges of the criminal district court were blocking his vice investigation and that "raises interesting questions about the racketeer influence on our eight vacation-minded judges." See R.A. Smolla, *Suing the Press* (New York: Oxford University Press, 1986).

41.  When the poll on Goldwater was underway, the medical director of the American Psychiatric Association made a public statement: "We alerted our officers, our district branches, to the mischief afoot and asked them to urge members not to write to *Fact* magazine but there was not time to reach all 14,000 members individually and, of course, many of them sent some form of a 'response'. . . I want to assure you that we will proceed with our plan to disavow the validity of any so-called psychiatric opinion of Mr. Goldwater's relative psychological fitness to be president that the magazine might publish." AP news-release, Sept. 30, 1964. Over 80 percent of the psychiatrists who were members of the American Psychiatric Association at that time did not respond to the questionnaire. Of the 20 percent who did respond, more than half said they either did not know enough about Sen. Goldwater to answer the questions or that they thought he was psychologically fit. In other words, less than half the responders and less than 10 percent of the membership of the APA expressed negative views of Sen. Goldwater's suitability for the presidency. Dr. Hubert Miller wrote to Ralph Ginzberg, the editor and publisher of *Fact* magazine, "If you will send me written authorization from Sen. Goldwater and arrange for an appointment, I shall be happy to send you a report concerning his mental status. The same goes for you." Dr. Stuart Keill wrote, "It takes a certain amount of psychopathology to become president and there is no evidence that Goldwater has any more

than any of his predecessors in the past 60 years." Quoted in A.L. Halpern (ltr.), "'Unfair Criticism' of Psychiatry," *Clin. Psychiatric News*, May 1992, p. 8.

42.   T.S. Szasz, "Mind Tapping: Psychiatric Subversion of Constitutional Rights," *Am. J. Psychiat.* 119:323, 1962. Of course, there is a difference between asking a question in order to obtain information relevant to the content of the question, and asking a question for purposes of psychological measurement. Questions on psychological tests about sexual behavior or religious belief, for example, may not be intended to discover anything about the subject's sexual experiences or religious beliefs. The questions are designed to measure psychological traits of flexibility, responsibility, psychological-mindedness, socialization, tolerance, and on. A test-taker's responses do not directly represent factual truth about himself.

43.   H. Silving, "Manipulation of the Unconscious in Criminal Cases," in L.A. Bear (ed.), *Law, Medicine, Science–And Justice*, (Springfield, Ill.: Thomas, 1964), p. 247; H. Silving, "Testing of the Unconscious in Criminal Cases," *Harv. L. Rev.* 69:683, 1956. Dr. Zigmond M. Lebensohn, then Chairman of the Committee on Public Information, American Psychiatric Association, presented testimony on the use of psychological tests in government before the Senate Subcommittee on Constitutional Rights, June 8, 1965, on behalf of the American Psychiatric Association. In part, he testified:

> I should now like to address myself briefly to one special aspect of the problem, namely, "invasion of privacy." It is my impression that this problem has been a major factor in stimulating these hearings in the first place. There is, of course, no blinking the fact that the more highly developed behavioral science becomes, the more sensitive becomes the question of invasion of privacy. If we are going to find out something about human behavior that will serve to advance mankind then obviously we have got to ask the right questions. We cannot settle for only those questions which might have been acceptable to our Victorian grandmothers. Our profession has long suffered, as this subcommittee well knows, from an understandable but mistaken belief on the part of the public that psychiatrists do little else but pry too closely into the more intimate aspects of a patient's life, with special emphasis on his sexual habits and religious concerns. It has been a cross for us to bear, so to speak, but we have looked upon it as an occupational hazard of psychiatric practice. It is gratifying to note however, that the public is gradually coming to accept the fact that if a psychiatrist is to uncover pathology and embark on corrective therapy, he cannot settle for information confined to "name, rank, and serial number." Fortunately, the confidentiality of information elicited in the doctor-patient relationship is reasonably well protected in our social and legal traditions–though not quite so well protected as we in psychiatry would like. Many of the states now have laws governing privileged communication which do prevent the physician and the psychiatrist

from divulging information about his patients without the patients' express permission. Even where such laws do not exist the patient still has the protection of a long and respected tradition, going back to Hippocrates, that the information he reveals to a physician will be held in strictest confidence.

The same degree of protection, unfortunately, does not yet pertain to government settings wherein employees who are tested may have the test results become a matter of record. Also, there is the possibility that the test results may be used by nonprofessional persons for purposes for which they were never intended. We do have a serious problem here and one to which I am certain this subcommittee will address its most thoughtful consideration. However, it is one thing to take steps to protect a patient or an employee against the misuse of confidential information elicited in a test or psychiatric interview, and quite another to discourage or prohibit the professional psychiatrist or psychologist from asking the questions in the first place. I make no particular plea for any particular questions that might be asked on these tests—for that is a scientific matter for professional workers in the field. I plead only for the principle that the questions which are asked are valid from the scientific point of view.

For example, in the Minnesota Multiphasic Personality Inventory Test [developed in 1942], a number of questions are asked about a person's attitude toward religion. Except for the fact that they are printed questions on a test form, they are not essentially different in their purpose from the kinds of questions that a psychiatrist might ask in more subtle ways in the course of several interviews. These questions are not for the purpose of prying into a person's normal and private religious life such as whether he is a Protestant, Catholic, or Jew. What these questions seek to elicit is the presence or absence of excessive "religiosity." Excessive religiosity may severely limit a person's usefulness on a job and may be a symptom of mental illness. Our mental hospitals are filled with patients suffering from paranoid disorders who think of themselves as prophets, saints, and saviors of the world. Some of them are very kind and harmless people but one would not want to appoint one of them as Ambassador to the Dominican Republic or as a member of the Peace Corps. It may be of special interest in this connection to note that for over 20 years the Methodist Board of Missions has made routine use of psychiatric and psychological evaluations for all applicants for overseas service....

In summary, I should like to say that psychological testing has long proved its usefulness in medicine, psychiatry, industry, and government agencies—especially in the Armed Forces. It holds great promise for making more effective use of personnel in our country. All possible encouragement should be given to its proper development. At the same time we must all be cognizant that safeguards must be developed which will protect persons seeking employment and advancement in government from inappropriate use of the tests and unjust verdicts based on isolated test results. It is imperative that the system under which the tests are given shall contain safeguards that are similar in their effectiveness to those that prevail in medical settings.

44. Of the widely used psychological test, the Minnesota Multiphasic Personality Inventory (MMPI), one critic alleged that "psychologists bicker interminably among themselves over the MMPI's 560-odd questions because no one seems able to agree what the answers mean." Although the MMPI's publisher (Psychological Corporation ) recommended against using the test as an employment-screening device, a number of government agencies insisted on doing so anyway. A critic said:

    Psychiatrists who hire out to the government need to take care what sort of program they get involved in, lest they end up making themselves and their profession look foolish. Infrequently the State Department requests employees it believes to be emotionally disturbed to see a psychiatrist, but there have been some complaints about the way the Department's consulting psychiatrist dispatches these cases. As a recent case illustrates, one twenty-five minute interview with a psychiatrist can mean the difference between holding a job in the Foreign Service or losing it.

45. "Potomac Perspective," *Prudential Securities Strategy Weekly,* June 12, 1996, p. 27. Stephen Hess, a distinguished scholar of the presidency at the Brookings Institution, says: "If it's a choice between bad character and good economic news, good economic news is always going to win," Quoted in E.C. Ladd, *op. cit. supra* note 7.

46. "Why Voters May Choose a Man They Don't Trust," *Wall Street Journal,* Sept. 20, 1996, p. 14.

# Chapter 4

# TEACHING AND WRITING

Let us assume that a psychiatrist is engaged in lighthearted talk at a gathering. He talks about a nonpatient, and by name, refers to him as a schizophrenic. Certainly, under these circumstances, the psychiatrist might be found to have slandered that person's character. The fact that the speaker happened to be a psychiatrist is of no moment in any action in defamation. The hazards are multiplied, though, where the psychiatrist has had a professional relationship with the person.[1]

The opening provision of the Bill of Rights is about freedom of speech—the First Amendment is the cornerstone of constitutional freedom—but it is cut across by restrictions. The right of free speech is not absolute at all times and under all circumstances. The lewd and obscene, the profane, the libelous, the insulting or "fighting" words, misrepresentation, perjury, false advertising, solicitation of crime, conspiracy, and the like are outside the area of protected speech.[2] The Supreme Court has said, "[S]uch utterances are no essential part of any exposition of ideas, and are of such slight social value as a step to truth that any benefit that may be derived from them is clearly outweighed by the social interest in order and morality."[3] These excluded areas do little or nothing to advance the central goal of the amendment, namely, "to assure a society in which 'uninhibited, robust, and wide open' public debate concerning matters of public interest would thrive."[4]

There is considerable doubt about the legal or ethical limitations on a psychiatrist making a disclosure about a patient or about a research subject, or about a person examined at the request of the court or an attorney, and it is having a chilling effect on publication. For example, at an annual winter meeting of the American Academy of Psychoanalysis, Dr. Edward A. Wolpert began his presentation of a paper, "Patients with the Personality of a Major Affective Disorder," observing that it is necessary to have the consent of a patient in order to present a case report, and not having that consent, he said that he would not present the paper he would have liked. Dr. Paul Chodoff, from the floor, interjected that consent is not necessary when the identity of the patient is concealed, but the question arose whether it is really possible to write a case report of a patient that would not lead to discovery. The next speaker, Dr. Silas L. Warner, addressing the audience on "Can Psychoanalytic Treatment Change Dreams?", said that he did not get the consent of his patient, and then wondered about whether he should have. In his presentation, Dr. Warner reported that his patient, when 20 years old, married a dull, kindly man (her boss). During the course of the marriage, she ran off, for a period of some two weeks, with the minister of her church. They both felt guilty about the adventure. He was transferred to another church and she felt branded with a scarlet A, and had dreams of being frightened by wild animals. Now, might not anyone (especially the patient) in Dr. Warner's home city, either reading or hearing the paper, discern the identity of the patient?[5]

In Philip Roth's novel, *My Life as a Man,* a patient in the waiting room of his psychiatrist's office opens a magazine and is upset on discovering an article written by the psychiatrist. It's about him! The patient's identity was changed from Jewish to Italian, but that was not much of a disguise.[6]

It was once said, in reference to a study of cases of suicided psychiatrists, that given three intimate personal facts, other psychiatrists would recognize the subjects. Dr. Maurice Grossman once reported a case study of the treatment of a "hopelessly" ill arthritic woman of some 50 years of age, whose illness (after 25 years of total disability) was mitigated by uncovering the psychopathologic factors perpetuating both the acute symptoms and disability. She returned to work, and continued her work until she retired on retirement pay. Professionals who attended the conference where the paper was presented immediately recognized the identity of the patient just by the factors listed here—age, sex, and physical illness history, which were all relevant and important for the conclusions being presented. Everything else, including geography, type of occupation, dates of the illness, factors of referral, where she was being treated for her arthritis, et cetera, were all altered to support the anonymity of the patient, yet she was recognized. As a result, Dr. Grossman did not submit his paper for publication in spite of the importance of the view of his colleagues who urged him to publish it.[7]

David Calof, a family therapist and hypnotherapist, writes in the opening of a book about his clients:[8]

> Writing a book about one's clients presents a quandary for a therapist. My clients share their secrets with me because they know those secrets are safe, and I in no way want to invalidate their trust. But at the same time I have witnessed remarkable demonstrations of human nature and behavior: in the course of a day I see things that most people never see, and it's hard not to want to share my experience with others. Ultimately, for two reasons, I decid-

ed in favor of telling. The first was that I realized I could disguise the individuals to the point where no one would recognize them, thus preserving their confidentiality. The second was that I believed that the stories are larger than the individuals themselves. In what they reveal about the workings of the human mind and body, they teach us a bit more about what it means to be human.

Legal and ethical issues also arise when a forensic expert publishes a book or article about a subject whom he has examined at the request of the court or attorney. While in this, as in the research situation, there is no physician-patient relationship, there is a fiduciary relationship. Among those pondering this kind of situation is one of the forensic psychiatrists who, on behalf of defense counsel, conducted a pretrial examination of John Gacy. Gacy was convicted in Chicago of murdering 33 young men and boys.[9] The psychiatrist would like to turn his notes into a book on Gacy, but Gacy would not give his permission. The question is posed: Is consent necessary in writing about an examinee? Must the examiner wait until the examinee dies? Is there a legal or ethical hazard when the examiner, or attorney, has an interest in the story value of the case?

There are also hazards when, even with the consent of the patient, the psychiatrist discloses a record made in the course of his office or hospital practice. It is generally known that disclosure to a third person, unless compelled by court order, requires the consent of the patient, but suppose the record contains statements that are defamatory about others, as for example, when a patient says that her husband is an alcoholic or is sexually abusing the children. Is there legal risk in the disclosure of confidential information, though done at the request of the patient, for such purposes as education, research, insurance, or litigation?

The following is a discussion of the legal and ethical issues involved in (1) writing an article or book or making a film about a patient, (2) writing about a research subject, (3) writing about a subject of a forensic examination on behalf of the court or attorney, and (4) writing in a medical record.

## 1. Writing an article or book or making a film about a patient

In writing an article or book about a patient, the nonpsychiatric physician usually has no difficulty, because the configuration of the body can be discussed without anyone recognizing the patient. Psychiatrists, on the other hand, are obliged to disguise their clinical data, even though it is detrimental to the scientific value of the material, in order to avoid the recognition of the patient. Freud, in his "Notes Upon a Case of Obsessional Neurosis," pointed out that the case history was not easy to compose, not only because of the inevitable compression, but also because of the need for greater discretion in print. His powers of presentation were taxed as the patient was well known in Vienna. Freud said, "How bungling are our attempts to reproduce an analysis; how pitifully we tear to pieces these great works of art Nature has created in the mental sphere." In his opening remarks, Freud explained how it is that intimate secrets could be more easily mentioned than the trivial details of personality by which a person could be readily identified, and yet it is just these details that play an essential part in tracing the individual steps in an analysis.

Freud published six case histories, now classic in psychoanalytic literature. The first of these, a case of hysteria, was turned down by the editor of the first journal to whom he sent it, apparently on the ground that it was a breach of discretion. In the fourth study, the actual name of the subject was used, but in this case, Freud had never seen him. In this study, based almost entirely on an autobiographical book, Freud apparently was unconcerned about public reprimand or a defamation suit, notwithstanding the fact that the subject, Dr. Daniel Paul Schreber, was a paranoid—the most litigious type of personality—and was the presiding judge in a division of an Appeals Court in Saxony and a member of a distinguished family. One might doubt that Freud would publish such an essay in today's climate even if Schreber were unsung or dead, or whether he were a public or private figure; one might have to contend with family members. Freud's other case histories are referred to as "The Case of Dora," "The Little Hans Case," "The Man with the Rats," "The Wolf-Man," and "A Case of Female Homosexuality."[10]

In 1964, in *Roe v. Doe*,[11] the United States Supreme Court accepted for review an action initiated by a psychiatric patient to prevent the publication of a book by her therapist. The patient, a university social work professor, claimed that the publication of the book, which appeared briefly before the suit was filed, violated her right of privacy and the confidential nature of the doctor-patient relationship. Giving credence to the defendant's claim that the disclosure was of scientific value, the trial court in New York formulated an innovative remedy. It enjoined only that portion of the book's distribution reasonably calculated to reach the nonscientific reader. The trial judge limited the book's distribution to the scientific community, that is, universities, medical schools, and other institutions of learning. The New York Appellate Court, however, found no justification for the distribution drawn by the trial court between "scientific readers" and the general public. It concluded that the plaintiff was entitled to either full protection or no protection at all and enjoined all distribution of the book.

The issue as presented to the United States Supreme Court was the propriety of a prior restraint on free expression in order to protect privacy or confidential information. In a relatively unusual action, after hearing oral arguments, the Supreme Court decided not to resolve the dispute. No reason was given for the dismissal, other than the usual recital that the order accepting the case had been "improvidently granted." The gossip has it that the case record was inadequate and confused. The *Roe v. Doe* case was not a suit for breach of contract, or a tort suit for malpractice, defamation, or invasion of privacy, which could occur in the event of distribution of the book.

The thought of writing a book about a patient may sharpen a therapist's interest in the patient, but there may be negative consequences. In disputes arising between a psychiatrist and a patient, the following questions are appropriate: Does the therapist unduly prolong treatment in order to obtain material for the book?[12] Is the treatment situation focused or skewed with interpretations in order to get material for the projected themes of the book? Was the note-taking done in order to supply material for the book, and did it inhibit the therapeutic relationship? And, inevitably, the writing about a patient will involve saying negative things, and what does that do to the ethical obligation of a doctor not to harm a patient? A book or article about a patient is not a public relations release: everything about the patient–healthy and unhealthy, holy and unholy, good and bad–must be in them. Thus, the psychiatrist's diagnosis, prognosis, comments, and conclusions create legal, ethical, and public relations problems.[13]

An examining psychiatrist who carries out an examination for forensic purposes–while not bound as is a treating psychiatrist by the ethical admonition of *primun non nocere* or by confidentiality–is confronted with the issue of potential harmful effects on the individual who hears a description of his psychodynamics in the adversarial context of a courtroom. Some forensic psychiatrists, out of concern for these effects, have requested the exclusion of the subjects of their testimony from the courtroom.[14]

What is decisive in cases such as *Roe v. Doe* is the patient's consent, or the lack of it, to the publication by the therapist. Without adequate disguise, consent of the patient to publication is required. The patient who consents with full knowledge may be considered like a joint venturer. The psychiatrist in *Roe v. Doe* claimed a verbal agreement. The complaint, however, argued that even if consent had been given, it should not be given effect because it was given during therapy. Consent at such time is meaningless, it was argued, for there is little likelihood of an informed or voluntary agreement in view of the patient's dependency upon the therapist and the submissive attitude that may be induced by the transference. And there is a question whether there is an "informed consent" when the patient has not seen the manuscript. In such cases, does one really know what one is consenting to? The law distinguishes between a particular retrospective waiver and a general waiver, holding the latter invalid.

In a case involving a famous multiple personality, Christine Costner Sizemore, whose life was the basis for the book (by psychiatrists C.H.

Thigpen and H.M. Cleckley) and subsequent movie classic (starring Joanne Woodward) "The Three Faces of Eve," challenged Twentieth Century Fox Film Corporation's claim that it holds the motion-picture rights to her life story. Actress Sissy Spacek had wanted to coproduce and star in a movie based on a new book by Sizemore, "In Sickness and Health," but negotiations bogged down when Fox claimed it held the rights to any movies about her. Fox claimed that it has owned those rights since 1956, when one of Sizemore's personalities signed over to Fox, "forever," the film rights to "all versions of my life story heretofore published or hereafter published" for $7,000. Sizemore's attorney contended that the original contract proves that Fox knew Sizemore was still deranged–beneath her signature were typed three more names: Eve White, Eve Black, and Jane. (The three Eves were timid "Eve White," flamboyant "Eve Black," and practical Jane.) In the new book, Sizemore details her life in the years following her development into an "integrated personality"–after her real self was distilled from the competing personalities through therapy. She alleged that she was unduly influenced in 1956 into signing away the rights to her life story by her then psychiatrist and author C.H. Thigpen.[15] The case has been settled.[16] Publishers are being advised to obtain the consent of all the multiples for the publication of a book by a person with MPD.[17]

What about writing about a patient who has died? The issue of psychiatric confidentiality in this situation leaped into public prominence when, on page one of the *New York Times*, it was reported that Dr. Martin Orne, who had treated the poet Anne Sexton for eight years, had turned over his complete files of the therapy, including more than 300 audiotapes of sessions with Sexton, to Diane Wood Middlebrook, a professor of English at Stanford University, for a biography.[18] Sexton killed herself by carbon-monoxide poisoning in 1974 after innumerable mental breakdowns. The release of the material ignited a firestorm of controversy and gasps of dismay.[19] Linda Sexton, the executor of her mother's estate, cooperated with the biographer and on the whole admired the end result, but some other members of the family were outraged. In a foreword to the book (some critics claim that writing a foreword to a book by a patient is unethical self-promotion at the expense of the patient), Dr. Orne said he gave Middlebrook the tapes only "after much soul-searching," and he added, "I also realized that Anne herself would have wanted to share this process–much as she did in her poetry, so that patients and therapist might learn from it." He wrote:[20]

> When Professor Diane Middlebrook requested an interview to discuss my work with Anne, it was uppermost in my mind how important it had been to Anne always to try to help others, especially in their writing. Although I had many misgivings about discussing any aspects of the therapy, which extended

over eight years, I also realized that Anne herself would have wanted to share this process—much as she did in her poetry—so that other patients and therapists might learn from it. After much soul-searching, and after being assured that Anne's family had given their encouragement and approval, I allowed Professor Middlebrook to have access to the audiotapes and my therapy file, including the early unpublished poems Anne brought to therapy. It is in the spirit of helping others that I also offer here a view of what I believe contributed to Anne's untimely death.

At a panel presentation at an annual meeting of the American Academy of Psychoanalysis, Dr. Paul Chodoff, coeditor of the book *Psychiatric Ethics*, asked for respect for Dr. Orne's judgment that release of the tapes served a useful purpose.[21] Middlebrook, who was modestly surprised by the furor, had expected far louder outcry over her report that Sexton's second therapist, a replacement after Dr. Orne moved away, not only slept with her but charged his regular fee for the time.[22] She notes that her biography of Sexton was not the first to use psychiatric records—Nancy Milford's biography of Zelda Fitzgerald (1970), Scott Donaldson's of John Cheever (1988), and Peter Pstwald's of Vaslav Nijinsky (1990) rely on extensive access to notes and interviews with psychiatrists who treated their subjects, to name only a few—but it was the first to use audiotapes of treatment, and that seems to have mattered most in shaping the critical opinions of commentators on the biographical use of these materials.[23]

Frederick Wiseman's film *Titicut Follies* contained scenes at Massachusetts Correctional Institution at Bridgewater to which "insane persons" charged with crime and "defective delinquents" were committed. He was enjoined from exhibition of the film in a proceeding brought by the state under its "obligation to protect the right of privacy of those committed to its custody." The decision is significant in that it protected the privacy of inmates at a correctional institution, who traditionally have been considered not to have any rights. The film depicts many inmates in situations which would be degrading to one of ordinary mentality and sensitivity. Although to a casual observer most of the inmates portrayed make little or no specific individual impression, others are shown in close-up pictures, sufficiently clearly exhibited (in some instances naked) to enable acquaintances to identify them. Wiseman contended that no asserted right of privacy may be protected from the publication of the film because the conditions at Bridgewater are matters of continuing public concern. Indeed, it was concern over conditions at Bridgewater which led various public officials a few years earlier to consider showing a documentary film in the hope that it might arouse public interest and lead to improvement. The court said, however, that a presentation to the public of conditions at an institution would not necessitate the inclusion of some episodes shown in the film, nor would it justify the depiction of identifiable inmates, who had not given valid written consents and releases, naked or in other embarrassing situations. No inmate shown in the film, by reason of past conduct, had any special news interest as a public figure.[24]

In a number of books, patients have written about their experiences in a mental hospital.[25] Some write about "oppression" in mental hospitals. Books by patients depicting their experience pose no problem of confidentiality, given that confidentiality is designed to protect the patient and the patient can consent to disclosure. But what about following discharge from a hospital, an individual seeks the records of his or her hospitalization to carry out the writing? The access is not sought for the purpose of further treatment (which would implement the concept of informed consent).

In *Godkin v. Miller*,[26] Janet Godkin had experienced several voluntary admissions for suicide attempts. Later she contracted to write a book about her experiences and wrote three hospitals for her records. Two refused and one ignored her request, so she brought a petition for declaratory relief, alleging a deprivation of property without due process. The court held, "We find no basis for the proposition that mental patients have a constitutionally protected property interest in the direct and...unrestricted access to their records which the appellants demand." And it said:[27]

> Nor do we find merit in [the] contention that the hospitals' refusal to disclose Mrs. Gotkin's records violated her right to privacy and control over her own body. This is not a case...in which a physician allegedly failed to disclose the risks which were involved in the course of treatment which he had prescribed. Mrs. Gotkin is not undergoing or contemplating treatment. She alleges that she wants the records to help her in the publication of her book, not to evaluate her medical condition. No serious interest in privacy or control over one's body is at issue.

If, however, Gotkin had sued the hospitals claiming malpractice in treatment, she could thereby have obtained the records. So hospitals, by and large, will accede to a patient's request for records, be it a past patient or not.

Dr. Roy R. Grinker, Jr. points out the extent that confidentiality was stressed in his father's analysis with Freud. "One day, Freud said he had heard from someone that Roy had repeated something from an analytic hour at the coffee-house. Roy suddenly burst into tears. Freud leaned over and said, 'Now, Dr. Grinker, you know what transference is.'"[28] Dr. Grinker Jr. encouraged his father to publish more about his relationship with Freud, but he consistently demurred on the grounds of confidentiality. "I disagreed with my father," he says. "Not only did he have interesting things to say, he truly was not bound by the rules of confidentiality. I can only imagine this was an unanalyzed piece of countertransference to Freud. My hunch is that my father had an 'idealizing-transference' to Freud, and that he felt special to him, and he wanted to keep it that way."[29] Dr. Grinker Jr., however, was told many anecdotes by his father about his analysis, including:[30]

> Freud was in the habit of having his and Anna's dogs in the consulting-room with the patient. If my father was telling a dream, or associating to it, and the dogs scratched at the door to be let out, Freud would do so. Then, when they scratched to get back in, a few minutes later, Freud would say, "Now the dogs are giving you another chance." He would open the door, they would rush at my father's genitals as he lay on the couch, nuzzling him. Roy could not remember which animal he was most terrified of, Anna's dog or Freud himself. One time, Freud, in his enthusiasm, got up to show Roy an Egyptian statute, tripped, fell forward on his nose, and lay there, clearly bleeding heavily. Roy the doctor knew he should do something; Roy the patient was too terrified to move. So Freud got up and took care of himself, leaving Roy with a dose of shame that has lasted over 50 years.

While respecting his father's wishes not to write about his analysis with Freud, Dr. Grinker Jr. says that he is delighted by the many books and TV shows about patients talking about their therapy. He says, "It is a breath of fresh air. I feel good that therapy is coming out of the closet. But I am all on the side of confidentiality—*from* the therapist, both before, during, and after therapy, including letters, memoranda, or tapes *á la* Martin Orne and Anne Sexton."[31]

## 2. *Writing about a research subject*

Publishing research studies or publishing clinical material in support of new insights or discovery is a professional obligation. The physician has an obligation not only to his patient but also to his profession and also to the general public. To satisfy both the obligations of service and education, there are many techniques used to disguise the identity of an individual or the nature of the material, but they are not always successful. Research studies, to test certain hypotheses, may require sensitive and intimate detail about the subjects, but in most cases the studies deal with statistical data, so that the published material does not lead to any individual, but sometimes the data is individually identifiable. The research project may require a follow-up, so in this event individual identification is necessary. Questionable practices have grown up gathering broad demographic data of intimate detail, hoping that significant trends will be developed by computer analysis. Many of these projects, containing intimate data about individuals, have later become public documents.

In an individual case study, be it of a patient or research subject, sometimes merely the author's byline leads to the individual's identification, so some authors use a pseudonym. Michael Crichton, while a student at Harvard Medical School, wrote potboiling paperbacks under the pseudonym Jeffery Hudson.[32] Crichton explains why he chose anonymity: "I thought I was going to be a practicing physician, and so I felt it necessary for my patients to come to me without worrying whether they'd appear in the next book. To allay those concerns, I decided not to disguise them but to disguise myself."[33]

The law, as noted, does not draw a distinction between material published in scientific journals or textbooks and that published in the lay press as magazine articles or books for the general public. The past chairman of the American Psychiatric Association's Committee on Confidentiality, Dr. Maurice Grossman, suggested, at least in the case of popular publications, that no matter how camouflaged the material, the project and the material should be discussed with the individual and permission obtained in writing.[34] Many researchers, however, find release forms not very satisfactory. When presented too soon to a research subject whose case is being investigated, it may frighten him and stiffen a relationship that is important to keep informal and friendly. But with an oral understanding the researcher may be caught as was one academic researcher, Dr. Jones, who is pseudonymous at his request.[35]

The case is question was referred for study to Dr. Jones because of his reputation for research in the area. The subject himself had sought consultation from a scientific investigator about his experiences, and it was upon this solicitation that Dr. Jones began his investigation of the case. He spent a lot of money, time, and energy on the investigation, and paid for the expenses of some special tests from his research funds. He had an oral understanding with the subject from a fairly early stage that he would be free, if he wished, to write and publish a scientific report of his investigation of the case, but no written agreement to that effect was signed.

After probing the case quite thoroughly, Dr. Jones thought that a report of it should be published. At this point, Dr. Jones raised the matter with the research subject and, for several years, the subject raised no objections to publication, but then the subject became concerned about the reaction of his family should they learn of his behavior. He wrote to Dr. Jones saying that he objected to publication. Dr. Jones, by telephone, gave him appropriate reassurances, and an oral agreement was reached.

Later yet another change of mind. The subject thought that publication of the study might generate publicity. At any rate, he asked Dr. Jones to postpone publishing his study until a later time. Some years went by. From time to time, Dr. Jones wrote to the subject, always to be told that the right time had not yet come. Eventually, Dr. Jones lost patience and decided that he had a right to publish his data. He wanted some return for all the work he had put into the study and he also had obligations to donors who had funded his research. He advised the subject, by letter, that he was going to proceed with publication but, as previously agreed, would conceal all identities with pseudonyms. There apparently was no reply.

Dr. Jones consulted his lawyer, because a third person passed on to him a threat that the subject would sue if he published. The advice was mixed: "There is a risk in proceeding with publication, but you have a right to use your data in publication."

The research eventually was published as a book. It included a certain amount of personal detail, but nearly all of it was considered essential in order to properly get the background for the case. Pseudonyms were used. The book, unexpectedly, generated a good deal of publicity. Some reporters succeeded in tracing the subject and tried to interview him. Friends who read newspaper stories telephoned the subject asking about the case and the newspaper reports. So the question arises: Might it be said that whenever a subject of a writing is discoverable, or in fact discovered, there has not been adequate disguise? *Post hoc, ergo propter hoc?* Should a researcher be responsible when a news reporter puts a spotlight to the case?

The subject filed suit against Dr. Jones and the publisher alleging invasion of privacy and also—much to the annoyance of Dr. Jones—medical malpractice. The subject had never had a physician-patient relationship with Dr. Jones at any time—Dr. Jones was solely involved in the case as a research investigator—but the attorney was probably seeking to reach into his medical malpractice insurance and perhaps also to embarrass Dr. Jones with his medical colleagues. Be that as it may, it ought to be noted that while a claim of medical malpractice may be embarrassing, it may be covered by a professional's insurance policy while an action for breach of contract or invasion of privacy may not be.[36] A complainant's attorney does the defendant a "favor" by alleging an action that is covered by insurance.[37]

Dr. Jones countersued, claiming breach of contract. He argued: there was an oral agreement on publication, the subject had benefited from his advice as a scientific consultant, and further, the subject was estopped from complaining by virtue of the fact that from a fairly early date he permitted, even encouraged him to spend much time and money in research of the case.

Finally, however, the parties agreed to an out-of-court settlement. The affair was costly to Dr. Jones, spending well over $35,000 out of pocket. His medical malpractice insurer did little or nothing about the case. He applied to his university to be allowed to pay his attorney fees out of his research funds but this was refused on the ground—perhaps reasonable, perhaps not—that it would set a precedent for academicians to make irresponsible statements and then ask for the use of their research funds to defend actions for defamation brought against them. Some universities, however, protect faculty members against "errors and omissions."

Naturally, Dr. Jones feels that he was treated very badly in this matter, both by the law and by the subject having gone back on his word to him, and on the other hand, the subject also feels aggrieved. In these matters how does one obtain an "informed consent" for publication? Does the patient or research subject actually know to what he or she is consenting? Does consent to participate in research include consent to publication of research? Can there be a valid, informed consent to publication without seeing the manuscript on completion? Consent to publication at the inception (be it oral or written) might not be said to be an informed consent.

Moreover, the doctrine of informed consent, in treatment or experimentation, includes a right to withdraw at any time. Typically, consent forms in treatment or experimentation expressly state the patient's or subject's right of withdrawal without explanation, but even when that is not made explicit, it remains implicit. Informed consent is thus deemed an ongoing condition of therapy or experimentation, and the patient or subject who has forgotten that consent was once given, or whatever, remains free to withdraw.[38] Under this doctrine, a research subject could say that he did not consent or could otherwise revoke the agreement. But many may argue that the doctrine of informed consent, as formulated, should not apply to research where the study itself is without risk, and that the general law on the performance of a promise ought to apply. The issue apparently has not been put to a test.

### 3. Writing about a subject of a forensic examination on behalf of the court or attorney

Writing about a subject of a forensic examination on behalf of the court or attorney may also present legal and ethical problems though the case is one of high profile. Trials generate public records, but there is need for the approval of those involved with regard to the use of information obtained as a result of a fiduciary relationship which is not a part of the public record. When an examination is court-ordered, the interviewer usually advises the accused that what is discussed will not be held confidential because a report will be written to the court (he does not advise that what is discussed will not be held confidential because he will write an article or book about him).[39] When an examination is at the request of an attorney, the confidentiality of the report is protected under the attorney-client privilege until such time as the attorney elects to use it.[40]

Consider the scenario. On being called to examine a person accused of crime, particularly a mass murder, the expert thinks, "This story would make

a very good article or book or movie." There arises a potentially serious conflict of interest. The danger is that the report may be prepared more to guarantee the value of the story—by making the case unnecessarily flamboyant,
or even ensuring the accused's conviction—than to secure the best legal
defense. The story may prove to be most valuable, in fact, if the client is executed. The pathway that may be good for literary purposes may not be for
the client. The expert with a book in mind would be interested in getting
extensive notes, far more than what would be required for a report (and
charging the attorney for the time spent on collecting the data). The adage,
"keep your eye on the ball," is likely violated when a situation is exploited.
Interviews are likely to be diverted from their necessary legal purpose when
the hidden agenda is writing about the subject. Suppose, though, the forensic expert says that the idea of writing about the subject did not come to him
until some time after the completion of the legal proceedings. It would surely be difficult, however, to monitor a subjective standard, for who can know
what was in the examiner's mind? Of course, anyone may make fair comment on what is a matter of public record, but the problem arises with inside
or nonpublic information.

It might also be said that the forensic expert who goes into a jail ostensi-
bly to prepare a report but with a book in mind commits a misrepresentation, and abuse of a special privilege. The general public does not have that
right of admission, and news gatherers are regarded no differently.[41] The
Supreme Court has ruled on a number of occasions that newsmen have no
right of access to prisons or to interviewing inmates beyond the rights generally extended to members of the public.[42] Prison wardens are on the alert
against the news media exploiting the career (or execution) of a criminal, and
they try to keep newsmen out. Norman Mailer writes in *The Executioner's
Song*:[43]

> The problem, which you could not explain to a newspaper man too exactly or
> to a judge either...was that tension in the prison often resulted from attention
> being focused on one inmate. He could get to be like a baseball star who
> wouldn't obey his manager. The risk of media exposure went deeper than
> [Gary] Gilmore being able to shoot off his mouth—the risk was in the reaction
> of other inmates. At any time a convict became bigger than the prison, it had
> to create disciplinary episodes all over the place.

The accused, however, has a right to see an attorney or one working under
him. Misrepresenting, attorneys have brought writers into prison alleging
that they are an associate. In the Gary Gilmore case, Norman Mailer used an
attorney (who was also a writer) to get material from Gilmore when he was
in prison. With a hidden recorder, he taped interviews that were used by

Mailer in the aforementioned book on Gilmore's life and death, *The Executioner's Song.*[44] In the case of Wayne Williams in Atlanta, his attorney, Mary Welcome, apparently ushered a freelance reporter into the jail by telling a guard, "She's with me"; the guard assumed the woman was part of the defense team.[45]

Now does it make a difference when the accused enters into an agreement to sell his story to the attorney, or expert, than when the story is obtained from him unknowingly? A series of cases over the past decade has prompted debate on several issues that arise when accused persons and their lawyers start talking about the literary or video value of their cases. There has been public debate on whether criminals should be limited in selling their own works, words, or thoughts about their crimes or court cases. Is there a danger when a defense attorney, or expert, has a direct interest in the story value of the case–either by taking the client's media rights as a fee, or by the attorney, or expert, arranging to write his own version of the case.[46] Norman Mailer has a passage in *The Executioner's Song* on this point:[47]

> [Lawyer] Bob Moody didn't think it would work to negotiate contracts for books or films while trying to advise Gary [Gilmore] on his legal situation. Suppose, at some point, Gary wished to change his mind and appeal, why then the rights for his life story would be considerably less. A potential conflict of interest existed right there. You just didn't want a situation where a lawyer might have to ask himself whether his client's death might be more profitable to him...A second lawyer would be necessary.

A number of courts have noted the danger in a defense attorney looking to profit from the client's story. There apparently has not been thus far litigation of a controversy involving a psychiatric expert in these matters, but the lawyer analogy is apropos. In the case of convicted mass killer Juan Corona, the California District Court of Appeals ordered a new trial on finding a conflict of interest in a fee arrangement in which Corona turned over the rights to his story to defense attorney Richard Hawk. Hawk had a writer participate in defense deliberations in order to detail Corona's conviction in the killing of 25 itinerant farm laborers. Hawk said he needed the money to fund a $50,000 defense, but the court ruled that on obtaining his client's literary rights, the attorney "was devoted to two masters with conflicting interests–he was forced to choose between his own pocketbook and the best interest of his client."[48]

Patricia Hearst, facing a charge of robbing a San Francisco bank, wanted the "best lawyer in America," F. Lee Bailey, she said, but he would undertake her defense only on the condition that he would have the rights to her story. That being the agreement, Bailey contracted with G.P. Putnam's Sons for a $225,000 payment for a manuscript and with *Ladies' Home Journal* for $40,000 for serial rights to a book called "The Defense of Patty Hearst." But on conviction, Patty Hearst sought a new trial claiming that decisions were made in her trial that favored Bailey's plan to write a book about the case. As we have noted, Bailey countered with a public statement that if Patty Hearst did not shut up, he would divulge information that she could be charged with crimes much more serious than the bank robbery of which she was convicted.[49]

The U.S. Court of Appeals for the Ninth Circuit refused to grant a new trial but said a hearing was called for on whether Bailey may have "pursued his own interest in publication rights rather than her interest in acquittal." The court pointed out the American Bar Association's caution against the "dangers inherent in simultaneous lawyering and authoring." The ABA's Code of Professional Responsibility states: "Prior to conclusion of all aspects of the matter giving rise to his employment, a lawyer shall not enter into any agreement or understanding with a client or a prospective client by which he acquires an interest in publication rights with respect to the subject matter of his employment or proposed employment."[50] The prohibition is rarely enforced, however, perhaps because it often turns out to be "victimless" in some sense of that word.[51]

The matter of criminals themselves, or in association, writing their stories for profit has given rise to some legislation on the subject. Prompted by the literary agents pursuing the inside story of the Son-of-Sam killings of couples in parked cars, New York State Senator Emanuel Gold introduced a bill formally titled, "Distribution of Moneys Received as a Result of the Commissions of Crime" (known as the Son-of-Sam law). In an interview, Senator Gold stated that "he developed the bill after reading a newspaper account during the hunt for the 'Son of Sam' stating that the killer 'stood to get rich' and that there would be people 'waiting at the precinct house to get him to sign a contract.'"[52] It was shocking also to read about Gary Gilmore disbursing thousands in royalties from his death cell, having mercilessly taken two lives for a handful of dollars. The New York Legislature was convinced–profits from the sale of a criminal's story should be made available to the victims of the crime.

The event which triggers the New York antiprofit statute is when a third party (be it a "person, firm, corporation, partnership, association or other legal entity") makes a contract with a person accused or convicted of a crime or with his representatives or assignee "with respect to the reenactment of such crime by way of movie, book, magazine article, tape recording, phonograph record, radio or television presentation, live entertainment of any kind, or from the expression of such accused or convicted person's thoughts, feelings, opinions of emotions regarding such crime."[53] The law adopted in

New York mandated that proceeds be kept in escrow for five years and then turned over to any victim who obtains a civil judgment against the criminal at that time. Even without such legislation, royalties provide a source to satisfy judgments obtained under common law or wrongful death statutes, but this law provided for keeping the moneys in escrow even before a judgment is obtained. The law also provided that in the event a criminal defendant sold his story before trial, and later won acquittal, the profits would be released to him. A similar law was adopted in a number of other states.[54]

Criminals writing their own stories, for profit or otherwise, is nothing new. They include classics by Anton Chekhov, Fedor Dostoyevsky, and Alexander Solzhenitsyn, who were at some point criminals in their societies. Prison inmates in the United States, while not reaching that level of literary attainment, have become authors of some notoriety. Caryl Chessman (the "Red Light Bandit"), sentenced to die in 1948 and executed in 1960, wrote three books while on death row. Three convicts on New Jersey's death row–Edgar Smith, Thomas Trantino, and Rubin "Hurricane" Carter–published memoirs within a few years of each other. During the last decade or so, at least six of those convicted of Watergate crimes wrote books about it. Jack Henry Abbott's correspondence as a convict with Norman Mailer became a literary celebration, "In the Belly of the Beast," and led to his parole.[55] More recently, Mumia Abu-Jamal, now in a Pennsylvania prison sentenced to death for the murder of a Philadelphia police officer, published a collection of his prison writings–an account of brutalities and humiliation of prison life and an indictment of racism and political bias in the American judicial system.[56]

The Son-of-Sam antiprofit law would not only deprive the convicted person of profiting from his crime, but it would also bar a defense attorney from gaining his legal fees, or funding the defense (including the compensating of experts), by selling his client's story. The New York Legislature, in 1981, enacted an amendment to its law allowing payments to representatives or attorneys of a convicted person up to one-fifth of the funds paid into an escrow account.[57]

In England, we may note, there has been the practice of certain newspapers buying the stories of persons charged with crimes, in some cases to help defray the cost of legal representation and expert witnesses. The practice, known as checkbook journalism, has been severely criticized and frowned on by the Press Council. In 1966, the Council issued its first declaration of principle against the practice. This declaration followed upon the growing disquiet surrounding checkbook journalism during the early 1960s. The Council's view, in essence, is that no person convicted of a criminal offense should profit from his crime by the publication of stories about him or his deeds, nor should any member of his family, nor should any arrangement be entered into which ultimately he or his family are the beneficiaries. The issue surfaced again in the case of Peter William Sutcliffe who was convicted in 1981 of the murder of thirteen women, but generally, since the Council's declaration in 1966, British newspapers have abided by its spirit. It is also to be noted that the use of payments to cover defense legal costs was more common before the introduction of legal aid. In any event, because checkbook journalism continues to occur, especially in notorious cases, the government in England has recently said it will be looking into the possibility of reclaiming some of the monies used in defense, in light of any subsequent income arising from newspaper and other sale of stories.[58]

The first application of the New York law came in 1981, four years after its passage in 1977, to reroute funds earmarked to John Wojtowicz, the bank robber played in the film "Dog Day Afternoon." The manager of the bank who was among the hostages nine years earlier in the robbery was awarded $20,000 out of the escrow account.[59] In another case, involving Son-of-Sam himself, David Berkowitz, the law was upheld by the appellate division of the New York Supreme Court over challenges on First Amendment and other grounds. The law also withstood another challenge, by Salvador Agron (known as the "Cape Man" murderer), that it deprived him of the right to make a contract.[60]

A number of legal commentators argue strongly that the statutes are objectionable on First Amendment and other grounds. One says: "To deprive the accused person of the ability to express his views and to fetter the other contracting party with such burdensome responsibilities that it will avoid publishing the speech of the accused person penalizes not only the accused person and the other contracting party, but also society as a whole."[61] Another says: "The [New York] statute acts as a disincentive to the accused criminal's writing of his history."[62]

In 1991, in *Simon & Schuster v. New York Crime Victims Board,*[63] the U.S. Supreme Court invalidated New York's "Son of Sam" law. According to the Court, the New York legislature did not narrowly tailor the statute to serve the purpose of providing compensation of crime victims but rather imposed a financial burden on speech based on its content. The Court noted that the New York statute applied to any work that expressed the criminal's thoughts about the crime, however incidentally or tangentially. Moreover, the Court noted, the statute applied to any author who admitted commission of a crime, regardless of whether the person was ever accused or convicted. The Court concluded that the "Son of Sam" law was overinclusive because it reached many works that did not enable criminals to profit from their crimes.[64]

A leaf from the case of lawyers writing about or in association with their clients may be applied to the case of the forensic psychiatrist writing about, or collaborating with, an examinee. There is involved the same potential conflict of interest and breach of fiduciary relationship. There is also another consideration. Once the defense counsel elects to use his examining expert's report, all of the notes of the expert would likely have to be made available to the prosecutor through discovery or otherwise (notwithstanding a contrary ruling by the trial court in the Hinckley trial).[65] In some cases, the notes may be legally advantageous to the client, but they may be legally harmful in other cases. They could be legally harmful, for example, if the notes indicate that the accused knew what he was doing at the time of the commission of the act.

## 4. Writing in a medical record

The laws in a number of states specifically provide that the patient's full medical record must be disclosed upon request by the patient to a person designated by him (such as to another doctor, insurance company, or employer).[66] Some doctors try to protect the privacy of third persons, as well as that of the patient, by providing only specific information or a summary of the record, which may be sufficient, or they mark out the statements about third persons, but this may appear to be a tampered record. By a review in chambers, the judge may enter such orders as may be necessary in order to protect the confidentiality, privacy, and safety of other persons.

Not very much attention has been given to the disclosure of sensitive information in a patient's record regarding persons other than the patient. Particularly in the case of the mentally ill, records may contain highly private information concerning the patient's relatives and associates. The information may have been provided by these other persons, or the patient may have talked about them in the course of treatment. Indeed, a psychiatric record devoid of sensitive and possibly inaccurate information about other persons is the exception rather than the rule. Disclosure may damage their reputation, or cause them severe emotional distress, or otherwise be harmful to them.[67]

So, even when a patient consents to release, the health care provider must be careful about releasing records containing information about others. It may constitute an invasion of their privacy, or may be defamatory about them. One who divulges an allegation by another may find himself liable, although he did not indicate his own belief in the truth of the statement. Unless privileged to make the disclosure, the health care provider is responsible even though the views clearly purport to be those of the patient. Each publication of a defamatory statement, including republication, is a separate tort.

## CONCLUSION

Freedom of speech is highly valued in American society, but there are limitations. The health care professional must be on the alert on the hazards in writing or disclosing information about a patient or nonpatient. It is somewhat a hazard even when the patient or nonpatient has died. The dead or their survivors do not have a cause of action for defamation or invasion of privacy, these being personal rights that die with the individual (even if a person is defamed while alive, the cause of action under common law dies with him), but there may be a cause of action when the words independently reflect upon and defame the survivors, as by calling a man's dead mother a whore.[68]

Two important interests are here pitted against each other–publication vs. confidentiality. Quite often the law is faced with a conflict between two competing positive values. The resolution of a conflict between good vs. good is often more difficult to resolve than a conflict of good vs. evil. In the matter at hand, the value in maintaining the confidentiality of a patient comes up against the value in educating members of one's profession and also the general public. Quite properly, physicians, especially those connected with educational institutions, are encouraged to write, report, teach, and they further the cause of good treatment thereby. The use of case material is essential in the education and training of future doctors. Collection of clinical data in research is necessary to find factors that relate to syndromes, and to determine efficacy of treatment approaches. In medicine, generally this is usually no problem, but in psychiatry all the material touches on the sensitive and personal.

The psychiatrist is entitled to protection, we would say, when he writes in a nonsensational way, and includes no names or easily recognized identities. Otherwise, we chill that robust discussion we so much prize under the First Amendment. Fear is very damaging, and it is not allayed by questionable insurance coverage. The pseudonymous Dr. Jones, like innumerable others, is now so jittery about a lawsuit that he acts and talks as though paralyzed. Like one who has had a gun put to his head, his mind has been cluttered with the trauma of litigation.

## NOTES

1. On the ethics of a psychiatrist expressing an opinion about an individual without an examination, see the discussion in Part IV, Chapter 3.
2. Chaplinsky v. New Hampshire, 315 U.S. 568 (1942); Koningsberg v. State Bar of California, 366 U.S. 36 (1961).

3. Chaplinsky v. New Hampshire, 315 U.S. at 571.

4. Buckley v. Valeo, 424 U.S. 1, 93 (1976).

5. Presentations at 25th Winter Meeting of the American Academy of Psychoanalysis, New York, Dec. 6, 1981.

6. P. Roth, *My Life as a Man* (New York: Bantam Books, 1975).

7. Correspondence from Dr. Maurice Grossman.

8. *The Couple Who Became Each Other/And Other Tales of Healing From a Hypnotherapist's Casebook* (New York: Bantam, 1996), p. 14.

9. J. Fritsch, "Gacy found guilty/jury turns down insanity defense," *Chicago Tribune*, March 13, 1980, p. 1; J. Fritsch, "Gacy sentenced to death," *Chicago Tribune*, March 14, 1980, p.1.

10. R. Slovenko, *Psychiatry and Law* (Boston: Little, Brown, 1973), pp. 438-439. It may be noted that subsequently, when Freud became famous, analysands came forward boasting proudly that they were patients of Freud.

11. 420 U.S. 307 (1975).

12. Jeffrey Toobin claims that attorney Robert Shapiro took on the O.J. Simpson defense with an eye on a book deal, and spent more effort on making himself look good than helping his client, to whom he proposed a plea bargain fairly late in the proceedings. J. Toobin, *The Run of His Life* (New York: Random House, 1996).

13. In a review of Dr. Irvin D. Yalon's book *Love's Executioner and Other Tales of Psychotherapy* (New York: Basic Books, 1989), Eileen Simpson writes: "The complaint sometimes voiced by readers of case histories written for the professional journals–that the analyst or psychiatrist is insufficiently candid about his countertransference (negative) feelings toward the patient–cannot be leveled against Dr. Yalom. In writing about Betty, for example, he says that he has always been repulsed by fat women, and that this 250-pounder is no exception. (When, at the end of treatment, she taunts him for hardly ever looking at her during the first six months of treatment, and demands a hug rather than a handshake in compensation, he says, 'When we embraced, I was surprised to find that I could get my arms all the way around her..') His need to confess his errors in technique is great. 'I had botched this case beyond belief,' he says. Or, 'This was one of my dumb, harebrained, manipulative ploys which always backfire....' Although Dr. Yalom says these case histories will 'be useful to therapists and/or other patients,' the use of the word 'tales' in the book's subtitle suggests that his primary desire is not to instruct but to entertain." E. Simpson, "'I Had Botched This Case Beyond Belief,'" *New York Times Book Review*, Sept. 4, 1989, p. 5.

14. See L.H. Strasburger, "'Crudely, without Any Finesse': The Defendant Hears His Psychiatric Evaluation," *Bull. Am. Acad. Psychiatry & Law* 15:229, 1987; E. Tanay, "The Expert Witness as a Teacher," *id.* 8:401, 1980; J. Gross, "Sutton and Dinkins: Labor of Law and Love," *New York Times*, Aug. 5, 1997, p. 1; see also the chapter on stigma of psychiatric discourse.

15. R.G. Blumenthal, "After All These Years, Here Is the Fourth Face of Eve: Plaintiff," *Wall Street Journal*, Feb. 1, 1989, p. B-1; N.J. Easton, "The real 'Eve'

faces court battle over biography," *Detroit News*, Feb. 13, 1989, p. B-3; D. Van Biema & M. Grant, "Three Faces of Eve Told Her Story, Now Chris Sizemore Is Battling a Major Studio Over Movie Rights and Wrongs," *People*, March 1989, p. 79.

16. "'Faces of Eve' Woman Settles Film Co. Lawsuit," *New York City Tribune*, June 21, 1990, p. 5.

17. "60 Minutes," CBS, Oct. 22, 1989.

18. *New York Times*, July 15, 1991, p. 1.

19. Special Section, "Anne Sexton and the Ethics of Psychotherapy," *J. Am. Acad. Psychoanalysis* 20:633-669, 1992; Symposium, "Privacy, Professionalism & Psychiatry," *Transaction/Society*, Jan/Feb. 1992, pp. 5-29; R.L. Goldstein, "Psychiatric Poetic License? Post-Mortem Disclosure of Confidential Information in the Anne Sexton Case," *Psychiatric Annals* 22:341, 1992; response, Ltrs., "The Anne Sexton Case: Protecting Confidentiality?" *Psychiatric Annals* 22:586, 1992; D. Gelman, "Secrets of the Couch," *Newsweek*, July 29, 1991, p. 54; J. E. Lifschutz, "The Anne Sexton Tapes: Confidentiality in Psychoanalysis and Psychotherapy," *Am. Psychoanalyst* 26:8, 1992; L. Morrow, "Pains of the Poet–and Miracles," *Time*, Sept. 23, 1991, p. 76; K. Hausma, "Psychiatrist Criticized Over Release of Poet's Psychotherapy Tapes," *Psychiatric News*, Sept. 6, 1991, p. 2; C. Sherman, "Biography Sparks Confidentiality Dispute," *Clinical Psychiatry News*, Sept. 1991, p. 1.

20. Foreword to D.W. Middlebrook, *Anne Sexton: A Biography* (New York: Houghton Mifflin, 1991), p. xvii.

21. N. Terestman, "Meeting Report/The Limits of Confidentiality: A Debate," *Academy Forum* (American Academy of Psychoanalysis), Fall 1992, p. 10.

22. H. Dudar, "The Author in the Middle of the Sexton-Tape Debate," *Wall Street Journal*, Sept. 24, 1991, p. 12.

23. D.W. Middlebrook, *Anne Sexton: A Biography*, at p. 402. And it might be added that books by physicians about their patients who have died abound. The medical writer Dennis L. Breo of the American Medical Association newspaper *American Medical News* provides from medical reports the medical care histories of the rich and the famous in the book *Extraordinary Care* (Chicago: Chicago Review Press, 1986). In the book *The Private Life of Chairman Mao* (New York: Random House, 1994), Dr. Li Zhisui, who describes himself as Mao's primary personal physician from 1954 to 1976, recounts Mao's appetite for young women and fatty pork, his addiction to sleeping pills, his adherence to esoteric Taoist sexual practices, his reluctance to bathe or brush his teeth. Apparently no reviewer of the book called into the question the propriety of a physician revealing a patient's private life albeit after the death of the patient. See, *e.g.*, P.G. Pickowicz, "Party Pathology: Mao's Doctor Speaks," *Wall Street Journal*, Nov. 21, 1994, p. 12; M. B. Hyoung, "The Parts Left Out of the Little Red Book, " *New York Times Book Review*, Nov. 27, 1994, p. 12.

   In France, Dr. Claude Gubler, President Francois Mitterand's personal physician, was given a suspended four-month sentence in prison for writing a book about him following his death. Mitterand's family complained about the book. M. Peyrot, "Le docteur Gubler condamné á quatre mois de prison avec sursis pour violation du secret professional," *Le Monde*, July 7/8, 1996, p. 18. In the book, Dr. Gubler disclosed that prostate cancer that eventually killed Mitterand had been with him from the start of his two presidential terms. Many Frenchmen reacted to the news that Mitterand had duped them about his health for more than a decade by condemning Dr. Gubler for betraying a confidence. C.R. Whitney, "The Secret Mitterrrand Couldn't Keep," *New York Times*, Jan. 17, 1996, p. 4.

24.  Commonwealth v. Wiseman, 356 Mass. 251, 249 N.E.2d 610 (1969); noted in *Colum. L. Rev.* 70:259, 1970; *Harv. L. Rev.* 83:1722, 1970; *Suffolk L. Rev.* 4:197, 1969. In a Reuters photo published worldwide, patients at Moscow's psychiatric hospital are shown close up as they registered to vote in Russia's presidential election in July 1996. Public interest about even mental patients voting in an unprecedented election in Russia apparently was considered to outweigh privacy. The photo appears among other places in the *Detroit News*, July 4, 1996, p. 9.

25.  See, *e.g.*, M. Glenn (ed.), *Voices from the Asylum* (New York: Harper & Row, 1974); C. Steir (ed.), *Blue Jolts/True Stories from the Cuckoo's Nest* (Washington, D.C.: New Republic Books, 1978). A classic book is Clifford Beers' *A Mind That Found Itself: An Autobiography* (New York: Doubleday, 1908). Another is *Memoirs of My Nervous Illness* (Cambridge: Harvard University Press, 1988 ed.) by Daniel Paul Schreber, a member of the High Court of Saxony who was hospitalized in the latter part of the 19th century. A recent book about Schreber based on hospital records and interviews is Z. Lothane, *In Defense of Schreber/Soul Murder and Psychiatry* (Hillsdale, N.J.: Analytic Press, 1992).

26.  514 F.2d 125 (2d Cir. 1975).

27.  514 F.2d at 130.

28.  R.R. Grinker, "Remarks at the Presentation of the Presidential Award for Distinguished Service and Scientific Contributions to Roy R. Grinker, Sr., M.D.," *J. Am. Acad. Psychoanal.* 22:321, 1994.

29.  Communication to author.

30.  R.R. Grinker, *op. cit. supra.*

31.  Communication to author.

32.  The real Hudson was a dwarf in the court of England's King Charles II; Crichton is 6 feet 9 inches.

33.  E. McDowell, "Behind the best sellers/Michael Crichton," *New York Times Book Review*, Feb. 8, 1981. p. 30.

34.  Personal communication.

35.  I am grateful to Dr. Jones for the information about the study.

36.  Many professional liability policies insuring doctors cover "claims based on professional services rendered in the practice of the insured's profession." This coverage may be said to be limited to the treatment context and thus would not cover research or publication. The professional liability insurance policy of the Medical Protective Company, for example, "would provide

protection for claims which arose out of research activities involving interviews of subjects and psychological testing, but would not provide coverage for claims arising from the publication of the information." Correspondence of March 8, 1982, from Robert J. Miller, Vice President of Medical Protective Company.

Other professional liability policies provide coverage for "injury resulting from professional services rendered...resulting from any claim or suit based upon...malpractice, error, negligence or mistake, assault, slander, libel [or] undue familiarity." The American Psychiatric Association policy (Chubb) covered "the publication or utterance of a libel or slander or of other defamatory or disparaging material or a publication or utterance in violation of an individual's right of privacy, except publications or utterances in the course of or related to advertising, broadcasting or telecasting activities conducted by or on behalf of the named insured."

Viking/Penguin decided in 1982 to provide its authors with free liability insurance coverage, and it is widely expected that other publishers will eventually do the same. The Media Professional Insurance Company is offering publishers a plan similar to Viking's, which carries the endorsement of the Authors League. The policy covers loss by libel, slander, invasion of privacy, plagiarism, copyright infringement or unfair competition. The Viking/Penguin plan, underwritten by the Employees Reinsurance Corporation, includes legal fees and is a $25,000 deductible policy, with the publisher covering all but $1,000 of the $25,000. The policy carries a $3 million maximum per claim or for all claims in any one year. E. McDowell, "Publishing: Free Insurance," *New York Times*, April 2, 1982, p. 23; R. Harris, "Insurance for writers," *The Nation*, April 3, 1982, p. 402.

The very insurability of intentional acts or punitive damages continues to produce a split among the courts deciding the issue. The insurability of intentional acts or punitive damages is often said to contravene public policy, despite specific coverage in a policy. To allow coverage, it is said, would defeat the purpose of such damages, namely, to punish the wrongdoer and deter similar conduct. M.T. Stoll, "Punitive Damages in Missouri," *Mo. L. Rev.* 42:593, 1977; "Punitive Damages," *For The Defense*, Sept. 1981, p. 6. Some courts, however, have ruled that although insurance companies may decline to offer coverage for punitive damages, public policy does not dictate non-coverage, See, *e.g.*, Harrell v. Travelers Indemnity Co., 279 Ore. 199, 567 P.2d 1013 (1977). Michigan courts in tort cases do not award punitive damages but they allow "exemplary" damages. Wise v. Daniel, 221 Mich. 229, 190 N.W. 746(1922). As a rule, a defendant's tort is usually classified as negligence rather than intentional, thereby bringing the defendant within insurance coverage.

37. See, *e.g.*, Security Insurance Group v. Wilkinson, 297 So.2d 113 (Fla. App. 1974).

38. B.M. Dickens, "Ethical Issues in Psychiatric Research," *Int'l J. Law & Psychiat.* 4:271, 1981.

39. The warning is set out, for example, in Commonwealth v. Lamb, 365 Mass. 265, 311 N.E.2d 47 (1974).

40. The American Psychiatric Association's Code of Ethics requires the examining psychiatrist to "fully describe the nature and purpose and lack of confidentiality of the examination at the beginning of the examination." *Psychiatric News,* June 4, 1982, p.8. The APA also states: "On occasion psychiatrists are asked for an opinion about an individual who is in the light of public attention, or who has disclosed information about himself/herself through public media. It is unethical for a psychiatrist to offer a professional opinion unless he/she conducted an examination and has been granted proper authorization for such a statement." APA, *The Principles of Medical Ethics With Annotations Especially Applicable to Psychiatry,* 1981 ed., sec. 7, no. 3; 1995 ed., sec. 7, annot. 3.

    The article, "Phases of Psychopathology After Assassination," in the *American Journal of Psychiatry* illustrates the doubt about the legal or ethical limitations on writing about a person accused or convicted of crime. The article, which is designed to recommend the computer method of diagnosis for medicolegal cases in which public opinion has been aroused and the specialist's objectivity may be impaired, has as its subject "a young man of Arabic origin who assassinated a prominent American political figure in 1968." There is a note to the article: "The Journal wishes to assure its readers that publication of this paper does not constitute a breach of ethics or of confidentiality, since the material discussed is part of a public record and is therefore in the public domain. In addition, approval for publication was obtained from the subject's lawyer and from attorneys for the American Psychiatric Association." F.C. Finney, D.E. Skeeters, C.D. Auvenshire, & D.F. Smith, "Phases of Psychopathology After Assassination" *Am J. Psychiat.* 130:1379, 1973

41. Thus, a photographer accompanying firemen and police onto fire-damaged premises commits a trespass and an invasion of privacy. Fletcher v. Florida Publishing Co., 319 So.2d 100 (Fla. 1975).

42. D. Carmody, "Reporters' rights to gather news facing increasing tests in court," *New York Times,* Nov. 19, 1976, p. B-2.

43. N. Mailer, *The Executioner's Song* (New York: Warner Books, 1979), p. 665.

44. N. Mailer, *op. cit. supra* at pp. 653, 690-691.

45. P. Lieberman & J. Stewart, "Making money off murder," *Student Lawyer,* Feb. 1982, p. 22. The view in Britain, and supported by the journalistic profession, is somewhat similar to that of the United States in respect of the rights of news gatherers, namely that they have no more rights than any member of the general public. There is, however, one ethical exception; subterfuge–which is not a right–may be used by a journalist if the information he gains and publishes by means of such action can be judged to be in the public interest. In this respect, the words "in the public interest" are critical as the view is taken that "in the public interest" is vastly different from what could be unacceptable, ethically, "of interest to the public." The case

of Mary Welcome ushering a reporter into jail under the guise of being a member of a defense team would be ruled by the British Press Council to be unethical conduct unless clearly there was no other way for the reporter to be present in the jail and most importantly, what he wrote after his visit could be ruled as being in the public interest. Personal communication from Raymond Swingler, Secretary of the British Press Council.

46. P. Lieberman & J. Stewart, *op. cit. supra.*
47. N. Mailer, *op. cit. supra* at pp. 623-624.
48. People v. Corona, 145 Cal. Rptr. 894 (Cal. App. 1978); J. Gibeaut, "Defend and Tell," *ABAJ* 82 (Dec. 1996):64.
49. "The Law: Hearst vs. Bailey", *Newsweek,* Aug. 21, 1978, p. 20; UPI news release, "A Swipe at Patty Hearst," Sept. 17, 1978.
50. Disciplinary Rule 5-104(b); see also ABA Model Rule 1.8(d). Today, 48 states use the Model Rules or the Model Code. Virginia has no rule but lists an ethical consideration on the subject. California permits lawyers to make media deals, subject to the client's waiver. O.J. Simpson's lead defense lawyer, Johnnie L. Cochran, Jr., has publicly suggested that colleagues Robert Shapiro and Robert Kardashian may have violated attorney-client confidences for money in post-trial publishing ventures.
51. Famed San Francisco lawyer Melvin Belli hurried to the defense of night-club owner Jack Ruby, who killed Lee Harvey Oswald, the suspected assassin of President Jack Kennedy, and as part of his fee, Belli was to receive the rights to Ruby's story. "The bar thought that was awful," said Geoffrey C. Hazard Jr., who served as a reporter for the commission which drafted the ABA Model Rules of Professional Conduct.
52. "Criminals' Revenues from Stories Curbed," *New York Times,* Aug. 13, 1977, p. 20.
53. N.Y. Exec. Law §632-a(1) (McKinney Supp. 1978). Questions arise whether the scope of the provision on "thoughts, feelings, opinions, or emotions regarding such crime" include a book depicting the criminal's childhood history with the crime as incidental, or a book telling of his repentance, or a book on the criminal justice system that mentions the crime. B.F. Wand, "Criminals-Turned-Authors: Victim's Rights vs. Freedom of Speech," *Indiana LJ.* 54:428, 1979.
54. P. Lieberman & J. Stewart, *op. cit. supra.*
55. The proceeds to the book, like any assets of a defendant in tort litigation, provide funds to compensate the family of the man he stabbed to death shortly following his release. P.L. Montgomery, "Abbott convicted of manslaughter in stabbing of East Village waiter," *New York Times,* Jan. 22, 1982, p. 1; D. Margolick, "Abbott case exploring ethics issue," *New York Times,* April 6, 1982, p. 19.
56. *Life From Death Row* (New York: Avon, 1995).
57. P. Lieberman & J. Stewart, *op cit. supra.*
58. I am grateful for the information on practices in England to Terrence Shaw, Daily Telegraph Legal Correspondent, John Greig, Times Assistant Managing Editor, and Raymond Seingler, Secretary of the Press Council.

59. "Some compensation for a 'dog day' victim," *New York Times*, Nov. 11, 1981, p. 17.

60. P. Lieberman & J. Stewart, *op. cit. supra.*

61. B.F. Wand, *op. cit. supra.*

62. R.A. Inz, "Compensating the Victim From the Proceeds of the Criminal's Story; The Constitutionality of the New York Approach," *Columbia J. of Law & Social Problems* 14:93, 1978.

63. 112 S. Ct. 501 (1991).

64. See S.B. Spencer, "Does Crime Pay–Can Probation Stop Katherine Ann Power From Selling Her Story?" *Bost. College L. Rev.* 35:1203, 1994; P.H. Webster, "*Simon & Schuster v. Crime Victims Board*: Unconstitutional Anti-Profit Statute Limits First Amendment Rights," *Wayne L. Rev.* 38:1983, 1992. See also J.C. Coffee, "The Morals of Marketing Simpson," *New York Times*, Oct. 8, 1995, p. F-10.

65. In the trial of John W. Hinckley Jr., charged with the shooting of President Reagan and three other men, Dr. Sally C. Johnson, a court-appointed psychiatrist, acknowledged that she had shredded "rough notes" of her interviews with Hinckley and others. She said she routinely shredded such notes after recording her observations in a permanent "medical record." Defense lawyers quickly moved that she be barred from testifying, because the unavailability of the notes would make it harder to test the basis for her conclusions. The trial judge denied the motion on the ground that there was no evidence that she had destroyed the notes out of any "evil intent." S. Taylor, "U.S., not defense, carries burden on Hinckley's sanity, judge says," *New York Times*, May 2, 1982, p. 14.

 The Minnesota Rules of Criminal Procedure, Rule 20.03, for example, provides that the defendant must turn over to the prosecutor "all medical reports and hospital and medical records" concerning his mental condition that the trial court determines are "relevant to the issue of the defense of [the defendant's] mental illness or mental deficiency." The Rule includes all such reports, "previously or thereafter made." The Rule limits the use of such records to use as evidence on the mental illness issue. The Comments to the Rule indicate that it "permits the disclosure to and use by the prosecution of medical reports and hospital and medical records that are relevant to the defense of mental illness or mental deficiency." Because the prosecution may "use" all reports and records that bear on the issue of mental illness, the Minnesota Supreme Court has ruled that the prosecution has the right to call a defense-retained psychiatrist (whom the defense has chosen not to use as a witness) to testify regarding his findings on the issue. State v. Dodis, 314 N.W.2d 233 (Minn. 1982). It has been ruled that a defendant does not have a constitutional right to prohibit his psychiatrist from being called as a witness by the prosecution. Edney v. Smith, 425 F. Supp. 1038 (E.D. N.Y. 1976), *aff'd mem.*, 556 F.2d 556 (2d Cir. 1977).

66. See, *e.g.*, Illinois Mental health and Development Disabilities Confidentiality Act, Ill. Ann. Stat. ch. 91 1/2 §810(b) (Smith-Hurd Supp. 1979).

67. G.A. Huber, & L.H. Roth, "Preserving the Confidentiality of Medical Record Information Regarding Nonpatients," *Va. L. Rev.* 66:583, 1980.

68. Eagles v. Liberty Weekly, 137 Misc. 575, 244 N.Y.S. 430 (1930). One commentator said: "[W]hen the historian is dealing with men whose children are still living there does not appear to be any good reason why he should enjoy an absolute immunity... [Admittedly] it is seldom that a writer *intends* to bring contempt on the families of those whose vices and peccadilloes he relates. What he intends to do is to sell his book, and if he can do this he does not care very much either about the reputation of the dead or the sensibilities of the living...It is true that the dead have no legal rights. But, it is equally true that a son has an interest in the reputation of his father and suffers if it is injured. Is there any adequate reason why this interest should not be protected by the law?" F.P. Watson, "Libel Upon the Dead and the Bath Club Case," *J. Comp. Leg. & Int. Law* 9:1, 1927.

# Chapter 5

# TREATMENT OF MINORS AND
# YOUNG ADULTS

L ike many adults, many youngsters are reluctant or ashamed to see a
counselor or therapist. Dr. Stephen Aaron, a staff psychologist at the private Dalton School in New York, explained that his office was on a high floor "so kids wouldn't be seen coming into my office."[1] Common problems among adolescents include learning difficulties, resentment of authority, eating disorders, depression and suicidal ideation, and drug and sexual experimentation.[2]

With the change in the character of the home and the family, schools have been asked to take on a variety of functions, such as mental health counseling, social rehabilitation, parental counseling, detecting cases of child abuse, preventing drug abuse, assimilating the student with AIDS, and dealing with the handicapped. In all too many instances, these many demands have impeded the school from carrying out its intended primary mission: to teach.

It may be noted here that, apart from any psychotherapist-patient privilege, a number of states have enacted legislation setting out a teacher-student privilege. To come under the privilege, the communication must be made in confidence.[3] The Michigan statute provides:[4]

> No teacher, guidance officer, school executive or other professional person engaged in character building in the public schools or in any other educational institution, including any clerical worker of such or schools and institutions, who maintains records of students' behavior who has records in his custody, or who receives in confidence communications from students or other juveniles, shall be allowed in any proceedings, civil or criminal, in any court of this state, to disclose any information obtained by him from the records of such communications; nor to produce records or transcript thereof, except that testimony may be given, with the consent of the person so confiding or to whom the records relate, if the person is 18 years of age or over, or, if the person is a minor, with the consent of his or her parent or legal guardian.

Most school children and high school students do not turn to a counselor or therapist unless they are forced to by parents and teachers. Lower school counselors spend little time on individual counseling; they consult with parents and teachers, and observe students in class. Years ago, R.A. Schermerhorn of Western Reserve University wrote:[5]

> Diagnostically, the school can do much with the aid of behavior specialists like psychologists, visiting teachers, counselors or psychiatrists. Such leaders, by organizing discussion groups of teachers and parents, can increase sensitivity to typical symptoms like truancy, sudden drop in grades, increased withdrawal, failure to participate, overaggressiveness, or warding off others because of expected unkindness. A special program then calls for reporting such problem cases to the key leader, who then arranges conferences with teacher, parents, principal, attendance officer or guidance personnel. This results in a mutual treatment process. The family becomes part of a collaborative team.

In Freud's famous case of "Little Hans," Freud did not see the boy, a 5-year-old, but treated him through his father. Hans had developed a "nervous disorder"–he became afraid to go out into the street for fear that a horse might bite him. He had a peculiarly lively interest in that portion of the body described as the "widdler." Years later, "a strapping youth of nineteen" came to Freud and announced that he was the "Little Hans" of the case study. He assured Freud that he was "perfectly well," and suffered from no troubles or inhibitions and had not only weathered puberty but also the divorce and remarriage of both his parents.[6]

Later, in Berlin, Melanie Klein, recognizing the problems of relying on verbal communication with young children (psychoanalysis was after all "the talking cure" and young children do not necessarily have a sufficient capacity to express their feelings adequately), developed a means of interpreting the play of children. Anna Freud and others also developed approaches to children along these lines.

In all cases, confidentiality is linked to the factual or legal competency of the patient to consent to treatment. With that as a given, how is the matter of confidentiality with a minor as patient to be handled in relation to parents or personnel of agencies who may have a legitimate interest in the minor? To whom is the clinician mainly responsible in the case of a minor with emotional difficulties? The American Psychiatric Association stated in its *Guidelines on Confidentiality*:[7]

> Parents and legal guardians are entitled to relevant medical information about children for whom they are responsible and, where appropriate, should be included in the  treatment. Minors themselves also have rights regarding confidentiality and must feel free to talk about their parents and other adults with-

out fear of reprisal. Extraneous information that the child would not want the parents to know should not be discussed with the parents or included in the chart. However, information that parents need to make informed decisions about their child's care must be provided to them. Child and adolescent patients should be informed about the nature of the information about them that may be shared with their parents. At a level appropriate to the child's age, he or she should also be informed about the limits to confidentiality in the particular therapeutic situation.

Minors (typically one under age 18) are not legally competent to act on their own. In *Parham v. J.R.*,[8] the U.S. Supreme Court addressed the constitutional requirements of due process for minors when parents or guardians seek to admit their children or wards for admission to mental hospitals. The Court held that the only process due minors in such situations was review of the minor's need for hospital treatment by the admitting physician, acting as a "neutral factfinder."[9]

Consent, express or implied, of a parent or guardian is necessary to authorize treatment or services for them.[10] To make an informed decision, as the APA Guidelines state, it is essential that the parents or guardian have relevant information. Absent parent or guardian consent, treatment, regardless of the outcome, constitutes a battery or possibly negligence. Disclosure to the parent or guardian in order to obtain consent is thus essential.

To the general rule about obtaining parental or guardian consent, there are a number of exceptions: (1) "parens patriae"; (2) emergencies; (3) emancipated minors; (4) mature minors; and (5) certain types of care. What follows is a discussion of these exceptions:

1. The state in its capacity as "parens patriae" (parent of the people) may protect the best interests of a minor in the face of parental refusal to consent to treatment deemed necessary to preserve the life or health of the minor. Under this authority, for example, the state can compel vaccination or fluoridation.[11] And the state may override parental consent. Even with parental consent, sterilization of a minor or the removal of an organ of a minor for a transplant for the sake of a sibling or other person is a procedure fraught with legal hazard, so court authorization is warranted.[12]

2. In an emergency where delay would produce serious risks for the minor, a physician may proceed with treatment without awaiting parental consent. Consent is implied from the emergency, which is defined as "a situation wherein, in competent medical judgment, the proposed surgical or medical treatment or procedures are immediately or imminently necessary and any delay occasioned by an attempt to obtain a consent would reasonably jeopardize the life, health or limb of the person affected, or would reasonably result in disfigurement or impairment of facilities."[13]

The courts give a broad interpretation to "emergency." Thus the treatment of a fracture has been deemed an emergency, though it was not life-saving but done to stop pain and suffering.[14] California, by statute, authorizes any minor age 12 or older to consent to outpatient care where such care is necessary to avert a danger of serious mental or physical harm or where there are allegations of incest or child abuse.

3. An emancipated minor—a minor who is free from the care, custody, and control of his or her parents—may give a legally valid consent. By dint of certain legislation, pregnancy amounts to emancipation.[15] This exception has mostly been applied to older minors whose parents were unavailable when the decision to treat had to be made, and involved relatively low-risk treatments clearly of benefit to the minor.[16]

4. A "mature minor" in some instances may give a valid consent. The usual standard, age, is easy of application, but maturity is a matter of dispute, it being a behavioral test.[17] One pediatrician has suggested that any child who could get to her Greenwich Village office by subway from the Bronx was, in her eyes, an adult. The mature minor doctrine has found application in cases where the minor is at least 15 years of age, the treatment is for the benefit of the minor, and the procedure is something less than major or serious in nature.[18]

5. In recent years, *ad hoc* exceptions have been made to parents' authority to consent, usually to help deal with problems that have high social costs, such as venereal disease, drug or alcohol abuse, contraception, and pregnancy. Underlying psychodynamics may be identical among individuals showing different symptoms or behavior, but it is only the named symptom or behavior that opens the door to care or treatment without parental consent. Some states set a minimum age for consent in these treatments or procedures. Many have suggested that programs involving parents in their children's lives are more worthy of support than those that isolate them, and they argue that such services should not be provided without parental consent, notice of consultation.[19] In any event, the majority of states have enacted statutes permitting minors to consent without parental notice or consultation, to receive treatment for venereal disease and drug or alcohol abuse, and to seek and receive counseling on and devices for birth control or contraception.[20] A number of state statutes also authorize minors to receive mental health treatment without parental consent. An Illinois statute provides, for example: "Any minor fourteen years of age or older may request and receive counseling services or psychotherapy on an outpatient basis. The consent of the parent, guardian, or person *in loco parentis* shall not be necessary to authorize outpatient counseling or psychotherapy."[21]

The U.S. Supreme Court has upheld the right of minors to obtain contraceptives without parental consent,[22] and in the wake of that decision, the

Sixth Circuit Court of Appeals ruled that contraceptives may be provided to minors even without the knowledge of their parents.[23] A number of state statutes specifically provide that records concerning the treatment of a minor for venereal disease or the performance of an abortion shall not be released or in any manner be made available to the parents. Other states require parental notification.[24] In any event, when a minor is using a family insurance plan to pay for service, the parents will learn about it when they receive a benefit report from the insurer.

In *Planned Parenthood of Missouri v. Danforth*,[25] the Supreme Court ruled that a parent may not veto a minor's decision to have an abortion, but the Court went on to say: "We emphasize that our holding...does not suggest every minor, regardless of age or maturity, may give effective consent for termination of her pregnancy." From this language it might be implied that "nonmature" or "noncompetent" minors would be required to have parental consent to abortion, even in the first trimester, as they would for any other procedure. That issue came to the Supreme Court in 1979 in *Bellotti v. Baird*.[26] In that case, the Court said that every minor has the right to go directly to a court without consulting her parents. Justice Powell said, "A pregnant minor is entitled in such a proceeding to show either: (1) that she is mature enough and well enough informed to make her abortion decision, in consultation with her physician, independently of her parents' wishes; or (2) that even if she is not able to make this decision independently, the desired abortion would be in her best interests."

Until 1981, it remained an open question whether a state could impose a requirement of parental notice (as opposed to consent or consultation) as a condition of a minor's receiving an abortion. Given notice, many have said, parents may be supportive and may dissuade their minor from having an abortion. Justice Stevens, in the *Bellotti* case in 1979, remarked in a footnote: "[Our previous decisions do not determine] the constitutionality of a statute which does no more than require notice to the parents, without affording them or any other third party an absolute veto." In 1981, the Supreme Court by a 6-3 vote upheld a Utah parental notification law. The Court said: "A statute setting out a 'mere requirement of parental notice' does not violate the constitutional rights of an immature, dependent minor. The Utah statute gives neither parents nor judges a veto power over the minor's abortion decision."[27] The Court's decision does not make parental notification mandatory nationwide but leaves it up to each state to decide whether to impose the requirement. In 1996, over a barbed dissent by Justice Antonin Scalia, the Court declined to hear South Dakota's appeal of a ruling that its law requiring teenagers seeking abortions to notify a parent 48 hours in advance was unconstitutional. There was no opinion for the Court, as is usual when it simply lets a lower court's opinion stand without review. In a dissent from the denial of review, Justice Scalia, with Chief Justice William Rehnquist and Justice Clarence Thomas joining, referred to the Court's approach to state abortion laws as an "ad hoc nullification machine."[28]

There are more than 400,000 abortions a year performed on teenagers in the United States, and an estimated one-quarter of these girls do not inform their parents about the pregnancy.[29] As a matter of practice, the procedure set out by the Court in the *Bellotti* case has been ignored. Abortion clinics around the country are carrying out abortions on minors just as on adults. No path is beaten to the courthouse door for a determination of maturity or best interests. Should there be complications, however, the minor will usually find that a hospital will not admit her without parental consent. Emergency care in a clearly life-saving situation may be available, but even then, the hospital (while administering such care) will as a matter of practice attempt to contact parent or guardian.

What actually is the hazard in treating a minor without parental consent? In general, physicians and other therapists appear to be overly fearful in the care and treatment of minors, leading quite often to tragic results. While the law defines an emergency broadly, many physicians and hospitals define it very narrowly. One publicized case involved a minor who split his lip and was spurting blood but the doctor in the emergency room refused to suture it without parental consent.[30] In actual fact, there is not a reported case in any state, apart from one transplant case, in which a physician or health facility has been held liable for treating a minor over age 15 without parental consent.[31]

And consent is no insulation against liability. Parental consent or no, there may be liability in the case of faulty treatment. Consent protects from a charge of battery, but not from negligence or malpractice. In the case where the treatment measures up to acceptable standard of care but there is no parental consent or applicable exception, the parents may claim that their expenses for the support and maintenance of their child were increased by an unfavorable result of the treatment, but that is not likely. Treatment of a minor without parental consent is technically a battery, but in these cases only for nominal damages, and the doctor is entitled to have the jury so instructed.[32] More likely, the court would allow the doctor payment for his services.[33]

Therapy with minors is rarely a strictly two-person arrangement. This is strikingly noted in Freud's treatment of "Little Hans." "Environmental manipulation," as it is called, may be essential in the treatment of minors. With some minors, especially young minors, it is particularly desirable or necessary to involve the parents in the treatment process. Effective therapy often depends upon cooperation with the parents. Moreover, teachers, in consultation with the psychiatrist, may contribute effectively to the child's treatment through the teacher-pupil relationship.[34]

The broad treatment approach, however, does not forsake the trust of the patient. The psychiatrist, as a matter of good practice, makes clear to both the minor (if old enough) and parents the type of rapport he will have with each. It is foolhardy for a therapist to promise absolute secrecy. Rather, wisdom dictates that the minor be advised that it may be necessary that certain information may be given to others. As the APA Guidelines provide, at a level appropriate to the minor's age, he or she as well as the parents should be informed about the limits of confidentiality. In this sense, confidentiality, or rather trust, is realistically maintained. There is no publication to the world. The psychiatrist in this situation is working with persons who are directly responsible for the patient and who can assist in the treatment. Parents, after all, are legally responsible for their children.

At times, however, it may be necessary to dismiss the parents, and to rely on others. The parents may be psychotic or otherwise disturbed. All physicians have encountered parents who deny treatment to an acutely ill minor or who are abusive. At times it is one's family against which one needs the most protection.[35]

The highly publicized "battered-child syndrome" has resulted in the passage of laws requiring that physicians and hospitals report cases of child abuse observed in the course of their professional practice. Without parental permission, they are permitted or obliged under these laws to take photos, skeletal surveys, and lab studies. Physical assaults on children may be a more frequent cause of death than such well-recognized and thoroughly studied diseases as leukemia, cystic fibrosis, and muscular dystrophy, and it may rank with automobile accidents. Many physicians have expressed the view that such laws would be useless without a provision protecting them from retaliation by irate parents who are investigated. Hence, the laws that have been enacted contain provisions protecting those reporting against any civil liability that might arise out of compliance with the statutory requirement.[36]

In a relatively short period of time, the various states enacted laws making it mandatory for physicians and institutions to report physical abuse of children to the appropriate police authority. The Children's Bureau of the Department of Health, Education and Welfare drafted a model bill based essentially on a California statute, and circulated it to state legislative members, health departments, hospitals, and some physicians. The recommendation was instrumental in obtaining passage of the laws. These laws do not require the reporting of "mental abuse," which may be much more devastating to the child. The percentage of such cases, serious in nature, can well be imagined to be multifold the number of cases of physical abuse.

A law requiring the reporting of "mental abuse," however, would be less workable than the "battered child law." One might consider that in custody cases and other cases involving minors it is often quite difficult to establish to the satisfaction of the judge that parents are so abusive to their children as to warrant judicial action, or when such a fact is established, there is little the court can do about it (except remove the child from their custody). While the court cannot command good parenthood, social casework in conjunction with legal action may sometimes help. It may happen that abusive parents will not bring their child to therapy out of fear of a report, or they may take their child out of therapy should abuse be reported. As it stands, the stigma of mental illness of a child prevents many cases from being treated before it is too late.

For a therapist to release information about a minor patient, the signature of either parent is generally adequate except in a case of divorce or custody, in which case the signature of a custodial parent or agency is required. The APA's "Model Law on Confidentiality of Health and Social Service Records" suggests that if no age is specified in a state statute, the psychiatrist may safely rely on the parent's consent alone for a child under 12. Illinois, by legislation, authorizes disclosure of records by parents alone for a minor under 12 years of age.[37] Other jurisdictions provide that a parent of a child under 14 may authorize disclosure.[38]

Given the right of access of patients to medical records, parents have this right with respect to their minor's records, but discretion may be exercised in the extent of disclosure. The concept of "therapeutic privilege" allowing the withholding of detrimental information may be applicable. In the case of involuntary civil commitment, whether or not the parent was the applicant for the commitment, the responsibility for the care and treatment of the patient becomes invested in the hospital or court, and so the parent has no right of access to the minor's records.[39]

With the recognition that most failures in school are due to emotional problems, the psychiatric aspect of counseling and student adjustment assumes greater importance in education. Programs focusing on self-esteem have been instituted in schools and universities. As an increasing number of educators have come to realize, emotional factors are just as significant as intellectual abilities for achievement in school. In a research study at Tulane University of medical students in two graduating classes, it was found that superior students generally are able to cope with emotional problems and resolve them in a positive manner, whereas students whose academic standings are low often allowed emotional factors to inhibit the progress of their studies. The poorer student "is apt to have neurotic work inhibitions resulting from the issue of competition, with prominent fears of failure or success." The researchers recommended "there should be greater evaluation of emotional factors at the time of admission," and "expanded counseling and psychiatric facilities are needed for students whose grades are off because they are facing emotional problems."[40]

In grade and high schools, some cities have psychiatric services within the school system (the services are also offered to the faculty who often feel that they are working in a war zone). On the university level, a number of universities have appointed psychiatrists as part of their health services to treat students. At one time, a number of schools required a report on nonreferral as well as on referral students, but as a result of protests by psychiatrists, this requirement of reporting has generally been dropped.[41]

Teachers, when they recognize that a problem exists, ought to make a referral as discreetly as possible, and that is all. Of course, teachers do intuitively adapt themselves and their methods of teaching to the varying personalities of students, but it is another thing to say that teaching should be officially based on therapy.[42] As Dr. D.W. Winnicott, a prominent figure in psychiatry, put it: "No one wants a teacher to take up a therapeutic attitude towards pupils. Pupils are not patients. At least, they are not patients in relation to the teacher while they are being taught."[43]

How should the mental health service consult with teachers or parents? What should teachers know? In litigation filed in federal court on the basis of diversity of citizenship, in *Iverson v. Frandsen*,[44] the parents brought their 9-year-old daughter to a mental hospital for help in overcoming her claustrophobia. As part of the examination, an IQ test and several other tests were administered and recorded by a staff psychologist in a standard hospital report. The report stated that she was a "feeble-minded," high-grade moron, and the report predicted that "at the time she is about sixteen, she should have progressed to about the fourth grade level in reading, arithmetic, writing, etc." Subsequently, on request of the guidance director of the child's school, a copy of the report was sent to the school, and a while later embarrassing rumors about the child's mental ability spread throughout the school. The parents, on behalf of their child, brought a libel action against the staff psychologist. The complaint alleged that the child was brought to the hospital for advice and treatment concerning claustrophobia; that the IQ testing was beyond the scope of the consultation. The court held that the psychologist had a conditional privilege to make ordinary hospital records of the test results, and to communicate this information to psychiatrists on the hospital staff who were also working on the case. The court held for the psychologist, as the report was made in accordance with standard procedures and intended only for hospital officials or professionally interested persons. The action was brought only against the psychologist. The hospital doctors, who were not sued, could reasonably believe that for the good of the child, information about her mental and emotional problems should be given, as was done, to the officials at her school.

While a medical report can at times assist teachers in planning special instruction for a child, teachers, generally speaking, have no need for a report from a mental health service. When scoring grades, for example, teachers ought to remain essentially unconcerned about the student's emotional problems. Does it matter that a student cannot take an examination because of a "neurosis"? Dr. Dana L. Farnsworth, then Director of the Harvard University Health Services, said:

> The task of the therapist is simplified if college officials do not make undue allowance for a student who is having emotional conflict–at least no more than would be given to a student suffering from any other type of disorder. The college should hold students who may be patients to the same ethical standards as it does all others. What is wrong is wrong, no matter who does it. Understanding the motive behind unacceptable or unsuitable behavior is not to be construed as condoning or excusing the behavior . . . The therapist and student patient work together in order that the latter may achieve self-control and a sense of responsibility. If the college administrators do not insist on their usual high standards for a student in emotional conflict, the therapist is handicapped and the student may become confused–or he may falsely assume that his illness entitles him to important secondary gains.

There is another side to the problem. There is a long tradition that, when things get rough, students get a doctor's certificate, or complain of sickness. In an earlier day, the complaint was mainly about a physical illness. Now, it is emotional distress. When it works to their advantage, students will advise teachers that they are in psychotherapy. But, understanding behavior does not mean that it ought to be condoned. Dr. Karl Menninger observed:[46]

> We psychiatrists have not made it sufficiently clear that attempting to understand an individual whom we treat is not necessarily to condone all the behavior of such an individual, or even to expect inevitable penalties for such behavior to be waived merely because he is in treatment . . . I think we psychiatrists have sometimes put ourselves in a bad light by giving the impression that if a man is taking treatment, he should be permitted some offensiveness without penalty.

What need parents know? Parents are legally responsible for their children, and consequently they have a right to know about them. As we have noted, under the law, a person is regarded as a minor until he is 18, and until that time (unless he is emancipated), the parents are legally responsible for his care and, in some states, for his misdemeanors. In psychotherapy, however, psychological age or the condition of the patient rather than chronological age, as we have noted, must determine the approach the therapist will have to take in dealing with parents.

In cases of physical illness, a surgeon operates on a minor only with the consent of the parents (or guardian), except in emergencies.[47] However, in psychotherapy, a minor may not wish that contact be made with his parents. The requirement that a school or a psychiatrist notify the parents of all minors who consult the psychiatrist would destroy service at once. As a consequence, university health services usually treat students as though they were adults.

Although the parents may afford private treatment, university clinics may treat students on a long-term basis at a nominal fee when they do not wish to contact the parents. Good practice would require that no one is told about treatment unless the student's permission is obtained or there is a problem involving suicide, potential homicide, or some kind of behavior which is going to handicap markedly the student or his parents. In any case, no action is taken without letting the student know, except in instances of acute psychosis or danger to life.

Some university health services, quite appropriately, notify students of exceptions to confidentiality in the following situations: when a student's mental condition is such that immediate action must be taken to protect the student or others from serious consequence of his illness; and when a student is referred for evaluation and an opinion or recommendation is requested.[48] In the first situation, immediate voluntary or involuntary hospitalization may be arranged and in such cases the college administration and parents are notified as quickly as possible. Cases in the second situation are called administrative referrals and in such cases the student is informed initially that a report will be made to the referring individual or agency, but the actual interview itself remains confidential as far as content is concerned.

Thus, the prevailing practice on notification of parents in the case of treatment of minors for mental illness is, curiously enough, just the opposite of the procedure generally followed, and approved by the law, in the case of treatment of minors for physical illness. In the former case, notification is made only in emergencies; in the latter case, lack of notification in emergencies is legally excused. Of course, the reason for the distinction is usually the element of time.

The treatment of a minor without parental consent is not a problem in private psychiatric practice; the parent usually brings the child for treatment. The problem of treating a minor without parental consent—a problem perhaps more theoretical than real—is discussed among therapists working in school clinics, community clinics, or outpatient services of a hospital. Generally speaking, parents do not protest, except possibly only briefly, when they learn that their child is in psychotherapy, and in any event, they do not sue the therapist. They are usually pleased that something is being done for the child. And what would happen if they protested treatment? The people who need and want therapy soon overwhelm any facility that offers it, and time is not spent on cases where there is objection to treatment.

For decades, psychiatrists have served as consultants to virtually every type of institution that deals with children or adolescents, most often apart from the school health system or the courts. Consultation is a way to provide help to a larger population than could be reached via direct treatment only. Usually, a consultation request involves a desire on the part of one professional for information from another professional who has expertise in a special area. The request for consultation comes not from a patient or parents but rather from another professional. Sometimes consultation is undertaken even though the patient or parents are unenthusiastic or resent it. The implication for confidentiality vary depending on the nature of the consultation.[49]

## NOTES

1. Quoted in S. Friedman, "Private School Shrinks: The Anxiety of Affluence," *New York Observer*, May 27, 1996, p. 10.

2. About two million teenagers a year attempt suicide and more than 2,000 carry it out. One-fourth of high school students across the nation have had serious suicidal thoughts. T. Ward, "Teens and Suicide/Stopping Suicide," *Oakland Press*, Feb. 17, 1997, p. 1. Dr. Joseph D. Noshpitz discusses the treatment of self-destructive adolescents and their inability to tolerate success in "Self-Destructiveness in Adolescence," *Am. J. Psychotherapy* 48:330, 1994; "Self-Destructiveness in Adolescence: Psychotherapeutic Issues," *id.* 48:347, 1994.

3. People v. Pitts, 548 N.W.2d 548 (Mich. App. 1996); W.P. Robinson, "Testimonial Privilege and the School Guidance Counselor," *Syracuse L. Rev.* 25:911, 1974; H. McDiarmid, "Students' statements in fight become confidentiality issue," *Detroit Free Press*, Feb. 4, 1997, p. B-6.

4. M.C.L., § 600.2165; M.S.A. § 27A.2165.

5. "Social Psychiatry," in A.M. Rose (ed.), *Mental Health and Mental Disorder/A Sociological Approach* (New York: W.W. Norton, 1955); reprinted from *Antioch Rev.* 13:67, 1953.

6. E. Jones, *The Life and Work of Sigmund Freud* (Middlesex: Harmondsworth, 1961), vol. 2, p. 258.

7. *Am. J. Psychiat.* 144:1522, 1987.

8. 442 U.S. 584 (1979).

9. See G. Melton, "Family and Mental Hospital as Myths: The Civil Commitment of Minors," in N. Reppucci, L. Weithorn, E. Mulvey & J. Monahan (eds.), *Children, Mental Health and the Law* (Beverly Hills, CA.: Sage, 1984), pp. 281-306; D.E. Cichon, "Developing a Mental Health Code for Minors," *Thomas M. Cooley L. Rev.* 13:529, 1996; L.A. Weithorn, "Mental Hospitalization of Troublesome Youth: An Analysis of Skyrocketing Admission Rates," *Stan. L. Rev.* 40:773, 1988.

In a scathing attack on private psychiatric hospitals, Joe Sharkey sets out a litany of scams and promotional claims and he notes the targeting of youngsters, resulting in lengthy hospitalizations of children and adolescents with essentially social problems. The profit margin for a psychiatric bed occupied by a youngster, he notes, is 30 percent compared with 20 percent for an adult because youngsters demand less service and attention. J. Sharkey, *Bedlam: Greed, Profiteering, and Fraud in a Mental Health System Gone Crazy* (New York: St. Martin's Press, 1994).

10.   In the psychiatric care of children and adolescents, medication is usually not appropriate but, on some occasions, it is claimed to be proper and necessary. Psychopharmacology may avoid having to suspend from school a youngster diagnosed with a conduct disorder or attention deficit hyperactivity. W.H. Green, *Child and Adolescent Clinical Psychopharmacology* (Baltimore: Williams & Wilkins, 2d ed. 1995). However, some professionals, and more often parents, feel that it will turn the youngsters into "zombies" or make them become drug addicts later on. Faced with suspension or special placement of a student, parents tend to consent to medication. Ritalin calms youngsters with attention deficit disorder, but it stirs up critics. See L.H. Diller, "The Run on Ritalin," *Hastings Center Report* 26(2):12, 1996; K. Livingston, "Ritalin: Miracle Drug or Cop-Out?" *Public Interest,* Spring 1997, p. 3; J.C. O'Leary, "An Analysis of the Legal Issues Surrounding the Forced Use of Ritalin: Protesting a Child's Right to 'Just Say No,'" *New Eng. L. Rev.* 27:1173, 1993; Cover story, "Ritalin/Are We Overmedicating Our Kids?" *Newsweek,* March 18, 1996, p. 51; M. Guttman, "The Ritalin Generation," *USA Weekend,* Oct. 27-29, 1995, p. 4; J. Merrow, "Reading, Writing and Ritalin," *New York Times,* Oct. 21, 1995, p. 15. Dr. Peter Breggin, longtime opponent of medication in psychiatry, suggests that Ritalin treats the needs of health professionals, parents and teachers rather than the needs of children. P.R. Breggin (ltr.), "Whose Attention Disorder Does Ritalin Treat?" *New York Times,* May 20, 1996, p. 14.

11.   W. Gerdes, "Parents fight radiation treatment for son," *Detroit Free Press,* Aug. 26, 1989, p. 1; M.L. Wald, "Parents in Connecticut Fight Ban on Pupils Needing Rubella Shots," *New York Times,* March 22, 1978, p. 37; AP news-release, "Therapy restored for boy denied care by parents," *Detroit Free Press,* March 24, 1978, p. 10.

12.   *In re* Guardianship of Pescinski, 67 Wis.2d 4, 226 N.W.2d 180 (1975); "A Brother's Sacrifice," *Time,* Nov. 7, 1969, p. 54.

13.   Mo. Ann. Stat. § 431.061.

14.   Greenspan v. Slate, 12 N.J. 426, 97 A.2d 390 (1953); Sullivan v. Montgomery, 155 Misc. 448, 279 N.Y.S. 575 (1935).

15.   *E.g.,* Alabama's statute provides: "Any minor who is married, or having been married is divorced, or has borne a child may give effective consent to any legally authorized medical, dental, health or mental health services for himself, his child or for herself or her child."

16. A tattoo does not fall in this category. In recent years, 15 states have adopted laws restricting or regulating tattooing. Minnesota, in 1996, tightened an old restriction to require the consent of both parents after a man's ex-wife allowed their 12-year-old son to get a tattoo on his arm. Supporters of legislation point to the risks of infection and possible allergic reactions as reasons to restrict tattooing. A. Petersen, "Parents Spur Laws Against Tattoos for Kids," *Wall Street Journal*, Sept. 16, 1996, p. B-1; K. Thomas, "Law requires parental consent for tattoos," *Detroit News*, March 1, 1995, p. B-8.

17. M. Oberman, "Minor Rights and Wrongs," *J. of Law, Medicine & Ethics* 24(2):127, 1996.

18. Mississippi by statute permits consent by a minor "of sufficient intelligence to understand and appreciate the consequences of the proposed surgical or medical treatments or procedures." Miss. Code Ann. § 41-41-3 (L). Idaho by statute provides that a minor may validly consent when he is of ordinary intelligence, sufficient to understand the need for, the nature of, and the significant risks of treatment." Idaho Code § 39-4302. In Cardwell v. Bechtol, 724 S.W.2d 739 (Tenn. 1987), the Tennessee Supreme Court explained that whether a minor is sufficiently mature "depends upon the age, ability, experience, education, training, and degree of maturity or judgment obtained by a minor, as well as upon the conduct and demeanor of the minor at the time of the incident involved." In this case a 17-year-old high school senior was held to be intelligent and mature enough to give valid consent to osteopathic treatment. See W. Gaylin, "The Competence of Children: No Longer All or None," *Hastings Center Report* 12(2):33, April 1982.

19. "Sex Value for Teens," *New York Times*, March 1, 1981, p. E-21.

20. I.N. Perr, "Confidentiality and Consent in Psychiatric Treatment of Minors," *J. Legal Medicine*, June 1976, p. 9.

21. Ill.-S.H.A. ch. 91 1/2, § 3-501(a).

22. Carey v. Population Services Int'l, 431 U.S. 678 (1977).

23. Doe v. Irwin, 615 F.2d 1162 (6th Cir. 1980).

24. N.Y. Public Health Law ch.763 (McKinney 1977).

25. 428 U.S. 52.

26. 428 U.S. 132.

27. H.L. v. Matheson, 101 S. Ct. 1164 (1981).

28. Janklow v. Planned Parenthood, 116 S. Ct. 1582 (1996); discussed in L. Greenhouse, "With Sharp Words, Court Refuses an Abortion Case," *New York Times*, April 30, 1996, p. 9.

29. L. Greenhouse, "Court Backs Law to Notify Parents Before an Abortion on a Teen-Ager," *New York Times*, March 24, 1981, p. 1.

30. S. Ramos, "Insuring Medical Aid If Parents Are Away," *New York Times*, Jan. 22, 1981, p. 15.

31. In the one case where liability has been imposed on a doctor for treating a minor without parental consent, a transplant operation was performed not for the benefit of the minor, a 15-year-old, but rather for the benefit of a cousin (consent was by an aunt), yet the case has been cited or relied upon

in discussions as to the need for parental consent in every situation. See H. Pilpel, "Minor's Rights to Medical Care," *Albany L. Rev.* 36:462, 1972.

32. Lacey v. Laird, 166 Ohio St. 1219, 129 N.E.2d 15 (1956) (plastic surgery).
33. Greenspan v. Slate, 12 N.J. 426, 97 A.2d 390 (1953) (fee awarded for X-raying a child's foot and applying a cast); cited *supra* note 14.
34. See M. Sugar (ed.), *Responding to Adolescent Needs* (Jamaica, N.Y.: Spectrum, 1980); C.P. Malmquist, "Problems of Confidentiality in Child Psychiatry," *Am. J. Orthopsychiat.* 35:787, 1965.
35. N. Kittrie, *The Right to be Different: Deviance and Enforced Therapy* (Baltimore: Penguin, 1971), pp. 66, 86.
36. "The key to solving the child-maltreatment problem," said St. Vincent's Dr. Fontana, "in the final analysis is in the hands of the lawmakers. Only they can protect the physician testifying in such cases from libel and malpractice charges. Only they can give the medical profession the means of preventing thousands of cases annually of permanent disability and death." "Parents Who Beat Children," *Sat. Eve. Post*, Oct. 6, 1962, p. 30. Under the law, parents have an obligation to care for their young in sickness and health. An infant is made a ward of the court, invading the parents' custody, where the life or health of the child is endangered by the medical neglect of its parents, such as where the parents are members of a faith healing group and refuse to consent to a blood transfusion or a surgical operation for their child. See People v. Labrenz, 411 Ill. 618, 104 N.E.2d 769 (1952).
37. Ill. Stat. § 740-7-110/5 (1993).
38. See Nagle v. Hooks, 295 Md. 123, 460 A.2d 49 (Md. App. 1983). What about when a minor over age 14 declines to authorize disclosure? Consider, for example, the case of the parent who arranges for private hospitalization for a minor child and anticipates that a substantial part of the cost will be paid by insurance coverage. The dependent patient may refuse to authorize the release of pertinent information. Dr. John Donnelly, then Medical Director of the Institute of Living, wrote about the situation where a minor declines to authorize disclosure:

> A number of these young persons have considerable difficulties with parents and express their resentment by refusing to authorize the release of information to the insurance company. When the patient is sufficiently psychotic that a Probate Court order of commitment or its equivalent may be obtained, the problem does not exist. But where the family, thinking of the future of the minor, hopes to avoid a record of a court commitment, wishes to provide continuation of therapy in the selected treatment setting, the psychiatrist is faced with a decision regarding the release of information. When a minor patient refuses to sign the release of information to an insurance company, what is the responsibility of the psychiatrist and the hospital to the parent and what is the exposure to suit if the information is transmitted? It is obvious that in such cases it may be impossible to establish the necessary therapeutic relationship since the therapist will be seen as the agent of

the parent if the information is released. On the other hand, failure to release the information necessitates the removal of the patient from the hospital. While it may be argued that treatment can be obtained under governmental auspices, the preferred treatment is seldom available in such situations.

J. Donnelly, "Medico-Legal Problems in Private Psychiatric Hospitals," *Am. J. Psychiat.* 121:465, 1964.

39. *In re* C.G., 144 N.J. Super. 579, 366 A.2d 733 (1976).

40. H. Lief, K. Young, V. Spruiell, R. Lancaster & N. Lief, "A Psychodynamic Study of Medical Students and Their Adaptational Problems," *J. Med. Ed.* 35:696, 1960. In a book that received wide attention, psychologist-author Daniel Goleman explains why many people with high IQs are less successful in their professions than those with lower scores: the former lack "emotional intelligence," abilities that include "self-control, zeal and persistence, and the ability to motivate oneself." To some degree these skills can be taught, he says, and should be both by parents and schools. D. Goleman, *Emotional Intelligence* (New York: Bantam, 1995); discussed in N. Gibbs (cover story), "The EQ Factor," *Time*, Oct. 2, 1995, p. 60.

41. Surprisingly, the problem of privacy has arisen in training analysis. Some psychoanalytic institutes ask an applicant's personal analyst for information regarding the applicant. Such inquiries from institutes constitute an invasion of privacy of the personal analysis, and is not compatible with psychoanalysis. T.S. Szasz, "The Problem of Privacy in Training Analysis," *Psychiatry* 25:195, 1962.

42. R. Slovenko, "Teaching Professional Responsibility: A Reply," *J. of Legal Ed.* 16:327, 1964.

43. D.W. Winnicott, *The Child and the Outside World* (London: Tavistock, 1957), p. 29.

44. 237 F.2d 898 (10th Cir. 1956).

45. D. Farnsworth, "The Psychotherapy of the College Student," in J. Masserman (ed.), *Current Psychiat. Therap.* 3:124, at 128, 1963.

46. J. Hall & K. Menninger, "'Psychiatry and the Law'—A Dual Review," *Iowa L. Rev.* 38:687, at 703, 1953.

47. The traditional idea that a child is the property of the parent has been drastically modified. The court now acts as *parens patriae.* In a number of cases, the courts have authorized medical treatment of minors over the protests of parents who refused such treatment. Thus, the court authorized a hospital to give a blood transfusion to an adult patient who had protested against it on religious grounds, and in so ordering, the judge made reference to the fact that the patient was the mother of an infant child and the judge suggested that his order was as much to protect the child's interest as for any other reason. Application of Georgetown College, 331 F.2d 1000 (D.C. 1964); see R. Slovenko, "The Psychiatric Patient, Liberty, and the Law," *Kan. L. Rev.* 13:59, 1964.

48. This is the policy generally agreed upon by university health centers. The university health service at Tulane University advises: "The student's con-

tacts with our services are strictly confidential. Absolutely no one in the University is notified of a student's visit, nor does it appear on any student's record. An exception would be if one of the deans or other administrative officials referred a student or faculty member to the clinic, in order that it might render an opinion concerning that person. One other exception would be where the clinic feels that the student is so upset, for instance, that he should leave school; then the clinic might notify the parents, but almost never over the student's objections." See generally, D. Farnsworth & P. Munter, "The Role of the College Psychiatrist," in G.B. Blaine & C.C. McArthur (eds.), *Emotional Problems of the Student* (New York: Appleton-Century-Crofts, 1961), p. 1; G.A. Peabody, "Campus Psychiatry," in J. Masserman (ed.), *Current Psychiat. Therap.* 1:1, 1961.

49.   G.K. Fritz, R.E. Mattison, B. Nurcombe & A. Spirito, *Child and Adolescent Mental Health Consultation in Hospitals, Schools, and Courts* (Washington, D.C.: American Psychiatric Press, 1993); D.T. Marsh & R.D. Magee, *Ethical and Legal Issues in Professional Practice with Families* (New York: Wiley, 1997).

# Chapter 6

# HOSPITAL CARE, CONSULTATION, SUPERVISION AND RESEARCH

Proper and efficient care of patients requires communications between various physicians and hospitals, or with others. A release of information to those interested in the care of the patient is usually cleared, generally in writing, with the patient.

A significant percentage of individuals who are hospitalized in general hospitals have coexisting psychiatric disorders, regressive symptoms in reaction to hospitalization, stress responses that exacerbate the illness, behavior patterns that complicate or impede treatment, or medication side effects or interactions. A major function of mental health professionals is providing consultation and liaison services.[1]

The existence of "health-care teams" means that information that previously had been held in confidence by an individual physician is now necessarily disseminated to many members of the team (not to mention chart reviewers, financial officers, insurance auditors, and quality-of-care assessors).[2] In response to a patient's concern about confidentiality, Dr. Mark Siegler of the University of Chicago School of Medicine enumerated the number of persons who had access to his hospital record: at least 25 and possibly as many as 100 health professionals and administrative personnel at the hospital. Despite his assurances that these people were all involved in providing or supporting his health-care services, the patient was distressed and retorted, "I always believed that medical confidentiality was part of a doctor's code of ethics. Perhaps you should tell me just what you people mean by 'confidentiality'!"

Following that experience, Dr. Siegler wrote in the *New England Journal of Medicine*:[3]

> The principle of medical confidentiality described in medical codes of ethics and still believed in by patients no longer exists. In this respect, it is a decrepit concept. Rather than perpetuate the myth of confidentiality and invest energy

403

vainly to preserve it, the public and the profession would be better served if they devoted their attention to determining which aspects of the original principle of confidentiality are worth retaining. Efforts could then be directed to salvaging those.

And he recommended: "Patients should be made aware of the large number of persons in the modern hospital who require access to the medical record in order to serve the patient's medical and financial interests."

Under a system similar to that of the military, records go (or should go) with a patient when transferred from a hospital to a clinic in the patient's community. In the event of another commitment or a transfer between hospitals, the record accompanies the patient. A coordinated mental health program requires a record system that places patient and family history at the fingertips of physicians, clinics, and hospitals.[4] One physician observed:[5]

> The celebrated doctor-patient relationship may become part of a triangle with the advent of computers in clinical medicine. We may now have to consider the doctor-patient-computer relationship, and the timeless ethical safeguards of a patient's privacy will take on new dimensions when almost any detail about almost any individual can be located electronically within the moment.

Does such a system violate confidentiality? The trend is toward interrelated medical centers and central medical records, and also collaboration with nursing homes, after-care homes, and other institutions. By undertaking treatment, to what extent does a patient implicitly give permission to other physicians and staff, and to researchers, recorders and others, to view the records? Apart from legal considerations, exchange and transfer of information should have the approval of the patient, otherwise the therapeutic relationship might be impaired. A patient will not likely protest a procedure designed to facilitate proper treatment.[6]

In making after-care placement or residential placement during treatment, the psychiatrist or social worker has the task of furnishing some information to the persons managing the home, or interpreting the patient's illness to them. The extent of disclosure must essentially be an individual determination. There are difficult questions. Should the family that will board the patient be advised, for example, that the patient has been suicidal, that he drinks excessively, that he is uncivil at the dinner table, or that he is a flirt?

## CASE CONFERENCES

Patients treated by medical students, interns, or residents are regularly presented at case conferences. It is quipped that a physician is a person who comes out of the middle class, learns on the lower class, and aspires to treat the upper class. This transition does not come easily—after all, one practices to a great extent as one has learned. Charity patients (and even patients in private hospitals) are often treated as objects—as physiological organisms without a mind. The patient may be depersonalized to "that kidney case in 103." Freud sought to change a patient's status from laboratory specimen to human being.

Individuals beginning psychotherapy at an educational institution usually, in their application, agree in advance to appear at a conference. It is explained as a part of the educational program, designed to help the patient as well as the therapist. Presentation before a conference, in fact, can be helpful not only for the training of the therapist, but also for the health of the patient. Conference presentation may result in a corrective emotional experience. The patient may derive a genuine sense of acceptability, not only by the therapist, but also by members of the group. Generally speaking, though, a patient who is reluctant to appear before a group, whether behind a one-way mirror or on closed-circuit TV, is not presented. The presentation of a patient, without his knowledge, is an affront to his dignity and might technically be said to violate his right of privacy.

## SUPERVISION AND PEER REVIEW

Confidentiality as an absolute principle would impede the "quality control" of care. Disclosure of information is essential for consultation, supervision or peer review.[7] The *Guidelines on Confidentiality* of the American Psychiatric Association states that "generally the sharing of clinical information between consultants directly involved in the care of a given patient does not require specific authorization, provided that the patient has approved of the consultation." "Similarly," it states, "letters of referral to other health care professionals, and letters in reply to such referrals, do not need specific authorization if the patient has approved the referral."

Without consent, the patient may feel aggrieved notably in the case where the patient has negative feelings about a consultant or supervisor. Consider the following complaint by a patient:[8]

> At the very beginning, and at various times throughout my therapy, I asked my psychiatrist if he talked to anyone about my case. He emphatically denied it. Later, when the therapy was terminated because he left town, I found out that he had been under supervision, supposedly on a private basis, for the entire therapy. Upon termination, the person he referred me to was the supervisor, an unlicensed psychotherapist. I was also on medication, which could not have

been given by the supervisor. I realize that leeway is given in regards to confidentiality between a therapist-supervisor. However, this was not a consultation, and more important, was not done in conjunction with any training program. Shouldn't I have been told from the beginning about the supervisor? Was his lying to me about not talking to anyone a breach of confidentiality?

In training settings, maintaining confidentiality often poses special problems. The APA's *Guidelines on Confidentiality* provide:[9]

All trainees should be informed of the professional responsibilities they are assuming and of their obligation to hold in confidence information they receive about patients. Special care must be taken by faculty and trainees alike not to discuss patients in corridors, elevators, or other public places where they may be overheard. When patients are presented at teaching conferences, their freely given consent must be obtained and care must be used not to identify them unnecessarily or to divulge sensitive material not directly pertinent to the presentation.

Training facilities should make their teaching role and its implications explicit in the documents that patients sign at the time of admission. Specific authorization is then not required for physicians to discuss the cases with trainees participating in programs approved by the institution. Trainees who make entries in patients' medical records should be instructed carefully about the issues of confidentiality involved and the need to exercise appropriate caution in what they include. Psychiatric residents who wish to make detailed "process" notes for discussion with their supervisors should generally keep these separate from official records and destroy such notes as soon as their use is over.

In training institutions, audio and video recordings of patients are occasionally made for teaching purposes. Disclosure of these recordings to persons not directly involved in the care of the patients cannot be made without the patients' written authorization. When making such recordings, it is wise to have patients authorize both the recordings themselves and the specific educational purposes for which they may be used, making provision for the patients to withdraw their consent at a later time if they so wish. Similarly, psychiatrists should take care not to disclose or make use of patients' artwork or other creative products in ways that would identify them in lectures and publications unless the patients' explicit permission is obtained.

Peer review, like supervision, calls for disclosure of information about the patient. All of these additional personnel are bound by the same ethics as the designated therapist. Judicially-ordained right-to-treatment envisions individualized treatment for institutionalized patients based on programs submitted for review to a mental health board.[10] Managed care may increase peer monitoring. Within a managed-care organization, providers have to compete on quality as well as cost, and this could well create a stronger incentive for them to monitor each other.

Professional standards review organizations (PSROs) were established in 1972 by the federal government in regard to services to Medicare patients but were terminated in 1982 because of lack of effectiveness.[11] In 1983, PSROs were replaced by peer review organizations (PROs). Federally financed and regulated but regionally operated by local contractors (approximately one per state), PROs are responsible for assuring the quality of services and eliminating unnecessary care. The PROs focus on reviewing high volume elective procedures, hospital admissions and stays, and transfers and readmissions. PROs emphasize retrospective review of records but also do some prospective review of selected procedures. The review is not based on an interview of a patient. The Omnibus Budget Reconciliation Act of 1986 expanded PRO activities to a variety of nonhospital settings, including ambulatory surgeries, nursing homes, home health care agencies, and health maintenance organizations.[12]

For physicians and hospitals not in the federal sector, the various states have enacted legislation granting immunity to peer review participants from liability and from testifying as to what transpired during peer review meetings, but some regulation does not discuss the discoverability of documents produced or created during these proceedings.[13]

Most states have enacted legislation providing that reports of professional review committees are privileged and confidential and are not discoverable in civil actions. Michigan's legislation provides that "the records, data, and knowledge collected for or by individuals or committees assigned a professional review function in a health facility or agency are confidential, shall be used only [for peer review], are not public records, and are not subject to court subpoena."[14]

For discovery, it is necessary to have a hearing (held *in camera*) to determine whether the information falls within the statutory protection. The mere submission of information to a peer review committee does not satisfy the collection requirement so as to bring the information within the protection of the statute.[15] Also, in deciding whether a particular committee assigned a review function so that information it collected is protected, the court may consider the hospital's bylaws and internal regulations, and whether the committee's function is one of current patient care or retrospective review.[16] Moreover, discovery and production of documents are restricted to those "relevant to the subject matter involved in the pending action."[17]

Various states have recognized a "self-analysis privilege" (also known as the privilege of self-critical analysis or the self-evaluation privilege) which affords a party in litigation the opportunity to shield from production an analysis critical of that party's conduct. The privilege is based on the rationale that it is in society's interests to allow a party's employees to engage in critical analysis and evaluation of the party's conduct, unfettered by the fear that such comments may be discoverable and used adversely to the party's interest in any ensuing litigation.[18]

The first case to articulate the self-analysis privilege was *Bredice v. Doctors Hospital*,[19] a medical malpractice action decided in 1970. In this case, the plaintiff sought production of minutes of a hospital peer review board meeting at which the death of plaintiff's decedent was discussed. The hospital objected to the production, arguing that the sole objective of the meetings was the improvement, through self-analysis, of the care and treatment of patients. The value of these discussions would be destroyed, said the hospital, if the staff meeting's participants knew that their constructive professional criticism could be used as evidence in a malpractice suit against their colleagues. The court agreed, finding that there "is an overwhelming public interest in having those staff meetings held on a confidential basis so that the flow of ideas and advice can continue unimpeded."[20]  The court reasoned:[21]

> The purpose of these staff meetings is the improvement, through self-analysis, of the efficiency of medical procedures and techniques. They are not a part of current patient care but are in the nature of a retrospective review of the effectiveness of certain medical procedures. The value of these discussions and reviews in the education of the doctors who participate, and the medical students who sit in, is undeniable. This value would be destroyed if the meetings and the names of those participating were to be opened to the discovery process.

The court then concluded that the meetings were entitled to a qualified privilege, one that can be overcome if the party seeking discovery can make a showing of extraordinary circumstances amounting to good cause for the production of the information.

The "extraordinary circumstances" test has not been widely followed; most courts have applied a balancing test to determine whether the privilege is applicable, to wit, the benefits that justify the privilege are weighed against societal interests involved in arriving at the truth. In *Gillman v. United States*,[22] the court found itself facing "the not uncommon dilemma of both sides being right."[23] The case involved the death of a mental patient at a Veterans Administration Hospital who had committed suicide by immolating himself after a self-dousing with turpentine. In the ensuing wrongful death action, the government contended that the board of inquiry report commissioned by the director of the Veterans Administration Hospital was privileged and not subject to disclosure.

The board of inquiry was convened to determine whether any disciplinary action should be taken against hospital personnel and whether any steps should be taken to change hospital procedure to prevent any recurrence. The government argued that the purposes of the board of inquiry would be thwarted if the proceedings were not accorded confidential status, claiming that neither the witnesses nor the board could speak freely if it were believed that the statements made could be used in a subsequent lawsuit by a prospective plaintiff. Indeed, the government argued that if such reports were discoverable, no such official inquiries would be undertaken, all to the detriment of patients.[24]

The plaintiff argued that without the report it would not be in a position to obtain information relevant to the facts surrounding the death. In weighing the claims of both sides and performing a balancing test as to whether the privilege should be allowed, the court allowed discovery of the statements of hospital personnel as to what in fact happened and denied discovery as to comments made for future improvements in hospital procedure.

In research, the principles to be observed are basically twofold. First, there is no justified objection to the use of data grouping statistics from many patients. Only data from one patient or subject can lead to identification of the individual. Second, in research requiring identification for follow up or other purposes, systems have been devised to achieve follow up that will protect the identity of the individuals. These methods have a review panel, separate from the researcher, that reviews the protocol to determine whether the project design has sufficient social merit to warrant using identifiable data without the consent of the subjects. This includes determining whether obtaining participant consent would vitiate the research design, or would be so cumbersome as to make it impractical (as in projects based on retrospective material). If the panel decides that obtaining permission would destroy a valuable project, then a broken-link set-up may be arranged. This approach centers on the treating source supplying the initial information with a coded number. The researcher or research unit would have no means to identify the subjects (and presumably ethically would make no effort to discover identities). For follow-up, the researcher would seek out the treating sources and the identifying code numbers, requesting that follow-up information be supplied. This system has been used in England, Ireland, and in some places in the United States.[25] The APA's *Guidelines on Confidentiality* provide:[26]

> Research studies that involve patients should not identify these patients in any way without their specific, written approval. Even then, care must be taken to limit access to confidential material and safeguard patients' privacy. Case material used for teaching purposes and in scholarly reports should be edited carefully to remove all identifying information about patients. When this cannot be done, patients' written authorization for use of the material should be obtained.

## NOTES

1. G.K. Fritz, R.E. Mattison, B. Nurcombe & A. Spirito, *Child and Adolescent Mental Health Consultation in Hospitals, Schools, and Courts* (Washington, D.C.: American Psychiatric Press, 1993).

2. The interdisciplinary team may involve the services of an attorney as in the case of the elderly. See B.V. Powell & R.C. Link, "The Sense of a Client: Confidentiality Issues in Representing the Elderly," *Fordham L. Rev.* 62:1197, 1994; H.A. Wydra, "Keeping Secrets Within the Team—Maintaining Client Confidentiality While Offering Interdisciplinary Services to the Elderly Client," *id.* 62:1517, 1994.

3. "Confidentiality in Medicine—A Decrepit Concept," *New Eng. J. of Med.* 307:1518, 1982.

4. Putting patients' records on the Internet's World Wide Web has already taken place. G.F. Knecht, "Click! Doctor to Post Patient Files on Net," *Wall Street Journal*, Feb. 20, 1996, p. B-1.

5. *Medical Tribune*, Nov. 26, 1962.

6. "Imagine you've been in a serious accident. You can't breathe. You are about to black out. Now how capable do you feel answering questions about your medical history? If you can't answer or if you don't know the answer, you run the risk of a possible life-threatening delay or a mistake. It's this mis-communication that leads to permanent injuries or even death to thousands of people each year." So begins the promotional announcement about the E.M.X. card, a form of electronic medical identification recently introduced in the New York area. When the card is passed through a device similar to a credit-card reader, emergency medical workers or doctors can, in seconds, get vital information, like the name of the patient's primary-care doctor, chronic illnesses or allergies, medications being taken, and even an image of the latest electrocardiogram. S. Gilbert, "Lifesaving Medical History Coming in a Flash," *New York Times*, Aug. 21, 1996, p. B-6. See Conn. Tit. 52, Ch. 889, 52-146f.

7. See A.K. Hess (ed.), *Psychotherapy Supervision/Theory, Research and Practice* (New York: Wiley, 1980).

8. Personal communication.

9. *Am. J. Psychiat.* 144:15-22 at 1529, 1987.

10. Wyatt v. Stickney, 344 F. Supp. 373 (M.D. Ala. 1972).

11. 42 U.S.C. §§ 1511 *et seq.* In 1979, Judge Gerhard Gesell of the U.S. District Court for the District of Columbia held that the PSRO entity was an "agency" of the Federal Government for purposes of the "Freedom of Information Act" and, further, that there was no statutory basis for with-holding peer review documents from the plaintiff. Public Citizens Health Research Group v. Dept. of HEW, 477 F. Supp. 595 (D.D.C. 1979).

12. D. Ermann, "Hospital Utilization Review: Past Experience, Future Directions," *J. Health Policy, Politics & Law* 13:683, 1988.

13. Louisiana's legislation (R.S. 40: 2205) provides:
    Notwithstanding any other provision of law, any health care provider licensed in this state who participates in quality of care or utilization reviews by a peer review committee, as a peer review committee member or a treating health care provider whose patients are subject to such review and have been contracted, employed or hired by a group purchaser shall be immune from liability for any act performed during such reviews of the activities of similarly licensed health care providers if such person acts without malice, makes a reasonable effort to obtain the facts and believes that the action taken is warranted by the facts. A peer review committee shall not be subject to discovery, and no person in attendance at such reviews shall be required to testify as to what transpired at such reviews. The utilization review requirements and administrative treatment guidelines of the peer review committee employed or hired by the group purchaser shall not fall below the appropriate standard of care and shall not impinge upon the independent medical judgment of the treating health care provider.
14. MCL 333.20175, 333.21515.
15. Monty v. Warren Hosp. Corp., 422 Mich. 138 (1985); Marchand v. Henry Ford Hosp., 398 Mich. 163, 247 N.W.2d 280 (1976). The court in Robinson v. Magovern, 83 F.R.D. 79 (1979) held that the State's Peer Review Protection Act does not shield from discovery events surrounding denial of staff privileges, including what occurred at meetings of the hospital's credentials committee and executive committees.
16. *Compare* Davidson v. Light, 79 FRD 137 (D. Colo. 1978),*with* Bredice v. Doctors Hospital, 50 FRD 249 (D.D.C. 1970), *aff'd without opinion*, 156 U.S. App. D.C. 199; 479 F.2d 920 (1973). See Coburn v. Seda, 101 Wash. 2d 270, 277, 677 P.2d 173, 180 (1984).
17. Mich. Gen. Court Rules 310.1(1).
18. M.J. Holland, "The Self-Analysis Privilege: Obscuring with the Truth but Safeguarding Improvement?" *The Brief* (Tort & Insurance Practice Section of American Bar Association), Fall 1995, vol. 25, no. 1, p. 52; see also Note, "The Privilege of Self-Critical Analysis," *Harv. L. Rev.* 96:1083, 1983.
19. 50 FRD 249 (D.D.C. 1970), *aff'd*, 479 F.2d 920 (D.C. Cir. 1973).
20. 50 FRD at 251.
21. 50 FRD at 250.
22. 53 FRD 316 (S.D. N.Y. 1971).
23. 53 FRD at 318.
24. *Ibid.*
25. See, *e.g.*, Michigan Health Code, M.C.L.A. §330.1748.
26. *Am. J. Psychiat.* 144:1522 at 1529, 1987.

# Chapter 7

# COMMUNICATIONS TO NONMEDICAL PERSONS IN RESPONSE TO INQUIRIES

In various situations, an individual is asked, and he may acknowledge, that he is seeing or has seen a physician or psychiatrist. Thereupon, the treating physician or psychiatrist may receive a request for information. The request may come from the family, an employer, insurance company, school or university, parole board, credit organization, motor vehicle department, professional organization, welfare department, the military, or others.

With deinstitutionalization, the emotional burden and continuous caring role of the mentally ill has been placed more on families. Management of the mentally ill patient needs to take into account the impact it has on the family. Helping families to cope with and manage the burden of caring requires consultation and planning. Educating about illness and supportive counseling help alleviate the stress on the family.

To qualify for Supplemental Security Income (SSI) benefits (which are provided to children with severe disabilities in low-income families), families need to obtain as much evidence about their child as possible. They must be able to show exactly how much the disability limits what the child can do at home, in school and elsewhere. Information from the child's physician, therapist, nurse, or teacher is very helpful. The child must have a physical or mental condition that can be medically proven and results in "marked and severe functional limitations" or substantial duration. The condition must meet a specific disability in the Social Security Administration's List of Impairments or be medically or functionally equal to the severity of a listed impairment. As guardian, parents are entitled to information about their child.

In other situations, families of patients complain about the reluctance of therapists to share information about the patient's illness out of concern about breaching confidentiality.[1] In the book *How to Live With a Mentally Ill Person*, Christine Adamec writes, "Issues of confidentiality can be a problem for caregivers because mental health professionals, fearing lawsuits or reprisals from their professional association, may refuse to provide information on medications, treatment, prognosis, and other issues involving adults who are mentally ill."[2]

Trust is confused with confidentiality. Dr. E. Fuller Torrey has this to say:[3]

> [S]uch confidentiality has been invoked to an absurd degree by professionals....[It] is a travesty of confidentiality. More often than not, such reluctance to share information under the guise of confidentiality simply reflects the disinterest of the mental illness professionals in having anything to do with nonprofessionals. It may also represent the lingering psychoanalytic orientation of the professionals with an implicit message: "You the family caused this disease, so now as punishment you have no right to know what is going on."

Some families threaten the therapist or hospital with a lawsuit based on the alleged ground that failure to provide them with needed information is malpractice.[4] In the *American Journal of Psychiatry*, Dr. Marc Hollender examined the relationship of the hospital psychiatrist with the family or sundry agencies that request or need information or recommendations. In part, he wrote:[5]

> Some hospital psychiatrists will provide information if it is "for the good of the patient," and then only if a release form has been signed....The psychiatrist is often the agent of the patient's family or the hospital as well as of the patient. Insofar as the patient is unable or unwilling to assume responsibility and to participate in decision-making concerning the treatment he will receive, this must be taken over by others, usually his family. To function in decision-making, the family must be provided with information. . . . This stands in sharp contrast to making decisions about the patient's ability to work or attend school after he has been discharged from the hospital. In the latter situation, the focus is on the good of an institution (company, school, etc.), whereas in the former, it is for the good of the patient.

And in the latter situations, what happens when psychiatric information is provided? Could not the institution do as well, or even better, by applying its usual method of selection, uncontaminated by data which may be understood poorly? The practice of supplying a label (*e.g.*, schizophrenia) may be unhelpful or misleading.

To "screen out misfits," it has been the practice of employers to ask prospective employees about personal finances, past employment, union activities, drinking record, physical and mental condition, police record, driving habits, sexual activities, political beliefs, and many other topics.[6] Many of these types of queries have been curtailed by the Americans with

Disabilities Act. Still today, some companies require present and prospective employees to sign a statement allowing the use of a lie detector.[7]

Administrative responsibility is often shifted onto psychiatrists or psychologists, directly or indirectly, by overweighing their opinions. For example, employees in Civil Service cannot be discharged merely for incompetence and inefficiency (how can one prove laziness, lack of interest, lack of devotion to a job, or inability to get along with supervisors or fellow workers?), hence a higher quality selection procedure is demanded.

In a competitive economy, employers want to choose employees who best fit the job and they need to monitor their work in order to maintain or improve productivity. Much of the broadened need for information derives from the expanded responsibilities of the employer in two important and costly areas: health insurance and liability. Health insurance costs have been cutting into profits at an exponential rate and the courts have held that an employer's "strong public interest" in containing health costs may outweigh an employee's right of privacy.

In the area of liability, under the tort of "negligent hiring," an employer can be held liable for failure to adequately check the past history of the employee.[8] To know which employees are high risk requires information, either from medical or psychological tests or personal questions and surveillance.[9]

The applicant must understand, in applying for employment or insurance, that when he is examined by a company physician or is referred for examination, the physician will report to the company. The examination does not create a physician-patient relationship. It is paid for and made solely for the benefit of the prospective employer or insurance company. In these circumstances, confidentiality cannot be expected, and the physician need not obtain the consent of the person examined before making the report. The situation is different, however, when the treating physician is asked for information.

In *Clark v. Geraci*,[10] an employee, an accountant, asked his physician to write a letter to the Air Force, his employer, verifying that the employee's frequent absences were due to illness. The physician did so, but he added that the illness was not a succession of colds, as the employee had reported, but alcoholism. The Air Force fired the employee. Thereupon, the employee brought suit for damages against the physician. By requesting the physician to make a report, the employee is held to have authorized the disclosure. The court ruled in favor of the physician.[11]

The U.S. Supreme Court denied a petition for a writ of certiorari in *Anonymous v. Kissinger*,[12] which involved a Peace Corps worker whose appointment to a supposedly sensitive State Department position was contingent on a security clearance. The applicant answered negatively to the standard question, "Have you ever had a nervous breakdown or have you ever had medical treatment for a mental condition?" Finding this to be a false answer, the State Department demanded disclosure of his medical records. He refused, and was dismissed.[13]

Commercial inquiries into the private affairs of individuals have become accepted as part of the price people pay for living in a credit-oriented society. As the amount of credit extended to consumers has grown, so has the business of investigating consumers' personal affairs. Such inquiries embrace not only debts and assets and buying habits but also employment records, medical records, and personal lives—the last often in astonishingly intimate detail. For the most part, such information is collected by private agencies on behalf of a widespread corporate clientele.

Generally, the agencies that specialize in collecting information on consumers are of two kinds—credit bureaus and consumer-investigation agencies. Credit bureaus report to their clients—department stores and other retailers, businessmen, banks, credit-card companies, finance companies—what is known as ledger information on consumers; that is, information from existing records on how a consumer who has applied for credit has been paying his bills.

The second kind of company—the consumer-investigation agency—sells an essentially different service, which is the compilation and dissemination of reports on applicants for various kinds of insurance and the claims arising out of such insurance; it also reports on applicants for employment with private companies, and some home mortgages and apartment leases. Many of the reports do more than verify applicants' answers to questionnaires; they purport to describe, among other things, the character, the reputation, the general style of life and work, the medical condition, the housekeeping habits, the drinking habits, and even the sexual habits of the people involved.

The following is a typical inquiry from an insurance company to a physician of a patient in treatment:

> Your patient has applied to us for needed insurance protection. In order to consider his application, we need information from you concerning his health history. To help determine this person's eligibility for insurance, will you please give us details of consultations for the past five years. Please furnish information on dates attended, complaints and abnormal physical findings, duration of illness, diagnosis, and describe treatment or operation. Please also give details of nervous disorders in full details, in addition to the other details for the past five years. Attached is a copy of the authorization form signed by the applicant. A prompt reply will help us give your patient prompt service and will be greatly appreciated.

Many inquiries are designed for the patient's benefit; they do not all come from an adversary.[14] When seeking payment under an existing insurance policy, a person must furnish information to the insurance company to justify the claim.[15] Insurers must be satisfied that the claim is legitimate. The information need not necessarily be very personal, but nonetheless the situation at times may pose difficulties.

The release of information regarding the psychiatric illness of a patient when insurance is involved is an issue of increasing importance. If insurance companies are to provide coverage for psychiatric illness, they must feel that they will get correct information to assess fairly the costs of their programs. Psychiatrists, however, generally feel that the insurer should accept the word of the physician and should not expect the same sort of information provided to them regarding physical disorders.

A survey of psychiatrists in northern California revealed that inquiries from insurance companies constitute the greatest third-party involvement.[16] Increased insurance coverage for health care precipitated the concern with confidentiality and the conceptual model of psychiatric practice. Out of concern about payment, there has been a resurgence in American psychiatry to link psychiatry more closely with medicine.[17]

In order to provide coverage for any treatment, an insurance carrier must be able to obtain information with which it can assess the administration and costs of programs. Statistics provide the predictability which is at the heart of the insurance process. By associating the medical model with psychiatry, insurers expect to receive information comparable to that for physical disorders. They expect reports "to verify that illness or disease is present." Indeed, some insurers use the same forms for cases involving surgery as for those involving psychiatric treatment—it is illustrative of how rhetoric not only expresses but shapes our ideas and actions.[18]

Freud noted that in psychotherapy, the doctor is not a doctor, and the patient is not a patient. Quite logically, then, if psychiatry were considered to be the reeducation of a demoralized individual rather than the treatment of a disease, a different type of report would be expected. Assume for a moment that education was an insured activity. Would the educator have to provide a diagnostic category and a report on the style of instruction? Probably not, but using the medical model, the insurer asks for this information and assumes that it is a safeguard. The assumption that the right name or label gets to the essence of and gives insight into the person or situation labeled pervades every aspect of life. Our national motto could be, "In Labels We Trust." Insurance carriers believe (or at least at one time believed) that psychiatric labeling assures that the psychiatrist "has control over the problem and knows what to do with it."

A diagnostic label, in theory, provides a description or diagnosis, an etiological explanation, and a prognosis. In considerable measure, a medical label, *e.g.*, diabetes, does furnish such a description, information about etiology, suggested treatment, and prognosis. Some assume that psychiatric labels do the same. In fact, a psychiatric label bears no relevance to the insurer's concerns and almost no relevance to clinical status, prognosis, or treatment. Given the same label, the treatment may be drug therapy, electroshock, or hospitalization. Psychiatrists are bemused by the question, "How long do you keep an average schizophrenic in the hospital?" Medicare asks for all of the records of Medicare patients of a therapist to ascertain whether they are receiving equal treatment.

Psychiatry has been debating whether its diagnostic categories are useful for psychiatry, but however that is resolved, labels assuredly are useful for neither law nor insurance. For example, since an insurer provides no coverage for treatment of "marital maladjustment," the psychiatrist searches for a classification that is covered, such as "anxiety neurosis." Consequently, the insurer increasingly asks for more information. Should the insurer ask how the transference and countertransference are developing? Not even a full psychiatric report would enlighten the insurer as already he does not know what to make of the information received.[19] With the increasing number of people covered by insurance, reports have become more and more bureaucratized and often have less and less meaning. The insurer's concern with overutilization of services may be alleviated by adequate supervision.[20]

Where the employer pays a part or all of the employee's insurance premium, the employer receives information to justify his cost (actually paid for by the employee through his labor). Through the efforts of the APA Task Force on Confidentiality, representatives of the Health Insurance Council agreed to supply employers with "experience reports" that omit any data identifying the employees who created the expenses on the program.[21] Though aggregate reporting is the prevailing practice, there are some instances when high-risk employees have been identified to the employer who then discharged them in order to obtain a lower premium. Such practice discourages an employee from seeking psychiatric help even though the costs are covered by insurance.[22]

An insurer, when called upon to pay disability benefits under a compensation plan, wants to know whether a condition exists that prevents the claimant from working at his usual job. For example, a person in the course of his employment loses an arm. He may be able to return to work using his other arm, but he may claim that he has developed a phobia about returning to the place. A psychiatric examination is requested. (One who visits a psychiatrist for the purpose of obtaining a report does not expect and does not receive a promise of confidentiality.) Other verification through witnesses is usually available, but the insurer finds it easier to substantiate the claim on the basis of a psychiatric report. In such cases, the psychiatric report often appears as stereotyped a production as the pleadings of an attorney.[23]

The general practice of insurers is that the confidentiality of records is maintained and information about a patient is guarded. Under prevailing practice, the records are confined to the medical department of the insurance company.[24] One wonders whether the concern over confidentiality, *vis-a-vis* a third-party payer, is designed to protect the interest of the patient or that of the therapist. The oaths of Hippocrates and Maimonides represent sacred commitments that they will, "as long as they live, protect not themselves nor their profession, but their patients."[25]

In law, as a general principle, the privacy of a fiduciary is justified only to the extent that it serves the interests of the beneficiary. Of the testimonial privilege, the courts have said that the privilege exists solely for the patient's benefit.[26] A person may want some things known by nobody; other things he may not mind having disclosed to strangers. To paraphrase George Orwell, some confidential matters are more confidential than others. The available evidence indicates that patients are not concerned about the divulgence of that type of information needed to justify a bill to a third-party payer, to review the competency of the therapist, or to provide material for follow-up and research.[27] The public is primarily concerned about the delivery, quality, and cost of health care (psychiatric or medical), and only marginally concerned about privacy.[28]

At least one psychiatrist has suggested that managed care's increasing invasion of confidentiality might be turned around and used for the benefit of therapists and their patients. By way of example, Dr. Helen Ullrich writes:[29]

> Discussions about the content of notes and of the information provided to managed care might contribute to the therapeutic alliance. In addition, patient education might decrease the solitude of illness and increase hope for a positive outcome. Documentation for dangerousness to self or others and severe disability (in which cases hospitalization may be necessary) might contribute to the therapeutic alliance for patient care. The patient may interpret this as physician concern. Moreover, *Diagnostic and Statistical Manual* documentation might hide much personal information.

In large measure, concern over privacy is a reflection of one's sense of security. Bob Slocum, the corporate executive, in Joseph Heller's *Something Happened* spends his working life fearing and distrusting his associates, all 120 of them. The insecurity or social paranoia upon which secrecy feeds, makes sharing of problems and learning to accept oneself difficult.[30]

Considering the social milieu, confidentiality in psychotherapy is essential, but to consider confidentiality as an absolute would impede the "quality control" of care. "Quality control" necessitates a review of individual patients and therapists and involves, not indiscriminate, but discriminate disclosure. The therapist in training must "breach" the confidence of his patient in order to discuss the case with his supervisor. Judicially ordained right-to-treatment envisions individualized treatment for institutionalized patients based on programs submitted for review to a mental health board.[31] In an attempt to insure that the data would not go beyond the board, a code system was used by some states to conceal the names of patients and therapists. The system proved unmanageable. (In any event, the value of supervision based on reports is dubious as such reports tend to be self-serving declarations.)

Confidentiality is also an obstacle to research. The Michigan Mental Health Code, for example, provides that information shall be disclosed:[32]

> as necessary for the purpose of outside research, evaluation, accreditation, or statistical compilation, provided that the person who is the subject of the information can be identified from the disclosed information only when such information is essential in order to achieve the purpose for which the information is sought or when preventing such identification would clearly be impractical, but in no event when the subject of the information is likely to be harmed by such identification.

With no time limit in which the request must be acknowledged, the researcher is often exhausted in his efforts to obtain any compliance. Year in and year out, law students meet a stone wall of resistance in their attempt to check on hospital or aftercare treatment programs.[33] Without the names and addresses of the patients, follow-up is impossible. Although most of the patients would be delighted to meet with the students, the hospital staff, perhaps understandably, is unwilling to expend the time and effort needed to contact the patients and obtain their approval. It is a foregone conclusion that the researcher will receive no cooperation from the private practitioner. Follow-up studies might focus on the allegation that psychotherapists "go merrily along from failure to failure." "If psychotherapy were a drug," it is said, "the FDA would ban it." As things stand, only the subpoena brings forth information, and then only when the patient becomes involved in litigation and his condition is in issue.

The FDA, recognizing the valuable role that hospitals play in the detection of adverse events and problems with medical products, views every active hospital monitoring program as a vital component of the national postmarketing surveillance system. Hospital reporting of adverse events, both within and outside an individual facility, is a mixture of voluntary and mandatory reporting.

Adverse event monitoring by hospitals is linked to Joint Commission on Accreditation of Healthcare Organizations (JCAHO) standards. In order to be accredited, JCAHO requires each hospital to monitor for adverse events involving pharmaceuticals and devices, with medication monitoring to be a continual collaborative function. JCAHO standards indicate that medical product adverse event reporting should be done per applicable law/regulation, including those of state/federal regulatory bodies.

The American Society of Health-System Pharmacists (ASHP) has also been instrumental in the evolution of active internal hospital adverse drug event (ADE)-monitoring systems. ASHP guidelines include delineated criteria for classifying an adverse drug reaction (ADR) as significant, unlike JCAHO standards, which do not mandate a specific definition for a serious ADE. ASHP guidelines specifically state serious or unexpected ADRs should be reported to FDA, manufacturer, or both.[34] As user facilities, hospitals are subject to mandatory federal medical device adverse event reporting.

Reporting by individual healthcare providers is essentially voluntary. However, manufacturers and distributors of FDA approved pharmaceuticals (drugs and biologicals) and medical devices, plus pharmaceutical packers and device user facilities, all have mandatory reporting requirements. The FDA acknowledges the concerns of health professionals regarding their confidentiality as reporters, and that of the patients whose cases they report. In order to encourage reporting of adverse events, FDA regulations offer substantial protection against disclosure of the identities of both reporters and patients. This was further strengthened in 1995, when a regulation went into effect extending this protection against disclosure by preempting state discovery laws regarding voluntary reports held by pharmaceutical, biological, and medical devise manufacturers.[35]

What about inquiries in regard to admission to universities or for professional licensure or appointment? A number of universities inquire whether the applicant has ever been under the care of a psychiatrist. When this is acknowledged, the student may be directed to have his complete psychiatric history transmitted to the university psychiatric consultant.[36]

Dr. Kay Redfield Jamison, now a professor of psychiatry at the Johns Hopkins University School of Medicine, devotes a good part of her book *An Unquiet Mind*[37] to a discussion of her concern about revealing her history of manic-depressive illness when she applied for licensure and academic appointment. In the application for clinical privileges, it was asked: "Are you currently suffering from, or receiving treatment for any disability or illness, including drug or alcohol abuse, that would impair the proper performance of your duties and responsibilities at this hospital?" The inquiry made her cringe, and she also cringed at the thought that those whom she would teach would, in deference to what they perceive to be her feelings, not say what they really think or not ask the questions that they otherwise should and would ask.

Jamison says that she was both fortunate and careful. She never had to give up her clinical privileges, although, on her own, she canceled or rescheduled appointments when she felt it would be in the best interests of patients. She writes:[38]

> The possibility always exists that my illness, or the illness of any clinician, for that matter, might interfere with clinical judgment. Questions about hospital privileges are neither unfair nor irrelevant. I don't like having to answer them, but they are completely reasonable. The privilege to practice is exactly that, a privilege; it is not a right. The real dangers, of course, come about from those clinicians (or, indeed, from those politicians, pilots, businessmen, or other individuals responsible for the welfare and lives of others) who—because of the stigma or the fear of suspension of their privileges or expulsion from medical school, graduate school, or residency—are hesitant to seek out psychiatric treatment. Left untreated, or unsupervised, many become ill, endangering not only their own lives but the lives of others; often, in an attempt to medicate their own moods, many doctors will also become alcoholics or drug abusers. It is not uncommon for depressed physicians to prescribe antidepressant medications for themselves; the results can be disastrous.

For the avowed purpose of safeguarding the public, the Board of Bar Examiners in various states have inquired of applicants to enter the bar about mental illness, alcoholism or substance abuse. In most states, some type of mental health question appears on their bar applications.[39] Eighteen states ask questions that are unlimited in scope or time, such as:

> Have you ever consulted a psychiatrist, psychologist, mental health counselor or medical practitioner for any mental, nervous, emotional condition or drug or alcohol use?
> Have you ever been diagnosed as having a nervous, mental, emotional condition or drug or alcohol problem?

Does the inquiry advance a determination of fitness to practice? In 1983, in a notable case, *Florida Board of Bar Examiners Re: Applicant*,[40] the applicant refused to answer a question on the bar application about treatment for mental disorders. The Florida Supreme Court, rejecting state and federal constitutional arguments, decided the state's interest in protecting the public outweighed the individual's privacy rights. The inquiry furthers a "legitimate state interest...The pressures placed on an attorney are enormous and his mental and emotional stability should be at such a level that he is able to handle his responsibilities," the court said.

Following that decision, the scope of inquiry expanded. At the same time, concerns about responding have caused applicants to avoid treatment or to answer falsely. They recognize that, even if admission is ultimately recommended, those who acknowledge that they have been in treatment face additional investigation and possible delay.

In the Florida case, the court recognized that there is "no precise list of medical conditions that may affect a person's fitness to practice law and no uniformity among people who suffer from those conditions." That is to say, the presence of a medical or psychiatric condition is not an accurate predictor of fitness, and individuals react differently to the same conditions. Nevertheless, the court did not reject questions inquiring about impairment.

Since then, in 1990, Congress passed the Americans with Disabilities Act (ADA). The ADA prohibits medical inquiries or exams during the interview process, but permits asking if an applicant can perform essential job functions. The ADA defines "disability" as "(A) a physical or mental impairment that substantially limits one or more of the major life activities of such individual; (B) a record of such an impairment; or (C) being regarded as having such an impairment."[41]

Under the ADA, an employer may not ask about the existence, nature, or severity of a disability and may not conduct medical examinations until after it makes a conditional job offer to the applicant. This prohibition ensures that the applicant's hidden disability is not considered prior to the assessment of the applicant's nonmedical qualifications. At this pre-offer stage, employers may ask about an applicant's ability to perform specific job-related functions and also may ask other questions that are not disability-related and may require examinations that are not medical.[42]

After a conditional offer is made, an employer may require medical examinations and may make disability-related inquiries if it does so for all entering employees in the job category. If an examination or inquiry screens out an individual because of disability, the exclusionary criterion must be job-related and consistent with business necessity. The employer also must show that the criterion cannot be satisfied and the essential functions cannot be performed with reasonable accommodation, though the employer can demand that an employee prove his right to an accommodation. Unless the disability is obvious, the employer is entitled to medical documentation, including information about the employee's functional limitations, so that he can determine how to accommodate them.[43]

Responding to an ADA challenge, U.S. District Judge James Cacheris for the Eastern District of Virginia in a lawsuit brought by Julie Ann Clark obliged the Virginia Board of Bar Examiners to withdraw the question "Have you within the past five years been treated or counseled for a mental, emotional or nervous disorder?"[44]

At trial, the Board of Bar Examiners offered the testimony of Dr. Charles Mutter, a psychiatrist and assistant professor at the University of Miami

School of Medicine. He insisted that broad mental health questions are essential to collect complete information on an applicant's fitness to practice law. Narrower inquiries allow applicants to filter their responses and provide self-promoting answers, he said.

For the applicant, Dr. Howard Zonana of the Department of Psychiatry of Yale University School of Medicine testified that the question is overbroad and ineffective in identifying those unfit to practice law. There is little evidence, he testified, to support the ability of bar examiners, or even mental health professionals, to predict inappropriate or irresponsible future behavior based on a person's history of mental health treatment.

Judge Cacheris concluded that Dr. Mutter's position is "unsupported by objective evidence and is discordant with a contemporary understanding of mental health questions under the ADA." Judge Cacheris did state, however, that some form of mental health inquiry is appropriate during the application process.

About a year earlier, in August 1994, the ABA's House of Delegates recommended that bar examiners narrowly tailor questions on mental health and treatment to "elicit information about current fitness to practice law." It stated:

> • BE IT RESOLVED, that the American Bar Association recommends that when making character and fitness determinations for the purpose of bar admission, state and territorial bar examiners, in carrying out their responsibilities to the public to admit only qualified applicants worthy of the public trust, should consider the privacy concerns of bar admission applicants, tailor questions concerning mental health and treatment narrowly in order to elicit information about current fitness to practice law, and take steps to ensure that their processes do not discourage those who would benefit from seeking professional assistance with personal problems and issues of mental health from doing so.

The American Psychiatric Association has no official position on state bar applications. The organization's work group on disclosure, however, has published guidelines that apply in such cases. "The only real issue is whether they are currently impaired to do the job at hand," said Dr. James H. Scully, Jr., deputy medical director of the APA.

Several other suits during the past few years have involved mental health inquiries on various applications. In at least eight states, suits involving bar applications were settled, and the states voluntarily narrowed the questions on the forms. Some ask only about hospitalization or institutionalization for mental problems, others ask about continuous treatment for mental or emotional disorder, and others ask about specific diagnosis or if mental disorder will affect ability to practice law.[45] Arizona and Massachusetts ask no mental health questions and five other states (Hawaii, Illinois, New Mexico, Pennsylvania, and Utah), without legal challenge, recently struck such questions from applications. Another 18 states, however, ask broad mental health questions, like the one challenged in Virginia.[46]

What mental condition, if any, warrants disqualification from the Bar? Paranoia? Psychosis? Attention deficit disorder (ADD)?[47] Over the last ten years, a Michigan lawyer regularly misplaced case files, missed appointments with clients, and failed to file the proper paperwork in dozens of appeals, most of them for criminal defendants. When the State Bar of Michigan moved to stop him from practicing, he explained that he had ADD, which prevented him from concentrating on deadlines. He took his case to the Sixth Circuit U.S. Court of Appeals, arguing that under the ADA, the state must allow him, distracted or not, to continue practice. He wanted the state to help him find a "structured setting" that would allow him to work despite his disorder. That, he argued, is the "reasonable accommodation" of a disability which the ADA requires. States have been obliged to give would-be lawyers with attention problems extra time to take the bar exam.

Traist such as irritability, chronic lateness, poor inpulse control or poor judgement are not deemed disabilities, but they may be manifestations of a mental impairment. In one case an emergency medical technician who was fired for "conduct unbecoming a paramedic and a history of rudeness to patients and colleagues" claimed that his obnoxiousness was a result of fluctuating blood sugar caused by diabetes. In his lawsuit he contended that he could have been accommodated by assignment to a less hectic work station. The district court dismissed the case, but the Sixth Circuit reversed, ruling that it was a "fact question" for the jury to decide whether he could function effectively with adequate accommodation. The court had to grapple with the ADA's definition of a disability as an impairment that "substantially limits one or more of the major life activities" of an individual. Did this plantiff's diabetes constitute such a "substantial limitation"? What if it could be controlled through a regimen of diet, medication and exercise? All three of the judges on the panel hald that the plaintiff should be able to sue, but two of the judges ruled that a claimant's ability to control his condition through medication or other medical devices should be taken into account in determining to what extent he is disabled. Under EEOC guidelines, the determination of whether a person is substantially limited in a major life activity is made without regard to the corrective effects of medication.

Figure 11. BIZARRO © By Dan Piraro. Reprinted with permission of Universal Press Syndicate. All rights reserved.

Harvard Law Professor Mary Ann Glendon recounts that when she was with a law firm, a young associate suffered from "a strange malady" which causes its victims to erupt in periodic outbursts of obscenities. A senior partner who happened to be on the board of the Menninger Foundation made sure, she says, that everyone knew that the associate's startling and unpredictable displays were the result of illness. The associate was given "back room" research work for a couple of years until hopes of a cure faded and another position could be found.[48]

The ADA does not excuse employees, though they may claim a disability, who violate rules of conduct (provided those rules are enforced uniformly).[49] The Joint Industry Board in New York was found to have acted legitimately when it fired an employee for his threatening, menacing behavior, despite the employee's claim that it was a symptom of his "general anxiety disorder."[50] Similarly, a federal court in Texas found that an employer did not violate the ADA when it fired an employee who had burned himself after failing to follow safety rules on handling hazardous chemicals. The employee had claimed his diabetes resulted in poor concentration.[51]

Paranoia is a dangerous condition, but at the same time it is a condition that is an asset for lawyers as it abets cross-examination. Long Island RR killer Colin Ferguson, though a layman, did, some believe, a rather good job in defending himself. Yet, as Thomas Friedman of the *New York Times* wrote about the O.J. Simpson trial, Simpson's lawyers have undermined public faith in the legal system by inventing government conspiracies behind every drop of spilt blood. Unlike Ferguson, they were not clinically mentally ill. In 1944, a New York appellate court denied a right-wing extremist admission to the Bar.

And what about psychosis, the condition asked about on the Michigan bar application? According to a song, the skies of Texas are not cloudy all day. Likewise, a person may not be psychotic all day, every day. People fall apart, and they pull themselves together. A client in a few minutes can detect whether a lawyer is psychotic. Indeed, under the law of evidence, a lay person is permitted to give an opinion on sanity. What is not obvious is the lawyer's competency or integrity.

Applicants are not denied licenses when they admit to a history of mental illness or addiction. Rather, it triggers an investigation and is considered with other evidence. But how does the inquiry on mental illness further the investigation and protect the public? Does it inform about competency or integrity? The most reliable predictor of future behavior is past behavior, and past behavior is a legitimate subject of inquiry. By focusing on diagnosis or the fact of treatment, instead of behavior that may be associated with it, an assessment of an individual would leave much to be desired.

Moreover, by requiring an individual to waive the privacy of a medical record would discourage seeking treatment. A study of the effect of asking about mental health treatment on state bar applications found that "students anticipating bar examinations and the extensive inquiry that accompanies them may avoid professional mental health consultation for fear of 'damaging' their record and delaying their admission while an investigation of fitness ensues."[52]

Ordinary citizens called for jury duty are asked numerous personal questions. The law offers no protection to jurors—unlike job applicants—from prying inquiries. On the contrary, in most cases judges require that potential jurors provide the information demanded. In the murder trial of O.J. Simpson, Judge Lance Ito asked potential jurors 302 written questions. The prosecutors and defense attorneys in the case believed that these questions were relevant in selecting a fair and impartial jury.[53] Postconviction relief based on an allegation of the dysfunction of the jury process on the ground of juror insanity is an elusive remedy.[54]

## NOTES

1. Therapists often claim that disclosure may be harmful to the patient. Pending Texas SB 72 would specifically provide that if a physician has reason to believe that disclosure to a legally authorized representative of a patient would be harmful to the patient's physical, mental, or emotional health, the physician may disclose to that representative only whether the requested records exist and whether the patient is in the facility. Where further disclosure is sought and denied, the physician must report this to the Department of Protective and Regulatory Services and seek a protective order on behalf of the patient. Where a hearing is held on the motion for a protective order, the court shall determine what information may be disclosed and what information shall remain confidential.

2. New York: Wiley, 1996, pp. 73-74.

3. *Surviving Schizophrenia* (New York: Harper Collins, 3d ed. 1995), pp. 311-312.

4. In Bellah v. Greenson, 81 Cal. App.3d 614, 146 Cal. Rptr. 535 (1978), the court found no duty of a psychiatrist to alert a patient's parents about suicidal propensity. It declined to extend the duty under *Tarasoff* to self-inflicted harm. See Part IV, Chapter 2.

5. "The Psychiatrist and the Release of Patient Information," *Am. J. Psychiat.* 116:828, 1960.

6. In 1997 the Netherlands enacted legislation placing limitations on medical examinations for job and insurance applicants. The legislation forbids medical examinations for job applicants except in situations where the position requires special physical abilities, such as in the case of pilots. The law also forbids testing applicants for incurable illnesses on the grounds that the individuals right "to not know" is more important than the possible advantages of such a test for employers and insurers. *Netherlander*, April 26, 1997, p. 2.

7. In the 1980s, lie detector testing was widely used. By 1987, an estimated 1.8 million polygraph tests were being conducted annually, with 75 percent of those being administered to job applicants. In 1988, Congress enacted the Employee Polygraph Protection Act (EPPA), which essentially bars the use of polygraphs, voice stress analyzers, and other physiological tests as job-screening devices by private employers. Exceptions were made for the pharmaceutical industry, security-guard companies, and government. Testing of employees suspected of specific incidents of theft is still permitted under the EPPA. See EPPA, 29 U.S.C. §2001 *et seq.*; E. Alderman & C. Kennedy, *The Right to Privacy* (New York: Knopf, 1995); J. Ridgeway, "The Snoops," *New Republic*, Dec. 19, 1964, p. 13.

8. In Foster v. The Loft, 26 Mass. App. 289, 526 N.E.2d 1309 (1988), a customer brought an action against an employer alleging negligent retention of an employee who injured the customer. The Massachusetts appellate court held that the employer was negligent in the retention of its employee, since the jury could find that the employer made no attempt to check on the employee's background or experience and made no inquiry of him as to job

or character references. In Copithorne v. Framingham Union Hospital, 401 Mass. 860, 520 N.E.2d 139 (1988), another Massachusetts case, a victim raped by a visiting staff physician at a hospital sued the physician and the hospital for injuries suffered during the rape. The Supreme Judicial Court of Massachusetts held that a material issue of fact existed as to whether the hospital's negligence in continuing the physician's staff privileges, after receiving actual notice of prior incidents in which the physician sexually assaulted patients, proximately caused the victim's injuries.

9. See E. Alderman & C. Kennedy, *The Right to Privacy* (New York: Knopf, 1995).

10. 28 Misc. 2d 791, 208 N.Y.S.2d 564 (1960).

11. The court said that the physician's "right, if not his duty, to his government to make a full disclosure of the facts superseded his duty to his patient to remain silent." This statement was contested. *Physician's Legal Brief*, Aug. 1962, vol. 4, no. 8.

12. 420 U.S. 990 (1975).

13. *Psychiatric News*, May 7, 1975, p. 1.

14. The U.S. Railroad Retirement Board, in communications with hospitals, asks about the payment of an insurance annuity: "In order that we might determine whether any benefits payable to this person might still be paid to him on his own account it is requested that you again advise us whether or not he is capable of understanding the act of endorsement." Social Security asks whether the patient is able to manage his funds or whether a curator should be appointed. See J. Lerner, "Confidentiality of Psychiatric Reports in Evaluating Social Security Disability Claims," *Am. J. Psychiat.* 120:992, 1964.

    Welfare departments question the physician about indigent patients whom he has treated. The welfare authorities need a report to learn the extent of attention the patient requires. By requesting and accepting welfare medical care, it is considered that the patient waives his right to secrecy. Physicians are cautioned to furnish information to organizations such as the Red Cross and the Cancer Society only upon written release from the patient. W. Eaton, "When to Violate a Patient's Confidence," *Med. Economics*, March 12, 1962, p. 147.

15. There is the requirement for medical certification of disability in order to qualify for workers' compensation or other type of disability insurance benefits. The disabled patient finds it to his pecuniary advantage to obtain such certification from his physician. However, it may occur that an employee who has been injured at work may request the physician not to make a report under the Workers' Compensation Act. Is a physician required to make such a report despite the patient's request? The terms of the Workers' Compensation Act in the particular state regulate the obligation of a physician to make such reports. A provision of a state act requiring a physician to make reports apparently would apply only if the employee makes a claim for compensation under the act. Thus, if the employee comes to the physi-

cian as a private patient who is paying his own bills without making any claim for compensation, the terms of the act would not appear to apply, even if the employee's injuries were received at work. *AMA News*, April 12, 1965, p. 14.

16.  M. Grossman, "Insurance Reports as a Threat to Confidentiality," *Am. J. Psychiat.* 128:64, 1971.

17.  P. Chodoff, "The Effect of Third-Party Payment on the Practice of Psychotherapy," *Am. J. Psychiat.* 129:540, 1972; R. Restak, "Psychiatry in Search of Identity," *New York Times*, Jan. 12, 1975, p. E-9.

18.  Special Section, "Insurance Coverage of Mental Disorders," *Am. J. Psychiat.* 126:667-705, 1969. On conditions constituting "disease" within terms of a life, accident, disability, or hospitalization insurance policy, see Annot., 61 A.L.R.3d 822 (1975). On the use—or misuse—of technical jargon, see I.D. Bross, "Prisoners of Jargon," *Am. J. Pub. Health* 54:918, 1964; M. Pilisuk, "Mental Health Mystification and Social Control," *Am. J. Orthopsychiat.* 45:414, 1975.

19.  Apropos is the story of one husband who said to his wife, "Dear, I've been working days and nights for 30 years. Henceforth, I'm going to spend my evenings with you." Within two or three hours of the first evening, the husband talking constantly, the wife exclaimed, "Stop! I can't stand it anymore. I can absorb no more. Leave me alone." Rather soon, insurance companies may be saying the same.

20.  *Psychiatric News*, Jan. 1, 1975, p. 1.

21.  M. Grossman, *Summary Report of the Task Force on Confidentiality as It Relates to Third Parties* (Washington, D.C.: July 1974).

22.  Holding that a self-insured employer's need for access to employee prescription records outweighs an employee's interest in keeping his AIDS-related drug purchases confidential, the Third U.S. Circuit Court of Appeals reversed a jury verdict in favor of the employee based on invasion of privacy. Southeastern Pennsylvania Transportation Authority (SEPTA) learned that an employee (John Doe) had AIDS through a regular audit of expensive prescription medications furnished to its employees through a contract with its supplier, Rite-Aid Drug Store. SEPTA put the audits in place to detect fraud, drug abuse and excessive costs in its employee benefits program. The audit contained John Doe's name and the drug Retrovir, which is used to treat AIDS. SEPTA's Chief Administrative Officer highlighted the names of patients taking HIV- or AIDS-related drugs on a list and quizzed SEPTA staff physicians on their illness, thus disclosing their condition without consent. The Third Circuit recognized an individual's limited right of privacy in the disclosure of his medical status, but applied a balancing test in determining that the impingement on Doe's privacy was insufficient to constitute a constitutional violation. The court reasoned that, although public knowledge of an AIDS affliction could result in social stigma, harassment, and discrimination, SEPTA's "strong public interest" in containing health costs outweighed the minimal intrusion on Doe's privacy, "especial-

ly given the lack of any economic loss, discrimination or harassment actually suffered by plaintiff." Doe v. Southeastern Pennsylvania Transportation Authority, 1995 WL 762891 (3d Cir. 1995).

23. An attorney representing the claimant-patient is entitled to see the report. Fundamentally, the issue at stake here is one of economics. As originally conceived, workers' compensation programs were designed to cover disabilities originating in the work environment. Many efforts are being made to convert the compensation from one of income protection for a person injured for whatever job-related cause to a welfare program for the worker and his family suffering from physical or nervous breakdown. Employers protest, saying that it would place upon them a disproportionate share of the welfare burden.

24. One insurance agent advises that to his knowledge there has been only one case where the health records of an insured were permitted to be seen indiscriminately by employees of the insurance company, and that dealt with the x-rays of Elizabeth Taylor's breasts which she insured for $13 million when going to Italy to film "Cleopatra." The insurance company people felt that "Miss Taylor's bosom was worth every cent of the policy."

25. J.A. Knight, "The Medical Connection," *Tulane Medicine* 6:7, 1974.

26. *In re* Lifschutz, 2 Cal.3d 415, 467 P.2d 557, 85 Cal. Rptr. 829 (1970).

27. H. Modlin, "How Private Is Privacy?," *Psychiatry Digest*, Feb. 1969, at 13.

28. It happens, when an analyst says, "Now just relax and say the first thing that comes to your mind," the analysand is thinking, "The money that this is costing me."

29. H.E. Ullrich, "The Myth of Confidentiality or The Empress' Clothes," *Newsletter of La. Psychiatric Med. Assn.* 31:22, Summer 1996.

30. Since the psychiatrist is often regarded as a modern-day confessor, it may be noted that in an earlier time, and still today in some societies, there was a practice of collective confession of sins. That practice is based on the idea that mankind is one, and therefore all men are bound up with each other. The collective confession made everyone fully aware of his own sins and also emphasized his share of guilt in the wrongs committed by others. Those confessions were not mere pro forma as is found in many churches today where there is a routine congregational confession of sin. The rise of individualism gave impetus to the penitent in isolation, and it has tended to dwarf mass confession as an effective method of relief from guilt. J. A. Knight, *Conscience and Guilt* (New York: Appleton-Century-Crofts, 1969), p. 118.

31. Wyatt v. Stickney, 344 F. Supp. 373, 387 (M.D. Ala. 1972), *aff'd in part, rev'd in part, remanded in part, sub nom.*, Wyatt v. Aderholt, 503 F.2d 1305 5th Cir.(1974).

32. Mich. Comp. Laws § 330.1748. See also Conn. Tit. 52, Ch. 299, §52-146g.

33. Consider the following example: "I am not at liberty to provide you with a listing of Community Living facilities servicing patients from this institution as this would violate our contract with the Community Living sponsors." Letter from office of the superintendent, Northville State Hospital,

Michigan, to Slovenko. On hospital practices, Herbert M. Silverberg, recalling his service as counsel for patients at St. Elizabeths Hospital, reports that one psychiatrist there sought commitment only of young women. This type of finding only comes about from a profile of practice, not from an individual study of a case. H.M. Silverberg, "Protecting the Human Rights of Mental Patients: One Lawyer's Experience in a World of Psychiatrists," *Barrister,* Fall 1974, p. 46. See also D.F. Greenberg, "Involuntary Psychiatric Commitments to Prevent Suicide," *N.Y.U.L. Rev.* 49:227, 1974; B. Sheridan, "Why the Lawyers Caught Nork and the Doctors Didn't," *Med. Economics,* July 22, 1974, p. 91.

34.  "ASHP Guidelines on Adverse Drug Reaction Monitoring and Reporting," *Am. J. Health Syst. Pharm.* 52:417, 1995.

35.  Fed. Regist. 60:16962-16968, 1995.

36.  To illustrate by an example (omitting names), the director of admissions of one university wrote to an applicant: "We note from your application form that you have been under the care of a psychiatrist or therapist within the past two years. Will you please arrange to have your doctor or psychologist write a letter to our consultant, giving a complete report of your condition, treatment, and prognosis. I might point out to you that this information will be kept in the consultant's medical file and will in no case be inserted in your University folder. This is a confidential professional report so it will be expected to be complete." Protesting, the applicant wrote to the President of the University:

> I applied for admission to your University as a nondegree student. In the application for admission I was asked if I had been treated by a doctor within the last two years, and for what condition. I replied I had been treated by a psychiatrist for an anxiety reaction. Next I received a letter from the director of admissions requesting a full, detailed case history to be sent to the psychiatric consultant at the University Hospital.
>
> Your institution has no legitimate right to this information. In the last few years when the American people have suffered greater and greater invasions of privacy for various "legitimate" reasons like applying for credit, a job, security clearance, insurance claims, and others, the university would seem the last stronghold of individual freedom. I was distressed, to say the least, then, to find that as a requirement for taking one evening course the psychiatrist who saw me was required to submit a complete report of my condition, treatment, and prognosis. Apparently, the question preceding the one regarding treatment is disregarded. It asks whether the applicant has any physical or emotional conditions which might interfere with the proper performance of scholastic duties. To it, I answered, no.
>
> The application form, itself, is deficient in various areas including performance in college and scholastic achievement after college. If the university is interested in my ability to perform in a classroom, it

might be a reasonable question to include on the form. If you are interested in my psychological health, I'd have no objections to taking a psychological test or being interviewed by your consultant. However, I strongly object to putting the most personal information that exists about myself in the hands of the University for your casual information. The medical profession takes extremely seriously what you seem to overlook, namely that a medical history is confidential information in many states between the patient and the doctor. Only a medical situation of great seriousness should induce disclosure of such a history, certainly not application to a university.

> Since I do not intend to comply with your requirements for application as your director of admissions has stated them, I withdraw my application for admission to nondegree status at your university.

In a communication to the author, the applicant advised that "the President's only response to the letter was to send me another catalogue." It is to be noted that the university initially had advised that the report would be kept in the consultant's medical file, and it is not to be ignored that the consultant could be of assistance to the applicant.

37.    New York: Knopf, 1995.
38.    Pp. 207-208.
39.    At issue, "Should bar applicants be asked about treatment for mental health?" *ABAJ*, Oct. 1994, p. 36.
40.    443 So.2d 71 (Fla. 1983).
41.    42 U.S.C. § 12102(2). See also P.S. Appelbaum, "Do the Mentally Disabled Have the Right to be Physicians?" in *Collected Articles from Hospital & Community Psychiatry* (Washington, D.C.: American Psychiatric Press, 1989), p. 17.
42.    The following examples are inquiries which are not disability-related: Can you perform the functions of this job (essential and/or marginal), with or without reasonable accommodation? Would you describe/demonstrate how you would perform these functions (essential and/or marginal)? Do you have a cold? Have you ever tried Tylenol® for fever? How did you break your leg? Can you meet the attendance requirements of this job? How many days did you take leave last year? Do you illegally use drugs? Have you used illegal drugs in the last two years? Do you have the required licenses to perform this job? How much do you weigh? How tall are you? Do you regularly eat three meals per day?

> The following are disability-related inquiries: Do you have AIDS? Do you have asthma? Do you have a disability which would interfere with the performance of your job? How many days were you sick last year? Have you ever filed for workers' compensation: Have you ever been injured on the job? How much alcohol do you drink each week? Have you ever been treated for alcohol problems? Have you ever been treated for mental health problems? What prescription drugs are you currently taking?

The following factors are used in determining whether any particular test is medical: whether the test is administered by a health care professional or trainee; whether the results of the test are interpreted by a health care professional or trainee; whether the test is designed to reveal an impairment or the state of an individual's physical or psychological health; whether the test is invasive (*e.g.*, requires drawing of blood, urine, breath, etc.); whether the test measures physiological/psychological responses (as opposed to performance of a task); whether the test is normally done in a medical setting; and whether medical equipment/devices are used for the test.

The following are tests which generally are not medical: physical agility/physical fitness tests which do not include medical monitoring; certain psychological tests, such as tests which simply concern an individual's skills or tastes; and tests for illegal use of drugs.

43. D.K. Fram, "What Employers Should Know About the ADA," *Wall Street Journal*, Sept. 16, 1996, p. 16. Any medical information obtained must be kept confidential by the employer. This means that the employer must collect and maintain the information on separate forms and in separate medical files. The employer may disclose the information only to persons and entities specified in the ADA.

44. Clark v. Virginia Bd. of Bar Examiners, 880 F. Supp. 430 (E.D. Va. 1995). The various approaches of bar examiners in the various states are set out in the opinion. 880 F. Supp. at 438-440.

45. The State Bar of Michigan asks the following:

• Are you now or have you ever been addicted to, dependent upon or undergone treatment for, or obtained professional counseling concerning the use of intoxicating liquor or narcotic or other drug substances, whether prescribed by a physician or not? If so, identify the involved substance, the nature and length of use and the names and addresses of involved physicians or other health care professionals, and institutions or consultants.

• (a) Have you ever had a mental illness, meaning a substantial disorder of thought or mood which significantly impaired your judgment, behavior, capacity to recognize reality, or ability to cope with the ordinary demands of life, to such extent that you required care and treatment for your own welfare, or the welfare of others or of the community?

• (b) Have you ever been found by appropriate clinical authorities to have a mental deficiency to such extent that you were incapable of managing yourself and your affairs? If the answer to either (a) or (b) is yes, provide the names and addresses of involved institutions, physicians or psychologists or other health care providers and describe the underlying circumstances or the diagnosis, treatment or hospitalization.

46. See S. Fedo & K.H. Brown, "Character and Fitness Review: Is It Legal to Ask About Addiction and Mental Disabilities?" *Bar Examiner* 61:40, 1992; D. Long, "A Professional Licensure, Mental Health Inquiries and the Americans with Disabilities Act," *Developments in Mental Health Law* (Institute of Law, Psychiatry and Public Policy of the University of Virginia) 15:1, Jan-June 1995; C.L. Reischel, "The Constitution, the Disability Act,

and Questions About Alcoholism, Addiction and Mental Health, *Bar Examiner* 61:10, 1992; W. Lambert, "Bar Debates Screening Out Mentally Ill," *Wall Street Journal*, March 10, 1995, p. B-1; K. Myers, "Privacy of Mental Health Records Poses Concern for Bar Applicants," *Nat'l L.J.*, July 11, 1994, p. 16.

47. See M.J. Place & S.L. Bloom, "Mental Fitness Requirements for the Practice of Law," *Buff. L. Rev.* 23:579, 1974; Anno., "Validity and Application of Regulation Requiring Suspension or Disbarment of Attorney Because of Mental or Emotional Illness," 50 A.L.R.3d 1259.

48. M.A. Glendon, *A Nation Under Lawyers* (Cambridge: Harvard University Press, 1994), p. 21. Why was the young associate's periodic outburst of obscenities called an illness? Professor Glendon says, "The associate was apparently afflicted with something like Tourette's syndrome–with a previous history of hospitalization for emotional problems. Of course, in those days, we were all pretty naive about these things. But the behavior was different from 'normal' swearing." Communication to author. The case discussed in the text involving the emergency medical technician is Gilday v. Mecosta Cy., 124 F.3d 760 (6th Cir. 1997). See M. Higgins, "No Sudden Impact," *ABAJ* 83 (Nov. 1997):24; see generally R.J. Bonnie & J. Monahan (eds.), *Mental Disorder, Work Disability and the Law* (Chicago: University of Chicago Press, 1997).

49. "'Poor judgement, irresponsible behavior and poor impulse control' do not amount to a medical condition that Congress intended to be considered an impairment" under the ADA. Daley v. Koch, 892 F.2d 212 (2d Cir. 1989).

50. Stola v. Joint Industry Bd., 889 F. Supp. 133 (S.D. N.Y. 1995).

51. Turco v. Hoeschst Celanese Corp., 101 F.3d 1090 (5th Cir. 1996); discussed in D.K. Fram, "What Employers Should Know About the ADA," *Wall Street Journal*, Sept. 16, 1996, p. 16.

52. G. Edson, "Mental Health Status Inquiries on Bar Applications: Overbroad and Intrusive," *U. Kan. L. Rev.* 43:869, 1995, citing S.T. Maher & L. Blum, "A Strategy for Increasing the Mental and Emotional Fitness of Bar Applicants," *Ind. L. Rev.* 23:821, 826-827, 1990.

53. N.N. Minow & F.H. Cate, "Justice for Jurors Too," *Christian Science Monitor*, Oct. 8, 1996, p. 18.

54. Sullivan v. Fogg, 613 F.2d 465 (2d Cir. 1980); N.B. Ledy & E. Lefkowitz, "Judgment by Your Peers? The Impeachment of Jury Verdicts and the Case of the Insane Juror," *N.Y. Law Forum* 21:57, 1975.

# Chapter 8

# FEE COLLECTION

There's a saying: "When you are in need of a physician, you esteem him like a god; when he has brought you out of danger, consider him a king; when you have been cured, he becomes human like yourself; when he sends you his bill, you think of him as a devil."

In early law, physicians could not maintain an action to recover fees for medical services. Fees were regarded as an honorarium, and not demandable of right. Times have changed–patients now sue physicians for malpractice and physicians sue patients for payment of their bills. In some states, the physician is allowed not only a cause of action, but also a ranking over other creditors.[1]

Yet, even in our "age of commercialism," the roles of creditor and debtor, issues of fairness of charges, promptness of payment especially at times of emotional tension, are generally considered not to promote "warm human relations" or "mutual confidence." Hostility generates hostility. If a patient is displeased with the therapy, instituting suit to collect a bill may trigger a retaliatory malpractice claim that a patient might not otherwise have brought.[2]

The psychiatrist must be particularly sensitive in collecting a bill. He has special problems in enforcing a claim for payment of a bill; he is as a rule reluctant to engage the services of a bill-collecting agency or to bring the matter to court. The Report of the Group for the Advancement of Psychiatry stated:[3]

> Psychiatrists are less likely to use such services since they tend to discuss financial matters with their patients more fully and reach agreements more often than do other physicians. While we will not argue the pros and cons of using such service, it should be pointed out that under some circumstances, when an account is turned over to an agency for collection, it may be a breach of the confidential relationship in that a patient should be able to control who knows he is in psychotherapy. This matter should be considered before such a step is taken.

The GAP report is cautious. It has traditionally been held in the law on privileges that confidentiality goes by the wayside in litigation between the parties.[4] Thus, when a patient sues a physician for malpractice, the physician may discuss diagnosis and treatment. By bringing suit, the patient waives his secrecy privilege in relation to the issue involved. The same principle applies in a suit brought by the physician for the patient's failure to perform his obligation under the contract, to wit, to pay for services rendered. The fact that a confidential communication privilege belongs to the patient does not prevent the physician from claiming payment in court for his services. The privilege precludes a third person from calling the physician as a witness against the patient; it is not applicable in suits between physician and patient (and similarly, between attorney and client). The Texas statute expressly makes an exception to privilege "when the purpose of the proceeding is to substantiate and collect on a claim for mental or emotional health services rendered to the patient/client."[5]

Furthermore, it is to be recalled that the medical privilege applies only to the communication itself, and not to the fact that a communication was made. Thus, under the orthodox medical privilege, the fact of a physician-patient relationship, that the person was under treatment, the number of visits, and the duration of treatment, are not privileged areas.[6] This may be all the information that may be needed to uphold a claim for payment. To turn over an entire record to an attorney or bill collector in order to obtain payment, even when the individual denies having consulted the therapist, would be indiscreet and a breach of confidentiality. Quite frequently, resort to a collection agency or litigation to obtain payment results in a counterclaim for malpractice.

The dynamics of behavior underlying failure to pay a bill surely are not to be ignored. Money has important meaning to everyone, on many levels of psychic functioning. A number of psychiatrists do not mail bills; they hand the bill to the patient in order to have the benefit of the interaction. The pattern of giving and receiving money is symbolic of many interpersonal transactions. Many of our personality traits and psychological problems find expression in our attitudes toward money.[7]

Lack of punctuality in the payment of fees may be a manifestation of temporary financial shortage, a problem in the patient related to money or to giving, an identification of money with "vulgarity" (excrement), or an indication of resentment toward the therapist and of a desire to frustrate him. Likewise, countertransference manifestations may reflect themselves in the therapist's attitude toward payment of fees. Conscious and unconscious conflicts may influence the therapist in determining his fee policy.

Unlike most other medical specialties, as GAP points out, a fee in psychotherapy is usually agreed upon at the outset. Billing for missed appointments is usually appropriate as long as the patient has been advised at the outset of treatment that this will be the psychiatrist's practice. The APA's ethical guidelines provide, "It is ethical for the psychiatrist to make a charge for a missed appointment when this falls within the terms of the specific contractual agreement with the patient." The American Medical Association has decided that interest may be charged on overdue accounts so long as patients are properly informed. A patient's disregard of a bill for a considerable period may indicate that the therapist himself is negligent in failing to bring to the patient's awareness possible avoidance of a responsibility which is part of the reality situation.

In practice, fees, financial ability to meet the costs, arrangements for credit if warranted, payment of installments, and all other related details ought to be discussed at the very outset of therapy as a baseline of reality. Attitudes about money, compulsive needs to pay, unconscious wishes or needs not to pay then become grist for the exploration of unconscious drives, whether in analysis or psychotherapy. The clarification that ensues usually makes non-payment of fees a rare occurrence. On infrequent occasions, a patient may not pay for months at a time. This gives impetus to the issue during therapy and eventually the bill gets paid. The infrequent losses of fee payments can then be absorbed without violating one's investment in protecting patients from disclosure to others.

## NOTES

1.  See La. Civil Code Art. 3191; R. Slovenko, "Psychotherapy and Informed Consent: A Search in Judicial Regulation," in W.E. Barton & C.J. Sanborn (eds.), *Law and the Mental Health Professions* (New York: International Universities Press, 1978), pp. 51-70.

2.  J.L. Klein, J.E. Macbeth & J.N. Onek, *Legal Issues in the Private Practice of Psychiatry* (Washington, D.C.: American Psychiatric Press, 1984), p. 56.

3.  GAP Report No. 45, *Confidentiality and Privileged Communication in the Practice of Psychiatry*, p. 105, 1960. On unreasonable debt collection as invasion of right of privacy, see Comment, *Villanova L. Rev.* 2:238, 1957.

4.  In Yoder v. Smith, 112 N.W.2d 862 (Iowa 1962), a former patient had a good-paying job, but was long past due on his bill, and showed no inclination to pay anything on the debt. The doctor resorted to a collection agency, which wrote the employer of the debtor for help in collecting the debt. The debtor thereupon sued, unsuccessfully, charging that his privacy had been invaded. The court held that contacting the debtor's employer was a reasonable way for the creditor "to pursue his debtor and persuade payment, although the steps taken may result in some invasion of the debtor's priva-

cy." In Patton v. Jacobs, 118 Ind. App. 358, 78 N.E.2d 789 (1948), the court denied a claim of invasion of privacy where a collection agency used by the physician notified the patient's employer of the bill owing the physician for medical services. However, unwarranted disclosure of indebtedness may be (and has been) treated as an invasion of privacy. See, *e.g.*, Brents v. Morgan, 221 Ky. 76S, 299 S.W. 967 (1927); Trammell v. Citizens News Co., 285 Ky. 529, 148 S.W.2d 708 (1941). It might be noted that the usual approach employed by collection agencies is, as one author put it, "to instill anxiety and yet remain on friendly terms with the debtor." H. Black, *Buy Now, Pay Later* (New York: Morrow, 1961), p. 53.

5. Texas Rules of Evidence, Rule 510(d)(3). Connecticut legislation provides: "[T]he name, address and fees for psychiatric services to a patient may be disclosed to individuals or agencies involved in the collection of fees for such services. In cases where a dispute arises over the fees or claims or where additional information is needed to substantiate the fee or claim, the disclosure of further information shall be limited to the following: (A) That the person was in fact a patient; (B) the diagnosis: (C) the dates and duration of treatment; and (D) a general description of the treatment, which shall include evidence that a treatment plan exists and has been carried out and evidence to substantiate the necessity for admission and length of stay in a health care institution or facility." Conn. Tit. 52, Ch. 899, §52-146f(3).

6. Compare United States v. Summe, 208 F. Supp. 925 (E.D. Ky. 1962), where an attorney, who had been called to appear at an investigation concerning the income tax returns of two of his clients, was asked certain questions concerning the preparation of the returns. The court held that the investigating special agents did not have unlimited authority to examine the attorney but were, rather, limited to questions which did not violate the attorney-client privilege.

7. W.G. Herron & S.R. Walt, *Money Matters/The Fee in Psychotherapy and Psychoanalysis* (New York: Guilford, 1992).

# Chapter 9

# CONSENT TO RELEASE OF INFORMATION

Release of medical information about a patient calls for the consent of the patient, or someone authorized to consent for him, if he is not competent, unless the disclosure is required by law or is vitally necessary for protection of the public interest. As we have discussed, a physician has an obligation to protect the confidentiality of the patient. Laws in various states provide that "no provider of health care shall disclose medical information regarding a patient of the provider without first obtaining an authorization."[1] The principles of ethics of the profession state that "A psychiatrist may release confidential information only with the authorization of the patient or under proper legal compulsion."[2]

A wise maxim for physicians is never to reveal information without a signed consent. While oral consent is sufficient, written authorization is more persuasive in the event the matter is ever contested (some states by statute require written consent).[3] Connecticut's statute on consent to disclosure provides: "Any consent given to waive the confidentiality shall specify to what person or agency the information is to be disclosed and to what use it will be put. Each patient shall be informed that his refusal to grant consent will not jeopardize his right to obtain present or future treatment except where disclosure of the communications and records is necessary for the treatment."[4]

For the truth to be told, records are often released without the consent of the patient. As is well-known among attorneys, record keepers at hospitals are often amenable to a bribe. In other cases, they released a record upon receiving a subpoena in the belief that it is a court order.

Insurers obtain access to records as a condition of coverage. "Blanket waivers" are required for enrollment in Medicare and Medicaid. The Blue Cross/Blue Shield has inscribed on its card: "The user of this card...consents to the release to and by BCBS of all medical, hospital and other information necessary for BCBS business purposes." There may be legislation that gives insurance companies as a payer of health services limited or full access to patient records. Under the Texas Medical Practice Act, according to legal counsel of the Texas Medical Association, it is assumed that patients who sign up for coverage under the Mental Health Blue Cross Network (74 percent of Texas physicians are providers in Blue Cross/Blue Shield plans) have given permission to the insurance company to have access to their records.[5] By way of complaint, Dr. Harry Wilmer of Texas wrote:[6]

> It is the ethical responsibility of a psychiatrist who has signed a managed care agreement to hand over patient records to tell the patient that the doctor's notes and records are not confidential and may get into the hands of the police, the FBI, his or her employer, or anyone hooked up to the national and international computer data bank of health care services, to say nothing of snoopers.

Under managed care, contracts of managed care companies with providers usually require the provider to allow the managed care company full access to patient records, but as patients are not parties to these agreements, their consent to the disclosure is necessary.

The Westhoff Memorial Hospital in Rockledge, Florida, considered the standard release form did not inform its patients sufficiently. It advised its patients:

> The Medical Records Department at this hospital has recently received a request from your insurance company for the medical records pertaining to your hospitalization.
>
> We are aware that you have signed a record release for your insurance company; however, we do not feel that you have been properly informed as to the nature of the records being requested. Your insurance company is asking for a copy of the discharge summary, the history, the physical examination, the progress notes and the nurses' notes, as well as some additional information. We want you to know that this material contains observations not only from your physician, but also from nurses, social workers and in some cases, aides who took part in the course of your hospitalization and treatment. These records contain day-to-day observations (sometimes even direct quotations) which were intended to be useful only to those people who were directly involved in your care.
>
> We feel that you should also know that other insurance companies generally require only a diagnosis for most non-psychiatric patients. In some other states, insurance companies have been restricted to obtaining only the diagnosis for use in their consideration of payment.
>
> If, after reading this, you still wish us to send the request medical records, please sign the informed consent enclosed. If you do not wish this, please discuss the matter with your insurance company representative or those people to whom the insurance premiums are paid.

On the horizon is the computerization and development of a birth-to-grave medical record. On the one hand, it would assist in the treatment of a patient and in preventive medicine. On the other hand, there is the concern over privacy.[7] Will medical records become transformed into commodities desired by insurers, employers, researchers, and police? Will the development of the records be done without the consent of the patient? Without a requirement of consent, a civil liberty has been lost.

Maryland has begun collecting information for a state database authorized to track every doctor-patient encounter—including psychotherapy sessions—without patient consent. The state is authorized to demand reporting of this information even if the patient pays "out-of-pocket."[8] To inform patients of that state of affairs, Dr. Jennifer Katze, a Baltimore psychiatrist and chair of an ad hoc committee on privacy and consent, gives new patients a two-page handout. (Her husband is an attorney who has become heavily involved in privacy/medical record ethics issues, including the legalities.)[9] Bemoaning the loss of privacy in psychiatric care, she wrote in *Psychiatric Times*:[10]

> Psychiatrists now live in the untenable position of coughing up the goods on their patients' most intimate information, or costing their patients reimbursement and permission for further "treatment approval" by the insurance carrier. True, patients sign release of information forms, but could they possibly anticipate all that we may be asked to divulge? And what choice do they really have if they need treatment and can't afford to pay out of pocket?
>
> Most psychiatrists have become psychologically worn down by this process. For 10 years or so we have been filling out progressively frequent and detailed "treatment plans" for more and more of our patients, as managed care corners a bigger share of the insurance market. What initially may have seemed like an ethical offense has become an everyday paperwork nuisance that we carry out with merely a small groan. We have become psychically numb.
>
> Our personal ethics are waning without our notice. By routinely relinquishing personal patient information, we are in grave danger of the apathy of the defeated.

Dr. Katze's two-page handout to her patients (quoted in pertinent part in the notes) is rather complex for the average person, as she readily admits, but she says that she serves "a hyper-educated clientele." How have the patients reacted to the handout? Mostly, in Dr. Katze's opinion, with appropriate concern, given Maryland's precedent-setting Medical Care Data Base. Some of her patients choose to pay out of pocket, some ask for vaguer treatment plans and then do personal battle with the insurance company if reimbursement is denied, some capitulate and accept the risks, some change insurers to indemnity plans (with less "management"), and some seem to just ignore her handout. She gives all of her patients their treatment plans to peruse and to decide whether to send them; she does not herself send the information directly to insurers. She also gives "accurate diagnoses," though veering towards the more benign if there is a grey-zone choice.[11]

The American Psychiatric Association's Resource Document on "Principles of Informed Consent in Psychiatry" has this to say about informed consent for psychotherapy and confidentiality:[12]

> Informed consent developed in the context of invasive procedures and has since been extended to treatment with medication. There has always been uncertainty as to the extent to which the doctrine of informed consent is applicable to psychotherapy. Whether or not required by law, it seems reasonable to encourage psychiatrists to discuss with their patients the nature of psychotherapy, likely benefits and risks (where applicable) and alternative approaches (both psychotherapeutic and non-psychotherapeutic) to their problems.
>
> Psychiatrists have been required by their ethical code to reveal to patients likely limitations on confidentiality in certain settings. Given the large number of exceptions to the general principle of confidentiality, it does not seem reasonable to ask psychiatrists to disclose them all. Rather, patients should be told at the outset of treatment about risks to confidentiality that are evident to the treating psychiatrist, and should be told in the course of treatment about additional risks as they appear to be relevant to their cases.

Would Freud today abandon his advice against "lengthy preliminary discussions" before the beginning of psychoanalytic treatment? To what extent?

## NOTES

1. Calif. Civil Code § 56.10(a). Connecticut law states: "'Consent' means consent given in writing by the patient or his authorized representative" and "Any consent given to waive the confidentiality shall specify to what person or agency the information is to be disclosed and to what use it will be put." Conn. Gen. Stat. §§ 52-146d(3), 52-146e(b).
2. "The Principles of Medical Ethics with Annotations Especially Applicable to Psychiatry" (1995 ed.).
3. Michigan's statute on the marriage counseling privilege calls for a written waiver. MCL 339.1509.
4. Conn. Gen. Stat. § 57-146e.
5. Texas Medical Practice Act, § 5.08(h)(6).
6. H.A. Wilmer, "Patient Confidentiality: A Vanishing Act," *Psychiatric News*, Sept. 1, 1995, p. 14.
7. P.K. Sutherland & G. Yarborough, "High-Tech Gossip/Physician-Patient Confidentiality and Computerized Managed Care," *Trial* 32 (11):58, Nov. 1996.

8.  B. McMenamin, "It can't happen here," *Forbes*, May 20, 1996, p. 252; J.A. Katze (ltr.), "Loss of Privacy," *Psychiatric Times*, Sept. 1996, p. 4.

9.  Dr. Katze's handout reads, in pertinent part:

> I bill and collect from you directly for my services, rather than dealing with your insurance company. If you have a reimbursable percentage, your insurer should pay that to you directly, since I am NOT a "participating" or "preferred" provider with any insurance companies or health maintenance organizations (HMOs). I will of course sign your claims forms and provide whatever information you need to complete them, returning them directly to you to mail off at your discretion, but I may charge for the far more extensive task of completing "treatment plans" which some insurers periodically require for reimbursement. I am not a participating provider in Medicare. At this stage of electronic data banking usage and sophistication, you should be aware that when you submit for insurance reimbursement, that information may be stored (including your social security number and any diagnosis you submit) in data banks possibly accessible to other insurers, such as life or disability insurance companies....Feel free to invite your internist or other physicians to coordinate care with me. For confidentiality purposes, I keep very minimal notes, so nothing is routinely available for forwarding to other health care providers.
>
> In the past two or three years there has been a galloping escalation in requests for "Treatment Plans" by insurance companies which they use to determine "Medical Necessity" for treatment. These treatment plans are reviewed by "Managed Care" companies with the intent of "cost containment" for the insurance company. The goal is to determine whether treatment is "necessary" by the managed care company's standards, which may be as restrictive as requiring dangerousness to self or others as a requisite for ongoing psychiatric treatment, if such treatment is to be approved and reimbursed by the insurance company.
>
> One of the crucial aspects of psychotherapy is the absolute assurance of full and guaranteed confidentiality. Any issue whatsoever must be open to discussion without fear of its becoming public knowledge. Treatment Plans, as required by Managed Care monitors, are progressively extensive documents which ask personal questions regarding both history and symptoms, as well as diagnoses and the content of treatment sessions. They are clear intrusions into the confidential nature of psychotherapy. Although every patient signs a "Release of Information" with his/her insurance company, granting the physician the legal right to answer such personal questions, few people truly may understand the extent of the information being requested. When the Treatment Plan is mailed to the Managed Care company, it may become part of a paper trail that is wholly beyond the control of either the patient or the physician. Each company has its own procedures for

handling and storing such sensitive and confidential paperwork, and there is no assurance that I can make that it will be handled with utmost discretion. At the same time, failure to submit such Treatment Plans, or submission of incomplete and overgeneralized information, may result in a denial of "medical necessity" and thus insurance reimbursement.

Because it is my belief that the psychotherapeutic relationship is a private one between the therapist and patient, without an insurance company or managed care reviewer as an intermediary party, I bill my patients directly, leaving it to each patient to decide whether he/she chooses to submit claims to the insurer. I have decided that it is only consistent that I should also deliver all requested Treatment Plans directly to my patients, for each to consider and submit, with full knowledge of what information is being divulged in order to try to procure insurance benefits. This decision has an extremely unpleasant and potentially painful, dehumanizing aspect. Treatment Plans need to be specific and direct, with use of jargon and diagnostic nomenclature to justify the need for treatment. The terms used and the "pathology" described is alien to a complete view of one's self, and emphasizes deficits rather than assets in a way that can be experienced as denigrating and demeaning. This is a terribly unfortunate by-product that can't be avoided if the Treatment Plan is to be an effective tool for procuring insurance reimbursement. I hope that the reactions you may have to such diagnostic descriptions will be something we can discuss together.

Dr. Katze also provides the following information to patients who use insurance, Medicare, or Medicaid:

As your physician, I think it's important to notify you that the state of Maryland enacted a law (HB 1359) in 1993 that is now having a direct impact on your right to privacy and to consent to the release of your medical information.

When physicians send information about you and your medical condition to your insurance company, they are permitted to do so only because you sign your consent. This is the way you are given an opportunity to know about and consent to the fact that physicians are sending information about you to the insurance company. This is done for the sole purpose of your getting reimbursement for your health care.

However, the State of Maryland now intends to gather personal medical information about all health care received by most citizens. It is collecting data directly from insurance companies and Medicare/Medicaid, without notice to you, and without your permission. The data being collected in the state computer data bank includes an encrypted social security number or other number developed by your insurance company. Your medical treatment and diagnoses, sex, zip code, and date of birth are included without encoding. Over time all your medical diagnoses and treatments will be accumulated. The state collects the data to do research on medical cost containment. Although physicians have always supported health care research, we strongly oppose governmental access to and electronic storage of medical information without patients' consent, because such private information belongs to each patient – not to anybody else, and because of the risk of confidentiality leaks.

The Health Care Access and Cost Commission is the branch of the Maryland state government that collects and studies the data collected. They believe they can protect the confidentiality of this information. Unfortunately, no computer security system is foolproof, and unauthorized leaks have occurred in other government data base systems. For that reason, the state data collection puts your medical privacy at risk. Since it is your private information your permission should always be obtained before it is exposed to such risk.

Confidentiality is the foundation of the trust between patient and physician. That's why physicians place such a high priority on protecting it. This year (1996), most physicians and many others concerned about privacy fought for new legislation that would have prevented medical information being collected by the state government without patients' consent. However, it was defeated. We will continue to advocate for laws that guarantee greater confidentiality.

Harper Hospital in Detriot has the following provision on release of information in the admission form to be signed by the patient: I authorized the Hospital and each physician who treated me, to release to any party responsible for payment for the patient's care, such information from the medical records as is required in order for the hospital/physician to obtain payment and to any participant in audits of such payments. This authorization to release information for purposes of payment, includes all records, including those records protected under the regulation in Code 42 of the Federal Regulations, Part 2, and Michigan Public Act 488 of 1988 of Alcohol and Drug Abuse and/or Treatment, records of psychological services, and records of social services, including communications made by the patient to a physician, social worker or psychologist as well as treatment for serious communicable diseases, including Acquired Immune Dificiency Syndrome, HIV Infection, AIDS Related Complex, and Hepatitis....In the event that I am transferred from this hospital to be treated or cared for at another hospital, extended care, or other facility, including each of the hospitals and subsidiaries of the Detroit Medical Center, I hereby consent and direct that medical and other information be released by Harper Hospital as may be necessary or useful in my obtaining such further care and treatment.

10. J. Katze, "Privacy: Lest We Forget What We're Losing," *Psychiatric News,* Sept. 6, 1996, p. 6.
11. Personal communication.
12. American Psychiatric Association Division of Government Relations, *State Update,* July/Aug. 1996, p. 4.

# Part V

# RECORDKEEPING AND ACCOUNTABILITY

Chapter 1. Recordkeeping
Chapter 2. Accountability and Abuse of
            Confidentiality
Chapter 3. The Stigma of Psychiatric Discourse

# Chapter 1

# RECORDKEEPING

The popular image of the psychiatrist is that of a doctor who spends his time taking extensive notes. Invariably, in the media, the psychiatrist is shown with a pad busily writing. Those who burglarized the office of Daniel Ellsberg's psychiatrist apparently thought they would find a gold mine of information. Ellsberg says the White House knew about his personal life (from his girlfriend), but they wanted to know something only his psychiatrist knew in order to blackmail him. Howard Hunt justified the break-in as an attempt to find out whether Ellsberg "might be a controlled agent of the Soviets."[1] As it turned out, the burglary produced no psychiatric or other material—the files were empty (and the billing records were at home).[2]

With wry humor, Gore Vidal fantasized Ellsberg saying to his psychiatrist, "I have these terrible headaches. They started just after I met my control Ivan and he said, 'Well, boychick, it's been five years now since you signed on as a controlled agent. Now I guess you know that if there's one thing we Sovs hate it's a non-producer so . . .' Doc, I hope you're writing all this down and not just staring out the window like last time."[3]

The idea that extensive records are kept in private medical offices, including psychiatric ones, is widespread. The popular notion is that they are absolutely essential to treatment. In consulting a psychiatrist, the patient expects the psychiatrist to take notes, and when this does not happen, the patient wonders whether he failed to say anything of importance.[4] Even I.F. Stone, the astute political columnist, urged a close study of the records of Soviet psychiatric institutions which had become available in order to determine whether individuals were committed for political reasons.[5] Stone must have expected to find the same copious records in a hospital ward as would be found in a bureaucrat's filing cabinet, and on top of that, accuracy and verity.

Psychiatry is unlike the legal or medical profession. In the courtroom, a stenographer is expected to record every word spoken by any participant.

Without such a record, an appellate system would lose much of its validity (though appellate court judges are not known to very much read the record). In medicine, too, there is emphasis on records that note somatic therapies and instructions to aides; medical doctors are indoctrinated to make records. Medical records constitute an integral and important part of the medical care process, transmitting information as well as facilitating memory.[6] To the extent that psychiatry is a medical discipline, the same need for records would be expected.[7] The order to search the office of Ellsberg's psychiatrist—"we want the medical files"—revealed a prevailing but unwarranted total identification of psychiatry with medicine.

There is a distinction to be drawn between psychoanalysis or intensive psychotherapy and other forms of psychiatric treatment, particularly institutional care, where somatic therapy is usually involved. In the practice of psychotherapy, it is customary to keep records of appointments and billings, but usually there are minimal records or notes of the patient's communications or evaluation. Most analytically-oriented therapists will insist that they do not need records to treat patients successfully, though to be sure, there is some variation. An individual who is blind could not perform as a surgeon, but he can perform very well indeed as a psychiatrist, without records.

Some therapists, as a therapy technique, occasionally videotape a session and later play it back to the patient (Erich Fromm found it provided perspective).

Teaching programs—for the purpose of training—require trainees to keep extensive write-ups, but the practice thereafter is different. For supervisory review, trainees need to make detailed records. If they try to relate cases from memory, all kinds of self-protective distortions creep in. Worse, they will distort material to fit preconceived theoretical constructs. The only pedagogical protection is to insist on a verbatim account of the content and of the interaction between the patient and the therapist. In training, what is not reported is as important as what is reported.

Some therapists may doodle in order to keep awake (or to listen with "the third ear").[8] Others may have a list of characters like that opening Tolstoy's *War and Peace*, to avoid calling someone by the wrong name.

Some therapists take notes in order to aid in decoding; the psychiatrist's role is, among other things, that of a translator and interpreter of a foreign language, so to speak. The psychiatrist looks for the latent or hidden message in a communication. For example, a person reports a dream about birds coming through the window attacking him; the dream and the interpretation—"You want to kill your baby"—may be recorded.

Others may write a scribble or a sentence to help discern continuity from one session to another. In all cases, the records appear as though written in Swahili.

Still other therapists say they keep no records in order to assure the privacy of the patient (particularly when treating, say, sexual deviation) or they skew the records as a protective device. For example, a patient revealed to her psychiatrist that she was having an affair but feared that this might come out in a custody action her husband was bringing against her as part of the couple's divorce. The psychiatrist in a book wrote about this incident, "I did not feel that I needed to write this down and agreed to keep it out of my record. Unless ordered to reveal it by a judge, I felt this patient's decision whether to reveal her affair to her husband was entirely her own and need not come out through my chart notes."[9]

"Do not take notes" is the title of a section on advice to therapists in Dr. Thomas Szasz's book *The Ethics of Psychoanalysis*.[10] He wrote:

> The psychoanalytic relationship is a personal encounter. You are not doing anything to the patient —at least no more than he is doing to you. You are not the observer and he the observed. Both of you play dual roles as participants in a relationship and as observers of it. What effect would note-taking have on your relationship with your mother, wife, or friend? Thus, do not be oblivious to the metacommunicative implications for the patient of your act of note-taking.
>
> In any case, ask yourself why you want to take notes. To help you remember what the patient tells you? It will not do that, but *not* taking notes might. To record a case history? What will you do with it? To record material for research purposes? You can jot down what you think you will need after the interview or at the end of the day. If you are uncertain about the sort of thing you will need, notes will serve no purpose; a detailed account of the patient's "productions" is a useless document.

In the same spirit, Dr. Emanuel Tanay said, "No useful purpose in psychotherapy would be served by records. Keep in mind that in intensive psychotherapy, there are rarely more than twelve patients treated by one psychotherapist; there is no problem in remembering. Besides, how can an intense emotional relationship be developed if one of the participants would be sitting and scribbling notes. Once you have those notes, what would you do with them?"[11] Dr. Eugene J. Stein said, "The only records I keep in my private practice are the dates of visits and any initial information such as psychological test results, relevant history, or other records forwarded to me. I do not need records for treatment."[12]

Dr. Stephen A. Appelbaum observed, "The taking of notes during hours is found more often in *New Yorker* cartoons than in the offices of responsible psychoanalytic practitioners. It is just such an activity that [tends] to separate therapist from patient, to shift the balance from feeling and experience to cognition and theory."[13]

Some therapists try to reconstruct the session after the patient has gone, and may make notes based on memory. Anyone who does will say that it is not possible to recall all the details chronologically. They find that as they write, the association memory brings back details that were at first over-looked. This helps (some therapists) in the treatment of the patient in two ways: the additional sensory input of details entailed in the writing as well as the listening reinforces the memory process. Even more important, details early in the session that rang no bell as significant take on meaning in connection with the trends later in the session. Originally, that material is heard without the key code that comes later. In reconstructing the session, review of the early material is then absorbed in full knowledge of the subsequent key that was supplied at the end of the hour. Occasionally, in trying to unravel a conflicted understanding, the therapist will go over past material.[14]

Unquestionably, in the use of chemotherapy, it is essential to have a record of what was prescribed; when and for what reasons; and subsequent changes in behavior in the broad sense. This is necessary as a guide to managing the chemotherapeutic regime.

Records are also necessary for research or teaching resources, or for publication. Sigmund Freud took copious notes as he was venturing into a new field and he planned to publish his case histories. Sandor Rado, one of the Freudian circle, never took notes except for dreams in which he had a particular interest.[15]

For clinicians who teach, it is important to have material that is freshly recorded. Clinical material makes theoretical concepts meaningful. Using one's memory without records for teaching resources tends to distortions that fit one's biases.

Thus one would assume that the scope or need of recordkeeping is linked to its purpose, and to what psychotherapy is all about. There are reports of over 200 varieties of psychotherapy, ranging from classical psychoanalysis to procedures administered in cult-like surroundings reminiscent of techniques used by preliterate peoples.[16] They may reflect the needs of various types of people. Some therapies stress cognitive learning, others behavior modification or affective experiencing; most use a combination of all three psychotherapeutic processes in which the crucial dimensions are the nature of the relationship, the emotional experience, and possibly, the content of the communication.

According to Szasz, psychotherapy is franchised talking;[17] for Jerome Frank, the restoration of morale;[18] for W. Schofield, the purchase of friendship.[19] Woody Allen, a veteran of over 22 years in psychoanalysis, said:[20]

> You don't learn anything in a dramatic rush. . . . But an hour a day, talking about your emotions, hopes, angers, disappointments, with someone who's trained to evaluate this material--over a period of years, you're bound to get more in touch with feelings than someone who makes no effort.

Woody Allen had a bout with the IRS over the deductibility of the cost as a medical expense. Unsuccessful, he then tried to declare it as a business deduction, but the IRS contended it was entertainment. They compromised by declaring it a religious contribution.

In psychotherapy, Freud observed, the doctor is not doctor and the patient is not a patient. Szasz says what is called mental illness is metaphorical illness, and psychiatry is metaphorical medicine. As earlier noted, in our discussion of response to inquiries, a different kind of report, quite logically, would be expected when psychiatry (psychotherapy) is considered the reeducation of a demoralized individual than when considered the treatment of a disease. Assuming education were an insured activity, what type of recordkeeping would be required? Would the insurer ask the educator for a diagnostic category and a report on the style of instruction? Nowadays elementary and secondary schools require the teachers to set out a daily outline, plans, goals and accomplishments on an overall, but not individual student, basis.

The prevailing logic on recordkeeping can be reduced to this: records are a medical necessity; medical doctors need records; psychiatrists are medical doctors; therefore, psychiatrists need records. Thus, records are considered absolutely vital for the care of the patient in psychiatry (even when there is no medication) or for the continuance of care later on or with another therapist. Thus, one lawyer was heard to say, "Years of psychoanalysis would irrevocably be lost if the therapist should die and leave no records." Consider the following testimony and cross-examination in a proceeding that alleged a cause of action on the theory psychiatry is the practice of medicine, and that the failure to maintain medical records would be negligence and a breach of contract with the patient:[21]

Q. Do you keep notes on your patients?

A. No, sir.

Q. None?

A. After the initial visit I keep everything in my head.

Q. Doctor, you mean to say that it is possible to have therapy without adequate records!

A. You have an erroneous idea about how things work in psychotherapy.

Q. Doctor, you go on trips, don't you? You leave your office occasionally, don't you?

A. No, sir. I sure don't.

Q. You never go on a vacation?

A. Not yet.

Q. In all your years of practice?

A. It's terrible.

Q. Nobody ever relieves you, you never have another psychiatrist relieve you when you go somewhere?

A. No, I haven't.

Q. If something were to happen to you then there would be no written record of any type to pass on to a colleague so that they could continue to give help to your patients?

A. [angrily] Sir, once again you demonstrate your lack of understanding of psychotherapy.

In another malpractice case, alleging sexual intimacy between the psychiatrist and the patient, the psychiatrist was asked for his records. He said he had none. The lawyer exclaimed: "You collected over $10,000 in fees and you kept no records? My lord, what kind of doctor are you!"

A number of articles in the law reviews advocate legislation to provide patients with the right of direct access to medical or psychiatric records, but no mention is made in these articles of the purpose of a record in psychiatry or the content of the record. The assumption is that a psychiatric record is as essential as a medical record for proper care. Thus in one law review article, "Access to Medical and Psychiatric Records: Proposed Legislation," the author stated:[22]

> Under the present order, it is often easier to find out, via an itemized bill, what has been done to one's car than to one's body. . . . [T]he [patient] ought to know about his physical or mental condition.

The astute therapist usually appreciates the dynamics of a case in the opening session or two, but what the patient integrates is picked up gradually. It is a continuous process involving the work of both. To be sure, the patient may wonder, "When am I going to get something out of all this?" If insights or getting to "know oneself" came so quickly, then patients could buy a book or consult "Dear Abby" about their concerns. Uncovering and absorption take time.[23]

If the view is taken that the documentation of sessions is of doubtful value for the psychiatric patient (except in the case of medication records which are crucial), why have records? There are now various record-generating pressures. Records are now being forced into existence where none were kept before. The demand for full and detailed records is increasing from legal and insurance sources. They are increasingly necessary for accountability. Quality assurance, accreditation, financial reimbursement, cost containment, and legal purposes call for the keeping of records.

Accountability implies a sharing of information, which involves, to some extent, a breach of confidentiality. The changing medical scene has impacted on confidentiality. Kirk B. Johnson, general counsel of the American Medical Association, put it thus:[24]

Confidentiality used to be a sacred principle in medicine, but it just isn't as sacred as it used to be. It is one of the things that got lost in the race to review everything in medicine and get it all computerized. The obsession with reviewing is so great and the techniques are so impersonal that it is difficult to establish rules that really protect the patient's privacy. Confidentiality is not a high priority for government regulators, third-party payers, insurers or utilization reviewers.

Sissela Bok had this to say:[25]

[T]he duty of confidentiality is no longer what it was when lawyers or doctors simply kept to themselves the confidences of those who sought their help. How can it be, when office personnel and collaborators and team members must have access to the information as well, and when clients and patients with numerous interdependent needs consult different professionals who must in turn communicate with one another? And how can it be, given the vast increase in information collected, stored, and retrievable that has expanded the opportunities for access by outsiders? How can it be, finally, when employers, school officials, law enforcement agencies, insurance companies, tax inspectors, and credit bureaus all press to see some of this confidential information?

The proposed "Fair Health Information Practices Act" would replace existing state laws governing confidentiality by a single, national standard. A version of this proposal was part of Hillary Clinton's comprehensive health care reform package that was defeated in 1995. The legislation would give law enforcement agencies access to medical records without a court order. In a related legislative proposal, national standards for the electronic transmission of health care information and the groundwork for a health information network would be established.[26]

Electronic recordkeeping is outdating paper recordkeeping, and is posing new problems of privacy. On promoting health care applications of the National Information Infrastructure, Vice President Al Gore wrote to Donna Shalala, Secretary of Health and Human Service, as follows, in part:[27]

As you know, new information and communications technologies will have a pervasive impact on the way we work, learn, live and communicate with each other. The emerging National Information Infrastructure will eventually allow Americans to send and receive voice, video images, and data with the same ease as we use telephones today.

Although the health sector is highly information-intensive, it has not capitalized on computers and information networks to the same extent as other sectors of the economy. Applications such as automated claims and payment transactions, telemedicine, computer-based patient records, and on-line access to the latest treatment and prevention information will help improve quality, expand access, and contain costs....

There is a developing consensus that everyone–consumers, industry, policy makers–would be better served by more uniform, shared standards for collection and transmission of health information. HHS has a unique opportunity to help create a national forum for the collaboration of all interested parties, with the long-term goal of increasing the interoperability of diverse health information systems. Such a forum could accelerate the development of a national health information infrastructure that dramatically reduces data collection and paperwork burdens and allows for multiple uses of data, while protecting the privacy of individuals....

A cornerstone for health applications of the NII must be strong privacy protection. Existing state and federal laws are not equipped to handle privacy and confidentiality in an electronic environment. The privacy policies of institutions that hold health information are of varying efficacy. Privacy policies should have procedural components (for example, determining who requires access for a given purpose) and technological components (for example, audit trails and encryption).

Accordingly, the Department should develop model institutional privacy policies and model state laws for health information. These models should be consistent with the privacy principles developed by the ITTF working group and informed by the advisory committee. A starting point for model institutional policies should be the most cost-effective policies in use in the private sector today. The model state laws should be designed to assist state legislatures, which will be struggling with these issues over the next few years.

The Administration should also consider what type of federal framework is needed to support these models. The framework could range from federal legislation to ideas for evaluating the efficacy of the suggested models....

Given the role that information and communications technologies can play in expanding access, increasing quality, and containing costs, I think it is imperative that the Department commit to making significant progress on these issues in the next year.

Consumer-credit reporting companies plan a series of networked regional and local medical data systems to provide everything from insurance claims and payment processing to record storage, outcomes research, and marketing advice. An editorial in *USA Today* exclaimed: "These days you may as well hire a health-care skywriter to transcribe your medical history. Because with each computer advance, your most private records are spreading farther and wider."[28]

## ACCOUNTABILITY TO THE PATIENT

Apart from whatever value records may have on treatment goals, one may say that good professional care dictates a system of establishing accountability to a patient about his care (and also to make it possible for the patient to obtain reimbursement from a third-party payer).[29] There is a story: "Do you love your wife as much as your money? Would you have your money in a bank that did not keep records? So would you have your wife treated without records?"

Citizens consumers' rights groups in other areas have demanded the right of a patient to examine his medical or psychiatric records; the patient is compared to a buyer of a product entitled to information. This right of access obviously would be an empty right if there were no record or nothing in the record or if the therapist has merely been a scrivener writing down nothing more than what the patient or client has said. A New Jersey court upheld the right of mental patients to obtain access to hospital records to help challenge their involuntary commitments and the quality of care they received.[30] Patients receiving medical care under the federally-administered Medicare program, all patients in Veterans Administration hospitals, and recipients of Social Security or Supplemental Security Income benefits under the Social Security Administration have right of access to their records.[31]

As the law has developed, the patient is given the right to inspect his own medical records, unless such divulgence can be shown to be detrimental to the patient's health. The general rule now is access (even in states without access statutes) except *"when a doctor can prove. . . .* that the disclosure would so seriously upset the patient that the patient would not [be] able to dispassionately weigh the risks of refusing to undergo the recommended treatment" (emphasis added).[32] As yet another court put it, the patient must be fully informed unless the physician can prove that "a complete disclosure . . . could so harm the patient that it would, In fact, constitute bad medical practice."[33]

## IMPLEMENTING THE RIGHT TO TREATMENT

The making of reports is necessary for the "right to treatment" which the courts have ruled for the institutionalized mental patient. In the well-known case of *Wyatt v. Stickney*, Judge Frank Johnson set out "minimum constitutional standards for adequate treatment of the mentally ill" and they included individualized treatment plans.[34] It is to be noted, however, that Chief Justice Burger, in a concurring opinion, pointed out that the High Court has never said that a patient has a constitutional right to treatment.[35]

## INSURANCE COVERAGE

Generating recordkeeping is the growth of insurance coverage for psychiatric care (now affecting 90 percent of care). Insurance is not a giveaway. Any system of reimbursement requires proof that services were necessary and were performed. An insurer must have information with which it can assess the administration and cost of programs. Using the medical model, insurers of psychiatric care expect to receive information comparable to that obtained for the care of physical disorders. According to medical standards, a record must be maintained for every patient which will serve as the basis for planning, and for continuity of care; provide a means of communication among the physician and any professionals who contribute to the patient's care; furnish documentary evidence of ordered and supervised treatments, observations of the patient's behavior, and his response to treatment; serve as a basis for review, study, and evaluation of the care rendered to the patient; assist in protecting the legal rights of the patient, the facility, and the professional staff; and provide data for use in research and education.

Insurers vary in their demand for information, but in general, they expect a report "to verify that illness or disease is present." For coverage there must be a diagnosis that appears in the World Health Organization's *International Classification of Diseases*, but experience has taught the insurance industry that a psychiatric diagnosis bears little or no relevance to the insurer's concern in setting a standard in setting rates for psychiatric coverage, and almost no relevance to clinical status, prognosis, or treatment. Given the same diagnosis, the treatment may be drug therapy, electroshock, or hospitalization. Psychiatrists are bemused by the question, "How long do you keep an average schizophrenic in the hospital?"[36]

The latest editions of the American Psychiatric Association's *Diagnostic and Statistical Manual of Mental Disorders* are designed to improve the reliability of diagnoses (their validity is another matter). In psychiatry there is debate whether its diagnostic categories are useful for psychiatry, but however that is resolved, the labels are not really helpful for law or insurance.[37] An insurer provides no coverage for treatment of "marital maladjustment" or "sexual dysfunction," so the psychiatrist searches for a classification that is covered, such as "adjustment to adult life." There is no coverage for a nasty smoking habit, but there is coverage if it is a symptom of an underlying disorder. Consequently, the insurer increasingly asks for more and more information, but indeed, what would fairly inform the third-party payer?

Like two drunks trying to shake hands but unable to meet, the third-party payer and the provider of treatment cannot meet on what ought to be in the record. The insurer increasingly wants data to justify payment, while the provider says essentially that the insurer ought to take his word for it. The third-party payer or managed care entity has no need for the communications of a patient with a therapist, but rather they have need to know about the condition of the patient. Patients rarely have concern about providing this type of information, and if there is misuse of it, an action under tort law can be instituted.[38]

There have been a substantial number of fraudulent and abusive practices, such as billing for services more extensive than those actually provided, billing for services not rendered, billing for multiple services to members of the same family on the same day, multiple referrals between practitioners when there is no real necessity for services, charging for physician's services actually provided by nonphysicians or paraprofessionals not eligible for reimbursement or full reimbursement, and billing more than one third-party for the same service.

The doctor's appointment book is one source of information to verify service, but sometimes the doctor has a number of appointment books, one for each insurer. The third-party payer finds it is engaged in something of a detective game trying to put together ledgers, records and appointment books. Trying to get adequate information is often like trying to get hold of a greased pig. There is insurance coverage for only a "treatable condition"; the condition must be "amenable to treatment." To convince the insurer that the treatment is worthwhile, the record must establish that the goal of treatment is being reached. In some cases, when a patient's coverage is exhausted, the name of a dependent is used as a cover for continued treatment of the patient. In the view of some therapists, insurance fraud is justified in order to continue treatment of a patient.

The standard of care, or how the "treatable condition" is treated, falls under the circumspection too of the third-party payer. Thus, for depression, the third-party payer does not cover a trip to the Bahamas or demon exorcism or a nude marathon, however therapeutic it may be. To be sure, the role of the fiscal third party in controlling "who gets what" is becoming increasingly controversial. The care must be of the type acceptable in the medical community. Thus, the third party payer looks for ways to pay less and less (and, if possible not to pay a claim at all, however justified it may be). The psychoanalytic or long-term approach is under attack by the AMA with its pill or surgery view of medicine, and by government and insurance companies because it is cheaper to control symptoms with drugs.[39] Economic accountability is increasingly determining the length of treatment, the length of hospitalization and the kinds of treatment.

In contrast to the passive role played by third-party payers under traditional indemnity insurance schemes, managed care entities play an active role in the delivery of health care. As a result, health care decisions are no longer made solely within the physician-patient relationship. While traditional insurers were satisfied with a diagnosis to justify coverage, managed care companies seek explicit information about the patient's symptoms and life experiences. The relationship of the therapist with the payer taxes the confidentiality of the relationship between the patient and the therapist in the prospective and concurrent review processes. There are various ways that managed care organizations structure and implement utilization review. The gatekeeper is usually a nurse or a social worker who evaluates the clinical presentation made by the therapist against a set of criteria, usually unknown to the therapist.

In cookbook fashion, one California insurer concocted a list of various diagnostic categories that were matched with treatment. This "standard of treatments" was formulated by Blue Shield in consultation with psychiatrists selected by them (not by any psychiatric organization), setting out rigid details of what constitutes indications for psychotherapy or hospitalization. For "depression," it was stated that "chemotherapy and electric shock therapy are the treatments of choice"; psychotherapy might be indicated in some cases.[40]

Blue Cross-Blue Shield periodically issue documentation guidelines and many managed care organizations do the same. They usually want progress notes, not the process notes of the clinician. They want information on the functioning of the patient. In some cases, there are computer-generated forms which have a place to check off "yes" or "no" in response to four questions: Depressed? Suicidal? Psychotic? Medication?

The denial of a claim works against the patient, not the provider, as the patient remains in the provider's debt.[41] To get around the limitations, the provider is moved to make a diagnosis that would provide the desired treatment. According to Dr. Maurice Grossman, reports were sent to Medi-Cal (California Medicaid) exaggerating the bizarre symptoms in order to qualify for authorization for extended treatment. Experience has shown that understated versions to protect the patient in the event of disclosure of his record results in rejection of the request.[42]

The underlying premise of mental health and other health agencies in seeking to extend care to a larger number of people is that "supervision" safeguards or improves the standard of care; it is said that even paraprofessionals can play an important and increasing role in health care if they have "appropriate training and supervision."[43] In this connection, the nature and structure of the Out-Patient Psychiatric Clinic (OPC) as devised in Michigan warrants examination.[44]

The OPC operation in Michigan was largely generated by the United Automobile Workers' attempt to expand the number of mental health personnel available to their members. Using a medical model, the services of psychologists and social workers were reimbursable only if they were "supervised" by a psychiatrist. Some called the supervision duplicity, others called it "fraud and abuse," still others called it "protection money." The UAW blamed the abuses on shoddy administration of its program by the insurer, and that raised the question of whether and to what extent a fiscal third party ought to set out standards and maintain supervision. Legislation was thereupon passed in Michigan mandating direct payment to psychologists.

In the OPC operation, the third-party payer considered a record as essential for the supervision that the psychiatrist is obliged to carry out, and for the third-party payer to ascertain who or what is being done in the clinic. "Without an adequate record, how would it be known what is going on?" That is what the third-party payer said. In fact, however, the length of the report was no assurance of anything. The supervising psychiatrist could sign a long record in the same time that he signs a short one. It just made for more paperwork by the underlings. There was much talk in Michigan about psychiatrists going from clinic to clinic signing papers and in some cases collecting over $1-million annually. The motivation for abuse was overwhelming. There was apparently no prosecution for insurance fraud as the I's and t's in the record were meticulously dotted and crossed.

## GOVERNMENTAL AND NONGOVERNMENTAL REGULATION

Yesterday it became necessary to keep records so that the patient could obtain reimbursement for his expenditures from a third-party payer. Today records must also be kept so that a governmental or nongovernmental agency can review whether the doctor's practice is in accord with its formula of medical indications. Inspecting teams and courts too take the attitude, "If it isn't written, it didn't happen." State licensing laws and regulatory agencies, such as the Division of Hospital Licensure or the Department of Health, set out requirements with which hospitals must comply. In addition, nongovernmental agencies, such as the Joint Commission on Accreditation of Healthcare Organizations (JCAHO), establish standards for the maintenance of records. The failure of a doctor to complete records provides a basis for his suspension from the hospital.[45]

Hospital and clinic care may be distinguished from that provided by an office practitioner. There is often involved a team approach, occupational and recreational activities, and somatic therapies. Traditionally, hospital and clinic records have consisted of identification data, admitting history, physical examination and laboratory data, mental status examination on admission, psychological testing, psychiatric evaluation, progress notes, and discharge summary. These records are often written by personnel from a variety of disciplines with varying amounts of training, *e.g.*, psychiatric residents, psychology interns, vocational rehabilitation counselors, social workers, registered nurses, licensed practical nurses, psychiatric aides, etc. These entries, while they may serve a useful purpose for the whole team, are often haphazard.

## Governmental Regulation

The Michigan Department of Mental Health, which may be taken as an example of state regulatory activity, requires in the public mental health system "a document prepared by an interdisciplinary team specifying for each mental health system client measurable objectives for service delivery, activities to be carried out to achieve objectives, the assignment of responsibility for performing activities, and criteria for evaluating the attainment of objectives." The code and regulations require a medical, psychiatric and social evaluation of the patient. The treatment plan documentation must reflect patient and family participation and understanding.[46]

Some years ago, the California Department of Mental Health demanded that all methadone clinics record fingerprints and photos of all patients, with a register centralized in Sacramento. The ostensible purpose was to discover patients who registered in more than one clinic to get extra drugs for street sale. The organization of clinic directors rebelled on grounds it would keep patients away, and they refused to comply. The state thereupon threatened to withhold funds. Some directors, capitulated; others did not.[47]

## Hospital Accreditation

The Joint Commission on Accreditation of Hospitals (JCAH) was formulated in 1951, now the Joint Commission on Healthcare Organizations (JCAHO), for the purpose of assessing the quality of care in treatment facilities. Each of its accreditation programs is monitored by national organizations committed to health care services for a variety of age and disability groups. The Accreditation Council for Psychiatric Facilities, which was established in 1970 to assess quality measures for health care services in psychiatry, made the patient record the source of assessment.[48]

## Professional Standards Review Organization Program

In 1972, Congress enacted the Professional Standards Review Organization (PSRO) Amendments to the Social Security Act "to promote the effective, efficient and economical delivery of health care services of proper quality" under fully or partially federally-funded programs.[49] As we have noted, it was found ineffective and it passed to the states for implementation.

Peer review is considered the only way to resolve the tension between quality assurance and cost containment—but the effectiveness of quality assurance is cut across by a limitation of peer review to inpatient care, and cost containment is cut across by a control that is based on the report of the one to be controlled. Peer review has been a review of records, not a personal review of patients, but now state reviewers and JCAHO surveyors talk with patients. When review is based on a record, it is very much a measure of how well one writes a record (and one may ask whether a psychotherapy process can be judged from a writing). Like a statement of expenses, the preparation of these reports is often creative writing at its best. But be it fiction or not, peers generally tend not to say that a colleague's treatment is unnecessary or inappropriate, particularly as that might lead not only to a claim of unnecessary services but also to an action in malpractice.[50] Information collected by individuals or committees in hospitals, HMOs, etc. for the purposes of a professional peer review function is confidential and may only be used for such review purposes.[51]

### Providing Legal Protection

A medical or business record is commonly called a "potential legal document." In the words of a director of JCAH, "Today, hospitals and physicians are increasingly subject to tort claims and lawsuits. The best protection against an unjustified lawsuit is a complete, accurate medical record."[52] There is an old saying: *si vis pacem, para bellum* (if you desire peace, prepare for war).

In the case of a suit against the physician, the medical record or hospital chart is very frequently the best and only proof of nonnegligent diagnosis or treatment. Properly kept, it may enable a physician to show that he used due care in a given case. A misjudgment may not be considered neglectful if it was well reasoned. The physician is advised to retain the record for longer than the time set out in the statute of limitations (generally 2 years), as that period does not begin to run until the patient appreciates that he has been harmed, or in the case of a minor, when he reaches majority.

The types of lawsuits most frequently involving psychiatric care are those in which the evidence shows the patient had a suicidal tendency of which the psychiatrist knew or should have been aware. The psychiatrist did not give proper attention to that history, failed to give appropriate orders to the hospital staff, or the hospital staff failed to carry out the orders. Other areas of litigation involve administration of electroshock, faulty diagnosis or screening, improper certification in commitment, harmful effects of psychotropic drugs, improper divulgence of information, and sexual intimacy with patients.[53] The facts in these or other legal actions are always in dispute, so it is helpful to have documentation to support one's version of the event.

As a result of the growing number of lawsuits by patients or their parents against therapists involving "revival of memory" of childhood sexual abuse, therapists are advised to take comprehensive notes on the process by which the memories were recovered. In litigation, a key question will be who first raised the issue of abuse, and how it was raised. Generally, the more outrageous, bizarre, or unusual the allegations of abuse, the more detailed the notes should be. The more bizarre the allegations, the more thoroughly the therapist must consider alternative explanations, such as that the memories being reported are metaphors and not literally true. The forensic expert, in evaluating the case, is expected to look for independent corroboration, such as medical, police, school, or therapist records at the time of the alleged abuse.

The record made by a therapist, however, is a double-edged sword. It may exculpate, but it may also inculpate. In general, tort liability is rarely imposed for the negligent practice of psychotherapy, because, given the nebulous nature of the psychotherapeutic process, a standard of care is all but impossible to define. Also there are problems establishing proximate causation and assessing nonphysical damages. In most of the cases where liability has been imposed, however, it has been where the record is very inadequate or indicates that suicidal precautions have not been followed.[54] An inadequate record of itself is taken to be indicative of poor care. As with inspecting teams, the courts consider that what is not documented is not done. In the courtroom, the record is the psychiatrist's Achilles' heel.

With standard of care difficult to establish in psychotherapy, taking an inadequate record as the equivalent of negligent care is the avenue increasingly taken to establish tort liability. It is a result of the many complaints that psychotherapists are singularly not accountable under tort law. A common saying is that when there is a wrong, there ought to be a remedy. Professional tort liability supposedly provides something akin to a certification service for the public as well as a remedy for wrong. Actually, in tort law, in some measure, the tail wags the dog. When insurance coverage is available, some theory is developed to provide an avenue of recovery. Tort claims are linked to insurance coverage.[55]

Inadequate recordkeeping contributing to malpractice liability may be illustrated by one case where the court said:[56]

The hospital record maintained by the State . . . was about as inadequate a record as we have ever examined. We find that said record did not conform to the standards in the community; and, that the inadequacies in this record militated against proper and competent psychiatric and ordinary medical care.... Therefore, to the extent that a hospital record develops information for subsequent treatment, it contributed to the inadequate treatment this claimant received. . . . [In] our opinion, it was so inadequate that even laymen could determine that fact.

In this case, the patient was kept in a state hospital over 12 years with virtually no written evidence of an adequate examination or treatment plan.

In patient suicide cases, the failure to note precautions in the record is taken as evidence warranting liability. In many of these cases, it is often a note written by a social worker or psychiatric aide indicating suicidal potential that establishes a case against the hospital or the attending psychiatrist. In training, social workers are taught to write down just about everything in a record, and that overflows in practice. But what is relevant in a social history? It often seems that everything is recorded, including news about the kitchen stove.[57] The "problem-oriented record," focusing on particular problems that the patient is experiencing, is an attempt to put boundaries on the notes placed in the record.[58]

## RECORDING CONSENT

Consent is essential in the treatment contract and in the passing on of information. Physicians generally have learned that if a patient claims that he did not consent to the treatment administered, a detailed and explicit form signed by the patient would likely establish that necessary disclosures had been made. Is a consent-to-treatment form also necessary for a psychotherapist to have in his dossier? Is it needed in practice, or in law? Freud, we recall, advised against "lengthy preliminary discussions" before the beginning of psychoanalytic treatment, but he did recommend that the patient be told of the difficulties and sacrifices which the treatment involves so that the patient would not be able "to say later on that he has been inveigled into a treatment whose extent and implications he did not realize."[59]

As far as the law is concerned in the purely verbal therapies, there is no possibility of a battery, there being no touching, so to that there is no need to consider a defense. It is putting the cart before the horse to consider defenses ahead of causes of action. And besides, consent would be implied in the case of psychotherapy by the fact of return; the patient has had a sample. Psychotherapy—unlike surgery—occurs over a period of time.

Failure to inform (lack of "informed consent") is also not likely to come up under negligence (malpractice) law in the case of psychotherapy. Would the therapist be obliged to point out the risks involved in the working through of transference feelings? Actually, as a matter of practice, psychotherapists follow the ancient wisdom of warning the patient that the cure will take a very long time.

In the use of medication, the patient under prevailing law is to be given information about a drug to the extent that such information does not in itself worsen the patient's emotional condition. As a matter of practice, what the patient is told should be documented in the record. If the patient could not be informed fully, because to do so would worsen his or her condition, then this fact too ought to be documented. The law does not require consent in writing, but the cautious physician, in addition to chart documentation, might nonetheless obtain consent in writing to medication as well as for other treatments.[60] In particular, in prescribing antipsychotic medication, periodic tongue checks for tardive dyskinesia ought to be documented.[61]

Under contract law, it is essential for the parties to agree on a price for services. Thus a therapist who tells a patient, "You have insurance, you have nothing to worry about," could not properly make a claim against the patient for services not covered by the insurance. Moreover, as we have noted, there may be an invasion-of-privacy tort action or a breach-of-contract action for an unauthorized disclosure of confidential information. To repeat, consent in writing is the best evidence, and is well advised, but, by and large, writing is not mandatory as a matter of law.[62] With the passage of time, though, who will remember what transpired? In one case, as discussed, where the therapist wrote a book about a patient not adequately disguised, the patient had given consent, withdrew it, consented, withdrew it, etc. The court noted that the consent "was there one day and not there another day." The court also observed, "Consent was sought while the [patient] was in therapy. It was never obtained in writing."[63]

On the use of records in a hospital, a patient gives permission by implication for all hospital personnel directly involved in the treatment to see the records, and they may also be viewed by hospital committees involved in monitoring quality of care. Legislation has been enacted that provides for the transmitting of information from one service entity of the state to another when the information is pertinent to providing services to the recipient. This sharing of information, which may be done without the patient's consent, is intended to aid service entities within a community mental health program to identify problems and help coordinate treatment and habilitation of recipients.[64] Under this scheme, the patient is regarded as a patient not of a particular clinic but of the state mental health system, an approach followed in a number of countries.

In the usual case, a patient authorizes a physician or psychiatrist to make the necessary disclosures in order to obtain payment for treatment and related services. Quite often there are no limitations in the forms on the extent of the information to be revealed, the time during which such information can be distributed, or the sharing of such information among various agencies. Such blank releases do not protect doctors who exceed the bounds of propriety.[65] Under various insurance plans, complete records are requested as a condition for payment.

At times, attorneys, investigators and others obtain records of a patient from the recordkeeper at a hospital by a bribe. At other times, they convince the recordkeeper that they have legal authority to have the records. It happens with more frequency than we would like to think.

## DISCUSSION

The concern over recordkeeping now clutters the psychiatrist's mind–what to put in the record, what to leave out, how to write what is put in, and when and to whom to release it. He wonders whether he can have a record that is just his, immune from demand. As a result of all of this, records in health care have become more and more bureaucratized. They are saying more, but actually telling less. The majority, if not all, of the treatment plans that are required in recordkeeping are what lawyers call "boilerplate" statements. They are as becoming as stereotyped a production as the pleadings of an attorney. And they have a life of their own, much like the records in Nikolai Gogol's *Dead Souls*.[66]

As long known by Peeping Toms, "The angle of observation has a good deal to do with the properties of the observed." The nature of the observer also has a good deal to do with what will be available to observe. When it is known that records will be reviewed by third parties, or by the patient, or by the patient's family, they will be written with that in mind.[67] This results in records that are worthless as clinical material for the patient's needs, or for teaching and research needs. More and more, they are written to protect the therapist or patient from all kinds of fantasied attacks.

To protect patients, many therapists consider it necessary to destroy records, or not make them in the first place, with the loss of whatever benefit they may have for treatment, research, or teaching.[68] Some therapists who feel a need for records in therapy have a two-record system–one for internal use, another for external use; they assume that internal or working records can be kept confidential. Some may call the internal record the "amoeba" or "personal notes." Just as a lawyer's "work product" is not subject to discovery, they believe that notes so classified might not be considered a record subject to demand.[69] Legislation was sought a few years ago that would protect the confidentiality of "personal notes."

Reports from physicians to schools have been watered down to be innocuous ever since the Buckley amendment requiring schools to reveal all their records to families. An analogous situation developed with regard to letters of recommendation to schools, colleges, and graduate schools.[70] It is a problem not only in psychiatry but in medicine generally—how does a pediatrician, for example, write to a school principal that the child's asthmatic attacks are related to the personality of the mother or father in response to an inquiry of the school that wishes to help the child while having to deal with the parents? These problems stem from legal views that legislate in a black and white manner, whereas medical or psychiatric practice does not lend itself to an either-or approach.

Of course, every institutionalized patient should have an individualized treatment plan, but where are the taxpayers who would support such a program in government hospitals that would make it possible? The doctor could write such notes and daily add details to suggest it is actually being carried out, but it would be meaningless, in terms of facilities and staff available. It would be an example of legal recordkeeping that in reality is a farce. Worse, with dedicated short-staffed therapists, it would deprive them of even more time that they would rather spend with the patient. And on the need to record the chief complaints of others regarding the patient as required in a much publicized case,[71] just imagine turning the records over to the patient who is acutely paranoid, or even with paranoid tendencies simmered down, and he reads what his family has said about him.[72]

The Michigan code and regulations mandating that treatment planning be done by assembling all the disciplines theoretically has value, but the problem is how to get these (high-priced) therapists to find enough time to work with patients after all of their mandatory planning sessions, on-job training seminars, administrative meetings, etc., have been arranged. There are ways that accomplish the intent of the regulations without going through all of the detail that regulation demands. Without such regulation, the staff is a happier and more effective group. Their morale grows, as they effectively treat patients, and not just sit around and talk about it.

## SUMMARY AND CONCLUSION

To summarize:

1. Most psychotherapists would claim they need no records for effective psychotherapy. Others say that the thinking that goes into writing a record,

apart from the keeping of the record, can increase effectiveness in therapy.

2.   Recordkeeping should be a foundation for effective research and teaching; even a well-analyzed therapist will have a memory distorted by bias.

3.   Any use of chemotherapy requires detailed recordkeeping. If it is an adjunct to psychotherapy, it requires psychotherapeutic notes to correlate with the drugs.

4.   Legal and economic encroachments on psychiatric practice have resulted in a self-protective need for recordkeeping. In some cases the result has been records that protect the therapist (or hospital) more than they serve the patient.

5.   Insurance is limited (Woody Allen would himself have to pay for his 22 or more years of psychoanalysis). Insurance coverage necessitates reports that range from billing data only to demand for photostats of all records. In a considerable number of cases, the records submitted are rejected as not detailed enough.

6.   The PRO has been a major record-generating pressure. The PRO does not really deal with quality of care, but functions primarily to determine if the cost of care is warranted, as measured by need, duration and frequency of treatment, and hospital utilization. Records are written to meet that criterion which has led to the formulation of "standards"–they are created as guidelines, but they are viewed primarily by nurses using them as rigid criteria. They result in "cookbook recipes" for medical or psychiatric care.

7.   Access by patients to their records has some advantages, but the tendency is to urge legislation allowing no leeway. Honest and meaningful records in psychiatry contain material that may be conjectures of the therapist as a working tool, and they contain confidential material from third parties, sometimes unsolicited by the therapist, but for legal reasons need to be recorded. Sometimes the patients have no memory of what they have related in treatment. Sometimes families coerce patients to demand their records. The mixture of the two can be like gasoline and fire being brought together. Sometimes patients have no insight into what they have revealed, at a time where understanding would be too threatening. The therapist may have recorded the meaning of the communication rather than the verbatim statements. Records cannot at one and the same time be adequate, accessible and confidential.

8.   Records are used to establish negligence in malpractice actions, though at other times they may be protective. However, records must not be regarded as absolute legal protection.

9.   Recording "consent" is a can of worms.

To conclude: The need for recordkeeping in the practice of psychiatry brings to mind a cartoon that showed a judge saying to the doctor, "I don't question your medical competence, Doctor--it's your paperwork!"[73] In the former U.S.S.R., a good part of the population was busily engaged in preparing reports that were sent to Moscow, no one apparently read them, and then people went about their business oblivious to the reports. In the U.S., it is mostly lawyers who spend most of their time preparing piles of papers that are rarely read, but are needed in a crisis. The doctor (or aide) must now engage in that kind of activity too.

Earl Long, when Governor of Louisiana, advised the heads of various state departments, "I will be sending you a lot of letters, I have to do it for the record, but pay no attention to them. If I need anything, I'll telephone." And that is the state of the psychiatric record. It is written—watered down and sanitized—to satisfy the patient, the third-party payer, the governmental and nongovernmental regulatory agencies. President Nixon's plumbers found no records when they burglarized the office of Ellsberg's psychiatrist; today they might find vacuous reports.

Like it or not, to survive in today's society, one must be bureaucratized. But sooner or later, Freud said, illusions come into conflict with some portion of reality, and are shattered against it. Recordkeeping in psychiatry is now very much an exercise in paperwork.[74]

For further discussion, see Part IV, Chapter 7 on communications with nonmedical persons in response to inquiries.

## NOTES

1. S.M. Hersh, "Nixon's Active Role on Plumbers: His Talks With Leaders Recalled," *New York Times*, Dec. 10, 1973, p. 30; *Time*, Aug. 27,1973, p. 18.
2. Obtaining psychiatric records in order to harass a patient was also revealed in documents the FBI seized from the Church of Scientology. The goal of the church, the document said, was "to get Paulette Cooper incarcerated in a mental institution or jail, or at least to hit so hard that she drops her attacks." G. Gordon, "Critic Framed by Scientologists," *New Orleans Times-Picayune*, Nov. 24, 1979, p. 2. Cooper, a New York writer, said the church began harassing her when it learned she was working on a book about the organization, *The Scandal of Scientology* (the book was published in 1971). The harassment got her so depressed that she sought psychiatric care. When beginning treatment, she told her psychiatrist not to take any notes, suspecting that the church would try to get them. She mused, "He must have thought I was paranoid!" He recorded only an innocuous statement that the church obtained by planting a typist. Communication from Paulette Cooper to author.
3. G. Vidal, "The Art and Arts of E. Howard Hunt," *New York Review of Books*, Dec. 13, 1973, p. 6.

4. A. Corman, *Kramer versus Kramer* (New York: Random House 1977), p. 106.

5. I.F. Stone, "Betrayal of Psychiatry," *New York Review of Books*, Feb. 10, 1972, p. 7.

6. At the same time, it must be noted that many medical records are written to comply with a ritual and as a result are meaningless. There are files on chronic patients so voluminous, no one ever reviews them, for treatment purposes or otherwise. The problem-oriented record is a step to make the record more valuable practically. In many situations, including hospitalization, the patient presents an acute problem, it is treated, cured, and no one ever looks at the record, except for a legal proceeding. With this in mind, the record is written for that purpose, not for the patient's benefit.

7. P. Chodoff, "Psychiatry and the Fiscal Third Party," *Am. J. Psychiat.* 134:114, 1978.

8. In a felicitous phrase, Freud said that the therapist should pay "hovering attention" to the patient, so as to be alert to one's own subjective responses while at the same time listening to the productions of the patient. Dr. Maurice Grossman put it this way: "In practice that is analytically oriented, the therapist does not focus on the details of the communications, but tries to 'listen' to the underlying trends; and relies on his or her own unconscious to find connections that clarify the underlying trends. . . . This need to avoid focusing on the current details is why some therapists smoke, doodle, knit, knot belts (done by an internationally known training analyst). This prevents a too rigid direct attention to the flowing details of the patient's free associations, while listening to it on a different level. Some take notes that are not really verbatim, as a hangover from student days when they had to have a detailed record for case supervision. Sometimes these notes serve the purpose of doodling." Personal communication.

9. J.M. Gorman, *The New Psychiatry* (New York: St. Martin's Press, 1996), p. 353.

10. T.S. Szasz, *The Ethics of Psychoanalysis* (New York: Basic Books, 1965), p. 220.

11. Personal communication.

12. Personal communication.

13. S.A. Appelbaum, *Out in Inner Space/A Psychoanalyst Explores the New Therapies* (New York: Doubleday, 1979), p. 66.

14. Dr. Maurice Grossman said (personal communication): "I find that my memory does get distorted at times, largely because later material creates a different image. If it were not for this, one could after reviewing a session discard whatever notes were made. So again it is not essential for effective therapy to keep the notes that constitute a record. However, I have had patients who completed therapy successfully, but return to therapy when changes in their life unlock other difficulties. Then the record is important for review, rather than depending recall of all the important details. I find after a patient leaves therapy that unconsciously I try to erase all memories other than generalities. Perhaps it is an outgrowth of my belief in the patient's privacy. So I am torn between keeping records and destroying them."

In the view of Mary S. Cerney, then staff psychologist at the Menninger Hospital, records are important in that they record changes in behavior or even the lack of change in behavior. She said (personal communication): "Our memories tend to play tricks on us. In my consultation work, I have been able to chart particular patterns of behavior and relate them to specific incidents or changes in medication, etc. Studying these patterns in greater depth has led to important decisions in regard to patients' treatment which would not have been possible if certain data were not recorded in the record. . . . In my own treatment of patients, I frequently go over the record (we have review conferences on our patients at least every six months, and more often) in order to detect patterns or look at the data from a different point of view. That is also one of the reasons we call in an outside consultant to help us review the cases at the review conferences, so as to get a different point of view, and perhaps help us find something we are missing. . . . I find records very important in preventing the repetition of treatment plans that have already proven to be ineffective with the patient. I feel that people who adequately study the treatment records and history of patients can make more appropriate treatment plans, and in the long run, shorten treatment of some patients." See also M.S. Cerney, "Record Keeping and Change," *Nat'l Assn. of Private Psychiatric Hospitals J.* (NAPPH) 10:42, 1978-1979.

15.   Dr. Grossman described his practice (communication to author): "Frequently I will detect a dynamic trend in a patient that seems to have significance. I will note this on an index card. As this same trend occurs in this patient, or other patients, I will make the notation that refers to the records of the specific session. In the course of this I have picked up confirmed trends that have been extremely valuable for treating the original patient. The extra dividend is that I can accept them as valid when they come up for future patients. This has nothing to do with publications for the benefit of others. Occasionally I will write of them; or more likely use them as material for an oral presentation."

16.   In 1976, *Saturday Review* stated that psychoanalysis is one of 130 therapies which compete in the "psychotherapy jungle." In 1979, Time raised the number of competing therapies to 200. See J. Kovel, *A Complete Guide to Therapy/From Psychoanalysis to Behavior Modification* (New York: Pantheon, 1976); M.G. Drellich, Editorial, "The Identity of the Psychoanalyst," *J. Amer. Acad. Psychoanal.* 7:475, 1979); S. Lesse, Editorial, "Caveat Emptor?–The Cornucopia of Current Psychotherapies," *Am. J. Psychotherapy* 33:329, 1979. Under the doctrine of informed consent, the doctor must tell the patient of the risks of treatment or of no treatment, and of the available alternatives. R. Slovenko, "Psychotherapy and Informed Consent: A Search in Judicial Regulation," in W.E. Barton & C.J. Sanborn (eds.), *Law and the Mental Health Professions* (New York: International Universities Press, 1978), p. 51.

17.   T. Szasz, *The Myth of Psychotherapy* (New York: Doubleday, 1978).

18.   J.D. Frank, *Persuasion and Healing: A Comparative Study of Psychotherapy* (Baltimore: Johns Hopkins University Press, 1961); "Mental Health in a

Fragmented Society: The Shattered Crystal Ball," *Am. J. Orthopsychiat.* 49:397, 1979.

19. W. Schofield, *Psychotherapy: The Purchase of Friendship* (Englewood Cliffs, N.J.: Prentice-Hall, 1964).

20. Quoted in N. Gittelson, "The Maturing of Woody Allen," *New York Times Magazine*, April 22, 1979, at 104. In the United States, an analysis usually takes 5 to 6 years, while in England, it takes about 10, but that is because, one wit suggested, the English take a longer time to catch on to a joke.

21. Dr. Grossman said, "When I have another psychiatrist stand in, I brief him on the patients who are in situations where crises or need for information would be necessary. For other situations the patient is able to tell the doctor what's what. This is also to preserve the confidentiality of intimate detail from others, including other doctors when revelation is not vital. In the case where something were to happen to me, based on many situations where patients have had to transfer based on just that, the patient would spell out in the first few hours the essential aspects of the preceding treatment. The previous doctor's notes would not supply the real ingredients necessary, that is, the unconscious storehouse of associations representing the communications. Even more important, notes would not shift over the transference relationship that had existed. It would begin automatically with the new therapist. I have found that not infrequently, a flow of feeling about the previous therapist would take place, things that were never revealed to him. And I am sure that when a patient of mine goes to another therapist the same thing happens because the resistance in the therapy had not been reduced enough at the time of severance." Personal communication.

22. E. Felch, "Access to Medical and Psychiatric Records: Proposed Legislation," *Albany L.Rev.* 40:581, 1976.

23. On the timing of interpretations in psychoanalytic psychotherapy, the aphorism is: "The analyst interprets resistances before contents, the surface before depths, ego before id, and, at the moment when `the unconscious becomes preconscious.'" R. Langs, "On the Formulation and Timing of Interventions," *J. Am. Acad. Psychoanal.* 7:477, 1979.

24. Quoted in M. Freudenheim, "Business and Health/Guarding Medical Confidentiality," *New York Times*, Jan. 1, 1991, p. 24.

25. S. Bok, "The Limits of Confidentiality," *Hastings Center Report*, Feb. 1983, p. 24; adapted from her book, *Secrets* (New York: Pantheon Books, 1982).

26. T. Lewin, "Questions of Privacy Roil Arena of Psychotherapy," *New York Times*, May 22, 1996, p. 1.

27. March 8, 1995.

28. Editorial, "Lack of medical privacy enough to make you sick," *USA Today*, Oct. 9, 1995, p. 12.

29. Dr. Herbert C. Schulberg observed: "The medical record is the window observing the quality of patient care. Rather than being the private working tool of clinicians alone, the medical record can also be used for evaluative and fiscal decisions. By studying the clinical record, a fellow practitioner or

carefully trained evaluator can reconstruct the course of treatment and estimate its quality." H.C. Schulberg, "Quality-of-Care Standards and Professional Norms," *Am. J. Psychiat.* 133:1049, 1976.

30. A.F. Westin, "Medical Records: Should Patients Have Access?" *Hastings Center Report* 7:23, 1977.

31. Federal Privacy Act of 1974.

32. Cobbs v. Grant, 104 Cal. Rptr. 505, 502 P.2d 1 (1972). Query: What constitutes proof? Possibly the only "proof" would be to disclose it to the patient and see whether or not the top of his head flies off. In demanding proof, the element of judgment is often ignored. The legal sense of righteousness takes place after the fact.

33. Natanson v. Kline, 186 Kan. 393, 350 P.2d 1093, *clarified on denial of rehearing*, 187 Kan. 186, 354 P.2d 670 (1960). While full disclosure to patients can reduce the quality of recordkeeping and cause the patient unnecessary distress, a substantial number of therapists feel there is something to be said for showing the patient a written summary, if she requests it. If the therapist goes over such a summary together with the patient, it can be therapeutic. And there is some ethical justification for sharing with a patient a report that will be sent to a third, nonmedical party, particularly if there is any reasonable likelihood that the contents of such a document will be revealed to the patient, or his or her family, or another party. See E.J. Stein, R.L. Furedy, M.J. Simonton & C.H. Neuffer, "Patient Access to Medical Records on a Psychiatric Inpatient Unit," *Am. J. Psychiat.* 163:327, 1979. See also G.A. Huber & L.H. Roth, "Preserving the Confidentiality of Medical Record Information Regarding Nonpatients," *Va. L. Rev.* 66:583, 1980.

34. Wyatt v. Stickney, 325 F.Supp. 781 (M.D. Ala. 1971), 344 F.Supp. 373 (M.D. Ala. 1972), *aff'd*, Wyatt v. Aderholt, 503 F.2d 1305 (5th Cir. 1974).

35. O'Connor v. Donaldson, 422 U.S. 563 (1975).

36. "Limitations of Modalities: What Therapy Is Best for This Patient?" *Roche Report: Frontiers of Psychiatry* (Nutley, N.J.: Roche Laboratories, Oct. 1979); see also F. Fromm-Reichmann, "Notes on the Development of Treatment of Schizophrenics by Psychoanalytic Psychotherapy," *Psychiatry* 11:263, 1948; M. Ostow, "Is It Useful to Combine Drug Therapy With Psychotherapy?" *Psychosomatics* 20:731, 1979.

37. See M. Grossman (Chairman), *Confidentiality and Third Parties: A Report on the APA Task Force on Confidentiality as It Relates to Third Parties* (Task Force Report 9) (Washington, D.C.: American Psychiatric Association, 1975). "A major problem in developing criteria is that diagnosis in psychiatry is less specific than in other medical specialties. Also, there is no consensus on the most effective treatment modalities for the various syndromes and symptoms. Because of the lack of validated treatment criteria, arbitrary and rigid standards of review cannot be justified. This places limitations on the auditing process and necessitates the difficult task of maintaining flexible norms while retaining acceptable standards based on the substantiated data that do exist." A.J. Gilandas, "Implications of the Problem-Oriented Record for

Utilization Review and Continuing Education," *Hosp. & Community Psychiatry* 25:22, 1974. See also "Symposium, Diagnosis and the Difference It Makes," Bull. Menninger Clinic 40:411-602, 1976; P. Williams, "Deciding How To Treat–The Relevance of Psychiatric Diagnosis," *Psychological Medicine* 9:179, 1979.

Dr. Karl Menninger in an appendix to his book *The Vital Balance* reviews psychiatric nosologies from early times. As Menninger would have it, various personality states or behaviors can be identified by studying stages of homeostatic disruption. K. Menninger (with M. Mayman & P. Pruyser), *The Vital Balance* (New York: Viking, 1963). Muhammad Ali, the boxer, claimed that there are four types of human personalities: the walnut (hard on the outside, soft on the inside); the prune (soft on the outside, hard on the inside); the pomegranate (hard on the outside, hard on the inside); and the grape (soft on the outside, soft on the inside). D. Kleiman, "A Lecture by Muhammad Ali: The Topic Is the Greatest," *New York Times*, Nov. 22, 1979, at B-3.

38. In Greenwood v. Taft, Stettinius & Hollister, 1995 WL 540221 (Ohio Ct. App. 1995), a gay employee amended his employee benefit forms to list his male partner as beneficiary and that information was allegedly shared with people with no responsibility for benefits administration. An Ohio appellate court held the employee could sue his employer for invasion of privacy. The court cited state case law recognizing the disclosure tort–the public disclosure of private facts where disclosure would be highly offensive and objectionable to a reasonable person. Here, it was not disputed that sexual orientation is a private fact. Further, a reasonable person wishing to keep his or her sexual orientation private could be highly offended by its disclosure. Consequently, the court remanded for a determination of whether the information was shared with outside persons.

39. At the same time, physicians are criticized for "over-prescribing" drugs. R.S. Mendelsohn, *Confessions of a Medical Heretic* (Chicago: Contemporary Books, 1979); R. Hughes & R. Brewin, *The Tranquilizing of America: Pill Popping and the American Way of Life* (New York: Harcourt, Brace & Jovanovich, 1979).

40. Personal communication from Dr. Maurice Grossman. Bertha Pappenheim (Freud's Anna O.) traveled for a while following her treatment and that helped her regain her mental balance. L. Freeman, "Immortal Anna O./From Freud to Feminism," *New York Sunday Magazine*, Nov. 11, 1979, p. 30. The voyage would not be covered under insurance. Moreover, a doctor's liability insurance covers only "standard treatments." Security Insurance Group v. Wilkinson, 297 So.2d 113 (Fla. App. 1974); Squires v. Hayes, 13 Mich. App. 449, 164 N.W.2d 565 (1968).

41. N.A. Jeffrey, "Doctors Can Leave You on Hook as Insurers Cut Back," *Wall Street Journal,* Jan. 26, 1996, p. C-1.

42. Personal communication.

43. P.G. Bourne (ltr.), *Am. J. Psychiat.* 135:1113, 1978.

44. R. Slovenko, "Legal Issues in Psychotherapy Supervision," in A. K. Hess (ed.), *Psychotherapy Supervision* (New York: Wiley, 1980).

45. Board of Trustees of Memorial Hospital v. Pratt, 262 P.2d 682 (Wyo. 1953).

46. *Michigan Mental Health Code* § 330.1746; *Michigan Department of Mental Health Administrative Manual*, chap. 14, § 220.

47. The U.S. Supreme Court upheld the constitutionality of a New York statute that required pharmacists to report to the state health department the name, address, and age of patients using certain scheduled drugs, and the name and dosage of the drug. The statute also required the reporting of the identity of the prescribing physician and of the pharmacy that filled the prescription and prohibited disclosure of the patient's identity by the state. The Court discounted the possibility of public disclosure of medical information in contravention of the statute, stating that "the remote possibility that judicial supervision of the evidentiary use of particular items of stored information will provide inadequate protection against unwarranted disclosures is surely not a sufficient reason for invalidating the entire patient identification program." Whalen v. Roe, 429 U.S. 589 (1977). See also S.P. Maguire, "OSHA Records and Privacy: Competing Interests in the Workplace," *American U. L. Rev.* 27:953, 1978.

48. See M. McAninch & R.D. Weedman, "The Purpose and Content of Psychiatric Records in Accreditation Procedures," NAPPH J. 1978:35.

49. 42 U.S.C.A. § 1320c *et seq.* (1974); see R.W. Gibson (ed.), *A Conference Report/Professional Responsibilities and Peer Review in Psychiatry* (Washington, D.C.: American Psychiatric Association, 1977); P.B. Goldblatt *et al.*, "A Chart-Review Checklist for Utilization Review in a Community Mental Health Center," *Hosp. & Community Psychiat.* 24:753, 1973.

50. Comment, "PSRO: Malpractice Liability and the Impact of the Civil Immunity Clause," *Georgetown L.J.* 62:1499, 1974; see also R.F. Holbrook & L.J. Dunn, "Medical Malpractice Litigation: Discoverability and Use of Hospital's Quality Assurance Committee Records," *Washburn L.J.* 16:54, 1976.

51. Mich. Compiled Laws 333.20175(8), 333.21515. In Swatch v. Treat, 41 Mass. App. 559, 671 N.E.2d 1004 (1996), the Massachusetts Court of Appeals ruled that documents from the National Association of Social Workers (NASW) Massachusetts Chapter's investigation of a client complaint against a member social worker could not be used in the client's subsequent civil suit. The case grew out of a client's complaint to NASW that a social worker treating her had violated the standards of ethical practice, including improper termination of treatment. An investigation by the NASW established that the social worker had not met her ethical duties. The client then filed a civil suit for damages against the social worker. In not allowing the peer review documents to be introduced into private judicial proceedings, the court said, "Peer review committees have a profound interest in the sanctity and protection of the confidentiality under which they operate. The ability of committee members to speak with candor and the willingness of persons called before them to be equally forthright would be seriously hampered by public release of proceedings or reports of the peer review body." 671 N.E.2d at 1007.

52. K. Babcock, Foreword to E. Hayt & J. Hayt, *Legal Aspects of Medical Records* (Berwyn, Ill.: Physicians' Record Company, 1964), p. viii.

53. R.J. Cohen, *Malpractice/A Guide for Mental Health Professionals* (New York: Free Press, 1979); D.J. Dawidoff, *The Malpractice of Psychiatrists* (Springfield, Ill.: Charles C. Thomas, 1973); R. Slovenko, *Psychiatry and Law* (Boston: Little, Brown, 1973); P.F. Slawson, "Psychiatric Malpractice: The California Experience," *Am. J. Psychiat.* 136:650, 1979.

54. R. Slovenko, *id.* at 565; L. Turner, "Presuit Investigation and Evaluation of Medical Malpractice Claims," in G.W. Holmes & M.I. Hiniker (eds.), *The Liability of Professionals: Malpractice* (Ann Arbor: Institute of Continuing Legal Education, 1976), p. 7. "On the whole, the record contained questions of fact as to supervision and whether or not any qualified medical judgment as to suicidal propensities and restraint was made in view of his behavior in the last part of his hospitalization. The failure to keep detailed and proper medical notes makes the present situation, under these circumstances, more than an error of judgment." Cohen v. State, 51 App. Div. 2d 494, 382 N.Y.S. 2d 128 (1976). "[Liability] does not rest upon either improper diagnosis or negligent treatment; but . . . is based on the failure of the specific duty of exercising reasonable care to safeguard and protect a patient with known suicidal tendencies from injuring herself." Kent v. Whitaker, 58 Wash.2d 569, 364 P.2d 556 (1961). See also Mounds Park Hospital v. Von Eye, 245 F.2d 756 (8th Cir. 1957) (note in record that the patient was to be "observed closely" not followed).

55. Providing insurance coverage for "bad advice" in pastoral counseling is opening a Pandora's box and encouraging suits. One suit given publicity, the box opens. "Labor Letter," *Wall Street Journal*, Nov. 6, 1979, p. 1. Insurance companies use the event to promote the sale of insurance. One advertisement reads: "Malpractice insurance: Don't go to work without it! Few events can be as catastrophic as a malpractice suit–defense costs alone may run to thousands, and successful claims have hit six figures. So even though the rising number of claims against psychotherapists seems to have hit a plateau, you shouldn't develop a case of false confidence. . . . With jury awards zooming, it's a mistake not to buy maximum coverage." *Am. J. Orthopsychiat.*, Oct. 1978 (inside cover). One event builds on the other in a circular fashion.

56. Whitree v. State, 56 Misc. 2d 693, 290 N.Y.S.2d 486 (N.Y. 1968).

57. S.J. Wilson, *Confidentiality in Social Work* (New York: Free Press, 1978), p. 36; see also S.J. Wilson, *Recording: Guidelines for Social Workers* (New York: Free Press, 1980). On nurses' entries in the record, see P.D. Andrade & J.C. Andrade, "Professional Liability of the Psychiatric Nurse," *J. Psychiatry & Law* 7:166, 1979.

58. See R.E. Sturdy & W. Falkowski, *The Problem-Oriented Psychiatric Record* (Welwyn Garden City, England: Smith, Kline & French, 1977); A.J. Gilandas, "Implications of the Problem-Oriented Record for Utilization Review and Continuing Education," *Hosp. & Community Psychiat.* 25:22,

1974; F. Hayes-Roth, F. Lingabaugh & R. Ryback, "The Problem-Oriented Medical Record and Psychiatry," *Brit. J. Psychiat.* 121:27, 1972; E. H. Liston, "Use of the Problem-Oriented Medical Record in Psychiatry: A Survey of University Based Residency Programs," *Am. J. Psychiat.* 133:700, 1976; G. Lowe, "The Problem-Oriented System in a Multi-Disciplinary Psychiatric Milieu," *Canadian Psychiat. Assn. J.* 20:585, 1975.

59. S. Freud, "On Beginning the Treatment" (1913), in J. Strachey (ed.), *Complete Psychological Works of Sigmund Freud* (London: Hogarth Press, 1958), vol. 1, p. 121.

60. However, the U.S. district court in Rennie v. Klein, 476 F.Supp. 1294 (D. N.J. 1979) said that "hospitals, whenever possible, [must] obtain specific, *written* consent from patients before they are medicated with any psychotropic drug" (emphasis added). 476 F.Supp. at 1307. "Whenever possible" means a nonemergency situation. What is an emergency? The court defined: "An emergency is a sudden, significant change in the patient's condition which creates danger to the patient himself or to others in the hospital." 476 F.Supp. at 1313. The form must state all known short-term and long-term side effects of the drug to be consented to, and may be supplemented by informal discussion by hospital staff with the patient concerning the risks and benefits of the drugs. Information on the rights of patients and the side effects of all psychotropic drugs used in a hospital are also to be posted or made available on each ward. 476 F.Supp. at 1313.

61. R. Slovenko, "On the Legal Aspects of Tardive Dyskinesia," *J. Psychiatry & Law* 7:295, 1979.

62. Routine practice of obtaining consent is admissible to establish consent on a particular occasion. See Rule 406, Federal Rules of Evidence; Wetherill v. University of Chicago, 570 F. Supp. 1124 (D. Ill. 1983). On consent to release of information, see Part IV, Chapter 9.

63. Doe v. Roe, 400 N.Y.S.2d 668, at 671 (N.Y. Co. 1977); discussed in Part IV, Chapter 4.

64. Michigan House Bill No. 4425 (April 5, 1979).

65. R. Shlensky, "Informed Consent and Confidentiality: Proposed New Approaches in Illinois," *Am. J. Psychiat.* 134:1416, 1977. A "blanket" consent form is "almost completely worthless" and could "have no possible weight." Rogers v. Lumberman's Mutual Casualty Co., 119 So.2d 649 (La. 1960). Medicaid patients sign a form permitting the psychiatrist to receive reimbursement for services, and giving Medicaid permission to examine and request any and all records or charts. It reads: "I certify that the service(s) covered by this claim has been received, and I request that payment be made on my behalf. I authorize any holder of medical or other information about me to release to the Division of Medical Assistance and Health Services or its authorized agents any information needed for this or a related claim." See H.J. Schwed, S.F. Kuvin & R.K. Baliga, "Medicaid Audit: Crisis in Confidentiality and the Patient-Psychiatrist Relationship," *Am. J. Psychiat.* 136:447, 1979. The federal district court in Hawaii observed: "It

would be unreasonable to hold that an indigent patient who signs a form stating that a provider may release certain medical records to the State exercises a knowing waiver of his interest in not having his most personal confidences to the psychiatrist disclosed. It is far more likely that, if he reads the form at all, a patient would assume that the records would include only billing information and similar non-confidential matters." Hawaii Psychiatric Society v. Ariyoski, 481 F. Supp. 1028 (D. Hawaii 1979).

66. In Czarist Russia, a landowner's wealth was reckoned by the number of male serfs listed in the census return for the head tax. Having pondered that the names of peasants who died were not taken off the lists, an astute swindler began to buy up the departed souls for a pittance and mortgage them to the State Bank at the going rate for live souls, producing a deed of purchase as evidence of ownership.

67. Thus, what might have been written at one time, "the patient is bothered by her junkie father," is now sanitized, "the patient has a family problem." To avoid controversy about reporting under child abuse laws, abuse is not recorded.

68. Mary S. Cerney, then staff psychologist at the Menninger Hospital, commented (personal communication):

> The problem with the high number of lawsuits and other issues around recordkeeping have led clinicians to put very little into their records. In that case they are not too helpful; however, on the other hand, if something is not recorded in the record, it is as if it were not done, even if it had been done. Record-keeping is becoming a burden because, on the one hand we have to do more of it, but on the other hand we have to be so careful about what we put in the record as it is so likely to be misunderstood by persons outside of the system that uses the record. . . . I do not personally like writing records to meet the requirements of an agency or third-party payer, as that limits, to a certain extent, what I can put in the record. I do realize that some mental health facilities do not give proper care. My preference would be that some of these regulations would be placed on them and not on everybody. Working at the Menninger Foundation, I am very aware of the dedication and self-sacrifice of my colleagues in working with extremely ill patients. Adding the burden of the paperwork requirements of outside agency or third-party payers is a frustrating, although perhaps necessary burden in today's culture.

69. In fact, any source of information can be subpoenaed (but disclosure may be resisted on the ground that the material is privileged, irrelevant, or unneeded). Dividing the patient's record into two or more charts is no guarantee that all of the recorded information will not become public. The physician who keeps no records can be subpoenaed for his memory of what happened, but in trial practice, an attorney tends not to ask a question unless he knows what answer will be forthcoming.

70. Waiver of the right of access to a record is now used extensively by many colleges throughout the country. Hospitals, like schools, might also provide waiver of access, but query as to its legality.

71. Wyatt v. Stickney, *supra* at p. 457.

72. At a prison riot in New Mexico, which took the lives of 39 inmates, the leaders of the riot broke into offices and found confidential files. The bloodbath began when inmates began rounding up and executing informers. *Wall Street Journal,* Feb. 5, 1980, p. 1.

73. *Medical Tribune,* March 15, 1978, p. 11.

74. See generally on recordkeeping: J.B. Sloan & B. Hall, "Confidentiality of Psychotherapeutic Records," *J. Legal Med.* 5:435, 1984; W. Winslade, "Confidentiality of Medical Records," *J. Legal Med.* 3:497, 1982.

# Chapter 2

# ACCOUNTABILITY AND ABUSE OF CONFIDENTIALITY

The accountability of health care practitioners is a highly controversial and significant issue. News stories reflect the growing concern about fraudulent and abusive health care practices.[1] State attorneys general and many physicians as well as journalists describe health care fraud as the biggest racket in the country.[2] Numerous congressional hearings, studies, and investigations have demonstrated that fraudulent and abusive practices associated with the provision of health services exist to a disturbing degree.[3] Psychiatric services are no exception. The following is a summary of fraudulent and abusive practices related to psychiatry:[4]

1. Billing for services more extensive than those actually provided (therapist sees a patient for five minutes and charges for a one-hour session).

2. Billing for services not rendered (a therapist bills a third party for treatment sessions that never occur).[5]

3. Billing for multiple services to members of the same family on the same day (a patient's family is encouraged to bring a patient in for treatment, and bills are submitted for "family therapy" or "individual therapy" for each member of the family or for services not actually rendered).

4. Multiple referrals between practitioners when there is no real necessity for services (a therapist automatically refers each patient to colleagues for tests and other forms of therapy and rehabilitation that are unnecessary).

5. Charging for physicians' services actually provided by professionals not eligible for reimbursement (a psychiatrist charges for services rendered by other professionals, paraprofessionals, or medical students).[6]

6. Offering or receiving kickbacks (a therapist refers patients to a psychologist for psychological testing and receives a percentage of the fee for each referral).[7]

7. Billing more than one third party for the same service (a therapist bills both Medicare and Medicaid for the same service given to a patient).

8. Dispensing drugs indiscriminately to anyone who can pay (a psychiatrist writes prescriptions for diazepam or phenobarbital for anyone including people who can then sell these drugs on the street for a profit).

9. Making excessive profits from a legitimate treatment (*e.g.*, a therapist charges each individual in a 10-person group the standard fee for an individual session and collects $1,000 or more for the hour of group therapy).

Methods for effectively detecting fraudulent and abusive practices are yet to be developed, notwithstanding the modern battalion of inspectors, regulators, and tabulators that visits hospitals with monotonous frequency. Some come from state, county, and local health departments; others represent the EEOC, ERISA, HEW, OSHA, PSRO, and IRS. However, when the state's attorney or other law-enforcement official seeks to investigate allegations of fraud and abuse, they are met with a claim of confidentiality. Confidentiality is asserted under the implied contract between patient and physician, the law of privacy, and the physician-patient testimonial privilege.

Recent years have been marked by significant legislative, regulatory and enforcement initiatives intended to induce desired behaviors on the part of health care providers and health insurers. Basically, all of the laws, old and new, are based on two basic premises: (1) that the provider should render all of the care that is appropriate, but only the care that is appropriate and (2) that the provider should receive compensation only for services rendered. On the federal level, in 1996 the Kennedy-Kassebaum Health Care bill was enacted providing for additional investigators and prosecutors to deal with health care fraud. Excepted from discovery are psychiatric records and drug and alcohol treatment programs.[8]

Confidentiality and accountability are entwined, and to some extent are at odds. The crucial questions are: What disclosure is necessary, and is that disclosure unfair? Are there situations in which confidentiality ought to be relaxed in the interest of the patient or in the interest of society at large? Is the privacy of the patient a fig leaf covering the naked self-interest of the therapist? Dr. Herbert Modlin of the Menninger Foundation wrote, "We should differentiate the privacy of the patient and the privacy of the doctor. Occasionally it might be that our secrets—not the patients'—are threatened by exposure."[9]

About confidentiality as an impediment to an investigation, the California Board of Behavioral Science once stated:[10]

> If a therapist is incompetent or grossly negligent in treating a client, the Board can investigate the particulars of that situation. However, it is virtually impossible for the Board to conduct such an investigation without the consent and cooperation of the actual client. The confidentiality of psychotherapeutic communication is protected by law and therapeutic treatment records cannot be obtained without a written release from the client, if the client is an adult.

Legislation has been enacted in regard to disciplinary actions. It is provided that physician-patient privilege does not apply "in any investigation or proceeding by a board or task force, a disciplinary subcommittee, a hearing examiner, the committee or the department acting within the scope of its authorization." The information is still deemed confidential, however, and shall only be disclosed to the extent necessary for the proceedings or pursuant to a valid court order.[11]

It is commonly recognized that the best safeguard for services is adequate supervision. Psychiatry, however, is largely an occupation in which practitioners work alone with no one observing them. When a surgeon operates on a patient, the result is known immediately among many people in the hospital. On the other hand, what happens in a psychotherapy session remains between therapist and patient except in instances of extreme emergency. In this way, the therapist carries on without checks other than those imposed by his sense of responsibility. There is always a danger of deterioration in work that takes place without the benefit of comparison or supervision.[12]

What about the patient himself monitoring the physician? In an ordinary commercial transaction the parties to it can be expected to act as a check on each other, but the ancient maxim of caveat emptor does not apply in a fiduciary relationship. One relying on a fiduciary relationship is not obliged to be on guard. In the nature of the relationship, a fiduciary is obligated to advance the best interests of the other at all times, and never to act adversely to it in any way. Moreover, in health care, there are many situations where the patient's disability impedes his providing the monitoring. For one thing, abuses in treatment may not be reported because patients do not know of any recourse. Indeed, they may not even know that they have been victims of abuse. Furthermore, when psychiatric treatment is involved, patients may feel intimidated by concern over privacy. Many psychiatric patients fear that they will become objects of stigma, censure and ridicule if even disclosure of the relationship is made.

The hospitalized psychiatric patient is a most vulnerable member of society, and even the patient of less incapacity may be unable to say whether the care that is itemized in a hospital bill has actually been rendered. A surgical patient, for example, due to the anesthetic administered, is unaware of much of the care that he has received. In any event, when the patient is personally responsible for payment, he has an incentive to be concerned about the charge, but when a third-party (government or private insurance company) pays, who cares? Not the patient, and not the insurer. Indeed, insurers seemed to encourage duplicity. Increases in claims and losses resulted in increased premium levels.[13] The process came to be known as "economic cannibalism."[14]

The rise in health care costs, coupled with the reduction in standard group health insurance benefit programs by employers, resulted in the rapid development and growth of health maintenance and preferred provider organizations. Until that development, quality was the chief concern of legal intervention in the health care system; cost factors rarely, if ever, were considered or at issue. The primary concern of the managed care HMO/PPO industry today is to contain the cost of health care while allegedly providing quality care.[15]

Under fee-for-service reimbursement, physicians were paid more for doing more. By defensive medicine, they could increase their income as well as lower the risks of tort liability, but under managed care, the situation is reversed. Physicians have a financial incentive to do less—capitation fees, bonuses, and fee withholds all reward physicians for seeing that care is kept to a minimum.

The role of a fiscal third-party in monitoring care is controversial. It is argued that the insurer as monitor would be an intruder in the physician-patient relationship. Should the insurer or HMO tell the doctor what drug to use and for what condition? Should the insurer or HMO question the school of therapy? Is the insurer or HMO competent to assess the quality or need for treatment? Does the interest of the insurer or HMO coincide with that of the patient? The insurer or HMO maintain that quality care will ultimately result through the denial of claims on the basis of overutilization, unnecessary service, or inappropriate charge.[16]

Having a supervisory role, the state's attorney—the guardian of the people—steps into the picture. The state's attorney may not be competent to assess the quality of care, but like any investigator, he may be able to assess health care fraud provided there is access to information. To what extent do the legal principles governing confidentiality preclude investigation? Should the patient expect the same degree of privacy when others are paying the bill as when he alone pays?[17]

One can understand the need of government, insurance companies or HMOs (on pain of economic cannibalism) to obtain verification.[18] Medicaid laws require the maintenance and disclosure of "such records fully to disclose the extent of the services provided to" Medicaid recipients.[19] In an effort to curb Medicaid fraud, the legislature of the State of Hawaii in 1978 adopted an administrative inspection scheme which required health providers to maintain records fully describing the care being provided to Medicaid recipients and to make such records available to authorized state officials. The statute authorized the issuance of administrative inspection warrants upon a showing of "probable cause." In *Hawaii Psychiatric Society v. Ariyoshi,*[20] a psychologist, together with the Hawaii Psychiatric Society, challenged the constitutionality of the search portion of the statute, both on its face and as applied to the psychologist. An administrative search warrant was issued authorizing the inspection of the psychologist's Medicaid records, including "therapeutic notes, patient history forms, medical records and reports, and diagnoses." The federal district court, in granting a preliminary injunction, concluded that it was highly probable that the statute violated constitutional prohibitions against invasion of privacy and unreasonable searches without the requisite compelling justification.[21]

In *Commonwealth v. Korbrin,*[22] the Massachusetts Supreme Judicial Court rejected the attorney general's request for access to "psychiatric records in their entirety" as a "wholesale assault on privacy." The Court pointed out that not all portions of psychiatric records are "necessary fully to disclose the extent of services provided." Rather, the court said, the extent of permissible disclosure depends on the purposes for which the disclosure is sought. The court observed that the Medicaid fraud investigation did not address the necessity for or quality of the psychiatric services rendered. If it did, the court implied, broader disclosure might be authorized. Instead, the central issue in the investigation was "whether the psychiatrist has accurately represented the number of patients seen, the frequency of patient visits, and the length of time per visit or psychotherapeutic session."[23]

Every relationship or transaction obliges the related persons to exchange an appropriate amount of information to establish eligibility. Sometimes the information is obvious and shared with many as when a bedraggled figure shows up for a free meal at the Salvation Army. To establish eligibility for psychiatric care, how much or what information is necessary? Assuredly, the fiscal third-party does not need to know the contents of the patient's communications or how the transference and countertransference are developing, but what is necessary and sufficient information? Insurers in the past tended to have faith in a psychiatric diagnosis, but verification on the basis of diagnosis was found to be an exercise in futility.[24]

Since it is clear that there would be no payment of bills unless a report is made, disclosure of some data about the patient, with patient consent, is made to the fiscal third party. Disclosure of the identity of patients is also made, without patient consent, when names and addresses are turned over to a secretary or bookkeeper for billing, or when delinquent accounts are turned over to collection agencies. yet, when there is a public investigation, the therapist balks at turning over the names of his patients. On this occasion, it is claimed that divulgence of the identity of persons in psychiatric care would be stigmatizing and damaging. But to carry out an investigation, the state's attorney may need the names of patients so as to inquire what, if any, treatment or consultation they have actually received.

There could be surveillance of a clinic or hospital to ascertain the identity of patients by posting an investigator on the premises, but in lieu of this cumbersome procedure, the state's attorney, in order to investigate allegations of fraud and abuse, asks for billing records which would lead him to the patients. In response, the psychiatrist or hospital claims confidentiality.

## INVESTIGATION OF CHICAGO LAKESHORE HOSPITAL

The investigation of the Chicago Lakeshore Hospital is a case in point. It is cited to illustrate the issues involved in discovery; we are not concerned here with the merits of the allegations of fraud and abuse. It was claimed that the hospital, a mental health treatment center, used unnecessary electroshock treatments, cruelly tied patients down for long periods, billed for psychotherapy sessions that were not given, and kept patients for overlong stays to mulct insurance companies. These charges came from members of Scientology, a gadfly of psychiatry, from patients, and from former members of the staff. Prompted by these allegations of patient abuse and insurance fraud, the state authorities commenced an investigation and sought the records of former patients at the hospital. The hospital, not surprisingly, denied the allegations, and refused to turn over its records. The hospital, however, was willing to allow the state's attorney to view the facility. The issue, it said, was the right of former mental patients to privacy regarding psychiatric treatment. When learning of the proposed investigation, two former patients contacted the hospital expressing their concern about the divulgence of their hospitalization. They feared the effects of their hospitalization being made public. "It would jeopardize my job, no doubt about it," said one of the patients anonymously. "If my name ever came out," said another, "I would never–never–go back into a hospital, even if I had another breakdown. I would die first." The state's attorney suggested that the hospital encouraged these two patients to complain. Reputedly, they were told, "Your hospital record will be plastered on page one of the *Chicago Tribune.*"[25]

The state's attorney took the matter to a grand jury and obtained a subpoena for the hospital's records for the two preceding years. After lawyers for the hospital and one of its psychiatrists complained that the grand jury was on a "fishing expedition," the court quashed the subpoena, ruling that it was too vague and too inclusive. The state's attorney then sought a new and restricted subpoena seeking only the hospital's billing records for the preceding eighteen months. Under Illinois law, the state's attorney is given the duty of enforcing the mental health codes which set standards for treatment. Other sections of Illinois law cloak the patient-psychiatrist relationship with privacy rights. Under a compromise proposed by the hospital, which was turned down by the state's attorney, the hospital would have forwarded letters to all former patients of the hospital in the last eighteen months informing them of the grand jury's interest and advising them to contact the state's attorney's office if they wished to give information. Questions arise: Would the patients understand the communication? Would they be unduly alarmed? Would it create a precedent that might hamper grand jury investigations? Would a psychiatric patient, unless approached skillfully and cautiously, likely come forward with information? Would the patient be upset by the mere suggestion that the therapist, in whom he has confided, is incompetent or untrustworthy? Would the patient fear embarrassment or involvement in a lawsuit? Would the patient be a credible witness, either for or against the therapist, considering the transference that has evolved? The trial court ruled that the hospital must comply with the grand jury's subpoena for patient-billing data for the preceding two years, but the issue will be with us for a long time.

## JURISPRUDENCE ON DIVULGING PATIENT IDENTITY

As we have discussed, the courts are divided on the issue of compelling the divulgence of patient identity. In fiscal matters, where there is no need to inquire into the nature of the patient's illness, disclosure is usually ordered. However, disclosure is much less likely to be compelled when it is sought to demonstrate incompetence or malpractice. If, as lawyers say, the malpractice action provides a certification service for the public, then that service is undercut by the restrictions on discovery.[26]

### A. Ordering Disclosure

One of the best known of the cases on the subject is *In re Albert Lindley Lee Memorial Hospital.*[27] In this case, a hospital and physician attempted to bar discovery by the Internal Revenue Service of names and addresses of the physician's patients, claiming that the information was privileged. In rejecting the claim, the court observed:[28]

> [The Internal Revenue agent] is not seeking privileged information as to the nature of a patient's illness; all he desires is information as to the names and addresses of the taxpayer's patients in order, no doubt, to interrogate the taxpayer or the patients, or both, as to the amounts received by the doctor in payment for professional services during the tax years under investigation. All that the order directs the hospital to disclose is the names and addresses of the appellant's patients. It is doubtless true, as the appellant vehemently argues, that subsequent interrogation of the patients at their homes, may cause embarrassment or humiliation, if the fact of their hospitalization should thus become known to their families or friends who are previously ignorant of it. But such embarrassment or humiliation would not result [from] the mere fact of hospitalization—that is no disgrace—but from the actual or suspected reason for the patient's need of hospitalization. The public interest in the collection of taxes

owing by a taxpayer outweighs the private interest of the patient to avoid embarrassment resulting from being required to give the revenue agent information as to fees paid the attending physician.

The hospital was instructed to take precautions to ensure that the treatment afforded any patient or the diagnosis of his illness would not be disclosed. The revenue agent was not to use the hospital records to learn the nature of a patient's illness.

The court gave two reasons for allowing a doctor to testify to the fact that he attended a patient professionally, while not disclosing the nature of the patient's illness. First, the court noted that the fact of hospitalization and the identity of the attending physician are "patent to anyone who sees a person in a hospital and observes what doctor is attending him. The patient does not enter the hospital secretly; nor does the attending physician conceal his identity. Facts which are plain to the observation of anyone are not within the prohibition of the privilege of confidential communication."[29] The lower court in *Albert Lindley Lee Memorial Hospital* had observed: "This court cannot understand how a person is injured by the disclosure of the fact that he has received the services and care of a hospital, and has been attended by a certain physician. These are every day incidents of life occurring openly and with notoriety. The patient does not secrete his entry into the hospital; neither does the doctor mask his identity when entering the home or the room of his patient. Any injury to the patient is hypothetical rather than actual."[30] The lower court also had noted that the information sought in the case was in fact necessary to lay a foundation supporting the objection that the information was privileged. In other words, as we shall discuss more fully, the patient-physician relationship must be shown before the privilege may be invoked.[31]

Another decision ordering the divulgence of patient identity is *Cranford v. Cranford*,[32] which arose out of a suit for alimony and child support. The husband, a psychologist, was asked to produce "all office receipt books, ledgers and other records which show any or all collections [in the past three years]." Contesting the order, the psychologist contended that the psychologist-client testimonial privilege protected his employment relationships as confidential. He reminded the court of the stigma affecting those who consult a psychologist should their identity be disclosed. The argument did not prevail. The court said that just as the name of a client in the attorney-client relationship is not privileged, the fact of employment is also not protected form disclosure under the psychologist privilege.[33]

In these cases, the information sought related solely to the fact of employment. Under general principles, where any documents sought to be produced contain a mixture of privileged and nonprivileged communication or information, the remedy is to delete the privileged matter. In a New York case, *Lewis v. Hynes*,[34] discovery of patient records was allowed for the purpose of investigating nursing home abuse, but the court, in considering the issue of the physician-patient privilege, directed that "insofar as the records of current residents and living former residents of the nursing home are concerned...the petitioners may excise from the medical charts of all those patients just described any record of communications from the patient which falls within the scope of the privilege." In this way, the court balanced the confidentiality rights of the individual patient and the duty of the state to monitor the care of handicapped individuals.

In a Texas malpractice action, where it was alleged that the doctor sexually exploited several women patients, the court ordered the divulgence of names of other patients. Evidence of a pattern would give credence to the allegations. The court based its decision on the fact that Texas had no medical privilege. The suggestion in the case is that privilege would have made a difference with respect to patient identity as well as to the content of the relationship.[35]

## B. Disallowing Disclosure

In a malpractice action, it is difficult if not impossible to obtain through discovery the names of other patients to whom the defendant physician gave treatment similar to that allegedly injuring the plaintiff. The Texas case cited above is relatively unique. In a California case, *Marcus v. Superior Court of Los Angeles County*,[36] a doctor and a hospital, defendants in a malpractice action, asked that a discovery order be set aside on the ground that it violated the physician-patient privilege. In this malpractice action, the plaintiff sought damages from the defendants for injuries allegedly sustained when the defendants performed various tests upon him. The plaintiff sought disclosure of the names and addresses of other persons to whom defendants had given the same (angiographic) tests. The purpose of giving plaintiff this information was to enable investigators to seek out and interrogate the attending physician's other patients and try to persuade them to discuss their experiences with the tests. The court, barring discovery, was of the opinion that if the defendant physician were required to list persons receiving such tests, he would necessarily be revealing confidential information.

The court referred to *Costa v. Regents of the University of California*,[37] where it was recognized that the disclosure of a patient's name and address did not necessarily violate the physician-patient privilege. However, requiring the physician to reveal the identity of other patients conjoined with the nature of their illnesses or treatment provided made the discovery order improper.

The *Costa* case was a malpractice action brought as a result of alleged negligence in connection with X-ray treatment. The court said that a physician may not be compelled to name another of his patients who had had similar results from the same type of X-ray treatment as this would violate the confidence between physician and patient.

In *Boddy v. Parker*,[38] a New York trial court directed the hospital to produce, for examination before trial, records of every hysterectomy performed by the doctor at the hospital during the two years prior to the alleged malpractice. This case was an action against a physician and hospital to recover damages for alleged malpractice in hysterectomy surgery. The appellate court ruled, however, that records of medical procedures performed on persons other than the plaintiff were privileged confidential communications which the defendant hospital could not divulge absent an express waiver by the third parties affected thereby.

In a New Jersey case, *Osterman v. Ehrenworth*,[39] a medical malpractice action involving prescription of a certain drug, interrogatories were directed to the physician seeking the identity of any other person who had ever previously been treated with that drug. Both names and addresses, as well as particular illnesses and treatment were requested. The appellate court held that disclosure of such information concerning third persons, individuals not parties to the litigation, would violate the physician-patient privilege and would, therefore, amount to judicial disregard of the legislatively expressed public policy.[40]

Not infrequently a doctor who has poorly managed his patients will dump them on other physicians or hospitals, or the patients on their own seek care elsewhere. The identity of these patients may help establish or refute an allegation of incompetency. The physician, taking on one or more of these patients, may feel moved to lodge a complaint with the licensure board about the competency of the previous physician.

In a Michigan case, *Schechet v. Kesten*,[41] suit was brought to recover damages resulting from an alleged defamatory report made by the defendant, then chairman of a department of surgery, to the credentials and executive committee of the hospital.[42] That report was critical, to say the least, of the plaintiff's surgical competence. It concluded with a recommendation that the plaintiff should be permanently suspended from the staff. The plaintiff submitted a series of interrogatories to the defendant, most of which demanded discovery of the sources of the information defendant conveyed to the committee. The court, in upholding privilege, stated: "[The] veil of privilege is the patient's right. It prohibits the physician from disclosing, in the course of any action wherein his patient or patients are not involved and do not consent, even the names of such non-involved patients."[43]

In the California case, *Division of Medical Quality, Board of Medical Quality Assurance v. Gherardini*,[44] a subpoena for records of patients was sought by the medical board pursuant to an investigation involving an allegation of gross negligence or incompetence in the treatment of patients by the named doctor. Just as the physician-patient privilege does not apply in litigation between physician and patient, it is usually inapplicable in an investigation by a medical board. Thus, the California Evidence Code provides: "There is no privilege under this article in a proceeding brought by a public entity to determine whether a right, authority, license, or privilege (including the right or privilege to be employed by the public entity or to hold public office) should be revoked, suspended, terminated, limited or conditioned."[45] However, the court ruled, the medical board must demonstrate "good cause" before it can invade a patient's right of privacy. The court, disallowing the subpoena, noted that the declaration in support of the subpoena alleged neither patient consent nor complaint. As in the Chicago Lakeshore case, the question remains whether or not an investigatory body can obtain at least the names of patients in order to establish fraud or incompetency.

Another question is presented: How may a doctor in a malpractice case who claims competency in similar operations be challenged? In an Iowa case, *Shephard v. McGinnis*,[46] the defendant-physician testified on direct examination about the number of major operations he had performed and about the limited number in which operative wound infections had occurred. On cross-examination, he was required, over objection, to testify concerning the specifics of those occasions and name the numerous patients involved. On appeal, however, the court stated that these matters were privileged.

Several years ago, for the purpose of a research program, a law professor and two students at the University of Washington sought to examine 189 randomly-selected, mental illness files. The stated purpose of the research was to investigate the involuntary commitment procedure in the state of Washington. It might equally have been a study of the competency of a therapist or the efficacy of treatment. The following data were to be obtained from the files: (1) the relationship (family, social, etc.) between the applicants for involuntary hospitalization and the alleged mentally ill persons; (2) the age, race, sex, marital status, and other characteristics of the allegedly mentally ill persons; (3) the relationship between the applicants' allegations of mental illness and the actual diagnoses; and (4) the character of mental disorders diagnosed in those persons for whom involuntary hospitalization was ordered. Under the state law closing mental illness files subject to examination on court order, the researchers obtained permission from a lower court to commence their research. However, on intervention of the county prosecutor, the Washington Supreme Court denied access. The decision rested upon two factors: (1) no notice was provided to anyone who had a direct "interest in preserving the privacy of the 189 mental illness files"; and (2) no adequate safeguards were established to ensure individual privacy and con-

fidentiality. The researchers had contended that although privacy was affected, the order by the lower court "reduced that effect to minimal, indeed negligible proportions." The lower court, in permitting the research, directed
anonymity and confidentiality; violation of confidentiality would have
resulted in a contempt citation.[47] The case, not involving a judicial or other
legal proceeding, would not be governed by the parameters of testimonial
privilege.

In recent years, legislation has been enacted in various states adding a significant number of reporting requirements both in terms of outside entities
required to report instances of misconduct to the state Department of
Commerce and reporting requirements made directly upon physicians. The
Public Health Codes of the various states now have a fairly traditional whis-
tle-blower requirement as well as self-reporting requirements for a physician.
Failure to self-report may result in independent disciplinary action apart
from the incident giving rise to self-reporting.[48]

Health care facilities are required to report all changes of staff which are a
result of "discipline"–a term of art.[49] Malpractice insurers are required to
report all settlements, awards, and verdicts. The clerks of the trial courts are
required to report malpractice verdicts within 10 days of entry; all felonies
and misdemeanors are to be reported. The reporter receives immunity and
confidentiality.[50] In addition, all PSROs are required to report any adverse
action. Finally, the Department of Commerce is on-line with the National
Physicians Data Bank and receives reports as well from other states through
the cooperation of the American Federation of Boards of Medicine.

Physicians are required to blow the whistle on fellow practitioners; the
immunity and confidentiality provisions also apply. A physician is required
to report, under this controversial provision, all violations within that physician's knowledge.[51] An exception exists if that knowledge was received while
providing professional services to an individual physician or if the information was received in the course of an ethics or peer-review committee, or a
professional review committee within a health facility.

Special reporting provisions have been adopted where an individual has
reason to believe a physician is impaired. Impairment is defined to mean
"the inability or immediately impending inability of a health professional to
practice his or her health profession in a manner that conforms to the minimum standards of acceptable and prevailing practice for that health profession due to the health professional's substance abuse, chemical dependency,
or mental illness or the health professional's use of drugs or alcohol that does
not constitute substance abuse or chemical dependency.[52] "Chemical dependency" is defined as "a group of cognitive, behavioral, and physiological
symptoms that indicate that an individual has a substantial lack of or no control over the individual's use of one or more psychoactive substances."
"Mental illness" means that term as defined in the mental health code.[53]

Under the Public Health Code as amended, a Health Professional Recovery Committee was established which contracts with a Health Recovery Program.[54] It is required to report all information received concerning health professionals if an impaired status leads to a threat to the public health, safety, and welfare. An exception exists in a genuine physician-patient relationship where the physician-patient is receiving treatment for the impaired status.[55] "Sex addiction" or "undue familiarity" with patients is considered a matter of morals, not impairment, hence a therapist in a recovery program for that reason would not be covered under its confidentiality provisions.

To deal with the problem of abuse of patients, some psychoanalytic institutes have set up Colleague Assistance Committees or Patients' Assistance Committees. They are designed to provide an avenue for patients or colleagues to bring up concerns about questionable overtures or initiated intimacies in therapy. There is concern about the confidentiality regarding the complaints and proceedings.[56]

## DISCUSSION

Whatever the scope of the testimonial privilege, it is not for the protection of the physician but rather for the protection of the patient.[57] The privilege, as oft-noted, belongs to the patient, but there is some recognition that it may not always be in the psychiatric patient's best interest to allow him the sole discretion to refuse to invoke or to waive the privilege as to communications made in the course of psychiatric care. Psychiatric patients may not be aware of the significance of the waiver or what is being waived. Thus, the Illinois Legislature conferred upon the psychiatrist the power not only to assert the privilege in behalf of the patient but also to preclude its waiver.[58] The motive of this legislation, however, has always been the protection of the patient and only the patient. Assuredly, it was not intended to be used as a shield against bona fide investigation of claims of patient abuse or fraud.[59] Illinois' Mental Health and Developmental Disabilities Confidentiality Act of 1979 specifically provided that when the therapist asserts the privilege, it must be in the best interest of the patient.[60] The phrase "best interest of the patient" is an attractive one, but what does it mean, and how is it established?

The very basis of psychotherapy is a trustful relationship, a working alliance. Psychiatrists are ethically "bound by an obligation" to establish such a "partnership."[61] The testimonial privilege is an aid in the preservation of the trust essential to the maintenance of the relationship. For example, no marital privilege is recognized as to communications or behavior concerning civil or criminal offenses committed by one spouse against the other.[62] Similarly, acts by a psychiatrist that abuse or exploit the relationship with his patient must be excluded from privileged status. The privilege may not be used to turn the relationship into a cradle of crime or fraud.

To ensure that hospital mental patients are given the care and protection required by the laws of the state, Illinois law, for example, authorizes the Director of the Department of Mental Health and the State's attorneys to examine institutional records.[63] That authority is in conflict to some degree with confidentiality. Illinois, in its 1979 Mental Health and Developmental Disabilities Confidentiality Act, included specific provisions related to accountability. The Illinois act, with some changes, was based on the Model Law on Confidentiality prepared jointly by the American Psychiatric Association Task Force on Confidentiality of Children's and Adolescents' Clinical Records and the APA Committee on Confidentiality.[64] The Illinois Confidentiality Act is a broad law covering matters of confidentiality in the courtroom and out of the courtroom. The opening section provides that a "confidential communication" includes information indicating that a person is a recipient of mental health or developmental disability services.[65]

The state's attorney in the Chicago Lakeshore Hospital investigation, while subsequently narrowing the scope of his subpoena to billings, originally sought patient records. Should records be made available when accountability of a therapist or hospital is at issue? To protect confidentiality, as we have noted, some therapists recommended keeping no records or minimal records. As one psychiatrist observed, "I treat homosexuals, so I don't keep records. I don't want them defamed." Other psychiatrists say they keep no records (except billings) because they are unnecessary in the practice of psychotherapy. This may surprise the general public considering that the psychiatrist is invariably sketched or caricatured with a writing pad.

But whether or not records are necessary as a clinical tool, they provide a means for audit and control. For that reason alone, recordkeeping may be deemed obligatory. Dr. Herbert C. Schulberg stated: "The medical record is the window for observing the quality of patient care. Rather than being the private working tool of clinicians alone, the medical record can also be used for evaluative and fiscal decisions. By studying the clinical record, a fellow practitioner or carefully trained evaluator can reconstruct the course of treatment and estimate its quality."[66]

Assuming that there are no records or that they are protested as confidential, may a discovery demand be made of billings or names of patients in the case of psychiatry? Given the context, disclosure of even a name may reveal a lot about the person. As noted, the courts are divided on whether the testimonial privilege shields information relating to the fact of a relationship, including the time of employment or the business aspects of the relationship. In the few cases on the subject, disclosure seems permissible when fiscal fraud is involved, but not when malpractice is sought to be established.

As a practical matter, however, it is also often necessary to prove a pattern of behavior in order to establish malpractice. The testimony of a psychiatric patient is likely to be considered the product of an unstable and infirm mind. Thus to establish a case, it is often crucial that a complainant obtain the names of other patients in order to show a pattern of behavior in order to impeach the credibility of the professional.

Recall the suit of Julie Roy against her psychiatrist, Dr. Renatus Hartogs. Roy claimed that Dr. Hartogs lured her into sex under the guise of therapy. The doctor, denying the claim, asserted that she was delusional and further testified that he was impotent during the last ten years due to a physical condition. The climax of the trial came when other women, reading about the case in the newspapers, came forward and testified that during this period of time they too were patients of the doctor and that he had had sexual intercourse with them.[67] The result was a judgment of $350,000 ($250,000 in compensatory and $100,000 in punitive damages). Without the testimony of these other women, that result would likely not have been reached.

At times, only a cross-sectional study may reveal incompetency or abuse. For example, there may be something amiss when a male psychiatrist at a hospital quickly discharges patients of his sex but holds onto young women for unusually long stays. The tendency to keep a harem would not be revealed by studying the case of a single individual who complains of unnecessary treatment or hospitalization.[68] Also, only by a cross-sectional study may it be shown that a therapist is incompetent to deal with particular classes of people—for example, women, homosexuals, or suicidal individuals. It may be significant, were it known—that an unusually large number of patients of a particular therapist obtain divorces or commit suicide. It may also be significant that an unusually large number of a therapist's patients are pushed on to other therapists or dropped when there is no longer insurance coverage. Proof in these cases would require divulgence of names of other patients. The Bible teaches that "By their fruits ye shall know them."[69]

The testimonial privilege, as it turns out, does not provide an adequate guideline as to whether a physician or psychiatrist, without the consent of patients who are not a party to litigation, may be compelled to respond to an inquiry in a legal proceeding which would reveal their identity. Under traditional law, a testimonial shield covers the content of communications or observations in certain protected relationships, not the fact of a relationship.[70] Indeed, as we have noted, a foundation must be established to show that the relationship is in a category (such as attorney-client or physician-patient) in which communications are privileged.[71] In general, a professional relationship must be established in order to claim the privilege of remaining silent. Thus, the privilege does not cover communications between best friends, however confidential or therapeutic the relationship may be.

But is the foundation argument germane to the problem at hand? Principles develop out of a situation but tend to be applied in a wooden manner in other circumstances. That the privilege does not cover the fact of a relationship arose out of the situation where the doctor or other fiduciary is put on the stand and the patient objects to his testifying on the ground of privilege. The objection depends on a physician-patient relationship, but in the case of accountability, the investigator wants the names of the physician's patients, not his friends or others. The existence of a physician-patient relationship is assumed; thus, the foundation argument would seem inapposite.

## NOTES

1.   The late columnist Sydney Harris wrote: "I am convinced that one of the great American scandals of our time, and perhaps of any time, is the systematic cheating and looting of government funds by the medical and health professions. Our present system of billing and payments is an open invitation to larceny...We might not extract sums for work not done from a private patient, but evidently no such compunction exists where a public body is involved...When you think of the enormous Medicare and Medicaid programs, and the full panoply of government-paid services in the health field (not forgetting for a moment the huge pharmaceutical aspect), what we have here is a monster of mass dishonesty that reduces Watergate to a pimple on the backside of the body politic." S. Harris (syndicated column), "Medical profession loots public funds," *Detroit Free Press*, April 24, 1979, p. B-7.

2.   Personal interviews with Attorneys General.

3.   Reference is often made that 10 percent of health care billing is fraudulent. Often cited to support this estimate are reports of the General Accounting Office. The GAO states, "Though no one knows for sure, health industry officials estimate that fraud and abuse contributes some 10% to the $77-plus billion in U.S. health care spending." Fraud is expansively defined to include reimbursement requests submitted in error, good faith disputes as to appropriate coding and other instances in which the provider is acting without an intent to deceive or to receive reimbursement to which it knows it is not entitled. See also Special Committee on Aging, U.S. Senate, *Fraud and Abuse Among Practitioners Participating in the Medicaid Program* (Washington, D.C.: Govt. Printing Office, 1976).

4.   The practices are discussed in O.B. Towery & S.S. Sharfstein, "Fraud and Abuse in Psychiatric Practice," *Am. J. Psychiat.* 135:92, 1978.

5.   It sometimes happens that a therapist will bill an insurance company for group sessions when treating a patient claiming multiple personalities. In

the treatment of a patient with allegedly 120 personalities, the psychiatric bill was $300,000. M. Jones, "Doctor accused of bogus therapy, bills," *Milwaukee Journal Sentinel,* Feb. 4, 1997, p. 1. See generally, D. Newman, "Outpatient Psychiatric Care: Corruption and Contempt," *Mich. Psychiatric Soc. Newsletter,* Jan./Feb. 1979, p. 1; "Of Privacy in Medicine and Abuse Detection," *New York Times,* Dec. 10, 1978, p. E-22.

6. D. Newman, *op. cit. supra.*

7. Another aspect is directing patients to a particular pharmacy (a psychiatrist urges all of his patients to go to a local pharmacist from whom he receives gifts and favors). O.B. Towery & S.S. Sharfstein, *op. cit. supra.*

8. The Civil False Claims Act, 31 U.S.C. §§ 3729-3733, applies to all federal health care funds–Medicare, Medicaid, Champus, and VA and Railroad Retirement. See also 42 U.S.C. § 1395; 31 U.S.C. § 3730.

9. H.C. Modlin, "How Private Is Privacy?", *Psychiatry Digest,* Feb. 1969, p. 13.

10. Quoted in *Newsletter of False Memory Syndrome Foundation,* May 3, 1994, p. 7.

11. Mich. Compiled Laws 333.16244(2).

12. R. Waelder, "The Function and the Pitfalls of Psychoanalytic Societies," *Bull. Philadelphia Assn. for Psychoanalysis* 5:1, 1955.

13. L.S. Seidman, "...And Paying Doctors' Bills," *New York Times,* March 27, 1979, p. 25.

14. E.F. Torrey, "A Merger of Oil Filters and Ids," *Psychology Today,* May 1979, p. 120. See also the comprehensive four-volume study by Daniel Hogan, *The Regulation of Psychotherapists* (Cambridge: Ballinger, 1979).

15. See C. Butler, "Preferred Provider Organization Liability for Physician Malpractice," *Am. J. Law & Med.* 11:345, 1985; W.A. Chittenden, "Malpractice Liability and Managed Health Care: History and Prognosis," *Tort & Insurance L.J.* 26:451, 1991; B. Furrow, "The Changing Role of Law in Promoting Quality in Health Care: From Sanctioning Outlaws to Managing Outcomes," *Houston L. Rev.* 26:151, 1989; L.C. Giordani, "A Cost Containment Malpractice Defense: Implications for the Standard of Care and for Indigent Patients," *Houston L. Rev.* 26:1007 (1989); D.J. Oakley & E.M. Kelley, "HMO Liability for Malpractice of Member Physicians: The Case of IPA Model HMOs," *Tort & Ins. L.J.* 22:624, 1988.

16. The fiscal third-party that engages in monitoring may be held responsible for the quality of care. Insurers have been held liable to workers (outside of workers' compensation) when they undertake an inspection of premises (albeit for its own benefit) and a worker is injured by a condition which it should have discovered. Nelson v. Union Wire Rope Corp., 31 Ill.2d 69, 199 N.E.2d 769 (1964). The greater number of decisions, as in Gerace v. Liberty Mut. Ins. Co., 264 F. Supp. 95 (D.D.C. 1966), have held the insurer not liable, although most of them have relied on provisions of the workers' compensation acts. See A.H. McCoid, "The Third Person in the Compensation Picture: A Study of the Liabilities and Rights of Non-Employers," *Tex. L. Rev.* 37:389, 1959; S.S. Boynton & H.B. Evans, "What Price Liability for Insurance Carriers Who Undertake Voluntary Safety Inspections?" *Notre Dame Law.* 43:193, 1967.

17.   H. Schwartz, "Why Should We Pay for Medical Criminals?" *New York Times*, Oct. 5, 1978, p. 20.

18.   "Insurance companies have a legitimate interest in determining whether claims made under their policies are claims which they are obligated to pay, and whether those already paid were in fact claims for which they were liable. Since they are expected to pay claims promptly, they should not be forced to make payment without such investigation as they deem necessary." Pyramid Life Ins. Co. v. Masonic Hosp. Assn., 191 F. Supp. 51 (W.D. Okla. 1961).

19.   42 U.S.C. § 1396a (a); similarly under state law, *e.g.*, Mass. Gen. Law c. 118E, § 20.

20.   481 F. Supp. 1028 (D. Hawaii 1979).

21.   481 F. Supp. at 1034.

22.   395 Mass. 284 (1985).

23.   The court made specific rulings as to the types of records that were and were not privileged. It ruled that those portions of the records documenting the times and lengths of patient appointments, fees, diagnoses, treatment plans and recommendations and somatic therapies are not protected, but that those portions of the records reflecting patients' thoughts, feelings, impressions, and psychotherapeutic conversations are. It directed submission of all the records to the trial court for an *in camera* inspection and determination. See R.G. Taranto, "The Psychiatrist-Patient Privilege and Third-Party Payers: *Commonwealth v. Kobrin*," *Law, Medicine & Health Care* 14:25, 1986.

24.   K. Sawyer, "Insuring the Bureaucracy's Mental Health; Insurers Seek Accountability But Patients Want Privacy," *Washington Post*, April 10, 1979, p. 1.

25.   Interview, Jan. 3, 1979, in office of Illinois Attorney General. The magazine *New Times* (Oct. 28, 1977, p. 12), wrote under the headline, "Nothing sacred in Chicago, including medical records": "Chicagoans beware. Those neuroses you've been unloading on your analyst are in danger of becoming courtroom evidence—public access gossip—if courts now hearing a landmark suit determine that the state's attempt to obtain evidence for a criminal prosecution outweighs a patient's right to privacy. County attorneys investigating alleged patient abuse and insurance fraud on the part of Chicago Lakeshore Hospital have subpoenaed the private records of 1,990 former patients of the institution. Two of the patients have joined their psychiatrist and the hospital in trying to quash the subpoenas."

26.   See Part II, Chapter 5, on identity of patient.

27.   209 F.2d 122 (2d Cir. 1953).

28.   209 F.2d at 124.

29.   209 F.2d at 123.

30.   115 F. Supp. 643 at 646 (N.D.N.Y. 1953).

31.   115 F. Supp. at 646. See also Sparer v. Travelers' Ins. Co., 185 App. Div. 861, 173 N.Y.S. 573 (1919).

32.   120 Ga. App. 470, 170 S.E.2d 844 (1969).

33. Under this line of jurisprudence, it has been held that place and date of treatment are also not privileged as they fall under "fact of treatment." Jenkins v. Metropolitan Life Ins. Co., 171 Ohio St. 557, 173 N.E.2d 122 (1961); Leeds v. Prudential Ins. Co., 128 N.D. 395, 258 N.W. 672 (1935); Pattern v. United Life and Accident Ins. Assn., 133 N.Y. 450, 31 N.E. 342 (1892).

34. 368 N.Y.S.2d 738 (1975).

35. In this litigation Suzanne Wood Brown of Austin, Texas, represented several women patients of John Abell, Ed.D., in civil actions against him for having had sexual relations with them. Abell admitted the sexual relations but denied that they were part of therapy. Even though the sexual activity took place in his office and he charged for the sessions, Abell claimed that he "dichotomized" the relationship so that the sexual intimacies were not part of the therapy. Attorney Brown was aware of several other women patients with whom Abell was sexually involved. In an effort to locate more, so as to show a pattern and get exemplary damages, Brown asked, in discovery, for the names of all of Abell's female patients with whom he had had sexual relations. The judge limited this to a certain time period and held Abell in contempt for refusing to furnish the names. Abell's petition for a writ of habeas corpus was denied in an unreported action by the Texas Supreme Court. *Ex parte* John M. Abell, No. B8055. The Texas Supreme Court relied upon its (also unreported) decision in *Reproductive Services v. Walker* in which it denied the motion of an abortion clinic, a defendant in a malpractice action, and its decision in a Texas Deceptive Trade Practices Act case, for a writ of mandamus to overturn the trial judge's order that it comply with a subpoena requiring it to divulge certain patient records (but permitting it to delete the patients' names). In the subsequent history of *Reproductive Services*, the applicants sought, unsuccessfully, to raise the question whether the names of abortion patients can be obtained by discovery for use in a civil suit against a person or clinic performing abortions where the parties have not agreed to a protective order to ensure the privacy of those patients. 58 L.Ed.2d 16, 61 (1978); 59 L. Ed.2d 96 (1979).

36. 18 Cal.App.3d 22, 95 Cal. Rptr. 545 (1971).

37. 116 Cal. App.2d 445, 254 P.2d 85 (1953).

38. 45 App. Div.2d 1000, 358 N.Y.S.2d 218 (1974).

39. 106 N.J. Super. 515, 256 A.2d 123 (1969).

40. In *Osterman* the New Jersey Superior Court rejected an earlier decision, Meyers v. St. Francis Hospital, 91 N.J. Super. 377, 220 A.2d 693 (App. Div. 1966), until then apparently the strongest decision in a malpractice action allowing discovery of information about nonparty patients. In this case it was held that interrogatories directed to the defendant-physician asking "The number of occasions he treated conditions similar to infant plaintiff's, inducing him to perform an exchange transfusion, the name, address, date and factual account of every patient for whom he performed an exchange transfusion in the preceding two years" must be answered to enable the

plaintiff "to cross-examine the doctor with respect to his qualifications and experience" and on his represented status as a specialist in the treatment of infant children. The court in a summary manner accounted for its departure from Meyers as due to the intervening legislative recognition of the physician-patient privilege in the state. 256 A.2d at 124.

41. 372 Mich. 346, 126 N.W.2d 718 (1964).

42. Several states now provide for immunity against civil action for a physician who supplies information concerning another practitioner to a licensure board. A couple of states go further and require a physician, on pain of licensure revocation, to report his observations regarding an impaired colleague. See S.C. Scheiber & B.B. Doyle (eds.), *The Impaired Physician* (New York: Plenum, 1983); W.C. Felch & A.L. Halpern, "Coping with Physician Incompetence," *N.Y. State J. Of Med.* 79:12, 1979.

43. In an analogous case involving the news reporter's privilege, the question has been raised: How does a public official or public figure suing for libel establish that the reporter knew the material was false or recklessly disregarded whether it was true, which is required as an element of proof, without having access to this kind of material? The U.S. Supreme Court has taken the view that there is not much danger to a free press in allowing persons suing for libel to find out how and why relevant editorial decisions were made. "Newsmen Dealt Blow on Defense in Suit for Libel," *New York Times*, April 19, 1979, p. 1.

44. 93 C.A.3d 669 (1979).

45. Calif. Evidence Code § 1007. For further discussion, see Part IV, Chapter 2.

46. 257 Iowa 35, 131 N.W.2d 475 (1964).

47. State *ex rel.* Carroll v. Junker, 79 Wn.2d 1, 48 P.2d 775 (1971), noted in *Gonzaga L. Rev.* 7:106, 1971.

48. See, *e.g.,* Michigan Public Health Code 1978 P.A. 368 as amended; MCL 333.1101 *et seq.*; MSA 14.15 (1101) *et seq.*

49. See Mich. Comp. Laws, MCL 331.20175.

50. MCL 333.16244, 16238.

51. MCL 333.16222; see also N.Y. Public Health Law, sec. 4, subdv. 11.

52. MCL 333.16106a.

53. Michigan Mental Health Code, Sec. 400a; MCL 330.1400a.

54. MCL 333.16165, 16168.

55. An impaired practitioner may receive an agreement for nondisciplinary, confidential treatment. MCL 33.16170, 16170a. The Department of Commerce and boards have adopted policies to guide the health professional recovery program as far as acceptance of an impaired physician into the program is concerned.

56. M. Margolis, "Analyst-Patient Sexual Involvement–Clinical Experiences and Institutional Responses" (presentation on Jan. 18, 1996 at meeting of Michigan Psychoanalytic Institute).

57. Tweith v. Duluth, M. & I.R. Ry. Co., 66 F. Supp. 427 (D. Minn. 1946); Heir v. Farmers Mut. Fire Ins. Co., 104 Mont. 471, 67 P.2d 831 (1937).

58. Ill. Rev. Stat., ch. 51, § 5.2 (1977).

59. J. Beigler, "The 1971 Amendment of the Illinois Statute on Confidentiality: A New Development in Privilege Law," *Am. J. Psychiat.* 129:87, 1972.

60. "When, contrary to the express wish of the recipient, the therapist asserts a privilege on behalf of and in the interest of a recipient, the court may require that the therapist, in an in-camera hearing, establish that disclosure is not in the best interest of the recipient. The court or agency may prevent disclosure or limit disclosure to the extent that other admissible evidence is sufficient to establish the facts in issue." Illinois Mental Health and Developmental Disabilities Confidentiality Act, Art. I, sec. 10(b).

61. F. Redlich & R.F. Mollica, "Overview: Ethical Issues in Contemporary Psychiatry," *Am. J. Psychiat.* 133:125, 1976.

62. "It would be simply monstrous to permit a party to assist his own fraud by such an objection. The rule he invokes was intended to subserve a very wise, wholesome, and holy purpose, but never to further such an end as that for which he invokes it." Henry v. Sneed, 99 Mo. 407, 1 S.W. 663 (1889).

63. Ill. Rev. Stat., Ch. 91-1/2, §§ 12.3, 129 (1975).

64. See J. Beigler, "Editorial - The APA Model Law on Confidentiality," *Am. J. Psychiat.* 136:71, 1979; S. Nye, "Commentary on Model Law on Confidentiality of Health and Social Service Records," *Am. J. Psychiat.* 136:145, 1979.

65. Illinois Mental Health and Developmental Disabilities Confidentiality Act, Art. I, Sec. 2(1).

66. H.C. Schulberg, "Quality-of-Care Standards and Professional Norms," *Am. J. Psychiat.* 133:1047, at 1049, 1976.

67. L. Freeman & J. Roy, *Betrayal* (New York: Stein & Day, (1976).

68. H.M. Silverberg, "Protecting the Human Rights of Mental Patients" *Barrister* 1:46; Comment, "Procedural Safeguards for Periodic Review: A New Commitment to Mental Patients' Rights," *Yale L.J.* 88:850, at 856, 1979.

69. Medication was cited in deaths of many mental patients at two of New York State's biggest mental institutions—were the deaths incidental or coincidental? "It's a very difficult question to resolve unless there is a clustering of deaths, or a pattern," said Dr. Michael Baden, then New York City Chief Medical Examiner, quoted in "Tranquilizers held an agent in deaths of mental patients," *New York Times,* July 17, 1978, p. D-8. A worker claiming disability compensation, in order to establish the necessary causal nexus between his ailment (say, lung disease) and the work environment, may need as evidence the health records of other people who worked in the place. "The claimant must show a reasonable relation of cause and effect between work and injury." Kostamo v. Marquette Iron Mining Co., 274 N.W.2d 411 (Mich. 1979).

The Occupational Safety and Health Administration (OSHA) requires employers to preserve records of employee exposure to toxic materials or harmful physical agents and other medical records so that "employees and their representatives may ultimately gain access to these records." The regulations also allow OSHA access to the records to monitor and enforce the rule. The courts have required employers to turn over employees' medical records to OSHA over the objection that employees' privacy would be invaded. DuPont v. Finklea, 442 F. Supp. 821 (S.D. W. Va. 1977).

70. There is some jurisprudence on client identity under the attorney-client privilege. In the usual case, the identity of the attorney's client is not a matter of confidence. The procedure of litigation ordinarily presupposes a disclosure of these facts; the client is identified and is a matter of public record upon the opponents. Some tax investigation cases have highlighted the issue of confidentiality of client identity under the attorney-client privilege. A noted case is Baird v. Koerner, 279 F.2d 623 (9th Cir. 1960). In United States v. Mintz, 39 A.F.T.R.2d 77 (1977), the attorneys for former Vice President Spiro T. Agnew were ordered to disclose their fee arrangements. The privilege was said not to cover this information.

71. *In re* Albert Lindley Lee Memorial Hosp., 209 F.2d 122 (2d Cir. 1953); see also Klein v. Prudential Ins. Co., 221 N.Y. 449, 117 N.E. 942 (1917).

# Chapter 3

# THE STIGMA OF PSYCHIATRIC DISCOURSE

The disclosure of a psychiatric record or the testimony of a psychiatrist or other psychotherapist has hazards to a patient arising just out of psychiatric discourse. Psychiatrists, by their very vocation, tend to pathologize as well as anatomize. The *Diagnostic and Statistical Manual of Mental Disorders* is called a description of "human life as a form of mental illness."[1] In some measure, psychiatric labeling or the psychiatric explanation of behavior impacts negatively on attitudes. "Psychiatrists use curse words," wrote Dr. Karl Menninger, the renowned dean of American psychiatry. By that, he meant that the labels used by psychiatrists have replaced curse words in common discourse and are now used to stigmatize.[2] He wrote:[3]

> Every profession has its own jargon, and we psychiatrists have ours. But while the strange terms a lawyer or an archaeologist uses are harmless enough–the worst they do is mystify outsiders–the terms psychiatrists use can hurt people and sometimes do. Instead of helping to comfort and counsel and heal people– which is the goal of psychiatry–the terms often cause despair.
>
> Words like "schizophrenia" and "manic-depressive" and "psychotic," for example, frighten patients and worry their anxious relatives and friends. The use of these alarming terms also affects us psychiatrists. They lead us back into the pessimism and helplessness of the days when mental illness . . . bore a formidable label and a gloomy prognosis. . . . I avoid using words like schizophrenia just as I avoid using words like "wop" and "nigger." Some angry people don't call their opponents liars or skunks anymore; they call them psychiatric names like "psychotics" or "psychopaths." Why? Because these technical words have become pejorative. They no longer mean merely psychiatric illness; they mean something despised.

What would Menninger substitute?, he was often asked even by fellow psychiatrists. "How should we testify or write reports?" "What do you want us to call these people–or these conditions?" These questioners missed

Menninger's point. He would not call them anything. He wanted psychiatry to emerge from the name-calling stage.

Dynamic psychiatrists like Menninger, as they are known, would spurn diagnosis in favor of attention to the "whole person" and his or her fit to the environment. Disease should be thought of, in Menninger's words, as a disturbance of the total economics of the personality.[4] He wrote:[5]

> With a number of other psychiatrists, I hold that the words "neurosis," "psychoneurosis," "psychopathic personality" and the like are [as] valueless [as the word "schizophrenia"]. I do not use them, and I try to prevent my students from using them, although the latter effort is almost futile once the psychiatrist discovers how conveniently ambiguous these terms really are.... In general, we hold that mental illness should be thought and spoken of less in terms of disease entities than in terms of personality disorganization. We can precisely define organization and disorganization; we cannot precisely define disease.... Of course one can describe a "manic" or a "depressed" or a "schizophrenic" constellation of symptoms, but what is most important about this constellation in each case? Not, we think, its curious external form, but rather what it indicates in regard to the process of disorganization and reorganization of a personality which is in a fluctuant state of attempted adjustment to environmental reality. Is the imbalance increasing or decreasing? To what is the stress related? What psychological factors are accessible to external modification? What latent capacities for satisfaction in work, play, love, creativity are discoverable for therapeutic planning? And this is language that can be understood. It is practical language and not language of incantation and exorcism.

In numerous writings, Dr. Thomas Szasz pointed to a fundamental distinction between the concepts of "mental illness" and conventional (*i.e.*, organic) illness. He protested against the use of medical terminology for "problems of living." He argues that "mental illness" is a form of social labeling that has dramatic and drastic consequences for individuals. The nosology of psychiatry, he claims, lacks reliability and validity and embodies a set of value judgments that imposes a particular view of reality. Psychiatry, for him, is merely an instrument of social control.[6] He sees psychiatric labeling as a pejorative social construction that depersonalizes people. Of the label "schizophrenic," he wrote:[7]

> When a priest blesses water, it turns into holy water—and thus becomes the carrier of the most beneficent powers. Similarly, when a psychiatrist curses a person, he turns into a schizophrenic—and thus becomes the carrier of the most maleficent powers. Like "divine" and "demonic," "schizophrenic" is a concept wonderfully vague in its content and terrifyingly awesome in its implications.

The resort to a diagnostic label, Dr. Walter Reich has written, is a natural turn when an explanation for unwanted behavior is needed, and is done every day, inside and outside the arena of psychiatry. Journalists and other observers turn to it for simplifying explanations of behavior. Still others call upon diagnostic explanations to justify forgiveness or elicit sympathy, or to reassure. It has the power to re-classify socially unacceptable behavior as the product of illness. In the hands of psychiatrists, diagnoses achieve status and recognition, and result in lasting effects which are not always salutary.[8]

So as to minimize the negative consequences of psychiatric discourse, various mental health organizations have participated in the development of nonstigmatizing media language about mental illness. The National Stigma Clearing House, headquartered in New York, is an organization particularly concerned with portrayals of people with mental illness. It tracks and, if necessary, protests terms and images in the media that "unintentionally hurt millions of Americans." Its goals:

> To end the exploitation of mental illness for humor, sensationalism, or in routine dramatic formulas.
> To promote the accurate use of medical terms associated with psychiatric disabilities.
> To encourage portrayals of people with mental illnesses as human beings rather than as caricatures.

The Stigma Clearinghouse points to the harm resulting from the stigmatization of mental illness: "[It] causes people to keep their condition a secret for fear of losing their jobs, health insurance, homes, even their families. It prevents many from seeking treatment. It adds needless pain to recovery and continues to inflict pain after recovery."

The Stigma Clearinghouse has scored many "stigma-busting coups." When it received complaints about Doug Marlette's Kudzu comic strip, it issued a "Stigma Busters Alert," accusing the cartoonist of "flippant treatment of depression, euthanasia and suicide in over a dozen strips." One Kudzu strip depicted a nerdy type saying, "I can't decide which feature I like best in Modern Depression magazine. . .the monthly column 'What's the Point?'...or the 'Suicide Notes to the Editor.'" The cartoonist form-letter response to protest mail was that he was not making fun of the mentally ill, but was making fun of feel-good gurus who exploit them.[9]

"Inmate escapes from asylum in Vermont," was the message in Oregon advertising Darigold's maple nut ice cream, and it prompted a protest from psychiatrist David Pollack and a number of relatives of the mentally ill. "The mentally ill are not 'nuts' to be mocked or 'escapees' to be feared. They should not be exploited to sell ice cream." Darigold removed the advertisement and made a public apology.[10]

The Federal Bureau of Investigation, responsible for collecting data about hate crimes involving race, ethnicity, religion, and sexual orientation, consulted the Stigma Clearinghouse when it was recently also given the category of physical and mental disability to track. It sought sensitive, neutral terminology it could use in training manuals and reports to describe people who are mentally ill, but it soon learned that there is nothing simple about the language of mental illness.[11]

According to the Stigma Clearinghouse, it is more respectful to refer to individuals as afflicted with mental disorders rather than as diagnostic categories. By a "people first" rule, the description would be "persons suffering from schizophrenia or depression" rather than "the schizophrenic" or "the depressive." Likewise, the "Guidelines for Bias-Free Writing" by Marilyn Schwartz and the Task Force on Bias-Free Language of the Association of American University Presses suggests putting "the person before the disability."

The American Psychiatric Association's *Diagnostic and Statistical Manual of Mental Disorders* states that it is "a classification of mental disorders, not of people." It thus avoids terms such as "a schizophrenic" and uses instead "a person with schizophrenia."

Mental health organizations also suggest that terms like "schizophrenia" not be used when unrelated to the illness itself, for example, "schizophrenic weather."[12] The Stigma Clearinghouse persuaded the John Deere company to stop ads on "the world's first schizophrenic lawn mower." It wrote, "Why is it that schizophrenia is fair game for comedians in a way that cancer, AIDS and drug addiction are not?" Clarion Car Audio ceased its "A Lot of Good an Airbag Will Do You If You Go Insane" campaign. Others capitulating include Nike sneakers, Wordstar software, and Planters foods.[13]

More often than not, the term "schizophrenia" when used in the media is taken to signify "split personality" or "multiple personality," whereas it means a separation between intellect and emotions. The misuse reflects back on individuals bearing a diagnosis of schizophrenia and they are regarded as another Dr. Jekyll and Mr. Hyde. An example of the misuse, among the many, is the title of Law Professor Michael Green's article on products liability, "The Schizophrenia of Risk-Benefit Analysis in Design Defect Litigation."[14] The *DSM* in a caveat cautions against the nonprofessional use of the terms in the manual, but to no avail.[15]

Mental health organizations are critical too of advertising that, they assert, portrays mental illness in an insensitively jocular fashion. In an award-winning advertisement which the organizations protested, Daffy's, a chain of discount clothing stores, advertised: "If you're paying over $100 for a dress shirt, may we suggest a jacket to go with it?" Next to those words was a picture of a mental patient in a straitjacket.

Mental health and patient advocacy groups were outraged by the promotions for the film titled "Crazy People," which carried the slogan, "Warning:

Crazy People Are Coming." In Philadelphia, a newspaper ran a promotion that offered free tickets to readers who could "prove to us you're crazy." A large sign with the "warning" that "crazy people are coming" was erected a few yards from a state psychiatric hospital in Pembroke Pines, Florida. As a result of the protests, the offending advertising campaign was ended.[16]

In investigating the savage murder of 52 men and women in the Soviet Union, the police's first reaction was to round up the usual suspects who included local psychiatric patients; the killer turned out to be Andrei Chikatilo, who did not have a history of psychiatric hospitalization but who was socially maladroit.[17]

In the media, mental illness is often identified with dangerousness.[18] Newspapers in particular stress a history of mental disorder when they find it in the backgrounds of people who commit crimes of violence. The fact that the individual is an "ex-mental patient" (or an "ex-con") is headlined.[19] A front page headline in the *Detroit Free Press*–"2 cops, mentally ill man slain"– stirred the ire of those attending a conference in Detroit on "Mental Health Partnerships and Strategies." The report detailed the case of a gunman who killed two police officers in a standoff before police fatally shot him. The man had been hospitalized for mental illness at least six times in the previous 19 years. "When you sensationalize, the public becomes full of fear and afraid of people who are mentally ill," said an administrator for several Detroit area group homes for the mentally ill.[20]

**MOTHER GOOSE & GRIMM** By Mike Peters

©1996 Grimmy, Inc. Distributed by Tribune Media Services.
All rights reserved. Reprinted with permission.

Over the years, researchers have been studying the relationship of mental illness and violence. Studies in the first half of the 20th century all found that mentally ill persons had a lower arrest rate than the general population, which led to the oft-quoted claim that the mentally ill are no more danger- ous than the general population–which was true prior to the era of deinsti- tutionalization because most potentially dangerous mentally ill persons were

kept in hospitals. In 1955, when the nation's total population was 164 million, there were 558,239 severely mentally ill persons in the nation's public
psychiatric hospitals, whereas in 1994, when the nation's population had
increased to 260 million, there were only 71,619 persons in the hospitals.
More recent studies indicate that the arrest and conviction rates for violent
crimes committed by mentally ill persons exceed general population rates.
At the same time, as research psychiatrist Dr. E. Fuller Torrey has pointed
out, it should be explicitly noted that the mentally ill as a group account for
only a small fraction of the violence in the country. America is a violent society, and the total contribution of the mentally ill is not large. Alcohol and
drug abuse, and the availability of lethal weapons, far outweigh mental illness in contributing to its high incidence of violence.[21]

And it is to be noted that correlation is not causation. As psychologists
John Monahan and Henry Steadman have written, "[M]ental disorder may
simply coexist with criminality, without having any causal significance, much
as an offender may have a toothache without arousing suspicions of dental
determinism." And, as they note, "[M]ental disorder may *inhibit* criminality,
as catatonia would inhibit a person who otherwise would commit rape."[22]
More often, the mentally ill are the victims of crime rather than the victim-
izers.

Support groups for people afflicted with Asperger's syndrome (an autism-
like disorder) expressed concern over suggestions by one forensic examiner
that the actions of Martin Bryant, who went on a rampage and killed 35 people in Australia in 1996, were due to his suffering from the disorder. Autism
centers in Australia reported a flood of inquiries from parents of children
with Asperger's as to whether their children could develop violent tendencies. One director of an autism center said that parents were "concerned that
aggression and Asperger's go hand-in-hand" and she thought society might
judge sufferers in the same light as Bryant. One mother of a 14-year-old son
with Asperger's feared people would "tar us all with the same brush." She
feared her son would be targeted by classmates as "another Bryant."[23]

Individuals who have been found not guilty by reason of insanity have
been known as "the criminally insane," but the term has been supplanted
recently in New York forensic psychiatric circles by the term "dangerously
mentally ill." The former was felt to be too pejorative, but the latter is hardly less so.[24] Dr. Dorothy Bernstein is puzzled why one would feign insanity
given that it is such a stigmatized condition.[25] Gary Gilmore, the Utah murderer who was executed, refused to plead insanity because of the stigma of
it.[26]

The terms used to describe "mental illness" have changed markedly over
the years, reflecting not only scientific shifts in explanation and treatment but
also efforts to rid "mental illness" of stigma. When not long ago the St.

Luke's-Roosevelt Hospital Center in New York opened a schizophrenia research clinic, naming it became an issue. Dr. Peter Weiden, its director, said, "We struggled whether to call the clinic the Neurobiologic Disorder Clinic or the Schizophrenic Research Clinic. The former was selected because patients were more comfortable with the neurobiological label," he admitted. "We chose to go politically correct, because we feel we have more to risk by alienating people who might be uncomfortable coming to our clinic."[27]

In 1996, the Michigan Department of Mental Health changed its name to "Department of Community Health." Simultaneously, it has been cutting back on public hospitals under a program of deinstitutionalization. The new name hardly reflects the reality—one must look long and hard for a "community" or for the "village" called for by Hillary Clinton.

Increasingly today patients are called "consumers" and therapists are called "providers" of "mental health services." Dr. Torrey, who is a member of the Public Citizens Health Research Group in Washington, D.C., recently changed the subtitle of the third edition of his book, *Surviving Schizophrenia*, from "A Family Manual" to "A Manual for Families, Consumers and Providers," though he resented having to make the change. In the preface, he tells readers that he "doesn't like the term *consumer* one bit." "I still call my patients 'patients' and I feel they do have a brain disease, but it is the choice of the majority of people with this disease that they wish to be called consumers," Torrey explained. "So I'm willing to call them consumers."[28]

The various terms have a different genesis or connotation. In the 17th and 18th centuries, the term "distraction" was used to signify a state of mental agitation and excitement short of complete madness. In the 18th and 19th centuries, "demoniac possession," "madness," "lunacy", and "insanity" were common descriptions of what is now called mental illness. The traditional belief about madness has been that it is a punishment visited by God on the sinner, and in the 19th century the medical model began to contest the dominance of theological explanations.

From biblical explanations came the term "demoniac"—a person possessed by the devil. "Lunacy" derived from the belief that mental condition is related to phases of the moon. The ancients worshiped the moon—appearing and disappearing in the skies, it became the symbol of mystery and magic. Man's deepest secrets, fears, and madnesses were ascribed to this force in the sky.

"Madness" is the more vernacular term and suggests wildness, a lack of restraint by reason, loss of emotional control, unpredictability. The idea behind the old tradition of stripping bare naked and painting one's entire body blue for combat (as illustrated in Mel Gibson's film "Braveheart") was to convince the enemy that they were mad men too crazy to be afraid.

The term "psychopathic," literally "psychically damaged," was introduced in 19th century Germany to cover all forms of psychopathology, but was later narrowed to refer to psychic anomalies which were not considered mental illnesses. In American psychiatry, the term has been used interchangeably with "sociopathic," a term denoting any form of socially deviant behavior, or in common parlance, an S.O.B. The terms "psychopath" or "sociopath" have disappeared from official nomenclatures, but they are commonly used.

Psychiatrists tend to avoid the term "madness" because it is an emotionally charged term, tinged with contempt. They prefer instead the more clinical "insanity," which literally means not "sane" (clean, health), but now they use terms that stress the medical nature of insanity—"mental illness," "mental disease," or "mental disorder." Dr. Frederick K. Goodwin, who has been at the forefront of national efforts to destigmatize mental illness, has stated a preference for the term "people with a mental illness or disorder" because, he said, it reinforces the notion that the condition is medical in nature.

At the same time, the use of the word "illness" has been harshly criticized on the ground that the use of this word implies acceptance of a "medical model" and acquiescence to modes of language dictated by the medical establishment. The classic critique of the medical model is, as we have noted, Thomas Szasz's book, *The Myth of Mental Illness.*[29] Against all this, some present and former mental patients have demanded to be called "mental patients."[30]

The word "mental," no less than the word "illness," has come into criticism. Focusing on the organic is looked upon as a way to avoid stigma (and also to link psychiatry with medicine). At the 1996 annual meeting of the American College of Forensic Psychiatry, Dr. Lewis Bloomingdale suggested that in the anticipation of a neurological origin for Attention Deficit Hyperactivity Disorder (ADHD), it should be considered neurological rather than psychiatric, and he said, "The stigma still attached to psychiatric disorders would become less of a burden to ADHD children and their parents."[31]

Dr. Stefan Lerner has stated that one of the most helpful things he can do for his patients is to explain that diseases of the brain are just as organic as— and no more "mental" than—diseases of other body organs. He clearly states to them that they are *not* "mentally" ill and are no different than the patients of the rheumatologist or dermatologist. He has found that this educational effort raises his patients' self-esteem and enables them to feel less stigmatized. He implores the American Psychiatric Association to do a risk-benefit analysis regarding the continued use of the words "mental illness" by the APA and its members.[32]

In the nature vs. nurture controversy, nurture prevailed following the end of World War II, with the defeat of the Nazis, but nature is returning to the fore as the primary determinant of personality.[33] George McGovern, the former Democratic Presidential contender, found some peace by accepting that alcoholism can be an inherited condition. His daughter Terry, at age 45, died on a frigid night when she fell in a drunken stupor from an addiction to alcohol and other drugs as well as depression since she was a teenager. He wrote: "To this day, practicing medical doctors, psychiatrists and specialists in alcoholism dispute the relative importance of physiological versus psychological factors as a basis for alcoholism. However, there is a growing consensus, which I share, that the basic cause of the disease is a physiological genetic structure inherited at birth."[34]

The terms "mental illness," "mental disease," or "mental defect" are the terms used in prevailing laws of criminal responsibility and civil commitment. At trial, if the term "insane" or "mad" is used, jurors become alarmed. They have more sympathy for an individual described as "mentally ill." Mental health professionals and defense attorneys object to the use of colloquial terms on grounds that they are unscientific and demeaning, but they have the greatest impact.

The number of colloquial expressions for mental illness is immense, but their fine nuances in conventional use are intuitively understood: apartment to let, bag of nerves, bananas, barmy, batty, berserk, beside oneself, bizarre, blow a fuse, bonkers, buggy, bugsy, bugs in the brain, cracked, crackpot, crazy, crazy as a bed bug, crazy-ass, cuckoo, daffy, deranged, dizzy, dope, fanatic, flaky, flipped out, freaked out, freaky, go ape, gone in the head, idiot, kooky, lamebrained, light's on but nobody's home, loco, loony, loose screw, loose up top, lost one's marbles, lost one's mind, lunatic, mad, *meshugge, non compos mentis,* not all there, not dealing with a full deck, nutty, oddball, off one's head, off one's rocker, off the deep end, off the rails, off the wall, out of your mind, out in left field, over the edge, psycho, queer, run amuck, scrambled, screwy, space cadet, stressed, unbalanced, unglued, unhinged, weird, wacky, wild-ass, zany.[35]

**MR. BOFFO** By Joe Martin

Reprinted with special permission of Universal Press Syndicate

In a malpractice case, *Aiken v. Clary*,[36] the defendant psychiatrist testified that his justification for making less than full disclosure of the hazards of insulin shock therapy to the patient was because he was suffering from "process schizophrenia" and that he was "real shook." The patient had contended that not he but his wife was "way out in left field."

Of the various terms, social historian Roy Porter, among others prefers "madness." In the opening of his book titled *Madness*, he writes:[37]

> Throughout this book, I shall use the term "madness" as an umbrella term. Psychiatrists today often object to such usage, suggesting that it is unscientific and somehow demeaning. Surely, however, it is the right term, because it conveys the richest resonances in everyday parlance. For it is widely applied to many people besides the clinically certifiable, and includes all manner of abnormalities and extremes of thought and emotion (I can be mad over you, mad at you, madly in love with you). No synonym or euphemism is half so evocative.

The language used to describe the institutions housing the mentally ill has also changed over the centuries. The names have included: insane asylum, feeble-minded colonies, imbecile asylums, idiot asylums, state hospitals, state farms, sanatoriums for nervous invalids, epileptic villages, psychopathic hospitals, psychiatric centers, psychiatric institutes, and retreats. Colloquial terms are booby hatch, bughouse, crazy house, funny farm, loony bin, and nut house (the human head is shaped like and is hard as a nut). "For the fun of it," says Meryl Streep in the film "Marvin's Room," "let's call the 'mental institution' a 'nuthouse' or 'loony bin.'"

And the language used to describe those who specialize in the treatment of the "mentally ill" has changed over the centuries. Today, as we have noted, they are called "providers" (for "clients" or "consumers"). The renaming is viewed as an attempt by insurance companies to frame psychiatry and medicine as another pure business field. Psychiatrists protest the label, "We do not like to be called providers, and patients do not like to be called customers, clients, or consumers."[38]

In the 18th century, physicians who ran asylums were called "mad doctors." In the wake of the asylum reform movement, which began in the late 1700s, the head of the new reform-minded institutions referred to themselves as "asylum doctors" or "asylum superintendents," and to their field of specialty as "asylum medicine." In common parlance, they are mostly called "shrinks."[39] Cinematic stereotypes have contributed to the stigmatization of psychiatrists as well as of patients–psychiatrists are frequently portrayed as libidinous lechers, eccentric buffoons, cold fish, repressive agents of society, and also as vindictive or of an evil mind.[40]

English specialists called themselves "alienists" because they treated abnormal or "alien" states of mind. The term "psychiatrist" first appeared in the mid-1800s in Germany and gradually came into use throughout Europe and the United States. The term "psychiatry" stems from the Greek *psyche*; in the ancient myth, Psyche is liberated from confinement.[41]

In the past, therapists underdiagnosed patients to avoid the stigma of a more severe diagnosis (like schizophrenia). They now tend to "overdiagnose" in order to justify treatment to a third-party payer. And most patients willingly go along with this or even suggest it, since they want the therapy or the benefit of a disability allowance. Given the concern about stigma, it is unintended irony.

Bruce Link, associate professor of public health at Columbia University and research scientist at the New York State Psychiatric Institute, argues "that labeling and stigma are 'social problems,' not 'individual troubles.'" In a nutshell, he says that individuals diagnosed with mental illness do not bring stigma onto themselves; the diagnosis itself does. Fear of stigma, he contends, can mean greater symptoms.[42]

However, based on a long-term study of mental patients and their families, sociologist John Clausen concluded that their feelings of stigmatization are not so much a consequence of the response of others to their having been hospitalized for mental illness or labeled mentally ill as of chronic manifestations of mental illness or self-doubts. Severe mental disorder, he found, evokes negative responses in those who must live with or deal with the affected person, whatever the label applied to that person or whatever the law on confidentiality. He writes, "By whatever name they are referred to, psychotic persons tend to be hard to live with. They are frequently unreasonable. Even when they pose no threat to self or others, they may be exquisitely sensitive to slights from others, and they often rage furiously against those who love them most."[43]

Of course, as the National Stigma Clearing House and socio-linguists point out, words are powerful, but even more powerful in evoking attitudes about a person is behavior. Changing a label does little in the long term to change attitudes. Before long, the new label carries the emotional baggage of the old. People who are odd or difficult generate stigma, no matter the label.[44]

The argument against referring to the mentally ill by the name of a disorder is that such usage implies that the disorder is all there is to the person, as if one were schizophrenic rather than human. No one assumes that a person with a poorly functioning bladder is all there is to the person, but the problem with schizophrenia or other mental disorder is not the appellation but the disorder, which sometimes is pervasive.[45]

A leaf may be taken from the Spanish language, which has two forms of the verb "to be": *estar,* for the conditional or temporary, and *ser,* for essence or permanency. Thus, one uses *estar* to say that a shirt is soiled but *ser* to say that a person is a homosexual.

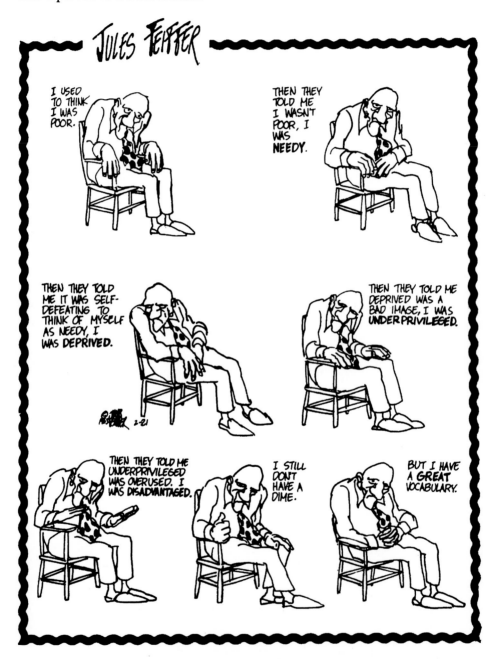

## NOTES

1. L.J. Davis, "The Encyclopedia of Insanity," *Harper's*, Feb. 1997, p. 61.
2. It is reported that Carl Jung, the renowned psychoanalyst, used traditional curse words as well as psychiatric language in describing his patients. He referred to one patient as a "slimy bastard," another as an "empty gasbag," and yet another "a pisspot of unconscious devils." F. McLynn, *Carl Gustav Jung* (New York: Bantam Press, 1996). In the cartoon strip "Dr. Katz" (Jan. 20, 1997), the receptionist informs the doctor, "Dr. Katz, the agitated paranoid neurotic is here." The patient becomes angry, "I have a name, you know."
3. "Speaking Out," *Sat. Eve. Post*, April 25, 1964, no. 237, p. 12.
4. Menninger suggested five levels of dysfunction. See K.A. Menninger, *The Vital Balance* (New York: Viking, 1963).
5. K. A. Menninger, "Communication and Mental Health," *Bull. Menninger Clin.* 26:43, 1962.
6. See T.S. Szasz, *The Myth of Mental Illness* (New York: Hoeber-Harper, 1961); *The Manufacture of Madness* (New York: Harper & Row, 1970); "The Classification of 'Mental Illness,'" *Psychiatric Q.* 33:77, 1959. Szasz does not deny the existence of the behaviors called "mental illness," as many critics have said, but rather he has challenged its conceptualization. See R.E. Vatz & L.S. Weinberg, "The Rhetorical Paradigm in Psychiatric History: Thomas Szasz and the Myth of Mental Illness," in M.S. Micale & R. Porter (eds.), *Discovering the History of Psychiatry* (New York: Oxford University Press, 1994), chap. 17, pp. 311-330. See also R. Slovenko, "Dr. Karl A. Menninger and Dr. Thomas Szasz: Were They Apart on 'Mental Illness'?", *Newsletter of Am. Acad. Psychiatry & Law* 16:21, April 1991.
7. T.S. Szasz, *Schizophrenia/The Sacred Symbol of Psychiatry* (New York: Basic Books, 1976), p. xiii.
8. W. Reich, "Psychiatric diagnosis as an ethical problem," in S. Bloch & P. Chodoff (eds.), *Psychiatric Ethics* (New York: Oxford University Press, 2d ed. 1991), chap. 7. At the trial of Malcolm Shabazz, the 12-year-old grandson of Malcolm X who set a fire that killed his grandmother, the psychiatric testimony described the boy as a paranoid schizophrenic, with episodes of psychosis and a preoccupation with fire. On the day of the psychiatric testimony, his lawyers kept him from the courtroom, saying they did not want him embarrassed by hearing the report. J. Gross, "Sutton and Dinkins: Labor of Law and Love," *New York Times*, Aug. 5, 1997, p. 1.
9. M. Winerip, "Humor to One, Pain to Another," *New York Times*, June 6, 1993, p. 21; J. Willwerth, "It Hurts Like CRAZY," *Time*, Feb. 15, 1993, p. 53.
10. "Offensive Ice Cream Ad Ignites Controversy in Oregon," *Psychiatric News*, Sept. 6, 1996, p. 2.
11. L.W. Foderaro, "There Is Little Consensus as the Mentally Ill Debate What to Call Themselves," *New York Times*, June 20, 1995, p. 12.

12. The film "Batman Forever" was reviewed as "a weird, wonder-inducing, profoundly schizophrenic film–madness was seeping right out from the screen into the audience." N. Andrews, "High-intensity junk," *Financial Times,* July 13, 1995, p. 5.

13. Then too among many others as the TV pitchman for the "Crazy Eddie" electronics chain who would wave his arms and screech that its prices were "inSAAANE!" The firm's founder, Eddie Antar, later became a fugitive from justice. M. Siconolfi, "It's Crazy Eddie, So the Idea May Be a Little Insane," *Wall Street Journal,* June 13, 1996, p. 1.

14. *Vand. L. Rev.* 48:609, 1995. In response to my query about the title, Professor Green responded (letter of June 10, 1996, quoted with permission): "You pointed out my incorrect usage in the title of my article and asked me about how I selected the title. I used the term 'schizophrenia' to connote a split view, one that contains some tension between the two. While I did not mean literally to invoke a mental illness, the tension that does exist between the two concepts I was concerned with is a troubling one, so that the allusion to mental illness was a felicitous byproduct. 'Split personality' (the second definition provided in my *Webster's Third New International Dictionary*) isn't quite what I had in mind, but my sense is that the common understanding of schizophrenia was close enough to what I describe that it would work tolerably well. While my usage was technically incorrect, since I was not trying to communicate with mental health professionals, I'd be inclined to use the term 'schizophrenia' in the same fashion again."

15. *DSM-IV*, p. xvii.

16. "Paramount Denies Wrongdoing in 'Crazy People' Ad Campaign," *Psychiatric News*, May 18, 1990, p. 9.

17. R. Cullen, *The Killer Department: The Eight-Year Hunt for the Most Savage Killer of Modern Times* (London: Orion, 1993).

18. Although there is general agreement that individuals with certain characteristics of mental disorder are more prone to violence than other individuals, there is still debate concerning the prevalence of violent behavior among various diagnostic groups. Current data suggest that acute paranoid schizophrenia, the manic phase of manic-depressive illness, and substance abuse, especially PCP, may all be associated with greater risk of serious violence. When the alleged Unabomer, Theodore John Kaczynski, was apprehended, Dr. James Kocsis, professor of psychiatry at Cornell University, mused (without an examination of Kaczynski), "It is safe to say that the guy is disturbed and that he has a severe personality disorder. The reason you could say he was at least psychotic is that he basically gave up all human relationships, never involved himself, as far as we know, in any romantic relationships, and had very few or no friends. He became a hermit, an isolated loner." A. Kuczynski (no relation), "The Unabomer on the Couch: New York Shrinks Go Nuts," *New York Observer*, April 15, 1996, p. 10. See also B. Duffy, "The Mad Bomber?" *U.S. News & World Report,* April 15, 1996, p. 29. See generally: R. Slovenko, *Psychiatry and Criminal Culpability* (New York:

Wiley, 1995); E.F. Torrey, "Violent Behavior by Individuals with Serious Mental Illness," *Hosp. & Comm. Psychiat.* 45:653, 1994.

19. The opening line of the news report about James Wilke shooting and killing his father and mother was, "James Wilke suffered from schizophrenia." D. Durfee, "Double murder and suicide shatter calm of Royal Oak," *Detroit News*, Aug. 4, 1996, p. 1. Reporters thereupon wrote stories about schizophrenia. "I hope this doesn't prejudice people against mental illness, because that's what it is, an illness," said Dr. Husseini Manji in an interview. "It's not a split personality." And Carol Vainer, a member of the Alliance for the Mentally Ill, said, "You're stigmatized if you let your child be taken care of by the state. And then if you keep him home and something happens–whoa!" W. Wendland, "Mental illness is treatable, experts say," *Detroit Free Press*, Aug. 5, 1996, p. B-1. Tom Sovine, executive director of the Michigan Mental Health Association, had this to say: "Schizophrenia. The word conjures up images of people who act strangely, who are tormented by voices in their heads or even become violent–like James Wilke. But most schizophrenics don't become violent. More often, they're the victims. They are vulnerable in so many ways. But it's the violent episodes that most often make headlines, further stigmatizing people who suffer from the illness." Quoted in J. DeHaven, "Schizophrenia is not always debilitating," *Detroit News*, Aug. 12, 1996, p. D-5. See also, *e.g.*, AP news release, "Australia Gunman Called a Loner With a Mental History," *New York Times*, April 30, 1996, p. 3.

20. "Group critical of headline," *Detroit Free Press*, Oct. 9, 1988, p. 14.

21. E. Fuller Torrey, *Out of the Shadows* (New York: Wiley, 1997).

22. "Crime and Mental Disorder: An Epidemiological Approach," in M. Tonry & N. Morris (eds.), *Crime and Justice: An Annual Review of Research* (Chicago,: University of Chicago Press), 4:145, 1983.

23. "Parents fear syndrome," *Australian*, Nov. 23, 1996, p. 4.

24. See D. Woychuk, *Attorney for the Damned/A Lawyer's Life With the Criminally Insane* (New York: Free Press, 1996). Woychuk calls the NGRI acquitees "patients." In 1981, Dr. Abraham Halpern, Dr. Stephen Rachlin, and Dr. Stanley Portnow strongly objected to the failure of "The Insanity Defense Reform Act of 1980," N.Y. Crim. Proc. Law § 330.20, to mention the word "patient" even once when referring to insanity acquittees; the law, instead, used the word "defendant" no fewer than 141 times. A.L. Halpern, S. Rachlin & S.L. Portnow, "New York's Insanity Defense Reform Act of 1980: A Forensic Psychiatric Perspective," *Albany L. Rev.* 45:661, 1981. See also V.P. Hans & D. Slater, "'Plain Crazy' Lay Definitions of Legal Insanity," *Int. J. Law & Psychiatry* 7:105, 1984; H. Tarpley, "Pejorative Psychiatry: Formula for Failure," *Am. J. For. Psychiatry* 12:29, 1991.

25. D.M. Bernstein, "Feigned Insanity: Early Manifestations," *Psychiatric News*, Aug. 16, 1996, p. 13.

26. N. Mailer, *The Executioner's Song* (Boston: Little, Brown, 1979).

27. M.J. Grinfeld, "What's in a Name?," *Psychiatric Times*, June 1995, p. 14.

28. E.F. Torrey, *Surviving Schizophrenia* (New York: Harper Collins, 3d ed. 1995).

29. New York: Hoeber-Harper, 1961.

30. *New York Times,* June 16, 1995, p. B-1.

31. "Is ADHD a Psychiatric or Neurological Disorder," at meeting on March 24, 1996, in New Orleans.

32. Ltr., "On the Words 'Mental Illness,'" *Am. J. Psychiatry* 152:1692, 1995.

33. E.F. Torrey, *Freudian Fraud* (New York: HarperCollins, 1992).

34. G. McGovern, *Terry/My Daughter's Life-and-Death Struggle With Alcoholism* (New York: Villard, 1996). See also C. Knapp, *Drinking* (New York: Dial Press, 1996).

35. Thomas Szasz in his book *A Lexicon of Lunacy* discusses the extraordinary profusion of terms for what is conventionally called "mental illness." T. Szasz, *A Lexicon of Lunacy, Metaphoric Malady, Moral Responsibility and Psychiatry* (New Brunswick, N.J.: Transaction, 1993). "Loco," for crazy, is the most commonly used term in Spanish-speaking countries. Abdala Bucaram, the ousted president of Ecuador, called himself, "El Loco," the crazy one. His campaign for office included a road show featuring him as a singer, dancer, and comedian. He sang a song from his CD, "A Crazy Man in Love." In office, he invited Lorena Bobbitt, the Ecuadorean famous for slashing off her American husband's penis, to an official lunch. D.J. Schemo, "As Ecuadorean Resists Ouster, 3 Claim to Rule," *New York Times*, Feb. 8, 1997, p. 1; "Ecuador president ousted for 'mental incapacity,'" *USA Today*, Feb. 7, 1997, p. 10. In a reprint of the *New York Times* article, the *Detroit Free Press* (Feb. 8, 1997) carried the headline, "Ecuador is in turmoil–El Loco tries to hang on."

36. 396 S.W.2d 668 (Mo. 1965).

37. R. Porter (ed.), *The Faber Book of Madness* (London: Faber & Faber, 1991).

38. B. Burstow & D. Weitz (eds.), *Shrink Resistant* (Vancouver: New Star Books, 1988).

39. C.S.J. Probert, T. Battock & J.F. Mayberry, "Consumer, Customer, Client, or Patient," *Lancet* 335:1466, 1990; N.C. Andreasen, Editorial, "Clients, Consumers, Providers, and Products: Where Will It All End?", *Am. J. Psychiat.* 152:1107, 1995.

40. See the discussion by Dr. Glen and Kim Gabbard in P.J. Fink & A. Tasman (eds.), *Stigma and Mental Illness* (Washington, D.C.: American Psychiatric Press, 1992).

41. In an attractive illustrated book, *Madness in America*" (Ithaca: Cornell University Press, 1995), Lynn Gamwell and Nancy Tomes set out the cultural and medical perceptions of mental illness before 1914.

42. B. Link, "The Effectiveness of Stigma Coping Orientations," *J. Health & Science Behavior* 32:303, 1991.

43. J.A. Clausen, "Stigma and Mental Disorder: Phenomena and Terminology," *Psychiatry* 44:287, 1981. Walter Gove also contends that more stigmatization results from the aberrant behavior of the mentally ill than from the labels placed upon them. W.R. Gove, "Societal Reaction as an Explanation of Mental Illness," *Am. Soc. Rev.* 35:873, 1970. See also P.J. Caplan, *They Say*

*You're Crazy* (Reading, MA.: Addison-Wesley, 1995); B. Link, F. Cullen, J. Frank & J. Wozniak, "The Social Rejection of Former Mental Patients: Understanding Why Labels Matter," *Am. J. Soc.* 92:1461, 1987; P.M. Marzuk, "Violence, Crime, and Mental Illness/How Strong a Link?" *Arch. Gen. Psychiat.* 53:481, 1996; J.G. Rabkin, "Criminal Behavior of Discharged Mental Patients: A Critical Appraisal of the Research," *Psychological Bull.* 86:1, 1979.

44. J.W. Trent, "Suffering Fools," *Sciences,* July/August 1995, p. 19. The ultimate in relabelling may have been reached in the film "Ghosts" when the politically correct psychiatrist observes, "You can call them ghosts or, as I prefer, the living impaired." One teacher says, "We don't use the word 'stealing' here. We call it 'uncooperative behavior.'" W. Herbert, "The Moral Child," *U.S. News & World Report,* June 3, 1996, p. 52.

45. P.D. Kramer, "Call Me Paranoid," *Psychiatric Times,* March 1996, p. 4.

46. See R. Slovenko, "Sexual Deviation: Response to an Adaptational Crisis," *U. Colo. L. Rev.* 40:222, 1968.

**Part VI**

# EVIDENTIAL VALUE OF THERAPIST VERSUS FORENSIC EXPERT TESTIMONY

The question is increasingly posed: Is a preference to be made between the testimony of a therapist and a forensic expert in the case of a psychiatric patient, past or present, who is involved in litigation? Who is in a more favorable position to provide accurate and honest testimony? Is there greater evidential value of the testimony of a therapist who, over a period of time, has had long opportunity to evaluate and understand the psychodynamics of the patient than that of the testimony of a forensic expert divorced from the therapeutic relationship?

Time and again, the contention is made that psychiatric testimony based on psychotherapy is incompetent or irrelevant for the legal process. If so, the need for privilege is moot. Privileges are needed only to exclude competent or relevant evidence–the basic criteria for the admissibility of evidence are competency and relevancy. Actually, some critics go so far as to suggest the exclusion of all psychiatric testimony–be it of a psychiatric examiner or of a treating psychiatrist. They call the testimony unhelpful or unnecessary. They call it "snake oil."[1]

In some measure, apart from ethical or therapy considerations, the claim of incompetency or irrelevancy of testimony of a treating psychiatrist is well taken. First, it may be urged, a therapist cannot within any reasonable degree of accuracy present to the court in a question and answer format, which is usually required in a courtroom, material produced over a period of time in therapy. At staff conferences, attended by persons experienced in the field, it takes considerable time to present a case report and it is done in narrative fashion. Moreover, in the courtroom, the psychiatrist faces a jury reluctant to accept psychiatric theories and unable to evaluate the testimony, particularly when it must be done in Q&A fashion. Indeed, nonpsychiatric physicians complain that psychiatrists talk in jargon, and have developed a tower of Babel, resulting in a communication gap between psychiatrists and even other physicians.[2] By and large, by dint of experience in the courtroom, a forensic examiner is better able to communicate with lawyers, judges, and juries.

In 1954, in the case of a housebreaker named Monte Durham, Judge David L. Bazelon of the U.S. D.C. Court of Appeals set out a new test of criminal responsibility–"An accused is not criminally responsible if his unlawful act was the product of mental disease or defect"—and he stated that the purpose of the new rule was to get good and complete psychiatric testimony. In effect, he wanted a forensic examiner to present the type of evidence that a therapist would present at a case conference. As it turned out, Bazelon rued the day that he handed down his ruling. Instead of serving as a bridge between law and psychiatry, it resulted in confusion, a plethora of appeals, and scholarly debates about the complexities of the defense.[3]

Second, data from free association, fantasies, or memories are not reliable for use in court as they represent the way the person experienced an event, and not necessarily how the event occurred. In law, by and large, a cigar is a cigar, but in psychotherapy a cigar is likely a phallic symbol. In fantasy life, a patient may tell of hidden treasures; its correspondence in reality is not of crucial importance in treatment. The tale of Cinderella reminds us that by projection all stepparents are cruel. In imaginary reality we never meet a good stepparent, no matter what they may do in actual reality.

**MOTHER GOOSE & GRIMM** By Mike Peters

© 1996 Grimmy, Inc. Distributed by Tribune Media Services.
All Rights Reserved. Reprinted with permission.

The material revealed in psychotherapy is not restricted to the reality of the outer world; hence it would likely make poor, even prejudicial, evidence. The material is often of childhood fantasies and not directly germane to current activities of the patient. A young girl who claims that she is having sexual relations with every male member of the family is sick, whether or not it is true. The therapist is not compelled to check on the outer reality, and the therapist does not cross-question the patient. In therapy, the important thing is how the patient looks at himself or herself and the world. But, in the courtroom, say, in a criminal case involving incest or contributing to the delinquency of a minor, it makes a world of difference whether the allegation is in the realm of fantasy or reality.

There are times when the psychotherapist deliberately participates in the psychosis of a patient by entering the fantasy and from that position attempting to pry the patient loose from his psychosis (John Rosen and Milton Wexler were among the notable exponents of this practice). The procedure, however, has been reported to get out of control. Robert Lindner reported the case where, as the patient was losing his delusion, larger and larger areas of Lindner's mind were being taken over by the fantasy.[4] Countertransference and identification with the patient may result in a loss of objectivity.

The Ethical Guidelines for the Practice of Forensic Psychiatry of the American Academy of Psychiatry and the Law (AAPL) call for honesty and striving for objectivity. By and large, by virtue of the greater distance and objectivity, an evaluation can be more helpful to the court than a psychiatrist who is treating or has treated the litigant. When a therapist testifies, he is biased for or against the litigant by virtue of countertransference feelings toward a patient. To be sure, an examining psychiatrist is something of an advocate for the side retaining his services, but the term "objective" does not mean only one right answer. It is critical to distinguish among honest differences of opinion, biases (conscious or unconscious) and "hired guns."

Consider a question put by a psychiatrist to the AAPL's Committee on Ethics: "I am treating an insurance company employee who for the past several years has been forging signatures on loan applications and running an illegal scheme at work. On two occasions, he has been admitted to the hospital because of stress. I will be testifying at a workers' compensation hearing regarding the employee's ability to work. Am I obliged to reveal these illegal activities as one major source of stress?"[5]

Would an examining psychiatrist be privy to information about the illegal schemes? In this case, the treating psychiatrist would likely be more helpful to the court than an evaluator. Likewise, a treating psychiatrist may be singularly aware that injuries complained about by a patient in a lawsuit predated the alleged cause of action.[6] The therapist is familiar with the patient's condition at the time of visitation—the therapist is an "eyeball witness"—and hence is qualified to testify about it, but discerning a past condition or what happened in the past (without corroboration) is dubious. The *Diagnostic and Statistical Manual of Mental Disorders* does not give etiology of the various disorders set out in the manual.

In a much publicized California case, a young girl who sought damages for emotional trauma allegedly resulting from an automobile collision, stated in the course of a deposition that prior to the collision she had no problems necessitating psychiatric care, but thereafter she had felt the need because she blamed herself for the accident in which her mother and brother were killed. The testimony and records of the psychiatrist, Dr. George Caesar, were thereupon sought. Dr. Caesar contended that an independent psychiatric evaluation by another psychiatrist, which had been done, could determine the specific effect of the collision on the plaintiff and would be more useful than his records. The effect of any disclosure by him, he urged, could prevent the continuation of therapy and might "conceivably result in even more catastrophic things like suicide attempt."[7] In contrast, Dr. Samuel D. Lipton argued: "Who is able to provide better evidence–the psychiatrist who examined her immediately after the accident and continued to treat her, or one who saw her for the first time much later?" The question, for him, was rhetorical.[8]

Then too, cases of factitious sexual harassment may only be recognized by access to medical records to show that an alleged event was fabricated. In a case where a patient is the victim of a homicide, as in the Iverson case, the therapist's testimony as to any statements of the patient as to whether or by whom threats against the patient were made would be helpful in a investigation or prosecution. In a civil action for the alleged wrongful death of a patient where the defendant contends that the deceased did not die as the result of any action of the defendant but was a suicide, the testimony of the therapist of the deceased would be helpful in discerning the cause of death. In cases of criminal responsibility of a patient, or the civil commitment of a patient, the therapist has what many consider a superior vantage point as to the patient's mental status, diagnosis and clinical condition. Reporting statutes are based on the assumption that therapists are aware, or reasonably so, of the veridical truth.

The problem is ascertaining those cases when a therapist can provide otherwise unavailable and relevant information. No witness has to hit a home run, so to speak, but might not the therapist in some cases advance the inquiry at least to first base? To make that determination prompts the demand for discovery of the therapist's records in all cases. At a minimum, it may be suggested, an evaluator would be remiss in not considering a therapist's report. The forensic examiners, for example, obtained the therapy records of John W. Hinckley, Jr., the would-be assassin of President Reagan.

Actually, there are areas of the law where an examiner is also expected or obliged to treat. In some states in workers' compensation cases the examiner is also obliged to provide treatment. In cases of competency to stand trial, the examiner often treats the individual as well as testifies on triability. In an evaluation in child custody cases, an examiner will not only make an examination but may also offer counseling. The Social Security Administration as well as other agencies require statements from treating psychiatrists in adjudicating patients' disability claims.

In the case of Lyle and Erik Menendez, who were charged with murdering their parents, there was an audiotape of a therapy session in which Lyle explained why he and his brother killed them. This information would be probative, it may be said, but there is no duty for a treating psychiatrist to obtain information from sources other than the patient. Unlike a therapeutic session that involves helping a patient as the primary purpose, a forensic evaluation may necessitate the exploration of areas that a litigant may prefer to avoid and finds upsetting. Therapists are concerned with the symptoms of a patient, not with legal causation. In therapy, bringing up certain matters may interfere with dealing with the symptoms.

To be sure, testifying conflicts with a therapeutic role. Even though therapy may be formally terminated, therapy never ends—it is in the mind, so the transference is always there. It is well known that heroes, even long after their death, can still influence and inspire. Ethical questions also arise when a treating psychiatrist takes on the role of an expert at trial. The roles of healer and examiner get confused. What should go in the report, and should a report be written? What is fantasy, and what is fact?

Because the therapist has firsthand knowledge of a patient's condition, the therapist may be called to testify as a "fact witness" (assuming the testimonial privilege is waived) but the therapist may also be qualified to testify as an expert and in that event the therapist may offer an opinion based on hearsay or other information. However, to be credible as an expert witness, the therapist must attempt to corroborate the patient's version of events. Testimony as a fact witness is often unavoidable and is harmful enough to treatment, but testimony as an expert on behalf of one's patient poses destruction of the treatment relationship and also poses great risk of professional embarrassment.[9] Dr. Martin Blinder writes:[10]

> [T]hough [I perform] both psychotherapy and forensic evaluations, [I] will not do *both*—for the same patient. It's one or the other. (If functioning in my forensic role with someone who needs psychiatric treatment, I will refer out, as I would a patient of mine who, during the course of treatment, finds that he or she needs a forensic evaluation and report.) In short, no psychiatrist can be an effective therapist if over treatment sessions there hangs the possibility that the patient's revelations might subsequently be shared with others. Accordingly, [I remain] unalterably opposed to the common practice of calling upon the treating doctor to testify on his patient's behalf; though assisting a plaintiff's legal case, it forever destroys his doctor's usefulness as his therapist. Defendants who have a financial investment in seeing a plaintiff successfully treated in as short a time as possible might also bear this in mind.

In a stunning admission during the penalty phase of the retrial of the Menendez brothers, Dr. William Vicary, who had treated Erik and also served as the forensic psychiatrist, said under oath that he had altered notes of his sessions at the request of defense attorney Leslie Abramson. The revelation set off a firestorm of controversy. According to Dr. Vicary, information that could have been critical to the prosecution was deleted from his notes because Abramson felt it would hurt the defense. Among the most important deletions, a statement by Erik a week before the murders that he hated his parents, and that he "wanted to kill them." Other deletions related to statements regarding Erik's homosexual conduct and an incestuous relationship with his mother that was "in his head" rather than real. The Ethical Guidelines of the American Academy of Psychiatry and Law discourage (but do not forbid) treating psychiatrists from acting as expert witnesses for their patients.

In a critical comment about Dr. Vicary's agreeing to be both therapist and expert witness for Eric Menendez, Dr. Diane Schetky wrote:[11]

> Dr. William Vicary is to be commended for owning up to his mistakes in the Menendez case,[12] but he minimizes the untenable position he put himself in by agreeing to be both therapist and expert witness for Eric Menendez. If there is a lesson to be learned from this case it is the perils of trying to serve two masters at one time....Amidst pressures to protect his patient, appease his attorney client and his belief that his testimony was critical to the case, he lost sight of the need for the psychiatrist at all times to testify truthfully. When we allow our integrity to be compromised by competing pressures, we do a disservice to our patients, the profession and the legal system.[13]

By way of response, Dr. Theodore Pearlman wrote:[14]

> Dr. Schetky pontificates about the perils of "serving two masters." There is nothing absolute in the American Academy of Psychiatry and Law ethical guidelines which precludes duality of service. The creditable psychiatrist serves no masters other than loyalty to his training, qualifications and integrity. Rigidly separating out the expert role from the treating role by no means guarantees ethical expert opinion. Lucrative fees for expert psychiatric services, known in one celebrated case to have amounted to $3,000 per day for the two-week duration of a trial, may well influence expert psychiatric opinion.
>
> The important question is this: Who is in a more favorable position to provide accurate and honest expert testimony in the case of a psychiatric patient under treatment who subsequently becomes involved in a question of law? [Is it the] nontreating forensic psychiatrist divorced from the therapeutic relationship, or the treating psychiatrist who, over a period of maybe many months, has seen the patient within the context of a therapeutic alliance and has had ample opportunity to not only objectively evaluate, but also understand the psychodynamics of the patient's mental illness, personality function, interpersonal relationships and patterns of behavior preceding the incident forming the basis of the legal inquiry? The conclusion is compelling that a judge and jury will afford greater weight to psychiatric testimony inclusive of retrospective evaluation and treatment than to the testimony of an expert evaluating the patient for the first time after the event constituting the basis for medico-legal inquiry.

In a number of instances when a forensic examination of a patient is undertaken, a treating psychiatrist (usually over objection) will sit in at the examination allegedly to provide emotional support to the patient. The therapist will at times also testify in deposition or at trial, and in these cases there is the suspicion that the therapist does so in the hope of obtaining a favorable judgment to provide funds for the payment of therapy, past or future. The bias is evident.

To be sure, there is bias among witnesses be they therapist or forensic examiner. They may be biased by virtue of philosophy.[15] Dr. Bernard Diamond, the late renowned forensic psychiatrist, testified only for the defense in criminal cases because of "the need of psychiatric testimony to humanize the law."[16] More experts are biased by the fee than by philosophy. The sobriquet "hired gun" is not without basis. Oft-quoted in discussions about expert testimony is the following testimony on cross-examination in a personal injury case: "Is that your conclusion that this man is a malingerer?" The expert responded, "I wouldn't be testifying if I didn't think so, unless I was on the other side, then it would be a post-traumatic condition."[17]

"I'm not a detective," therapists say when their counselling is challenged in litigation. This issue has taken on special social significance in view of the attention now given to childhood incest and abuse. When Richard and Cheryl Althaus together with their 19-year-old daughter, Nicole, brought a malpractice lawsuit charging Dr. Judith Cohen with failure to evaluate properly the girl's accusations of parental sex abuse, Dr. Cohen argued that her job was to treat her patient, not investigate her accusations, and she contended that challenging her patient's claims during therapy could have deepened her depression and undermined her confidence. Dr. Cohen had diagnosed Nicole's condition as posttraumatic stress disorder brought on by sexual abuse. Before their daughter recanted, the parents were arrested and charged with sex abuse. A Pittsburgh jury awarded them $272,000.[18]

If Dr. Cohen were to act as a detective, Professor Alan Scheflin asks, what should she have done? According to the lawsuit, it was wrong for the therapy to be conducted according to the narrative developed by the patient, rather than the alleged historical truth which Dr. Cohen should have known by completely disbelieving her patient and totally ignoring her claims and expressed needs. And if a therapist is to be a detective, Professor Scheflin asks: Should the patient be told that the therapist is conducting an investigation? How does the therapist investigate without breaking the patient's confidentiality? How thorough an investigation must be conducted? What should the therapist tell the patient about the investigation? What should the therapist do if the therapist reasonably concludes that the patient is telling the truth, or is not telling the truth? Should therapists receive training in investigation?[19]

During a flashback experience, patients vividly reexperience aspects of a traumatic response while feeling detached from their surrounding environment. While some flashbacks may be accurate depictions of a traumatic situation, others have unreal or distorted qualities, similar to dreams.[20] In any event, the most reliable memories of trauma are those that have been present throughout the patient's life. Recollections of childhood traumata that come up for the first time in therapy are not credible evidence of actual events.[21]

In California, seven months before the Althaus case, Gary Ramona obtained a judgment against a medical center and a pair of psychotherapists who he claimed created false memories in his daughter of his sexually abusing her as a child. The therapists had suggested to the daughter that her eating disorder was caused by childhood sexual abuse, the memory of which she had repressed. Together with the therapists, the daughter confronted her father with an allegation that he had raped her between the age of five and eight. Again, the therapists contended that they were not detectives, and had no obligation to make a factual investigation.[22]

The daughter was told that if she recovered a memory of abuse under sodium amytal, the memory of abuse would be historically accurate.[23] The father maintained that the daughter had succumbed to suggestion by manipulative therapists. "The only time she had memories of her father abusing her was when the doctors told her after the amythal," testified Dr. Park Dietz, an expert witness for the plaintiff. "Before the amytal she couldn't remember for sure who it was in those images she was having."[24] Dr. Harrison G. Pope, Jr., on the basis of research he had done on bulimia nervosa, testified for the plaintiff that evidence is wanting of a link between sexual abuse (even if it had occurred) and eating disorders.[25]

In a case in Dallas, a jury held a psychiatrist, Dr. Wayne C. Jones, liable for slander in the amount of $350,000 when in a joint family encounter he accused a couple, Edward and LaVerne Khatain, of sexual abuse against their grown daughter, his patient. (Under the law of defamation "publication" does not mean publicity but merely communication of the defamatory words to some one other than the person defamed.) The jury awarded the couple $350,000. The psychiatrist's claim was based on interviews with the daughter using the "truth serum" amobarbital sodium. The daughter later recanted her allegations. The couple charged that the psychiatrist elicited false memories in her and failed to investigate the truthfulness of her allegations before revealing them to her family. As in the other cases, the psychiatrist claimed he was under no obligation to investigate the truthfulness of the patient's allegations, since such an investigation would have violated patient confidentiality. The psychiatrist's attorney said, "When [the patient] does not consent to having [the doctor] contact her parents, he can't investigate." Furthermore, he said, "if he does outside investigation—which he's not trained to do—he takes off his therapeutic hat and puts on his investigator's hat, and potentially damages his therapeutic relationship with his patient."[26]

Psychoanalysis or other psychotherapy is not an archeological dig, but a search for a regenerative story. In psychoanalytic psychotherapy, as oft said, mental reality is more important than objective reality. Punctilious history taking is not necessary for therapy. A patient does not—and need not—take an oath, like a witness, to tell the truth, the whole truth, and nothing but the truth. Psychiatrists neither have nor need investigators to determine the objective reality. Indeed, traditionally oriented psychotherapists are usually careful to guard against obtaining information from outside sources, lest it undermine the therapeutic alliance.[27]

In making an assessment in litigation, in contrast, it is important to obtain information from all medical records, vocational evaluations, and educational and psychological records. It is also important to gather history from parties known to the evaluee, including information from teachers and school records. In some circumstances it may be appropriate to go so far as to read books read by the evaluee as well as material written by him.[28] Dr. Paul Appelbaum and Dr. Thomas Gutheil have noted that whereas the treating clinician "must always begin by attempting to see the world through the patient's eyes—non-critically, non-challenging, non-judgmentally"—the forensic examiner, in contrast, "must always assume that an examinee may cherish covert goals, under the general rubric of 'secondary gain,' which inevitably attend most forensic examinations."[29]

In the psychotherapeutic dialogue, on the other hand, attention is focused on continuity and coherence, not on historical truth. What patients tell a therapist about their childhood is not necessarily related to what actually happened. Dr. Judith Herman writes, "[The therapist's] role is to be an open-minded, compassionate witness, not a detective."[30]

Time and again, therapists say that they have "no problem whatsoever" dealing with memories, be they accurate or not. Memories, they say, contribute to the process of healing and help patients build a "compelling personal narrative" that makes sense to them even though not historically correct. Therapists operate as "literary critics," focusing on enduring themes emerging from the patient's self-narrative.[31]

The literal truth of a patient's story about the past may be only tangentially related to improvement in therapy. Clinicians are concerned with clinical utility. They lift resistance to memories which are used in treatment if they have efficacy, regardless of their historical accuracy; but historical accuracy is essential in a courtroom. It is also important when third parties will be affected as they are in the case of allegations of sexual abuse.

The perception of psychoanalysis as an archeological dig stems out of Sigmund Freud's case studies. Take Freud's celebrated analysis of the "Wolf

Man." Sergei Petrov Tankieff was 26 when he began treatment with Freud. He reported that at age four he began having a recurrent dream in which several white wolves with bushy tails stared at him from the branches of a walnut tree. He awoke in terror. Freud's interpretation was that the dream was a reconstructed version of another "terrifying" memory hidden deep in the boy's unconscious: at age 18 months, while sleeping in his parents' bedroom, young Sergei witnessed the primal scene–his father, erect, penetrating his crouching mother. The revelation did not result in a cure. In fact, Tankieff, a Russian aristocrat ruined by the revolution, spent the rest of his life with psychoanalysts, among them Anna Freud.

Sigmund Freud eventually arrived at the view that he would never know the historical truth concerning any particular patient's experience. To the question whether the "Wolf Man" actually saw his parents in a primal scene, Freud concluded that in therapy the important concern is the construct in the patient's mind.

The "revival of memory" controversy is a rebirth of an issue that has long been abandoned by responsible psychotherapists. The "affect-trauma" theory emphasized recovery of memories as curative in itself (one lanced the abscess and the neurotic pus drained out), but contemporary theory de-emphasizes memory recovery because it rarely works in itself. Hollywood took it over as the "Aha!" theory of psychotherapy–"Aha! I remember now, and I'm cured!"[32]

Psychoanalyst Theodor Reik argued that psychoanalysis has no contribution to make in ascertaining the truth, as it is concerned with mental (inner) reality rather than material (outer) reality.[33] The psychoanalyst–ordinarily concerned with the patient's view of reality rather than with what reality actually is–does not cross-examine the patient. Indeed, some psychoanalysts say that outside information about the patient actually interferes with their clinical work, and they prefer to close their eyes to it. By and large, they learn the "truth" only through the eyes of the patient.

**REX MORGAN, M.D.**

Reprinted with special permission of King Features Syndicate

Dr. Gutheil said, "The distinction between what is true and what is real [is not crucial]. The debate about whether to believe a patient . . . is wholly misguided: The matter is irrelevant. If a patient in therapy says something, assume it is true—*i.e.*, that it captures some fundamental (but perhaps metaphoric or symbolic) truth about that person; but do not delude yourself that it is real, *i.e.*, veridical, or that you know whether or not it actually happened just that way."[34]

But does "I'm not a detective" mean no responsibility for the historical accuracy of recovered memory claims? The fundamental standard of physicians is, "First, do no harm," from the Oath of Hippocrates. Allegations of childhood sexual abuse rupture the family and deprive the patient of a support group. These recovered memory therapists ("RMT" as they are known) do not help reconcile a patient and the family.[35] Indeed, without corroborating evidence, they encourage their patients to confront their parents. "Confront your abuser," they say.[36]

All therapy, of course, involves memory and, as therapists say, they are not detectives. Investigation, as they say, would interfere with therapy. The duty of the therapist, after all, is to see the world through the patient's eyes. But many therapists have departed far from mainstream practice. Almost every symptom of dysphoria is taken as probative of early abuse, and unlike the traditional neutrality of psychoanalysts, these therapists become advocates and encourage confrontation. Many of them file affidavits or testify on behalf of the patient in the civil or criminal case. Many lose perspective because of their own abuse histories.

In assessing the validity of sexual abuse allegations, it is an error to rely on the child's history or on an adult's "revival of memory" without interviewing family members and others having information about the home environment. Dr. Paul McHugh, chief of the Johns Hopkins Department of Psychiatry, would in cases of "recovered memory" of childhood sexual abuse call attention to the genesis of the memory, consider its content, seek its confirmation with external informants, and attend to the accompanying mental symptoms that may be influencing a patient's beliefs.[37] In view of the controversy surrounding adult delayed recall, an ad hoc committee was set up by the American Academy of Psychiatry and Law to make a statement about the role of forensic examiners in repressed memory lawsuits. It recommended that all claims of repressed memory be independently corroborated. Actually, in making an assessment for litigation, it is incumbent upon an examiner in all cases to obtain corroboration.[38]

Bewildering in many cases of "recovered memory" is the prosecutor's acceptance of bizarre allegations of childhood sexual abuse. A prosecutor, unlike a therapist, *is* supposed to be a detective who searches for the historical reality. In the Pittsburgh case the prosecutor dropped the charges against the parents only when the daughter refused to testify against them. The daughter had also claimed that her grandmother flew about on a broom, that she had been tortured with a medieval thumbscrew device, that she had borne three children who were killed, and that she had been raped in view of diners in a crowded restaurant.

THE WALL STREET JOURNAL

HAVE YOU BEEN ABDUCTED BY ALIENS?

KNOW YOUR RIGHTS! LEGAL HELP IS AVAILABLE. CALL THE LAW OFFICE OF JANE WILLS AT 555-7900

From the Wall Street Journal – Permission, Cartoon Features Syndicate.

Various state crime compensation funds have been tapped on the "revival of memory" of childhood sexual abuse and, incredibly, revival of memory has served as the sole evidence in lawsuits against parents and others. Some have been found guilty on criminal charges on the basis of nothing more than the uncorroborated testimony of adult children and their therapists. By and large, the discovery rule is applied to prevent the running of the statute of limitations on a claim of childhood sexual abuse during the time that the victim did not have memory of the sexual abuse.[39] In general, a cause of action accrues when the plaintiff discovers or, through the exercise of reasonable diligence, should have discovered the injury and its likely cause. Blocking an incident (or incidents) from conscious memory is analogized to other disabilities warranting a tolling of the statute of limitations.[40] In some states, to remove any doubt about the applicability of the discovery rule in sexual abuse cases, the statute of limitations has been changed to specifically provide that a lawsuit can be filed within three years after the "memories" emerge.

Virginia in 1991 enacted special legislation permitting an action in cases of sexual abuse from the time "when the fact of the injury and its causal connection to the sexual abuse is first communicated [to the patient] by a licensed physician, psychologist, or clinical psychologist."[41] The Virginia statute posits the situation of a therapist revealing a connection between emotional distress and past sexual abuse. The statute of limitations begins to run from the time of such communication by the therapist to the patient.[42] The statute rests on the assumption that therapy uncovers legally relevant "facts" connecting past trauma to current distress.

Under the widely followed *Frye* rule, first enunciated in 1923, general acceptance in the relevant scientific community is a prerequisite to the admissibility of scientific evidence.[43] Like all standards, the *Frye* rule could be bent, and it often was. The question of what is the "relevant scientific community" arose frequently, and was not always answered intelligently.

Under the U.S. Supreme Court's decision in 1993 in *Daubert v. Merrill Dow Pharmaceuticals*,[44] trial judges should be active gatekeepers who insure that "any and all scientific testimony or evidence admitted is not only relevant but reliable." Under *Daubert*, general acceptance within the relevant field of science is but one consideration in ascertaining reliability; the court may also consider: Is the theory or technique testable, and has it been tested? Has the theory or technique been subjected to peer review and publication? What is the known or potential error rate for the technique, and are these standards controlling the technique's operation?

By and large, however, the courts are interpreting the *Daubert* criteria not in the conjunctive, as might have been expected, but in the disjunctive. *Daubert* too, like *Frye,* is often bent. (*Daubert* is applicable in federal courts and has been adopted in a number of states). Under *Daubert*, the admissibility of recovered memory evidence will depend upon the rigor with which the court addresses the criteria.[45] The concepts of repression and dissociation are accepted in the scientific community (though there is some disagreement about both), but the determination of historical reality is another matter. Not being a detective, a therapist giving testimony on historical reality, it can be argued, is unwarranted under either the *Frye* or *Daubert* test of admissibility.[46]

A number of courts hold, however, that these tests do not apply to the "soft sciences" (like the behavioral sciences).[47] Furthermore, a number of courts have held that *Daubert* does not apply to "technical" or "specialized" knowledge that falls short of qualifying as "scientific" knowledge. The Federal Rules of Evidence of 1975 and their counterpart in the various states allow "scientific, technical, or other specialized knowledge [that] will assist the trier of fact to understand the evidence or to determine a fact."[48] Quite often, *Daubert* is being restricted to a definition of "scientific evidence" as not including "technical" or "specialized" knowledge as well as not including the behavioral sciences.[49] Time and again, psychoanalysis or psychotherapy is called an art, not science.[50]

Though the therapist is not a fact-finder, and therapists when asked for objective evidence say, "I'm not a detective," lawsuits have been built on what comes out of the therapy. The accusations are made without physical evidence, medical records, diaries, or interviews with family members. It may be compared to a witch hunt. It is pure speculation to suggest that a person can forget, then years later remember traumatic events of childhood, especially a series of events such as incest.[51] While generally defending psychoanalysis, philosophy professor Richard Rorty writes, "Freudian ideas have encouraged such abominations as the imprisonment of innocent parents on the basis of 'repressed memories' of abuse, solicited from young children [or adults] by eager therapists."[52]

The case that can be said to have put "revival of memory" on the map, as it were, involved Eileen Franklin Lipsker who claimed to have had a sudden recollection that her father, George Franklin, murdered her eight-year-old friend Susan twenty years before. When the story first aired in 1990, it became a media sensation. On the strength of her new-found memory, her father was convicted and sentenced to a life term. Then, in 1995, a federal judge overturned the conviction on the ground, *inter alia*, that the trial judge wrongly prevented the defense from introducing evidence that the details of the killing that Eileen Franklin Lipsker recalled had been reported in the media. The prosecution argued at trial that only an eyewitness could have known the specifics of the murder.[53] Franklin was not retried—DNA testing by the prosecutor's office showed that Franklin could not have been involved and additionally, Eileen Franklin Lipsker's sister recently stated that she and her sister "lied at the first trial."[54]

Early in 1994, the New Hampshire Supreme Court called for external validation of memory repression when the case is tried on the merits.[55] The case involved a 50-year-old daughter who sued her 80-year-old parents for abuse which allegedly took place 35 years earlier and allegedly remained repressed until she attended a therapy workshop on child abuse. The trial court denied the defendant's motion to dismiss which argued that the suit was barred by the statute of limitations. That decision resulted in an interlocutory appeal which reached the state's supreme court. The court allowed the discovery rule without independent corroborative evidence for the purpose of tolling the statute of limitations but, at trial on the merits, the court said, "[T]he plaintiff still carries the burden to substantiate her allegations of abuse, and, if challenged, to validate the phenomenon of memory repression itself and the admissibility of evidence flowing therefrom."[56] California and Louisiana by recent legislation require a certificate of merit as a prerequisite to the filing of a lawsuit involving revival of memory.[57] Ohio, by legislation, calls for "objective and verifiable evidence" to toll the statute of limitations. The Michigan Supreme Court has held that "repression of memory" does not (like insanity) toll the statute of limitations.[58] To toll the statute of limitations without corroboration opens the door to wasteful and anguishing trials.[59]

## CONCLUSION

It is widely considered that a treating psychiatrist, seeing the patient over a period of time when the patient would have no apparent motive to deceive, has more to offer the court than an examining psychiatrist. In fact, probably more often than not, a psychiatrist appointed to carry out an examination obtains in a few hours (without a promise of confidentiality) more information related to the legal issues than a treating psychiatrist who may have seen the patient over a period of years. The examiner conducts an interview with the legal issues directly in mind, whereas in therapy the subject may never come up or, if it does, it may be diluted with fantasy and association.

In any event, the issue is not really one of privilege but rather the relevancy or materiality of communication, and in some cases, where the psychiatrist is an agent of the state, constitutional limitations on the use of evidence. Among other countries, notably in France, confidentiality of communications with a physician is given much more respect than in the United States. Whenever medical information is needed, reliance is placed on an examiner, not on the treating doctor.

## NOTES

1.  M.A. Hagen, *Whores of the Court/The Fraud of Psychiatric Testimony and the Rape of American Justice* (New York: HarperCollins, 1997); J. Ziskin, *Coping with Psychiatric and Psychological Testimony* (Marine del Rey, CA.: Law and Psychology Press, 1988). See the discussion in R. Slovenko, *Psychiatry and Criminal Culpability* (New York: Wiley, 1995, chap. 12); see also R. Slovenko, "Surveying the Attacks on Psychiatry in the Legal Process," *Int'l J. of Evidence & Proof* 1:48, 1996.

2.  L.H. Bartemeier, "American Medicine and the Development of Psychiatry," *J.A.M.A.* 163:95, 1957.

3.  See R. Slovenko, *Psychiatry and Criminal Culpability* (New York: Wiley, 1995).

4.  R. Lindner, *50-Minute Hour* ("The Jet-Propelled Couch") (New York: Reinhart, 1954).

5.  R. Weinstock, "AAPL's Committee on Ethics–Additional Opinions," *Newsletter of Am. Acad. of Psychiat. and Law*, 20(2):49, Aug. 1995.

6.  For example, consider the case reported by Dr. Jack M. Gorman of a patient who suffered back trouble for many years preceding a car accident that she claimed in litigation hurt her back. *The New Psychiatry* (New York: St. Martin's Press, 1996), p. 353.

7.  In line with prevailing law, the court ruled that there is no privilege for a communication relevant to an issue concerning mental or emotional condition tendered by the patient. The court reiterated that it would not permit the disclosure of irrelevant evidence or the exposure of a litigant to humiliation. Murphy v. Hall, Calif. Court of Appeal, Oct. 19, 1971, reported in *Psychiat. News*, Feb. 2; May 17, 1972; Mar. 7, 1973, p. 1. The test of the limits of the therapist's privilege in this case went on for several years, beginning in 1972, at various court levels. The latest episode came in 1976, when the U.S. Court of Appeals for the Ninth Circuit affirmed the district court's denial of Dr. Caesar's petition for writ of habeas corpus. H. Foster, "The Devil's Advocate," *Bull. Am. Acad. of Psychiat. & Law* 4: 248, 1976; *Psychiat. News*, Nov. 5, 1976, p. 1.

8.  Ltr., *Psychiat. News*, March 15, 1972, p. 2.

9.  R. Schouten, "Pitfalls of Clinical Practice: The Treating Clinician as Expert Witness," *Harv. Rev. Psychiatry* 1:64, 1993. In a *New Yorker* cartoon by Leo Cullum, an analysand asks of his analyst, "Can I count on your testimony?"

10. *Psychiatry in the Everyday Practice of Law* (Deerfield, IL.: Clark Boardman Callaghan, 3d ed. 1992), §2.6, p. 75

11. Ltr., "A Question of Ethics," *Psychiatric Times*, Sept. 1996, p. 4.

12. Dr. Vickary's statement appears in Ltr., Psychiatric Times, June 1996.

13. For another criticism, see M.J. Grinfeld, "No Excuses from Menendez Psychiatrist," *Psychiatric Times*, June 1996, p. 1.

14. Ltr., "In Defense of Dual Roles," *Psychiatric Times*, Nov. 1996, p. 5.

15. The bias of child sexual abuse experts is discussed in T.M. Horner, M.J. Guyer & N.M. Kalter, "The Biases of Child Sexual Abuse Experts: Believing is Seeing," *Bull. Am. Acad. Psychiatry & Law* 21:281, 1983.

16. Personal communication; and see J.M. Quen (ed.), *The Psychiatrist in the Courtroom: Selected papers of Bernard L. Diamond, M.D.* (Hillsdale, N.J.: Analytic Press, 1994).

17. Ladner v. Higgins, 71 So.2d 242, 244 (La.App. 1954).

18. Case No. GD 92-20893 (Court of Common Pleas, Allegheny County, Pa., 1994). AP news-release, "Jury Finds for Parents Who Sued Psychiatrist in a Sex-Abuse Case," *New York Times*, Dec. 17, 1994, p. 7; S. Barlas, "Psychiatrists Unraveling Memories of Abuse Walk on Tenuous Ground," *Psychiatric Times*, March 1995, p. 44.

19. A.W. Scheflin, "Narrative Truth, Historical Truth and Forensic Truth: Implications for the Mental Health Clinician in Court," in L. Lifson & R.I. Simon (eds.), *Practicing Psychiatry Without Fear: A Clinician's Guide to Liability Prevention* (Cambridge: Harvard University Press, 1997).

20. J.H. Krystal, S.M. Southwick & D.S. Charney, "Post Traumatic Stress Disorder: Psychobiological Mechanisms of Traumatic Remembrance," in D.L. Schacter, *Memory Distortion* (Cambridge: Harvard University Press, 1995).

21. R. Pies, "Should We Forget About Recovered Memory?" *Psychiatric Times*, Sept. 1996, p. 53.

22. Ramona v. Isabella, Rose & Western Medical Center, case no. C61898 (1994); see also discussion at p. 125.

23. J. Goss, "Suit Asks, Does 'Memory Therapy' Heal or Harm?" *New York Times*, April 8, 1994, p. 1.

24. Quoted in B. Hewitt & L. Mullen, "A Father Fights Back," *People*, May 16, 1994, p. 52; see also J. Gross, "Heated Closing Arguments In 'Recovered Memory' Case," *New York Times*, May 12, 1994, p. 12.

25. An Interview with Harrison G. Pope Jr., M.D., "'Recovered Memories': Recent Events and Review of Evidence," *Currents in Affective Illness* 13:5, July 1994. See H.G. Pope, B. Mangweth, A.B. Negrao, J.I. Hudson & T.A. Cordas, "Childhood Sexual Abuse and Bulimia Nervosa: A Comparison of American, Austrian, and Brazilian Women," *Am. J. Psychiat.* 151:732, 1994.

26. S.J. Brown, "Recovered Memory Case Ends With $350,000 Decision Against Psychiatrist," *Clin. Psychiatry News*, Jan. 1995, p. 1; K. Hausman, "Psychiatrist Commits Slander In 'Recovered' Memories Case," *Psychiatric News*, Jan. 20, 1995, p. 10.

27. R. Schaefer, *Retelling a Life/Narration and Dialogue in Psychoanalysis* (New York: Basic Books, 1992).

28. D.J. Bourne, "Truth Beyond History: Pitfalls and Challenges," *Psychiatric Annals* 24:155, 1994; P.E. Dietz, "The Quest for Excellence in Forensic Psychiatry," *Bull. Am. Acad. Psychiatry & Law* 24:153, 1996.

29. *Clinical Handbook of Psychiatry and the Law* (Baltimore: Williams & Wilkins, 2d ed. 1991).

30. *Trauma and Recovery* (New York: Basic Books, 1992); see also "Crime and Memory," *Bull. Am. Acad. Psychiatry & Law* 23:5, 1995. David Calof says, "I am a therapist, not a detective....I use hypnosis all the time, but rarely to discover 'what really happened.' In fact, a patient may lose the legal right to testify as a witness if his or her memories have been hypnotically refreshed." D. Calof, "Facing the Truth About False Memory," *Family Therapy Networker*, Sept./Oct. 1993, p. 39.

31. D.P. Spence, *Narrative Truth and Historical Truth: Meaning and Interpretation in Psychoanalysis* (New York: Norton, 1982); I.D. Yalom, *Lying on the Couch* (New York: Basic Books, 1996); P.R. McHugh, "What's the Story?", *American Scholar* 64:191, 1995; S. Rose, "Two Types of Truth," *New York Times Book Review*, Feb. 26, 1995, p. 20. Psychoanalyst Milton Viederman writes: "It was only years later that the patient was able to confirm from external sources that a real incident had occurred. Clearly, in the absence of external confirmation it was impossible to determine whether fantasy or memory of actual trauma was emerging. In practice, the analyst often has the luxury of ignoring this distinction, and indeed it generally is not considered his task to make such a judgment. However, it has been noted that analysts frequently develop views about the reality or truth value of what the patients tell them." M. Viederman, "The Reconstruction of Repressed Sexual Molestation Fifty Years Later," *J. Amer. Psycholanal. Assn.* 43:1169, 1995. Dr. Charles V. Ford, author of *Lies! Lies!! Lies!!!/The Psychology of Deceit* (Washington, D.C.: American Psychiatric Press, 1996), says, "Many patients who lie and lie during psychotherapy have severe disturbances in their sense of self. Vigorous confrontation leads only to narcissistic injury and subsequent rage and frequently the patient finds it necessary to leave therapy. It is necessary for the therapist to maintain neutrality. Any therapist who is confident that he or she can determine reality through some sixth sense or through intuition is, in my way of thinking, only self-deceptive." Communication to author. Dr. Ethel Person and Dr. Howard Klar say that "distinguishing repressed memories from fantasies is often difficult and sometimes impossible," but they hypothesize that "repressed memories and conscious fantasies can often be distinguished insofar as they may be 'stored' or encoded differently, and that subsequently the sequelae of trauma and fantasy often, but not always, can be disentangled." E.S. Person & H. Klar, "Establishing Trauma: the Difficulty Distinguishing Between Memories and Fantasies," *J. Amer. Psychoanal. Assn.* 42:1055, 1994.

32. M.G. Goldzband, "The Hottest Topic," *Psychiat. Annals* 25:477, Aug. 1995.

33. T. Reik, *The Unknown Murderer* (1930), reprinted as part one of *The Compulsion to Confess* (New York: Farrar, Straus & Cudahy, 1959).

34. T.G. Gutheil (ltr.), "Assessing Satanic Cult Abuse," *Psychiatric Times*, July 1992, p. 9.

35. C. Wassil-Grimm, *Diagnosis for Disaster/The Devastating Truth About False Memory Syndrome and Its Impact on Accusers and Families* (New York: Overlook Press, 1995).

36.  In his book *The Meaning of Mind* (Westport, CT.: Praeger, 1996), Dr. Thomas Szasz absolves the therapist and casts the responsibility on the patient. The use of narratives or metaphors that cause harm, however, is irresponsible. Dr. Harold Merskey of Canada puts it this way: "It has been all right to treat patients on the basis of dynamic notions of repression so long as the concept was only one which was exchanged between therapist and patient and merely served to revise, in a positive fashion, the patient's view of himself or herself in the world. Using repression as an idea which works to the detriment of other people, disrupts families, wipes out the life savings of parents, abolishes their contact with children and grandchildren, and embroils some in painful legal battles, is another matter altogether and not compatible with the old principle 'first do no harm.'" "Multiple Personality Disorder and False Memory Syndrome," *Brit. J. Psychiat.* 166:281, 1995.

37.  P.R. McHugh, "The Do's and Don't's for the Clinician Managing Memories of Abuse," address at conference "Memory and Reality: Reconciliation," Baltimore, Dec. 10, 1994; see also K.S. Pope, "Memory, Abuse, and Science," *Am. Psychologist* 51:957, 1996, adapted from K.S. Pope & L.S. Brown, *Recovered Memories of Abuse: Assessment, Therapy, Forensics* (Washington, D.C.: American Psychological Assn., 1996); "When a Patient 'Recovers' Memories of Abuse," *Clinical Psychiatric News*, Jan. 1995.

38.  K. Maurer, "APAs Sidestepped Recovery Memory Issue," *Clin. Psychiatry News*, April 1996, p. 14.

39.  See R. Slovenko, "The 'Revival of Memory' of Childhood Sexual Abuse: Is the Tolling of the Statute of Limitations Justified?" *J. Psychiatry & Law* 21:7, 1993. A list of law review articles on statutes of limitations in repressed memory cases appears in Farris v. Compton, 652 A.2d 49 (D.C. App. 1994), at p. 59 n. 14.

40.  The District of Columbia Court of Appeals in Farris v. Compton, 652 A.2d 49 (D.C. App. 1994) put it thus: "Suppose that the defendant threw acid in a plaintiff's face and blinded her. As a result of her blindness, which was caused by the defendant, the plaintiff has become disabled from making an identification, and no other evidence is available. Twenty-five years later, however, a new procedure restores the plaintiff's 20:20 eyesight. She identifies the defendant as her assailant from a photograph taken of the defendant on the day of the assault. To apply the statute of limitations against the plaintiff in such a case to defeat recovery would surely be intolerable, for to do so would permit the assailant to profit from his own wrong." 652 A.2d at 58-59.

41.  1991 Va. Acts ch. 674, Va. Code Ann. §8.01-249.

42.  P.A. Lombardo, "Turning Back the Clock on Sexual Abuse of Children: Amending Virginia's Statute of Limitations," *Developments in Mental Health Law/University of Virginia* 12:21, 1992.

43.  In *Frye*, the D.C. Circuit Court wrote, "Just when a scientific principle or discovery crosses the line between experimental and demonstrable stages is difficult to define. Somewhere in this twilight zone the evidential force of the

principle must be recognized, and while the courts will go a long way in admitting expert testimony deduced from a well recognized scientific principle or discovery, the thing from which the deduction is made must be sufficiently established to have general acceptance in the particular field in which it belongs." United States v. Frye, 293 Fed. 1013 (D.C. Cir. 1923).

44. 113 S. Ct. 2786 (1993).

45. Shahzade v. Gregory, 923 F. Supp. 286, 930 F. Supp. 673 (D. Mass. 1996) (acceptance of phenomenon of repressed memory). In a number of cases involving relatively undeveloped technical theories in the mechanical design and engineering field, the courts citing *Daubert* found the proferred testimony insufficiently reliable for admission. See A.J. McElaney, "Practical Aspects of Presenting and Excluding Expert Testimony," *ABA Brief* 26(2):40, 1997; see also T.L. Bohan & E.J. Heels, "The Case Against *Daubert*: The New Scientific Evidence 'Standard' and the Standards of the Several States," *J. For. Sci.* 40:1030, 1995; G.M. Fenner, "The Daubert Handbook: The Case, Its Essential Dilemma, and Its Progeny," *Creighton L. Rev.* 29:939, 1996; B.D. Sales, D.W. Shuman & M. O'Connor, "In a Dim Light: Admissibility of Child Sexual Abuse Memories," *Applied Cognitive Psychology* 8:399, 1994; Comment, "The Necessity of Memory Experts for the Defense in Prosecutions for Child Sexual Abuse Based Upon Repressed Memories," *Am. Crim. L. Rev.* 32:69, 1994.

46. Judge Gerald Rosen in Isley v. Capuchin Province, 877 F. Supp. 1055 (E.D. Mich. 1995), accepted the concept of repression but not the competency of therapist testimony on historical reality. Shortly after rendering the decision, Judge Rosen in a conference at the Wayne State University Law School said that trial judges are not in a position to carry out the mandate of the *Daubert* decision, and as a consequence more evidence would be found admissible than under the *Frye* test where the judge would defer to the scientific community.

The Ninth U.S. Court of Appeals has held that the *per se* rule that unstipulated polygraph evidence is inadmissible in civil or criminal trials is set aside in light of *Daubert*. The court reasoned that the rule is inconsistent with the flexible inquiry posed by *Daubert*. The court nonetheless made clear that "we are not expressing new enthusiasm for admission of unstipulated polygraph evidence," but stated it would leave the question of admissibility to the trial judge. United States v. Cordoba, 1997 WL 3317 (9th Cir. 1997).

47. Thus, the Michigan Supreme Court said: "Psychologists, when called as experts, do not talk about things or objects; they talk about people. They do not dehumanize people with whom they deal by treating them as objects composed of interacting biological systems. Rather, they speak of the whole person. Thus, it is difficult to fit the behavioral professions within the application and definition of *Frye*." People v. Beckley, 434 Mich. 691, 456 N.W.2d 391 (1990). *Contra*: Doe v. Maskell, 679 A.2d 1087 (Md. 1996).

In State v. Randle, 484 N.W.2d 220 (Iowa App. 1992), the Iowa Court of Appeals, over a dissent, admitted the results of a Minnesota Multiphasic

Personality Inventory test, taken a few days after the alleged offense, to show that the victim was experiencing little stress or anxiety at that time. In a dissent, Judge Allen Donielson said, "I find the MMPI test is no more reliable as an evidentiary tool than the polygraph test is....Psychologists should be encouraged to use the MMPI test as a clinical tool for the diagnosis and treatment of the alleged victim, and prosecutors should be encouraged to use this test as an investigatory tool in determining the veracity of the complaining witness's account. Until the test's reliability is more clearly established, however, it should not be used to generate evidence for introduction at trial." 484 N.W.2d at 223.

See R.S. Hanson, "James Alphonzo Frye Is 65 Years Old: Should He Retire?," *West. St. U. L. Rev.* 16:357, 1989; D. Lynch, "Post-Daubert Admissibility of repressed Memories," *Champion* 20(9):14, Nov. 1996; R.N. Jonakait, "Real Science and Forensic Science," *Shepard's Expert & Sci. Evid. Q.* 1:435, 1994; Note, *Loyola of L.A. L. Rev.* 30:1379, 1997.

48. Rule 702, Federal Rules of Evidence.
49. In United States v. Starzecpyzel, 880 F. Supp. 1027 (S.D. N.Y. 1995), the district court was asked to pass on the admissibility of testimony by questioned-document examiners. The court concluded that questioned-document testimony is not scientific knowledge under *Daubert* because there is a lack of systematic empirical validation for many of the assumptions in questioned-document examination.

In Compton v. Subaru of America , 82 F.3d 1513 (10th Cir. 1996), the Tenth Circuit stated, "[A]pplication of the *Daubert* factors is unwarranted in cases where expert testimony is based solely upon experience or training." The court went on to quote the *Daubert* ruling by saying that "in such cases, Rule 702 merely requires the trial court to make a preliminary finding that proffered expert testimony is both relevant and reliable while taking into account '[t]he inquiry envisioned by Rule 702 is...a flexible one.' Subsequent to *Daubert*, we have continued to apply essentially the same Rule 702 analysis except in cases involving unique, untested, or controversial methodologies or techniques." 82 F.3d at 1519. See E.J. Imwinkelried, "Admissibility of Nonscientific Expert Testimony," *Trial*, Oct. 1996, p. 58.

50. See, *e.g.*, A.A. Stone, "Where Will Psychoanalysis Survive," *Harvard Magazine*, Jan.-Feb. 1997, p. 35.
51. In a two-part series, "The Revenge of the Repressed," in *The New York Review of Books*, Nov. 17, 1994, p. 54; Dec. 1, 1994, p. 49, Professor Frederick Crews reviewed a number of recently published books about "repressed memory," and he wrote, "Throughout the past decade or so, a shock wave has been sweeping across North American psychotherapy, and in the process causing major repercussions within our families, courts, and hospitals. A single diagnosis for miscellaneous complaints–that of unconsciously repressed sexual abuse in childhood–has grown in this brief span from virtual nonexistence to epidemic frequency." The two-part series has been published as a book by the *New York Review of Books*.

Of the recent books about "repressed memory," investigative journalist Mark Pendergrast's *Victims of Memory* (Hinesburg, Vt.: Upper Access, 1995) is the most comprehensive as well as the most emotionally committed, a gripping account of a national tragedy. Devastated by the sudden alienation from his two adult daughters, and determined to understand the social phenomenon behind it, he spent over two years researching and writing his book.

52.   R. Rorty, "Sigmund on the Couch," *New York Times Book Review*, Sept. 22, 1996, p. 42.

53.   Franklin v. Duncan, 1995 U.S. Dist. LEXIS 4955; T. Lewin, "Judge Upsets Conviction in 'Repressed Memory' Case," *New York Times*, April 5, 1995, p. 14. See L. Wright, *Remembering Satan/A Tragic Case of Recovered Memory* (New York: Random House, 1994).

54.   "Retrial Dropped in First Repressed Memory Case," *Clinical Psychiatry News*, Sept. 1996, p. 5.

55.   McCollum v. D'Arcy, 138 N.H. 285, 638 A.2d 797 (1994). A superior court in New Hampshire later in 1994 excluded "revival of memory" as not meeting the test of scientific reliability. The court said, "Before any evidence flowing from the phenomenon of memory repression can be admitted, the validity of the phenomenon must be validated." State v. Hungerford, 1995 WL 378571 (N.H. Sup. Ct., May 23, 1995); discussed in C. Gorman, "Memory on Trial," *Time*, April 17, 1995, p. 54. In a subsequent proceeding in the case, after hearing more than a week of testimony from the accusers of the two men and several experts in psychology and psychiatry, Hillsborough Superior Court Judge William J. Groff ruled that testimony derived from repressed memories cannot be used because experts disagree on whether such recollections are scientifically reliable. He wrote, "The phenomenon of memory repression and the process of therapy used in these cases to recover the memories have not gained general acceptance in the field of psychology and are not scientifically reliable." "Judge in New Hampshire Bars Repressed-Memory Prosecutions," *New York Times*, May 26, 1995, p. 12. The N.H. Supreme Court affirmed in 697 A.2d 916 (N.H. 1997).

56.   638 A.2d at 800.

57.   California legislation provides that a plaintiff 26 years of age or older at the time an action is filed for damages suffered as a result of childhood sexual abuse must append a certificate of merit that the attorney has reviewed the facts of the case and that the attorney has consulted with at least one mental health practitioner who is not a party to the litigation. Cal. Code Civ. Proc. § 340.1 (1995).

58.   Lemmerman v. Fealk, 534 N.W.2d 695 (Mich. 1995).

59.   See R. Gardner, *Sex Abuse Hysteria: Salem Witch Trials Revisited* (Cresskill, N.J.: Creative Therapeutics, 1991); M.D. Yapko, *Suggestions of Abuse* (New York: Simon & Schuster, 1994); C. Gorman, "Memory on Trial," *Time*, April 17, 1995, p. 54;   see also J.W. Schutte, "Repressed Memory Lawsuits: Potential Verdict Predictors," *Behavioral Sciences & Law* 12:409, 1994.

# CONCLUSION

There being a compelling state interest in maintaining the privacy and confidentiality of the psychiatric relationship, the law provides protection under the doctrines of privacy, the contractual duty (express or implied) to maintain confidentiality, and testimonial privilege. The protection given is distinguished by the areas covered by each of these formulas.[1] To be sure, there are times when the court eschews formulas and declares simply "what justice requires."[2]

The right of privacy takes several forms, one of which is "the right to have one's private facts kept private."[3] The breach of the right of privacy gives rise to an action in tort. It also gives rise to an action for breach of contract, given the implied covenant not to disclose. As one court observed, "Almost every member of the public is aware of the promise of discretion contained in the Hippocratic oath and every patient has a right to rely upon this warranty of silence. The promise of secrecy is as much an expressed warranty as the advertisement of the commercial entrepreneur."[4]

The invasion-of-privacy tort action or the breach-of-contract action provide protection against inexcusable or promiscuous disclosures of confidential information that occur outside the testimonial arena. In the usual case, the patient authorizes the physician or psychiatrist to make the necessary disclosure in order to obtain payment for treatment and related services. When signing a waiver and giving consent, however, the patient rarely reads the form. There are usually no limitations in the form on the extent of information to be revealed, the time during which such information can be distributed, or the sharing of such information between various agencies. Such blank releases, however, do not protect doctors who exceed the bounds of propriety.[5]

The testimonial privilege is designed to protect privacy or confidentiality in the judicial arena or other investigation at law. The privilege sets out the scope of privacy when testimony or records are sought in that arena. The limitations of privilege law would be rendered meaningless if the "right of privacy" were allowed to stand broadly as a shield against judicial investigation. Yet this is precisely what the Pennsylvania Supreme Court did in *In re B.*[6] In a 4-3 opinion, it reversed a lower court decision holding a psychiatrist, Dr. Loren Roth, in contempt for failure to disclose a patient's records when requested by the court to help determine placement of the patient's juvenile son. The majority opinion held that although the state's doctor-patient privilege statute does not prohibit disclosure in this case, the right of privacy guaranteed by the constitution does.[7] The court said:[8]

> There can be no question that American jurisprudence recognizes the right of privacy; the only question being its limits....We conclude that in Pennsylvania, an individual's interest in preventing the disclosure of information revealed in the context of a psychotherapist-patient relationship has deeper roots than the Pennsylvania doctor-patient privilege statute, and that the patient's right to prevent disclosure of such information is constitutionally based.

In general, the word "privilege" connotes inequality and unfairness, or special comforts, but a "privilege" to maintain confidentiality in the law of evidence has a different meaning. It stems from our aversion of forcing a person to testify against himself. A confidential communication privilege, fundamentally, represents a civilized standard of behavior. To reveal a confidence in or out of the courtroom is not the way of a person who acts decently. It is betrayal. Children and adults alike cherish their secrets and their confidences.

An individual who consults a professional person expects a high standard of conduct. Good professionalism is ethical professionalism. At some level of consciousness, confidentiality is expected. In some cases, privilege, like insurance, is not considered until the need for it arises; then, we are reminded of its importance. In other cases, a person may come to the therapeutic situation expressing the fear that unauthorized persons may learn of his disclosure. Whether or not the patient is paranoid, fear of disclosure may be reduced by assurance that information will not be passed on. The therapist must make good on this assertion. The maintenance of confidentiality, however, is a matter of considerable delicacy in view of the prevailing law on privilege. Ultimately, the therapist's promise of confidentiality must rest on reality. Is the therapist willing to maintain secrecy at the risk of a contempt citation? Can the patient really be assured of such confidentiality? Can the patient trust the therapist?

Georgia, in 1959, and Connecticut, in 1961, were the first states to enact statutes specifically providing privileged communication for the psychotherapist-patient relationship. Following its abandonment of an earlier recommendation, the Group for the Advancement of Psychiatry recommended the Connecticut statute as a model for all states. Unlike the initial GAP proposal and the Georgia statute, the Connecticut statute was detailed in its provisions. Like later statutes, it was attenuated by exceptions and by narrow interpretation by the courts.

Without full and fair acceptance by the courts, statutes come to naught. The example that psychiatrists themselves show in maintaining the privacy of the patient would best convince the courts, and the general public, of the importance of confidentiality in psychotherapy.

The criticisms directed against the traditional medical privilege are inapposite to the psychotherapist-patient relationship. It is true that mind and body are related, as psychosomatic illnesses so clearly point out, and all physicians to some extent or other may employ psychotherapy but, nevertheless, it is essential in the law of evidence to discriminate between the types of practice and their peculiar requirements. A privilege for those receiving psychotherapy is necessary if psychiatry and allied professions are to fulfill their responsibility to their patients.

If the law of a state recognizes that psychiatrists and other psychotherapists perform a useful function by legalizing their practice, it would appear that the law would recognize the confidentiality or trust which is essential to their practice. Without the legal sanctity of a privilege, treatment may be effectively fettered by the fear of the patient that what is said in therapy may be compelled in the courtroom. Weighing the conflicting values, the benefit of preserving the confidence inviolate seemingly outbalances the possible benefit of permitting litigation to prosper, significant as is that consideration.

Privileges bar the admission of evidence which may thwart the ascertainment of truth in any given litigation, but this is not too great a price to pay for the value of secrecy in certain human relationships. Every testimonial privilege inevitably results in the suppression of material and relevant evidence, but the public policy behind some privileges outweighs the public policy behind the unfettered search for the truth. The problem in the law is where to draw the line separating the privileged from the unprivileged. Wigmore's four conditions warranting a privilege would appear to be satisfied in the practice of psychotherapy.

Should there be exceptions to confidentiality? When should the privilege be terminated or waived? Does the choice lie between a privilege of complete secrecy on the one hand, and on the other hand, compulsory disclosure without restriction? Judge Edgerton suggested that "a communication made in reasonable confidence that it will not be disclosed, and in such circumstances that disclosure is shocking to the moral sense of the community, should not be disclosed in a judicial proceeding, whether the trusted person is or is not a wife, husband, doctor, lawyer, or minister." This approach apparently prevailed centuries ago, but is unlikely to be followed today, although the law does preclude wiretapping of private conversations, irrespective of the relationship of the parties.

The medical privilege originated at a time when contagious or infectious diseases were prevalent. Today, mental illness–especially schizophrenia–is the "loathsome disease." Of course, schizophrenia or psychosis–unlike a venereal disease–is readily apparent to one and all. In any event, surveys indicate that a person seeing a psychiatrist is looked upon with distrust or suspicion. The public generally feels or acts differently toward a psychiatric patient. This is reflected in the law of defamation where it is provided that a statement that a person is mentally ill is an "imputation of want of ability to discharge the duties" of that person's business, profession, vocation, trade, or calling, and thus slander on its face.[10]

There is still considerable stigma in receiving mental health services. According to a GAP report, one prominent psychiatrist in Washington, D.C., has never been able to maintain, in his long experience, a member of Congress in psychotherapy for more than a few months.[11] The very-important-person fears that disclosure of his treatment would jeopardize his status and position. A notable example is the disclosure of Senator Thomas Eagleton's history as a mental patient and the type of treatment he received (electroshock) which resulted in his being dropped as the Democratic vice-presidential candidate.

The fate of the psychotherapist-patient privilege illustrates the old adage that history repeats itself. The psychotherapist-patient privilege, like the medical privilege before it, offers a shield that looks more like a sieve. Like the medical privilege, virtually nothing that is relevant about a patient in litigation is shielded by the shield.

Given the exceptions, the privilege provides more atmosphere than substance, though atmosphere has its purpose. Various publications such as *Psychiatric News* of the American Psychiatric Association and *Clinical Psychiatry News* as well as the *New York Times* heralded the U.S. Supreme Court decision in 1996 in *Jaffee v. Redmond* as upholding privilege, but without mentioning the exceptions to the privilege, it reinforced the mistaken belief about the privilege as a shield. As is often the case, what appears as gold is actually an alloy, but for those unaware of the exclusions, the belief in privilege has a placebo effect. Belief in God has effect whether or not God exists.

In any event, more often than not, the doctrine of relevancy provides protection against intrusion into confidential communications made in the course of psychotherapy. Moreover, even though proffered evidence may be relevant, several other factors may move the court to exclude it: first, the danger that the facts offered may unduly arouse in the jury emotions of prejudice, hostility, or sympathy; second, the probability that the proof and the answering evidence that it provokes may create a side-issue that will unduly distract the jury from the main issues; and third, the likelihood that the evidence offered and the counterproof will consume an undue amount of time. Also, when evidence is burdensome or cumbersome to obtain, and alternate sources of the information exist, then production is usually not ordered. In other words, confidentiality will be undermined only when the evidence is relevant, material, or necessary to make out a defense. Put negatively, if the information is irrelevant or immaterial or unnecessary, then disclosure cannot or ought not to be mandated.[12]

The available evidence indicates that patients, by and large, are not concerned about the divulgence of that type of information needed to justify a bill to a third-party payer, to review the competency of the therapist, or to provide material for follow-up and research. The public is primarily concerned about the delivery and quality of health care (psychiatric or medical), and only secondarily concerned about privacy.[13]

The brief on behalf of the Chicago Lakeshore Hospital when it was being investigated opens with a quotation of a passage of mine written years ago that a person sees a psychiatrist, by and large, with the same secrecy that a man goes to a bawdy house.[14] Though with less intensity, there are still strong feelings of shame even though just about every middle or upper class American family has had some contact with a psychotherapist. One must wonder, if everyone is in the same boat, why the shame or need for concealment?

The testimonial medical or psychotherapy privilege may offer a sense of security but it serves essentially only as a placebo. When push comes to shove, the privilege has served the patient in litigation little, if at all, in shielding the contents of communications. Judicial interpretations or legislatively adopted exceptions to the privilege have shrunk the occasion of its application to the vanishing point. It is the other concepts in the law (relevancy or prejudice) that substantially protected confidentiality. In application, the privilege tends to accomplish little more than obstruct accountability of the professional, something not intended by proponents of the privilege.

All things considered, no firm principle on confidentiality can be offered. The general principle is confidentiality, but inevitably there will be exceptions which must be handled case-by-case. Here, as in everything else, the law is faced with a conflict of interests, and has to decide where to draw the dividing line. Benefits and risks in every instance must be balanced. To borrow an old saying, it must depend upon the circumstances of each case.

Actually, it is trust—not absolute confidentiality—that is the cornerstone of psychotherapy. Talking about a patient or writing about him without his knowledge or consent would be a breach of trust. But imposing control where self-control breaks down, as in the case of a patient posing a danger, is not a breach of trust when it is not deceptive. And it is not necessary to be deceptive. Indeed, it requires a stretch of the imagination to posit a case where it would be necessary to exercise control without first discussing it with the patient. As a last resort, the therapist typically says something like, "You are afraid of losing control, I'm going to prevent you from doing it."

The patient is told, or ought to be told, that there will be a disclosure, what kind of disclosure, and to whom.[15]

Psychotherapists who proclaim a need for confidentiality can best achieve it by acting accordingly. They might borrow a leaf from the priest-penitent relationship or from pastoral counseling. The number of cases where clerics have been sued for breach of confidentiality is incredibly small.[16] By and large, clerics do not reveal confidences (except when sued or prosecuted for sexual abuse). They do not discuss members of their congregation with journalists or authors. They do not sue to collect a fee. They insist on confidentiality even when their supplicants ask them to disclose. Rev. Percy Rex of Delaware, for example, stood firm against making a disclosure notwithstanding the wishes of his supplicant.

Almost singularly, Dr. Joseph Lifschutz of California took the same position as Rev. Rex. He argued a right of privacy separate from that of any individual patient, a right derived from what he saw as a duty not to a particular patient alone but to all patients; that, he urged, takes precedence over any waiver of privilege. Sooner or later, with a reputation that psychotherapists stand firm on confidentiality, society will likely back them up and lawyers will hesitate to make a demand on them for information, just as they do not as a rule make a demand on a cleric.

Even in states without a priest-penitent privilege, a demand on a cleric to disclose a communication is rare indeed. As a trial tactic, it would boomerang. Until the psychotherapist-patient relationship is regarded in the same light as that of the priest-penitent relationship, demands will be made on the therapist for disclosure and exceptions to privilege will be made.

The prescription of the venerable Greek physician Hippocrates in his oath of ethics remains the physician's best guide even for the space age.

## NOTES

1. Note, "Action for Breach of Medical Secrecy Outside the Courtroom," *U. Cin. L. Rev.* 36:103, 1967.

2. See People v. Smith, 275 N.W.2d 466 at 472 (Mich. 1979). In this spirit, Alexander Solzhenitsyn said in his address on June 8, 1979, at Harvard University: "I have spent all my life under a communist regime and I will tell you that a society without any objective scale is a terrible one indeed. But a society with no other scale but the legal one is also less than worthy of man. A society based on the letter of the law and never reaching any higher fails to take advantage of the full range of human possibilities. The letter of the law is too cold and formal to have a beneficial influence on society. Whenever the issue of life is woven of legalistic relationships, this cre-

ates an atmosphere of spiritual mediocrity that paralyzes man's noblest impulses."

3. The seminal article is S.D. Warren & L.D. Brandeis, "The Right to Privacy," *Harv. L. Rev.* 4:195, 1890. It is doubtful if any other law review article, before or since, has achieved greater fame. Perhaps the most striking thing about the right to privacy is that nobody seems to have any clear idea what it is or its scope. For contrasting views, see E. Alderman & C. Kennedy, *The Right to Privacy* (New York: Knopf, 1995); R.H. Bork, *The Tempting of America* (New York: Free Pres, 1990); E.J. Bloustein, "Privacy as an Aspect of Human Dignity; An Answer to Dean Prosser," *N.Y.U.L. Rev.* 39:962, 1964; F. Davis, "What Do We Mean by 'Right to Privacy'?", *S. Dak. L. Rev.* 4:1, 1959; W. Prosser, "Privacy," *Calif. L. Rev.* 48:383, 1960; Symposium, "The Right to Privacy," *Philosophy & Public Affairs* 4:295, 1975.

4. Hammond v. Aetna Casualty Surety Co., 243 F. Supp. 793 at 801 (N.D. Ohio 1965).

5. See R. Shlensky, "Informed Consent and Confidentiality: Proposed New Approaches in Illinois," *Am. J. Psychiat.* 134:1416, 1977.

6. 394 A.2d 419 (Pa. 1978). See also Falcon v. Alaska Public Offices Commission, 570 P.2d 469 (Alaska 1977).

7. Dr. Roth's counsel inserted the privacy argument as an afterthought in a footnote (appellant's brief, footnote 9), and lo and behold, the court protected confidentiality on that ground. The case was talked about as the "footnote 9" decision.

8. 394 A.2d at 425. In a concurring opinion, one Justice noted that alternative means of obtaining the needed information did exist, such as the mother's demonstrated willingness to submit to psychiatric examination by the family court psychiatrist. The relevant and probative material required by the court was available from legislatively unprotected sources. The case could have been decided on that ground. 394 A.2d at 427.

9. Dictum by Judge Edgerton in Mullen v. United States, 263 F.2d 275, 281 (D.C. 1958).

10. L. H. Eldredge, *The Law of Defamation* (Indianapolis: Bobbs-Merrill, 1978), p. 149. The statement that one is "recovering from mental illness" was held defamatory in Cooper v. Vannier, 20 Ill. App.2d 499, 156 N.E.2d 761 (1959).

11. Group for the Advancement of Psychiatry, *The VIP with Psychiatric Impairment* (Washington, D.C.: American Psychiatric Assn., 1973).

12. What is more, the lawyer is not likely to put a witness on the stand not knowing what he is going to say. By and large, psychiatrists would assert that lying is justified to protect a confidence. They would say that their oath and honor mandate it.

13. Professor David Mechanic, director of the Center for Medical Sociology and Health Services Research at the University of Wisconsin, said: "The goals of accountability and confidentiality conflict to some degree... Such conflict in valuable goals is no unique situation, and in my view the goals of confidentiality and accountability are not incompatible...[The extent to which people

are concerned about privacy] is an empirical question. Certainly those who care less about privacy would readily give release to auditors to review the medical care they have received. Moreover, privacy and confidentiality do not imply necessarily that auditors cannot have access to privileged information for the performance of specified functions such as research or review of the quality of medical care. I realize the latter is a highly debated point at this time, but it seems to me that this is more a reflection of the politics of the situation than of what is possible. We do fairly large-scale epidemiological surveys here which require access to people's medical and psychiatric records, and we find that most people are willing to grant us such release when we provide a reasonable explanation for what we wish to do. It strikes me as quite likely that patients who are concerned about the quality of care they receive would be equally willing to give auditors the right to evaluate the care they receive through review of their medical records." Personal communication.

14. R. Slovenko, "Psychiatry and a Second Look at the Medical Privilege," *Wayne L. Rev.* 6:175 at n. 46, 1960.

15. Dr. John R. Lion states the proposition that "violent patients are frightened of their own hostile urges and desperately seek help in preventing a loss of control." He writes:

> [V]iolent patients are very much afraid of their own impulses. The homicidal patient . . . wants control furnished so that he will not kill. Therefore, . . . the psychiatrist should assure him that he will not be allowed to act upon his feelings. . . . [The psychiatrist] elicits the emotions and some of the accompanying fantasy, but firmly conveys to the patient that he will be prevented from any violent act. The latter statement is usually most reassuring to the violent patient.

J. Lion, *Evaluation and Management of the Violent Patient* (Springfield, Ill: Thomas, 1972), p. 5. See also L. Salzman, "Truth, Honesty, and the Therapeutic Process," *Am. J. Psychiat.* 130:1280, 1973.

16. Could it be that cleric confidentiality is changing? Sheridan Anne Edwards filed a civil suit against her Episcopal priest charging that he violated the secrecy of her confession that as treasurer she had embezzled church funds. The priest maintained that she had not made the divulgence during a formal confession. K. Bishop, "Suit Accuses Priest of Disclosing Theft Confession," *New York Times*, Aug. 8, 1985, p. 12. Because the criminal case against Edwards ended in conviction, the civil case did not proceed. Personal communication from attorney Patrick R. McMahon (Dec. 19, 1995).

The issue of clergy confidentiality is at the center of a lawsuit in Royal Oak, Michigan, filed by David Smith against his pastor, Mark Byers of Calvary Christian Church, for revealing to the congregation his confession about his sexual past. Byers admits to revealing the information to dozens of parishioners but he says it was part of an agreement he and Smith had made regarding Smith's conditional reinstatement in the church. According to Byers, Smith agreed in 1991 to confess his past behavior to his wife and the entire congregation as part of his repentance. Smith did tell his wife and appeared to be making progress, Byers says, so they agreed Smith did not need to tell the congregation, but as time passed, Smith began to act out, says Byers, who has accused Smith of disrupting church services, slapping and punching parishioners and visitors, making threats and attempting to divide the congregation. "The agreement was to expose him if he became unruly and divisive again," Byers says. Upon being sued, Byers said on television that Smith was possessed by the devil. J. Chambers, "Ex-member sues pastor over revelation," *Oakland Press*, Feb. 12, 1997, p. 1.

# APPENDIX

Statutes on Medical and Psychotherapy Privilege

Oral Argument in U.S. Supreme Court in *Jaffee v. Redmond*

U.S. Supreme Court Decision in *Jaffee v. Redmond*

# STATUTES ON MEDICAL AND
# PSYCHOTHERAPY PRIVILEGE

*Alabama*
Ala. Code §08.86.200 (psychologist and psychological associates); §08.95.900 (clinical social workers); §§09.25.230 & 12.45.049 (Supp 1992) (domestic violence and sexual assault victim counselors); Alaska R. Evid. 504 (physicians and psychotherapists).

*Arizona*
Ariz. Rev. Stat. Ann §12-2235 (physicians); §32-2085 (psychologists); Ariz. R. Evid. 501.

*Arkansas*
Ark. Code Ann. §16-41-101 (Rule 503) (physicians, psychotherapists & chiropractors); §17-24-308 (1992) (counselors); §17-39-107 (social workers).

*California*
Cal. Evid. Code §§990-1007 (physicians); §§1010-1027 (psychotherapists, clinical social workers, and school psychologists); §§1035-1036.2 (sexual assault victim counselors); §§1037-1037.7 (domestic violence victim counselors).

*Colorado*
Colo. Rev. Stat. §13-90-107(d) & (g) (physicians, surgeons, psychiatrists, psychologists and their employees, registered nurses and group therapy participants).

*Connecticut*
Conn. Gen. Stat. Ann. §52-146c (psychologists); §§52-146d to -146g (psychiatrists); §52-146k (battered women's and sexual assault counselors); §52-146o (physicians, surgeons, or health care providers).

*Delaware*
Del. R. Evid. 503 (physicians and psychotherapists).

*District of Columbia*
D.C. Code Ann. §14-307 (physicians, surgeons, and mental health professionals, including psychologists, social workers, marriage and family counselors, and psychiatric nurses).

### Florida
Fla. Stat. Ann §90.503 (psychotherapists); §90.5035 (sexual assault counselors).

### Georgia
Ga. Code. Ann. §24-9-21(5) (psychiatrists and psychologists); §§24-9-40 to -45 (physicians); §26-5-17 (drug abuse clinics); §43-39-16 (psychologists); §24-9-29 (veterinarians).

### Hawaii
Haw. R. Evid. 504 (physicians); 504.1 (psychologists).

### Idaho
Idaho Code §9-203.4 (physicians or surgeons); §9-203.6 (counselors, psychologists, or psychological examiners); §54-2314 (psychologists); §54-3213 (social workers); §54-3410 (counselors); Idaho R. Evid. 503 (physicians and psychotherapists); 516 (school counselors); 517 (counselors); 518 (social workers).

### Illinois
Ill. Ann. Stat. ch 91fi ¶¶802-810 (psychiatrists, physicians, psychologists, social workers, or nurses); ch. 110, ¶8-802.1 (rape crisis counselors and personnel); ch. 110, ¶8-802.2 (violent crime victim counselors and personnel); ch. 111, ¶5355 (psychologists); ch 111, ¶6366 (social workers).

### Indiana
Ind. Code Ann. §34-1-14-5 (physicians and chiropractors); id. §34-4-12.4-1 to 34-4-12.4-4 (mental health service providers); §25-33-1-17 (psychologists); §25-23.6-6-1 (social workers); §25-23.6-9-1 (marriage and family therapists); §25-26-13-15 (pharmacists); §20-6.1-6-15 (school counselors); §35-37-6 (victim counselors).

### Iowa
Iowa Code Ann. §622.10 (physicians, surgeons, physician's assistants, mental health professionals, dentists, all personnel, psychologists, psychotherapists, and school guidance counselors).

### Kansas
Kan. Stat. Ann §60-427 (physicians and other practitioners of the "healing arts"); §74-5323 (psychologists); §65-5601 (treatment facility personnel); §65-1525 (optometrists); §65-5810 (counselors); §65-6410 (marriage & family therapists).

### Kentucky
Ky. R. Evid. 506 (school counselors, clinical social workers, sexual assault counselors, drug abuse counselors, and alcohol abuse counselors); 507 (psychotherapists).

### Louisiana
La. Code. Evid. Ann. Art. 510 (health care providers, including physicians, psychotherapists, and their representatives).

### Maine
Me. R. Evid. 503 (physicians and psychotherapists); Me. Rev. Stat. Ann. tit. 22, §4015 (physicians and psychotherapists); tit. 20-A, §4008 (school counselors and school social workers); tit. 32, §7005 (social workers); tit 32, §1092-A (dentists); tit. 16, §53-A (sexual assault counselors); tit. 32, §13862 (counseling professionals).

### Maryland
Md. Code Ann. Cts. & Jud. Proc. §9-109 (psychiatrists and psychologists); §9-109.1 (psychiatric-mental health nursing specialists); §9-121 (social workers).

### Massachusetts
Mass. Gen. Laws Ann ch 233, §20B (psychotherapists); ch. 233, §20J (sexual assault counselors); ch. 233, §20K (domestic violence counselors); ch. 112, §§135, 135A, & 135B (social workers); ch. 112, §129A (psychologists); ch. 112, §172 (mental health and human services professionals).

### Michigan
Mich. Mental Health Code MCL 330.1750; MCLA §600.2157 (physicians, surgeons, psychiatrists, and psychologists); id. §333.18237 (psychologists); §333.16648 (dentists); §333.18117 (licensed professional counselors); §339.1507 (marriage counselors); §339.1610 (social workers).

### Minnesota
Minn. Stat. Ann. §595.02 (physicians, surgeons, dentists, chiropractors, psychologists, registered nurses, chemical dependency counselors, and sexual assault counselors).

### Mississippi
Miss. Code Ann. § 13-1-21 (physicians, surgeons, osteopaths, dentists, hospitals, nurses, pharmacists, podiatrists, optometrists, and chiropractors); § 73-31-29 (psychologists); § 73-30-17 (licensed professional counselors).

### Missouri
Mo. Ann. Stat. §491.060(5) (physicians, dentists, and psychologists); §337.055 (psychologists); §337.540 (counselors); §337.636 (social workers).

### Montana
Mont. Code Ann. §26-1-805 (1991) (physicians, surgeons and dentists); §26-1-806 (speech pathologists and audiologists); §26-1-807 (psychologists); §26-1-809 (school counselors, psychologists, nurses, and teachers); § 37-23-301 (counselors).

### Nebraska
Neb. Rev. Stat. §27-504 (physicians and psychologists).

### Nevada
Nev. Rev. Stat. §§49.215-.245 (physicians, dentists, osteopaths, psychologists and psychiatric social workers); §§49.426-.249 (marriage and family therapists); §49.290 (school counselors and psychologists); §49.291 (teachers); §§49.251-254 (social workers).

### New Hampshire
N.H. Rev. Stat. Ann. §396.26 (physicians and surgeons); §330-A (psychologists).

### New Jersey
N.J. Stat. Ann. §§2A:84A-22.1 to 22.7 (physicians); §§2A:84A-22.13-16 (victim counselors); §45:8B-29 (marriage counselors); §45:14B-28 (psychologists and group therapy participants); §45:15BB-13 (social workers).

### New Mexico
N.M.R. Evid. 11-504 (psychotherapists); 11-509 (probation officers and social service workers in juvenile proceedings); N.M. Stat. Ann. §61-31-24 (social workers).

### New York
N.Y. Civ. Prac. L&R §4504 (physicians, dentists, podiatrists, chiropractors and nurses); §4507 (psychologists); §4508 (social workers).

### North Carolina
N.C. Gen. Stat. §8-53 (physicians); §8-53.3 (psychologists); §8-53.4 (school counselors); §8-53.5 (marital and family therapists); §8-53.7 (social workers); §8-53.8 (counselors).

### North Dakota
N.D. R. Evid. 503 (physicians and psychotherapists); N.D. Cent. Code §31-01-06.1 (school counselors); §§31-01-06.3 to -.06.6 (addiction counselors).

### Ohio
Ohio Rev. Code Ann. §2317.02(B) (physicians, osteopaths, dentists and podiatrists); §2317.02(G) (school guidance counselors, counselor assistants, social workers, and social work assistants); §4732.19 (psychologists).

### Oklahoma
Okla. Stat. Ann. tit. 12, §2503 (physicians, including naturopathic and chiropractic physicians, and psychotherapists); tit. 59, §1261.6 (social workers); tit. 59, §1910 (counselors); tit. 59, §1272.1 (social workers)); tit. 59, § 1925.11 (marriage and family therapists).

### Oregon
Or. Rev. Stat. Ann. §40.230 (psychotherapists); §40.235 (physicians, licensed or certified naturopaths, and chiropractors); §40.240 (1988) (nurses); §40.245 (school employees and counselors); §40.250 (1988 & Supp 1992) (clinical social workers); §40.262 (Supp. 1992) (counselors).

### Pennsylvania
42 Pa. Cons. Stat. Ann. §5929 (physicians); §5944 (psychologists); §5945 (school personnel); §5945.1 (sexual assault counselors).

### Rhode Island
R.I. Gen. Laws §§5-37.3-3 to-4 (physicians, hospitals, intermediate care facilities or other health care facilities, dentists, nurses, optometrists, podiatrists, physical therapists, psychiatric social workers, psychologists, any person licensed to provide health care services, and officers, employees or agents of such providers).

### South Carolina
S.C. Code Ann. §19-11-95 (psychologists, counselors, marital and family therapists, social workers, and registered nurses working in the mental health field).

### South Dakota
S.D. Codified Laws Ann §§19-13-6 to -11 (Rule 503(a) (physicians and psychotherapists); §§19-13-21.1 to -21.2 (1987) (school counselors); §36-26-30 (social workers) (1986); §36-32-27 (counselors).

### Tennessee
Tenn. Code Ann. §24-1-207 (Supp. 1992) (psychiatrists); id. §63-11-213 (psychologists); §63-22-114 (professional counselors and marriage and family therapists); §63-23-107 (1990) (social workers).

### Texas
Tex. R. Civ. Evid. 509 (physicians); 510 (mental health professionals).

### Utah
Utah Code Ann §78-24-8(4) (1992) (physicians and surgeons); §78-24-8(6) (1992 & Supp 1992) (sexual assault counselors); §§78-3c-1 to -4 (sexual assault counselors); §58-25a-8 (1990) (psychologists); id. §58-41-16 (speech-language pathologists and audiologists); §58-35-12 (social workers); §58-39-10 (1990) (marriage and family therapists).

### Vermont
Vt. Stat. Ann. tit. 12, §1612 (physicians, chiropractors, dentists, nurses and mental health professionals); Vt. R. Evid. 503 (mental health professionals, including physicians, dentists, nurses, psychologists and social workers).

### Virginia
Va. Code Ann. §8.01-399 (physicians); §8.01-400.2 (counselors, psychologists, and social workers).

### Washington
Wash. Rev. Code Ann. §5.60.060(4) (physicians, surgeons, and osteopaths); §5.62.010 (registered nurses); §18.83.110 (1993) (psychologists); §18.53.200 (1989) (optometrists).

### West Virginia
W. Va. Code §27-3-1 (1992) (information obtained in the course of treatment or evaluation of patients at mental health facilities); §30-30-12 (1986) (social workers); §30-31-13 (professional counselors).

### Wisconsin
Wis. Stat. Ann. §905.04 (physicians, registered nurses, chiropractors, psychologists, social workers, marriage and family therapists and professional counselors).

### Wyoming
Wyo. Stat. §1-12-101(a)(I) (physicians); §1-12-116 (1988) (family violence or sexual assault advocates); §33-27-103 (psychologists and their secretaries, stenographers, or clerks); §33-38-109 (professional counselors, marriage and family therapists, social workers, and chemical dependency specialists).

# ORAL ARGUMENT
# IN *JAFFEE v. REDMOND*
# BEFORE THE UNITED STATES
# SUPREME COURT

## IN THE SUPREME COURT OF THE UNITED STATES

Carrie Jaffee, Special Administrator for Ricky Allen, Sr.,
Deceased Petitioner,
v.
Marylu Redmond, et al.
No. 95-266
Monday, February 26, 1996
Washington, D.C.

The above-entitled matter came on for oral argument before the Supreme Court of the United States at 10:02 a.m.

APPEARANCES:

KENNETH N. FLAXMAN ESQ., Chicago, Ill.; on behalf of the Petitioner.

GREGORY E. ROGUS, ESQ., Chicago, Ill.; on behalf of the Respondents.

JAMES A. FELDMAN, ESQ., Assistant to the Solicitor General, Department of Justice, Washington, D.C.; on behalf of the United States, as amicus curiae, supporting the Respondents.

## PROCEEDINGS

Chief Justice William H. Rehnquist: We'll hear argument first this morning in No. 95-266, *Carrie Jaffee v. Marylu Redmond.* Mr. Flaxman.

### ORAL ARGUMENT OF KENNETH N. FLAXMAN ON
### BEHALF OF THE PETITIONER

*MR. FLAXMAN*: Mr. Chief Justice, and may it please the court:

In Rule 501 of the Federal Rules of Evidence Congress delegated to this Court the power to recognize new evidentiary privileges consistent with the principles of the common law as interpreted in the light of reason and experience.

Even before Rule 501, when this Court had full common law power to recognize privileges, the Court was very parsimonious in the privileges that it would recognize. The Court recognized a common law privilege for trade secrets, a common law privilege for informants, a common law privilege for military secrets. The Court rejected a news gatherer's privilege, and an accountant's privilege.

Following the adoption of the Federal Rules of Evidence, the Court has continued to be very reluctant to establish new privileges. The Court rejected an editorialist privilege, a state legislator's privilege, an accountant's work product privilege, and an academic peer review privilege.

*JUSTICE REHNQUIST*: When were the Federal Rules of Evidence adopted, Mr. Flaxman?

*MR. FLAXMAN*: 1973, I believe.

*JUSTICE REHNQUIST*: Thank you.

*MR. FLAXMAN*: And the Court limited spousal privileges. The respondents in this case ask the Court to fashion a new, broad privilege that would apply to any mental health professional engaged in psychotherapy or counseling. The number of persons engaged in these professions is countless, and the number of conversations that would be protected by this new privilege are countless.

*JUSTICE ANTHONY M. KENNEDY*: Well, it's not countless if they're licensed and we confine the privilege to those who are licensed. I assume you could go to every state and count how many licenses there are.

*MR. FLAXMAN*: Well, except the states are each day creating new counselor status positions. I think that in California, somebody after two years of an associate's degree can becomes a certified alcoholic counselor.

*JUSTICE KENNEDY*: But are they licensed, or do they have some state certification, or is there some document?

*MR. FLAXMAN*: Yes. They receive a state license, and they're—

*Q*: Well then, I assume they could be counted.

*MR. FLAXMAN*: They can be counted, but it would be a very large number.

*JUSTICE RUTH BADER GINSBURG*: And Mr. Flaxman, they would be counted in a diversity case, is that not right?

*MR. FLAXMAN*: That's absolutely correct. In a diversity case, the Rules of Evidence require the federal courts to apply state law in determining privileges. This case was not a diversity case. There was a federal civil rights claim.

*JUSTICE GINSBURG*: Wasn't there one state claim? In addition, there was a wrongful death claim under state law?

*MR. FLAXMAN*: There was a supplemental claim brought under state law. The principle that was applied by the district court that was not questioned by the district court is that when there is a state law claim and a federal claim, that for the federal claim, there being no federal privilege, the rule would be to admit the evidence.

*JUSTICE GINSBURG*: Is there precedent that holds that the state—

*MR. FLAXMAN*: That principle is recognized, I think uniformly within the circuits. It's consistent with the legislative history. I don't think it's been ruled on by this Court. It was not challenged by the respondents in the court of appeals, and I don't believe it's within the questions that are presented in the petition for certiorari. I think the question here is that the agreed question is whether there should be a federal privilege for this kind of evidence, and this kind of evidence that we're focusing on is not confidential communications about dreams or feelings.

*JUSTICE DAVID H. SOUTER*: Well, is it different in kind from the kind of evidence that would be privileged–under a privilege for clinical psychologists? Does the social worker here learn something different in sort of standard counseling–

*MR. FLAXMAN*: Well–

*JUSTICE SOUTER*: From what a clinical psychologist learns and hears?

*MR. FLAXMAN*: Well, we don't know, on this record, what kind of therapy was actually being administered. As a general rule, I think a legislature could make a rational distinction between social workers and clinical psychologists and psychiatrists.

*JUSTICE SOUTER*: Because?

*MR. FLAXMAN*: Because they'd be different kinds of therapy.

*JUSTICE SOUTER*: Well, what is the difference?

*MR. FLAXMAN*: Well, I think as a rational distinction a legislature could say that a psychiatrist and a clinical psychologist are going to be more concerned wi.th psychic reality, and a social worker would be more concerned with helping somebody deal with problems that they're facing.

*JUSTICE SOUTER*: I mean, that sounds very sensible just based on the language we're using. As a matter of positive knowledge, is that correct?

*MR. FLAXMAN*: It's–

*JUSTICE SOUTER*: It sounds like a reasonable answer, but is it true, I guess is what I'm saying.

(Laughter.)

*MR. FLAXMAN*: Unlike the number of people who are licensed, that's a question that can't really be ascertained. It can be debated by scholars. It can be debated by interest groups.

*JUSTICE SOUTER*: Can we say that there simply are no clear, standard cases on which we can answer that question? In other words, psychiatric social workers do all sorts of things. Who knows what they're doing, is that sort of what you're saying?

*MR. FLAXMAN*: That's correct. Our approach.

*JUSTICE KENNEDY*: The brief of the American Psychiatric Association I take it, correct me if I'm wrong, supports the Respondent here, and they don't ask that we draw the line that you're suggesting in this colloquy with Justice Souter.

*MR. FLAXMAN*: That brief–

*JUSTICE KENNEDY*: Or am I incorrect?

*MR. FLAXMAN*: No, I think you're absolutely correct, but I think they're incorrect in reading the record in this case. The record in this case doesn't support the claim.that there was psychoanalytic counseling going on with the social worker and respondent Redmond. The record in this case doesn't reflect anything about the type of therapy–

*JUSTICE KENNEDY*: Well, but I infer from their position that formal psychiatric or psychoanalytic sessions are not necessarily different in their objectives than clinical counseling in the more ordinary sense, assuming there's an aura of confidentiality about it, where the confidentiality is expected on both sides.

*MR. FLAXMAN*: No, perhaps I'm misreading their brief, but I think they make a distinction between psychoanalysis and counseling. Psychoanalysis is dealing with psychic truth. Not with what really happened, but with a person's feelings and emotions and dreams about what happened, and about someone's childhood.

*JUSTICE SANDRA DAY O'CONNOR*: Well, Mr. Flaxman, I take it you would not extend in a federal case a privilege to a psychiatrist.

*MR. FLAXMAN*: That's correct. Our primary position is that there should not be any privilege.

*JUSTICE O'CONNOR*: Right.

*MR. FLAXMAN*: That when there are confidential interests, and we–

*JUSTICE O'CONNOR*: Regardless of what differences there might be?

*MR. FLAXMAN*: Right.

*JUSTICE O'CONNOR*: In the therapy or the nature of the questions?

*MR. FLAXMAN*: That's our primary position, that the confidential interest–and we concede that there are confidential interests in counseling and therapy.

*JUSTICE O'CONNOR*: And yet all 50 states recognize some form of privilege in this area.

*MR. FLAXMAN*: Well, some of them--they recognize some form of privilege. Some of those privileges amount to nothing more than the balancing test, the district judge's, the trial judge's discretion that we're seeking in this case, and the states have made different exceptions, and many states–

*JUSTICE O'CONNOR*: Now, the court below didn't adopt a clear rule of privilege and that's that. It went on to balance the need for the evidence?

*MR. FLAXMAN*: Well, the court below adopted a very unconventional definition of cumulative. It said, I think, that because there were four witnesses who were family members of the deceased, and one police officer on the other side in the civil rights case, our learning what the police officer told the social worker, our learning that the police officer had had memory problems, would be cumulative.

*JUSTICE O'CONNOR*: In the area of privileged communications do federal courts typically engage in a balancing whether to apply the privilege or not?

*MR. FLAXMAN*: The one circuit that has expressly adopted a balancing test, and describes the privilege that it was adopting as nothing more than a requirement that the district judge balance the privacy interest with the opponent's need to know.

*CHIEF JUSTICE REHNQUIST*: Well, that's really not much of a privilege, is it, if everything is going to be balanced at the time the evidence is sought to be admitted. The time the privilege is supposed to work is when the person either feels free or does not feel free to confide to the professional therapist.

*MR. FLAXMAN*: Well, we're not seeking disclosures about confidences about feelings or about dreams. We want to know what the client–what the respondent told the social worker about the the incident. The district judge said that's all we can get.

*CHIEF JUSTICE REHNQUIST*: Well, but that may be a very difficult line to draw. You say you don't want the person's mental reflections and that sort of thing, but it's not always easy to separate those from an account of what happened.

*MR. FLAXMAN*: Well, the district judge and the magistrate judge who supervised the deposition of the respondent didn't have any trouble dealing with that. It was very clear that we could ask, what did you say about the incident, and when we tried--

*JUSTICE GINSBURG*: Mr. Flaxman, correct me if I'm wrong about this, but I thought that part of what you were asking did involve mental impressions to the extent that you were asking for the notes of the social worker.

*MR. FLAXMAN*: The notes of the social worker only came up after the respondent testified that she could not recall any of her conversations with the social worker.

*JUSTICE GINSBURG*: Are you now conceding that mental impressions of the social worker, mental impressions reflected in her notes, are things to which you do not have access?

*MR. FLAXMAN*: As a matter of relevancy, that's correct, and the district judge said that we could not get her notes when he was ruling on the relevancy question. The district judge said we could get notes that relate to conversations about the incident. It was after--

JUSTICE GINSBURG: But the conversations, the notes, mix in, as lawyer's notes do, the social worker's own mental impressions with things that the patient or client said about what happened.

*MR. FLAXMAN*: Well, we were given three pages of heavily redacted notes which made clear the things that the client had said about the incident.

*JUSTICE GINSBURG*: But I--please just straighten me out on what your position is. I thought you were objecting to the reactions.

*MR. FLAXMAN*: Well--

*JUSTICE GINSBURG*: I thought you were saying, we want her notes, without the editing.

*MR. FLAXMAN*: We objected to that. The district judge ruled against us, and we're not challenging the district judge's ruling on that, and we've never challenged the district judge's ruling on the reactions. The district judge held a hearing to inquire about these. I don't recall that came from respondent Redmond when she was asked about the contents of conversations with the social worker.

After hearing and observing the character and demeanor of the witness, the district judge said these denials are wholly incredible, and the only way to refresh her recollection is to review all of the notes, and the review just for counsel's eyes only. That order about production of the notes wasn't about a privilege or about confidentiality, it was to help us cross-examine her. It was sanctioned for this meeting.

*JUSTICE KENNEDY*: The propriety of that particular resolution I'm not sure is before us, or seems to me very odd. It's standard for you to ask a witness, have you talked to your attorney, and the unprepared witnesses will say, oh, no. Well, everybody knows that that's incredible, but if the witness responds in that incredible way, that isn't an open door to then inquire about all the conversations with the attorney.

*MR. FLAXMAN*: That's correct. The attorney-client--

*JUSTICE KENNEDY*: And it seems to me that if this is any kind of a privilege, that the same rule should apply here. If she makes a statement that's incredible that she didn't go to a social worker or that she didn't discuss the event, I don't think that necessarily opens the door under the trial judge's ruling to explore everything that was said under any conventional privilege. Now, if you want to have some different sort of privilege here, I suppose that's something altogether separate.

MR. FLAXMAN: Well, there's a vast difference between conferring with an attorney who is an officer of the court, who is interested in following the law and not helping somebody change their recollections of an incident, to going into therapy.

CHIEF JUSTICE REHNQUIST: You say an attorney isn't always interested in changing someone's recollections of an incident?

(Laughter.)

MR. FLAXMAN: An attorney should not be helping somebody change their recollections and commit perjury, and if an attorney does that, then the attorney is subject to sanctions.

If a therapist does that, and helps somebody sleep at night after they did a horrible thing, then the therapist has succeeded. The goals of therapy are quite different than the goals of an attorney. An attorney is ultimately answerable to the court as an officer.

JUSTICE ANTONIN SCALIA: Mr. Flaxman, you said earlier that the privilege recognized by some states, which amounts to a balancing of the importance of the information versus the--I guess, what, the confidentiality of it, that that isn't much different from what would be applied anyway in the absence of a privilege.

MR. FLAXMAN: In some states there is a judicial override. There's a privilege, there are exceptions to the privilege, then there's a final exception that provided, however, the trial court may in the exercise of its discretion–

JUSTICE SCALIA: Allow it in.

MR. FLAXMAN: Or allow it to be disclosed.

JUSTICE SCALIA: Yes, but that still is a privilege of sorts, isn't it?

MR. FLAXMAN: It's a privilege–

JUSTICE SCALIA: I mean, it's different from the rule which would be applied otherwise.

MR. FLAXMAN: That's correct. It's like the Second Circuit's privilege that's just a balancing test.

JUSTICE SCALIA: Now, of these privileges that exist in the states, has any of them been adopted judicially, as a matter of common law? Are they all legislated?

MR. FLAXMAN: The Alaska Supreme Court adopted it, and also the Arizona Supreme Court. Other than that, all of the privileges have been adopted by legislative action.

JUSTICE SCALIA: What is the nature of the Alaska and the Arizona privilege ?

MR. FLAXMAN: The Alaska privilege applied to psychologists and psychiatrists and did not extend to social workers, and the Arizona–

JUSTICE SCALIA: Absolute?

MR. FLAXMAN: That's correct.

JUSTICE SCALIA: It's an absolute privilege?

MR. FLAXMAN: No. Well, I think all of the privileges have been limited with the duty to disclose that someone is dangerous, or that there's a child abuse admission. There are no absolute privileges in psychotherapy in any state in this–

JUSTICE SCALIA: And that includes Alaska and Arizona?

*MR. FLAXMAN*: That's correct. There are always instances where a therapist is required by law to make disclosures, and so there can't be this guarantee of absolute privilege which the American Psychiatric Association would urge and would seek.

*JUSTICE SCALIA*: You asked us to recognize a line between statements about fact and statements about feeling, and I confess that I'm skeptical that we could do that. What if somebody says to the social worker or the psychologist, "I feel bad about killing somebody." Is that on one side of the line or the other?

*MR. FLAXMAN*: I think that's on the side that we don't get. I feel bad is–

*JUSTICE SOUTER*: Even though there's an implicit admission in it?

*MR. FLAXMAN*: That's right. I think that invades the–

*JUSTICE SCALIA*: Why is "feeling about killing somebody" fact?

*MR. FLAXMAN*: Because the district judge could say that kind of response is the response that anybody would feel, even if it was justifiable, and the probative value of that statement that I feel bad-

*JUSTICE SCALIA*: What if he says, "I didn't do it"?

*MR. FLAXMAN*: The statement, "I didn't–

*JUSTICE SCALIA*: "I didn't kill anybody." That's his defense. "I did not kill anybody."

*MR. FLAXMAN*: "I didn't kill anybody" is a statement about the incident. That should be disclosed.

*JUSTICE SCALIA*: No, I'm saying that's his legal position, "I did not kill the decedent whom I am accused of killing." Go back to our statement, "I feel bad about killing somebody." Is it subject to the privilege? Would it be subject to a privilege or not?

*MR. FLAXMAN*: I would say that a district judge would require that that denial would have to be disclosed, that it wouldn't be privileged, it should not be hidden from the Government in a criminal case, or from a plaintiff in a civil case.

*JUSTICE SOUTER*: So there's no analytical distinction then between the fact and the feeling.

*MR. FLAXMAN*: That's why we believe this should be a question for the district judge, who can balance all of these factors. In your hypothetical--

*JUSTICE SOUTER*: Yes, but even on your balancing theory I thought the judge was supposed to draw a line between fact and feeling. Maybe I misunderstood you.

*MR. FLAXMAN*: No, I--

*JUSTICE SOUTER*: Balancing the appropriateness of admitting the fact as against other interests?

*MR. FLAXMAN*: I think that's one of the things that the trial judge could be balancing, whether it's fact or feeling, but also the need for the evidence.

*JUSTICE SCALIA*: I don't understand that, "the need for the evidence"? You come here saying there is no privilege, but you're going to let the court balance the need for the evidence?

*MR. FLAXMAN*: With the confidentiality interests that are involved in therapy.

*JUSTICE SCALIA*: Oh, okay, so you're not denying there ought to be a privilege?

*MR. FLAXMAN*: I–

*JUSTICE SCALIA*: We're just arguing about what the scope of it ought to be.

*MR. FLAXMAN:* No, I am denying there should be--if there's a privilege, then--

*JUSTICE SCALIA:* You see, I thought you were arguing on the basis of relevance before. I thought you were saying, the facts come in because they're relevant, the feelings don't come in because they're not, because they aren't relevant.

*MR. FLAXMAN:* That's–

*JUSTICE SCALIA:* There's no balancing there at all. There's a determination of what's fact and what's feeling.

*MR. FLAXMAN:* Well

*JUSTICE SCALIA:* But now you say there is a balancing, so you're willing to acknowledge that some stuff doesn't get in because it's subject to--

*MR. FLAXMAN:* No, what I'm willing to say is that in an appropriate case the district judge could say that these feelings have so little probative value, even if they are relevant they should not come in.

If there was a case where there are five police officers who each say that the officer who shot did so because the man had a knife and was about to plunge it into the back of another man, the therapy admissions or therapy statements of that fifth police officer who did the shooting would have so little probative value that the confidentiality should not be invaded.

*CHIEF JUSTICE REHNQUIST:* That really isn't much of a privilege at all.

*MR. FLAXMAN:* We are saying that there should not be a privilege, that the district judge should consider relevancy, should consider the confidential interests, should consider the impact of disclosure on the person who's in therapy--

*JUSTICE SCALIA:* Why?

*MR. FLAXMAN:* Because there are confidential interests involved in therapy.

*JUSTICE SCALIA:* Privilege?

*MR. FLAXMAN:* Not privilege, just--

*JUSTICE SCALIA:* No, not a privilege, just confidential interests. You want us just to call it a confidential interest instead of a privilege, is that it?

*MR. FLAXMAN:* If there is a privilege, then the burden shifts to one who has to pierce the privilege.

In this case, what happened is that the respondent came forward and said, I don't have to demonstrate that it was psychotherapy. I don't have to demonstrate that there was a promise of confidentiality. I don't have to demonstrate that disclosure would interfere with the counseling relationship. All I have to do is to say, I saw a social worker and discussed things with her.

*JUSTICE STEPHEN BREYER:* If you wouldn't have to say that, why, in fact, are you saying that there should not be a privilege? I'm not interested in the semantics. I'm interested in this--If a woman goes to a doctor and has a physical problem, there is a privilege for confidential communications between the patient and her doctor made for the purposes of diagnosis or treatment if the doctor is licensed by the state to perform that diagnosis or treatment. Why should there not be precisely the same privilege where the doctor is engaged in diagnosis or treatment of a mental or emotional condition? Why should there be a distinction--

*MR. FLAXMAN:* Well–

*JUSTICE BREYER:* Why a distinction between a doctor who diagnoses or treats a mental or emotional condition and a doctor who treats a physical condition, provided that the state licenses the individual to engage in that diagnostic or treatment profession?

*MR. FLAXMAN:* The lower federal courts, and this Court has never reached the question--

*JUSTICE BREYER:* I'm not saying what the lower--

*MR. FLAXMAN:* Have--

*JUSTICE BREYER:* I'm saying what reason is there--

*MR. FLAXMAN:* Well--

*JUSTICE BREYER:* Why in logic or policy make that distinction?

*MR. FLAXMAN:* There is no reason for a physician-patient privilege and that privilege is not recognized in the federal courts.

*JUSTICE BREYER:* No, look, I'm asking why is it any different where, instead of seeing the doctor for purposes of diagnosis or treatment of your itch, or cancer, or worse, you see that doctor or psychologist or social worker licensed to engage in psychotherapy because you have a very serious, or less serious, mental or emotional problem? Why in reason or logic or policy should one try to make such a distinction?

*MR. FLAXMAN:* Well, there are many distinctions that can be made, but the fundamental reason why there's no need to make that distinction is because there is no privilege for when you go to a doctor and say "I've a broken foot."

*JUSTICE BREYER:* I'11 try once more. I'm not saying what there is. I'm asking what there should be.

*MR. FLAXMAN:* Well--

*JUSTICE BREYER:* And what I'm asking is--it's only me who's interested, perhaps, but I am interested--is there any reason in logic or policy, is there any reason, other than what the courts have held? I'm not interested, for this question, what courts have held in the past. I'm interested in whether there is a reason in logic or policy for drawing the line that I just referred to.

*MR. FLAXMAN:* There's no reason for drawing the line. If the respondent had gone to a physician and in the course of getting treatment for a broken finger said, "I can't remember pulling the trigger," that statement should be admissible in the Federal--

*JUSTICE BREYER:* Am I not being clear? I'm saying, what is the difference whether you go to a physician to diagnose your cancer, skin disease or whatever, or if you go to a licensed psychologist or psychotherapist or psychiatrist for diagnosis or treatment of a mental or emotional condition? That's the line I'm talking about. What's the reason for drawing that line?

*MR. FLAXMAN:* If the Court is willing to recognize a privilege for physician-patient communications, then the Court should recognize a psychotherapist privilege. The Court has never recognized the doctor-patient privilege, and the Court should not recognize the psychotherapist-client privilege. In *Upjohn v. United States* [449 U.S. 383 (1981)], the Chief Justice, then Justice, wrote that the Court doesn't lay down broad rules but decides only the case before it.

*JUSTICE SCALIA:* I suppose if we did recognize a doctor's privilege, which we haven't, it would be a lot less expensive, wouldn't it? Very few people go to a doctor in order to get treatment and say, "I just killed somebody," whereas a lot of people go to psychiatrists and say, "I just killed somebody. I feel really bad about it."

*MR. FLAXMAN*: I don't think that–

*JUSTICE SCALIA*: I mean, don't you think the cost of the psychiatrist privilege would be a lot higher than the cost of the medical doctor's privilege?

*MR. FLAXMAN*: Oh, it would be specially in a case like this, where we've had the disclosures made in November 1991, which is five or six months after the incident, that respondent Redmond was unable to recall pulling the trigger. That kind of information, which is relevant to her believability and her ability to come into court and recall and recount what happened, is the kind of information that would be shielded from us by the broad privilege that's sought in this case.

*JUSTICE BREYER*: How many states have a physician's privilege, by the way?

*MR. FLAXMAN*: Virtually all states.

*JUSTICE BREYER*: Virtually all of them, and yet we don't in federal courts?

*MR. FLAXMAN*: That's correct.

*JUSTICE BREYER*: Has this Court affirmatively disavowed a medical doctor's privilege, or has it just never passed on it?

*MR. FLAXMAN*: The Court has never passed on it, and--

*JUSTICE BREYER*: And how about the circuits?

*MR. FLAXMAN*: The circuits have uniformly rejected a physician privilege. The circuits have generally recognized a clergyperson privilege, and this Court has in dicta suggested that there should be such a privilege, and that privilege is quite different than the privilege with the therapist. If somebody goes to a clergyperson and talks about having done a horrible thing, the clergyperson probably will not engage in 50 or 75 therapy sessions to help the memory.

*JUSTICE KENNEDY*: Suppose the clergyperson is also a licensed social worker?

*MR. FLAXMAN*: The question then is whether the sessions were clerical in nature or counseling in nature. My understanding of clerical-

*JUSTICE KENNEDY*: Suppose the answer is both?

*MR. FLAXMAN*: That would be a difficult question for the district judge to balance.

(Laughter.)

*MR. FLAXMAN*: If the clergyperson was doing therapy and was helping somebody recall memories, or get a sharper recollection of what happened, then it would not be what the organized religion probably would recognize as clerical-penitent counseling, and I think that it's more likely that a clerical person who's confronted with someone who's confessing to a horrible thing would encourage that person to go turn him- or herself in rather than helping them process it in their mind so they remember it differently. I'd like to reserve the rest of my time.

*CHIEF JUSTICE REHNQUIST*: Very well, Mr. Flaxman.

## ORAL ARGUMENT OF GREGORY E. ROGUS ON
## BEHALF OF THE RESPONDENTS

*MR. ROGUS*: Mr. Chief Justice, and may it please the Court:

In enacting Rule 501, Congress declared that the federal courts are to look to reason and experience in determining evidentiary privileges. The intent behind the rule as evidenced both in the legislative history and as acknowledged by this Court in the *Trammel v. United States* [445 U.S. 40 (1980)] was not to freeze the law of privilege as it existed but to allow the courts flexibility to develop rules of privilege, once again in line with reason and experience.

Now, it is true, as Mr. Flaxman has mentioned, that decisions of this Court have counseled caution in terms of the recognition of privilege. However, this Court has also stated that when a privilege promotes sufficiently important interests to outweigh the need for probative evidence, recognition and implementation of a privilege is proper.

Now, in this case the Seventh Circuit acted consistent with its authority under Rule 501 and consistent with this Court's directive in *Trammel,* and determined that reason and experience justified a recognition—

*JUSTICE O'CONNOR:* Mr. Rogus, did the court also balance need for the evidence with its notion of the privilege?

*MR. ROGUS:* The court did engage in balancing.

*JUSTICE O'CONNOR:* Is that the way that federal courts normally approach the exercise of a privilege?

*MR. ROGUS:* That is a technique and approach that was mentioned by the Second Circuit in the *Doe* case [*In re* Doe, 964 F.2d 1325 (1992)]. In actuality, what's at work here—

*JUSTICE O'CONNOR:* Do you defend that as an appropriate approach?

*MR. ROGUS:* The need for balancing is appropriate particularly with respect to determining when an exception to a privilege should come into play.

*JUSTICE O'CONNOR:* Well, would that be the approach in the case of an attorney-client privilege, for example? You balance the need?

*MR. ROGUS:* Well, I think that has been done in the sense of the recognition of the privilege, for example, in the crime or fraud exception. While the attorney-client privilege is recognized, there are no exceptions that come to mind immediately. The crime fraud exception—

*JUSTICE KENNEDY:* But that's not balancing. That's a boundary to the privilege. It prevents the abuse of the privilege. It has nothing to do with the requirements or the exigencies of, and the necessities of producing the information in a particular case, and I'm quite surprised that you support the balancing idea. I should have thought you would say the privilege either should be granted or it shouldn't.

*MR. ROGUS:* Well, the underlying privilege should be granted. The balancing that we refer to is the balancing of the important interests that are served by recognition of the privilege against the need for probative—

*CHIEF JUSTICE REHNQUIST:* Is that a case-by-case balancing?

*MR. ROGUS:* No, not a case-by-case balancing. It's a balancing at the policy level weighing the interests, the important interests against the need for probative evidence.

*CHIEF JUSTICE REHNQUIST:* Well, is it possible--

*JUSTICE SCALIA:* You mean, it wouldn't matter if it's the only source of this evidence available in this particular case? I had thought that some of the state courts that do balancing would consider that this thing couldn't be obtained from any other source, it's crucial to the defense or the plaintiff's--

*MR. ROGUS*: If it were the only evidence available on a material element of the cause of action, that would certainly affect the balancing.

*JUSTICE SCALIA*: Well, I'd consider that case-by-case, myself.

*CHIEF JUSTICE REHNQUIST*: If you subscribe to what Justice Scalia just said, the purpose of the privilege is to enable the attorney or the doctor, whoever, to tell a person, I suppose, that what you say here is confidential, and if instead he has to say, what you say here may be confidential, depending on how some future court may balance the need for your testimony, that's much less disposed to get people to confide.

*MR. ROGUS*: Well, in this instance, psychotherapists do need to tell their patients that their communications are confidential.

*JUSTICE SCALIA*: So you're in effect starting with a presumption of confidentiality subject to case-by-case balancing on the issue of exception?

*MR. ROGUS*: A presumption of confidentiality, yes.

*JUSTICE SCALIA*: Okay.

*MR. ROGUS*: In this–

*CHIEF JUSTICE REHNQUIST*: That's a much weaker sense of privilege, then, than the sort of classic privileges.

*MR. ROGUS*: We did not and we are not asking for recognition of an absolute privilege.

*CHIEF JUSTICE REHNQUIST*: Okay.

*JUSTICE BREYER*: Well, how does it stack up with the doctor? I'm thinking now about the other side. They're saying, well, it should be the same as the doctor who is diagnosing you for cancer and so forth.

*JUSTICE BREYER*: Are you asking for a psychiatric privilege where the doctor with the physical injury wouldn't have one? Are you saying treat both alike? What is the relationship?

*MR. ROGUS*: I'm saying if anything the psychotherapist-patient privilege should be recognized more readily than the doctor-patient because of, once again, the nature of the privacy interests involved, the types of things that people go to see psychotherapists for, the types of things that people discuss with psychotherapists that touch upon very--not always, but very frequently very highly private personal concerns, so if anything there's more reason to recognize the psychotherapist–

*JUSTICE O'CONNOR*: And you think that the doctor doesn't receive communications of a very private nature from a patient?

*MR. ROGUS*: I am not saying that a doctor does not.

*JUSTICE O'CONNOR*: Do you concede that there is no doctor-patient privilege recognized in the federal courts?

*MR. ROGUS*: I believe that it has not been recognized, but that is not–

*JUSTICE O'CONNOR*: And that that is the general rule in the courts, in the circuits?

*MR. ROGUS*: I believe that is correct.

*JUSTICE BREYER*: So what are we supposed to do about that? That's what I mean. Are we supposed to say that just a psychiatrist and psychoanalyst have it? What are we supposed to do about doctors in general?

MR. ROGUS: Psychotherapists should have the privilege. We are looking at a function—psychotherapy—which has not always coincided with medical practice. There is some overlap, but it does not always coincide. We are zeroing in on the function of psychotherapy, the treatment and diagnosis of mental and emotional conditions and disorders.

JUSTICE SOUTER: You keep speaking of the function, and if you speak in terms of the function, then there's never any question as to whether, if a privilege for psychotherapy is recognized, it would cover social workers, as in this case. Let's assume that I agree that there ought to be a privilege so far as communications back and forth between the patient and a psychiatrist are concerned and the patient and a clinical psychologist are concerned. Is there a difference between what the clinical psychologist does in the kind of standard case and what the psychiatric social worker does?

MR. ROGUS: My understanding, based upon what was developed in the record, and the research, and the information provided by the amici, is that the training, the education, and the functioning of clinical social workers approaches if not equates to what clinical psychologists do in terms of performing the psycho-therapeutic function, of doing psychotherapy.

JUSTICE SOUTER: But they don't have the advanced only clearly standardized difference.

MR. ROGUS: Well, I wouldn't say that one degree is more advanced than another. There are a lot of Ph.D.'s, for example, in the clinical social work field, just as there are Ph.D. advanced degrees in psychology. Much of the training, the clinical experience, as I believe was developed in the record with respect to Ms. Beyer, the clinical social worker who was involved in this particular case, demonstrates the amount of experience, the quality, the type of experience she had, much of which overlapped with that which a clinical psychologist--

JUSTICE KENNEDY: I take it, in line with Justice Souter's questioning, that most states license clinical social workers and they pass some sort of an examination.

MR. ROGUS: It is our understanding that of the 50 states that recognize privileges, 44 of them do, in fact, extend that privilege to clinical social workers.

JUSTICE KENNEDY: And do those persons who hold that privilege have a duty of confidentiality under their own professional ethical standards?

MR. ROGUS: Yes, they do. That's set forth--

JUSTICE KENNEDY: But you're saying that the courts should not recognize what is generally understood as a duty of confidentiality, even in degree. That's the patient-doctor relation, much less this.

MR. ROGUS: If that is what my previous remarks sounded like, that is not what I meant to say. They should recognize privilege.

JUSTICE SCALIA: I suppose I have a duty of confidentiality. If somebody comes up to me and, let's say, my nephew comes up to and says, you know, Unc, I want to tell you something in strictest confidence, and I say yes, you tell me that, I promise you I won't tell this to anybody. Is that enough that I've undertaken a duty of confidentiality to justify the creation of a privilege?

*MR. ROGUS*: But you are not engaging, under the facts as you've laid them out, in a psychotherapeutic situation.

*JUSTICE SCALIA*: No, I understand that, but I just don't see the relevance of the fact that there is a duty of confidentiality here. There are duties of confidentiality in a lot of situations which we've simply, utterly ignored. Parent-child, there's no parent-child privilege, for Pete's sake. That's certainly a very confidential relationship.

*MR. ROGUS*: This arises in the setting of a professional approach to psychotherapy and the importance and value that society puts in--

*JUSTICE SCALIA*: Yes, but --

*MR. ROGUS*: Having and maintaining such a profession for the purpose of aiding members of society, and in this particular--

*JUSTICE SCALIA*: That allows us--

*JUSTICE KENNEDY*: The fact that a client expects that his communications to an attorney are going to be confidential is relevant in our creation of the privilege, is it not?

*MR. ROGUS*: It certainly is, an expectation of confidentiality, and there is an expectation of confidentiality and the protection of private communications when a patient engages in a psycho-therapeutic--

*JUSTICE SOUTER*: Okay, so we can draw the line simply by saying the line's got to be drawn somewhere, and we're going to draw it at the point at which the person receiving the communication is licensed by the state. But in principle, apart from that line-drawing methodology, there's no reason to draw it there, is there? I have had law clerks tell me things in confidence, and I presume they felt better after telling me. (Laughter.) I assume there was some value to it, but you would not recognize the privilege in that case, but there's no reason in principle why you shouldn't, is there?

*MR. ROGUS*: Once again, we are talking about a particular function here.

*JUSTICE SOUTER*: Well, the function is feeling better, and I don't denigrate that, by telling somebody something, and so the function is being performed--talk about poor man's psychiatrist, but the function is being performed when they.tell me, and so it seems to me there's no reason in principle why I shouldn't be able to claim the privilege. And your--I think your answer is, well, we've got to draw the line somewhere, judge.

MR. ROGUS: And the difference would be, once again, not only what--how the person feels when they have talked to you, brought to you whatever is on their mind, what they're feeling, et cetera, but what you, in turn, can tell them and help them.

*JUSTICE SOUTER*: What can the psychiatrist tell--even the full-dress psychiatrist, if we grant the sort of privilege that you want us to grant? What can he tell the patient?

*MR. ROGUS*: Well, my--

*JUSTICE SCALIA*: What you tell me will, what, probably, most likely, be held in confidence?

*MR. ROGUS*: What you will tell me will be held in confidence.

*JUSTICE SCALIA*: He can't say that. You acknowledge exceptions.

*MR. ROGUS*: There are some exceptions that have been noted by the courts based on--

*JUSTICE SCALIA*: Is there any state that has no exceptions?

*MR. ROGUS*: No. I believe they all have at least one exception.

*JUSTICE SCALIA*: And some have very broad exceptions. If it's important enough, you can get it in, right?

*MR. ROGUS*: That would be correct.

*JUSTICE SCALIA*: Well, what could a psychiatrist possibly comfort his patient with, what kind of assurance could he possibly comfort his patient with in that kind of state?

*MR. ROGUS*: Because the exception should be--

*JUSTICE SCALIA*: Very little.

*MR. ROGUS*: Very narrowly and--there should be very few exceptions, and they should be very narrowly drawn to fit only certain categorical situations. For--

*JUSTICE SCALIA*: If--

*MR. ROGUS*: For example, I think one of the instances that was referred to during Mr. Flaxman's argument was if something should be mentioned in terms of a definite threat of harm to a specifically identified individual, if a person goes in, talks to their therapist and says, "I'm going to kill Joe Smith," and there is no reason for the clinician to doubt that that person is in fact capable of and will, and would carry out that specific threat to Joe Smith. In that instance, most of the states I believe have recognized a very narrowly drawn privilege, once again, arising out of the fact that that very specific threat to that one very specific individual is there.

*JUSTICE SOUTER*: But I take it even on your scheme if Smith is dead, and an admission has been made to a psychiatric social worker and to no one else, and a case cannot be proven without that beyond a reasonable doubt, without that admission, you would let the admission in, wouldn't you?

*MR. ROGUS*: Under the--if it were the only evidence--

*JUSTICE SOUTER*: Right. My hypo. My hypo.

*MR. ROGUS*: They--

*JUSTICE SOUTER*: You'd let it in.

*MR. ROGUS*: There have been cases that allow that testimony in under--

*JUSTICE SOUTER*: So whatever the value of being able to assure the patient of confidentiality may be, on your theory that value would be absent, because the social worker, the psychiatrist, the psychologist could not say, "What you tell me is in confidence." All he could say is, "What you tell me will be kept confidential unless they need it badly enough."

*MR. ROGUS*: Yes, in a sense.

*JUSTICE SOUTER*: All right.

*MR. ROGUS*: Based on--

*JUSTICE SOUTER*: Now, what about a case like this, in which there is a claim that memory enhancement may be involved? Given the possibility that the memory enhancement in fact is memory change, I would suppose that that kind of evidence could be just as crucial as the unique evidence of guilt. Why shouldn't an exception be recognized for cases in which there is a colorable claim that memory enhancement went on?

*MR. ROGUS:* Several points in response to that. First of all, the record does not give any indication whatsoever that there was such enhancement. Secondly, as the Court--

*JUSTICE SOUTER:* But there are grounds for some suspicion.

*JUSTICE O'CONNOR:* Would state law in this case have allowed an exception for this evidence to come in?

*MR. ROGUS:* Whether under the law of the state it would have been privileged?

*JUSTICE O'CONNOR:* And you don't rely, apparently, in giving your responses, on what state law allows or doesn't allow? You're going to have us decide it on the basis of whether it would be needed or not?

*MR. ROGUS:* As the Court indicated in *trammel*, we certainly, in terms of formulating the federal rule, can look to state law for guidance, but inasmuch as there was a federal question involved in this case, and under the language of 501, we can look to state law for guidance, but state law as state law would not control the question.

*JUSTICE O'CONNOR:* All right. Well, what does 501 tell us? It tells us that the privilege of a witness shall be governed by the principles of the common law as they may be interpreted by the courts of the United States in the light of reason and experience. Now, what do you think the common law provides?

*MR. ROGUS:* At the common law prior to the early seventies there was no vast body of case law indicating one way or the other whether there was a psychotherapist-patient privilege or not There were courts that were starting to entertain the notion of a psychotherapist-patient privilege. Based on the analysis provided by many of the commentators, it was at about that same time that many of the courts were getting involved in addressing that issue that many of the legislatures simultaneously also began to take action in terms of not only looking at, for example, the social work profession and stepping up the amount of state regulation of the profession itself, but also enacting provisions providing for privilege.

*JUSTICE O'CONNOR:* What do we look to for determining what the principles of the common law are here?

*MR. ROGUS:* Basically we would look to the development of the law through cases and court decisions, that is correct, and as of the time was enacted.

*JUSTICE JOHN PAUL STEVENS:* Mr. Rogus, do you know if there are any states that recognize a psychotherapist privilege and do not recognize a doctor-patient privilege?

*MR. ROGUS:* Off-hand I do not know the answer to that question.

*JUSTICE GINSBURG:* Mr. Rogus, Mr. Flaxman said there were two states that had this privilege by virtue of court decisions. You've just explained that the legislatures were responding with kind of a dialogue. Do you know--in how many states the privilege notion began in the courts, that there was first a court declaration and then there was legislative codification?

*MR. ROGUS:* I do not know specifically how many. It was very few. Very few. My understanding is, just a handful of states where that is the case.

*JUSTICE SCALIA:* Why shouldn't we do the same? I mean, I have no doubt we have the power to pronounce a common law rule, but the variety of rules in the states is so diverse.

*MR. ROGUS*: And in that--

*JUSTICE SCALIA*: I wouldn't know which common law rule to adopt. Why shouldn't we say, you know, it looks like pretty much a policy call that different states have gone different ways, and I don't know why we should pick one of these infinite varieties of laws and impose them on the federal courts.

*MR. ROGUS*: But the basic thrust of what has been going on in the states is to recognize the privilege and, given once again that--

*JUSTICE SCALIA*: It doesn't get you anywhere. You don't even know what privilege means. I mean, as you've described to us, in some states it means very little. It means only, we'll think about whether it's important enough, and if it is, you can't– if it isn't important enough, you can't get it. It–I don't view this as a solid basis for saying yes, the common law has developed in a certain way.

*MR. ROGUS*: Thank you.

*CHIEF JUSTICE REHNQUIST*: Thank you, Mr. Rogus.

## ORAL ARGUMENT OF JAMES A. FELDMAN
## ON BEHALF OF THE UNITED STATES, AS AMICUS CURIAE,
## SUPPORTING THE RESPONDENTS

*MR. FELDMAN*: Mr. Chief Justice, and may it please the Court:

Rule 501 provides that the privilege of a witness shall be governed by the principles--not the specific privileges, but the principles of the common law as interpreted by the courts of the United States in the light of reason and experience. In our view, the most significant feature to look to in determining what reason and experience tells us here is the fact that all 50 states have recognized the privilege in one form or--

*JUSTICE SOUTER*: Well, they recognize something. I mean, your brother was just saying, I think, that what we should recognize is a presumption of confidentiality subject to exception by weighing. If we go no further than to do that, is it even worth the trouble?

*MR. FELDMAN*: I--

*JUSTICE SOUTER*: Why bother? Of the kind of presumption that he was arguing for, is that worth the trouble?

*MR. FELDMAN*: I think it would have some incremental value in increasing the confidence of patients that their communications would be confidential, but I don't think it would have the kind of value that the states generally have recognized when they've adopted–

*JUSTICE SOUTER*: If that's all we did, should we do it at all?

*MR. FELDMAN*: Yes. I think that that would be something useful to do. It's not our position that that's what the courts ought to do. I think under Rule 501, the federal courts ought to take a cautious view towards the recognition of privileges. It ought to be sure to recognize the general policy of the Federal Rules in favor of the admissibility of evidence, but where a privilege is justified, and especially where the 50 states have at least uniformly recognized the important interests that are at stake in a case like this, I think the federal courts should do likewise. The fact that all 50 states have recognized it I think shows that they recognize the importance of psychotherapy in the relief of mental and psychological distress for people. I think they've recognized the need for confidentiality, the very strong need for confidentiality.

*JUSTICE GINSBURG*: Mr. Feldman, how could you justify a psychologist-social worker privilege without recognizing a medical doctor privilege?

*MR. FELDMAN*: In our view the case for medical doctor privilege has not yet been compellingly enough made, and I'11 tell you why. First, there are fewer states that recognize it. Second, if you look at the way the states recognize it, it generally has even more exceptions, and there's less of it than with respect to a psychotherapist-patient privilege.

As the Advisory Committee on the proposed rules in 1973, or around there, recognized, if you look at their commentary on the psychotherapist-patient privilege, which was in those proposed rules, and the doctor-patient privilege was not, they noted that confidential communications are even more important for the successful practice of psychotherapy than for the successful practice of medicine.

*JUSTICE BREYER*: Well, what can I read to find out about this? I mean, I'm used to, as many of us, having diversity cases, where, of course, there is the privilege you're arguing for and also a medical doctor privilege. That's the normal case. I don't know how you distinguish between a patient who comes in with a gunshot wound, and the doctor's got to find out what happened, and a psychiatric social worker who says, I'd like you to tell me what your problem was in this case, or some other. How can you do the one without the other? And what were the objections to the doctor privilege? Why wasn't a rule written on that? What do I read to find out about this It didn't seem to me very fully developed in the briefs.

*MR. FELDMAN*: In the Advisory Committee notes on proposed Rule 504, they do specifically go into that question, and they cite a previous paper that was issued by the Group for the Advancement of Psychology [Psychiatry] that explored the subject more fully. There's also been a number of other things that are cited throughout the amicus briefs about it. But the general point, and the general reason why the states have seen fit to recognize one to a greater extent than the other is that, although confidentiality is no doubt important for the practice of medicine, it's important for the practice of many things. It's probably important for accountants. It's generally an important value, but the extraordinary level of confidentiality that a privilege involves, that step should only be taken where it's clearly justified.

*JUSTICE SCALIA*: Mr. Feldman, let's assume that the consultation occurs in a state that has under state law, the very negligible privilege that you said it's worth adopting, but it won't do a whole lot of good, so all that that person can tell the client is, you know, under state law, you have very little assurance of confidentiality.

Why should a federal court accord to that social worker or psychiatrist a greater degree of confidentiality than the state itself? Shouldn't the maximum federal protection be, where the consultation has occurred in State X, whatever confidentiality the courts of State X accord? I can't see any federal justification for going further than that, or any use, for that matter.

*MR. FELDMAN*: It would certainly be a possible rule to set the federal ceiling at the state floor.

*JUSTICE SCALIA*: Well, wonderful, but can we do that under the federal rule? It seems to me the federal rule has to be uniform, so isn't this eminently an area that we should leave to legislation?

*MR. FELDMAN*: I've two answers. First of all, I think Congress has made it quite clear and the Court has said in its opinions that this is something that the courts have to grapple with one way or the other. A decision not to recognize a privilege in a state that has a very strong privilege, for example, is going to do some damage to that state's policies, and what that state has recognized as necessary for the advancement of--

*JUSTICE KENNEDY*: Well, it's not just that state's policy. It's according to the licensing system of the state, more dignity than the state itself gives...

*MR. FELDMAN*: But–

*JUSTICE KENNEDY*: – and I have the same trouble as Justice Scalia does. I'm not sure how to handle that.

*MR. FELDMAN*: I wanted to get to the second point, which was that in our brief we suggest that the key question is whether a confidential relationship is formed. On that question, since states are the primary level of government that governs the relationships of psychotherapists and patients, as with most other professions, the question of whether a confidential relationship, a highly confidential, an extraordinarily confidential relationship is formed, I think it's reasonable to look to state law for that.

*JUSTICE KENNEDY*: So you look to licensing, plus the extent of privilege, state by state?

*MR. FELDMAN*: I think you'd look to the question of whether the privilege extends to this kind of a relationship. As far as the specific narrow exceptions to the state...

*JUSTICE KENNEDY*: Under the rubric of whether or not there's a reasonable justification to believe that the communication is confidential?

*MR. FELDMAN*: A necessity for the application of any privilege is that a confidential relationship is formed. In attorney-client privilege, the state gets to determine who's a member of the bar. If you're not a member of the bar, there's no question that you don't have a privilege in federal court, and similarly with the marital privilege and other kinds of privilege. In the same way, it's up to the state to determine whether a confidential relationship has been formed, and that's a prerequisite for the application of the federal privilege. Once you have that, I think the exceptions in the states follow enough of a pattern that...

*JUSTICE STEVENS*: Mr. Feldman, in this case would Illinois have recognized a privilege for what's at issue here?

*MR. FELDMAN*: Yes, the Seventh Circuit so held, in fact.

*JUSTICE STEVENS*: I was unclear on your answer a moment ago. Are you still arguing for a uniform federal rule on privilege?

*MR. FELDMAN*: Yes.

*JUSTICE SOUTER*: So you're not arguing for a rule that would vary from state to state.

*MR. FELDMAN*: It would--no more--

*JUSTICE SOUTER*: Okay. But let me tell you why I ask the question. Part of the premise of your argument is, the value of recognizing the privilege depends upon the value of the confidentiality in the relationship. Now, we can't tell what the value of the confidentiality in the relationship is unless we go state-by-state and find out which states have strong privileges, which states have just weak privileges.

And so I guess what we would have to do is to say, well, if a majority of the states have really strong privileges, that would probably justify our recognition of the strong privilege, but if a majority of the states have a weak privilege, it wouldn't do any good for us, at least in those states, to recognize a strong privilege because it would have no effect on the relationship.

The social worker would have to say, I can't guarantee much. Is that what we should do, is sort of do a nose count and find out whether we're going to get much for our privilege or a little for our privilege?

*MR. FELDMAN*: I think not quite. What the federal court should do is look to see whether the state recognizes, for instance, a relationship between a psychiatric social worker and a client as being one that's entitled to a very high confidentiality protection and accords it a privilege. If in that state the state has said, social workers in this state--you can go to see a social worker, but we're not going to accord it any privilege at all, it's just not that confidential a relationship. It would be like going to see somebody about a legal problem who's not a lawyer. You can do it, I suppose, but-- it's not going to be privileged.

*JUSTICE SOUTER*: Yes, but on your understanding, if there were 45 states that recognized a social worker's privilege and five that didn't, you would say we ought to recognize it, right?

*MR. FELDMAN*: I think–

*JUSTICE SOUTER*: As a uniform federal rule?

*MR. FELDMAN*: No. I think–

*JUSTICE SOUTER*: No?

*MR. FELDMAN*: The federal rule should be that where the state recognizes a confidential relationship, recognizes a privilege with respect to a given category of provider, that in those cases I think there is enough uniformity in the states to say that a federal privilege is also warranted.

CHIEF JUSTICE REHNQUIST: Thank you, Mr. Feldman. Mr. Flaxman, you have three minutes remaining.

## REBUTTAL ARGUMENT OF KENNETH N. FLAXMAN
## ON BEHALF OF THE PETITIONER

*MR. FLAXMAN*: Thank you. I have always been tantalized by the idea that if you tell someone, you tell this to me I'11 keep it a secret, that that could be a privilege, that the court should enforce that kind of promise, and as a matter of fact, that used to be the law. It used to be called the gentleman's privilege. I think in about the 17th century to 18th century, courts stopped enforcing that privilege. In *Branzburg v. Hayes* [408 U.S. 665 (1972)], this Court explicitly recognized that that used to be the law and it is no longer the law.

The question of whether the confidential communication should be protected by a privilege or protected by case-by-case balancing I think should be answered in favor of case-by-case balancing.

*JUSTICE BREYER*: Could I ask a question about state law? I assume that even in Illinois, the Illinois psychiatrist or social worker could not give assurance that even a state law action would not require it. And it would depend upon where the action came up. I assume that an Indiana court would apply Indiana's rules; isn't that right? So that if the lawsuit were in Indiana, the Illinois social worker, by reason of being an Illinois social worker, wouldn't have a special privilege in Indiana.

*MR. FLAXMAN*: That's what I believe the Court should do. The question about–

*JUSTICE BREYER*: No, I'm not saying what it should do, but isn't that the way things work? These are forum rules, so that Illinois can only assure that an Illinois social worker will not be compelled to testify in an Illinois forum.

*MR. FLAXMAN*: That's correct, but Illinois can't even make that assurance, because the common law trend of courts has not been to create privileges, it's been to create exceptions to broad statutory privileges. We've seen that in Illinois, where there aren't exceptions, or evidence that might be relevant in a criminal case, where courts have created an exception.

*JUSTICE BREYER*: Do you agree that this communication would be privileged in the Illinois courts? You don't, do you?

*MR. FLAXMAN*: I agree that we don't know, and we wouldn't know unless we litigated it in the Illinois courts. There was just a recent amendment to the Illinois statute which says that the social worker could reveal confidential communications to her employer, and if this was in state court we would argue that this exception and all the other exceptions require the courts, when the evidence is crucial, to fashion yet another exception.

*JUSTICE BREYER*: And is it true that the rule they apply is governed by the law in the state where the conversation occurred, rather than where the case is being tried?

*MR. FLAXMAN*: I think it's where the case is being tried, rather than where the conversation occurred. But these questions have not arisen--

*JUSTICE BREYER*: Why has it never arisen, in §1983 [Civil Rights Act, 42 U.S.C. § 1983] cases. Has no one ever tried to subpoena medical records from a hospital or a medical doctor's private records? Why have we never had to face the problem of the gunshot wound or the medical doctor who's dealing with physical problems?

*MR. FLAXMAN*: We don't face that problem because the district judges uniformly say there's no privilege. If it's relevant--

*JUSTICE BREYER*: But wouldn't you think some doctor somewhere or a hospital somewhere would have faced a subpoena for some confidential patient records and would have asked us?

*MR. FLAXMAN*: That hasn't happened, it's just routinely accepted.

*CHIEF JUSTICE REHNQUIST*: The case is submitted. Thank you, Mr. Flaxman. (Whereupon, at 11:02 a.m. the case was submitted.)

# THE UNITED STATES SUPREME COURT DECISION IN
## *JAFFEE v. REDMOND*

116 S. Ct. 1923 (1996)

Supreme Court of the United States
No. 95-266
Jaffee v. Redmond
On writ of certiorari to the United States Court of Appeals for the Seventh
Circuit
Decided June 13, 1996

Justice STEVENS delivered the opinion of the Court.

After a traumatic incident in which she shot and killed a man, a police officer received extensive counseling from a licensed clinical social worker. The question we address is whether statements the officer made to her therapist during the counseling sessions are protected from compelled disclosure in a federal civil action brought by the family of the deceased. Stated otherwise, the question is whether it is appropriate for federal courts to recognize a "psychotherapist privilege" under Rule 501 of the Federal Rules of Evidence.

I

Petitioner is the administrator of the estate of Ricky Allen. Respondents are Mary Lu Redmond, a former police officer, and the Village of Hoffman Estates, Illinois her employer during the time that she served in the police force. Petitioner commenced this action against respondents after Redmond shot and killed Allen while on patrol duty.

On June 27, 1991, Redmond was the first officer to respond to a "fight in progress" call at an apartment complex. As she arrived at the scene, two of Allen's sisters ran toward her squad car, waving their arms and shouting that there had been a stabbing in one of the apartments. Redmond testified at trial that she relayed this information to her dispatcher and requested an ambulance. She then exited her car and walked toward the apartment building. Before Redmond reached the building, several men ran out, one waving a pipe. When the men ignored her order to get on the ground, Redmond drew her service revolver. Two other men then burst out of the building, one, Ricky Allen, chasing the other. According to Redmond, Allen was brandishing a butcher knife and disregarded her repeated commands to drop the weapon. Redmond shot Allen when she believed he was about to stab the man he was chasing. Allen died at the scene. Redmond testified that before other officers arrived to provide support, "people came pouring out of the buildings," and a threatening confrontation between her and the crowd ensued.

Petitioner filed suit in Federal District Court alleging that Redmond had violated Allen's constitutional rights by using excessive force during the encounter at the apartment complex. The complaint sought damages under...42 U.S.C. § 1983 and the Illinois wrongful death statute... At trial, petitioner presented testimony from members of Allen's family that conflicted with Redmond's version of the incident in several important respects. They testified, for example, that Redmond drew her gun before exiting her squad car and that Allen was unarmed when he emerged from the apartment building.

During pretrial discovery petitioner learned that after the shooting Redmond had participated in about 50 counseling sessions with Karen Beyer, a clinical social worker licensed by the State of Illinois and employed at that time by the Village of Hoffman Estates. Petitioner sought access to Beyer's notes concerning the sessions for use in cross-examining Redmond. Respondents vigorously resisted the discovery. They asserted that the contents of the conversations between Beyer and Redmond were protected against involuntary disclosure by the psychotherapist-patient privilege. The district judge rejected this argument. Neither Beyer nor Redmond, however, complied with his order to disclose the contents of Beyer's notes. At depositions and on the witness stand both either refused to answer certain questions or professed an inability to recall details of their conversations.

In his instructions at the end of the trial, the judge advised the jury that the refusal to turn over Beyer's notes has no "legal justification" and that the jury could therefore presume that the contents of the notes would have been unfavorable to respondents. The jury awarded petitioner $45,000 on the federal claim and $500,000 on her state-law claim.

The Court of Appeals for the Seventh Circuit reversed and remanded for a new trial. Addressing the issue for the first time, the court concluded that "reason and experience," the touchstones for acceptance of a privilege under Rule 501 of the Federal Rules of Evidence, compelled recognition of a psychotherapist-patient privilege. 51 F.3d 1346, 1355 (1955). "Reason tells us that psychotherapists and patients share a unique relationship, in which the ability to communicate freely without the fear of public disclosure is the key to successful treatment." *Id,.* at 1355-1356. As to experience, the court observed that all 50 States have adopted some form of the psychotherapist-patient privilege. *Id.,* at 1356. The court attached particular significance to the fact that Illinois law expressly extends such a privilege to social workers like Karen Beyer. *Id.,* at 1357. The court also noted that, with one exception, the federal decision rejecting the privilege were more than five years old and that the "need and demand for counseling services has skyrocketed during the past several years." *Id.,* at 1355-1356.

The Court of Appeals qualified its recognition of the privilege by stating that it would not apply if "in the interest of justice, the evidentiary need for the disclosure of the contents of a patient's counseling sessions outweighs that patient's privacy interests." *Id.,* at 1357. Balancing those conflicting interests, the court observed, on the one hand, that the evidentiary need for the contents of the confidential conversations was diminished in this case because there were numerous eyewitnesses to the shooting, and, on the other hand, that Officer Redmond's privacy interests were substantial. *Id.,* at 1358. Based on this assessment, the court concluded that the trial court had erred by refusing to afford protection to the confidential communications between Redmond and Beyer.

The United States courts of appeals do not uniformly agree that the federal courts should recognize a psychotherapist privilege under Rule 501...Because of the conflict among the courts of appeals and the importance of the question, we granted certiorari. We affirm.

## II

Rule 501 of the Federal Rules of Evidence authorizes federal courts to define new privileges by interpreting "common law principles... in the light of reason and experience." The authors of the Rule borrowed this phrase from our opinion in *Wolfe v. United States*, 291 U.S. 7, 12 (1934), which in turn referred to the oft-repeated observation that "the common law is not immutable but flexible, and by its own principles adapts itself to varying conditions," *Funk v. United States*, 290 U.S. 371 (1933). See also *Hawkins v. United States*, 358 U.S. 74 (1958) (changes in privileges may be "dictated by 'reason and experience'"). The Senate Report accompanying the 1975 adoption of the Rules indicates that Rule 501 "should be understood as reflecting the view that the recognition of a privilege based on a confidential relationship...should be determined on a case-by-case basis." S.Rep. No. 93-1277, p. 13 (1974); U.S.Code Cong. & Admin.News 1974, pp. 7051, 7059. The Rule thus did not freeze the law governing the privileges of witnesses in federal trials at a particular point in our history, but rather directed federal courts to "continue the evolutionary development of testimonial privileges." *Trammel v. United States*, 445 U.S. 40, 47 (1980)...

The common-law principles underlying the recognition of testimonial privileges can be states simply. "'For more than three centuries it has now been recognized as a fundamental maxim that the public...has a right to every man's evidence. When we come to examine the various claims of exemption, we start with the primary assumption that there is a general duty to give what testimony one is capable of giving, and that any exemptions which may exist are distinctly exceptional, being so many derogations from a positive general rule.'"... Exceptions from the general rule disfavoring testimonial privileges may be justified, however, by a "'public good transcending the normally predominant principle of utilizing all rational means for ascertaining the truth.'" *Trammel*, 445 U.S. at 50, quoting *Elkins v. United States*, 364 U.S. 206, 234 (1960) (Frankfurter, J., dissenting).

Guided by these principles, the question we address today is whether a privilege protecting confidential communications between a psychotherapist and her patient "promotes sufficiently important interests to outweigh the need for probative evidence...." 445 U.S., at 51. Both "reason and experience" persuade us that it does.

### III

Like the spousal and attorney-client privileges, the psychotherapist-patient privilege is "rooted in the imperative need for confidence and trust." *Trammel*, 445 U.S. at 51. Treatment by a physician for physical ailments can often proceed successfully on the basis of a physical examination, objective information supplied by the patient, and the results of diagnostic tests. Effective psychotherapy, by contrast, depends upon an atmosphere of confidence and trust in which the patient is willing to make a frank and complete disclosure of facts, emotions, memories, and fears. Because of the sensitive nature of the problems for which individuals consult psychotherapists, disclosure of confidential communications made during counseling sessions may cause embarrassment or disgrace. For this reason, the mere possibilities of disclosure may impede development of the confidential relationship necessary for successful treatment. As the Judicial Conference Advisory Committee observed in 1972 when it recommended that Congress recognize a psychotherapist privilege as part of the Proposed Federal Rules of Evidence, a psychiatrist's ability to help her patients "is completely dependent upon [the patients'] willingness and ability to talk freely. This makes it difficult if not impossible for [a psychiatrist] to function without being able to assure...patients of confidentiality and, indeed, privileged communication. Where there may be exceptions to this general rule..., there is wide agreement that confidentiality is a *sine qua non* for successful psychiatric treatment." Advisory Committee's Notes to Proposed Rules, 56 F.R.D. 183, 242 (1972) (quoting Group for the Advancement of Psychiatry, Report No. 45, Confidentiality and Privileged Communication in the Practice of Psychiatry 92 (June 1960)). By protecting confidential communications between a psychotherapist and her patient from involuntary disclosure, the proposed privilege thus serves important private interests.

Our cases make clear that an asserted privilege must also "serv[e] public ends." *Upjohn Co. v. United States*, 449 U.S. 383, 389 (1981). Thus, the purpose of the attorney-client privilege is to "encourage full and frank communication between attorneys and their clients and thereby promote broader public interests in the observance of law and administration of justice." *Ibid.* And the spousal privilege, as modified in *Trammel*, is justified because it "furthers the important public interest in marital harmony," 445 U.S. at 53. See also *United States v. Nixon*, 418 U.S. at 705; *Wolfe v. United States*, 291 U.S. at 14. The psychotherapist privilege serves the public interest by facilitating the provision of appropriate treatment for individuals suffering the effects of a mental or emotional problem. The mental health of our citizenry, no less than its physical health is a public good of transcendent importance [1].

In contrast to the significant public and private interests supporting recognition of the privilege, the likely evidentiary benefit that would result from the denial of the privilege is modest. If the privilege were rejected, confidential conversations between psychotherapists and their patients would surely be chilled, particularly when it is obvious that the circumstances that give rise to the need for treatment will probably result in litigation. Without a privilege, much of the desirable evidence to which litigants such as petitioner seek access--for example, admissions against interest by a party--is unlikely to come into being. This unspoken "evidence" will therefore serve no greater truth-seeking function than if it had been spoken and privileged.

That it is appropriate for the federal courts to recognize a psychotherapist privilege under Rule 501 is confirmed by the fact that all 50 States and the District of Columbia have enacted into law some form of psychotherapist privilege. We have previously observed that the policy decisions of the States bear on the question whether federal courts should recognize a new privilege or amend the coverage of an existing one. See *Trammel*, 445 U.S. at 48-50; *United States v. Gillock*, 445 U.S. 360, 368, n. 8 (1980). Because state legislatures are fully aware of the need to protect the integrity of the fact finding functions of their courts, the existence of the consensus among the States indicates that "reason and experience" support recognition of the

---

1. This case amply demonstrates the importance of allowing individuals to receive confidential counseling. Police officers engaged in the dangerous and difficult tasks associated with protecting the safety of our communities not only confront the risk of physical harm but also face stressful circumstances that may give rise to anxiety, depression, fear or anger. The entire community may suffer if police officers are not able to receive effective counseling and treatment after traumatic incidents, either because trained officers leave the profession prematurely or because those in need of treatment remain on the job. [The footnotes are by the Court. Some are omitted.]

privilege. In addition, given the importance of the patient's understanding that her communications with her therapist will not be publicly disclosed, any State's promise of confidentiality would have little value if the patient were aware that the privilege would not be honored in a federal court. Denial of the federal privilege therefore would frustrate the purposes of the state legislation that was enacted to foster these confidential communications.

It is of no consequence that recognition of the privilege in the vast majority of States is the product of legislative action rather than judicial decision. Although common-law rulings may once have been the primary source of new developments in federal privilege law, that is no longer the case. In *Funk v. United States*, 290 U.S. 371 (1933), we recognized that it is appropriate to treat a consistent body of policy determinations by state legislatures as reflecting both "reason" and "experience." *Id.*, at 376-381. That rule is properly respectful of the States and at the same time reflects the fact that once a state legislature has enacted a privilege there is no longer an opportunity for common-law creation of the protection. The history of the psychotherapist privilege illustrates the latter point. In 1972 the members of the Judicial Conference Advisory Committee noted that the common law "had indicated a disposition to recognize a psychotherapist-patient privilege when legislatures began moving into the field." Proposed Rules, 56 F.R.D. at 242 (citation omitted). The present unanimous acceptance of the privilege shows that the state lawmakers moved quickly. That the privilege may have developed faster legislatively than it would have in the courts demonstrates only that the States rapidly recognized the wisdom of the rule as the field of psychotherapy developed.

The uniform judgement of the States is reinforced by the fact that a psychotherapist privilege was among the nine specific privileges recommended by the Advisory Committee in its proposed privilege rules. In *United States v. Gillock*, 445 U.S. 360, 367-368 (1980), our holding that Rule 501 did not include a state legislative privilege relied, in part, on the fact that no such privilege was included in the Advisory Committee's draft. The reasoning in *Gillock* thus supports the opposite conclusion in this case. In rejecting the proposed draft that had specifically identified each privilege rule and substituting the present more open-ended Rule 501, the Senate Judiciary Committee explicitly stated that its action "should not be understood as disapproving any recognition of the psychiatrist-patient...privilege contained in the [proposed] rules." S.Rep. No. 93-1277, at 13; U.S.Code Cong. & Admin.News 1974, pp. 7051, 7059.

Because we agree with the judgement of the state legislatures and the Advisory Committee that a psychotherapist-patient privilege will serve a "public good transcending the normally predominant principle of utilizing all rational means for ascertaining truth," *Trammel*, 445 U.S. at 50, we hold that confidential communications between a licensed psychotherapist and her patients in the course of diagnosis or treatment are protected from compelled disclosure under Rule 501 of the Federal Rules of Evidence.

## IV

All agree that a psychotherapist privilege covers confidential communications made to licensed psychiatrists and psychologists. We have no hesitation in concluding in this case that the federal privilege should also extend to confidential communications made to licensed social workers in the course of psychotherapy. The reasons for recognizing a privilege for treatment by psychiatrists and psychologists apply with equal force to treatment by a clinical social worker such as Karen Beyer. Today, social workers provide a significant amount of mental health treatment. Their clients often include the poor and those of modest means who could not afford the assistance of a psychiatrist or psychologist, but whose counseling sessions serve the same public goals. Perhaps in recognition of these circumstances, the vast majority of States explicitly extend a testimonial privilege to licensed social workers. We therefore agree with the Court of Appeals that "[d]rawing a distinction between the counseling provided by costly psychotherapists and the counseling provided by more readily accessible social workers serves no discernible public purpose." 51 F.3d at 1358, n. 19.

We part company with the Court of Appeals on a separate point. We reject the balancing component of the privilege implemented by that court and a small number of States. Making the promise of confidentiality contingent upon a trial judge's later evaluation of the relative importance of the patient's interest in privacy and the evidentiary need for disclosure would eviscerate the effectiveness of the privilege. As we explained in *Upjohn*, if the purpose of the privilege is to be served, the participants in the confidential conversation "must be able to predict with some degree of certainty whether particular discussions will be protected. An uncertain privilege, or one which purports to be certain but results in widely varying applications by the courts, is little better than no privilege at all." 449 U.S. at 393.

These considerations are all that is necessary for decision of this case. A rule that authorizes the recognition of new privileges on a case-by-case basis makes it appropriate to define the details of new privileges in a like manner. Because this is the first case in which we have recognized a psychotherapist privilege, it is neither necessary nor feasible to delineate its full contours in a way that would "govern all conceivable future questions in this area." *Id.*, at 386.[2]

V

The conversations between Officer Redmond and Karen Beyer and the notes taken during their counseling sessions are protected from the compelled disclosure under Rule 501 of the Federal Rules of Evidence. The judgement of the Court of Appeals is affirmed.

It is so ordered.

Justice SCALIA, with whom THE CHIEF JUSTICE joins as to Part III, dissenting.
The Court has discussed at some length the benefit that will be purchased by creation of the evidentiary privilege in this case: the encouragement of psychoanalytic

---

2. Although it would be premature to speculate about most future developments in the federal psychotherapist privilege, we do not doubt that there are situations in which the privilege must give way, for example, if a serious threat of harm to the patient or to others can be averted only by means of a disclosure by the therapist.

counseling. It has not mentioned the purchase price: occasional injustice. That is the cost of every rule which excludes reliable and probative evidence–or at least every one categorical enough to achieve its announced policy objective. In the case of some of these rules, such as the one excluding confessions that have not been properly "Mirandized,:" see *Miranda v. Arizona*, 384 U.S. 436 (1966), the victim of the injustice is always the impersonal State or the faceless "public at large." For the rule proposed here, the victim is more likely to be some individual who is prevented from proving a valid claim–or (worse still) prevented from establishing a valid defense. The latter is particularly unpalatable for those who love justice, because it causes the courts of law not merely to let stand a wrong, but to become themselves the instruments of wrong.

In the past, this Court has well understood that the particular value the courts are distinctively charged with preserving–justice–is severely harmed by contravention of "the fundamental principle that 'the public...has a right to every man's evidence.'" *Trammel v. United States*, 445 U.S. 40, 50 (1980). Testimonial privileges, it has said, "are not likely created nor expansively construed, for they are in derogation of the search for truth." *United States v. Nixon*, 418 U.S. 683, 710 (1974) (emphasis added). Adherence to that principle has caused us, in the Rule 501 cases we have considered to date, to reject new privileges, see *University of Pennsylvania v. EEOC*, 493 U.S. 182 (1990) (privilege against disclosure of academic peer review materials); *United States v. Gillock*, 445 U.S. 360, (1980) (privilege against disclosure of "legislative acts" by member of state legislature), and even to construe narrowly the scope of existing privileges, see, *e.g., United States v. Zolin*, 491 U.S. 554, 568-570 (1989) (permitting *in camera* review of documents alleged to come within crime-fraud exception to attorney-client privilege); *Trammel, supra* (holding that voluntary testimony by spouse is not covered by husband-wife privilege). The Court today ignores this traditional judicial preference for the truth, and ends up creating a privilege that is new, vast, and ill-defined. I respectfully dissent.

# I

The case before us involves confidential communications made by a police officer to a state-licensed clinical social worker in the course of psychotherapeutic counseling. Before proceeding to a legal analysis of the case, I must observe that the Court makes its task deceptively simple by the manner in which it proceeds. It begins by characterizing the issue as "whether it is appropriate for federal courts to recognize a 'psychotherapist privilege,'" and devotes almost all if its opinion to that question. Having answered that question (to its satisfaction) in the affirmative, it then devotes *less than a page of text* to answering in the affirmative the small remaining question whether "the federal privilege should also extend to confidential communications made to licensed social workers in the course of psychotherapy."

Of course the prototypical evidentiary privilege analogous to the one asserted here–the lawyer-client privilege– is not identified by the broad area of advice-giving practiced by the person to whom the privileged communication is given, but rather by the professional status of that person. Hence, it seems a long step from a lawyer-client privilege to a tax advisor-client or accountant-client privilege. But if one recharacterizes it as a "legal advisor" privilege, the extension seems like the most natural thing in the world. That is the illusion the Court has produced here: It first frames an overly general question ("Should there be a psychotherapist privilege?") that can be answered in the negative only by excluding from protection office consultations with professional psychiatrists (*i.e.*, doctors) and clinical psychologists. And then, having answered that in the affirmative, it comes to the only question that the facts of this case present ("Should there be a social worker-client privilege with regard to psychotherapeutic counseling?") with the answer seemingly a foregone conclusion. At that point, to conclude against the privilege one must subscribe to the difficult proposition, "Yes, there is a psychotherapist privilege, but not if the psychotherapist is a social worker."

Relegating the question actually posed by this case to an afterthought makes the impossible possible in a number of wonderful ways. For example, it enables the Court to treat the Proposed Federal Rules of Evidence developed in 1972 by the Judicial Conference Advisory Committee as strong support for its holding, whereas they in fact counsel clearly and directly against it. The Committee did indeed recommend a "psychotherapist privilege" of sorts; but more precisely, and more relevantly, it recommended a privilege for psychotherapy conducted by "a person authorized to practice medicine' or "a person licensed or certified as a psychologist," Proposed Rule of Evidence 504, 56 F.R.D. 183, 240 (1972), which is to say that it recommended against the privilege at issue here. That condemnation is obscured, and even converted into an endorsement, by pushing a "psychotherapist privilege" into the center ring. The Proposed Rule figures prominently in the Court's explanation of why that privilege deserves recognition, and is ignored in the single page devoted to the sideshow which happens to be the issue presented for decision.

This is the most egregious and readily explainable example of how the Court's misdirection of its analysis makes the difficult seem easy; others will become apparent when I give the social-worker question the fuller consideration it deserves. My initial point, however, is that the Court's very methodology–giving serious consideration only to the more general, and much easier, question–is in violation of our duty to proceed cautiously when erecting barriers between us and the truth.

## II

To say that the Court devotes the bulk of its opinion to the much easier question of psychotherapist-patient privilege is not to say that its answer to that question is convincing. At bottom, the Court's decision to recognize such a privilege is based on its view that "successful [psychotherapeutic] treatment" serves "important private interests" (namely those of patients undergoing psychotherapy) as well as the "public good" of "[t]he mental health of our citizenry." I have no quarrel with these premises. Effective psychotherapy undoubtedly is beneficial to individuals with mental problems, and surely serves some larger social interest in maintaining a mentally stable society. But merely mentioning these values does not answer the critical question: are they of such importance, and is the contribution of psychotherapy to them so distinctive, and is the application of normal evidentiary rules so destructive to psychotherapy, as to justify making our federal courts occasional instruments of injustice? On that central question I find the Court's analysis insufficiently convincing to satisfy the high standard we have set for rules that "are in derogation of the search for truth." *Nixon*, 418 U.S. at 710.

When is it, one must wonder, that the psychotherapist came to play such an indispensable role in the maintenance of the citizenry's mental health? For most of history, men and women have worked out their difficulties by talking to, *inter alios*, parents, siblings, best friends and bartenders—none of whom was awarded a privilege against testifying in court. Ask the average citizen: Would your mental health be more significantly impaired by preventing you from seeing a psychotherapist, or by preventing you from getting advice from your mom? I have little doubt what the answer would be. Yet there is no mother-child privilege.

How likely is it that a person will be deterred from seeking psychological counseling, or from being completely truthful in the course of such counseling, because of fear of later disclosure in litigation? And even more pertinent to today's decision, to what extent will the evidentiary privilege reduce that deterrent? The Court does not try to answer the first of these questions; and it cannot possibly have any notion of what the answer is to the second, since that depends entirely upon the scope of the privilege, which the Court amazingly finds it "neither necessary nor feasible to delineate." If, for example, the psychotherapist can give the patient no more assurance than "A court will not be able to make me disclose what you tell me, unless you tell me about a harmful act," I doubt whether there would be much benefit from the privilege at all. That is not a fanciful example, at least with respect to extension of the psychotherapist privilege to social workers. See Del.Code Ann., Tit. 24, § 3913(2) (1987); Idaho Code § 54-3213(2) (1994).

Even where it is certain that absence of the psychotherapist privilege will inhibit disclosure of the information, it is not clear to me that that is an unacceptable state of affairs. Let us assume the very worst in the circumstances of the present case: that to be truthful about what was troubling her, the police officer who sought counseling would have to confess that she shot without reason, and wounded an innocent man. If (again to assume the worst) such an act constituted the crime of negligent wounding under Illinois law, the officer would of course have the absolute right not to admit that she shot without reason in criminal court. But I see no reason why she should be enabled *both* not to admit it in criminal court (as a good citizen should), *and* to get the benefits of psychotherapy by admitting it to a therapist who cannot tell anyone else. And even less reason why she should be enabled to *deny* her guilt in the criminal trial—or in a civil trial for negligence—while yet obtaining the benefits of psychotherapy by confessing guilt to a social worker who cannot testify. It seems to me entirely fair to say that if she wishes the benefits of telling the truth she must also accept the adverse consequences. To be sure, in most cases the statements to the psychotherapist will be only marginally relevant, and one of the purposes of the privilege (though not one relied upon by the Court) may be simply to spare patients needless intrusion upon their privacy, and to spare psychotherapists needless expenditure of their time in deposition and trial. But surely this can be achieved by means short of excluding even evidence that is of the most direct and conclusive effect.

The Court confidently asserts that not much truth-finding capacity would be destroyed by the privilege anyway, since "[w]ithout a privilege, much of the desirable evidence to which litigants such as petitioner seek access...is unlikely to come into being." If that is so, how come psychotherapy got to be a thriving practice before the "psychotherapist privilege" was invented? Were the patients paying money to lie to their analysts all those years? Of course the evidence-generating effect of the privilege (if any) depends entirely upon its scope to be the broadest possible, is it really true that most, or even many, of those who seek psychological counseling have the worry of litigation in the back of their minds? I doubt that, and the Court provides no evidence to support it.

The Court suggests one last policy justification: since psychotherapist privilege statutes exist in all the States, the failure to recognize a privilege in federal courts "would frustrate the purpose of the state legislation that was enacted to foster these confidential communications." This is a novel argument indeed. A sort of inverse pre-emption: the trust-seeking functions of federal courts must be adjusted so as not to conflict with the policies of the States. This reasoning cannot be squared with *Gillock*, which declined to recognize an evidentiary privilege for Tennessee legislators in federal prosecutions, even though the Tennessee Constitution guaranteed it in state criminal proceedings, *Gillock*, 445 U.S. at 368. Moreover, since as I shall discuss, state policies regarding the psychotherapist privilege vary considerably from State to State, *no* uniform federal policy can possibly honor most of them. If furtherance of state policies is the name of the game, rules of privilege in federal courts should vary from State to State, *á la Erie.*

The Courts failure to put forward a convincing justification of its own could perhaps be excused if it were relying upon the unanimous conclusion of state courts in the reasoned development of their common law. It cannot do that, since *no* State has such a privilege apart from legislation. What it relies upon, instead, is "the fact that all 50 States and the District of Columbia have enacted into law some form of psychotherapist privilege." Let us consider both the verb and its object: The fact that all 50 States have enacted this privilege argues not *for*, but *against*, our adopting the privilege judicially. At best it suggests that the matter has been found not to lend itself to judicial treatment–perhaps because the pros and cons of adopting the privilege, or of giving it one or another shape, are not that clear; or perhaps because the rapidly evolving uses of psychotherapy demand a flexibility that only legislation can provide. At worst it suggests that the privilege commends itself only to decisionmaking bodies in which reason is tempered, so to speak, by political pressure from organized interest groups (such as psychologists and social workers), and decisionmaking bodies that are not overwhelmingly concerned (as courts of law are and should be) with justice.

And the phrase "some form of psychotherapist privilege" covers a multitude of difficulties. The Court concedes that there is "divergence among the States concerning the types of therapy relationships protected and the exceptions recognized." To rest a newly announced federal common-law psychotherapist privilege, assertible from this day forward in all federal courts, upon "the States' *unanimous judgment* that some form of psychotherapist privilege is appropriate," is rather like announcing a new, immediately applicable, federal common law of torts, based upon the States' "unanimous judgment" that *some* form of tort law is appropriate. In the one case as in the other, the state laws vary to such a degree that the parties and lower federal judges confronted by the new "common law" have barely a clue as to what its content might be.

## III

Turning from the general question that was not involved in this case to the specific one that is: The Court's conclusion that a social-worker psychotherapist privilege deserves recognition is even less persuasive. In approaching this question, the fact that five of the state legislatures that have seen fit to enact "some form" of psychotherapist privilege have elected not to extend any form of privilege to social workers, ought to give one pause. So should the fact that the Judicial Conference Advisory Committee was similarly discriminating in its conferral of the proposed Rule 504 privilege, see *supra*. The Court, however, has "no hesitation in concluding...that the federal privilege should also extend" to social workers, and goes on to prove that by polishing off the reasoned analysis with a topic sentence and two sentences of discussion, as follows (omitting citations and nongermane footnote): "The reasons for recognizing a privilege for treatment by psychiatrists and psychologists apply with equal force to treatment by a clinical social worker such as Karen Beyer. Today, social workers provide a significant amount of mental health treatment. Their clients often include the poor and those of modest means who could not afford the assistance of a psychiatrist or psychologist, but whose counseling sessions serve the same public goals." So much for the rule that privileges are to be narrowly construed.

Of course this brief analysis–like the earlier, more extensive, discussion of the general psychotherapist privilege–contains no explanation of why the psychotherapy provided by social workers is a public good of such transcendent importance as to be purchased at the price of occasional injustice. Moreover, it considers only the respects in which social workers providing therapeutic services are similar to licensed psychiatrists and psychologists; not a word about the respects in which they are different. A licensed psychiatrist or psychologist is an expert in psychotherapy–and that may suffice (though I think it not so clear that this Court should make the judgment) to justify the use of extraordinary means to encourage counseling with him, as opposed to counseling with one's rabbi, minister, family or friends. One must presume that a social worker does not bring this greatly heightened degree of skill to bear, which is alone a reason for not encouraging that consultation as generously. Does a social worker bring to bear at least a significantly heightened degree of skill– more than a minister or rabbi, for example? I have no idea, and neither does the Court. The social worker in the present case, Karen Beyer, was a "licensed clinical social worker" in Illinois, a job title whose training requirements consist of "master's degree in social work from an approved program," and "3,000 hours of satisfactory, supervised clinical professional experience." Ill. Comp. Stat., ch. 225 § 20/9 (1994). It is not clear that the degree in social work requires *any* training in psychotherapy. The "clinical professional experience" apparently will impart some such training, but only of the vaguest sort, judging from the Illinois Code's definition of "[c]linical social work practice," viz., "the providing of mental health service for the evaluation, treatment, and prevention of mental and emotional disorders in individuals, families and groups based on knowledge and theory of psychosocial development, behavior, psychopathology, unconscious motivation, interpersonal relationships, and environmental stress." Ch. 225, § 20/3(5). But the rule the Court announces today–like the Illinois evidentiary privilege which that rule purports to respect, Ch. 225 § 20/16–is not limited to "licensed clinical social workers," but includes all "licensed social workers." "Licensed social workers" may also provide "mental health services" as described in § 20/3(5), so long as it is done under supervision of a licensed clinical social worker. And the training requirement for a "licensed social worker" consists of either (a) "a degree from a graduate program of social work" approved by the State, or (b) "a degree in social work from an undergraduate program" approved by the State, plus "3 years of supervised professional experience." Ch. 225, § 20/9A. With due respect, it does not seem to me that any of this training is comparable in its rigor (or indeed in the precision of its subject) to the training of the other experts (lawyers) to whom this Court has accorded a privilege, or even the experts (psychiatrists and psychologists) to whom the Advisory Committee and this Court proposed extension of a privilege in 1972. Of course these are only Illinois' requirements for "social workers." Those of other States, for all we know, may be even less demanding. Indeed, I am not even sure there is a nationally accepted definition of "social worker," as there is of psychiatrist and psychologist. It seems to me quite irresponsible to extend the so-called "psychotherapist privilege" to all licensed social workers, nationwide, without exploring these issues.

Another critical distinction between psychiatrists and psychologists, on the one hand, and social workers, on the other, is that the former professionals, in their consultations with patients, do nothing but psychotherapy. Social workers, on the other hand, interview people for a multitude of reasons. The Illinois definition of "[l]icensed social worker," for example, is as follows: "'Licensed social worker' means a person who holds a license authorizing the practice of social work, which includes social services to individuals, groups or communities in any one or more of the fields of social casework, social group work, community organization for social welfare, social work research, social welfare administration or social work education." Ch.225, § 20/3(9).

Thus, in applying the "social worker" variant of the "psychotherapist" privilege, it will be necessary to know whether the information provided to the social worker was provided to him in his capacity as a psychotherapist, or in his capacity as an administrator of social welfare, a community organizer, etc. Worse still, if the privilege is to have its desired effect (and is not to mislead the client), it will presumably be necessary for the social caseworker to advise, as the conversation with his welfare client proceeds, which portions are privileged and which are not.

Having concluded its three sentences of reasoned analysis, the Court then invokes, as it did when considering the psychotherapist privilege, the "experience" of the States–once again an experience I consider irrelevant (if not counter-indicative) because it consists entirely of legislation rather than common-law decision. It says that "the vast majority of States explicitly extend a testimonial privilege to licensed social workers." There are two elements of this impressive statistic, however, that the Court does not reveal.

First—and utterly conclusive of the irrelevance of this supposed consensus to the question before us—the majority of the States that accord a privilege to social workers do *not* do so as a subpart of a "psychotherapist" privilege. The privilege applies to all confidences imparted to social workers, and not just those provided in the course of psychotherapy. In Oklahoma, for example, the social-worker-privilege statute prohibits a licensed social worker from disclosing, or being compelled to disclose, "*any information* acquired from persons consulting the licensed social worker in his or her professional capacity" (with certain exceptions to be discussed *infra*). Okla. Stat., Tit. 59, § 1261.6 (1991) (emphasis added). The social worker's "professional capacity" is expansive, for the "practice of social work" in Oklahoma is defined as:

"[T]he professional activity of helping individuals, groups or communities enhance or restore their capacity for physical, social and economic functioning and the professional application of social work values, principles and techniques in areas such as clinical social work, social service administration, social planning, social work consultation and social work research to one or more of the following ends: Helping people obtain tangible services; counseling with individuals, families and groups; helping communities or groups provide or improve social and health services; and participating in relevant social action. The practice of social work requires knowledge of human development and behavior; of social, economic and cultural institutions and forces; and of the interaction of all of these factors. Social work practice includes the teaching of relevant subject matter and of conducting research into problems of human behavior and conflict." Tit. 59, § 1250.1(2) (1991).

Thus, in Oklahoma, as in most other States having a social-worker privilege, it is not a subpart or even a derivative of the psychotherapist privilege, but rather a piece of special legislation similar to that achieved by many other groups, from accountants, see, *e.g.*, Miss. Code Ann. § 73-33-16(2) (1995) (certified public accountant "shall not be required by any court of this state to disclose, and shall not voluntarily disclose" client information), to private detectives, see, *e.g.*, Mich. Comp. Laws § 338.840 (1979) ("Any communications...furnished by a professional man or client to a [licensed private detective], or any information secured in connection with an assignment for a client, shall be deemed privileged with the same authority and dignity as are other privileged communications recognized by the courts of this state"). These social-worker statutes give no support, therefore, to the theory (importance of psychotherapy) upon which the Court rests its disposition.

Second, the Court does not reveal the enormous degree of disagreement among the States as to the scope of the privilege. It concedes that the laws of four States are subject to such gaping exceptions that they are "'little better than no privilege at all,'" ...so that they should more appropriately be categorized with the five States whose laws contradict the action taken today. I would add another State to those whose privilege is illusory. See Wash. Rev.Code § 18.19.180 (1994) (disclosure of information required "[i]n response to a subpoena from a court of law"). In adopting *any* sort of a social worker privilege, then, the Court can at most claim that it is following the legislative "experience" of 40 States, and contradicting the "experience" of 10.

But turning to those States that do have an appreciable privilege of some sort, the diversity is vast. In Illinois and Wisconsin, the social-worker privilege does not apply when the confidential information pertains to homicide, see Ill. Comp. Stat., ch. 740, § 110/10(a)(9) (1994); Wis. Stat. § 905.04(4)(d) (1993-1994), and in the District of Columbia when it pertains to any crime "inflicting injuries" upon persons, see D.C.Code § 14-307(b)(1) (1995). In Missouri, the privilege is suspended as to information that pertains to a criminal act, see Mo.Rev.Stat. § 337.636(2) (1994), and in Texas when the information is sought in any criminal prosecution, compare Tex. Rule Civ. Evid. 510(d) with Tex. Rule Crim. Evid. 501 *et seq.* In Kansas and Oklahoma, the privilege yields when the information pertains to "violations of any law," see Kan. Stat. Ann. § 65-6315(a)(2) (Supp.1990); Okla. Stat., Tit. 59, § 1261.6(2) (1991); in Indiana, when it reveals a "serious harmful act," see Ind.Code Ann. § 25-23.6-6-1(2) (1995); and in Delaware and Idaho, when it pertains t any "harmful act," see Del.Code Ann., Tit. 24, § 3913(2) (1987); Idaho Code § 54-3213(2) (1994). In Oregon, a state-employed social worker like Karen Beyer loses the privilege where her supervisor determines that her testimony "is necessary in the performance of the duty of the social worker as a public employee." See Ore.Rev.Stat.§ 40.250(5) (1991). In South Carolina, a social worker is forced to disclose confidences "when required by statutory law or by court order for good cause shown to the extent that the patient's care and treatment or the nature and extent of his mental illness or emotional condition are reasonably at issue in a preceding," See S.C.Code Ann. § 19-11-95(D)(1) (Sup. 1995). The majority of social-worker-privilege States declare the privilege inapplicable to information relating to child abuse. And the States that do not fall into any of the above categories provide exceptions for commitment proceedings, for proceedings in which the patient relies on his mental or emotional condition as an element of his claim or defense, or for communications made in the course of a court-ordered examination of the mental or emotional condition of the patient.

Thus, although the Court is technically correct that "the vast majority of States explicitly extend a testimonial privilege to licensed social workers," that uniformity exists only at the most superficial level. No State has adopted the privilege without restriction; the nature of the restrictions varies enormously from jurisdiction to jurisdiction; and 10 States, I reiterate, effectively reject the privilege entirely. It is fair to say that there is scant national consensus even at to the propriety of a social-worker psychotherapist privilege, and none whatever as to its appropriate scope. In other words, the state laws to which the Court appeals for support demonstrate most convincingly that adoption of a social-worker psychotherapist privilege is a job for Congress.

\*\*\*

The question before us today is not whether there should be an evidentiary privilege for social workers providing therapeutic services. Perhaps there should. But the question before us is whether (1) the need for that privilege is so clear, and (2) the desirable contours of that privilege are so evident, that it is appropriate for this Court to craft it in common-law fashion, under Rule 501. Even if we were writing on a clean slate, I think the answer to that question would be clear. But given our extensive precedent to the effect that new privileges "in derogation of the search for truth" "are not lightly created," *United States v. Nixon*, 418 U.S. at 710, the answer the Court gives today is inexplicable.

In its consideration of this case, the court was the beneficiary of no fewer than 14 *amicus* briefs supporting respondents, most of which came from such organizations as the American Psychiatric Association, the American Psychoanalytic Association, the American Association of State Social Work Boards, the Employee Assistance Professionals Association, Inc., the American Counseling Association, and the National Association of Social Workers. Not a single *amicus* brief was filed in support of petitioner. That is no surprise. There is no self-interested organization out there devoted to pursuit of the truth in the federal courts. The expectation is, however, that this Court will have that interest prominently—indeed, primarily—in mind. Today we have failed that expectation, and that responsibility. It is no small matter to say that, in some cases, our federal courts will be the tools of injustice rather than unearth the truth where it is available to be found. The common law has identified a few instances where that is tolerable. Perhaps Congress may conclude that is is also tolerable for the purpose of encouraging psychotherapy by social workers. But that conclusion assuredly does not burst upon the mind with such clarity that a judgement in favor of suppressing the truth ought to be pronounced by this honorable Court. I respectfully dissent.

# TABLE OF CASES

A.B. v. C.D., 317
Abell, J., *Ex parte*, 146, 499
Abety v. Abety, 22
Adams v. Ludorf, 296
Aiken v. Clary, 512
A.J.S., Matter of, 112
Al-Kanani, People v., 173
Alar v. Mercy Memorial Hospital, 327
Albert Lindley Lee Memorial Hospital, *In re*, 487, 488, 502
Alexander v. Knight, 128
Allen, State v., 146
Allred v. State, 14
Amato v. Porter, 199
American Motorcycle Assn. v. Superior Court, 328
Anderson v. Strong Memorial Hospital, 149
Andring, State v., 174, 215
Anonymous v. Kissinger, 414
Antill, State v., 33
Antrade v. Superior Court of Los Angeles County, 24
Application of _____, *see name of party*
A.R.A., *In re*, 112
Atwood v. Atwood, 113, 114
Axelson, State of Florida v., 67

B, *In re*, 547
Baird v. Koerner, 502
Banks, United States v., 173
Barber v. Time, 149
Barefoot v. Estelle, 301
Bartley v. Kremens, 268
Bassil v. Ford Motor Co., 216
Beardsley, People v., xv
Beatty v. Baston, 268
Beaver v. Alaska, 185
Beckley, People v., 542
Behnke, State v., 181
Bellah v. Greenson, 427

Bellotti v. Baird, 390, 391
Bercier, United States v., 22
Berry v. Moench, 317
Betty J.B. v. Division of Social Services, 114
Binder v. Ruvell, 105
Bindrim v. Mitchell, 215
Blue Cross v. Superior Court & Blair, 215
Blunt v. State, 169
Board of Trustees of Memorial Hospital v. Pratt, 476
Boddy v. Parker, 147, 490
Boofar, State v., 213
Bounds, State v., 169
Boyd v. Wynn, xv, 31
Boyd v. United States, 157
Boyles v. Cora, 23
Brady v. Hopper, 294, 311
Bredice v. Doctors Hospital, 408, 411
Brennan v. Orban, 104
Brents v. Morgan, 438
Brewster v. Martin Marietta Aluminum Sales, 120
Britt v. Superior Court, 116
Britton v. Soltes, 322
Brown v. Northville Regional Psychiatric Hosp., 333
Bryson v. Tillinghast, 268
Brzonkala v. Virginia Polytechnic Institute, 104
Buckley v. Valeo, 378
Burtrum, United States v., 69
Burzynski Cancer Research Inst., United States v., 22
Butler v. Acme Markets, 341
Butler, United States v., 254
Byers, United States v., 154, 171, 173

C.G., *In re*, 401
Cansler v. State, 332
Cardwell v. Bechtol, 399

Carey v. Population Services Int'l, 399
Carr v. Allison Gas Turbine Div., 132
Carr v. Watkins, 268, 317
Carroll v. Junker, 500
Carson v. Beatley, 33
Cathey, *In re*, 73
Chambers v. Mississippi, 178
Chaplinsky v. New Hampshire, 377, 378
Cheatham v. Rogers, 70
Chitty v. Fitzgerald, 112
Chrisos, United States v., 183
Christy Bros. Circus v. Turnage, 136
Circuit Court, State ex rel. Green Bay Newspaper Co. v., 146
Cisneros, State v., 180
City & County of San Francisco v. Superior Court, 24, 88, 174
City of Alhambra v. Superior Court, 117, 146
Clark v. Geraci, 264, 414
Clark v. People, 175
Clark v. Virginia Bd. of Bar Examiners, 433
Clarke v. Whittemore, 321
Claus Von Bulow, *In re*, 247
Clayman v. Bernstein, 149
Cobbs v. Grant, 474
Coburn v. Seda, 411
Coddington, Matter of, 248
Cohen v. State, 477
Collins v. Augur, 173
Combes, People v., 31
Commonwealth v._____, *see opposing party*
Compton v. Subaru of America, 543
Cooper v. Vannier, 553
Copithorne v. Framingham Union Hospital, 428
Cordoba, United States v., 542
Cornona, People v., 383
Corona, United States v., 69
Costa v. Regents of the University of California, 147, 489
Cranford v. Cranford, 488
Crews, United States v., 176
Crims, State v., 179
Critchlow v. Critchlow, 113
Cunningham v. Southlake Ctr. for Mental Health, 69
Currie v. United States, 308
Curry v. Corn, 268
Cutter v. Brownbridge, 249

D. v. D., 112
D.F., United States v., 152
D.W.H., *In re*, 188
Daley v. Koch, 434
Daubert v. Merrill Dow Pharmaceuticals, 535, 536, 542
Davidson v. Light, 411
Davis v. Alaska, 178
Davis v. Allied Supermarkets, 341
Davis, State v., 179
Davis v. Lhim, 294, 295, 299, 337
Dean, State v., 169
DeAngelis v. El Paso Mun. Police Off. Assn., 131
DeMay v. Roberts, xiii
Denaro v. Prudential Ins. Co., 32
Dillon v. Legg, 333
DiMarco v. Lynch Homes, 322
Ditson, People v., 31
Division of Medical Quality, Board of Medical Quality Assurance v. Gherardini, 490
Dixon, People v., 14
Dodis, State v., 384
Doe v. Doe, 104
Doe v. Irwin, 399
Doe v. Maskell, 542
Doe v. Mills, 147
Doe v. Roe, 149, 267, 478
Doe v. S.E. Pa. Transp. Authority, 430
Doe, *In re*, 68
Doll v. Equitable Life Assur. Soc, 22
Domako v. Rowe, 138, 249
Donner v. Edelstein, 180
Dorris v. Detroit Osteopathic Hosp., 141, 142
Dulger, People v., 183
DuPont v. Finklea, 502
Dutton, People v., 169
Duvall v. Goldin, 335
Dyer v. State, 30

Eagles v. Liberty Weekly, 385
Easter v. McDonald, 129, 136, 248
Eberle v. Savon Food Stores, 70
Edney v. Smith, 384
Eide, United States v., 23
Ellis v. D'Angelo, 328
Ellis v. Ellis, 216
Ellison v. Brady, 132

Elsbach, People v., 185
Emmett v. Eastern Dispensary & Cas. Hosp., 199, 248
Enright v. Eli Lilly, 323
Estelle v. Smith, 155, 171
Ex parte_____, *see name of party*

Fair v. United States, 277, 322
Falcon v. Alaska Public Offices Commission, 553
Farrell L. v. Superior Court, 182, 215
Farris v. Compton, 541
Farrow, Matter of, 189
Feeney v. Young, 148
Feldman v. Feldman, 113
First Federal Sav. & Loan Assn. v. Oppenheim, Appel, Dixon & Co., 255
First Trust Co. of St. Paul v. Kansas City Life Ins. Co., 88
Fisher v. United States, 157
Fitzgerald, People v., 14, 112
Fletcher v. Florida Pub. Co., 382
Florida Board of Bar Examiners Re: Applicant, 421
Fontana, State v., 174
Foster v. The Loft, 428
Franklin v. Duncan, 544
Free v. State, 169
Freese v. Lemmon, 335
Frye, United States v., 535, 536, 541, 542
Furness v. Fitchett, 187, 268

Garland, People v., 174
Georgetown College, Application of, 40
Gerace v. Liberty Mut. Ins. Co., 497
Gesiberger v. Willuhn, 268
Gilbreath v. Guadalupe Hospital Foundation, 69
Gilchrist v. Mystic Workers, 34
Gilday v. Mecosta, 434
Gillman v. United States, 408
Godkin v. Miller, 366
Gonzales, State of New Mexico v., 182, 249
Grand Jury Proceedings, *In re*, 69
Grand Jury Subpoena, *In re*, 146, 169
Grand Jury Subpoena Duces Tecum, *In re*, 69, 146
Grand Jury Subpoena (Psychological Treatment records), *In re*, 169

Grand Rapids v. Impens, 331
Green Bay Newspaper Co. v. Circuit Court, 146
Greenspan v. Slate, 398, 400
Greenwood v. Taft, Stettinius & Hollister, 475
Grey v. Los Angeles Superior Court, 129
Greyhound v. Superior Court of Merced County, 199
Griggs v. Griggs, 32, 114
Grosslight v. Superior Court, 119
Guardianship of Pescinski, *In re*, 398

H.B. *ex rel.* Clarke v. Whittemore, 321
H.L. v. Matheson, 399
Hague v. Williams, 260
Hall v. Hall, 113
Hamilton v. Verdow, 137
Hammond v. Aetna Casualty Surety Co., 268, 553
Hancock v. Dodson, 22, 69
Haney v. Mizell Memorial Hosp., 134
Hansen, United States v., 179
Harrel v. Travelers Indemnity Co., 381
Harris v. Forklift Systems, 120, 122
Harris v. International Paper Co., 132
Hawaii Psychiatric Society v. Ariyoshi, 479, 484
Hedlund v. Superior Court of Orange County, 297, 311
Heir v. Farmers Mut. Fire Ins. Co., 500
Henry v. Sneed, 501
Herring, People v., 134
Hicks v. United States, 328
Hillman v. Columbia County, 327
Hinckley, United States v., 173
Hoffman v. Blackmon, 323
Homere v. State, 277, 322
Hopkins, People v., 136
Horne v. Patton, xv, 260, 263,
Horton v. California, 177
Hudlow, State v., 179
Humphrey, Matter of, 216
Hungerford, State of New Hampshire v., 544
Hurlburt v. Hurlburt, 216
Husgen v. Stussie, 114
Hyman v. Jewish Chronic Disease Hospital of Brooklyn, 197

Iacona v. Schrupp, 322
Imlay, State of Montana v., 185
Imlay, Montana v., 185
*In re,*_____, *see name of party*
Isley v. Capuchin Province, 542
Iverson v. Frandsen, 147, 394

Jablonski v. United States, 296, 302
Jackson v. New Center Community Mental Health Services, 296, 333
Jacobs, Government of Virgin Islands v.,
Jaffee v. Redmond, 9, 41, 42, 53, 54, 60, 68, 69, 84, 117, 550, 565, 586
Jane Doe v. John Doe, 104
Janklow v. Planned Parenthood, 399
Jenkins v. Metropolitan Life Ins. Co., 499
Jess v. Herman, 328
John M. Abell, *Ex parte*, 499
Jones v. State of New York, 277, 322
Jones v. Shek, 319
Jones v. Superior Court, 127
Junker, State *ex rel.* Carroll, 500

Kaiser v. Suburban Transportation System, 335
Kent v. Whitaker, 477
Kilarjian v. Horwath, 74
Kim v. Bardoni, 337
Kinsella v. Kinsella, 104
Kinsman, Petition of, 324
Klein v. Prudential Ins. Co., 502
Kobrin, Commonwealth v., 485
Koningsberg v. State Bar of California, 377
Kostamo v. Marquette Iron Mining Co., 501

Labrenz, People v., 400
Lacey v. Laird, 400
Lacy v. G.D. Searle & Co., 267
Ladner v. Higgins, 539
Lamb, Commonwealth v., 382
Landelius v. University of Michigan, 137
Landelius v. Sackellares, 137
Landelius v. Rafko, 137
Landeros v. Flood, 329
Lank v. Steiner, 267
Lawless v. Schoenaker, 216
Lawrence v. Bay Osteopathic Hosp., 249
Layton, United States v., 322
Lee v. County Court of Erie County, 173

Leeds v. Prudential Ins. Co., 499
Lemmerman v. Fealk, 544
Lessard v. Schmidt, 143
Leusink v. O'Donnell, 88
Lewis v. Hynes, 489
Ley v. Dall, 146
Leyra v. Denno, 171
Lifschutz, *In re*, 66, 70, 74, 116, 129, 291, 331, 430
Linch v. Thomas-Davis Medical Centers, 177
Lindsay v. Lipson, 24, 88
Lindstrom, United States v., 23, 161
Lipari v. Sears, Roebuck, 297, 301
Locke, State v., 88, 174
Long Beach City Employees Assn. v. City of Long Beach, 53
Love v. Johnson, 182
Lukaszewicz v. Ortho Pharmaceutical Corp., 173
Lynch v. Des Moines, 132

M.M., *In re*, 114
Madred, United States v., 173
Magwood v. State, 173
Marchand v. Henry Ford Hosp., 74, 411
Marcus v. Superior Court of Los Angeles County, 147, 489
Marr v. Yousif, 319
Martin, People v., 172, 174
Matter of _____, *see name of party*
Mavroudis v. Superior Court for County of San Mateo, 336
M.C., *In re*, 114
McCollum v. D'Arcy, 544
McDonald v. Clinger, 263, 267
McDonough v. Director of Patuxent Institution, 170
McDougall v. Schanz, 30
McDougall v. Eliuk, 190
McGarry v. Mercier Co., 199
McIntosh v. Milano, 297, 298, 303
McIntyre v. McIntyre, 114
Meagher, United States v., 23, 69
Meeboer, People v., 178
Menendez v. Superior Court, 157, 175
Merchants National Bank & Trust Co. of Fargo v. United States, 277, 322
Meritor Savings Bank v. Vinson, 132

Meyerhofer v. Empire Fire & Marine Ins. Co., 254

Meyers v. St. Francis Hospital, 499

Michaelson, *In re*, 146

Miller, State v., 174

Mintz, United States v., 502

Miragliv v. Miragliv, 113

Miranda v. Arizona, 331

Mississippi State Board of Psychological Examiners v. Hosford, 249

Modla v. Parker, 147

Molien v. Kaiser Foundation Hospital, 282, 283

Monty v. Warren Hosp. Corp., 411

Morgan v. State, 183

Moulin v. Monteleone, 104

Mounds Park Hospital v. von Eye, 477

Mullen v. United States, 14, 553

Mulrine, State v., 174

Munoz, State of Wisconsin v., 181

Murphy v. Hall, 538

Myers v. Quesenberry, 323

Nagle v. Hooks, 400

Naidu v. Laird, 298

Nallan v. Helmsley-Spear, 341

Nash v. Overholser, 104

Nasser v. Parker, 325

Natanson v. Kline, 474

Navarre v. Navarre, 113

Nelson v. Union Wire Rope Corp., 497

Nichols v. Frank, 132

Nixon v. Pittsburgh Plate Glass Co., 130

Nixon, United States v., 12, 182

Noggle v. Marshall, 174, 249

North Carolina v. Alford, 185

Novak v. Rathman, 337

O'Barr v. Feist, 147

O'Connor v. Donaldson, 474

Oakland County Prosecutor v. Department of Corrections, 185

Oaks v. People, 171

Olson v. Court of Honor, 248

Omer v. Edhren, 267

Osterlind v. Hill, 325

Osterman v. Ehrenworth, 490, 499

Ostrowski v. Mockridge, 32, 88

Palay v. Superior Court, 137

Palsgraf v. Long Island RR, 281, 335

Parham v. J.R., 388

Patnaude, State v., 179

Pattern v. United Life and Accident Ins. Assn., 499

Patton v. Jacobs, 438

Peck v. Counseling Service of Addison County, 332, 336, 337

Peisach v. Antuna, 113, 114

Pena, People v., 181

People v. _____, *see opposing party*

Perin v. Peuler, 190

Perkins, Illinois v., 171

Perry v. Fiumano, 112

Peterson v. State, 298

Petition of _____, *see name of party*

Pierce v. Penman, 199

Pitts, People v., 397

Pittsburgh Action Against Rape, Matter of, 179

Planned Parenthood of Missouri v. Danforth, 390

Plummer, People v., 173

Poddar, People v., 320

Popovitch v. Kasperlik, 255

Porter v. Michigan Osteopathic Hosp. Assn., 142

Porterfield, People v., 332

Prink v. Rockefeller Center, 116

Prudential Life Ins. Co. v. Koslowski, 32

Prudhomme, State v., 55

Pruitt v. Payton, 254

Public Citizens Health Research Group v. Dept. of HEW,

Pyramid Life Ins. Co. v. Masonic Hosp. Assn., 498

Queen, Application of, 22

Radtke v. Everett, 131

Ramona v. Isabella, Rose & Western Medical Center, 125, 126, 136, 530, 539

Randa v. Bear, 24, 34

Randle, State v., 542

Rea v. Pardo, 134

Reisner v. Regents of University of California, 283, 323

Rennie v. Klein, 478

Renslow v. Mennonite Hosp., 322
Renville, United States v., 178
Renzi v. Morrison, 104, 245
Reproductive Services v. Walker, 499
Ritchie, State of Pennsylvania v., 178
Rizzuto v. Employer Liability Assurance Corp., 130
Robinson v. Magovern, 411
Robinson, State v., 178
Roe v. Doe, 362, 363
Rogers v. Lumberman's Mutual Casualty Co.,
Roper v. Roper, 113, 114
Rost v. State Bd. of Psychology, 250, 267
Rowland v. Christian, 328
Roy v. Hartogs, 140
Roy, West Virginia v., 180
Rudnick v. Superior Court of Kern County, 146
Ryan v. New York Central R.R. Co., 322, 324

Samson v. Saginaw Professional Bldg., 341
Sanders, People v., 152
Sandoval v. Acevedo, 179
Saunders, United States v., 179
Saur v. Probes, 189, 249
Schaffer v. Soucerm, 249
Schaffer v. Spicer, 268
Schechet v. Kesten, 141, 490
Schlagenhauf v. Holder, 103, 120
Schreiber, State v., 169
Schuler v. United States, 249
Schulz v. Pennsylvania Railroad Co., 320
Schuster v. Altenberg, 321, 334, 338
Schwarz, State *ex rel.* Warren v., 185
Security Insurance Group v. Wilkinson, 381, 475
Seibel v. Kembel, 328
Seltrecht v. Bremer, 137
Shahzade v. Gregory, 542
Shartzer v. Israels, 178
Shepard v. United States,
Shephard v. McGinnis, 491
Shiffra, State of Wisconsin v., 180, 181
Sibbach v. Wilson & Co., 119
Simon & Schuster v. New York Crime Victims Board, 375
Simonsen v. Swenson, 317

Sims v. State, 87
Sizemore v. Smock, 332
Skidmore v. Baltimore & O.R.R., xv
Skillings v. Allen, 323
Smith, People v., 552
Smith v. Driscoll, 249
Smith v. Illinois, 178
Smith v. Superior Court, 147
Smith v. United States, 183
Solberg, State v., 180
Soutear v. United States, 303
Sparer v. Travelers' Ins. Co., 498
Spartan Steel, 324
Spikes v. Michigan Parole Board, 185
Squires v. Hayes, 475
Stadler v. Cross, 322
Stanaway, People v., 180
Starzecpyzel, United States v., 543
State v _____, *see opposing party*
State Farm Fire & Cas. Co. v. Wicka, 355
Stevens, People v., 170
Stewart v. Wulf, 324
Stola v. Joint Industry Bd., 434
Stuart v. Stuart, 104
Stussie, State *ex. rel.* Husgen, v., 114
Sudtelgte v. Reno, 132
Sullivan v. Chesier, 136
Sullivan v. Fogg, 434
Sullivan v. Montgomery, 398
Summe, United States v., 438
Swatch v. Treat, 476
Sweeney v. Green, 146

Talley, United States v., 24, 174
Tarasoff v. Regents of University of California, xvii, 151, 176, 208, 209, 236, 262, *274*, 276, 277, 280, 284, 285, 288, 289, 293, 295, 298, 300, 301, 303, 304, 307, 309, 311, 313, 314, 317, 319, 320, 321
Taylor v. United States, 53
Thigpen, United States v., 55
Thing v. LaChusa, 322, 324
Thomas v. Hogan, 196
Thomas v. Morris, 197
Thompson v. County of Alameda, 293, 294, 298
Thomsen v. Mayo Foundation, 249
Tobin v. Grossman, 333
Trammel v. United States, 13, 60, 590

Trammell v. Citizens News Co., 438
Trotta v. Ward Baking Co., 34
Turco v. Hoeschst Celanese Corp., 434
Tweith v. Duluth, M. & I.R. Ry. Co., 500
Tylitski v. Triple X Service, 70, 248

United States v. _____, *see opposing party*
Urseth v. City of Dayton, 249

Van Wie v. United States, 23, 33
Vaughn, State v., 179
Vega-Penarete, United States v., 173
Vitek v. Jones, 147
Viviano v. Stewart, 285
von Dameck v. St. Paul Fire & Marine Ins.,
  129
von Goyt, Matter of, 113, 144
von Bulow by Auersperq v. von Bulow, 247

Wallace v. University Hospitals of Cleveland,
  199
Wallace v. Hurlburt, 216
Watkins v. United States, 299
Weatherford v. Bursey, 216
Webb, People v., 162
Weisbeck v. Hess, 147, 324
Welke v. Kuzilla, 299, 332
Wetherill v. University of Chicago, 478

Whalen, People v., 89
Whalen v. Roe, 215, 476
Wharton, People v., 175
Whitree v. State, 477
Whyte v. Connecticut Mut. Life Ins. Co., 23
Wichansky v. Wichansky, 215
Wiles v. Wiles, 87
Williams v. Cunningham Drug Stores, 341
Williams v. New York, 183
Wilson, State v., 31
Wilson v. Upell, 113
Winstead, *In re*, 189
Wise v. Daniel, 381
Wiseman, Commonwealth v., 149, 380
Witt, United States v., 169
Wood, People v., 88
Wood v. Alaska, 179
Woody, People v., 173
Wyatt v. Aderholt, 430, 474
Wyatt v. Stickney, 410, 430, 457, 474, 480

Yaron v. Yaron, 216
Yoder v. Smith, 437
Youngberg v. Romeo, 336

Zolin, United States v., 177
Zuniga, *In re*, 68, 69, 146

# NAME INDEX

Aaron, S., 386
Abbott, J.H., 374
Abel, G.G., 12
Abell, J., 499
Abramson, L., 527
Abu-Jamal, M., 374
Adamec, C., 412
Adler, G., 327
Agnew, S.T., 502
Agron, S., 375
Aichhorn, A., 88
Alar, C., 287
Alderman, E., 427, 428, 553
Alexander, S., 217
Alexander, R., 15
Ali, M., 475
Alibrandi, T., 176
Allen, J., 168
Allen, R., 55, 139, 140
Allen, R.C., 22
Allen, W., xiv, 91, 452, 453, 469
Althaus, C., 529
Althaus, R., 529
Altman, L.K., 353, 354
Alverson, L., 43
Alves, J.T., 88
Anderson, T., 353
Andrade, J.C., 477
Andrade, P.D., 477
Andreasen, N.C., 518
Andrews, N., 516
Anna O., 475
Annas, G.J., 268
Anslinger, H.J., 33
Antar, E., 516
Antilla, S., 134
Appelbaum, P.S., 53, 54, 136, 173, 176, 215, 292, 306, 332, 336, 337, 340, 341, 432, 531
Appelbaum, S.A., 451, 471
Arabian, J., 63

Argiroff, A., 104
Ariès, P., xi
Armani, F.H., 176
Arterton, J., 104
Austad, C.S., 54
Auvenshire, C.D., 382
Avery, L., 308

Babcock, K., 477
Baden, M., 501
Bailey, F.L., 253, 373
Bakken, G.M., 318
Baldwin, R.W., 30
Balinga, R.K., 478
Bar-Levav, R., xv
Barbaree, H.E., 12
Barkin, E.N., 183
Barlas, S., 199, 539
Barrett, P.M., 69, 129
Barrett, W., 96
Barron, J., 330
Barrymore, J., 212
Bartemeier, L.H., 538
Barton, W.E., 269, 437
Battani, M., 113
Battock, T., 518
Bauer, L.M., 14
Baumoel, J., 175
Bazelon, D.L., 144, 152, 523, 524
Bean-Bayog, M., 251, 254
Bear, L.A., 247
Beck, J., 332
Beck, J.C., 292, 318, 326
Becker, E.R., 184
Becker, S.J., 145, 148
Beer, C., 380
Beigler, J., 501
Bellak, L., 335, 344, 345
Belli, M., 383
Bemmann, K.C., 329

Bentley, S., 84
Benzien, J., 75
Berger, J., 213
Berger, M.A., 24
Bergstrom, R.E., 128
Berke, R.L., 352
Berkowitz, D., 375
Bernstein, D.M., 508, 517
Berry, R., 271
Beschloss, M., 344
Besharov, D.J., 327, 329
Bhavsar, R.N., xvii
Binder, R., 339, 340
Bindrim, P., 214
Bird, R.E., 329
Bisbing, S.B., 136, 140, 329
Bishop, K., 554
Biskupic, J., 53, 72
Black, C.L., 13
Black, H., 438
Blaine, G.B., 402
Blinder, M., 527
Blitch, C.L., 318
Bloch, F., 212
Bloch, S., xiv, 184, 317, 515
Bloom, C., 99
Bloom, J.D., 326
Bloom, L.H., 178
Bloom, S.L., 434
Bloom, V., 124, 135
Bloomingdale, L., 510
Bloustein, E.J., 553
Blum, D., 320, 321, 335
Blum, L., 434
Blumenthal, R.G., 378
Blyn, A., 206
Boffitt, L., 518
Bohan, T.L., 542
Bok, S., xiii, 42, 53, 455, 473
Bollas, C., 40, 53, 241
Bonnie, R.J., 434
Boochever, R., 14
Booth, J.W., 28
Boothe, M., 271
Bork, R.H., 553
Bouhoutos, J., 329
Bourne, P.G., 475
Bourne, D.J., 539
Bowers, W.J., 318

Bowman, C.G., 136
Bowman, R.G., 199
Boynton, S.S., 497
Brandeis, L.D., 57, 67, 553
Brando, M., 144
Bray, T.J., 353
Breaskin, J., 30
Breggin, P., 398
Breitel, C.D., 333
Breo, D.L., 379
Brewin, R., 475
Brewster, J., 120
Breyer, S., 10, 72
Brinkley, D., 354
Brodsky, A.M., 75, 136
Brogger, S., xi
Brosman, J., 144
Bross, I.D., 429
Brower, M., 338, 339
Brown, S.W., 499, 539
Brown, K.H., 433
Brown, L.S., 541
Brown, S.J., 539
Browne, K.R., 132
Bruni, F., 170
Bryant, M., 508
Brzonkala, C., 104
Bucaram, A., 518
Buchwald, A., 144, 145
Buckley, W.F., 13
Bull, R., 54
Burger, W., 457
Burstein, A., 354
Burstow, B., 518
Bush, G., 343, 344, 349
Butler, C., 497
Butler, K., 136, 539
Butler, R.N., 12
Byers, B., 152
Byers, M., 554

Cacheris, J., 422, 423
Caesar, G., 54, 525, 538
Caesar, S., 118, 144
Cahill, T., 10
Callahan, C.C., 23
Calof, D., 360, 540
Cannon, J., 344
Caplan, P.J., 518

Capoccia, R.M., 182
Capper, A., 94
Capper, B.G., 299
Cardamone, R., 242
Cardozo, B., 281
Carmody, D., 382
Carroll, L., 51
Cartensen, P.C., 325
Carter, R., 374
Carter, J., 344, 346, 348
Cathey, *In re*, 188
Cate, F.H., 434
Catherine of Russia, 63
Cavanagh, M., 287
Cecil, H., 217, 218
Cellini, H.R., 185
Cerney, M.S., 472, 479
Chafee, Z., 18, 19, 24, 29, 34, 129
Chaimp, C.L., 104
Chaleby, K., 319
Chambers, J., 555
Chaplin, C., 51, 55, 351
Charney, D.S., 539
Chase, T., 144
Chaucer, vii
Chayet, N.L., 325
Cheever, J., 365
Chekhov, A., 374
Chessman, C., 374
Chikatilo, A., 507
Chiles, L., 145
Chittenden, W.A., 497
Chodoff, P., 184, 359, 365, 429, 471, 515
Choi, A., 214
Cichon, D.E., 397
Clark, D.C., 44
Clark, J.A., 422
Clark, W., 289
Clausen, J.A., 196, 513, 518
Cleary, E., 215
Cleckley, H.M., 364
Clinton, W., 7, 343, 346, 349, 350, 353
Clinton, H.,
Coady, M., xiv, 317
Cochran, J.L., 383
Cocozza, J.J., 335
Coffee, J.C., 384
Cohen, R.J., 477
Cohen, J., 529

Cole, K., 103
Coleman, L., 127
Commons, M.L., 176
Connor, R.G., 14
Cooper, P., 470
Copper, H.H.A., 173
Corcoran, J.F.T., 30
Cordas, T.A., 539
Corman, A., 471
Cornwall, J., 137
Corona, J., 372
Court, H.L., 30
Cox, P., 208, 213
Crancer, A., 46, 326, 543
Crews, F., 46
Cribbs, U., 297
Crichton, M., 368, 380
Crocker, E.M., 318
Cronkite, K., 148
Cross, H.L., 196
Cross, W., 215
Cullen, F., 518
Cullen, R., 516
Cullum, L., 538
Curd, T.H.S., 23

Dahmer, J., 153
Dain, N., 32
Daley, S., 75
Dallek, R., 344
Dann, L.W., 309, 338
Dann, R., 309
Darrow, C., 164
Davidson, H., 54, 103
Davis, F., 553
Davis, L.J., 515
Davis, R., 328
Dawidoff, D.J., 477
DeBenedictis, D.J., 175
DeHaven, J., 177, 517
Delonas, S., 344
Demming, Lord, 324
DeParle, J., 354
Dershowitz, A., 162, 179, 241, 242
Dession, G., 183
DeWitt, C., 31
Diamond, B., 52, 88
Diaz-Plaja, F., 210, 218
Dickens, B.M., 327, 381

Dickens, C., 295
Dietz, P.E., 153, 530, 539
Diller, L.H., 398
Dillinger, J., 28
DiRenzo, G.J., 354
Dobie, S., 213, 219
Dodd, C., 347
Doege, T.C., 326
Dole, E., 352
Dole, R., 344, 346, 352
Donaldson, S., 365
Donielson, A., 543
Donnelly, J., 400, 401
Dooling, R., 132
Dorris, D., 141
Dostoyevsky, F., 374
Douecek, H.J., 321
Douglas, M., 349
Douglas, W.O., 130, 131
Dowd, M., 353
Doyle, B.B., 500
Drake, S., 102
Drellich, M.G., 266, 472
Drob, S.L., 332
Dudar, H., 379
Duffy, B., 516
Dukakis, K., 144, 148
Duke, P., 144, 148
Dunn, L.J., 476
Dunne, D., 175
Duque, H., 23
Durfee, D., 517
Durham, M., 523
D.W.H., In re, 188
Dyer, A.R., 318, 331
Dykstra, M.J., 318
Dysken, M.W., 327

Eagleton , T., 349, 378, 550
Easton, N.J., 378
Eaton, W., 428
Edelstein, L., 273, 317
Edelwich, J., 136
Edgerton, H., 9, 10, 14, 43, 549, 553
Edson, G., 434
Edstrom, E., 316
Eisenhower, D.W., 346
Eissler, K., 176
Eist, H.I., xiv, 40

Eldredge, L.H., 553
Elizabeth, Duchess of Kingston, 16
Ellsberg, D., 449, 450, 470
Engelberg, A.L., 326
English, D.M., 189
Ennis, B.J., 143, 335
Epstein, R.S., 345, 353
Erard, B.H., 137
Ermann, D., 410
Eth, S., 175, 340, 341
Evans, H.B., 497
Evrard, J.R., 179
Ewalt, J.R., 37, 52
Eysenck, H., 343, 352

Falkowski, W., 477
Farber, L.H., 207, 216
Farnsworth, D.L., 37, 52, 395, 401, 402
Fazzio, A.M., 114
Fedo, S., 433
Feiffer, J., 91, 92, 514
Felch, E., 473, 500
Feldman, M.D., 134
Felix, R., 198
Felsenthal, E., 148
Felstiner, W.L.F., 103
Felthous, A.R., 318, 325
Fenichel, O., 266
Fenner, G.M., 542
Fenton, N., 87, 167, 185
Ferguson, C., 426
Ferguson, E.E., 23
Ferster, E.Z., 22
Fines, B.G., 104
Fink, P.J., 518
Finkelstein, L., 160, 177
Finney, F.C., 382
Fisch, E.L., 173
Fischer, A., 87
Fischoff, J., xvii
Fisher, H., 100, 101
Fisher, R.M., 14
Fitzgerald, Z., 365
Flaxman, K., 64, 565
Fleming, J.G., 304, 321, 332
Flores, P.J., 212
Flynn, E., 350
Foderaro, L.W., 515

Fontana, C., 400
Forbes, S., 343
Ford, B., 144, 145
Ford, C.V., 134, 540
Ford, G., 344, 349
Foreman, P., 252
Forer, L., 353
Forrester, W.R., 275
Forward, S., 244
Foster, H., 538
Foster, L.M., 201, 213
Fox, J., xiv
Fram, D.K., 433, 434
Frank, J., 353
Frank, J.D., 85, 452, 472
Frank, L., 103
Franklin, B., 202, 213
Franklin, G., 536
Franklin, T., 341
Franks, B., 164
Frazer, J.G., xv
Frederick, C.J., 336
Frederico, M., 213
Freedman, A.M., 124, 135, 266
Freeman, B., 144
Freeman, C., 282, 322
Freeman, L., 144, 475, 501
Freud, A., 387, 532
Freud, S., 27, 42, 43, 46, 50, 55, 88,
    164, 338, 350, 361, 362, 367, 387,
    391, 442, 452, 453, 470, 471, 478,
    531, 532
Freudenheim, M., 473
Friedland, S.I., 134
Friedman, L., 115
Friedman, L.M., 128
Friedman, S., 397
Friedman, T., 426
Frimer, D.I., 104, 130
Fritsch, J., 378
Fritz, G.K., 402, 410
Fromm, E., 450
Fromm-Reichmann, F., 474
Frye, J.A., 543
Fryer, W.T., 174
Fuhrman, M., 62
Furedy, R.L., 474
Furrow, B., 497

Gabbard, K., 518
Gacy, J., 361
Gallagher, M., 92, 103
Gallup, G., 9
Gamwell, L., 518
Garbo, G., 212
Garces, 144
Gard, S.A., 62, 69
Gardner, R., 544
Garrison, J., 355
Gaylin, W., 173, 399
Gediman, H.K., 134
Geller, J.J., 148, 201
Gelman, D., 379
George III, 143, 295
Gerard, J.B., 132
Gerdes, W., 398
Gesell, G., 410
Gibbs, N., 105, 401
Gibeaut, J., 383
Gibson, M., 509
Gibson, R.W., 476
Giffs, N., 175
Gigot, P.A., 351
Gilandas, A.J., 474, 477
Gilbert, S., 410
Gilmore, G., 371, 372, 508
Ginzberg, R., 355
Ginsberg, R.B., 72
Giordani, L.C., 497
Gittelson, N., 473
Givelber, D., 318
Glantz, L.H., 268
Glaser, R.A., 137
Glendon, M.A., 425, 434
Glenn, M., 380
Glickfield, B., 133
Godard, S.L., 326
Godkin, J., 366
Godsell-Stytz, G., 287
Goffman, E., 52
Gogol, N., 467
Goin, M.K., 267
Gold, E., 373
Gold, P., 54
Gold, J.H., 53
Gold, S., 279
Goldberg, B.A., 18
Goldblatt, P.B., 476

Goldin, S., 196
Goldman, M., 176
Goldman, R., 244
Goldstein, J., 59, 68, 88, 159, 177, 187, 190
Goldstein, R.L., 248
Goldwater, B., 347, 348, 355
Goldzband, M.G., 114, 540
Goleman, D., 401
Goodman, T.A., 318, 332
Goodwin, F.K., 510
Goodwin, J., 329
Gordon, G., 470
Gordon, J.M.,
Gordon, M.R.,
Gore, A., 144, 455
Gore, T., 144
Gorman, C., 544
Gorman, J.M., 128, 145, 148, 471, 538
Goss, J., 539
Gostin, L.O., 137, 342, 352
Gould, D., xv
Gove, W.R., 518
Graham, M.H., 136
Grano, J.D., viii, xiii
Grant, M., 379, 506, 516
Grant, U.S., 349
Green, P., xviii
Green, W.H., 398
Greenberg, D.F., 431
Greenberg, J.A., 324
Greenberg, S.A., 75
Greene, G., 144
Greenhouse, L., 53, 69, 354, 399
Greenwald, H., 144
Greer, A., 215
Greig, J., 383
Grigson, J.P., 335, 348
Grigson, R., 171
Grinfeld, M.J., 248, 517, 538
Grinker, R.R., 100, 366, 367, 380
Grob, G., 32
Grobe, J., 46, 54
Groff, W.J., 55
Gross, J., 378, 515, 539
Gross, M.L., 347
Grossman, M., xvii, 67, 250, 267, 304, 360, 368, 378, 429, 460, 471, 472, 473, 474, 475

Gruber, D., 333
Gruenberg, P.B., 146
Gubler, C., 379, 380
Guernsey, T.F., 114, 136
Gunn, J., 326
Gurevitz, H., 340
Gutheil, T.G., 75, 176, 196, 306, 337, 531, 533, 540
Guttmacher, M., 24, 31, 183, 247, 270, 317
Guttman, M., 398
Guyer, M.J., 539

Hagen, M.A., 538
Haines, R.A., 198
Hall, B., 480
Hall, J., 177, 401
Halleck, N.H., 55
Halleck, S.L., 55, 337, 339
Halpern, A.L., xvii, 124, 135, 247, 345, 356, 500, 517
Hans, V.P., 517
Hanson, R.S., 543
Hardie, W.H., 323
Hardwicke, Lord, 12
Hare, A., 129
Harper, F.V., 328
Harris, R., 381
Harris, S., 496
Hartogs, G., 349
Hartogs, R., 495
Hartstein, N.B., 103
Hassard, H., 130, 172, 248
Hathaway, J., xvii
Hausma, K., 379
Hausman, K., 539
Hawk, R., 372
Hay, P., 354
Hayes-Roth, F., 478
Hayt, E., 196, 477
Hayt, J., 477
Hazard, G.C., 383
Hearst, P., 253, 373
Hedlund, J.L., 335
Heels, E.J., 542
Heilman, S.C., xv
Heller, J., xv, 418
Hellewell, J.S., 271
Henry, P., 91

Herbert, W., 519
Herbert, A.P., 132
Herman, J., 531
Herron, W.G., 438
Hersh, S.M., 470
Hertzberg, H., 344
Hess, A.K., 410, 475
Hess, S., 358
Hewitt, B., 539
Heyman, K., 144
Heywood, A., 151
Hicks, D.W., 30
Hicks, M., 168
Higgins, M., 434
Hillel, ix
Himmelwright, G.O., 268
Hinckley, J.W., 154, 294, 384, 526
Hiniker, M.I., 477
Hippocrates, 202, 269, 273, 317, 533, 547, 552
Hobbs, G.E., 326
Hochman, G., 148
Hoffman, J., 217
Hoffman, L., 65
Hogan, D., 497
Hogan, M.B., 179
Hogan, M.W., 248
Hoge, S.K., 55, 194
Holbrook, R.F., 476
Holland, M.J., 411
Hollender, M., 413
Holmes, G.W., 477
Holmes, O.W., 14, 315, 341
Holzman, D., 54
Homan, K., 178
Hoover, J.E., 270
Horner, T.M., 539
Housek, J., 63
Howard, E.B., 61
Huber, G.A., 385, 474
Hudson, J., 368, 539
Hughes, R., 475
Hunt, H., 449
Hunt, W., 81
Hutelmyer, D., 105
Hutschnecker, A.A., 52, 67
Hwang, S.L., 214
Hyoung, M.B., 379

Illich, I., 89, 90
Imlay, D., 167
Imwinkelried, E.J., 69, 543
Inz, R.A., 384
Ito, L., 426
Iverson, D., 160
Iverson, R., 177

Jackson, J., 143
Jackson, M., 251
Jacobs, J., 54
Jamison, K.R., 145, 420, 421
Jansen, K., 287
Jefferson, T., 354
Jeffrey, N.A., 475, 198
Jesus, 143
Johnson, A., 28
Johnson, D., 103
Johnson, F., 457
Johnson, J., 137
Johnson, K.B., 454
Johnson, L.B., 343, 344, 346
Johnson, M., 136
Johnson, S., 341, 384
Joiner, C., 30
Jonakait, R.N., 543
Jones, E., 88, 397
Jones, J., 322
Jones, M., 497
Jones, W.C., 530
Jorgenson, L.M., 125, 136, 140, 329
Joseph, 59
Judd, N., 145
Jung, C., 46, 515

Kaczynski, T.J., 516
Kaiser, B.L., 198
Kaiser, D., 54
Kal, E.F., 124, 134, 135
Kalichman, S.C., 321
Kalter, N.M., 539
Kant, I., 240
Kapen, G., 53, 54
Kaplan, H.I., 213
Kaplan, J., 338
Kardashian, R., 383
Karel, R., 53
Kass, J., 338
Kass, L.R., 103

Katz, B.F., 268
Katz, J., 59, 68, 88, 159, 177, 187, 190
Katze, J.A., 441, 443, 444, 445
Kaye, M., 199
Keables, K., 178
Keill, S., 355
Kelley, E.M., 497
Kelly, J.A., 137
Kemp, J., 346
Kennedy, A., 72
Kennedy, C., 427, 428, 553
Kennedy, J.F., 295, 343, 346, 383
Kermani, E.J., 332
Kevles, D.J., 53
Khatain, E., 530
Khatain, L., 530
Kidder, M., 40
Kime, P.M., 328
King, L., 145
King, M.L., 252
Kinsey, A.C., 6, 12
Kirkpatrick, L.C., 177, 216
Kiser, J., 104
Kittrie, N., 400
Kizer, K.W., 327
Klar, H., 540
Klee, P., 300
Kleiman, D., 475
Klein, J., 350, 353
Klein, J.L., 437
Klein, M., 387
Knapp, C., 518
Knapp, S., 275, 319, 331
Knecht, G.F., 410
Knight, J.A., 30, 430
Knowles, M.F., 114
Kocsis, J., 516
Kolakowski, L., 263
Kolata, G., 352
Korner, O., 273
Kovel, J., 472
Kramer, P., 48, 519
Krattenmarker, T.G., 33
Kresnak, J., 113
Krystal, J.H., 539
Kurland, A.A., 196
Kuvin, S.F., 478
Kuzilla, S.M., 299

Ladd, E.C., 353, 358
Ladd, M., 24
Laird, G., 299
Lakin, M., 320
Lambert, W., 434
Lancaster, R., 401
Landelius, J., 126
Langs, R., 473
Larkin, M.A., 30
Lasswell, H.D., 354
Laughton, C., 350
Laughran, C.W., 318
Laumann, L.A., 327
Lawrence, J., 353
Laws, D.R., 12
Lawson, M., 353
Lebensohn, Z.M., 356
Ledy, N.B., 434
Lee, P., 176
Lees-Haley, P.R., 132
Lefkowitz, E., 434
Leibovich, M., 200
Leigh, M., xi
Leiter, L., 338
Leong, G.B., 73, 175, 179
Leopold, N., 164
Lerner, J., 55, 428
Lerner, S., 510
Levine, M., 321
Levy, D., 354
Lewin, T., 473, 544
Lewis, M.B., 338
Lidz, C., 53, 54
Lieberman, P., 382, 383, 384
Lieberman, J.S., 134
Lief, N., 401
Lief, H., 401
Lifschutz, J.E., 54, 63, 71, 72, 118, 240, 379, 552
Lifson, L., 539
Lincoln, A., 28, 349
Lindner, R., 525, 538
Lindsay, S.D., 54
Lingabaugh, F., 478
Link, B., 513, 518
Link, R.C., 410
Lion, J.R., 336, 337, 554
Lipscomb, H.S., 23
Lipsker, E.F., 536

Lipton, S.D., 526
Lister, M., 103
Liston, E.H., 478
Little, R.B., 317
Litwack, T.R., 335
Livingston, K., 398
Loeb, R., 164
Loftus, E.F., 136
Logan, J., 144
Lombardo, P.A., 541
Long, D., 434
Long, E., 470
Lorand, S., 144
Lorenger, L., xvii
Losoncy, L., 15
Lothane, Z., 380
Louisell, D., 52, 53, 88, 146
Loupos, N., 89
Lowe, G., 478
Lozano, P., 251
Luby, E., xvii, 303
Luce, C.B., 348
Lund, C.C., 198
Lupos, N., 15
Lynch, D., 543

Macbeth, J.E., 326, 327, 437
MacCormick, A., 184, 217
MacDonald, J.M., 49
MacInnes, M., 199
Madden, D.J., 337
Magee, R.D., 402
Maguire, S.P., 476
Maher, S.T., 434
Maier, G.J., 199
Mailer, N., 371, 372, 374, 382, 383, 517
Maimonides, 418
Malcolm, A.H., 14
Malmquist, C.P., 113, 400
Mangweth, B., 539
Manji, H., 517
Mao, 379
Marcus, F.F., 326
Margolick, D., 383
Margolis, M., 500
Marlette, D., 505
Marsh, D.T., 402
Marshall, W.L., 12
Martin, J., 178, 511

Martin, P.R., 212
Martin, C.E., 12
Martin, W.H., 270
Mason, J., viii
Masserman, J.H., 217, 401, 402
Masters & Johnson, 236
Mastrangel, P.J., 114
Matthew, 143
Mattison, R.E., 402, 410
Maurer, K., 541
Maximov, B., 304, 332
May, C., 28
Mayberry, J.F., 518
Mayman, M., 475
McAninch, M., 476
McArthur, C.C., 114, 402
McCall, D., 264
McCarthy, C.C., 114
McCarthy, J.F., 90
McCoid, A.H., ,497
McCormick, C., 20, 24, 52, 196, 204, 205, 215
McCurry, M., 353
McDiarmid, H., 397
McDonald, J.J., 132, 133
McDonald, J.M., 49
McDowell, E., 380, 381
McElaney, A.J., 542
McFarlane, W.J.G., 199
McGovern, G., 349, 355, 510, 518
McGovern, T., 511
McHugh, P., 317, 533, 540, 541
McKray, G.A., 327
McLynn, F., 515
McMahon, P.R., 554
McManus, M., 103
McMenamin, B., 443
McNaughton, J., 12
McNeil, D., 339
McPherson, J., 97
Meadows, J., 144
Mechanic, D., 553
Medini, G., xv
Mehlman, M. J., 148
Mehta, S.N., 185
Meisel, A., 179, 199
Meister, K.E., 172
Melcher, M.L., 351
Melton, G.B., 318, 328, 397

Memon, A., 54
Mencken, H.L., 43
Mendelsohn, R.S., 475
Menendez, E., 156, 175, 526, 527, 528
Menendez, L., 156, 175, 526
Menlowe, M.A., 319, 338
Menninger, K.A., 67, 159, 177, 199, 272, 285,
    317, 395, 401, 475, 503, 504, 515
Menninger, W.C., 144
Menninger, W.W., 41
Merchior, K.W., 71
Merrow, J., 398
Merskey, H., 541
Mertz, E., 136
Meyers, C.J., 318
Meyers, W., 198
Micale, M.S., 515
Michels, R., 250
Middlebrook, D.W., 364, 365, 379
Middlebrook, S.B., 328
Milford, N., 365
Miller, A., 353
Miller, H., 355
Miller, H.A., 105
Miller, M.H., 55
Miller, R., 55, 194, 199
Miller, R.J., 381
Mills, M.J., 275, 319, 340, 341
Minow, N.N., 434
Mitchell, A., 12
Mitchell, B.F., 316
Mitchell, G.D., 214
Mitchell, V.F., 270
Mitterand, F., 380
Modlin, H.C., xv, 303, 430, 482, 497
Moench, L., 271, 272
Mollica, R.F., 501
Monahan, J., 335, 397, 434, 508
Montgomery, P.L., 383
Moody, B., 372
Moore, L., 278, 279, 280
Moore, H., 300
Moore, R.F., 212
Moreno, J.L., 202, 213
Morgan, E., 23, 247
Morgan, J., xv
Morris, G.H., 328
Morris, N., 517
Morris, R., 7

Morrison, H., 245, 246
Morrison, J.K., 203, 213, 214
Morrow, B., 199
Morrow, L., 379
Morse, W., 348
Morton, D., 53
Mosk, S., 294, 301
Mudd, N., 33
Mudd, S., 28, 33
Mueller, C.B., 146, 171, 177, 216
Mueller, G., 171
Mullen, L., 539
Mulvey, E., 397
Munoz, S., 181
Munster, J.H., 30
Munter, P., 402
Muravchik, E., 14
Murray, C., 320
Mutter, C., 423
Myers, K., 434
Mykel, N., 215

Nabokov, V., 47
Naidu, V., 299
Negrao, A.B., 539
Neuffer, C.H., 474
Newman, D., 497
Newman, J.R., 89
Nijinsky, V., 365
Nixon, R.M., 12, 73, 210, 343, 344,
    346, 470
Nizer, L., 98
Noah, C., 142
Noonan, P., 344
Noshpitz, J.D., 397
Nurcombe, B., 402, 410
Nye, S., 501

O'Connor, M., 542
O'Connor, S.D., 72
O'Leary, J.C., 398
Oakley, D.J., 497
Oberman, M., 399
Oldham, T.C., 30
Omestad, T., 355
Onek, J.N., 248, 326, 327, 437
Orenstein, A., 184
Orley, L., 113
Orne, M., 364, 365, 367

Orwell, G., 418
Ostow, M., 474
Oswald, L.H., 383
Oziel, L.R., 156, 157, 175

Packwood, B., 157
Paddock, J.R., 136
Palmiere, D., xvii
Palsgraf, 281
Panetta, L., 91
Papajohn, G., 338
Pappenheim, B., 475
Parks, C., 180
Parsons, J.B., 183
Peabody, G.A., 402
Pearlman, T., 528
Pendergrast, M., 544
Perlez, J., 217
Perlman, S.D., 53
Perot, R., 348
Perr, I.N., 268, 318, 399
Person, E., 540
Peters, M., 507, 524
Peters, R., 5
Petersen, A., 399
Petrila, J., 318, 328
Peyrot, M., 380
Phelan, M.E., 173
Phillips, M.C., 103
Pickowicz, P.G., 379
Pierpont, C.R., 132
Pies, R., 539
Pilisuk, M., 429
Pilpel, H., 103, 400
Piorkowski, J.D., 327
Piraro, D., 425
Place, M.J., 434
Poddar, P., 278, 279, 280, 288, 306, 309, 321
Pollack, D., 505
Pollina, A., 144
Pollock, E.J., 30, 53, 180
Pollock, J., 350
Polreis, R., 75
Pomeroy, W.B., 12
Poole, D.A., 54
Pope, H.G., 530, 539
Pope, K.S., 329, 541
Porter, R., 512, 515, 518

Portnow, S., 517
Posner, R., 53
Post, J.M., 348, 354, 355
Powell, L.,390
Powell, C., 346, 347
Powell, B.V., 410
Powelson, H., 280
Power, K.A., 384
Poythress, N.G., 318, 328
Price, J., 317
Probert, C.S.J., 518
Proctor, M.L., 146
Prosser, W., 553
Pruyser, P., 475
Pstwald, P., 365
Puente, M., 103
Purrington, W.A., 23
Putney, H., 298

Quattrocchi, M.R., 318
Quen, J.M., 539
Quinn, K.M., 341
Quiring, D.L., 326

Rabkin, J.G., 518
Rachlin, S., 75, 517
Radauskas, B., 196
Radin, M., 239, 247
Rado, S., 266
Raduyev, S., 33
Raffle, P.A.B., 326
Rafko, P., 126
Ramona, G., 125, 530
Ramos, S., 399
Randles, R.M., 136, 329
Rappeport, J., 52, 73, 184, 310
Rather, D., 151, 171
Rauma, A., 338
Ray, J.E., 252
Reagan, R., 154, 294, 343, 344, 346, 526
Reagan, N., 346
Redlich, F., 501
Redmount, R.S., 353
Reed, J.D., 53
Reed, T.J., 213
Reeves, R., 343
Regan, M.C., 13
Rehnquist, W., 72, 118, 171, 391

Reich, R., 91
Reich, R.B., 103
Reich, W.T., 30, 504, 515
Reid, W.H., 337
Reik, T., 532, 540
Reinhold, R., 175
Reischel, C.L., 434
Reisner, R., 336
Renzi, D., 245, 246
Renzi, N., 245, 246
Reppucci, N., 397
Restak, R., 429
Rex, P., 14, 241, 247, 552
Rice, P., 254
Riddell, Lord, vii
Ridgeway, J., 427
Roback, H.B., 201, 212
Robertson, J.D., 319
Robinson , K., 54
Robinson, W.P., 397
Rock, S.F., 137
Rodman, D., 143
Rooney, A., 151
Roosevelt, F.D., 346
Ropiequet, J., 137, 138
Rorty, R., 544
Rose, A.M., 397
Rose, S., 540
Rosen, G., 542
Rosen, J., 525
Rosenberg, E.H., xv
Rosenthal, A.M., 354
Rosenthal, H.J., 213
Rosner, R., 318
Ross, H.A., 197
Ross, J.W., 320
Rossi, A.M., 336
Rossiaud, J., 340
Rotello, G., 330
Roth, L.H., 53, 54, 195, 199, 360, 385, 474, 547, 553
Roth, M., 330
Roth, P., 99, 100, 378
Rottunda, S.J., 327
Rouleau, J. L., 12
Rowlands, S., 7
Roy, J., 495, 501
Royce, E., 308
Roz, R., 140

Rubin, E., 176
Rubin, J.G., 22
Ruby, J., 383
Rueveni, U., 217
Ryan, L.J., 322
Ryback, R., 478

Sacks, H., 41
Sadock, B.J., 213
Sadoff, R.L., 55
Safire, W., 7, 12, 346, 354
St. James, M., 7
Sales, B.D., 542
Salter, A., 55
Salzman, L., 554
Sanborn, C.J., 437
Sarat, A., 103
Sawyer, D., 70
Sawyer, K., 498
Scalia, A., 10, 11, 14, 42, 72, 118, 122, 154, 390, 391
Scarmeas, C.J., 179
Schacter, D.L., 539
Schaefer, R., 539
Scheflin, A.W., 529, 539
Scheiber, S.C., 500
Schemo, D.J., 518
Schermerhorn, R.A., 387
Schetky, D., 528
Schine, E., 148
Schlit, C., 316
Schneider, C.D., xv
Schofield, W., 452, 473
Schopp, R.F., 318
Schorrig, S.F., xvii, 123, 133
Schouten, R., 538
Schreber, D.P., 362, 380
Schulberg, H.C., 473, 474, 494, 501
Schulhofer, S.J., 184
Schutte, J.W., 544
Schwartz, B.K., 185
Schwartz, H., 498
Schwartz, M., 506
Schwartz, R.D., 12
Schwartz, V.E., 99, 104
Schwarzberg, K.A., 114
Schwed, H.J., 478
Scully, J.H., 423
Seelye, K.Q., 50, 75

Seidman, L.S., 497
Seingler, R., 383
Sesser, S., 327
Sexton, A., 364, 367, 379
Sexton, L., 364
Shabazz, M., 515
Shah, S.A., 335
Shakespeare, W., 85, 103, 143
Shalala, D., 455
Shammai, ix
Shapire, D.L., 320
Shapiro, R., 378, 383
Sharfstein, S.S., 496, 497
Sharkey, J., 398
Sharp, L.J., 183
Shartzer, S., 178
Shaw, T., 383
Sheedy, C.E., 171
Shelton, M., 212
Sheridan, B., 431
Sherman, C., 379
Shlensky, R., 478
Shuman, D.W., xvii, 24, 31, 41, 42, 53, 70, 75, 173, 338, 542
Siconolfi, M., 516
Sidel, V., xiv, 159, 177, 316, 317
Siegel, R.B., 104
Siegler, M, 403
Silbaugh, K., 53
Silva, J. A., 73, 175, 179
Silverberg, H.M., 431, 501
Silving, H., 247, 338, 356
Simon, R.I., 114, 172, 325, 329, 340, 539
Simonton, M.J., 474
Simpson, E., 378
Simpson, N. B., 244
Simpson, O.J., 62, 164, 244, 383, 426
Sims, C., 148
Sither, J.W., 326, 327
Sizemore, C.C., 363, 364
Skeeters, D.E., 382
Sklar, R., xiv
Slater, D., 517
Slaughter, M.E., 147
Slawson, P.F., 477
Sloan, J.B., 480
Slobogin, C., 318, 328, 335, 336

Slovenko, R., 23, 31, 55, 70, 90, 103, 134, 136, 147, 173, 176, 185, 197, 219, 250, 312, 322, 325, 327, 332, 341, 378, 401, 431, 437, 475, 477, 478, 515, 516, 519, 538, 541, 554
Smith, A.E., 322
Smith, A.M., 319, 338
Smith, D., 554
Smith, D.F., 382
Smith, E., 374
Smith, H., xv
Smith, H.W., 198
Smith, J.C., 321
Smith, J.T., 318
Smith, M., 338
Smith, P.J., 104
Smith, S.R., 70
Smithbell, M., xv
Smolla, R.A., 355
Smyth, J., 175
Soffin, E.S., 146
Solomon, J., 148
Solzhenitsyn, A., 312, 374, 552
Souter, D., 72, 84
Southwick, S.M., 539
Sovine, T., 517
Sowell, T., 353
Sowle, C., 171
Spacek, S., 364
Sparks, T., 168
Speck, R.V., 217
Spence, D.P., 540
Spencer, S.B., 384
Spikes, K., 185
Spingarn, N.D., 201
Spirito, A., 402, 410
Spratling, C., 103
Spruiell, V., 401
Steadman, H., 335, 508
Stein, E.J., 451, 474
Steinbeck, J., 89
Steinberg, K.L., 321
Steir, C., 380
Stevens, J.P., 64, 65, 72, 84, 118, 354, 390
Stewart, D.M., 285, 325, 326
Stewart, J., 382, 383, 384
Stoll, M.T., 381

Stone, S.H., 22
Stone, M.H., 134
Stone, I.F.,449, 471
Stone, A.A., 312, 336, 340, 341
Stone, R., 343, 353
Strachey, J., 478
Strasburger, L.H., 75, 136, 329, 378
Strecker, E.A., 317
Streep, M., 512
Streisand, B., 144
Streseman, K.D., 132
Styron, W., 144
Sturdy, R.E., 477
Suarez, J.M., 103
Sugar, M., 400
Sugarman, S.D., 320
Sullivan, G., 340, 341
Sundelson, D., 40, 53, 241
Super, W., 197
Sutcliffe, P.W., 375
Sutherland, P.K., 136, 140, 329, 442
Swingler, R., 383
Swisher, P.N., 105
Szasz, T.S., 82, 87, 240, 247, 356, 401,
    451, 452, 453, 471, 472, 504, 510, 515,
    518, 541

Tager, W., 151, 171
Tanay, E., 276, 327, 378, 451
Tankieff, S.P., 532
Taranto, R.G., 498
Tarasoff, A., 280
Tarasoff, T., 278, 279, 280, 306, 315
Tardiff, K., 337
Tarpley, H., 517
Tasman, A., 518
Taub, S., 137
Taylor, E., 430
Taylor, P.J., 326
Taylor, R.K., 22
Taylor, S., 384
Terestman, N., 379
Thigpen, C.H., 364
Thomas, C., 72, 391
Thomas, M.M., 12
Thomas, K., 399
Thomma, S., 353
Thomsen, R.C., 183
Thoreau, H.D., 52

Thornton, H., 175
Thurber, J., 209
Tierney, J., 15
Tillman, W.A., 326
Tobriner, M.O., 71, 289, 294, 298,
    329
Toles, 352
Tolstoy, L., 450
Tomes, N., 518
Toney, S., 103
Tonry, M., 517
Toobin, J., 70, 378
Torrey, E.F., 217, 413, 497, 508,
    509, 517, 518
Towery, O.B., 496, 497
Trantino, T., 374
Trent, J.W., 519
Tsongas, P., 346
Turkington, R.C., 31, 88
Turner, L., 477
Tybor, J.R., 338

Ullrich, H.E., 430
Usdin, G.L., xvii, 248

Vainer, C., 517
Van Biema, D., 379
VandeCreek, L., 275, 319, 331
Vatz, R.E., 515
Vicary, W., 527, 528, 538
Vickery, A.B., 267
Vidal, G., 449, 470
Viederman, M., 540
Viviano, B., 285
Volokh, E., 132
von Bulow, C., 241, 242, 247, 264

Wachtler, S., 54, 352
Waelder, R., 497
Wahl, C.W., 54
Wald, M.L., 398
Wallace, M., 145
Wallerstein, J., 98, 103
Walt, S.R., 438
Walters, B., 53, 54, 355
Wand, B.F., 383, 384
Ward, T., 397
Warner, S.L., 360
Warren, S.D., 553

Wassil-Grimm, C., 540
Waterhouse, G.J., 212
Watkins, J.D., 330
Watson, F.P., 385
Webster, R., 53
Webster, P.H., 384
Weedman, R.D., 476
Weiden, P., 509
Weihofen, H., 52, 88, 248
Weinapple, M., 268
Weinberg, M.G., 178
Weinberg, L.S., 515
Weiner, M.F., 41, 42, 53
Weinreb, E.J., 322
Weinstein, R.H., 56
Weinstein, J.B., 24
Weinstein, F., 248
Weinstein, J., 90
Weinstock, R., 73, 170, 179, 538
Weiss, J., 30
Weithorn, L., 397
Weitz, D., 38
Welcome, M., 372, 383
Wendland, W., 148, 517
Wesbacker, J., 127
West, M., 132
Westin, A.F., 474
Weston, N.L., 103
Weston, W.I., 105
Wettstein, R.M., 335
Wexler, D.B., 306, 337
Wexler, M., 525
Wheeler, A.M., 326, 327
Whitehead, B.D., 103
Whitford, W.C., 86
Whitney, C.R., 380
Wicker, T., 89, 344
Wicker, V.D., 285, 325
Wickham, D., 147
Wiesel, E., xiv
Wigand, J., 214
Wigmore, J., 7, 12, 13, 18, 20, 23, 24, 36, 37, 51, 154, 173
Wilke, J., 517
Wilkerson, I., 330
Wilkinson, J.H., xv
Will, D.E., 176

Williams, T., 44, 144
Williams, W., 372
Williams, P., 475
Willwerth, J., 175, 515
Wilmer, H.A., 440, 442
Wilson, L., 297
Wilson, R., 343
Wilson, S., 297
Wilson, S.J., 88, 477
Wilson, T., 305
Wilson, W., 346
Winerip, M., 515
Winick, B.J., 53
Winnicott, D.W., 394, 401
Winslade, W.J., xv, 320, 480
Winstead, In re, 189
Wise, T.B., 331
Wiseman, F., 365
Wojtowicz, J., 375
Wolf, A., 202
Wolford, J., 199
Wolpert, E.A., 359
Woods, R.M., 210
Woodward, J., 364
Woychuk, D., 517
Wozniak, J., 518
Wright, L., 544
Wright, L.B., 137
Wydra, H.A., 410
Wysocky, K., 338

Yalom, I.D., 378, 540
Yapko, M.D., 544
Yarborough, G., 442
Yeltsin, B., 345
Young, C., 104
Young, D., 102
Young, K., 401
Young, R., 40

Zappert, L.T., 132
Zavin, T., 103
Zenoff, E., 52
Zhisui, L., 379
Ziskin, J., 538
Zolteck-Jick, R., 136
Zonana, H., 423

# SUBJECT INDEX

Abortion, 390

Abuse of confidentiality, 481

Accountability (*see also* Records, Identity of patients)
    abuses, 140 , 481
    generally, 456, 461, 463, 481
    investigation of Chicago Lakeshore Hospital, 486, 494, 551
    monitoring by fiscal third-party, 453, 456, 483
    surveillance, 485

Accountants, 6

Adverse drug reactions, reporting, 420

Advocacy groups (*see* Identity of patient)

*Advocate's Devil, The*, 162

After-care placement, 412

Agent of attorney, 21, 156 (*see also* Attorney - client privilege)

AIDS, 120, 286, 290, 310, 323, 330, 327

Alabama privilege statute, 59

Alcohol and drug abuse, 33, 79, 81, 86, 151, 307, 566

Alcoholics Anonymous, 208, 212, 213

Alford plea, 185

Alien abduction, 534

Alienation of affections, 91, 100, 228 (*see also* Marriage)

Alienists, 46, 513

American Academy of Psychiatry and Law, 525, 528

American Bar Association Model Rules of Professional Conduct, 289, 373

American Civil Liberties Union, 9

American Group Psychotherapy Association, 204, 207 (*see also* Group therapy)

American Law Institute proposal, 21, 253

American Medical Association, xii

*American President, The*, 349

Americans with Disabilities Act, 422, 432

American Psychiatric Association:

Diagnostic & Statistical Manual of Mental Disorders, 458, 503, 506, 525

Guidelines on Confidentiality, 211, 244, 387, 393, 405, 406, 409, 442

Model Law on Confidentiality of Health and Social Service Records, 393

Principles of Informed Consent in Psychiatry, 442

Principles of Medical Ethics, 40, 290

*Anmchara*, 11

*Annie Hall*, 91

*An Unquiet Mind*, 420

Archeological dig, therapy as, 531

Architects, 6

Assertion of privilege by therapist, 141, 246, 549

Assumption of confidentiality, vii, 37

Asylum doctors, 512

Attention Deficit Hyperactivity Disorder, 510

Attitudes toward mental illness, 47 (*see also* Stigma)

Attorney-client privilege:
    examiner as agent of attorney, 21, 156
    generally, 6, 8, 52, 68, 590, 591, 594
    ownership of, 239
    Roman law, 239
    secretary, 31

Automobiles, danger in driving, 270, 286, 326, 334

Barroom therapy, 14, 596

Bar examiners, reporting to, 421

Battered child syndrome, 392

Bedisde manner, 19, 35

Berkley High School, 144

Best interest of child (*see* Child custody)

*Beyond Bedlam*, 46

Bias - free language, 506

Bias of witness, 529

Bigamy trial, 16
Bill of rights for patients, x
*Bizarro*, 121, 425
*Blondie*, 48, 102
Borda Psychiatric Hospital, 144
*Brain Watchers, The*, 347
*Braveheart*, 509
Breach of confidentiality, remedies, xiii, 158, 259, 547
Breach of fiduciary duty, 259
Buckley amendment, 468

California privilege statute, 63, 70
Call-girls, 7
"Cape Man" murderer, 375
Caricaturing psychiatry, 46, 512
Case conferences, 404
Case files in social agencies, 412
Celebrities, revelation by, 342
*Character Above All*, 343
Chaucer, vii
Chicago Lakeshore Hospital, 486, 494, 551
Child abuse reporting, 24
  resident manager, duty to report, 321
Child abuse, 24
Child custody:
  (*see also* Minors)
  best interest of child, 106
  generally, 106
  health issues, 109
  mental health records, 110
Christian Science practitioners, 19
*Cinderella*, 524
Civil commitment, 172, 186,188, 279, 307, 508
Civil Rights Act, 117, 120, 122, 123
Clergy privilege, 6, 8, 9, 13, 241, 552, 554, 574, 598
*Close to Home*, 97
Codes of ethics, *ix*, 274, 285, 348, 382
Colloguialisms, 512
Common law,16, 21
Communal living, xi
Communications with non-medical persons:
  (*see also* Consent to release of information, Tort cases, Criminal cases)
  bar examiners, 421
  blanket waivers, IV-9-2
  commercial inquiries, 415

consent, 439, 442
consumer agencies, 415, 456
disability benefits, 417, 428
duty to maintain, 259
employers, 414, 417, 429
families, sharing information with, 259, 395, 400
generally, 412
handout to patients, 443
informed consent, 439
insurers, 415, 417
jury duty, 426
managed care, 45, 418, 440, 443, 484
Maryland tracking program, 441
Michigan, requirement of written waiver, 442
minors, treatment of, 386
parole board, 168, 412
professional licensure, 421
recording consent, 439
release of information, 415, 439
remedies for breach, 158, 259
requirement of written waiver, 442
Texas Medical Practice Act, 439
treatment of minors, 386
universities, 396
welfare departments, 428
workers' compensation, 29, 428
Community attitudes, 47, 50, 503, 511
Compelling examination, 98, 170 (*see also* Torts cases)
Confessional:
  (*see also* Clergy privilege)
  ritual, 38
  talk shows, 145
Confidentiality, expectation of, vii, 37, 547
  (*see also* Need for confidentiality)
Conflict of laws, 17
Conjoint family therapy, 98, 306
Connecticut privilege statute, 68, 59, 82, 160, 243,439, 548
Consent to release of information, 362, 368, 415, 439,442, 465
Consultation, 387, 397
Consumer credit reporting, 412
*Consumer Reports*, 48
Contractual waiver, 29
Controversy between parties, 123, 253

Correctional institutions, therapy in (*see* Criminal cases)
Counsellors (*see* Therapists covered by privilege)
Court opinions, understanding of, 275
Covenant marriage (*see* Marriage)
Creation of privilege, criteria, 7, 35
Crime (*see* Criminal cases, Duty to report, Mental illness)
Criminal cases:
  community-based programs, 167
  correctional institution, therapy in, 166
  diminished capacity, 164
  discovery by accused, 161
  discovery by law-enforcement officials, 156, 166
  driving under influence of alcohol, 150
  *Durham* test of criminal responsibility, 524
  duty to report danger, *xii*, 160, 236
  evaluation for sentencing, 164
  exceptions from privilege, 26, 31, 150, 601
  Federal Rules of Criminal Procedure, 165
  Fifth Amendment, 157
  fraud, 28, 44, 140, 150
  future crime or fraud, xii, 28, 44, 159, 160, 209
  generally, xii, 150, 158, 508
  *in camera* review, 161, 163
  limitation on examiner's findings, 151
  *Miranda* warning, 153, 171, 291, 442, 594
  misprision of a felony, 158, 176
  narcotics, 151
  not guilty by reason of insanity plea, 115, 151, 154, 156, 158, 526
  patient as victim of crime, 160
  parole, 168
  plea of insanity, 115, 151, 154, 156, 158, 526
  post-trial proceedings, 164
  pre-sentence report, 183
  prison psychiatry, 166, 184
  privilege against self-incrimination, 151
  probation, 82, 165
  rape crisis center, 162
  reporting crime, 158, 176, 221, 270
  search warrant, 156, 160, 177
  sentencing, 165
  statements to examiner, 151, 155
  surreptitious psychiatric interrogation, 152, 171

  therapeutic seduction, 153
  threat to patient, 160
Criminally insane, 151, 154, 156, 158 (*see also* Criminal cases)
Criteria for enacting privilege, 7, 35
Cross-examination, right of, 39, 182

*Dagwood Bumstead*, 48, 102
Dalton School, 386
Danger, assessment of, 301
Dangerous individuals (*see* Duty to report)
*Daubert* rule, 535, 542
*Dead Souls*, 467
Death of patient, 29, 160, 242, 243, 364
Death penalty, 155, 171
Debt collection, 435
Declarations:
  Hawaii, x
  Madrid, x
  Vienna, x
Decorum, 85
Defamation, 530
Demon possession, 45
Deontological analysis, 41
Detective, therapist as, 531, 540
Determination of applicability, 28
Diagnostic labeling:
  manipulating, 458
  overdiagnosis, 459
  purpose of, 416, 458
  stigma of labeling, 50, 503, 511
Direct victim theory, 282, 342 (*see also* Revival of memory therapy)
Disability benefits, 417
Disclosure, qualified privilege, 194, 262
Dissociation, 535
Dissociative identity disorder (*see* Multiple personality disorder)
Dissolution of marriage (*see* Divorce)
Diversity cases, 566
Divorce:
  generally, 91
  Italian style, 93
  state law as governing, 94
  tort suit for emotional damages, 99
DNA testing, 536
*Dog Day Afternoon*, 375
Domestic violence victims (*see* Criminal cases)

*Dr. Jekyll and Mr. Hyde*, 49
*Dr. Katz*, 515
Drug use (*see* Alcohol and drug abuse)
Duty to aid, 271, 284
Duty to protect, 304 (*see* Duty to report)
Duty to report:
  adverse drug reactions, 420
  AIDS, 286, 290, 330, 327
  attorneys, duty of, 24
  child abuse, 24 ,321
  crime, xi, xii, 64, 158
  danger, 159, 175, 249,  264, 270, 274, 287,
    301
  duty to testify, 157
  espionage, 270
  firearms, 33, 286
  foreseeability of victim, 293, 311
  fugitive, 28, 33
  generally, xii, 44, 158, 270
  group therapy, 208
  gun or knife wounds, 33
  identifiable victim, 293, 311
  imminent danger, 64, 285
  impaired physician, 290, 493
  law-enforcement officials, 166
  legislation, 310, 311, 313
  motor vehicles, danger in driving, 262, 270,
    286, 326, 334
  narcotics, procuring, 33, 86
  prediction of violence, 300
  public health matters, xii, xv, 271
  sexual relations with patient, 290
  special relationship, giving rise to duty, 281,
    283, 287, 300, 321
  standard of care in assessing danger, 281,
    287, 300
  standard of care in disclosing duty, 304, 312
  suicide risk, 308, 427
  suspicious death, 33
  treasonous activities, 33, 270
  undue familiarity with patient, 290
Duty to rescue, 271, 314
Duty to testify, 157
Duty to third persons, 126, 136 (*see also* Duty
  to report)
Dyadic relationships, coverage of privilege,
  26, 79

Eli Lilly, suit against, 127

Empirical research, 41
Espionage (*see* Duty to report)
Ethics, codes of, vii, xii, 274, 525, 528
*Ethics of Psychoanalysis, The*, 451
*Everyone Says I Love You*, xiv
Evidence, manner of obtaining, 6, 49, 74
Examination, compelling, 98 (*see also* Torts
  case)
Examiner as agent of attorney, 21
Exceptions to privilege:
  child custody, 62, 106
  criminal cases, 62
  future crime or fraud, 140, 158
  generally, 62
  hospitalization, 62, 186
  no-fault automobile insurance, 62
  patient-litigant exception, 20, 62, 115, 128
  self-defense exception, 251
  tort cases, 20, 62, 70, 116
  waiver, 29, 34, 239
  expertation of confidentiality, vii
*Executioner's Song, The*, 371, 372
*Ex parte* interview, 128, 137
Experts:
  competency of psychiatric testimony, 521
  disclosure of information to the media, 151
  ethical guidelines of American Academy of
    Psychiatry and Law, 525, 528
  "hired guns," 75
  surreptious examination, 152
  therapist as expert witness, 75, 129, 521
  therapist as fact witness, xiii, 75, 129, 521
  therapist vs. forensic expert testimony, xiii,
    75, 129, 521
  use of opponent's expert, 24
Expectation of confidentiality, vii, 37, 547

Fact of treatment under privilege, 44, 139
*Fact* magazine poll, 347, 350
Fair Health Information Practices Act, 455
Families, sharing information with, 148, 395,
  400, 427
Family therapy, 98, 211, 306
Fear of physician,  ix
Federal Rules of Civil Procedure, Rule 35(a),
  120
Federal Rules of Evidence:
  exclusion of medical privilege, 60
  generally, 10, 17, 20, 41, 60, 66, 117, 565

proposed rule 60, 504
reason and experience, 60, 565, 589
Rule 403, 40
Rule 501, 17, 60, 117, 565, 588, 589
Rule 504, 116, 84, 80 63, 60
scientific evidence, 535, 542
Federal Tort Claims Act (*see* Torts cases)
Federally assisted treatment of substance abusers, 79
Fee collection, 435
Fiduciary duty, 259
First Amendment, 8, 265, 359, 374, 377
Fiscal third party, monitoring by (*see* Accountability)
"Fishing expedition," 120, 130
Flashback experience, 530
Forensic examiner, duty to report danger, 289, 328
Fostering therapist-patient relationship, 46
Fraud (*see* Accountability, Tort cases, Criminal cases)
Free association data, 49
Freedom of Information Act, 168
Freedom of speech (*see* First Amendment)
Friend as confidant, 9, 10, 84, 549, 596
*Frye* rule, 535
Future crime or fraud (*see* Accountability, Tort cases, Criminal cases)

Georgia privilege statute, 59, 80, 548
Gobbledygook, 55
Governmental and nongovernmental regulations, 461
Gresham's Law, 350
Group for Advancement of Psychiatry, proposals of, 9, 51, 59, 68, 80, 251, 435, 548, 550
Group therapy:
  Alcoholics Anonymous, 212, 213
  American Group Psychotherapy Association, 204, 207
  Christian Passion Plays, 217
  communal living, xi
  concern of therapists, 200
  contractual agreement, 203
  correctional settings, 167
  danger posed by member, 208
  definition of group, 207
  encounter groups, 86

generally, 200
  interview of group members, 219
  liquidated damages clause, 203
  tribal in nature, xi
  types of groups, 207
Guardianship, 186,189
Guidance counsellor, 387
Guidelines on confidentiality, 244, 387, 393, 405, 406, 409
Guns, 33, 286, 315
Gunshot wounds, 33 (*see also* Duty to report)

Hairdresser therapy, 15
Harm to therapy by disclosure, 40
"Head shrinker," ix
Health Maintenance Organizations (HMO), 19
Hearsay exception, 161
*Herb & Jamal*, 84
Hippocratic oath, ix, x, 17, 18, 202, 269, 273, 317, 418, 533, 547, 552
HIV, 120, 286, 290, 310, 323, 327, 330
Homosexuality:
  fear of, 50, 350, 528
  outing, 145
  reporting in military, 30
  stigma, 50, 350, 528
Hospital accreditation, 419, 462
Hospital and office records, 191, 232, 403, 449
Hospital care, 403, 419
Hospital case conferences, 404
Hospitalization:
  judicial record, 188
  proceedings for, 186, 188
  suicide risk, 308, 427
*How the Irish Saved Civilization*, 10
*How to Live With a Mentally Ill Person*, 412
Human immunodeficiency virus (HIV), 120, 286, 290, 310, 323, 330, 327
Husband-wife privilege (*see* Marital privilege)
Hypnosis, 152
Hypochondriacs, 19

Identity of patient, 39, 139, 487, 495
  (*see also* Accountability)
  advocacy groups, 145
  confessional talk shows, 145

discovery demand, 139
fact of treatment, 44
picketing therapist's office, 142
revelations by celebrities, II-5-10
undue familiarity, 140
Illinois privilege statute, 150, 246, 494
Immunity for disclosure in court, 246
Impact of insurance on litigation, 115
Impaired physician, 290, 493
Incompetency proceeding, 193
Informants, 270
Information from family of patient, 119
Insanity defense, 115, 151, 154, 156, 158, 526
(*see also* Criminal cases)
Insurance coverage, demand for information, 124, 415, 458
Insurance policies, 34, 124, 415
Insurers, 124, 415
Interspousal suits, 99
Interview of members in group therapy, 219
Invasion of privacy (*see* Privacy, Teaching and writing)
Investigation of Chicago Lakeshore Hospital, 486, 494, 551
Involuntary hospitalization, 186, 508

Janus, 62
Jeopardy to patient or others (*see* Duty to report)
Jewish story, ix, 36
Journalist privilege, 6
Judicial interpretation, general rule of, 21
Judicial record on commitment, 188
Junk science, 535, 542
Jury duty, qualification for, 426
Justice, evidence as basis, 5, 19, 42, 49, 594

*Kramer v. Kramer*, 471
*Kudzu*, 505

Law of forum, 17, 22
Law-enforcement officials, duty to report, 166
Law script, 90
Liability for unauthorized disclosures (*see* Breach of confidentiality)
Licensing, 421
Lie detector, 542
Life and accident insurance policies, 29

*Listening to Prozac*, 48
Literary critic, therapist as, 531
"Little Hans," 387, 391
*Little Murders*, 92
*Lois Lane*, 40
*Lolita*, 47
Loony Radio, 144

*Macbeth*, 143
*Madness*, 512
Madness as label, 509
Malpractice insurer, notifying, 124
Managed care, 45, 418, 440, 443, 484
Mann Act, 94
Manner of obtaining evidence, importance of, 6
Marital offender, 99
Marital privilege, 6, 8, 19, 60, 200, 566, 580, 590
Marital tort claims, 99
Marriage:
alienation of affections, 91, 100
covenant marriage, 93
divorce, 91
limitations on, 95
"Marriage savers," 95
premarital counseling, 96
Russian folk saying, 91
state law, 94
tort claims against spouse, 99
"Marriage savers," 95
*Marvin's Room*, 512
Maryland tracking program, 441
Materiality as guideline (*see* Relevancy as guideline)
Media, divulgence to, 151
Medical model, 503, 510
Medical privilege:
criticisms of, 16, 18, 549
generally, 24, 28, 572, 576, 580,
loathsome diseases, 17, 19, 286, 290, 330, 327
New York statute, 16, 17, 23
restrictions, 25
states without, 16, 22, 580
Medicare, 417
Medication, as disinhibiting, 127
*Memory Wars, The*, 46
Mnemonic device, xiii

Mental illness:
 crime, link to, 507, 508, 513, 518
 dangerousness, relation to, 507, 508, 513, 518
 definition, 492
 labeling, 503
 stigma, 45, 54, 58, 143, 144, 196, 352, 393, 503
 terms used to describe, 50, 503, 511
Mental institutions, terms to describe, 512
Military law, 25, 30
Minors:
 (*see also* Child custody)
 abortion, 390
 *ad hoc* exceptions to parental authority, 388, 389
 alcohol or drug abuse treatment, 389
 APA Guidelines on Confidentiality, 387
 battered child syndrome, 392
 Buckley amendment, 468
 child abuse reporting, 24, 321
 consent to treatment, 386
 consultants to teachers, 386, 394
 contraceptives, 389
 emancipated minor, 389, 398
 Illinois statute, 389
 "Little Hans," 387, 391
 mature minor, 389
 medication, 398
 mental health treatment, 389
 *parens patriae* doctrine, 388
 parents, informing, 395, 400
 reporting child abuse, 24, 321
 teacher-student privilege, 386
 treatment of, 386
 treatment without parental consent, 388
 university health services, 396
*Miranda* warning, 153, 171, 291, 313, 442, 594 (*see also* Criminal cases)
Misguided hope in privilege, 57
Misprision of a felony, 158, 176
*Mr. Boffo*, 511
Monitoring (*see* Accountability)
Moral significance of privilege, 41
Model Code of Evidence, 21, 253
*Mother Goose & Grimm*, 524
Motion in limine, 245
Motion to quash, 73
Motor vehicles, 262, 270, 286, 326, 334

Multiple personality disorder, 364, 541
*My Life as a Man*, 360
*Myth of Mental Illness, The*, 510

Narcotics (*see* Alcohol and drug abuse)
National Coalition of Free Men, 92
National Commission on Confidentiality of Health Records, 201
National Self-Help Clearinghouse, 208
National Physicians Data Bank, 492
National security, 270, 287
National Stigma Clearing House, 505, 513
Nebraska privilege statute, 80, 87, 150
Need for confidentiality, 35, 40, 42 (*see also* Confidentiallity, expectation of)
*New Informants, The*, 241
New York statute, 16, 17, 22, 23
News reporter privilege, 6, 192
Notifying malpractice insurer, 124
Nurses, 26, 31, 32
Nursing homes, 412

Office records (*see* Records)
Old Testament, 59
Opinion without examination, 348
Oral argument on privilege in U.S. Supreme Court, 565
Outing, homosexuality, 145
Outpatient clinic operation in Michigan, 460
Ownership of privilege, 141, 246, 549
Ownership of records (*see* Records)

Paranoia, 426
Pastoral counseling (*see* Clergy privilege)
Parent - child privilege, 10, 14, 209, 596
Parents, informing about child, 395
Parole, 168
Patient advocate in hospital, duty of reporting, IV-2-37
Patient as victim of crime, 160
Patient, definition of, 85
Patient identifying information (*see* Accountability, Identity of patient)
Patient - litigant exception (*see* Exceptions to privilege)
Peer review, 405, 406
*Persona*, 38
Personal notes, 467

Personal injury litigation (*see* Exception to privilege, Tort cases)
Personality testing, 354
Pharmacists, 26
Photos of Podder and Tarasoff, 279
Physician, definition of, 26, 27, 35, 79
Physician, wife, 268
Picketing therapist's office, 142 (*see also* Identity of patient)
Placebo effect, belief in privilege, 550
Polygraph evidence, 542
Political candidates:
  character, 342
  informing the public, 342, 349
  selection of, 342
Pollution of privilege, 26, 27, 168, 204
*Poor Richard's Almanac,* 202
Prediction of violence, 300
Premarital counseling (*see* Marriage)
Premises liability, 314
Presence of third party (*see* Pollution of privilege)
Priest-patient privilege (*see* Clergy privilege)
Primum non nocere, 67
Prison psychiatry (*see* Criminal cases)
Privacy:
  concept of, xi, 63, 547
  history of, xi
  political candidates, 345
  right to, xi, 63, 547
  teaching and writing, 359
Privacy Protection Study Commission, viii
*Privata lex,* privilege as, 25, 79, 548
Private detectives, communications to, 600
Privilege, meaning of, 25, 79, 548
Probation (*see* Criminal cases)
Probative value of evidence, 65, 74
Procedural or substantive Law, nature of privilege, 22, 566
Proceedings to hospitalize, 186
Professional licensure, reporting on, 421
Professional negligence, 259
Professional standards review organizations, 407, 462
Protection and Advocacy for Mentally Ill Individuals Act, 83
Psychiatric discourse (*see* Stigma)
*Psychiatric Ethics,* 365
Psychic reality vs. outer reality, 531

Psychoanalysis, status of, 47, 79
Psychohistory, 348
Psychotherapist, definition of, 11
Psychologists (*see* Therapists covered by privilege)
Public health matters, 17, 196, 271, 549 (*see also* Duty to report)

Qualified privilege:
  to disclose, 262
  to withhold information, 194
Quality control, 405

*Radio La Colifata,* 144
Rape crisis center (*see* Criminal cases)
Rape shield laws, 133
Reconciliation of Episcopal Church, 241
Records:
  accountability, 453, 456, 463, 481
  bribing hospital recordkeeper, 467
  deceased physician, 196
  electronic, 455
  generally, 449
  hospital and office records, 191, 232, 403, 449
  implementing right to treatment, 457
  involuntary hospitalizations records, 188
  insurance coverage, 124, 415, 458
  not keeping, 232, 451, 453, 464
  note-taking, styles of, 232, 451
  ownership of, 195, 366, 376
  police records, 188
  political candidates, 342
  recording consent, 465
  right of patient to see, 366, 376
  subpoena of, 58, 157, 246
Refusal to undergo examination, 98
Relational privileges:
  common law, 5
  generally, 5
Release of information (*see* Consent)
Relevancy as guideline, 65, 108, 506, 569
Remedies for breach of confidentiality, 158, 259
Reporting duties (*see* Duty to report)
Repressed memories (*see* Revival of memory Therapy)
Repression, concept of, 535, 541
Research, 6, 419

Research study of medical students, 393
Residential placement, 262, 404
Responsibility to public, 44, 221, 270
*Restatement of Law of Torts*, 328
Restrictions on medical privilege, 25
*Reversal of Fortune*, 241
Revival of memory therapy, 46, 80, 125, 464, 530 (*see also* Direct victim theory)
*Rex Morgan, M.D.*, 532
Right of patient to see records, II-8-6
Right to privacy (*see* Privacy)
Roman god Janus, 62
Roman Law, 239
Royal Australian & New Zealand College of Psychiatrists, code of ethics, 274

School counseling, 6
Scientific evidence, use in court, 535, 542
Scripts of situations, 85
Search for truth, 6, 535, 596
Search warrants, 156, 160, 161, 177
*Second Chances*, 98
Secretary-employer relationship, 210
Secrecy:
  as cover for wrongdoing, xi, 57
  confessional, 8
  danger in, 5, 57
  fashion and trends, xi
  maintaining, 548
Self-analysis privilege, 407
Self-critical analysis, 407
Self-defense exception, 125, 251
Self-evaluation privilege, 407
Sentencing (*see* Criminal cases)
Sex discrimination (*see* Tort cases)
Sex offender treatment programs, 185
Sex research, 6
Sex with patient, 140, 495
Sexual abuse allegations, 530
Sexual assault victims (*see* Criminal cases)
Sexual harassment (*see* Tort cases)
*Sherlock Holmes*, ix
Social Security benefits, 150, 412
Social significance of privilege, 41
Social workers (*see* Therapists covered by privilege)
*Something Happened*, xv, 418
Soul-friend, 10
South Africa Truth and Reconciliation Commission, 75

Sovereign immunity, 295
*Spaniard and the Seven Deadly Sins, The*, 210
Spanish language, *estar* or *ser* distinction, 513
Special relationship, giving rise to duty to report (*see* Duty to report)
Stalking law, 307
Statutes, 559
Statutory, definition of, 22
Stenographer, 6, 26
Stereotypes, 512
Sterilization, 95
Stigma Clearinghouse, 505
Stigma:
  mental illness, 45, 54, 66, 143, 144, 196, 352, 393
  psychiatric discourse, 50, 503
Student - teacher privilege, 386
Subpoena, significance of, 58, 157, 246, 261
Substance abuse treatment programs, 79. (*see* Alcohol and substance abuse)
Suicide of patient, 161
*Superman*, 40
Supervision, 405
Supplemental Security Income benefits, 150, 412
Surreptious examination, 152, 171
Sword or shield, privilege as, 18, 29, 115

Teacher-student privilege, 386
Teaching and writing (*see also* Records)
  anti-profit statutes, 373
  articles or books about a patient, 241, 361
  consent to writing, 241, 362, 369
  deceased patient, writing about, 364
  film about patient, 361
  First Amendment, 359, 374, 377
  forensic experts, writings by, 363, 370
  Freud's case histories, 361
  generally, 359
  medical record, 376
  multiple personality disorder, 363
  note-taking, 449
  records sought by patient, 366, 376
  research subject, writing about, 367
  "Son of Sam" law, 373
Teaching programs, 406
Team approach in treatment, II-1-8
Termination of privilege (*see also* Exceptions to privilege)

by pollution, 26, 31, 168
death of patient, 29, 160, 242, 243, 364
generally, 111, 127, 237, 242
waiver by contract, 29, 34
Territorial imperative, 37
Testaments, 28, 29, 243, 244
Testimonial privileges, types of, 5
Therapeutic privilege, 194
Therapist as detective, 535
Therapist as expert witness, xiii, 75, 129, 521
Therapist as fact witness, xiii, 75, 129, 521
Therapists covered by privilege:
  alcoholic counselor, 566
  counselors, 82
  generally, 11, 15, 19, 27, 35, 36, 50, 79, 80, 82, 416
  marriage counselors, 83
  nonmedical therapists, 27, 416
  nurses, 26, 31, 32
  psychiatrists, 79
  psychologists, 26, 67, 82, 567
  psychotherapists, 79
  social workers, 6, 82, 84, 88, 565, 587, 598
  unlicensed therapists, 80
Therapy as purchase of friendship, 10
Therapy in correctional institutions, 166
Therapy, types of, 11, 472
Third party, definition of, 26, 8 (*see also* Pollution of privilege)
*Titicut Follies*, 365
Title VII of Civil Rights Act, 117, 120
Timely assertion of privilege, need for, 245
Torah, ix
Tort cases:
  dangerous patient exception to privilege, 125
  disputes between therapist and patient, 123, 253
  *ex parte* interviewing of therapist, 127
  examination of defendant, 103, 104, 117, 120, 130
  exceptions to privilege, 116, 125
  factitious sexual harassment, 123, 526
  Federal Tort Claims Act, 296
  frequency of, 115
  genetic information about parent, 127
  gross negligence, 302, 336
  impact rule, 136
  information about third party, 125, 127

information from family of patient, 127
  medication, as disinhibiting, 127
  notifying insurer, 124
  patient-litigant exception, 116
  Rule 35(a) of Federal Rules of Civil Procedure, 120
  sex discrimination, 122
  sexual harassment, 120, 122, 131, 214
  significance of privilege, 115
  suicide, 117
  third-party suit against therapist, 125
  Title VII of the Civil Rights Act, 120
  undue familiarity with patient, 125
  waiver of privilege, 127
  wrongful death, 116, 117
*Touching*, 214
Training setting, IV-6-6, V-1-3
Treating a fugitive, 28
Treatment plans, 468
Trust, importance of, 41, 273, 292, 413, 493, 551
Truth vs. privilege, 5, 19, 292, 413, 551
Types of therapy, 11, 472

U.S. Air Force Academy, reporting to, 264, 287
U.S. Supreme Court on therapy privilege, xi, 5, 10, 11, 41, 60, 84, 117, 565, 587
Undue familiarity with patient, 123, 125, 140, 495
Uniform Rules of Evidence, 20
Uniform State Laws, 20
Universities, reporting to, 396
Unlicensed therapists, 80

Very Important Persons:
  (*see also* Privacy, Stigma)
  candidate's spouse, 346
  disclosure of medical records, 342
  private life, relevance in governance, 349
  right of privacy, 345, 356
  stigma, 54, 352
  treatment of, 342
Vital statistics, 26
Voluntary disclosure in court, 245

Waiver (*see* Exceptions to privilege, Termination of privilege, Tort cases)
*Walden*, 52

Watergate, xiv, 57, 348
*War and Peace*, 450
Westhoff Memorial Hospital, 440
Wills (*see* Testaments, 29, 129)
Witchdoctor, ix
Witness bias, 529
Witness, therapist as, xiii, 29, 75, 129, 521
Witnesses, credibility of, 70
"Wolf Man," 532
Workers' compensation, 29, 428, 526
World Medical Association, x
Writing about a patient (*see* Teaching and writing)
Writing by a patient, 144
Wrongful death (*see* Tort cases)

*Ziggy*, 305

# ABOUT THE AUTHOR

**Ralph Slovenko** is Professor of Law and Psychiatry at Wayne State University in Michigan. He received B.E., LL.B., M.A., and Ph.D. degrees from Tulane University. He was editor-in-chief of the Tulane Law Review, and a varsity sports letterman at Tulane University. He served as law clerk to the Louisiana Supreme Court, and as senior assistant district attorney under Jim Garrison in New Orleans. He was a Fulbright scholar to France. A professor of law at Tulane University from 1954 to 1964, he was also a member of the faculty of the Tulane University Department of Psychiatry and Neurology. At the invitation of Dr. Robert G. Heath, chairman of the Tulane University Department of Psychiatry and Neurology, he did a residency in psychiatry, one of two persons to do so without a medical degree.

He held a joint appointment, from 1965 to 1968, at the Menninger Foundation and the University of Kansas School of Law. Since then, he has been at Wayne State University. He has lectured widely in the United States and also in Australia, Canada, France, Holland, Israel, Japan, Russia (Soviet Union), and South Africa. He was visiting professor in South Africa in 1976 and 1989, and he occupied the Rood Eminent Scholar Chair in 1991 at the University of Florida College of Law. He is a frequent visitor to Poland, Russia and South Africa, and has written extensively about them. He has frequently served as an expert witness.

He is a member of the American, Kansas, Louisiana and Michigan Bar Associations, and a scientific associate of the American Academy of Psychoanalysis and amicus of the American Academy of Psychiatry and Law. He is the author of numerous books and articles. His book *Psychiatry and Law* received the 1974 Manfred Guttmacher award of the American Psychiatric Association and was a selection of the Behaviorial Science Book Club. His most recent book, *Psychiatry and Criminal Culpability*, was runner-up for the 1995 Guttmacher Award. He is a regular commentator in the *Journal of Psychiatry and Law* and is editor of the American

Series in Behavioral Science and Law. He is on the Board of Editors of the *International Journal of Offender Therapy and Comparative Criminology, Journal of the American Academy of Psychiatry and Law, Journal of Psychiatry and Law*, and *Medicine and Law*. He writes a weekly column in the *Detroit Legal News*.